ninth edition

Psychology Applied to Modern Life

ADJUSTMENT IN THE 21ST CENTURY

WAYNE WEITEN
University of Nevada, Las Vegas

MARGARET A. LLOYD
Georgia Southern University

DANA S. DUNN
Moravian College

ELIZABETH YOST HAMMER
Xavier University of Louisiana

WADSWORTH
CENGAGE Learning™

Australia • Brazil • Japan • Korea • Mexico • Singapore •
Spain • United Kingdom • United States

WADSWORTH
CENGAGE Learning™

Psychology Applied to Modern Life: Adjustment in the 21st Century, **Ninth Edition**
Wayne Weiten, Margaret A. Lloyd, Dana S. Dunn, Elizabeth Yost Hammer

Publisher: Michele Sordi
Development Editor:
  Kristin Makarewycz
Assistant Editor: Magnolia Molcan
Editorial Assistant: Erin Miskelly
Technology Project Manager:
  Lauren Keyes
Marketing Manager: Kim Russell
Marketing Assistant: Melanie Cregger
Marketing Communications Manager:
  Linda Yip
Project Manager, Editorial Production:
  Jennie Redwitz
Creative Director: Rob Hugel
Art Director: Vernon Boes
Print Buyer: Karen Hunt
Permissions Editors: Linda L. Rill,
  Bob Kauser
Production Service: Tom Dorsaneo
Text Designer: Liz Harasymczuk
Photo Researcher: Linda L. Rill
Copy Editor: Jackie Estrada
Illustrator: Carol Zuber-Mallison
Cover Designer: Liz Harasymczuk
Cover Image: "Inner Peace" by Jennifer
  Main, mixed media on canvas, 2005
  www.jennifermaingallery.com
Compositor: Thompson Type

For product information and technology assistance, contact us at
Cengage Learning Academic Resource Center, 1-800-423-0563
For permission to use material from this text or product, submit all requests online at **www.cengage.com/permissions**. Further permissions questions can be e-mailed to **permissionrequest@cengage.com**.

Library of Congress Control Number: 2007930881

Student Edition:
ISBN-13: 978-0-495-55339-7
ISBN-10: 0-495-55339-5

Loose-leaf Edition:
ISBN-13: 978-0-495-50535-8
ISBN-10: 0-495-50535-8

Wadsworth Cengage Learning
10 Davis Drive
Belmont, CA 94002-3098
USA

Cengage Learning products are represented in Canada by Nelson Education, Ltd.

For your course and learning solutions, visit
academic.cengage.com.

Purchase any of our products at your local college store or at our preferred online store **www.ichapters.com**.

Printed in the United States of America
1 2 3 4 5 6 7 12 11 10 09 08

Cover Image: "Inner Peace" by Jennifer Main, mixed media on canvas, 2005
www.jennifermaingallery.com

About the Authors

WAYNE WEITEN is a graduate of Bradley University and received his Ph.D. in social psychology from the University of Illinois, Chicago in 1981. He currently teaches at the University of Nevada, Las Vegas. He has received distinguished teaching awards from Division Two of the American Psychological Association (APA) and from the College of DuPage, where he taught until 1991. He is a Fellow of Divisions 1 and 2 of the American Psychological Association. In 1991, he helped chair the APA National Conference on Enhancing the Quality of Undergraduate Education in Psychology and in 1996–1997 he served as President of the Society for the Teaching of Psychology. Weiten has conducted research on a wide range of topics, including educational measurement, jury decision-making, attribution theory, stress, and cerebral specialization. His recent interests have included pressure as a form of stress and the technology of textbooks. He is also the author of *Psychology: Themes & Variations* (2007) and the creator of an educational CD-ROM titled *PsykTrek: A Multimedia Introduction to Psychology.*

MARGARET (MARKY) A. LLOYD received her B.A. from the University of Denver and her M.A. and Ph.D. in psychology from the University of Arizona. She is the author of *Adolescence* (1985). She has served as chair of the psychology departments at Suffolk University and Georgia Southern University and is the founding Chair of the Council for Undergraduate Psychology Programs. She is a past President of the Society for the Teaching of Psychology (Division 2 of the American Psychological Association), past Executive Director of the Society's Office of Teaching Resources in Psychology, and currently serves on APA's Council of Representatives for the Society. She is a Fellow of Divisions 1 and 2 of the American Psychological Association. She is Emerita Professor and Chair of Psychology at Georgia Southern University and a recipient of that institution's Award for Excellence for Contributions to Instruction.

DANA S. DUNN earned his B.A. in psychology from Carnegie Mellon University and received his Ph.D. in social psychology from the University of Virginia. He is currently professor of psychology and director of the Learning in Common Curriculum at Moravian College, Bethlehem, PA. He chaired the psychology department at Moravian for 6 years. A Fellow of the American Psychological Association (APA), Dunn is active in the Society for the Teaching of Psychology and frequently presents at national and regional disciplinary conferences. Dunn has written numerous articles, chapters, and book reviews concerning his areas of research interest: the teaching of psychology, social psychology, and rehabilitation psychology. He is the author or editor of several books, including *Research Methods for Social Psychology* (in press) and *A Short Guide to Writing about Psychology* (2008).

ELIZABETH YOST HAMMER earned her B.S. in psychology from Troy State University and received her Ph.D. in social psychology from Tulane University. She is currently professor of psychology and director of the Center for the Advancement of Teaching at Xavier University of Louisiana in New Orleans. She is a Fellow of Division Two of the American Psychological Association (APA) and is a past President of Psi Chi, the National Honor Society in Psychology. Recently, she was elected as treasurer for the Society for the Teaching of Psychology. She is passionate about teaching and has published on collaborative learning, service learning, the application of social psychological theories to the classroom, and mentoring students. After her experience with Hurricane Katrina, she developed a Psychology of Disasters course and is currently co-authoring a book of the same title.

To the Instructor

Many students enter adjustment courses with great expectations. They've ambled through their local bookstores, and in the "Psychology" section they've seen numerous self-help books that offer highly touted recipes for achieving happiness for a mere $12.95. After paying far more money to enroll in a college course that deals with the same issues as the self-help books, many students expect a revelatory experience. However, the majority of us with professional training in psychology or counseling take a rather dim view of self-help books and the pop psychology they represent. Psychology professors tend to see this literature as oversimplified, intellectually dishonest, and opportunistic and often summarily dismiss the pop psychology that so many students have embraced. Instructors try to supplant pop psychology with more sophisticated academic psychology, which is more complex and less accessible.

In this textbook, we have tried to come to grips with this problem of differing expectations between student and teacher. Our goal has been to produce a comprehensive, serious, research-oriented treatment of the topic of adjustment that also acknowledges the existence of popular psychology and looks critically at its contributions.

In Chapter 1 we confront the phenomenon of popular self-help books. We try to take the student beneath the seductive surface of such books and analyze some of their typical flaws. Our goal is to make the student a more critical consumer of this type of literature.

While encouraging a more critical attitude toward self-help books, we do not suggest that all of them should be dismissed. Instead, we acknowledge that some of them offer authentic insights. In fact, we highlight some of the better books in Recommended Reading boxes sprinkled throughout the text. These recommended books tie in with the adjacent topical coverage and show the student the interface between academic and popular psychology.

Throughout the book we try to provide the student with a better appreciation of the merits of the empirical approach. This effort to clarify the role of research, which is rare for an adjustment text, appears in the first chapter.

Recognizing that adjustment students want to leave the course with concrete, personally useful information, we end each chapter with an application section. The Applications are "how to" discussions that address everyday problems. While they focus on issues that are relevant to the content of the particular chapter, they contain more explicit advice than the text proper.

In summary, we have tried to make this book both rigorous and applied. We hope that our approach will help students to better appreciate the value of scientific psychology.

Philosophy

A certain philosophy is inherent in any systematic treatment of the topic of adjustment. Our philosophy can be summarized as follows:

▶ We believe that an adjustment text should be a resource book for students. We have tried to design this book so that it encourages and facilitates the pursuit of additional information on adjustment-related topics. It should serve as a point of departure for more learning.

▶ We believe in theoretical eclecticism. This book will not indoctrinate your students along the lines of any single theoretical orientation. The psychodynamic, behavioral, and humanistic schools of thought are all treated with respect, as are cognitive, biological, evolutionary, and other perspectives.

▶ We believe that effective adjustment requires taking charge of one's own life. Throughout the book we try to promote the notion that active coping efforts are generally superior to passivity and complacency.

Changes in the Ninth Edition

One of the exciting things about psychology is that it is not a stagnant discipline. It continues to progress at what seems a faster and faster pace. A good textbook must evolve with the discipline. Although the professors and students who used the earlier editions of this book did not clamor for change, we have made countless content changes to keep up with new developments in psychology—adding and deleting some topics, condensing and reorganizing others, and updating everything (there are 1,082 new references). A brief overview of some of these changes, listed chapter by chapter, can be found on pages ix–xi following this introduction.

The most significant change in this edition is the addition of two new co-authors to the *Psychology Applied to Modern Life* team. Dana Dunn and Elizabeth Yost Hammer each contributed revisions of four chapters to this edition. We brought Dana and Elizabeth on board because Marky Lloyd intends to fully embrace retirement after this edition. This gradual transition in authorship has gone smoothly, as Dana and Elizabeth have brought fresh perspectives to the topics in their chapters, reenergizing the revision process and producing a great deal of new coverage.

Writing Style

This book has been written with the student reader in mind. We have tried to integrate the technical jargon of our discipline into a relatively informal and down-to-earth writing style. We use concrete examples extensively to clarify complex concepts and to help maintain student interest. Although we now have four authors, the original author of this book (Wayne Weiten) continues to do the final rewrite of all 16 chapters to ensure stylistic consistency.

Features

This text contains a number of features intended to stimulate interest and enhance students' learning. These special features include Applications, Recommended Reading boxes, Web Links, Practice Tests, a didactic illustration program, and cartoons.

Applications

The Applications should be of special interest to most students. They are tied to chapter content in a way that should show students how practical applications emerge out of theory and research. Although some of the material covered in these sections shows up frequently in adjustment texts, much of it is unique. Among the Application topics are

- Understanding Intimate Violence
- Monitoring Your Stress
- Understanding Eating Disorders
- Getting Ahead in the Job Game
- Building Self-Esteem
- Enhancing Sexual Relationships
- Bridging the Gender Gap in Communication

Recommended Reading Boxes

Recognizing students' interest in self-help books, we have sifted through hundreds of them to identify some that may be especially useful. These books are featured in boxes that briefly review some of the higher-quality books. These Recommended Reading boxes are placed where they are germane to the material being covered in the text. Some of the recommended books are well known, while others are obscure. Although we make it clear that we don't endorse every idea in every book, we think they all have something worthwhile to offer. This feature replaces the conventional suggested readings lists that usually appear at the ends of text chapters, where they are almost universally ignored by students.

Living in Today's World Boxes

The Living in Today's World boxes were originally developed to address issues that surfaced in the aftermath of the 9/11 terrorist attacks in the United States. Continuing in this vein, many of the boxes in this edition deal with concerns raised by the threat of terrorism in today's world. For example, we discuss how people tend to be affected by traumatic events, how people can cope more effectively with personal trauma, and how people can think more rationally about the threat of terrorism. However, we have broadened the scope of coverage in these boxes to include adjustment issues that are especially pertinent in light of current events, such as sexual interactions over the Internet, the controversy over whether the government should promote marriage, and difficulties coping with unemployment. We hope these digressions on pressing, contemporary issues prove helpful to students.

Web Links

The Internet is rapidly altering the landscape of modern life, and students clearly need help dealing with the information explosion in cyberspace. To assist them, we recruited web expert Vincent Hevern (Le Moyne College) to evaluate hundreds of psychology- and adjustment-related sites on the web and to come up with some recommended sites that appear to provide reasonably accurate, balanced, and empirically sound information. Short descriptions of these recommended websites are dispersed throughout the chapters, adjacent to related topical coverage. Because URLs change frequently, we have not included the URLs for the Web Links in the book. Insofar as students are interested in visiting these sites, we recommend that they do so through the *Psychology Applied to Modern Life* home page at the Wadsworth Psychology website (academic.cengage.com/psychology/weiten). Links to all the recommended websites are maintained there, and the Wadsworth webmaster periodically updates the URLs. Of course, students can also use search engines such as Google to locate the recommended websites.

Practice Tests

Each chapter ends with a ten-item multiple-choice Practice Test that should give students a fairly realistic assessment of their mastery of that chapter and valuable practice in taking the type of test that many of them will face in the classroom (if the instructor uses the *Test Bank*). This feature grew out of research on students' use of textbook pedagogical devices (see Weiten, Guadagno, & Beck, 1996). This research indicated that students pay scant attention to some standard pedagogical devices. When students were grilled to gain a better understanding of this perplexing finding, it quickly became apparent that students are pragmatic about pedagogy. Essentially, their refrain was, "We want study aids that will help us pass the next test." With this mandate in mind, we added the Practice Tests. They should be very realistic, as many of the items came from the *Test Bank* for previous editions (these items do not appear in the *Test Bank* for the current edition).

Didactic Illustration Program

The illustration program is once again in full color, and many new figures have been added along with extensive redrawing of many graphics. Although the illustrations are intended to make the book attractive and to help maintain student interest, they are not merely decorative: They have been carefully selected and crafted for their didactic value to enhance the educational goals of the text.

Cartoons

A little comic relief usually helps keep a student interested, so we've sprinkled numerous cartoons throughout the book. Like the figures, most of them have been chosen to reinforce ideas in the text.

Learning Aids

Because this book is rigorous, substantive, and sizable, a number of learning aids have been incorporated into the text to help the reader digest the wealth of material:

▶ The *outline* at the beginning of each chapter provides the student with a preview and overview of what will be covered.

▶ *Headings* are used extensively to keep material well organized.

▶ To help alert your students to key points, *learning objectives* are distributed throughout the chapters, after the first-level headings.

▶ *Key terms* are identified with **blue italicized boldface type** to indicate that these are important vocabulary items that are part of psychology's technical language.

▶ An *integrated running glossary* provides an on-the-spot definition of each key term as it is introduced in the text. Each formal definition is printed in **blue boldface** type.

▶ An *alphabetical glossary* is found in the back of the book, as key terms are usually defined in the integrated running glossary only when they are first introduced.

▶ *Italics* are used liberally throughout the text to emphasize important points.

▶ A *chapter review* is found at the end of each chapter. Each review includes a concise but thorough summary of the chapter's key ideas, a list of the key terms that were introduced in the chapter, and a list of important theorists and researchers who were discussed in the chapter.

Supplementary Materials

A complete teaching/learning package has been developed to supplement *Psychology Applied to Modern Life*. These supplementary materials have been carefully coordinated to provide effective support for the text. Supplements are available to qualified adopters. Please consult your local sales representative for details.

Personal Explorations Workbook

The *Personal Explorations Workbook* is a small booklet assembled by John Pulver of the College of Southern Nevada and Wayne Weiten. It contains experiential exercises for each text chapter, designed to help your students achieve personal insights. The questionnaires are psychological tests or scales that your students can administer and score for themselves. The "Personal Probes" consist of questions intended to help students think about themselves in relation to issues raised in the text. In addition to generating student interest, these exercises can be fruitful in stimulating class discussion. The *Personal Explorations Workbook* can be ordered shrinkwrapped with the text.

Instructor's Manual

The *Instructor's Manual,* revised by Lenore Frigo of Shasta College, is available as a convenient aid for your educational endeavors. It provides a thorough overview of each chapter, along with a list of relevant films and InfoTrac College Edition integration. It also includes a wealth of suggestions for lecture topics, class demonstrations, exercises, and discussion questions, organized around the content of each chapter in the text.

Test Bank

The *Test Bank,* revised by Joan Thomas-Spiegel of Los Angeles Harbor College, contains an extensive collection of multiple-choice questions for objective tests, all closely tied to the learning objectives found in the text chapters. We're confident that you will find this to be a dependable and usable test bank.

ExamView® Computerized Testing

Preloaded with all of the questions in the *Test Bank,* ExamView allows you to create, deliver, and customize tests and study guides (both print and online) in minutes. ExamView offers both a Quick Test Wizard and an Online Test Wizard that guides you step by step through the process of creating tests, while its unique "what you see is what you get" capability allows you to see the test you are creating onscreen exactly as it will print or display online. You can build tests of up to 250 questions using up to 12 question types. Using ExamView's complete word-processing capabilities, you can enter an unlimited number of new questions or edit existing questions.

PowerLecture with JoinIn™ and ExamView

This one-stop lecture and class preparation tool makes it easy for you to assemble, edit, publish, and present custom lectures for your course using Microsoft® PowerPoint®. PowerLecture lets you bring together text-specific lecture outlines written by Lisa Garner of Tallahassee Community College with art from the text, along with video and animations from the web or your own materials—culminating in powerful, personalized, media-enhanced presentations. The CD-ROM also contains the full *Instructor's Manual, Test Bank,* and other instructor resources. The CD-ROM also includes software that lets you pose book-specific questions and display students' answers seamlessly within the Microsoft® PowerPoint® slides of your own lecture, in conjunction with the "clicker" hardware of your choice, as well as the ExamView assessment and tutorial system, which guides you step by step through the process of creating tests.

Study Guide

The *Study Guide,* written by William Addison of Eastern Illinois University, is designed to help students master the information contained in the text. It contains a programmed review of learning objectives, quiz boxes, and a self-test for each chapter. Your students should find it helpful in their study efforts.

Culture and Modern Life

Culture and Modern Life is a small paperback intended to help your students appreciate how cultural factors moderate psychological processes and how the viewpoint of one's own culture can distort one's interpretation of the behavior of people from other cultures. Written by David Matsumoto (San Francisco State University), a leading authority on cross-cultural psychology, this supplementary book should greatly enhance your students' understanding of how culture can influence adjustment. *Culture and Modern Life* can be ordered shrinkwrapped with the text.

Critical Thinking Exercises

A set of critical thinking exercises can be found at the *Psychology Applied to Modern Life* website (academic. cengage.com/psychology/weiten). These exercises are intended to introduce students to specific critical thinking skills such as recognizing extraneous variables, sampling bias, and fallacies in reasoning. The exercises also challenge students to apply these skills to adjustment-related topics on a chapter-by-chapter basis.

Highlights of Content Changes in the Ninth Edition

To help professors who have used this book over many editions, we are providing an overview of the content changes in the current edition. The following list is not exhaustive, but it should alert faculty to most of the major changes in the book.

Chapter 1 Adjusting to Modern Life

In discussion of the paradox of progress, new material on how work follows people home and how the modern time crunch fosters an epidemic of sleep deprivation

In discussion of the paradox of progress, new material on compulsive buying syndrome

New discussion of modern "makeover culture," and the widespread obsession with self-improvement

New coverage of Salerno's critique and expose of self-help gurus.

New discussion of how self-help books often encourage a self-centered, exploitive approach to interpersonal relationships

New discussion of the surprisingly modest association between actual wealth and subjective perceptions of finances, and other new research on income and happiness

New coverage of the heritability of subjective well-being

New discussion of Gilbert's work on how people are surprisingly bad at predicting what will make them happy

New research on the degree to which the hedonic treadmill makes it difficult for people to enhance their happiness

Chapter 2 Theories of Personality

Discussion of trait models now includes explanation of the role of factor analysis

New research relating the Big Five traits to various aspects of behavior

Expanded coverage of relations between self-efficacy and specific behaviors

New discussion of Nettle's evolutionary analysis of the adaptive implications of the Big Five traits

New discussion of how hindsight bias presents problems for evolutionary theories of personality

New research on terror management theory and reactions to abstract art

New research relating terror management theory to psychological discomfort about bodily processes, including sexuality

New section on culture and personality examines the cross-cultural relevance of the five-factor model

New research on cultural variations in scores on Big Five traits and the inaccuracy of national character stereotypes

Revised, more critical evaluation of projective tests

Chapter 3 Stress and Its Effects

New discussion of recent research on the impact of stress appraisals, specifically on children's responses to the 9/11 terrorist attacks

Updated research using the City Stress Inventory as an index of urban environmental stress

New coverage of perceived discrimination as a source of stress

Discussion of acculturation as a form of stress

Streamlined coverage of conflict and vacillation

New description of the role of depleted self-control in test anxiety

Added description of posttraumatic shame and guilt

Expanded discussion of stress and memory

Coverage of new research on posttraumatic growth

Inclusion of 9/11 data on rescue workers and PTSD

Chapter 4 Coping Processes

New discussion of the importance of being flexible in choosing coping strategies

Expanded discussion of how exposure to media violence increases aggressive behavior

New data on the ramifications of self-blame as coping strategy

New, more contemporary introduction to using humor as a coping strategy

New discussion of cultural variations in the tendency to seek social support

New findings on personality factors related to procrastination

New discussion of the thinking underlying college students' procrastination on academic assignments

New coverage of the distinction between people who are future-oriented versus present-oriented in relation to time management

New section on exercise as an emotion-focused coping strategy

New advice on factors promoting effective exercise

Streamlined, reorganized coverage of meditation and relaxation

Chapter 5 The Self

New opening vignette illustrating self-reflection

Expanded discussion of efforts to cope with self-discrepancies

Expanded coverage of social comparison processes, including current versus past selves, reference group appraisal, and upward and downward comparisons

New section on the impact of social context as a factor shaping self-concept

New discussion of the self, cultural values, and focus on interpersonal agency

New discussion of trait versus state self-esteem

New material concerning secure high self-esteem and defensive high self-esteem

Broadened discussion of terror management theory and beliefs about terrorism in relation to self-esteem

New comparison drawn between self-handicapping and defensive pessimism

Additional details concerning predictors of self-handicapping

New Recommended Reading on defensive pessimism

Addition of negative acknowledgment as an impression management strategy

Chapter 6 Social Thinking and Social Influence

New opening vignette showing person perception in action

New discussion of how bad can be stronger than good in person perception

Extension of the confirmation bias to group behavior

Broader discussion of the attractiveness stereotype and its impact on romance

Added discussion regarding why the fundamental attribution error is hard to avoid

Additional discussion concerning why prejudice does not always lead to discrimination

Coverage of new topic, aversive racism

New material on a prejudiced personality style called the social dominance orientation

New discussion of mood and the need for cognition as receiver factors in persuasion

Additional consideration of the Asch study's impact

Introduction of how the foot-in-the-door technique can also be used for socially beneficial goals

Chapter 7 Interpersonal Communication

New material on net lingo and cyberspeak

New point about how nonverbal communication plays an important role in conveying emotions

New data on people's ability to detect deception in others

New material on nonverbal sensitivity, including gender differences

New discussion of the role of nonverbal communication in self-disclosure

Added visualization as a treatment for speech anxiety

New big-picture conclusion for the main body of the chapter

New box on communication in an adversarial culture

Chapter 8 Friendship and Love

New material on the use of online dating sites

New discussion of deception in online romantic interactions

New material on changing body ideals for men

New discussion of special friendship issues for gay males and lesbians

New data on Sternberg's triangular theory of love

Revised conceptualization of attachment styles in terms of continuous dimensions

New material on the contribution of increased social isolation to trends in loneliness

Added information on the emotional costs of receiving social support

Chapter 9 Marriage and Intimate Relationships

New discussion of polygamy

Expanded discussion of interracial marriages

Revised coverage of age at marriage as a predictor of marital success

New material on the importance of positive emotions in premarital interactions

New data on the most common problems in marriages in later life

Expanded discussion of positive and negative work-to-family spillover

New findings on maternal employment and child development

New material on adjusting to divorce

Increased discussion of same-sex relationships

Chapter 10 Gender and Behavior

New chapter introduction focuses on Harvard President Lawrence Summers' controversial remarks regarding gender differences in math and science

Expanded discussion of the concept of gender

New discussion of androcentrism in science literature

Added discussion of Hyde's gender similarities hypothesis

Streamlined coverage of gender differences in personality and social behavior

Added data of gender differences in PTSD

Expanded coverage of gender role socialization through children's literature

Expanded coverage of the role of TV in gender role socialization

New discussion of the role of new media (video games, software) in gender role socialization

New evidence on gender differences in pressure to succeed

Inclusion of the double jeopardy status for harassment of minority women in the workplace

New discussion of differentiated androgyny

Chapter 11 Development in Adolescence and Adulthood

New opening vignette illustrating the importance of developmental perspectives

Expanded discussion of adolescent autonomy and its positive impact on relations with parents

Lengthened discussion of parasuicide in adolescence

New material on the proposed stage of development known as emerging adulthood

New Recommended Reading on a book outlining research on emerging adulthood

More specific and up-to-date characterization of Erikson's concept of generativity

More on mid-life as a construct of modern cultures

Additional coverage of the "empty nest syndrome"

New discussion of belief in adaptive control in relation to mid-life adjustment

Additional coverage of women and the notion of the mid-life crisis

More detail on the role friendship and social support networks play in later life

Addition of new material on gender and ethnicity as risk factors for Alzheimer's disease

Supplementary discussion concerning adapting to grief across time

New Recommended Reading on the funeral industry and green burials

Chapter 12 Careers and Work

Revised chapter opener to be a more involving vignette

Extensive discussion of contemporary technological tools throughout

Streamlined coverage of Super's stages of vocational development

New material on sexual orientation disclosure and employment discrimination

New research on the glass ceiling for women, especially minority women

Updated discussion of family-friendly workplace policies

New findings on the benefits of leisure activities

New material on video résumés and on the perils of résumé padding

New Recommended Reading box profiles book on making the transition from college to career

Chapter 13 Development and Expression of Sexuality

Revised chapter opener to be a more engaging vignette

Updated material on peers as a socializing influence on sexual behavior

Revised discussion of how the media acts as a socializing influence on sexuality

Revised coverage of sexual identity development

New scheme for understanding motives for engaging in sex

New data on gender differences in comfort with "hooking up"

Revised discussion of constraints on effective contraception

Updated discussion of new contraceptive methods

Added information on the new vaccine for HPV

Chapter 14 Psychology and Physical Health

New opening vignette illustrating the connections between behavior and physical health

Expanded discussion of influential factors in the biopsychosocial model

Greater detail on how personality can be linked to physical health

New material on the interaction of race and hostility in relation to cardiovascular risk

Expanded discussion of the relation between low social support and heart disease

Discussion of problems in the prediction of heart disease posed by conceptual overlap of depression, anger, and anxiety

New description of the cancer prone or Type C personality

Updated discussion of stress and immune suppression

New research showing that merely thinking about alcohol can prime aggressive thoughts and behaviors

More detail on the link between sedentary lifestyle and weight gain

New material on demographic factors and obesity

Added detail regarding the benefits of exercise at any age

New discussion of age as a factor in treatment seeking

Chapter 15 Psychological Disorders

New discussion of how psychiatric views of homosexuality have changed over time, illustrating the value-laden nature of judgments of abnormality

New discussion of the process to develop DSM-V

New coverage of controversy surrounding recent high estimates of the prevalence of mental illness

New findings on personality and somatoform disorders

Updated discussion of diagnostic patterns for dissociative identity disorder

New discussion of genetic mapping findings in relation to the etiology of mood disorders

New coverage of innovative theory that attributes depression to suppressed neurogenesis in the hippocampus

Updated coverage of how interpersonal factors contribute to depressive disorders

New box on understanding and preventing suicide

Updated coverage of the prevalence of eating disorders

Application on eating disorders now includes description of binge-eating disorder

Chapter 16 Psychotherapy

Updated discussion of psychologists' efforts to obtain prescription privileges

New data on who seeks and receives professional treatment

New information on how hypnosis and dream interpretation may contribute to recovered memories of abuse in therapy

Coverage of cognitive therapy moved from section on insight therapies to section on behavioral treatments

Revised discussion of the effectiveness of insight therapies

New discussion of the cost effectiveness of newer atypical antipsychotics in comparison to conventional antipsychotics

New Recommended Reading box profiling the book *Crazy*, which provides a chilling and disturbing portrait of America's mental health system

Streamlined Application on looking for a therapist

Acknowledgments

This book has been an enormous undertaking, and we want to express our gratitude to the innumerable people who have influenced its evolution. To begin with, we must cite the contribution of our students who have taken the adjustment course. It is trite to say that they have been a continuing inspiration—but they have.

We also want to express our appreciation for the time and effort invested by the authors of various ancillary books and materials: Vinny Hevern (Le Moyne College), Bill Addison (Eastern Illinois University), Jeffry Ricker (Scottsdale Community College), John Pulver (Community College of Southern Nevada), David Matsumoto (San Francisco State University), Lenore Frigo (Shasta College), Lisa Garner (Tallahassee Community College), and Joan Thomas-Spiegel (Los Angeles Harbor College). In spite of tight schedules, they all did commendable work.

The quality of a textbook depends greatly on the quality of the prepublication reviews by psychology professors around the country. The reviewers listed on pages xiii–xiv have contributed to the development of this book by providing constructive reviews of various portions of the manuscript in this or earlier editions. We are grateful to all of them.

We would also like to thank Michele Sordi, who has served as editor of this edition. She has done a wonderful job following in the footsteps of Claire Verduin, Eileen Murphy, and Edith Beard Brady, to whom we remain indebted. We are also grateful to Jackie Estrada, who did an excellent job of copy editing and indexing; Tom Dorsaneo, who performed superbly as our production editor; Liz Harasymczuk, who created the colorful, inviting design; Linda Rill, who provided outstanding photo and permissions research; Carol Zuber-Mallison, who created the new graphics; Alma Bell of Thompson Type who oversaw the composition; and Fiorella Ljunggren, who shepherded previous editions into existence. Others who have made significant contributions to this project include Jennie Redwitz (project manager), Kristin Makarewycz (development editor), Magnolia Molcan (ancillaries editor), Kim Russell (marketing manager), Erin Miskelly (editorial assistant), Lauren Keyes (technology projects), and Vernon Boes (art director).

In addition, Wayne Weiten would like to thank his wife, Beth Traylor, who has been a steady source of emotional support despite the demands of her medical career, and his 14-year-old son, T. J., who adds a wealth of laughter to his dad's life. He is also grateful to his former colleagues at the College of DuPage and at Santa Clara University for their counsel and assistance, and to Melissa Lanctot for her assistance with the references. Marky Lloyd would like to thank Sarah Goss for her suggestions of popular songs and Judith A. Holleman for her assistance and support. Dana Dunn thanks his wife, editor Sarah Dunn, for making suggestions on drafts of the manuscript. As always, his children, Jake and Hannah, were happy distractions during the writing process. He also thanks one of his former students, Jessica Barkhausen, for suggesting and tracking down reference materials. Elizabeth Yost Hammer would like to thank Elliott Hammer—her constant source of inspiration, encouragement, and support—for far too much to list here. She is grateful to Samantha Hagler, Lyse Jackson, Alise Olivio, and Emily Santiago for their research assistance. She is also grateful to Kendall Eskine for his assistance with the reference list. Finally, she wishes to thank Wayne Weiten for inviting her to be part of this project.

Wayne Weiten
Margaret A. Lloyd
Dana S. Dunn
Elizabeth Yost Hammer

Reviewers

Bette Ackerman
Rhodes College

David W. Alfano
Community College of Rhode Island

Jeff Banks
Pepperdine University

Marsha K. Beauchamp
Mt. San Antonio College

John R. Blakemore
Monterey Peninsula College

Barbara A. Boccaccio
Tunxis Community College

Paul Bowers
Grayson County College

Tamara L. Brown
University of Kentucky

George Bryant
East Texas State University

James F. Calhoun
University of Georgia

Robert Cameron
Fairmont State College

Bernardo J. Carducci
Indiana University, Southeast

M. K. Clampit
Bentley College

Meg Clark
California State Polytechnic University-Pomona

Stephen S. Coccia
Orange County Community College

Dennis Coon
Santa Barbara City College

Katherine A. Couch
Eastern Oklahoma State College

Tori Crews
American River College

Salvatore Cullari
Lebanon Valley College

Kenneth S. Davidson
Wayne State University

Lugenia Dixon
Bainbridge College

Jean Egan
Asnuntuck Community College

Richard Fuhrer
University of Wisconsin-Eau Claire

R. Kirkland Gable
California Lutheran University

Lee Gills
Georgia College

Lawrence Grebstein
University of Rhode Island

Bryan Gros
Louisiana State University

Kyle Max Hancock
Utah State University

Barbara Hansen Lemme
College of DuPage

Robert Helm
Oklahoma State University

Barbara Hermann
Gainesville College

Jeanne L. Higbee
University of Minnesota

Robert Higgins
Central Missouri State University

Clara E. Hill
University of Maryland

Michael Hirt
Kent State University

Fred J. Hitti
Monroe Community College

William M. Hooper
Clayton College and State University

Joseph Horvat
Weber State University

Kathy Howard
Harding University

Teresa A. Hutchens
University of Tennessee-Knoxville

Jerry Jensen
Minneapolis Community & Technical College

Walter Jones
College of DuPage

Wayne Joose
Calvin College

Bradley Karlin
Texas A&M University

Margaret Karolyi
University of Akron

Lambros Karris
Husson College

Martha Kuehn
Central Lakes College

Susan Kupisch
Austin Peay State University

Robert Lawyer
Delgado Community College

Jimi Leopold
Tarleton State University

Harold List
Massachusetts Bay Community College

Corliss A. Littlefield
Morgan Community College

Louis A. Martone
Miami Dade Community College

Richard Maslow
San Joaquin Delta College

Sherri McCarthy
Northern Arizona University

William T. McReynolds
University of Tampa

Fred Medway
University of South Carolina-Columbia

Frederick Meeker
California State Polytechnic University-Pomona

Mitchell Metzger
Pennsylvania State University-Shenago Campus

John Moritsugu
Pacific Lutheran University

Jeanne O'Kon
Tallahassee Community College

Gary Oliver
College of DuPage

William Penrod
Middle Tennessee State University

Joseph Philbrick
California State Polytechnic University-Pomona

Barbara M. Powell
Eastern Illinois University

James Prochaska
University of Rhode Island

Megan Benoit Ratcliff
University of Georgia

Katherine Elaine Royal
Middle Tennessee State University

Joan Royce
Riverside Community College

Joan Rykiel
Ocean County College

John Sample
Slippery Rock University

Thomas K. Savill
Metropolitan State College of Denver

Patricia Sawyer
Middlesex Community College

Carol Schachat
De Anza College

Norman R. Schultz
Clemson University

Dale Simmons
  Oregon State University
Sangeeta Singg
  Angelo State University
Valerie Smead
  Western Illinois University
Dolores K. Sutter
  Tarrant County College-Northeast
Karl Swain
  Community College of Southern Nevada
Diane Teske
  Penn State Harrisburg

Kenneth L. Thompson
  Central Missouri State University
David L. Watson
  University of Hawaii
Deborah S. Weber
  University of Akron
Clair Wiederholt
  Madison Area Technical College
J. Oscar Williams
  Diablo Valley College
Raymond Wolf
  Moraine Park Technical College

Raymond Wolfe
  State University of New York at Geneseo
Michael Wolff
  Southwestern Oklahoma State University
Madeleine E. Wright
  Houston Community College
Norbert Yager
  Henry Ford Community College

Brief Contents

Contents

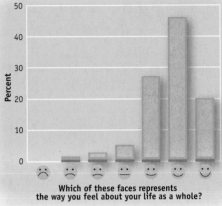

Which of these faces represents the way you feel about your life as a whole?

Successful students

Always or almost always in class
84%

Sometimes absent
8%

Often absent
8%

Unsuccessful students

Sometimes absent
8%

Always or almost always in class
47%

Often absent
45%

CHAPTER 2 Theories of Personality 32

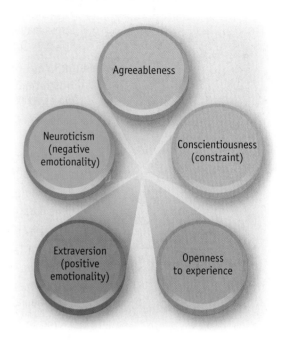

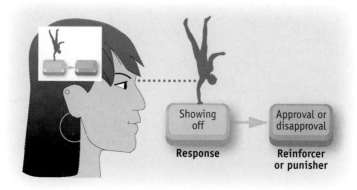

CHAPTER 4 Coping Processes 104

PART TWO

The Interpersonal Realm

CHAPTER 5   The Self   140

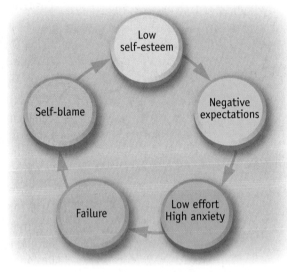

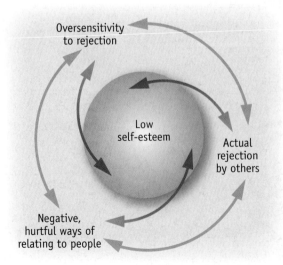

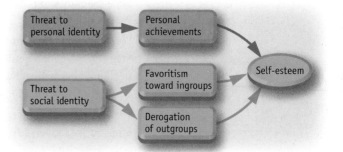

Where men and women tend to be touched
by friends of the . . .

Same gender   **Other gender**

Seldom (0–25%)
Quite often (26–50%)
Often (51–75%)
Very often (51–75%)

© Richard Flood/DK Stock/Getty Images

CHAPTER 8 Friendship and Love 236

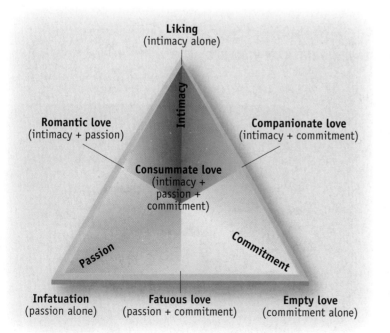

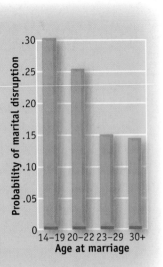

© Matthew McVay/Corbis Saba

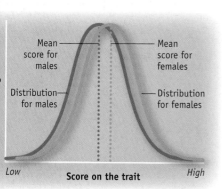

© Paul Wood/Alamy

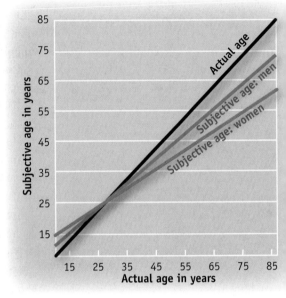

CHAPTER 12 Careers and Work 372

Percentage of respondents who . . .
- get a sense of identity from job
- work just to earn a living

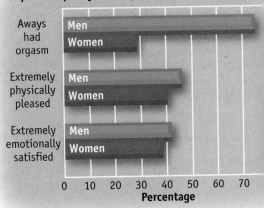

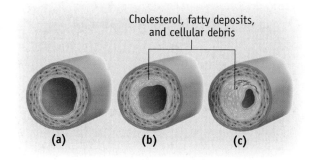
Cholesterol, fatty deposits, and cellular debris

(a)   (b)   (c)

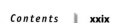

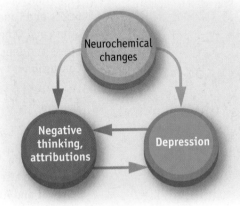

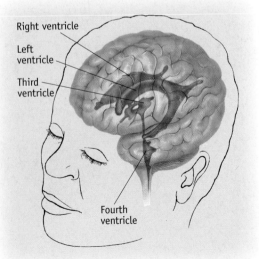

CHAPTER 16 Psychotherapy 514

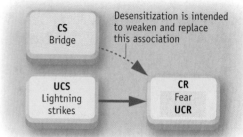

© Bruce Ayres/Stone/Getty Images

To the Student

In most college courses students spend more time with their textbooks than with their professors. Given this reality, it helps if you like your textbook. Making textbooks likable, however, is a tricky proposition. By its very nature, a textbook must introduce a great many new concepts, ideas, and theories. If it doesn't, it isn't much of a textbook, and instructors won't choose to use it—so you'll never see it anyway. Consequently, we have tried to make this book as likable as possible without compromising the academic content that your instructor demands. Thus, we have tried to make the book lively, informal, engaging, well organized, easy to read, practical, and occasionally humorous. Before you plunge into Chapter 1, let us explain some of the key features that can help you get the most out of the book.

Learning Aids

Mastering the content of this text involves digesting a great deal of information. To facilitate this learning process, we've incorporated a number of instructional aids into the book:

▶ *Outlines* at the beginning of each chapter provide you with both a preview and an overview of what will be covered. Think of the outlines as road maps, and bear in mind that it's easier to reach a destination if you know where you're going.

▶ *Headings* are used extensively to keep material well organized.

▶ To help alert you to key points, *learning objectives* are found throughout the chapters, immediately after the first-level headings.

▶ *Key terms* are identified with **blue italicized boldface** type to indicate that these are important vocabulary items that are part of psychology's technical language.

▶ An *integrated running glossary* provides an on-the-spot definition of each key term as it's introduced in the text. These formal definitions are printed in **blue boldface** type. It is often difficult for students to adapt to the jargon used by scientific disciplines. However, learning this terminology is an essential part of your educational experience. The integrated running glossary is meant to make this learning process as painless as possible.

▶ An *alphabetical glossary* is provided in the back of the book, as key terms are usually defined in the run-

ning glossary only when they are first introduced. If you run into a technical term that was introduced in an earlier chapter and you can't remember its meaning, you can look it up in the alphabetical glossary instead of backtracking to find the place where it first appeared.

▶ *Italics* are used liberally throughout the book to emphasize important points.

▶ A *chapter review* near the end of each chapter includes a thorough summary of the chapter and lists key terms and important theorists, with page references. Making use of these review materials can help ensure that you've digested the key points in the chapter.

▶ Each chapter ends with a ten-item *practice test* that should give you a realistic assessment of your mastery of that chapter and valuable practice taking multiple-choice tests that will probably be representative of what you will see in class (if your instructor uses the test bank designed for this book).

Recommended Reading Boxes

This text serves as a resource book. To facilitate this goal, particularly interesting self-help books on various topics are highlighted in boxes within the chapters. Each box provides a brief description of the book. We do not agree with everything in these recommended books, but all of them are potentially useful or intriguing. The main purpose of this feature is to introduce you to some of the better self-help books that are available.

Living in Today's World Boxes

These boxes were originally developed to address issues that surfaced in the aftermath of the 9/11 terrorist attacks in the United States. Continuing in this vein, many of the boxes in this edition deal with concerns raised by the threat of terrorism in today's world. For example, we discuss how people tend to be affected by traumatic events, how people can cope more effectively with personal trauma, and how people can think more rationally about the threat of terrorism. However, we have since broadened the scope of coverage in these boxes to include additional adjustment issues that are especially pertinent in light of current events, such as sexual interactions over the Internet, the controversy over whether government should promote marriage, and difficulties coping with unemployment. We hope these digressions on pressing, contemporary issues prove helpful.

Web Links

To help make this book a rich resource guide, we have included Web Links, which are recommended websites that can provide you with additional information on adjustment-related topics. The recommended sites were selected by Vincent Hevern, the former Internet editor for the Society for the Teaching of Psychology. Professor Hevern sought out sites that are interesting, that are relevant to adjustment, and that provide accurate, empirically sound information. As with the Recommended Reading boxes, we cannot say that we agree with everything posted on these web pages, but we think they have some real value. The Web Links are dispersed throughout the chapters, adjacent to related topical coverage. Because URLs change frequently, we have not included the URLs for the Web Links in the book. If you are interested in visiting these sites, we recommend that you do so through the *Psychology Applied to Modern Life* home page at the Wadsworth Psychology website (academic.cengage.com/psychology/weiten). Links to all the recommended websites are maintained there, and the Wadsworth webmaster periodically updates the URLs. Of course, you can also use a search engine such as Google to locate the recommended websites.

Study Guide

The *Study Guide* that accompanies this text, written by William Addison of Eastern Illinois University, is an excellent resource designed to assist you in mastering the information contained in the book. It includes a wealth of review exercises to help you organize information and a self-test for assessing your content mastery. You should be able to purchase it at your college bookstore, or you can order it online at www.ichapters.com.

Personal Explorations Workbook

The *Personal Explorations Workbook* is a small booklet that contains interesting, thought-provoking experiential exercises for each text chapter. These exercises are designed to help you achieve personal insights. The Questionnaires are psychological tests or scales that you can take to see how you score on various traits discussed in the text. The Personal Probes consist of questions intended to help you think about issues in your personal life in relation to concepts and ideas discussed in the text. Many students find these exercises to be quite interesting, even fun. Hence, we encourage you to use the *Personal Explorations Workbook*. The exercises related to each chapter are listed at the end of each text chapter on the same page as the Practice Test.

A Concluding Note

We sincerely hope that you find this book enjoyable. If you have any comments or advice that might help us improve the next edition, please write to us in care of the publisher, Wadsworth Cengage Learning, 10 Davis Drive, Belmont, California 94002. There is a form in the back of the book that you can use to provide feedback. Finally, let us wish you good luck. We hope you enjoy your course and learn a great deal.

Wayne Weiten
Margaret A. Lloyd
Dana S. Dunn
Elizabeth Yost Hammer

Psychology Applied to Modern Life

ADJUSTMENT IN THE 21ST CENTURY

Adjusting to Modern Life

The immense Boeing 747 lumbers into position to accept its human cargo. The eager passengers-to-be scurry on board. In a tower a few hundred yards away, air traffic controllers diligently monitor radar screens, radio transmissions, and digital readouts of weather information. At the reservation desks in the airport terminal, clerks punch up the appropriate ticket information on their computer terminals and quickly process the steady stream of passengers. Mounted on the wall are video terminals displaying up-to-the-minute information on flight arrivals, departures, and delays. Back in the cockpit of the plane, the flight crew calmly scans the complex array of dials, meters, and lights to assess the aircraft's readiness for flight. In a few minutes, the airplane will slice into the cloudy, snow-laden skies above Chicago. In a little over three hours its passengers will be transported from the piercing cold of a Chicago winter to the balmy beaches of the Bahamas. Another everyday triumph for technology will have taken place.

The Paradox of Progress

LEARNING OBJECTIVES

▶ *Describe four examples of the paradox of progress.*

▶ *Explain what is meant by the paradox of progress and how theorists have explained it.*

We are the children of technology. We take for granted such impressive feats as transporting 300 people over 1500 miles in a matter of hours. After all, we live in a time of unparalleled progress. Our modern Western society has made extraordinary strides in transportation, energy, communication, agriculture, and medicine. Yet despite our technological progress, social problems and personal difficulties seem more prevalent and more prominent than ever before. This paradox is evident in many aspects of contemporary life, as seen in the following examples.

Point. Modern technology has provided us with countless time-saving devices—automobiles, telephones, vacuum cleaners, dishwashers, photocopiers, personal computers. Today, cell phones allow people to talk to friends or colleagues and battle rush hour at the same time. In a matter of seconds a personal computer can perform calculations that would take months if done by hand.

Counterpoint. Nonetheless, most of us complain about not having enough time. Our schedules overflow with appointments, commitments, and plans. Surveys suggest that a majority of people subjectively feel that they suffer from a *time famine*—that they have less and less time for themselves (Robinson & Godbey, 1997). Time has become such a precious commodity, one national survey found that 51% of the adult respondents would rather have more time than more money (Weil & Rosen, 1997). As social critic Jeremy Rifkin (1989) notes, "It is ironic in a culture so committed to saving time that we feel increasingly deprived of the very thing we value" (p. 19). Part of the problem is that in our modern society, work follows people home. Thus, Peter Whybrow (2005) comments, "citizens find themselves tethered to their jobs around the clock by the same nomadic tools—cell phones, pagers, wireless e-mail— that were heralded first as instruments of liberation" (p. 158). To deal with this time crunch, more and more people are cutting back on their sleep as they attempt to juggle work, family, and household responsibilities, leading noted sleep researcher William Dement to comment that "most Americans no longer know what it feels like to be fully alert" (Toufexis, 1990, p. 79). Sleep experts assert that American society suffers from an epidemic of sleep deprivation (Walsh, Dement, & Dinges, 2005). Unfortunately, research indicates that chronic sleep loss can have significant negative effects on individuals' daytime functioning, as well as their mental and physical health (Dinges, Rogers, & Baynard, 2005).

Point. Thanks in large part to technological advances, we live in extraordinary affluence. Undeniably, there are pockets of genuine poverty, but social critics, such as Paul Wachtel (1989), David Myers (2000), Gregg Easterbrook (2003), Paul Ransome (2005), and Peter Whybrow (2005) argue convincingly that in North America and Europe the middle and upper classes are larger and wealthier than ever before. Most of us take for granted things that were once considered luxuries, such as color television and air conditioning. People spend vast amounts of money on expensive automobiles, audio systems, computers, flat panel TVs, clothing, and vacations. In the late 1990s, the amount of money spent on luxury goods increased four times faster than overall spending (Frank, 1999). Wachtel quotes a New York museum director who asserts that "shopping is the chief cultural activity in the United States" (p. 23). Symptomatic of this trend, research suggests that many people in modern society are troubled by a *compulsive buying syndrome,* characterized by uncontrollable, impulsive, excessive shopping for things they don't need and often can't afford (Faber, 2003). One recent study estimated that 5%–6% of the U. S. population may have problems with this syndrome (Koran et al., 2006). Some clinical experts argue that compulsive buying should be viewed as a new psychiatric disorder (Hollander & Allen, 2006).

Counterpoint. In spite of this economic abundance, research suggests that most people do not feel very good about their financial well-being. For example, when one survey inquired about Americans' satisfaction with 13 aspects of their lives, the results showed that people were least satisfied with their finances (Myers, 2000). In his book titled *The High Price of Materialism,* Tim Kasser (2002) summarizes research showing that people who are especially concerned with money and possessions tend to report lower levels of happiness than others. Why are people so dissatisfied with their economic well-being? One problem is that advertising helps foster an insatiable thirst for consumption and the belief that material goods are the key to happiness (Kanner & Soule, 2004; Kasser et al., 2004). As Kasser

Life May Never Be the Same Again: Implications for Adjustment

The citizens of the United States received a gigantic wake-up call on September 11, 2001, in the form of the horrific, tragic terrorist attacks on the World Trade Center and the Pentagon. Life in the United States and much of the Western world may never be quite the same again. The specter of terrorism has psychological repercussions for virtually everyone in the United States (Danieli, Engdahl, & Schlenger, 2004; McCauley, 2007). People are upset over losing many things that they used to take for granted but have lost, such as being able to fly to a business meeting without a second thought, to pick up mail without worrying about contamination, to walk into a tall building without being searched, and to interact with strangers without being suspicious. They are angry about the injustice of it all, disgusted by the senseless violence, and anxious about what future terrorist attacks might bring. Above all else, Americans have lost their sense of invulnerability.

In light of the fundamental ways in which our lives have been changed, you might wonder whether the principal premise of this book—that the basic challenge of modern life is the quest for meaning and direction—might suddenly seem irrelevant. In reality, the situation is quite the opposite. Perhaps more than before, because of the threat of terrorism, people are questioning the meaning of their lives. Americans are wondering whether what they do matters, whether what they cherish is important, and whether what they have worked for has been worth it. The terrorist-induced jolt to our collective psyche has made the search for a sense of direction even more relevant to contemporary life.

That said, the threat of terrorism raises some important issues that an adjustment textbook should attempt to address. Fortunately, the field of psychology has much to contribute to the battle against terrorism (Bongar,

2007; Marsella, 2004). After all, terrorism is *psychological* warfare (Breckenridge & Zimbardo, 2007; Levant, Barbanel, & DeLeon, 2004). The goal of terrorism is to provoke psychological vulnerability and agitation in a population. The death, destruction, and havoc wreaked by terrorists is not an end in itself, but a means to an end—the creation of widespread anxiety, alarm, and panic.

In each chapter you will find boxes labeled "Living in Today's World" that address some of the adjustment issues raised by the threat of terrorism itself, related problems spawned by terrorism, and a variety of other challenges unique to our modern world. These boxes discuss such topics as how people tend to react to traumatic events, how people can cope more effectively with personal trauma, whether the government should promote marriage, how resilience can be enhanced in children, how workers can cope with unemployment, and other contemporary issues. We sincerely hope that this feature proves helpful.

(2004) puts it, "Everyday and in many ways people are bombarded with powerful, psychologically sophisticated proclamations that the good life is 'the goods life'" (p. 55). Thus, studies find that the gap between what people have and what they desire is greater in the material domain than in other areas of life (Solberg, Diener, & Robinson, 2004).

Point. The range of life choices available to people in modern societies has increased exponentially in recent

decades. For example, Barry Schwartz (2004) describes how a simple visit to a local supermarket can require a consumer to choose from 285 varieties of cookies, 61 suntan lotions, 150 lipsticks, and 175 salad dressings. Although increased choice is most tangible in the realm of consumer goods and services, Schwartz argues that it also extends into more significant domains of life. Today, people tend to have unprecedented opportunities to make choices about how they will be educated (e.g., vastly more flexible college curricula are available), how and where they will work (e.g., telecommuting presents employees with all sorts of new choices about how to accomplish their work), how their intimate relationships will unfold (e.g., people have increased freedom to delay marriage, cohabit, not have children, and so forth), and even how they will look (advances in plastic surgery have made personal appearance a matter of choice).

Counterpoint.   Although increased freedom of choice sounds attractive, Schwartz (2004) argues that the overabundance of choices in modern life has unexpected costs. He argues that people routinely make errors even when choosing among a handful of alternatives and that errors become much more likely when decisions become vastly more complex. And he explains how having more alternatives increases the potential for rumination, postdecision regret, and anticipated regret. Ultimately, he argues, the malaise associated with choice overload undermines individuals' happiness and contributes to depression. Consistent with this analysis, studies have found that the incidence of depressive disorders has increased dramatically—perhaps tenfold—over the last 50 years (Kessler, 2002). Average anxiety levels have also gone up substantially in recent decades (Twenge, 2000). It is hard to say whether choice overload is the chief culprit underlying these trends, but it is clear that increased freedom of choice has not resulted in enhanced tranquillity or improved mental health.

Point.   Modern technology has gradually provided us with unprecedented control over the world around us. Advances in agriculture have dramatically increased food production, and biotechnology advocates claim that genetically modified crops will make our food supply more reliable that ever before. Elaborate water supply systems, made up of hundreds of miles of canals, tunnels, and pipelines, along with dams, reservoirs, and pumping stations, permit massive metropolitan areas to grow in inhospitable deserts. Thanks to progress in medicine, doctors can reattach severed limbs, use lasers to correct microscopic defects in the eye, and even replace the human heart.

Counterpoint.   Unfortunately, modern technology has also had a devastating negative impact on the world around us, leading to environmental problems such as global warming, destruction of the ozone layer, deforestation, exhaustion of much of the world's fisheries, widespread air and water pollution, and extensive exposure of plants and animals to toxic chemicals (Oskamp, 2000). Many experts worry that in a few generations the earth's resources will be too depleted to sustain an adequate quality of life (Winter, 2004). To most people, these crises sound like technical problems that call for technological answers, but they are also behavioral problems in that they are fueled by overpopulation and overconsumption (Howard, 2000). In North America, the crucial problem is excessive consumption of the world's natural resources. For example, the United States houses 5% of the world's population but guzzles 25% of its commercial energy and fuel (Flavin & Dunn, 1999).

All these apparent contradictions reflect the same theme: *The technological advances of the past century, impressive though they may be, have not led to perceptible improvement in our collective health and happiness.* Indeed, many social critics argue that the quality of our lives and our sense of personal fulfillment have declined rather than increased. This is the paradox of progress.

Barry Schwartz argues that people in modern societies suffer from choice overload. He maintains that the endless choices people are presented with lead them to waste countless hours weighing trivial decisions and ruminating about whether their decisions were optimal.

What is the cause of this paradox? Many explanations have been offered. Erich Fromm (1963, 1981) has argued that the progress we value so much has scrambled our value systems and undermined our traditional sources of emotional security, such as family, community, and religion. Alvin Toffler (1970, 1980) attributes our collective alienation and distress to our being overwhelmed by rapidly accelerating cultural change. Robert Kegan (1994) maintains that the mental demands of modern life have become so complex, confusing, and contradictory that most of us are "in over our heads." Tim Kasser (2002) speculates that excessive materialism weakens the social ties that bind us, stokes the fires of insecurity, and undermines our collective sense of well-being. Micki McGee (2005) suggests that modern changes in gender roles, diminished job stability, and other social trends have fostered an obsession with self-improvement that ultimately undermines many individuals' sense of security and their satisfaction with their identity. According to McGee, our "makeover culture," nourishes the belief that we can all reinvent ourselves as needed, but this assumption can create tremendous pressures on people that "foster rather than quell their anxieties" (p. 17)).

Whatever the explanation, many theorists, working from varied perspectives, agree that *the basic challenge of modern life has become the search for meaning, a sense of direction, and a personal philosophy* (Dolby, 2005; Emmons, 2003; Naylor, Willimon, & Naylor, 1994; Sagiv, Roccas, & Hazan, 2004). This search involves struggling with such problems as forming a solid sense of identity, arriving at a coherent set of values, and developing a clear vision of a future that realistically promises fulfillment. Centuries ago, problems of this kind were probably much simpler. As we'll see in the next section, today it appears that many of us are floundering in a sea of confusion.

The Search for Direction

LEARNING OBJECTIVES
▶ *Provide some examples of people's search for direction.*
▶ *Describe four problems that are common to popular self-help books.*
▶ *Summarize advice about what to look for in quality self-help books.*
▶ *Summarize the philosophy underlying this textbook.*

We live in a time of unparalleled social and technological mutation. According to a number of social critics, the kaleidoscope of change that we see around us creates feelings of anxiety and uncertainty, which we try to alleviate by searching for a sense of direction. This search, which sometimes goes awry, manifests itself in many ways.

For example, we could discuss how hundreds of thousands of Americans have invested large sums of money to enroll in "self-realization" programs such as *est* training, Scientology, Silva Mind Control, John Gray's Mars and Venus relationship seminars, and Tony Robbins's Life Mastery seminars. These programs typically promise to provide profound enlightenment and quickly turn one's life around. Many participants claim that the programs have revolutionized their lives. However, most experts characterize such programs as intellectually bankrupt, and book and magazine exposés reveal them as simply lucrative money-making schemes (Behar, 1991; Pressman, 1993). In a particularly scathing analysis of these programs, Steve Salerno (2005) outlines the enormous financial benefits reaped by their inventors, such as Tony Robbins ($80 million in annual income), Dr. Phil ($20 million in annual income) and John Gray ($50,000 per speech). In his critique, Salerno also attacks the hypocrisy and inflated credentials of many leading self-help gurus. For example, he asserts that John Gray's doctorate came from a nonaccredited correspondence college; that Dr. Phil has a history of alleged marital infidelity and that some of his video segments are contrived to a degree that would make Jerry Springer proud; and that Dr. Laura is "a critic of premarital and extramarital sex who's indulged in both" (p. 44). More than anything else, the enormous success of these self-help gurus and self-realization programs demonstrates just how desperate some people are for a sense of direction and purpose in their lives.

We could also discuss how a host of unorthodox religious groups—commonly called *cults*—have attracted countless converts who voluntarily embrace a life of regimentation, obedience, and zealous ideology. One study suggested that more than 2 million young adults are involved with cults in the U.S. (Robinson, Frye, & Bradley, 1997). Most of these cults flourish in obscurity, unless bizarre incidents—such as the 1997 mass suicide of the Heaven's Gate cult near San Diego— attract public attention. It is widely believed that cults use brainwashing and mind control to seduce lonely outsiders, but in reality converts are a diverse array of normal people who are swayed by ordinary—albeit sophisticated—social-influence strategies (Baron, 2000;

There are many manifestations of our search for a sense of direction, including the emergence of cults, such as the Raelian UFO cult, and the astonishing popularity of "Dr. Laura."

Anthony, 1999; Zimbardo, 2002). According to Philip Zimbardo (1992), people join cults because these groups appear to provide simple solutions to complex problems, a sense of purpose, and a structured lifestyle that reduces feelings of uncertainty. Hunter (1998) emphasizes how alienation, identity confusion, and weak community ties make some people particularly vulnerable to seduction by cults.

And, if you would like a mundane, everyday example of people's search for direction, you need look no farther than your radio, where you will find that the hottest nationally syndicated personality is "Dr. Laura," who doles out advice to more than 15 million listeners a week over a network of nearly 300 stations. Even though only seven or eight people get through to her during each show, an astonishing 75,000 people call each day to seek her unique brand of blunt, outspoken, judgmental advice. Dr. Laura, who is not a psychologist or psychiatrist (her doctorate is in physiology), analyzes callers' problems in more of a moral than psychological framework. Unlike most therapists, she unabashedly preaches to her audience about how they ought to lead their lives. In many instances she is insulting and abusive to her callers, models remarkable intolerance, and provides terrible advice (Epstein, 2001). In an editorial in *Psychology Today*, Robert Epstein (2001) concludes that "no legitimate mental health professional would ever give the kind of hateful, divisive advice that Schlessinger doles out daily" (p. 5). Yet, the remarkable popularity of her highly prescriptive advice demonstrates once again that many people are eager for guidance and direction.

Although we might choose to examine any of these examples of people's search for a sense of direction, we will reserve our in-depth analysis for a manifestation of this search that is even more germane to our focus on everyday adjustment: the spectacular success of best-selling "self-help" books.

Self-Help Books

In 2003, Americans spent roughly $650 million on "self-help books" that offer do-it-yourself treatments for

---

Web Link 1.1 **Psychological Self-Help**

Clinical psychologist and professor Clayton E. Tucker-Ladd has spent some 25 years exploring how individuals can help themselves deal with personal issues and problems from a psychological perspective. Here he has assembled an online 12-chapter book, grounded in up-to-date research, that complements this textbook extremely well.
Note: The URLs (addresses) for the Web Links can be found on the website for this text (academic.cengage.com/psychology/weiten), or you can find them using a search engine such as Google.

common personal problems (Arkowitz & Lilienfeld, 2006). If you include self-help audiotapes, CDs, DVDs, software, Internet sites, lectures, seminars, and life coaching, self-improvement appears to be a $2.5 billion-a-year industry (McGee, 2005). This fascination with self-improvement is nothing new. For decades American readers have displayed a voracious appetite for self-help books such as *I'm OK—You're OK* (Harris, 1967), *Your Erroneous Zones* (Dyer, 1976), *How to Be Awake and Alive* (Newman & Berkowitz, 1976), *Living, Loving & Learning* (Buscaglia, 1982), *The Seven Habits of Highly Effective People* (Covey, 1989), *Men Are from Mars, Women Are from Venus* (Gray, 1992), *Ageless Body, Timeless Mind* (Chopra, 1993), *Don't Sweat the Small Stuff . . . and It's All Small Stuff* (Carlson, 1997), *Life Strategies* (McGraw, 1999), *Making Peace with Your Past* (Bloomfield, 2000), *Self-Nurture* (Domar & Dreher, 2000), and *The Purpose Driven Life* (Warren, 2002). With their simple recipes for achieving happiness, these books have generally not been timid about promising to change the quality of the reader's life. Consider the following excerpt from the back cover of a self-help book titled *Self Creation* (Weinberg, 1979):

More than any book ever written, Self Creation *shows you who you are and reveals the secret to controlling your own life. It contains an action blueprint built around a clear-cut principle as basic and revolutionary as the law of gravity. With it you will discover how to conquer bad habits, solve sexual problems, overcome depression and shyness, deal with infuriating people, be decisive, enhance your career, increase creativity. And it will show you how to love and be loved. You created you. Now you can start to reap the boundless benefits of self-confidence, self-reliance, self-determination with* Self Creation.

If only it were that easy! If only someone could hand you a book that would solve all your problems! Unfortunately, it is not that simple. Merely reading a book is not likely to turn your life around. If the consumption of these literary narcotics were even remotely as helpful as their publishers claim, we would be a na-

tion of serene, happy, well-adjusted people. It is clear, however, that serenity is not the dominant national mood. Quite the contrary, as already noted, in recent decades Americans' average anxiety level has moved upward (Twenge, 2000), and the prevalence of depression has increased as well (Kessler, 2002). The multitude of self-help books that crowd bookstore shelves represent just one more symptom of our collective distress and our search for the elusive secret of happiness.

The Value of Self-Help Books

It is somewhat unfair to lump all self-help books together for a critique, because they vary widely in quality (Fried & Schultis, 1995; Norcross et al., 2003). Surveys exploring psychotherapists' opinions of self-help books suggest that there are some excellent books that offer authentic insights and sound advice (Starker, 1990, 1992). Many therapists encourage their patients to read carefully selected self-help books (Campbell & Smith, 2003). A few books have even been tested in clinical trials with favorable results (Floyd, 2003; Gregory et al., 2004), although the studies have often had methodological weaknesses (Arkowitz & Lilienfeld, 2006). Thus, it would be foolish to dismiss all these books as shallow drivel. In fact, some of the better self-help books are highlighted in the Recommended Reading boxes that appear throughout this text. Unfortunately, however, the gems are easily lost in the

The newest rage in self-help books is The Secret, *written by Australian Rhonda Byrne, shown here at a* Time *magazine gala publicizing the magazine's selection of the 100 most influential people in the world. Byrne's (2006) book, DVD, and CDs have been flying off the shelves of American bookstores. The marketing campaign for the book has been absolutely brilliant (who can resist the opportunity to learn* the secret *to life?). What is Byrne's captivating thesis? The former television producer asserts that "Your current thoughts are creating your future life. What you think about the most or focus on the most will appear as your life" (p. 25). In other words, just think more about earning that "A" in Biochemistry, losing weight, or taking that expensive vacation, and events will go your way (no need to study, exercise, or save money). Characterized by psychologist John Norcross as "pseudoscientific, psychospiritual babble," (Adler, 2007),* The Secret *provides a remarkable demonstration of how seductive self-help books can be.*

Recommended READING

The Paradox of Choice: Why More Is Less
by Barry Schwartz (HarperCollins, 2004)

In *The Paradox of Choice,* Barry Schwartz argues that people in modern, affluent societies suffer a variety of negative consequences because they face an over-abundance of choices in their personal lives (see pp. 2–3). Schwartz recognizes that his argument seems counterintuitive, as most people cherish their freedom of choice. But he maintains that "the fact that *some* choice is good doesn't necessarily mean that *more* choice is better" (p. 3). In perhaps the most interesting part of the book, Schwartz outlines the differences between *maximizers* and *satisficers*. Maximizers need to feel confident that virtually every decision they make yields the best possible outcome. In contrast, satisficers are frequently willing to settle for outcomes that are good enough. He emphasizes that satisficers try to meet certain standards—sometimes very high standards—in making their decisions, but they do not feel compelled to select the *best* possible printer, mattress, vacation, and so forth. Although maximizing sounds like an admirable goal, Schwartz reports that high maximization scores are associated with reduced optimism and happiness and increased depression—and he raises doubts about whether maximizing tends to lead to better decisions.

Does Schwartz have a solution for the problem of excessive choice? Yes, his final chapter offers advice for making the overabundance of choices in our modern world less painful. Among other things, he suggests that people should (1) decide which choices really matter, (2) satisfice more and maximize less, (3) avoid rumination about decisions, (4) let go of decision regrets, and (5) recognize that constraints on choice can sometimes be liberating. Schwartz's writing is clear, concise, and engaging. The book is loaded with charming anecdotes that provide real-life examples of the issues discussed, but Schwartz's conclusions are based on research rather than anecdotal evidence. In the final analysis, *The Paradox of Choice* delivers an enticing two-for-one bargain: It is a thought-provoking essay in social criticism and a sound, realistic self-help book.

mountains of rubbish. A great many self-help books offer little of real value to the reader. Generally, they suffer from four fundamental shortcomings.

First, they are dominated by "psychobabble." The term *psychobabble*, coined by R. D. Rosen (1977), seems appropriate to describe the "hip" but hopelessly vague language used in many of these books. Statements such as "It's beautiful if you're unhappy," "You've got to get in touch with yourself," "You have to be up front," "You gotta be you 'cause you're you," and "You need a real high-energy experience" are typical examples of this language. At best, such terminology is ill-defined; at worst, it is meaningless. Consider the following example, taken from a question/answer booklet promoting *est* training:

The EST training doesn't change the content of anyone's life, nor does it change what anyone knows. It deals with the context or the way we hold the content. . . . Transformation occurs as a recontextualization. . . . "Getting it" means being able to discover when you have been maintaining (or are stuck with) a position which costs you more in aliveness than it is worth, realizing that you are the source of that position, and being able to choose to give up that position or hold it in a way that expands the quality of your life.

What exactly does this paragraph say? Who knows? The statements are so ambiguous and enigmatic that you can read virtually any meaning into them. Therein lies the problem with psychobabble; it is often so obscure as to be unintelligible. Clarity is sacrificed in favor of a hip jargon that prevents, rather than enhances, effective communication.

A second problem is that self-help books tend to place more emphasis on sales than on scientific soundness. The advice offered in these books is far too rarely based on solid, scientific research (Ellis, 1993; Paul, 2001; Rosen, 1987, 1993). Instead, the ideas are frequently based on the authors' intuitive analyses, which may be highly speculative. Even when books are based on well-researched therapeutic programs, interventions that are effective in clinical settings with professional supervision may not be effective when self-administered without professional guidance (Rosen, Glasgow, & Moore, 2003). Moreover, even when responsible authors provide scientifically valid advice and are careful not to mislead their readers, sales-hungry publishers routinely slap outrageous, irresponsible promises on the books' covers, often to the dismay of the authors (Rosen et al., 2003).

The third shortcoming is that self-help books don't usually provide explicit directions about how to change your behavior. These books tend to be smoothly written and "touchingly human" in tone. They often strike responsive chords in the reader by aptly describing a common problem that many of us experience. The reader says, "Yes, that's me!" Unfortunately, when the book focuses on how to deal with the problem, it usually provides only a vague distillation of simple common sense, which could be covered in 2 rather than 200 pages. These books often fall back on inspirational cheerleading in the absence of sound, explicit advice.

Fourth, many of these books encourage a remarkably self-centered approach to life (Justman, 2005). Although there are plenty of exceptions, the basic message in many self-help books is "Do whatever you feel like doing, and don't worry about the consequences for other people." According to McGee (2005), this mentality began to creep into books in the 1970s, as "bald proposals that one ought to 'look out for #1' or 'win through intimidation' marked a new ruthlessness in the self-help landscape" (p. 50). This "me first" philosophy emphasizes self-determined ethics and an exploitive approach to interpersonal relationships.

What to Look for in Self-Help Books

Because self-help books vary so widely in quality, it seems a good idea to provide you with some guidelines about what to look for in seeking genuinely helpful books. The following thoughts give you some criteria for judging books of this type.

1. Clarity in communication is essential. Advice won't do you much good if you can't understand it. Try to avoid drowning in the murky depths of psychobabble.

2. This may sound backward, but look for books that do not promise too much in the way of immediate change. The truly useful books tend to be appropriately cautious in their promises and realistic about the challenge of altering your behavior. As Arkowitz and Lilienfeld (2006, p. 79) put it, "Be wary of books that make promises that they obviously cannot keep, such as curing a phobia in five minutes or fixing a failing marriage in a week."

Web Link 1.2 **Quackwatch**

Stephen Barrett, a retired psychiatrist, has sought to alert the public to "health-related frauds, myths, fads, and fallacies" for over 30 years. This site offers no-holds-barred evaluations of Internet-based medical resources that Barrett and his board of scientific and technical advisers judge to be dubious, fraudulent, or dangerous to one's health.

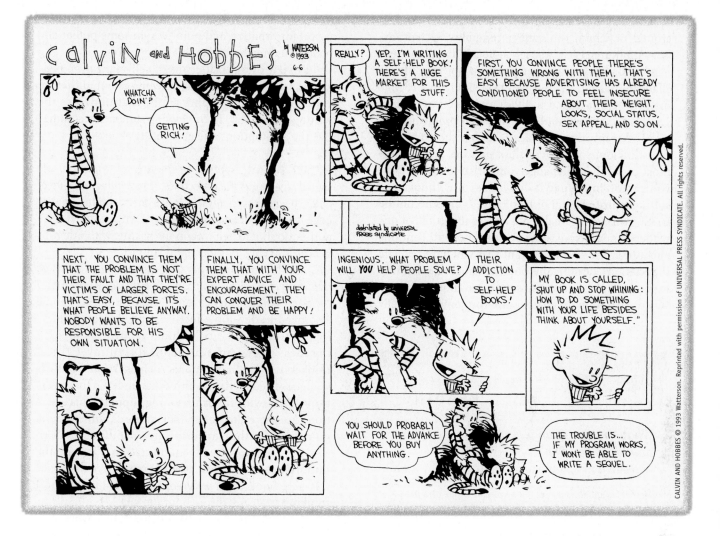

3. Try to check out the credentials of the author or authors. Book jackets will often exaggerate the expertise of authors, but these days a quick Internet search can often yield more objective biographical information and perhaps some perceptive reviews of the book.

4. Try to select books that mention, at least briefly, the theoretical or research basis for the program they advocate. It is understandable that you may not be interested in a detailed summary of research that supports a particular piece of advice. However, you should be interested in whether the advice is based on published research, widely accepted theory, anecdotal evidence, clinical interactions with patients, or pure speculation by the author. Books that are based on more than personal anecdotes and speculation should have a list of references in the back (or at the end of each chapter).

5. Look for books that provide detailed, explicit directions about how to alter your behavior. Generally, these directions represent the crucial core of the book. If they are inadequate in detail, you have been shortchanged.

6. More often than not, books that focus on a particular kind of problem, such as overeating, loneliness, or marital difficulties, deliver more than those that promise to cure all of life's problems with a few simple ideas. Books that cover everything are usually superficial and disappointing. Books that devote a great deal of thought to a particular topic tend to be written by authors with genuine expertise on that topic. Such books are more likely to pay off for you.

The Approach of This Textbook

Clearly, in spite of our impressive technological progress, we are a people beset by a great variety of personal problems. Living in our complex, modern society is a formidable challenge. This book is about that challenge. It is about you. It is about life. Specifically, it summarizes for you the scientific research on human behavior that appears relevant to the challenge of living effectively in contemporary society. It draws primarily, but not exclusively, from the science we call psychology.

This text deals with the same kinds of problems addressed by self-help books, self-realization programs, and Dr. Laura: anxiety, stress, interpersonal relationships, frustration, loneliness, depression, self-control. However, it makes no boldly seductive promises about solving your personal problems, turning your life around, or helping you achieve tranquility. Such promises simply aren't realistic. Psychologists have long recognized that changing a person's behavior is a difficult challenge, fraught with frustration and failure (Seligman, 1994). Troubled individuals sometimes spend years in therapy without resolving their problems.

This reality does not mean that you should be pessimistic about your potential for personal growth. You most certainly can change your behavior. Moreover, you can often change it on your own without consulting a professional psychologist. We would not be writing this text if we did not believe that some of our readers could derive some personal benefit from this encounter. But it is important that you have realistic expectations. Reading this book will not be a revelatory experience. No mysterious secrets are about to be unveiled. All this book can do is give you some potentially useful information and point you in some potentially beneficial directions. The rest is up to you.

In view of our criticisms of self-realization programs and self-help books, it seems essential that we explicitly lay out the philosophy that underlies the writing of this text. The following statements summarize the assumptions and goals of this book.

1. *This text is based on the premise that accurate knowledge about the principles of psychology can be of value to you in everyday life.* It has been said that knowledge is power. Greater awareness of why people behave as they do should help you in interacting with others as well as in trying to understand yourself.

2. *This text attempts to foster a critical attitude about psychological issues and to enhance your critical thinking skills.* Information is important, but people also need to develop effective strategies for evaluating information. Critical thinking involves subjecting ideas to systematic, skeptical scrutiny. Critical thinkers ask tough questions, such as: What exactly is being asserted? What assumptions underlie this assertion? What evidence or reasoning supports this assertion? Are there alternative explanations? Some general guidelines for thinking critically are outlined in **Figure 1.1**. We have already attempted to illustrate the importance of a critical attitude in our evaluation of self-help books, and we'll continue to model critical thinking strategies throughout the text.

3. *This text should open doors.* The coverage in this book is broad; we tackle many topics. Therefore, in some places it may lack the depth or detail that you would like. However, you should think of it as a resource book that can introduce you to other books or techniques or therapies, which you can then pursue on your own.

4. *This text assumes that the key to effective adjustment is to take charge of your own life.* If you are dissatisfied with some aspect of your life, it does no good to sit around and mope about it. You have to take an active role in attempting to improve the quality of your life. Doing so may involve learning a new skill or pursuing a particular kind of help. In any case, it is generally best to meet problems head-on rather than trying to avoid them.

Recommended READING

What You Can Change and What You Can't
by Martin E. P. Seligman (Knopf, 1994)

Martin Seligman is a prominent psychologist who has conducted influential research on learned helplessness, attributional style, optimism, depression, and phobias. He is also one of the chief architects of the new positive psychology movement (see Chapter 3). In this book he synthesizes research on a variety of issues to help people understand what they can and cannot change about themselves. Seligman points out that self-improvement programs of all types—from meditation, to self-help books, to professional therapy—are predicated on the assumption that people can permanently change themselves for the better. He notes, however, that recent, highly publicized research in biological psychiatry is at odds with this assumption. This research suggests that personality, intelligence, physique, and vulnerability to psychological disorders are predominantly determined by genetic inheritance and hence are largely unchangeable. Seligman asserts that both viewpoints are too extreme—that the architects of self-improvement programs are too optimistic while the authorities on biological psychiatry are too pessimistic about people's capacity for change. Thus, he sets out to review the empirical evidence on what can be modified with reasonable success, and what can't be. Seligman covers such wide-ranging topics as treatments for sexual difficulties, alcoholism, weight problems, anxiety, depression, obsessions, and posttraumatic stress syndrome. His discussions are lively, readable, objective, sophisticated, and thoroughly grounded in research.

Web Link 1.3 **Foundation for Critical Thinking**

How can students best develop those skills that go beyond merely acquiring information to actively weighing and judging information? The many resources of the Foundation for Critical Thinking at Sonoma State University are directed primarily toward teachers at every level to help them develop their students' critical thinking abilities.

Guidelines for Thinking Critically

1 **Ask questions; be willing to wonder.** To think critically you must be willing to think creatively — that is, to be curious about the puzzles of human behavior, to wonder why people act the way they do, and to question conventional explanations and examine new ones.

2 **Define the problem.** Identify the issues involved in clear and concrete terms, rather than vague generalities such as "happiness," "potential," or "meaningfulness." What does meaningfulness mean, exactly?

3 **Examine the evidence.** Consider the nature of the evidence that supports all aspects of the problem under examination. Is it reliable? Valid? Is it someone's personal assertion or speculation? Does the evidence come from one or two narrow studies, or from repeated research?

4 **Analyze biases and assumptions** — your own and those of others. What prejudices, deeply held values, and other personal biases do you bring to your evaluation of a problem? Are you willing to consider evidence that contradicts your beliefs? Be sure you can identify the bias of others, in order to evaluate their arguments as well.

5 **Avoid emotional reasoning** ("If I feel this way, it must be true"). Remember that everyone holds convictions and ideas about how the world should operate and that your opponents are as serious about their convictions as you are about yours. Feelings are important, but they should not substitute for careful appraisal of arguments and evidence.

6 **Don't oversimplify.** Look beyond the obvious. Reject simplistic, either-or thinking. Look for logical contradictions in arguments. Be wary of "arguments by anecdote."

7 **Consider other interpretations.** Before you leap to conclusions, think about other explanations. Be especially careful about assertions of cause and effect.

8 **Tolerate uncertainty.** This may be the hardest step in becoming a critical thinker, for it requires the ability to accept some guiding ideas and beliefs — yet the willingness to give them up when evidence and experience contradict them.

Figure1.1

Guidelines for thinking critically. Critical thinking should not be equated with criticism; it's not a matter of learning how to tear down others' ideas. Rather, critical thinkers carefully subject others' ideas — and their own — to careful, systematic, objective evaluation. The guidelines shown here, taken from Wade and Tavris (1990), provide a succinct overview of what it means to think critically.

From Wade, C., & Tavris, C. (1990). *Learning to Think Critically: A Handbook to Accompany Psychology.* New York: Harper & Row. Copyright © 1990 by Harper & Row Publishers, Inc. Reprinted by permission of Pearson Education, Inc.

The Psychology of Adjustment

LEARNING OBJECTIVES

► *Describe the two key facets of psychology.*

► *Explain the concept of adjustment.*

Now that we have spelled out our approach in writing this text, it is time to turn to the task of introducing you to some basic concepts. In this section, we'll discuss the nature of psychology and the concept of adjustment.

What Is Psychology?

Psychology **is the science that studies behavior and the physiological and mental processes that underlie it, and it is the profession that applies the accumulated knowledge of this science to practical problems.** Psychology leads a complex dual existence as both a *science* and a *profession.* Let's examine the science first. Psychology is an area of scientific study, much like biology or physics. Whereas biology focuses on life processes and physics focuses on matter and energy, psychology focuses on *behavior* and *related mental and physiological processes.*

Behavior **is any overt (observable) response or activity by an organism.** Psychology does *not* confine itself to the study of human behavior. Many psycholo-

gists believe that the principles of behavior are much the same for all animals, including humans. As a result, these psychologists often prefer to study animals — mainly because they can exert more control over the factors influencing the animals' behavior.

Psychology is also interested in the mental processes — the thoughts, feelings, and wishes — that accompany behavior. Mental processes are more difficult to study than behavior because they are private and not directly observable. However, they exert critical influence over human behavior, so psychologists have strived to improve their ability to "look inside the mind."

Finally, psychology includes the study of the physiological processes that underlie behavior. Thus, some psychologists try to figure out how bodily processes such as neural impulses, hormonal secretions, and genetic coding regulate behavior.

Practically speaking, all this means that psychologists study a great variety of phenomena. Psychologists are interested in maze running in rats, salivation in dogs, and brain functioning in cats, as well as visual perception in humans, play in children, and social interaction in adults.

As you probably know, psychology is not all pure science. It has a highly practical side, represented by the many psychologists who provide a variety of professional services to the public. Although the profession of psychology is quite prominent today, this aspect of psychology was actually slow to develop. Until the 1950s psychologists were found almost exclusively in the halls of academia, teaching and doing research. However, the demands of World War II in the 1940s stimulated rapid growth in psychology's first professional specialty—clinical psychology. *Clinical psychology* **is the branch of psychology concerned with the diagnosis and treatment of psychological problems and disorders.** During World War II, a multitude of academic psychologists were pressed into service as clinicians to screen military recruits and treat soldiers suffering from trauma. Many found their clinical work interesting and returned from the war to set up training programs to meet the continued high demand for clinical services. Soon, about half of the new Ph.D.'s in psychology were specializing in clinical work. Psychology had come of age as a profession.

What Is Adjustment?

We have used the term *adjustment* several times without clarifying its exact meaning. The concept of adjustment was originally borrowed from biology. It was modeled after the biological term *adaptation,* which refers to efforts by a species to adjust to changes in its environment. Just as a field mouse has to adapt to an unusually brutal winter, a person has to adjust to changes in circumstances such as a new job, a financial setback, or the loss of a loved one. Thus, *adjustment* **refers to the psychological processes through which people manage or cope with the demands and challenges of everyday life.**

The demands of everyday life are diverse, so in studying the process of adjustment we will encounter a broad variety of topics. In the first section of this book, "The Dynamics of Adjustment," we discuss general issues, such as how personality affects people's patterns of adjustment, how individuals are affected by stress, and how they use coping strategies to deal with stress. In the second section, "The Interpersonal Realm," we examine the adjustments that people make in their social relationships, exploring such topics as individuals' perceptions of others, interpersonal communication, behavior in groups, friendship, and intimate relationships. In the third section, "Developmental Transitions," we look at how individuals adjust to changing demands as they grow older. We discuss such topics as the development of gender roles, the emergence of sexuality, phases of adult development, and transitions in the world of work. Finally, in the fourth section, "Mental and Physical Health," we discuss how the process of adjustment influences a person's psychological and physical wellness.

As you can see, the study of adjustment delves into nearly every corner of people's lives, and we'll be discussing a diverse array of issues and topics. Before we begin considering these topics in earnest, however, we need to take a closer look at psychology's approach to investigating behavior—the scientific method.

The Scientific Approach to Behavior

LEARNING OBJECTIVES
▶ *Explain the nature of empiricism.*
▶ *Explain two advantages of the scientific approach to understanding behavior.*
▶ *Describe the experimental method, distinguishing between independent and dependent variables and between experimental and control groups.*

▶ *Distinguish between positive and negative correlation and explain what the size of a correlation coefficient means.*
▶ *Describe three correlational research methods.*
▶ *Compare the advantages and disadvantages of experimental versus correlational research.*

We all expend a great deal of effort in trying to understand our own behavior as well as the behavior of others. We wonder about any number of behavioral questions: Why am I so anxious when I interact with new people? Why is Sam always trying to be the center of attention at the office? Why does Joanna cheat on her wonderful husband? Are extraverts happier than introverts? Is depression more common during the Christmas holidays? Given that psychologists' principal goal is to explain behavior, how are their efforts different from everyone else's? The key difference is that psychology is a *science,* committed to *empiricism.*

The Commitment to Empiricism

Empiricism **is the premise that knowledge should be acquired through observation.** When we say that scientific psychology is empirical, we mean that its conclusions are based on systematic observation rather than on reasoning, speculation, traditional beliefs, or common sense. Scientists are not content with having ideas that sound plausible; they must conduct research to *test* their ideas. Whereas our everyday speculations are informal, unsystematic, and highly subjective, scientists' investigations are formal, systematic, and objective.

In these investigations, scientists formulate hypotheses (the ideas they want to test), gather data (make observations) relevant to their hypotheses, use statistics to analyze these data, and report their results to the public and other scientists, typically by publishing their findings in a technical journal. The process of publishing scientific studies allows other experts to evaluate and critique new research findings.

Advantages of the Scientific Approach

Science is certainly not the only method that can be used to draw conclusions about behavior. We can also turn to logic, casual observation, and good old-fashioned common sense. Because the scientific method often requires painstaking effort, it seems reasonable to ask: What exactly are the advantages of the empirical approach?

The scientific approach offers two major advantages. The first is its clarity and precision. Commonsense notions about behavior tend to be vague and ambiguous. Consider the old truism "Spare the rod and spoil the child." What does this generalization about childrearing amount to? How severely should children be punished if parents are not to "spare the rod"? How do parents assess whether a child qualifies as "spoiled"? Such statements can have different meanings to different people. When people disagree about this assertion, it may be because they are talking about entirely different things. In contrast, the empirical approach requires that scientists specify *exactly* what they are talking about when they formulate hypotheses. This clarity and precision enhance communication about important ideas.

The second advantage offered by the scientific approach is its relative intolerance of error. Scientists subject their ideas to empirical tests. They also scrutinize one another's findings with a critical eye. They demand objective data and thorough documentation before they accept ideas. When the findings of two studies conflict, they try to figure out why the studies reached different conclusions, usually by conducting additional research. In contrast, common sense and casual observation often tolerate contradictory generalizations, such as "Opposites attract" and "Birds of a feather flock together." Furthermore, commonsense analyses involve little effort to verify ideas or detect errors, so that many myths about behavior come to be widely believed.

All this is not to say that science has a copyright on truth. However, the scientific approach does tend to yield more accurate and dependable information than casual analyses and armchair speculation. Knowledge of empirical data can thus provide a useful benchmark against which to judge claims and information from other kinds of sources.

Now that we have an overview of how the scientific enterprise works, we can look at some of the specific research methods that psychologists depend on most. The two main types of research methods in psychology are *experimental* and *correlational*. We discuss them separately because there is an important distinction between them.

Experimental Research: Looking for Causes

Does misery love company? This question intrigued social psychologist Stanley Schachter. When people feel anxious, do they want to be left alone, or do they prefer to have others around? Schachter's hypothesis was that increases in anxiety would cause increases in the desire to be with others, which psychologists call the *need for affiliation*. To test this hypothesis, Schachter (1959) designed a clever experiment. **The *experiment* is a research method in which the investigator manipulates one (independent) variable under carefully controlled conditions and observes whether any changes occur in a second (dependent) variable as a result.** Psychologists depend on this method more than any other.

Independent and Dependent Variables

An experiment is designed to find out whether changes in one variable (let's call it x) cause changes in another variable (let's call it y). To put it more concisely, we want to know how x affects y. In this formulation, we refer to x as the independent variable, and we call y the dependent variable. **An *independent variable* is a condition or event that an experimenter varies in order to see its impact on another variable.** The independent variable is the variable that the experimenter controls or manipulates. It is hypothesized to have some effect on the dependent variable. The experiment is conducted to verify this effect. **The *dependent variable* is the variable that is thought to be affected by the manipulations of the independent variable.** In psychology studies, the dependent variable usually is a measurement of some aspect of the subjects' behavior.

In Schachter's experiment, *the independent variable was the participants' anxiety level*, which he manipulated in the following way. Subjects assembled in his laboratory were told by a Dr. Zilstein that they would be participating in a study on the physiological effects of electric shock and that they would receive a series of shocks. Half of the participants were warned that the shocks would be very painful. They made up the *high-anxiety* group. The other half of the participants, assigned to the *low-anxiety* group, were told that the shocks would be mild and painless. These procedures were simply intended to evoke different levels of anxiety. In reality, no one was actually shocked at any time. Instead, the experimenter indicated that there would be a delay while he prepared the shock apparatus for use. The participants were asked whether they would prefer to wait alone or in the company of others. *This measure of the subjects' desire to affiliate with others was the dependent variable.*

Experimental and Control Groups

To conduct an experiment, an investigator typically assembles two groups of participants who are treated differently in regard to the independent variable. We call these groups the experimental and control groups. **The *experimental group* consists of the subjects who receive some special treatment in regard to the independent variable. The *control group* consists of similar subjects who do not receive the special treatment given to the experimental group.**

Let's return to the Schachter study to illustrate. In this study, the participants in the high-anxiety condition were the experimental group. They received a special treatment designed to create an unusually high level of anxiety. The participants in the low-anxiety condition were the control group.

It is crucial that the experimental and control groups be similar except for the different treatment they receive in regard to the independent variable. This stipulation brings us to the logic that underlies the experimental method. If the two groups are alike in all respects *except for the variation created by the manipulation of the independent variable,* then any differences between the two groups on the dependent variable *must be due to this manipulation of the independent variable.* In this way researchers isolate the effect of the independent variable on the dependent variable. In his experiment, Schachter isolated the impact of anxiety on need for affiliation. What did he find? As predicted, he found that increased anxiety led to increased affiliation. The percentage of people who wanted to wait with others was nearly twice as high in the high-anxiety group as in the low-anxiety group.

The logic of the experimental method rests heavily on the assumption that the experimental and control groups are alike in all important matters except for their different treatment with regard to the independent variable. Any other differences between the two groups cloud the situation and make it difficult to draw solid conclusions about the relationship between the independent variable and the dependent variable. To summarize our discussion of the experimental method, **Figure 1.2** provides an overview of the vari-

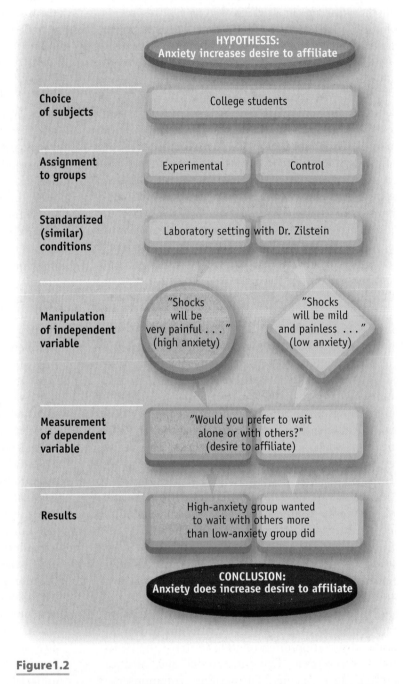

Figure1.2

The basic elements of an experiment. This diagram provides an overview of the key features of the experimental method, as illustrated by Schachter's study of anxiety and affiliation. The logic of the experiment rests on treating the experimental and control groups alike except for the manipulation of the independent variable.

ous elements in an experiment, using Schachter's study as an example.

Advantages and Disadvantages

The experiment is a powerful research method. Its principal advantage is that it allows scientists to draw conclusions about cause-and-effect relationships between variables. Researchers can draw these conclusions about causation because the precise control available in the experiment permits them to isolate the relationship between the independent variable and the dependent variable. No other research method can duplicate this advantage.

For all its power, however, the experimental method has its limitations. One disadvantage is that researchers are often interested in the effects of variables that cannot be manipulated (as independent variables) because of ethical concerns or practical realities. For example, you might want to know whether being brought up in an urban area as opposed to a rural area affects people's values. A true experiment would require you to assign similar families to live in urban and rural areas, which obviously is impossible to do. To explore this question, you would have to use correlational research methods, which we turn to next.

Correlational Research: Looking for Links

As we just noted, in some situations psychologists cannot exert experimental control over the variables they want to study. In such situations, all a researcher can do is make systematic observations to see whether a link or association exists between the variables of interest. Such an association is called a correlation. **A *correlation* exists when two variables are related to each other.** The definitive aspect of correlational studies is that the researchers cannot control the variables under study.

Measuring Correlation

The results of correlational research are often summarized with a statistic called the *correlation coefficient.*

Web Link 1.4 **Research Methods Tutorials**

Bill Trochim's classes in research and program design at Cornell University have assembled tutorial guides for undergraduate and graduate students for more than 50 topics at this subpage of the Web Center for Social Research Methods. Students new to research design may find these tutorials particularly helpful.

We'll be referring to this widely used statistic frequently as we discuss studies throughout the remainder of this text. **A *correlation coefficient* is a numerical index of the degree of relationship that exists between two variables.** A correlation coefficient indicates (1) how strongly related two variables are and (2) the direction (positive or negative) of the relationship.

Two kinds of relationships can be described by a correlation. A *positive* correlation indicates that two variables co-vary in the same direction. This means that high scores on variable x are associated with high scores on variable y and that low scores on variable x are associated with low scores on variable y. For example, there is a positive correlation between high school grade point average (GPA) and subsequent college GPA. That is, people who do well in high school tend to do well in college, and those who perform poorly in high school tend to perform poorly in college (see **Figure 1.3**).

In contrast, a *negative* correlation indicates that two variables co-vary in the opposite direction. This means that people who score high on variable x tend to score low on variable y, whereas those who score low on x tend to score high on y. For example, in most college courses, there is a negative correlation between how frequently a student is absent and how well the student performs on exams. Students who have a high number of absences tend to earn low exam scores, while students who have a low number of absences tend to get higher exam scores (see **Figure 1.3**).

While the positive or negative sign indicates whether an association is direct or inverse, the *size* of the coefficient indicates the *strength* of the association between

Figure 1.3

Positive and negative correlations. Variables are positively correlated if they tend to increase and decrease together and are negatively correlated if one variable tends to increase when the other decreases. Hence, the terms *positive correlation* and *negative correlation* refer to the *direction* of the relationship between two variables.

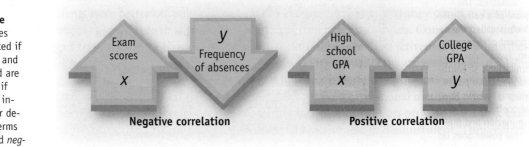

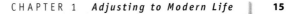

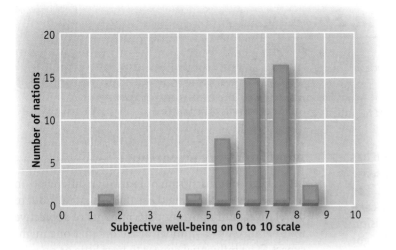

Figure1.9

The subjective well-being of nations. Veenhoven (1993) combined the results of almost 1000 surveys to calculate the average subjective well-being reported by representative samples from 43 nations. The mean happiness scores clearly pile up at the positive end of the distribution, with only two scores falling below the neutral point of 5. (Data adapted from Diener and Diener, 1996)

being very poor can make people unhappy, but once people ascend above the poverty level, there is little relation between income and happiness. On the average, even very wealthy people are only marginally happier than those in the middle classes. One reason for this weak association is that a disconnect seems to exist between actual income and how people feel about their financial situation. Recent research (Johnson & Krueger, 2006) suggests that the correlation between actual wealth and people's subjective perceptions of whether they have enough money to meet their needs is surprisingly modest (around .30).

Another problem with money is that in this era of voracious consumption, rising income contributes to escalating material desires (Frey & Stutzer, 2002). When these growing material desires outstrip what people can afford, dissatisfaction is likely (Solberg et al., 2002). Thus, complaints about not having enough money are routine even among people who earn hefty six-figure incomes. Interestingly, there is some evidence that people who place an especially strong emphasis on the pursuit of wealth and materialistic goals tend to be somewhat less happy than others (Ryan & Deci, 2001; Van Boven, 2005). Perhaps they are so fo-

cused on financial success that they derive less satisfaction from other aspects of their lives (Nickerson et al, 2003). Consistent with this view, a recent study (Kahneman et al., 2006) found that higher income was associated with working longer hours and allocating fewer hours to leisure pursuits (see **Figure 1.10**). Insofar as money does foster happiness, it appears to do so by reducing the negative impact of life's setbacks, allowing wealthier people to feel like they have a little more control over their lives (Johnson & Krueger, 2006; Smith et al., 2005).

Age. Age and happiness are consistently found to be unrelated (Lykken, 1999). Age accounts for less than 1% of the variation in people's happiness (Inglehart, 1990; Myers & Diener, 1997). The key factors influencing subjective well-being may shift some as people grow older—work becomes less important, health more so—but people's average level of happiness tends to remain remarkably stable over the life span.

Gender. Women are treated for depressive disorders about twice as often as men (Nolen-Hoeksema, 2002), so one might expect that women are less happy on the

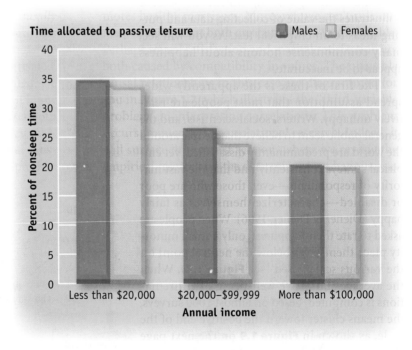

Figure1.10

Income and leisure. In an influential study of happiness, Nobel laureate Daniel Kahneman and his colleagues (2006) attempted to shed light on why the association between income and subjective well-being is so weak. One of their key findings was that as income goes up, the time devoted to work increases, and hence, the time left for leisure declines. This graph shows the percentage of nonsleep time devoted to passive leisure activities for three levels of income. (Data from Kahneman et al., 2006)

average. And Lykken (1999) notes that "men still tend to have better jobs than women do, and get higher pay for the same jobs . . . but they [women] report well-being levels as high as those of men" (p. 181). Thus, like age, gender accounts for less than 1% of the variation in people's subjective well-being (Myers, 1992).

Parenthood.   Children can be a tremendous source of joy and fulfillment, but they can also be a tremendous source of headaches and hassles. Compared to childless couples, parents worry more and experience more marital problems (Argyle, 1987). Apparently, the good and bad aspects of parenthood balance each other out, because the evidence indicates that people who have children are neither more nor less happy than people without children (Argyle, 2001).

Intelligence.   Intelligence is a highly valued trait in modern society, but researchers have not found an association between IQ scores and happiness (Diener, 1984). Educational attainment also appears to be unrelated to life satisfaction (Ross & Van Willigen, 1997).

Physical attractiveness.   Good-looking people enjoy a variety of advantages in comparison to unattractive people. Given that physical attractiveness is an important resource in Western society, we might expect attractive people to be happier than others, but the available data indicate that the correlation between attractiveness and happiness is negligible (Diener, Wolsic, & Fujita, 1995).

What Is Somewhat Important?

Research has identified three facets of life that appear to have a moderate impact on subjective well-being: health, social activity, and religious belief.

Health.   Good physical health would seem to be an essential requirement for happiness, but people adapt to health problems. Research reveals that individuals who develop serious, disabling health conditions aren't as unhappy as one might guess (Myers, 1992; Riis et al., 2005). Good health may not, by itself, produce happiness, because people tend to take good health for granted. Such considerations may help explain why researchers find only a moderate positive correlation (average = .32) between health status and subjective well-being (Argyle, 1999).

Social activity.   Humans are social animals, and people's interpersonal relations *do* appear to contribute to their happiness. People who are satisfied with their friendship networks and who are socially active report

above-average levels of happiness (Diener & Seligman, 2004; Myers, 1999). And people who score as exceptionally happy tend to report greater satisfaction with their social relations than others (Diener & Seligman, 2002).

Religion.   The link between religiosity and subjective well-being is modest, but a number of surveys suggest that people with heartfelt religious convictions are more likely to be happy than people who characterize themselves as nonreligious (Abdel-Khalek, 2006; Argyle, 1999; Ferriss, 2002). Researchers aren't sure how religious faith fosters happiness, but Myers (1992) offers some interesting conjectures. Among other things, he discusses how religion can give people a sense of purpose and meaning in their lives, help them accept their setbacks gracefully, connect them to a caring, supportive community, and comfort them by putting their ultimate mortality in perspective.

Recommended
READING

The Pursuit of Happiness
by David G. Myers (William Morrow, 1992)

The Pursuit of Happiness provides a thorough, accurate review of empirical research on the determinants of happiness, seasoned nicely with personal anecdotes and low-key, practical advice. Myers is a respected social psychologist and hard-nosed scientist who acknowledges that his reflections on happiness are "colored by Christian values and spirituality." Emphasizing the finding that objective circumstances have limited impact on happiness, Myers discusses how people might alter their subjective assessments of their lives to foster greater happiness. Working from the insight that happiness is relative, he offers suggestions for managing our comparisons to others and restraining our expectations to enhance our well-being.

Myers's book is a superb example of what self-help books could and should be, but rarely are. It is clearly written and appropriately cautious about the limits of our knowledge. It is carefully documented, and assertions are closely tied to research and theory. The author's conjectures—which are often fascinating—are accurately presented as learned speculation rather than scientific fact, and readers are encouraged to think for themselves. Complicated issues are not reduced to sound bites and bumper sticker slogans. Myers does not encourage a self-centered approach to life (quite the opposite!), nor does he offer simple prescriptions about how to live. Given these realities, *The Pursuit of Happiness* has not topped any best-seller lists, but it is well worth reading.

What Is Very Important?

The list of factors that turn out to be very important ingredients of happiness is surprisingly short. Only a few variables are strongly related to overall happiness.

Love and marriage. Romantic relationships can be stressful, but people consistently rate being in love as one of the most critical ingredients of happiness (Myers, 1999). Furthermore, although people complain a lot about their marriages, the evidence indicates that marital status is a key correlate of happiness. Among both men and women, married people are happier than people who are single or divorced (see **Figure 1.11**; Myers & Diener, 1995) and this relationship holds around the world in widely different cultures (Diener et al., 2000). However, the causal relations underlying this correlation are unclear. It may be that happiness causes marital satisfaction more than marital satisfaction promotes happiness. Perhaps people who are happy tend to have better intimate relationships and more stable marriages, while people who are unhappy have greater difficulty finding and keeping mates.

Work. Given the way people often complain about their jobs, we might not expect work to be a key source of happiness, but it is. Although less critical than love and marriage, job satisfaction is strongly associated with general happiness (Warr, 1999). Studies also show that unemployment has strong negative effects on subjective well-being (Lucas et al., 2004). It is difficult to sort out whether job satisfaction causes happiness or vice versa, but evidence suggests that causation flows both ways (Argyle, 2001).

Genetics and personality. The best predictor of individuals' future happiness is their past happiness (Diener & Lucas, 1999). Some people seem destined to be happy and others unhappy, regardless of their triumphs or setbacks. The limited influence of life events was highlighted in a fascinating study that found only modest differences in overall happiness between recent lottery winners and recent accident victims who became quadriplegics (Brickman, Coates, & Janoff-Bulman, 1978). Investigators were amazed that extremely fortuitous and horrible events like these didn't have a dramatic impact on happiness. Actually, *several* lines of evidence suggest that happiness does not depend on external circumstances—buying a nice house, getting promoted—as much as on internal factors, such as one's outlook on life (Lykken & Tellegen, 1996; Lyubomirsky, Sheldon, & Schkade, 2005).

With this reality in mind, researchers have investigated whether there might be a hereditary basis for variations in happiness. These studies suggest that people's genetic predispositions account for a substantial portion of the variance in happiness, perhaps as much as 50% (Lyubomirsky et al., 2005; Stubbe et al., 2005). How can one's genes influence one's happiness? Presumably, by shaping one's temperament and personality, which are known to be highly heritable. Hence, researchers have begun to look for links between personality and subjective well-being, and they have found some relatively strong correlations. For example, *extraversion* (sometimes referred to as *positive emotionality*) is one of the better predictors of happiness. People who are outgoing, upbeat, and sociable tend to be happier than others (Fleeson, Malanos, & Achille, 2002). Additional personality correlates of happiness include high

Figure1.11

Happiness and marital status. This graph shows the percentage of adults characterizing themselves as "very happy" as a function of marital status. Among both women and men, happiness shows up more in those who are married as opposed to those who are separated, who are divorced, or who have never married. These data and many other findings suggest that marital satisfaction is a key ingredient of happiness.

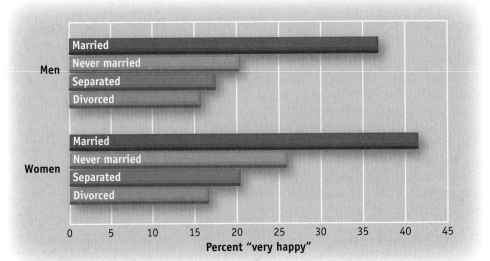

Adapted from Myers, D. G. (1999). Close relationships and quality of life. In D. Kahneman, E. Diener, & N. Schwarz (Eds.), *Well-being: The foundations of hedonic psychology*. New York: Russell Sage Foundation. Copyright © 1999. Reprinted by permission of the Russell Sage Foundation.

Research on the correlates of happiness suggests that two key ingredients of happiness are a rewarding work life and satisfaction in intimate relationships.

self-esteem and optimism (Lucas, Diener, & Suh, 1996; Lyubomirsky, Tkach, & DiMatteo, 2006).

Conclusions

We must be cautious in drawing inferences about the causes of happiness, because most of the available data are correlational data (see **Figure 1.12**). Nonetheless, the empirical evidence suggests that many popular beliefs about the sources of happiness are unfounded. The data also demonstrate that happiness is shaped by a complex constellation of variables. Despite this complexity, however, a number of worthwhile insights about human adjustment can be gleaned from research on the correlates of subjective well-being.

First, research on happiness demonstrates that the determinants of subjective well-being are precisely that: subjective. *Objective realities are not as important as subjective feelings.* In other words, your health, your wealth, your job, and your age are not as influential as how you *feel* about your health, wealth, job, and age (Schwarz & Strack, 1999).

Second, *when it comes to happiness, everything is relative* (Argyle, 1999; Hagerty, 2000). In other words, you evaluate what you have relative to what the people around you have. Thus, people who are wealthy assess what they have by comparing themselves with their wealthy friends and neighbors. This is one reason for the low correlation between wealth and happiness. You might have a lovely home, but if it sits next to a neighbor's palatial mansion, it might be a source of more dissatisfaction than happiness. People's evaluations are also made relative to their *expectations*. Research suggests that bad outcomes feel worse when unexpected than when expected, while good outcomes feel better when unexpected than when expected (Shepperd & McNulty, 2002). Thus, the same objective event, such as a pay raise of $2000 annually, may generate positive feelings in someone who wasn't expecting a raise and

negative feelings in someone expecting a much larger increase.

Third, *research on happiness has shown that people are surprisingly bad at predicting what will make them happy.* We assume that we know what is best for us and that we can accurately forecast our emotional reactions to future events, but scores of studies suggest otherwise (Gilbert, 2006; Hsee & Hastie, 2005; Wilson & Gilbert, 2005). People routinely overestimate the pleasure that they will derive from buying an expensive automobile, taking an exotic vacation, earning an important promotion, moving to a beautiful coastal city, or building their dream home. Likewise, people tend to overestimate the misery and regret that they will experience if

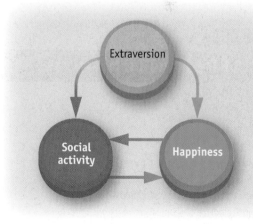

Figure 1.12

Possible causal relations among the correlates of happiness. Although we have considerable data on the correlates of happiness, it is difficult to untangle the possible causal relationships. For example, we know that a moderate positive correlation exists between social activity and happiness, but we can't say for sure whether high social activity causes happiness or whether happiness causes people to be more socially active. Moreover, in light of the finding that a third variable—extraversion—correlates with both variables, we have to consider the possibility that extraversion causes both greater social activity and greater happiness.

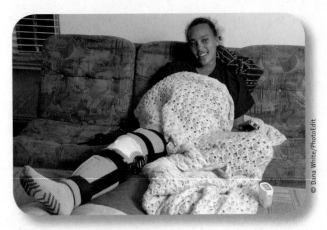

Research shows that happiness does not depend on people's positive and negative experiences as much as one would expect. Some people, presumably because of their personality, seem destined to be happy in spite of major setbacks, and others seem destined to cling to unhappiness even though their lives seem reasonably pleasant.

their neutral point, or baseline for comparison, is changed. Unfortunately, when people's experiences improve, hedonic adaptation may *sometimes* put them on a *hedonic treadmill*—their baseline moves upward, so that the improvements yield no real benefits (Kahneman, 1999). However, when people have to grapple with major setbacks, hedonic adaptation probably helps protect their mental and physical health. For example, people who are sent to prison and people who develop debilitating diseases are not as unhappy as one might assume because they adapt to their changed situations and evaluate events from a new perspective (Frederick & Loewenstein, 1999).

That's not to say that hedonic adaptation in the face of life's difficulties is inevitable or complete (Lucas et al., 2003). People who suffer major setbacks, such as the death of a spouse or serious illness, often are not as happy as they were before the setback, but generally they are not nearly as unhappy as they or others would have predicted (Diener & Oishi, 2005). The downside to the concept of hedonic adaptation is that it suggests that there is nothing people can do to increase their happiness. Fortunately, recent research on the hedonic treadmill is not as pessimistic as earlier research (Diener, Lucas, & Scollon, 2006). Although, this research has provided additional evidence that the hedonic treadmill is a genuine and common phenomenon, it has also shown that people vary considerably in the degree to which they experience hedonic adaptation and that enduring increases in individuals' set points for happiness can be achieved.

they experience a romantic breakup, don't get into the college they want, fail to get a promotion, or develop a serious illness. Thus, the roadmap to happiness is less clearly marked than widely assumed.

Fourth, *research on subjective well-being indicates that people often adapt to their circumstances.* This adaptation effect is one reason that an increase in income doesn't necessarily bring an increase in happiness. Thus, *hedonic adaptation* occurs when the mental scale that people use to judge the pleasantness-unpleasantness of their experiences shifts so that

Improving Academic Performance

LEARNING OBJECTIVES

▶ List three steps for developing sound study habits.
▶ Describe the SQ3R method of effective reading.
▶ Summarize advice on how to get more out of lectures.

▶ Summarize how memory is influenced by practice, interference, depth of processing, and organization.
▶ Describe several verbal and visual mnemonic devices.

Answer the following "true" or "false."

____ **1.** If you have a professor who delivers chaotic, hard-to-follow lectures, there is little point in attending class.

____ **2.** Cramming the night before an exam is an efficient way to study.

____ **3.** In taking lecture notes, you should try to be a "human tape recorder" (that is, take down everything exactly as said by your professor).

____ **4.** Outlining reading assignments is a waste of time.

As you will soon learn, all of these statements are false. If you answered them all correctly, you may already have acquired the kinds of skills and habits that lead to academic success. If so, however, you are not typical. Today, a huge number of students enter college with remarkably poor study skills and habits—and it's not entirely their fault. The U.S. educational system generally does not provide much in the way of formal instruction on good study techniques. In this first Application, we will try to remedy this deficiency to some extent by sharing some insights that psychology can provide on how to improve your academic performance. We will discuss how to promote better study habits, how to enhance reading efforts, how to get more out of lectures, and how to make your memory more effective.

Developing Sound Study Habits

Effective study is crucial to success in college. You may run into a few classmates who boast about getting good grades without studying, but you can be sure that if they perform well on exams, they study. Students who claim otherwise simply want to be viewed as extremely bright rather than as studious.

Learning can be immensely gratifying, but studying usually involves hard work. The first step toward effective study habits is to face this reality. You don't have to feel guilty if you don't look forward to studying. Most students don't. Once you accept the premise that studying doesn't come naturally, it should be clear that you need to set up an organized program to promote adequate study. Such a program should include the following three considerations (Siebert, 1995).

Set up a schedule for studying.   Research on the differences between successful and unsuccessful college students suggests that successful students monitor and regulate their use of time more effectively (Allgood et al., 2000). If you wait until the urge to study hits you, you may still be waiting when the exam rolls around. Thus, it is important to allocate definite times to studying. Review your time obligations (work, housekeeping, and so on) and figure out in advance when you can study. In allotting certain times to studying, keep in mind that you need to be wide awake and alert. Be realistic, too, about how long you can study at one time before you wear down from fatigue. Allow time for study breaks; they can revive sagging concentration.

It's important to write down your study schedule. Doing so serves as a reminder and increases your commitment to the schedule. As shown in **Figure 1.13** on the next page, you should begin by setting up a general schedule for the quarter or semester. Then, at the beginning of each week, plan the specific assignments that you intend to work on during each study session. This approach should help you to avoid cramming for exams at the last minute.

In planning your weekly schedule, try to avoid the tendency to put off working on major tasks such as term papers and reports. Time management experts such as Alan Lakein (1996) point out that many of us tend to tackle simple, routine tasks first, saving larger tasks for later, when we supposedly will have more time. This common tendency leads many of us to delay working on major assignments until it's too late to do

a good job. You can avoid this trap by breaking major assignments into smaller component tasks that you schedule individually.

Find a place to study where you can concentrate. Where you study is also important. The key is to find a place where distractions are likely to be minimal. Most people cannot study effectively while watching TV, listening to loud music, or overhearing conversations. Don't depend on willpower to carry you through these distractions. It's much easier to plan ahead and avoid the distractions altogether. Some learning theorists believe that it is wise to set up one or two specific places used solely for study (Hettich, 1998).

Reward your studying.   One of the reasons it is so difficult to motivate oneself to study regularly is that the payoffs for studying often lie in the distant future. The ultimate reward, a degree, may be years away. Even shorter-term rewards, such as an A in the course, may be weeks or months off. To combat this problem, it helps to give yourself immediate rewards for studying. It is easier to motivate yourself to study if you reward yourself with a tangible payoff, such as a snack, TV show, or phone call to a friend, when you finish. Thus, you should set realistic study goals and then reward yourself when you meet them. This systematic manipulation of rewards involves harnessing the principles of *behavior modification*, which are described in some detail in the Chapter 4 Application.

Improving Your Reading

Much of your study time is spent reading and absorbing information. *These efforts must be active.* If you engage in passive reading, the information will pass right through you. Many students deceive themselves into thinking that they are studying if they run a marker through a few sentences here and there in their text. If such highlighting isn't done with thoughtful selectivity, the student is simply turning a textbook into a coloring book. Research suggests that highlighting selected textbook material *is* a useful strategy—if students are reasonably effective in identifying the main ideas in the material and if they subsequently review the main

Web Link 1.6 **Sites to Promote Academic Success**

This site provides links to a number of other sites that provide advice on a diverse array of study-related topics, such as time management, effective note taking, memory-improvement strategies, and test-taking skills. Developed by Linda Walsh, a psychology professor at the University of Northern Iowa, it is an invaluable resource for students seeking to improve their chances of academic success.

	Mon	Tues	Wed	Thurs	Fri	Sat	Sun
8 A.M.						Work	
9 A.M.	History	Study	History	Study	History	Work	
10 A.M.	Psych		Psych		Psych	Work	
11 A.M.	Study	French	Study	French	Study	Work	
Noon	Math	Study	Math	Study	Math	Work	Study
1 P.M.							Study
2 P.M.	Study		Study		Study		Study
3 P.M.	Study	English	Study	English	Study		Study
4 P.M.							
5 P.M.							
6 P.M.	Work	Study	Work				Study
7 P.M.	Work	Study	Work				Study
8 P.M.	Work	Study	Work				Study
9 P.M.	Work	Study	Work				Study
10 P.M.	Work		Work				

Figure1.13

Example of an activity schedule. One student's general activity schedule for a semester is shown here. Each week the student fills in the specific assignments to work on during the upcoming study sessions.

ideas they have highlighted (Caverly, Orlando, & Mullen, 2000).

You can choose from a number of methods for actively attacking your reading assignments. One of the more worthwhile strategies is Robinson's (1970) SQ3R method. *SQ3R is a study system designed to promote effective reading that includes five steps: survey, question, read, recite, and review.* Its name is an abbreviation for the five steps in the procedure:

Step 1: Survey
Before you plunge into the actual reading, glance over the topic headings in the chapter and try to get an overview of the material. Try to understand how the various chapter segments are related. If there is a chapter outline or summary, consult it to get a feel for the chapter. If you know where the chapter is going, you can better appreciate and organize the information you are about to read.

Step 2: Question
Once you have an overview of your reading assignment, proceed through it one section at a time. Take a look at the heading of the first section and convert it into a question. This is usually quite simple. If the heading is "Prenatal Risk Factors," your question should be "What are sources of risk during prenatal development?" If the heading is "Stereotyping," your question should be "What is stereotyping?" Asking these questions gets

you actively involved in your reading and helps you identify the main ideas.

Step 3: Read
Only now, in the third step, are you ready to sink your teeth into the reading. Read only the specific section that you have decided to tackle. Read it with an eye toward answering the question that you just formulated. If necessary, reread the section until you can answer that question. Decide whether the segment addresses any other important questions and answer them as well.

Step 4: Recite
Now that you can answer the key question for the section, recite it out loud to yourself. Use your own words for the answer, because that requires understanding instead of simple memorization. Don't move on to the next section until you understand the main idea(s) of the current section. You may want to write down these ideas for review later. When you have fully digested the first section, go on to the next. Repeat steps 2 through 4 with the next section. Once you have mastered the crucial points there, you can continue. Keep repeating steps 2 through 4, section by section, until you finish the chapter.

Step 5: Review
When you have read the chapter, test and refresh your memory by going back over the key points. Repeat your questions and try to answer them without consulting your book or notes. This review should fortify your retention of the main ideas and alert you to any

Although some students downplay the importance of study efforts, the reality is that effective study habits are crucial to academic success.

key ideas that you haven't mastered. It should also help you to see the relationships between the main ideas.

The SQ3R method does not have to be applied rigidly. For example, it is often wise to break your reading assignment into smaller segments than those separated by section headings. In fact, you should probably apply SQ3R to many texts on a paragraph by paragraph basis. Obviously, doing so will require you to formulate some questions without the benefit of topic headings. However, the headings are not absolutely necessary to use this technique. If you don't have enough headings, you can simply reverse the order of steps 2 and 3. Read the paragraph first and then formulate a question that addresses the basic idea of the paragraph. The point is that you can be flexible in your use of the SQ3R technique.

Using the SQ3R method does not automatically lead to improved mastery of textbook reading assignments. It won't be effective unless it is applied diligently and skillfully and it tends to be more helpful to students with low to medium reading ability (Caverly, Orlando, & Mullen, 2000). Any strategy that facilitates active processing of text material, the identification of key ideas, and effective review of these ideas should enhance your reading.

Getting More Out of Lectures

Although lectures are sometimes boring and tedious, it is a simple fact that poor class attendance is associated with poor grades. For example, in one study, Lindgren (1969) found that absences from class were much more common among "unsuccessful" students (grade average of C– or below) than among "successful" students (grade average of B or above), as is shown in **Figure 1.14**. Even when you have an instructor who delivers hard-to-follow lectures from which you learn virtually nothing, it is still important to go to class. If nothing else, you'll get a feel for how the instructor thinks. Doing so can help you anticipate the content of exams and respond in the manner your professor expects.

Fortunately, most lectures are reasonably coherent. Studies indicate that attentive note taking *is* associated with enhanced learning and performance in college classes (Titsworth & Kiewra, 2004; Williams & Eggert, 2002). However, research also shows that many students' lecture notes are surprisingly incomplete, with the average student often recording less than 40% of the crucial ideas in a lecture (Armbruster,

2000). Thus, the key to getting more out of lectures is to stay motivated, stay attentive, and expend the effort to make your notes as complete as possible. Books on study skills (Longman & Atkinson, 2005; Sotiriou, 2002) offer a number of suggestions on how to take good-quality lecture notes. These suggestions include:

▶ Use *active listening procedures*. With active listening, you focus full attention on the speaker. Try to anticipate what's coming and search for deeper meanings. Pay attention to nonverbal signals that may serve to further clarify the lecturer's intent or meaning.

▶ When course material is especially complex and difficult, it is a good idea to prepare for the lecture by reading ahead on the scheduled subject in your text. Then you have less information to digest that is brand new.

▶ Don't try to be a human tape recorder. Instead, try to write down the lecturer's thoughts in your own words. Doing so forces you to organize the ideas in a way that makes sense to you. In taking notes, look for subtle and not-so-subtle clues about what the instructor considers to be important. These clues may range from simply repeating main points to saying things like "You'll run into this again."

▶ Ask questions during lectures. Doing so keeps you actively involved and allows you to clarify points you may have misunderstood. Many students are more bashful about asking questions than they should be. They don't realize that most professors welcome questions.

Applying Memory Principles

Scientific investigation of memory processes dates back to 1885, when Hermann Ebbinghaus published a series

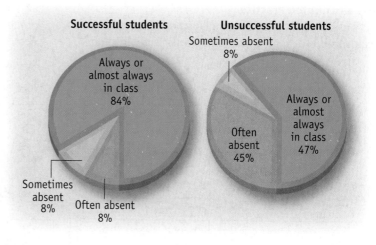

Figure 1.14

Successful and unsuccessful students' class attendance. Lindgren (1969) found that attendance was much better among successful students than unsuccessful students. (Data from Lindgren, 1969)

of insightful studies. Since then, psychologists have discovered a number of principles about memory that are relevant to helping you improve your study skills.

Engage in Adequate Practice

Practice makes perfect, or so you've heard. In reality, practice is not likely to guarantee perfection, but repeatedly reviewing information usually leads to improved retention. Studies show that retention improves with increased rehearsal (Greene, 1992). Continued rehearsal may also pay off by improving your *understanding* of assigned material (Bromage & Mayer, 1986). Although the benefits of practice are well known, people have a curious tendency to overestimate their knowledge of a topic and how well they will perform on a subsequent memory test of this knowledge (Koriat & Bjork, 2005). That's why it is a good idea to informally test yourself on information that you think you have mastered before confronting a real test (for example, by taking the Practice Tests in this text or additional tests available on the website for the book).

Evidence suggests that it even pays to overlearn material (Driskell, Wilis, & Copper, 1992). **Overlearning is continued rehearsal of material after you have first appeared to master it.** In one study, after participants mastered a list of nouns (they recited the list without error), Krueger (1929) required them to continue rehearsing for 50% or 100% more trials (repetitions). Measuring retention at intervals of up to 28 days, Kreuger found that overlearning led to better recall of the list. Modern studies have also shown that overlearning can enhance performance on an exam that occurs within a week, although the evidence on its long-term benefits (months later) is inconsistent (Peladeau, Forget, & Gagne, 2003; Rohrer et al., 2005).

Use Distributed Practice

Let's assume that you are going to study 9 hours for an exam. Is it better to "cram" all of your study into one 9-hour period (massed practice) or distribute it among, say, three 3-hour periods on successive days (distributed practice)? The evidence indicates that retention tends to be greater after distributed practice than massed practice (Payne & Wenger, 1996; Seabrook, Brown, & Solity, 2005). This advantage is especially apparent if the intervals between practice periods are fairly long, such as 24 hours (Zechmeister & Nyberg, 1982). The inefficiency of massed practice means that cramming is an ill-advised study strategy for most students (Dempster, 1996). Cramming will strain your memorization capabilities and tax your energy level. It may also stoke the fires of test anxiety.

Organize Information

Retention tends to be greater when information is well organized (Einstein & McDaniel, 2004). Hierarchical organization is particularly helpful when it is applicable (Tigner, 1999). Thus, it may be a good idea to *outline* reading assignments for school. Consistent with this reasoning, there is some empirical evidence that outlining material from textbooks can enhance retention of the material (McDaniel, Waddill, & Shakesby, 1996).

Emphasize Deep Processing

Research suggests that how *often* you go over material is less critical than the *depth* of processing that you engage in (Craik & Tulving, 1975). Thus, if you expect to remember what you read, you have to wrestle fully with its meaning (Einstein & McDaniel, 2004). Many students could probably benefit if they spent less time on rote repetition and devoted more effort to actually paying attention to and analyzing the meaning of their reading assignments. In particular, it is useful to make material *personally* meaningful. When you read your textbooks, try to relate information to your own life and experience. For example, if you're reading in your psychology text about the personality trait of assertiveness, you can think about which people you know who

DOONESBURY © G. B. Trudeau. Reprinted with permission of UNIVERSAL PRESS SYNDICATE. All rights reserved.

are particularly assertive and why you would characterize them as being that way.

Use Verbal Mnemonics

Of course, it's not always easy to make something personally meaningful. When you study chemistry, you may have a hard time relating to polymers at a personal level. This problem has led to the development of many **mnemonic devices, or strategies for enhancing memory,** that are designed to make abstract material more meaningful.

Acrostics and acronyms. *Acrostics* are phrases (or poems) in which the first letter of each word (or line) functions as a cue to help you recall the abstract words that begin with the same letter. For instance, you may remember the order of musical notes with the saying "Every good boy does fine" (or "deserves favor"). A variation on acrostics is the *acronym*—a word formed out of the first letters of a series of words. Students memorizing the order of colors in the light spectrum often store the name "Roy G. Biv" to remember red, orange, yellow, green, blue, indigo, and violet. Acrostics and acronyms that individuals create for themselves can be effective memory tools (Hermann et al., 2002).

Rhymes. Another verbal mnemonic that people often rely on is rhyming. You've probably repeated, "I before E except after C" thousands of times. Perhaps you also remember the number of days in each month with the old standby, "Thirty days hath September . . ." Rhyming something to remember it is an old and useful trick.

Use Visual Mnemonics

Memory can be improved through the use of visual imagery. One influential theory (Paivio, 1986) proposes that visual images create a second memory code and that two codes are better than one. Many popular mnemonic devices depend on visual imagery, including the link method and the method of loci.

Link method. The *link method* involves forming a mental image of items to be remembered in a way that links them together. For instance, suppose that you are going to stop at the drugstore on the way home and you need to remember to pick up a news magazine, shaving cream, film, and pens. To remember these items, you might visualize a public figure likely to be in the magazine shaving with a pen while being photographed. Some researchers suggest that the more bizarre the images, the better they will be remembered (Iaccino, 1996; Worthen, 1997).

Method of loci. The *method of loci* involves taking an imaginary walk along a familiar path where you have associated images of items you want to remember with certain locations. The first step is to commit to memory a series of loci, or places along a path. Usually these loci are specific locations in your home or neighborhood. Then envision each thing you want to remember in one of these locations. Try to form distinctive, vivid images. When you need to remember the items, imagine yourself walking along the path. The various loci on your path should serve as retrieval cues for the images that you formed (see **Figure 1.15**). The method of loci assures that items are remembered in their correct order because the order is determined by the sequence of locations along the pathway. Empirical studies have supported the value of this method for memorizing lists (Moe & De Beni, 2004).

Figure 1.15

The method of loci. In this example from Bower (1970), a person about to go shopping pairs items to be remembered with familiar places (loci) arranged in a natural sequence: (1) hot dogs/driveway; (2) cat food/garage; (3) tomatoes/front door; (4) bananas/coat closet; (5) whiskey/kitchen sink. As the last panel shows, the shopper recalls the items by mentally touring the loci associated with them.

Adapted from Bower, G. H. (1970). Analysis of a mnemonic device. *American Scientist, 58*, 496–499. Copyright © 1970 by Scientific Research Society. Reprinted by permission.

KEY IDEAS

The Paradox of Progress

▶ Although our modern era has seen great technological progress, personal problems have not diminished. In spite of many time-saving devices, people tend to have less free time. Although affluence is widespread, most people worry about economic decline, and materialism seems to undermine well-being.

▶ The life choices available to people have increased greatly, but Schwartz argues that choice overload undermines individuals' happiness. Although we have unprecedented control over the world around us, we seem to create as many problems as we solve. Thus, many theorists argue that technological progress has brought new, and possibly more difficult, adjustment problems.

The Search for Direction

▶ According to many theorists, the basic challenge of modern life has become the search for a sense of direction and meaning. This search has many manifestations, including the appeal of self-realization programs, religious cults, and media "therapists" such as Dr. Laura.

▶ The enormous popularity of self-help books is an interesting manifestation of people's struggle to find a sense of direction. Some self-help books offer worthwhile advice, but most are dominated by psychobabble and are not based on scientific research. Many also lack explicit advice on how to change behavior and some encourage a self-centered approach to interpersonal interactions.

▶ Although this text deals with many of the same issues as self-realization programs, self-help books, and other types of pop psychology, its philosophy and approach are quite different.

The Psychology of Adjustment

▶ Psychology is both a science and a profession that focuses on behavior and related mental and physiological processes.

▶ Adjustment is a broad area of study in psychology concerned with how people adapt effectively or ineffectively to the demands and pressures of everyday life.

The Scientific Approach to Behavior

▶ The scientific approach to understanding behavior is empirical. Psychologists base their conclusions on formal, systematic, objective tests of their hypotheses, rather than reasoning, speculation, or common sense. The scientific approach is advantageous in that it puts a premium on clarity and has little tolerance for error.

▶ Experimental research involves manipulating an independent variable to discover its effects on a dependent variable. The experimenter usually does so by comparing experimental and control groups, which must be alike except for the variation created by the manipulation of the independent variable. Experiments permit conclusions about cause-effect relationships between variables, but this method isn't usable for the study of many questions.

▶ Psychologists conduct correlational research when they are unable to exert control over the variables they want to study. The correlation coefficient is a numerical index of the degree of relationship between two variables. Correlational research methods include naturalistic observation, case studies, and surveys. Correlational research facilitates the investigation of many issues that are not open to experimental study, but it cannot demonstrate that two variables are causally related.

The Roots of Happiness: An Empirical Analysis

▶ A scientific analysis of happiness reveals that many commonsense notions about the roots of happiness appear to be incorrect, including the notion that most people are unhappy. Factors such as money, age, gender, parenthood, intelligence, and attractiveness are not correlated with subjective well-being.

▶ Physical health, social relationships, and religious faith appear to have a modest impact on feelings of happiness. The only factors that are clearly and strongly related to happiness are love and marriage, work satisfaction, and personality, which probably reflects the influence of heredity.

▶ Happiness is a relative concept mediated by people's highly subjective assessments of their lives. People are surprisingly bad at predicting what will make them happy. Individuals adapt to both positive and negative events in their lives, which creates a hedonic treadmill effect.

Application: Improving Academic Performance

▶ To foster sound study habits, you should devise a written study schedule and reward yourself for following it. You should also try to find places for studying that are relatively free of distractions.

▶ You should use active reading techniques, such as SQ3R, to select the most important ideas from the material you read. Good note taking can help you get more out of lectures. It's important to use active listening techniques and to record lecturers' ideas in your own words.

▶ Rehearsal, even when it involves overlearning, facilitates retention. Distributed practice and deeper processing tend to improve memory. Evidence also suggests that organization facilitates retention, so outlining reading assignments can be valuable.

▶ Meaningfulness can be enhanced through the use of verbal mnemonics such as acrostics and acronyms. The link method and the method of loci are mnemonic devices that depend on the value of visual imagery.

KEY TERMS

Adjustment   p. 12
Behavior   p. 11
Case study   p. 16
Clinical psychology   p. 12
Control group   p. 14
Correlation   p. 15
Correlation coefficient   p. 15
Dependent variable   p. 13
Empiricism   p. 12
Experiment   p. 13
Experimental group   p. 14

Hedonic adaptation   p. 24
Independent variable   p. 13
Mnemonic devices   p. 29
Naturalistic
   observation   p. 16
Overlearning   p. 28
Psychology   p. 11
SQ3R   p. 26
Subjective well-being   p. 19
Surveys   p. 17

KEY PEOPLE

David Myers   p. 21
Barry Schwartz   pp. 2–3, 7

Martin Seligman   p. 10

1. Technological advances have not led to perceptible improvement in our collective health and happiness. This statement defines
   a. escape from freedom.
   b. the point/counterpoint phenomenon.
   c. modern society.
   d. the paradox of progress.

2. Kasser argues that the correlation between happiness and materialism (a strong focus on money and possessions) is
   a. positive.
   b. negative.
   c. zero.
   d. about +1.24.

3. Which of the following is *not* offered in the text as a criticism of self-help books?
   a. They are infrequently based on solid research.
   b. Most don't provide explicit directions for changing behavior.
   c. The topics they cover are often quite narrow.
   d. Many are dominated by psychobabble.

4. The adaptation of animals when environments change is similar to _____ in humans.
   a. orientation
   b. assimilation
   c. evolution
   d. adjustment

5. An experiment is a research method in which the investigator manipulates the _____ variable and observes whether changes occur in a (an) _____ variable as a result.
   a. independent; dependent
   b. control; experimental
   c. experimental; control
   d. dependent; independent

6. A researcher wants to determine whether a certain diet causes children to learn better in school. In the study, the independent variable is
   a. the type of diet.
   b. a measure of learning performance.
   c. the age or grade level of the children.
   d. the intelligence level of the children.

7. A psychologist collected background information about a psychopathic killer, talked to him and people who knew him, and gave him psychological tests. Which research method was she using?
   a. Case study
   b. Naturalistic observation
   c. Survey
   d. Experiment

8. The principal advantage of experimental research is that
   a. it has a scientific basis and is therefore convincing to people.
   b. experiments replicate real-life situations.
   c. an experiment can be designed for any research problem.
   d. it allows the researcher to draw cause-and-effect conclusions.

9. Research has shown that which of the following is moderately correlated with happiness?
   a. Income
   b. Intelligence
   c. Parenthood
   d. Social activity

10. A good reason for taking notes in your own words, rather than verbatim, is that
    a. most lecturers are quite wordy.
    b. "translating" on the spot is good mental exercise.
    c. it reduces the likelihood that you'll later engage in plagiarism.
    d. it forces you to assimilate the information in a way that makes sense to you.

Book Companion Website

Visit the Book Companion Website at **academic.cengage. com/psychology/weiten,** where you will find tutorial quizzes, flash cards, and web links for every chapter, a final exam, and more! You can also link to the Psychology Resource Center (accessible directly at **academic.cengage.com/login**) for a range of psychology-related resources.

Personal Explorations Workbook

The following exercises in your *Personal Explorations Workbook* may enhance your self-understanding in relation to issues raised in this chapter. **Questionnaire 1.1:** Testwiseness Scale. **Personal Probe 1.1:** What Are Your Study Habits Like? **Personal Probe 1.2:** What Factors Affect Your Current Adjustment in Life?

1. d Pages 1–3
2. b Page 1
3. c Pages 7–8
4. d Page 12
5. a Page 13
6. a Pages 13–14
7. a Pages 16–17
8. d Page 15
9. d Pages 19–21
10. d Page 27

Figure 2.7

A behavioral view of personality. Behaviorists devote little attention to the structure of personality because it is unobservable, but they implicitly view personality as an individual's collection of response tendencies. A possible hierarchy of response tendencies for a specific stimulus situation is shown here. In the behavioral view, personality is made up of countless response hierarchies for various situations.

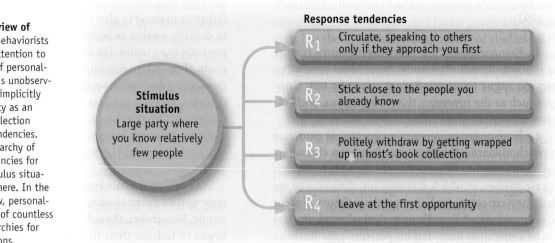

Response tendencies

Stimulus situation
Large party where you know relatively few people

R₁ — Circulate, speaking to others only if they approach you first

R₂ — Stick close to the people you already know

R₃ — Politely withdraw by getting wrapped up in host's book collection

R₄ — Leave at the first opportunity

---

anxious when you're around important people? When you're driving, does your heart skip a beat at the sight of a police car—even when you're driving under the speed limit? If so, you probably acquired these common responses through classical conditioning. *Classical conditioning* **is a type of learning in which a neutral stimulus acquires the capacity to evoke a response that was originally evoked by another stimulus.** This process was first described back in 1903 by Ivan Pavlov.

Pavlov was a prominent Russian physiologist who did Nobel Prize–winning research on digestion. He was a dedicated scientist who was obsessed with his research. Legend has it that Pavlov severely reprimanded an assistant who was late for an experiment because he was trying to avoid street fighting in the midst of the Russian Revolution. The assistant defended his tardiness, saying, "But Professor, there's a revolution going on, with shooting in the streets!" Pavlov supposedly replied, "Next time there's a revolution, get up earlier!" (Fancher, 1979; Gantt, 1975).

Ivan Pavlov

© Bettmann/Corbis

The Conditioned Reflex

Pavlov (1906) was studying digestive processes in dogs when he discovered that the dogs could be trained to salivate in response to the sound of a tone. What was so significant about a dog salivating when a tone was presented? The key was that the tone started out as a *neutral* stimulus; that is, originally it did not produce the response of salivation (after all, why should it?). However, Pavlov managed to change that by pairing the tone with a stimulus (meat powder) that did produce the salivation response. Through this process, the tone

acquired the capacity to trigger the response of salivation. What Pavlov had demonstrated was *how learned reflexes are acquired.*

At this point we need to introduce the special vocabulary of classical conditioning (see **Figure 2.8**). In Pavlov's experiment the bond between the meat powder and salivation was a natural association that was not created through conditioning. In unconditioned bonds, **the *unconditioned stimulus (UCS)* is a stimulus that evokes an unconditioned response without previous conditioning. The *unconditioned response (UCR)* is an unlearned reaction to an unconditioned stimulus that occurs without previous conditioning.**

In contrast, the link between the tone and salivation was established through conditioning. In conditioned bonds, **the *conditioned stimulus (CS)* is a previously neutral stimulus that has acquired the capacity to evoke a conditioned response through conditioning. The *conditioned response (CR)* is a learned reaction to a conditioned stimulus that occurs because of previous conditioning.** Note that the unconditioned response and conditioned response often involve the same behavior (although there may be subtle differences). In Pavlov's initial demonstration, salivation was an unconditioned response when evoked by the UCS (meat powder) and a conditioned response when evoked by the CS (the tone). The procedures involved in classical conditioning are outlined in **Figure 2.8**.

Web Link 2.3 **Behavior Analysis and Learning**

A multitude of annotated links, all focusing on learning through conditioning, have been compiled at the excellent Psychology Centre site at Athabasca University (Alberta, Canada).

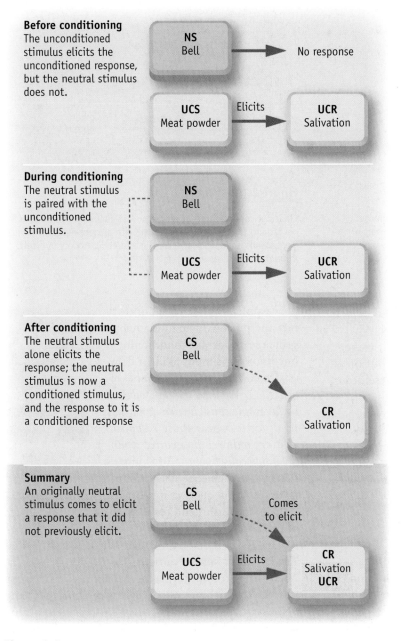

Before conditioning
The unconditioned stimulus elicits the unconditioned response, but the neutral stimulus does not.

NS Bell → No response

UCS Meat powder —Elicits→ **UCR** Salivation

During conditioning
The neutral stimulus is paired with the unconditioned stimulus.

NS Bell

UCS Meat powder —Elicits→ **UCR** Salivation

After conditioning
The neutral stimulus alone elicits the response; the neutral stimulus is now a conditioned stimulus, and the response to it is a conditioned response

CS Bell

CR Salivation

Summary
An originally neutral stimulus comes to elicit a response that it did not previously elicit.

CS Bell —Comes to elicit→ **CR** Salivation **UCR**

UCS Meat powder —Elicits→

Figure 2.8

The process of classical conditioning. The sequence of events in classical conditioning is outlined here. As we encounter new examples of classical conditioning throughout the book, you will see diagrams like that shown in the bottom panel, which summarizes the process.

Pavlov's discovery came to be called the *conditioned reflex.* Classically conditioned responses are viewed as reflexes because most of them are relatively involuntary. Responses that are a product of classical conditioning are said to be *elicited.* This word is meant to convey the idea that these responses are triggered automatically.

Classical Conditioning in Everyday Life

What is the role of classical conditioning in shaping personality in everyday life? Among other things, it contributes to the acquisition of emotional responses, such as anxieties, fears, and phobias (Antony & McCabe, 2003; Ayres, 1998). This is a relatively small but important class of responses, as maladaptive emotional reactions underlie many adjustment problems. For example, one middle-aged woman reported being troubled by a bridge phobia so severe that she couldn't drive on interstate highways because of all the viaducts she would have to cross. She was able to pinpoint the source of her phobia. Back in her childhood, whenever her family would drive to visit her grandmother, they had to cross a little-used, rickety, dilapidated bridge out in the countryside. Her father, in a misguided attempt at humor, made a major production out of these crossings. He would stop short of the bridge and carry on about the enormous danger of the crossing. Obviously, he thought the bridge was safe or he wouldn't have driven across it. However, the naive young girl was terrified by her father's scare tactics, and the bridge became a conditioned stimulus eliciting great fear (see **Figure 2.9** on the next page). Unfortunately, the fear spilled over to all bridges, and 40 years later she was still carrying the burden of this phobia. Although a number of processes can cause phobias, it is clear that classical conditioning is responsible for many people's irrational fears.

Classical conditioning also appears to account for more realistic and moderate anxiety responses. For example, imagine a news reporter in a high-pressure job where he consistently gets negative feedback about his work from his bosses. The negative comments from his supervisors function as a UCS eliciting anxiety. These reprimands are paired with the noise and sight of the newsroom, so that the newsroom becomes a CS triggering anxiety, even when his supervisors are absent (see **Figure 2.10** on the next page). Our poor reporter might even reach a point at which the mere *thought* of the newsroom elicits anxiety when he is elsewhere.

Fortunately, not every frightening experience leaves a conditioned fear in its wake. A variety of factors influence whether a conditioned response is acquired in a particular situation. Furthermore, a newly formed stimulus-response bond does not necessarily last indefinitely. The right circumstances can lead

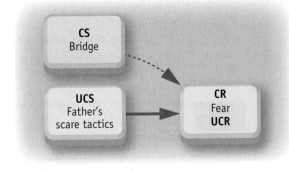

Figure 2.9

Classical conditioning of a phobia. Many emotional responses that would otherwise be puzzling can be explained as a result of classical conditioning. In the case of one woman's bridge phobia, the fear originally elicited by her father's scare tactics became a conditioned response to the stimulus of bridges.

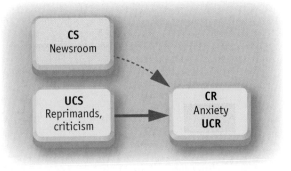

Figure 2.10

Classical conditioning of anxiety. A stimulus (in this case, a newsroom) that is frequently paired with anxiety-arousing events (reprimands and criticism) may come to elicit anxiety by itself, through classical conditioning.

to *extinction*—**the gradual weakening and disappearance of a conditioned response tendency.** What leads to extinction in classical conditioning? It is the consistent presentation of the CS *alone,* without the UCS. For example, when Pavlov consistently presented *only* the tone to a previously conditioned dog, the tone gradually stopped eliciting the response of salivation. How long it takes to extinguish a conditioned response depends on many factors. Foremost among them is the strength of the conditioned bond when extinction begins. Some conditioned responses extinguish quickly, while others are difficult to weaken.

Skinner's Operant Conditioning

Even Pavlov recognized that classical conditioning is not the only form of conditioning. Classical conditioning best explains reflexive responding controlled by stimuli that *precede* the response. However, both animals and humans make many responses that don't fit this description. Consider the response you are engaging in right now—studying. It is definitely not a reflex (life might be easier if it were). The stimuli that govern it (exams and grades) do not precede it. Instead, your studying response is mainly influenced by events that follow it—specifically, its *consequences.*

This kind of learning is called *operant conditioning. Operant conditioning* **is a form of learning in which voluntary responses come to be controlled by their consequences.** Operant conditioning probably governs a larger share of human behavior than classical conditioning, since most human responses are voluntary rather than reflexive. Because they are voluntary, operant responses are said to be *emitted* rather than *elicited.*

The study of operant conditioning was led by B. F. Skinner (1953, 1974, 1990), a Harvard University psychologist who spent most of his career studying sim-

ple responses made by laboratory rats and pigeons. The fundamental principle of operant conditioning is uncommonly simple. Skinner demonstrated that *organisms tend to repeat those responses that are followed by favorable consequences, and they tend not to repeat those responses that are followed by neutral or unfavorable consequences.* In Skinner's scheme, favorable, neutral, and unfavorable consequences involve reinforcement, extinction, and punishment, respectively. We'll look at each of these concepts in turn.

B. F. Skinner

Courtesy of B. F. Skinner

The Power of Reinforcement

According to Skinner, reinforcement can occur in two ways, which he called *positive reinforcement* and *negative reinforcement. Positive reinforcement* **occurs when a response is strengthened (increases in frequency) because it is followed by the arrival of a (presumably) pleasant stimulus.** Positive reinforcement is roughly synonymous with the concept of reward. Notice, however, that reinforcement is defined *after the fact,* in terms of its effect on behavior. Why? Because reinforcement is subjective. Something that serves as a reinforcer for one person may not function as a reinforcer for another. For example, peer approval is a potent reinforcer for most people, but not all.

Positive reinforcement motivates much of everyday behavior. You study hard because good grades are likely to follow as a result. You go to work because this behavior produces paychecks. Perhaps you work extra hard in the hopes of winning a promotion or a pay raise. In each of these examples, certain responses occur because they have led to positive outcomes in the past.

Positive reinforcement influences personality development in a straightforward way. Responses fol-

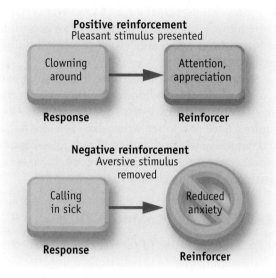

Positive reinforcement
Pleasant stimulus presented

| Clowning around | → | Attention, appreciation |
| Response | | Reinforcer |

Negative reinforcement
Aversive stimulus removed

| Calling in sick | → | Reduced anxiety |
| Response | | Reinforcer |

Figure 2.11

Positive and negative reinforcement in operant conditioning.
Positive reinforcement occurs when a response is followed by
a favorable outcome, so that the response is strengthened. In
negative reinforcement, the removal (symbolized here by the "No"
sign) of an aversive stimulus serves as a reinforcer. Negative reinforcement produces the same result as positive reinforcement:
The person's tendency to emit the reinforced response is strengthened (the response becomes more frequent).

lowed by pleasant outcomes are strengthened and tend
to become habitual patterns of behavior. For example,
a youngster might clown around in class and gain ap-
preciative comments and smiles from schoolmates.
This social approval will probably reinforce clowning-
around behavior (see **Figure 2.11**). If such behavior is
reinforced with some regularity, it will gradually become an integral element of the youth's personality.

Similarly, whether or not a youngster develops traits
such as independence, assertiveness, or selfishness depends on whether the child is reinforced for such behaviors by parents and by other influential persons.

Negative reinforcement **occurs when a response
is strengthened (increases in frequency) because it is
followed by the removal of a (presumably) unpleasant
stimulus.** Don't let the word *negative* here confuse you.
Negative reinforcement *is* reinforcement. Like positive
reinforcement, it strengthens a response. However, this
strengthening occurs because the response gets rid of
an aversive stimulus. Consider a few examples: You rush
home in the winter to get out of the cold. You clean your
house to get rid of a mess. Parents give in to their child's
begging to halt his whining.

Negative reinforcement plays a major role in the
development of avoidance tendencies. As you may
have noticed, many people tend to avoid facing up to
awkward situations and sticky personal problems. This
personality trait typically develops because avoidance
behavior gets rid of anxiety and is therefore negatively
reinforced. Recall our imaginary newspaper reporter
whose work environment (the newsroom) elicits anxiety
(as a result of classical conditioning). He might notice
that on days when he calls in sick, his anxiety evaporates,
so this response is gradually strengthened—through
negative reinforcement (shown in **Figure 2.11**). If his
avoidance behavior continues to be successful in reducing his anxiety, it might carry over into other areas of
his life and become a central aspect of his personality.

Extinction and Punishment

Like the effects of classical conditioning, the effects
of operant conditioning may not last forever. In both
types of conditioning, *extinction* refers to the gradual

*The behavioral approach to personal-
ity centers around the principle of
reinforcement—behaviors that are
followed by favorable outcomes, such
as attention, laughter, approval, and
appreciation, tend to be strengthened
and become more frequent.*

© Big Shot/Digital Vision/Getty Images

weakening and disappearance of a response. In operant conditioning, extinction begins when a previously reinforced response stops producing positive consequences. As extinction progresses, the response typically becomes less and less frequent and eventually disappears.

Thus, the response tendencies that make up one's personality are not necessarily permanent. For example, the youngster who found that his classmates reinforced clowning around in grade school might find that his attempts at comedy earn nothing but indifferent stares in high school. This termination of reinforcement would probably lead to the gradual extinction of the clowning-around behavior. How quickly an operant response extinguishes depends on many factors in the person's earlier reinforcement history.

Some responses may be weakened by punishment. In Skinner's scheme, **punishment occurs when a response is weakened (decreases in frequency) because it is followed by the arrival of a (presumably) unpleasant stimulus.** The concept of punishment in operant conditioning confuses many students on two counts. First, it is often mixed up with negative reinforcement because both involve aversive (unpleasant) stimuli. Please note, however, that they are altogether different events with opposite outcomes! In negative reinforcement, a response leads to the removal of something aversive, and this response is strengthened. In punishment, a response leads to the arrival of something aversive, and this response tends to be weakened.

The second source of confusion involves the tendency to view punishment as only a disciplinary procedure used by parents, teachers, and other authority figures. In the operant model, punishment occurs whenever a response leads to negative consequences. Defined in this way, the concept goes far beyond actions such as parents spanking children or teachers handing out detentions. For example, if you wear a new outfit and your friends make fun of it and hurt your feelings, your behavior has been punished, and your tendency to wear this clothing will decline. Similarly, if you go to a restaurant and have a horrible meal, in Skinner's terminology your response has led to punishment, and you are unlikely to return.

The impact of punishment on personality development is just the opposite of reinforcement. Generally speaking, those patterns of behavior that lead to punishing (that is, negative) consequences tend to be weakened. For instance, if your impulsive decisions always backfire, your tendency to be impulsive should decline.

According to Skinner (1987), conditioning in humans operates much as it does in the rats and pigeons that he has studied in his laboratory. Hence, he assumes that conditioning strengthens and weakens people's response tendencies "mechanically"—that is, without their conscious participation. Like John Watson (1913) before him, Skinner asserted that we can explain behavior without being concerned about individuals' mental processes.

Skinner's ideas continue to be influential, but his mechanical view of conditioning has not gone unchallenged by other behaviorists. Theorists such as Albert Bandura have developed somewhat different behavioral models in which cognition plays a role. *Cognition* is another name for the thought processes that behaviorists have traditionally shown little interest in.

Bandura's Social Cognitive Theory

Albert Bandura is one of several theorists who have added a cognitive flavor to behaviorism since the 1960s. Bandura (1977), Walter Mischel (1973), and Julian Rotter (1982) take issue with Skinner's view. They point out that humans obviously are conscious, thinking, feeling beings. Moreover, these theorists argue that in neglecting cognitive processes, Skinner ignores the most distinctive and important feature of human behavior. Bandura and like-minded theorists originally called their modified brand of behaviorism *social learning theory*. Today, Bandura refers to his model as *social cognitive theory*.

Bandura (1986, 1999b) agrees with the basic thrust of behaviorism in that he believes that personality is largely shaped through learning. However, he contends that conditioning is not a mechanical process in which people are passive participants. Instead, he maintains that individuals actively seek out and process information about their environment in order to maximize their favorable outcomes.

Albert Bandura

Observational Learning

Bandura's foremost theoretical contribution has been his description of observational learning. **Observational learning occurs when an organism's responding is influenced by the observation of others, who are called models.** Bandura does not view observational learning as entirely separate from classical and operant conditioning. Instead, he asserts that both classical and operant conditioning can take place indirectly when one person observes another's conditioning (see **Figure 2.12**).

To illustrate, suppose you observe a friend behaving assertively with a car salesman. Let's say that her assertiveness is reinforced by the exceptionally good buy she gets on the car. Your own tendency to behave assertively with salespeople might well be strengthened as a result. Notice that the favorable consequence

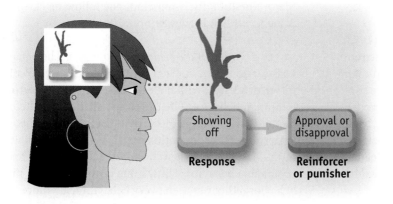

Figure 2.12

Observational learning. In observational learning, an observer attends to and stores a mental representation of a model's behavior (for example, showing off) and its consequences (such as approval or disapproval from others). According to social cognitive theory, many of our characteristic responses are acquired through observation of others' behavior.

is experienced by your friend, not you. Your friend's tendency to bargain assertively should be reinforced directly. But your tendency to bargain assertively may also be strengthened indirectly.

The theories of Skinner and Pavlov make no allowance for this type of indirect learning. After all, observational learning requires that you pay *attention* to your friend's behavior, that you *understand* its consequences, and that you store this *information* in *memory*. Obviously, attention, understanding, information, and memory involve cognition, which behaviorists used to ignore.

As social cognitive theory has been refined, it has become apparent that some models tend to be more influential than others (Bandura, 1986). Both children and adults tend to imitate people they like or respect more so than people they don't. People are also especially prone to imitate the behavior of those they consider attractive or powerful (such as celebrities). In addition, imitation is more likely when individuals see similarity between the model and themselves. Thus, children imitate same-sex role models somewhat more than other-sex models. Finally, as noted before, people are more likely to copy a model if they see the model's behavior leading to positive outcomes.

According to social cognitive theory, models have a great impact on personality development. Children learn to be assertive, conscientious, self-sufficient, dependable, easygoing, and so forth by observing others behaving in these ways. Parents, teachers, relatives, siblings, and peers serve as models for young children. Bandura and his colleagues have done extensive research showing how models influence the development of aggressiveness, gender roles, and moral standards in children (Bandura, 1973; Bussey & Bandura, 1984, 2004;

Mischel & Mischel, 1976). Their research on modeling and aggression has been particularly influential.

Self-Efficacy

Bandura (1993, 1997, 2004) believes that *self-efficacy* is a crucial element of personality. **Self-efficacy is one's belief about one's ability to perform behaviors that should lead to expected outcomes.** When a person's self-efficacy is high, he or she feels confident in executing the responses necessary to earn reinforcers. When self-efficacy is low, the individual worries that the necessary responses may be beyond her or his abilities. Perceptions of self-efficacy are subjective and specific to different kinds of tasks. For instance, you might feel extremely confident about your ability to handle difficult social situations but doubtful about your ability to handle academic challenges.

Perceptions of self-efficacy can influence which challenges people tackle and how well they perform. Studies have found that feelings of greater self-efficacy are associated with reduced procrastination (Steel, 2007); greater success in giving up smoking (Boudreaux et al., 1998); greater adherence to an exercise regimen (Rimal, 2001); more effective weight-loss efforts (Linde et al., 2006); better outcomes in substance abuse treatment (Bandura, 1999a); more success in coping with medical rehabilitation (Waldrop et al., 2001); better self-care among diabetics (Williams & Bond, 2002); reduced disability from problems with chronic pain (Hadjistavropoulos et al., 2007); greater persistence and effort in academic pursuits (Zimmerman, 1995); higher levels of academic performance (Chemers, Hu, & Garcia, 2001); reduced vulnerability to anxiety and depression in childhood (Muris, 2002); less jealousy in romantic relationships (Hu, Zhang, & Li, 2005); enhanced performance in athletic competition (Kane et al., 1996); greater receptiveness to technological training (Christoph, Schoenfeld, & Tansky, 1998); greater success in searching for a new job (Saks, 2006); higher work-related performance (Stajkovic & Luthans, 1998); reduced strain from occupational stress (Grau, Salanova, Peiro, 2001); and greater resistance to stress (Jex et al., 2001), among many other things.

Evaluating Behavioral Perspectives

Behavioral theories are firmly rooted in empirical research rather than clinical intuition. Pavlov's model has shed light on how conditioning can account for people's sometimes troublesome emotional responses. Skinner's work has demonstrated how personality is shaped by the consequences of behavior. Bandura's social cognitive theory has shown how people's observations mold their characteristic behavior.

Behaviorists, in particular Walter Mischel (1973, 1990), have also provided the most thorough account of why people are only moderately consistent in their behavior. For example, a person who is shy in one context might be quite outgoing in another. Other models of personality largely ignore this inconsistency. The behaviorists have shown that this inconsistency occurs because people behave in ways they think will lead to reinforcement in the situation at hand. In other words, situational factors are important determinants of behavior. Thus, a major contribution of the behavioral perspective has been its demonstration that personality factors and situational factors jointly and interactively shape behavior (Fleeson, 2004; Roberts & Pomerantz, 2004)

Of course, each theoretical approach has its shortcomings, and the behavioral approach is no exception.

Major lines of criticism include the following (Liebert & Liebert, 1998; Pervin & John, 2001):

1. *Dilution of the behavioral approach.* The behaviorists used to be criticized because they neglected cognitive processes, which clearly are important factors in human behavior. The rise of social cognitive theory blunted this criticism. However, social cognitive theory undermines the foundation on which behaviorism was built—the idea that psychologists should study only observable behavior. Thus, some critics complain that behavioral theories aren't very behavioral anymore.

2. *Overdependence on animal research.* Many principles in behavioral theories were discovered through research on animals. Some critics, especially humanistic theorists, argue that behaviorists depend too much on animal research and that they indiscriminately generalize from the behavior of animals to the behavior of humans.

Humanistic Perspectives

LEARNING OBJECTIVES

▶ *Discuss humanism as a school of thought in psychology.*

▶ *Explain Rogers's views on self-concept, development, and defensive behavior.*

▶ *Describe Maslow's hierarchy of needs, and summarize his findings on self-actualizing persons.*

▶ *Evaluate the strengths and weaknesses of humanistic theories of personality.*

Humanistic theory emerged in the 1950s as something of a backlash against the behavioral and psychodynamic theories (Cassel, 2000; DeCarvalho, 1991). The principal charge hurled at these two models was that they were dehumanizing. Freudian theory was criticized for its belief that primitive, animalistic drives dominate behavior. Behaviorism was criticized for its preoccupation with animal research. Critics argued that both schools view people as helpless pawns controlled by their environment and their past, with little capacity for self-direction. Many of these critics blended into a loose alliance that came to be known as "humanism" because of its exclusive interest in human behavior. **Humanism is a theoretical orientation that emphasizes the unique qualities of humans, especially their free will and their potential for personal growth.** Humanistic psychologists do not believe that we can learn anything of significance about the human condition from animal research.

Humanistic theorists take an optimistic view of human nature. In contrast to most psychodynamic and behavioral theorists, humanistic theorists believe that (1) human nature includes an innate drive toward personal growth, (2) individuals have the freedom to chart their courses of action and are not pawns of their environment, and (3) humans are largely conscious and rational beings who are not dominated by unconscious, irrational needs and conflicts. Humanistic theorists also maintain that one's subjective view of the world is more important than objective reality. According to this notion, if you *think* you are homely, or bright, or sociable, these beliefs will influence your behavior more than the actual realities of how homely, bright, or sociable you are.

The humanistic approach clearly provides a different perspective on personality than either the psychodynamic or behavioral approach. In this section we'll review the ideas of the two most influential humanistic theorists, Carl Rogers and Abraham Maslow.

Rogers's Person-Centered Theory

Carl Rogers (1951, 1961, 1980) was one of the founders of the human potential movement, which emphasizes personal growth through sensitivity training, encounter groups, and other exercises intended to help people get in touch with their true selves. Working at the University of Chicago in the 1940s, Rogers devised a major new approach to psychotherapy. Like Freud, Rogers based his personality theory on his extensive

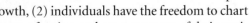

therapeutic interactions with many clients. Because of his emphasis on a person's subjective point of view, Rogers called his approach a *person-centered theory.*

The Self and Its Development

Rogers viewed personality structure in terms of just one construct. He called this construct the *self,* although it is more widely known today as the *self-concept.* **A *self-concept* is a collection of beliefs about one's own nature, unique qualities, and typical behavior.** Your self-concept is your mental picture of yourself. It is a collection of self-perceptions. For example, a self-concept might include such beliefs as "I am easygoing" or "I am pretty" or "I am hardworking."

Rogers stressed the subjective nature of the self-concept. Your self-concept may not be entirely consistent with your actual experiences. To put it more bluntly, your self-concept may be inaccurate. Most people are prone to distort their experiences to some extent to promote a relatively favorable self-concept. For example, you may believe that you are quite bright academically, but your grade transcript might suggest otherwise. Rogers used the term ***incongruence* to refer to the disparity between one's self-concept and one's actual experience.** In contrast, if a person's self-concept is reasonably accurate, it is said to be *congruent* with reality. Everyone experiences *some* incongruence; the crucial issue is how much (see **Figure 2.13**). Rogers maintained that a great deal of incongruence undermines a person's psychological well-being.

In terms of personality development, Rogers was concerned with how childhood experiences promote congruence or incongruence. According to Rogers, everyone has a strong need for affection, love, and acceptance from others. Early in life, parents provide most of this affection. Rogers maintained that some parents make their affection *conditional.* That is, they make it depend on the child's behaving well and living up to expectations. When parental love seems conditional, children often distort and block out of their self-concept those experiences that make them feel unworthy of love. At the other end of the spectrum, Rogers asserted that some parents make their affection *unconditional.* Their children have less need to block out unworthy experiences because they have been assured that they are worthy of affection no matter what they do.

Rogers believed that unconditional love from parents fosters congruence and that conditional love fosters incongruence. He further theorized that individuals who grow up believing that affection from others (besides their parents) is conditional go on to distort more and more of their experiences to feel worthy of

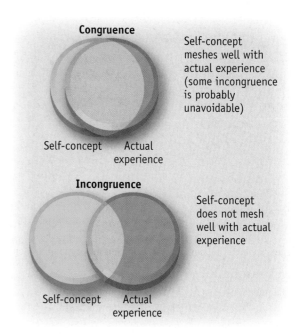
Photo caption: Carl Rogers · Carl Rogers Memorial Library

Figure 2.13

Rogers's view of personality structure. In Rogers's model, the self-concept is the only important structural construct. However, Rogers acknowledged that one's self-concept may not jell with the realities of one's actual experience—a condition called incongruence. Different people have varied amounts of incongruence between their self-concept and reality.

acceptance from a wider and wider array of people, making the incongruence grow.

Anxiety and Defense

According to Rogers, experiences that threaten people's personal views of themselves are the principal cause of troublesome anxiety. The more inaccurate your self-concept, the more likely you are to have experiences that clash with your self-perceptions. Thus, people with highly incongruent self-concepts are especially likely to be plagued by recurrent anxiety (see **Figure 2.14** on the next page).

To ward off this anxiety, such people often behave defensively. Thus, they ignore, deny, and twist reality to protect their self-concept. Consider a young woman who, like most of us, considers herself a "nice person." Let us suppose that in reality she is rather conceited and selfish, and she gets feedback from both boyfriends and

Web Link 2.4 **Personality Theories**

C. George Boeree, who teaches personality theory at Shippensburg University, has assembled an online textbook that discusses more than 20 important personality theorists in depth. All of the important figures cited in this chapter (except for the behaviorists such as Skinner and Pavlov) receive attention at this valuable site.

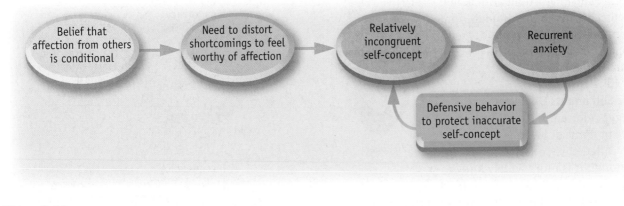

Figure 2.14

Rogers's view of personality development and dynamics. Rogers's theory of development posits that conditional love leads to a need to distort experiences, which fosters an incongruent self-concept. Incongruence makes one prone to recurrent anxiety, which triggers defensive behavior, which fuels more incongruence.

girlfriends that she is a "self-centered, snotty brat." How might she react to protect her self-concept? She might ignore or block out those occasions when she behaves selfishly and then deny the accusations by her friends that she is self-centered. She might also attribute her girlfriends' negative comments to their jealousy of her good looks and blame the boyfriends' negative remarks on their disappointment because she won't get more serious with them. Meanwhile, she might start doing some kind of charity work to show everyone (including herself) that she really is a nice person. As you can see, people often go to great lengths to defend their self-concept.

Rogers's theory can explain defensive behavior and personality disturbances, but he also emphasized the importance of psychological health. Rogers held that psychological health is rooted in a congruent self-concept. In turn, congruence is rooted in a sense of personal worth, which stems from a childhood saturated with unconditional affection from parents and others. These themes are similar to those emphasized by the other major humanistic theorist, Abraham Maslow.

Maslow's Theory of Self-Actualization

Abraham Maslow grew up in Brooklyn and spent much of his career at Brandeis University, where he provided crucial leadership for the fledgling humanistic movement. Like Rogers, Maslow (1968, 1970) argued that psychology should take a greater interest in the nature of the healthy personality, instead of dwelling on the causes of disorders. "To oversimplify the matter somewhat," he said, "it is as if Freud supplied to us the sick half of psychology and we must now fill it out with the healthy half" (Maslow, 1968, p. 5). Maslow's key contributions were his analysis of how motives are organized hierarchically and his description of the healthy personality.

Abraham Maslow

Hierarchy of Needs

Maslow proposed that human motives are organized into a *hierarchy of needs*—**a systematic arrangement**

Recommended READING

**Three Psychologies:
Perspectives from Freud, Skinner, and Rogers**
by Robert D. Nye (Wadsworth, 2000)

One would be hard pressed to identify anyone who has had more influence over the evolution of psychology in the 20th century than the three theorists profiled in this book: Sigmund Freud, B. F. Skinner, and Carl Rogers. In this concise (159 pages), highly readable book, Robert Nye gives readers a simple—but not oversimplified—introduction to the theories of Freud, Rogers, and Skinner. After providing a brief overview of all three theories—the psychodynamic, behavioral, and humanistic—in the first chapter, Nye devotes a chapter to each theorist, attempting to present each man's ideas as convincingly as possible, holding criticisms until later. These chapters include short biographical sketches of each man and discuss practical examples and real-world implications of each theorist's provocative ideas. In the final chapter, Nye systematically compares the three theorists, reviews criticism of each, and adds his own personal comments. All in all, this is a superb introduction to the three major perspectives that have shaped contemporary psychology.

Figure 2.15

Maslow's hierarchy of needs. According to Maslow, human needs are arranged in a hierarchy, and individuals must satisfy their basic needs first, before they progress to higher needs. In the diagram, higher levels in the pyramid represent progressively less basic needs. People progress upward in the hierarchy when lower needs are satisfied reasonably well, but they may regress back to lower levels if basic needs cease to be satisfied.

Need for self-actualization:
Realization of potential

Progression if lower needs are satisfied

Aesthetic needs:
Order and beauty

Cognitive needs:
Knowledge and understanding

Esteem needs:
Achievement and gaining of recognition

Belongingness and love needs:
Affiliation and acceptance

Regression if lower needs are not being satisfied

Safety and security needs:
Long-term survival and stability

Physiological needs:
Hunger, thirst, and so forth

Web Link 2.5 **The Personality Project**

William Revelle, director of the graduate program in personality at Northwestern University's Psychology Department, has assembled a directory to many Internet-based resources in the study of personality.

of needs, according to priority, in which basic needs must be met before less basic needs are aroused. This hierarchical arrangement is usually portrayed as a pyramid (see **Figure 2.15**). The needs toward the bottom of the pyramid, such as physiological or security needs, are the most basic. Higher levels in the pyramid consist of progressively less basic needs. When a person manages to satisfy a level of needs reasonably well (complete satisfaction is not necessary), *this satisfaction activates needs at the next level.*

Like Rogers, Maslow argued that humans have an innate drive toward personal growth—that is, evolution toward a higher state of being. Thus, he described the needs in the uppermost reaches of his hierarchy as *growth*

needs. These include the needs for knowledge, understanding, order, and aesthetic beauty. Foremost among the growth needs is the ***need for self-actualization, which is the need to fulfill one's potential;*** it is the highest need in Maslow's motivational hierarchy. Maslow summarized this concept with a simple statement: "What a man *can* be, he *must* be." According to Maslow, people will be frustrated if they are unable to fully utilize their talents or pursue their true interests. For example, if you have great musical talent but must work as an accountant, or if you have scholarly interests but must work as a sales clerk, your need for self-actualization will be thwarted.

The Healthy Personality

Because of his interest in self-actualization, Maslow set out to discover the nature of the healthy personality. He tried to identify people of exceptional mental health so that he could investigate their characteristics. In one case, he used psychological tests and interviews to sort out the healthiest 1 percent of a sizable population of college students. He also studied admired historical figures (such as Thomas Jefferson and

PEANUTS reprinted by permission of United Feature Syndicate, Inc.

psychologist-philosopher William James) and personal acquaintances characterized by superior adjustment. Over a period of years, he accumulated his case histories and gradually sketched, in broad strokes, a picture of ideal psychological health.

Maslow called people with exceptionally healthy personalities *self-actualizing persons* because of their commitment to continued personal growth. He identified various traits characteristic of self-actualizing people, which are listed in **Figure 2.16**. In brief, Maslow found that self-actualizers are accurately tuned in to reality and are at peace with themselves. He found that they are open and spontaneous and that they retain a fresh appreciation of the world around them. Socially, they are sensitive to others' needs and enjoy rewarding interpersonal relations. However, they are not dependent on others for approval, nor are they uncomfortable with solitude. They thrive on their work, and they enjoy their sense of humor. Maslow also noted that they have "peak experiences" (profound emotional highs) more often than others. Finally, he found that they strike a nice balance between many polarities in personality, in that they can be both childlike and mature, rational and intuitive, conforming and rebellious.

Evaluating Humanistic Perspectives

The humanists added a refreshing perspective to the study of personality. Their argument that a person's subjective views may be more important than objective reality has proven compelling. Today, even behavioral theorists have begun to consider subjective personal factors such as beliefs and expectations. The humanistic approach also deserves credit for making the self-concept an important construct in psychology. Finally, one could argue that the humanists' optimistic, growth, and health-oriented approach laid the foundation for the emergence of the positive psychology movement that is increasingly influential in contemporary psychology (Sheldon & Kasser, 2001b; Taylor, 2001).

Of course, there is a negative side to the balance sheet as well. Critics have identified some weaknesses in the humanistic approach to personality, including the following (Burger, 2004; Carducci, 1998):

1. *Poor testability.* Like psychodynamic theorists, the humanists have been criticized for proposing hypotheses that are difficult to put to a scientific test. Humanistic concepts such as personal growth and self-actualization are difficult to define and measure.

Characteristics of Self-Actualizing People

- Clear, efficient perception of reality and comfortable relations with it
- Spontaneity, simplicity, and naturalness
- Problem centering (having something outside themselves they "must" do as a mission)
- Detachment and need for privacy
- Autonomy, independence of culture and environment
- Continued freshness of appreciation
- Mystical and peak experiences
- Feelings of kinship and identification with the human race
- Strong friendships, but limited in number
- Democratic character structure
- Ethical discrimination between means and ends, between good and evil
- Philosophical, unhostile sense of humor
- Balance between polarities in personality

Figure 2.16

Characteristics of self-actualizing people. Humanistic theorists emphasize psychological health instead of maladjustment. Maslow's sketch of the self-actualizing person provides a provocative picture of the healthy personality.

2. *Unrealistic view of human nature.* Critics also charge that the humanists have been overly optimistic in their assumptions about human nature and unrealistic in their descriptions of the healthy personality. For instance, Maslow's self-actualizing people sound *perfect*. In reality, Maslow had a hard time finding self-actualizing persons. When he searched among the living, the results were so disappointing that he turned to the study of historical figures. Thus, humanistic portraits of psychological health are perhaps a bit unrealistic.

3. *Inadequate evidence.* Humanistic theories are based primarily on discerning but uncontrolled observations in clinical settings. Case studies can be valuable in generating ideas, but they are ill-suited for building a solid database. More experimental research is needed to catch up with the theorizing in the humanistic camp. This situation is precisely the opposite of the one you'll encounter in the next section, on biological perspectives, where more theorizing is needed to catch up with the research.

Biological Perspectives

LEARNING OBJECTIVES

▶ *Describe Eysenck's views on personality structure and development.*

▶ *Summarize recent twin studies that support the idea that personality is largely inherited.*

▶ *Summarize evolutionary analyses of why certain personality traits appear to be important.*

▶ *Evaluate the strengths and weaknesses of biological theories of personality.*

Like many identical twins reared apart, Jim Lewis and Jim Springer found they had been leading eerily similar lives. Separated four weeks after birth in 1940, the Jim twins grew up 45 miles apart in Ohio and were reunited in 1979. Eventually, they discovered that both drove the same model blue Chevrolet, chain-smoked Salems, chewed their fingernails, and owned dogs named Toy. Each had spent a good deal of time vacationing at the same three-block strip of beach in Florida. More important, when tested for such personality traits as flexibility, self-control, and sociability, the twins responded almost exactly alike. (Leo, 1987, p. 63)

So began a *Time* magazine summary of a major twin study conducted at the University of Minnesota, where investigators have been exploring the hereditary roots of personality. The research team has managed to locate and complete testing on 44 rare pairs of identical twins separated early in life. Not all the twin pairs have been as similar as Jim Lewis and Jim Springer, but many of the parallels have been uncanny (Lykken et al., 1992). Identical twins Oskar Stohr and Jack Yufe were separated soon after birth. Oskar was sent to a Nazi-run school in Czechoslovakia, while Jack was raised in a Jewish home on a Caribbean island. When they were reunited for the first time during middle age, they both showed up wearing similar mustaches, haircuts, shirts, and wire-rimmed glasses. A pair of previously sepa-

rated female twins both arrived at the Minneapolis airport wearing seven rings on their fingers. One had a son named Richard Andrew, and the other had a son named Andrew Richard!

Could personality be largely inherited? These anecdotal reports of striking resemblances between identical twins reared apart certainly raise this possibility. In this section we'll discuss Hans Eysenck's theory, which emphasizes the influence of heredity, and look at behavioral genetics and evolutionary perspectives on personality.

Eysenck's Theory

Hans Eysenck was born in Germany but fled to London during the era of Nazi rule. He went on to become one of Britain's most prominent psychologists. According to Eysenck (1967), "Personality is determined to a large extent by a person's genes" (p. 20). How is heredity linked to personality in Eysenck's model? In part, through conditioning concepts borrowed from behavioral theory. Eysenck (1967, 1982, 1991) theorizes that some people can be conditioned more readily than others because of inherited differences in

Hans Eysenck

Is personality largely inherited? The story of these identical twins would certainly suggest so. Although they were reared apart from 4 weeks after their birth, Jim Lewis (left) and Jim Springer (right) exhibit remarkable correspondence in personality. Some of the similarities in their lives—such as the benches built around trees in their yards—seem uncanny.

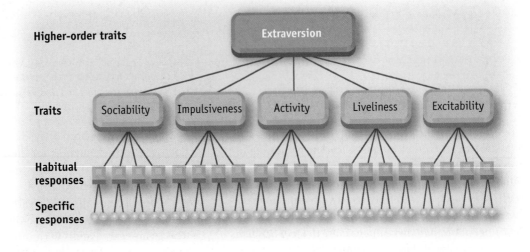

Higher-order traits   **Extraversion**

Traits   Sociability   Impulsiveness   Activity   Liveliness   Excitability

Habitual responses

Specific responses

Figure 2.17

Eysenck's model of personality structure. Eysenck describes personality structure as a hierarchy of traits. In this scheme, a few higher-order traits (such as extraversion) determine a host of lower-order traits (such as sociability), which determine one's habitual responses (such as going to lots of parties).

From Eysenck, H. J. (1967). *The biological basis of personality*, p. 36. Springfield, IL: Charles C. Thomas. Courtesy of Charles C. Thomas.

their physiological functioning (specifically, their level of arousal). These variations in "conditionability" are assumed to influence the personality traits that people acquire through conditioning.

Eysenck views personality structure as a hierarchy of traits. Numerous superficial traits are derived from a smaller number of more basic traits, which are derived from a handful of fundamental higher-order traits, as shown in **Figure 2.17**. Eysenck has shown a special interest in explaining variations in *extraversion-introversion*, the trait dimension first described years earlier by Carl Jung. He has proposed that introverts tend to have higher levels of physiological arousal than extraverts. This higher arousal purportedly motivates them to avoid social situations that will further elevate their arousal and makes them more easily conditioned than extraverts. According to Eysenck, people who condition easily acquire more conditioned inhibitions than others. These inhibitions, coupled with their relatively high arousal, make them more bashful, tentative, and uneasy in social situations. This social discomfort leads them to turn inward. Hence, they become introverted.

Recent Research in Behavioral Genetics

Recent twin studies have provided impressive support for Eysenck's hypothesis that personality is largely inherited. In *twin studies* researchers assess hereditary influence by comparing the resemblance of identical twins and fraternal twins on a trait. The logic underlying this comparison is as follows. *Identical twins* emerge from one egg that splits, so that their genetic makeup is exactly the same (100% overlap).

Fraternal twins result when two eggs are fertilized simultaneously; their genetic overlap is only 50%. Both types of twins *usually* grow up in the same home, at the same time, exposed to the same relatives, neighbors, peers, teachers, events, and so forth. Thus, both kinds of twins normally develop under similar environmental conditions, but identical twins share more genetic kinship. Hence, if sets of identical twins exhibit more personality resemblance than sets of fraternal twins, this greater similarity is probably attributable to heredity rather than to environment. The results of twin studies can be used to estimate the heritability of personality traits and other characteristics. **A heritability ratio is an estimate of the proportion of trait variability in a population that is determined by variations in genetic inheritance.** Heritability can be estimated for any trait. For example, the heritability of height is estimated to be around 90% (Plomin, 1994), whereas the heritability of intelligence appears to be about 50%–70% (Petrill, 2005; Plomin & Spinath, 2004).

The accumulating evidence from twin studies suggests that heredity exerts considerable influence over many personality traits (Livesley, Jang, & Vernon, 2003; Rowe & van den Oord, 2005). For instance, in research on the Big Five personality traits, identical twins have been found to be much more similar than fraternal twins on all five traits (Loehlin, 1992). Some skeptics still wonder whether identical twins might exhibit more personality resemblance than fraternal twins because they are raised more similarly. In other words, they wonder whether environmental factors (rather than heredity) could be responsible for identical twins' greater similarity. This nagging question can be answered only by studying identical twins who have been reared apart. Which is why the twin study at the University of Minnesota has been so important.

The Minnesota study (Tellegen et al., 1988) was the first to administer the same personality test to identical and fraternal twins reared together as well as apart. Most of the twins reared apart were separated quite early in life (median age of 2.5 months) and remained separated for a long time (median period of almost 34 years). Nonetheless, on all three of the higher-order traits examined, the identical twins reared apart displayed more personality resemblance than fraternal twins reared together. Based on the pattern of correlations observed, the researchers estimated that the heritability of personality is around 50%. Another large-scale twin study of the Big Five traits conducted in Germany and Poland yielded similar conclusions (Riemann, Angleitner, & Strelau, 1997). The heritability estimates based on the data from this study, which are shown in **Figure 2.18**, are in the same range as the estimates from the Minnesota study.

Research on the genetic bases of personality has inadvertently turned up another interesting finding that is apparent in the data shown in **Figure 2.18**. A number of recent studies have found that shared family environment has surprisingly little impact on personality (Beer, Arnold, & Loehlin, 1998; Rowe & van den Oord, 2005). This finding is surprising in that social scientists have long assumed that the family environment shared by children growing up together led to some personality resemblance among them. *These findings have led some theorists to conclude that parents don't matter— that they wield very little influence over how their children develop* (Cohen, 1999; Harris, 1998; Rowe, 1994).

Web Link 2.6 **Great Ideas in Personality**

At this site, personality psychologist G. Scott Acton demonstrates that scientific research programs in personality generate broad and compelling ideas about what it is to be a human being. He charts the contours of 12 research perspectives, including behaviorism, behavioral genetics, and sociobiology, and supports them with extensive links to published and online resources associated with each perspective.

Although the assertion that "parents don't matter" seems premature and overstated (Collins et al., 2000; Maccoby, 2000; Turkheimer & Waldron, 2000), the perplexing findings in behavioral genetics studies of personality have led researchers to investigate why children from the same family are often so different. Thus far, the evidence suggests that children in the same family experience home environments that are not nearly as homogeneous as previously assumed (Hetherington, Reiss, & Plomin, 1994; Pike et al., 2000). Children in the same home may be treated quite differently, because gender and birth order can influence parents' approaches to childrearing. Temperamental differences between children may also evoke differences in parenting. Focusing on how environmental factors vary *within* families represents a promising new way to explore the determinants of personality.

The Evolutionary Approach to Personality

In the realm of biological approaches to personality, the most recent development has been the emergence

Figure 2.18

Heritability and environmental variance for the Big Five traits. Based on the twin study data of Riemann et al. (1997), Plomin and Caspi (1999) estimated the heritability of each of the Big Five traits. The data also allowed them to estimate the amount of variance on each trait attributable to shared environment and nonshared environment. As you can see, the heritability estimates hovered in the vicinity of 40%, with two exceeding 50%. As in other studies, the influence of shared environment was very modest.

Based on Plomin, R., & Caspi, A. (1999). Behavioral genetics and personality. In L. A. Pervin & O. P. John (Eds.), *Handbook of Personality: Theory and Research*. New York: The Guilford Press. Adapted by permission.

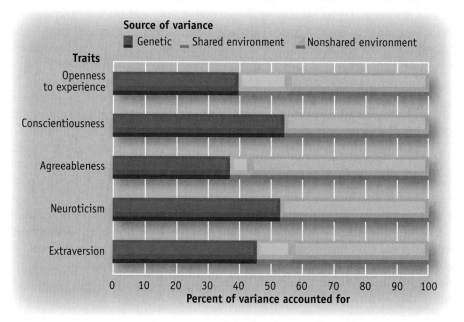

of an evolutionary perspective. Evolutionary psychologists assert that the patterns of behavior seen in a species are products of evolution in the same way that anatomical characteristics are. ***Evolutionary psychology examines behavioral processes in terms of their adaptive value for members of a species over the course of many generations.*** The basic premise of evolutionary psychology is that natural selection favors behaviors that enhance organisms' reproductive success—that is, passing on genes to the next generation. Evolutionary theorists assert that personality has a biological basis because natural selection has favored certain personality traits over the course of human history (Figueredo et al., 2005). Thus, evolutionary analyses of personality focus on how various traits—and the ability to recognize these traits in others—may have contributed to reproductive fitness in ancestral human populations.

For example, David Buss (1991, 1995, 1997) has argued that the Big Five personality traits stand out as important dimensions of personality across a variety of cultures because those traits have had significant adaptive implications. Buss points out that humans have historically depended heavily on groups, which afford protection from predators or enemies, opportunities for sharing food, and a diverse array of other benefits. In the context of these group interactions, people have had to make difficult but crucial judgments about the characteristics of others, asking such questions as: Who will make a good member of my coalition? Who can I depend on when in need? Who will share their resources? Thus, Buss (1995) argues, "Those individuals able to accurately discern and act upon these individual differences likely enjoyed a considerable reproductive advantage" (p. 22). According to Buss, the Big Five emerge as fundamental dimensions of personality because humans have evolved special sensitivity to variations in the ability to bond with others (extraversion), the willingness to cooperate and collaborate (agreeableness), the tendency to be reliable and ethical (conscientiousness), the capacity to be an innovative problem solver (openness to experience), and the ability to handle stress (low neuroticism). In a nutshell, Buss argues that the Big Five reflect the most salient features of others' adaptive behavior over the course of evolutionary history.

Daniel Nettle (2006) takes this line of thinking one step further, asserting that the traits themselves (as opposed to the ability to recognize them in others) are products of evolution that were adaptive in ancestral environments. For example, he discusses how extraversion could have promoted mating success, how neuroticism could have fueled competitiveness and avoidance of dangers, how agreeableness could have fostered the effective building of coalitions, and so forth. Nettle also discusses how each of the Big Five traits may have had adaptive costs (extraversion, for example, is associated with risky behavior) as well as benefits. Thus, he argues that evolutionary analyses of personality need to weigh the *trade-offs* between the adaptive advantages and disadvantages of the Big Five traits.

Evaluating Biological Perspectives

Recent research in behavioral genetics has provided convincing evidence that biological factors help shape personality. Evolutionary theorists have developed thought-provoking hypotheses about how natural selection may have sculpted the basic architecture of personality. Nonetheless, we must take note of some weaknesses in biological approaches to personality:

1. *Problems with estimates of hereditary influence.* Efforts to carve personality into genetic and environmental components with statistics are ultimately artificial. The effects of heredity and environment are twisted together in complicated interactions that can't be separated cleanly (Funder, 2001; Sternberg et al., 2005). Although heritability ratios sound precise, they are estimates based on a complicated chain of inferences that are subject to debate.

2. *Hindsight bias in evolutionary theory.* **Hindsight bias—the common tendency to mold one's interpretation of the past to fit how events actually turned out**—presents thorny problems for evolutionary theorists, who generally work backward from known outcomes to reason out how adaptive pressures in humans' ancestral past may have led to those outcomes (Cornell, 1997). Evolutionary theorists' assertion that the Big Five traits had major adaptive implications over the course of human history seems plausible, but what would have happened if other traits, such as dominance or sensation seeking, had shown up in the Big Five? With the luxury of hindsight, evolutionary theorists surely could have constructed plausible explanations for how these traits promoted reproductive success in the distant past. Thus, some critics have argued that evolutionary explanations are post-hoc, speculative accounts contaminated by hindsight bias.

3. *Lack of adequate theory.* At present there is no comprehensive biological theory of personality. Eysenck's model does not provide a systematic overview of how biological factors govern personality development (and it was never intended to). Evolutionary analyses of personality are even more limited in scope. Additional theoretical work is needed to catch up with recent empirical findings on the biological basis for personality.

A Contemporary Empirical Approach: Terror Management Theory

LEARNING OBJECTIVES

▶ Explain the chief concepts and hypotheses of terror management theory.

▶ Describe how reminders of death influence people's behavior.

So far, our coverage has been largely devoted to grand, panoramic theories of personality. In this section we'll examine a new approach to understanding personality functioning that has a narrower focus than the classic theories of personality. *Terror management theory* emerged as an influential perspective in the 1990s. Although the theory borrows from Freudian and evolutionary formulations, it provides its own unique analysis of the human condition. Developed by Sheldon Solomon, Jeff Greenberg, and Tom Pyszczynski (1991, 2004b), this fresh perspective is currently generating a huge volume of research, much of which seems especially relevant to contemporary adjustment issues.

Essentials of Terror Management Theory

One of the chief goals of terror management theory is to explain why people need self-esteem (Solomon, Greenberg, & Pyszczynski, 1991). The theory begins with the assumption that humans share an evolutionary heritage with other animals that includes an instinctive drive for self-preservation. However, unlike other animals, humans have evolved complex cognitive abilities that permit self-awareness and contemplation of the future. These cognitive capacities make humans keenly aware of the inevitability of death—they appreciate that life can be snuffed out unpredictably at any time. The collision between humans' self-preservation instinct and their awareness of the inevitability of death creates the potential for experiencing anxiety, alarm, and terror when people think about their mortality (see **Figure 2.19**).

How do humans deal with this potential for terror? According to terror management theory, "What saves us is culture. Cultures provide ways to view the world—worldviews—that 'solve' the existential crisis engendered by the awareness of death" (Pyszczynski, Solomon, & Greenberg, 2003, p. 16). Cultural worldviews diminish anxiety by providing answers to universal questions such as Why am I here? and What is the meaning of life? Cultures create stories, traditions, and institutions that give their members a sense of being part of an enduring legacy through their contributions to their families, tribes, schools, churches, professions, and so forth. Thus, faith in a cultural worldview can give people a sense of order, meaning, and context that can soothe their fear of death.

Where does self-esteem fit into the picture? Self-esteem is viewed as a sense of personal worth that depends on one's confidence in the validity of one's cultural worldview and the belief that one is living up to the standards prescribed by that worldview. "It is the feeling that one is a valuable contributor to a meaningful universe" (Pyszczynski, Solomon, & Greenberg, 2004, p. 437). Hence, self-esteem buffers people from the profound anxiety associated with the awareness that they are transient animals destined to die. In other words, self-esteem serves a *terror management* function (refer to **Figure 2.19**).

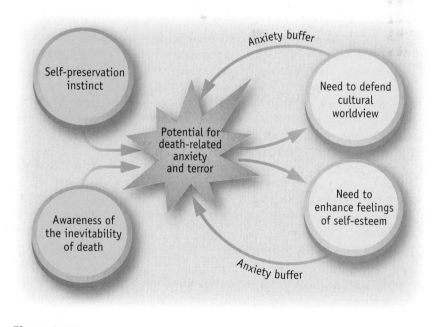

Figure 2.19

Overview of terror management theory. This graphic maps out the relations among the key concepts proposed by terror management theory. The theory asserts that humans' unique awareness of the inevitability of death fosters a need to defend one's cultural worldview and one's self-esteem, which serve to protect one from mortality-related anxiety.

Understanding Reactions to Terrorist Attacks

Although its name might suggest otherwise, terror management theory was not developed to deal with the phenomenon of terrorism in the aftermath of 9/11. Terror management theory has been around since the mid-1980s, and as the text explains, it is a wide-ranging theory that analyzes the many ramifications of humans' existential struggle with the inevitability of death (see pp. 59–62). Nonetheless, given its central focus on the effects of reminding people of their mortality, the theory can help us understand the psychological impact of terrorist attacks in today's world.

In their book *In the Wake of 9/11*, Tom Pyszczynski, Sheldon Solomon, and Jeff Greenberg (2003) point out that the tragic events of 9/11 produced a powerful, nationwide manipulation of mortality salience. The televised images of death and destruction seen that day made most Americans feel extremely vulnerable. According to the architects of terror management theory, many of the reactions seen across the country after 9/11 were exactly what one would expect based on their theory. These reactions included the following:

Reaffirmation of cultural worldviews. When mortality salience is elevated, terror management theory predicts that people will embrace their cultural worldviews even more strongly than before. Consistent with this prediction, in the months following 9/11, church attendance and the sale of bibles both increased dramatically. Thus, people reaffirmed their faith in organized religion, which represents the foundation of many individuals' cultural worldview. People also became much more overtly patriotic. Flags flew everywhere, patriotic songs were all over the radio, and corporate logos were redesigned in red, white, and blue. Thus, people proudly proclaimed their faith in the American way.

Reduced tolerance. Research has shown that when death anxiety is heightened, people become less tolerant of opposing views and more prejudiced against those who are different. Consistent with this analysis, in the aftermath of 9/11 individuals who questioned government policies met more hostility than usual.

Increased altruism. Altruism, which consists of unselfish concern for the welfare of others, is a highly respected virtue in most cultures. Behaving in an altruistic manner makes people feel like they are good citizens, thus reaffirming their commitment to their cultural worldview and enhancing their self-esteem. Terror management theory would anticipate that increased mortality salience would stimulate increased altruism, which clearly was seen in the months after the terrorist assaults. Many people traveled to New York or Washington to help in whatever way they could after the attacks. Blood donations reached unprecedented levels, and charitable giving skyrocketed.

Intensified need for heroes. Research indicates that reminders of mortality increase the tendency to admire those who uphold cultural standards. More than ever, people need heroes who personify cultural values. This need was apparent in the aftermath of 9/11 in the way the media made firefighters into larger-than-life heroes. This analysis is not meant to suggest that firefighters did not deserve to be characterized as heroic. Rather, the point is that firefighters had a long history of heroic behavior that largely went unrecognized until a massive increase in mortality salience created an urgent need for uplifting heroes.

Admittedly, some of the reactions to 9/11 predicted by terror management theory could also be explained by other theoretical perspectives. Nonetheless, terror management theory seems to provide a perspective that is uniquely well suited to understanding some of the effects of terrorism on our collective psyche.

The notion that self-esteem functions as an *anxiety buffer* has been supported by numerous studies (Pyszczynski et al., 2004). In many of these experiments, researchers have manipulated what they call *mortality salience* (the degree to which subjects' mortality is prominent in their minds), usually by asking participants to briefly think about their own future death. Consistent with the anxiety buffer hypothesis, reminding people of their mortality leads subjects to engage in a variety of behaviors that are likely to bolster their self-esteem, thus reducing anxiety (see Chapter 5 for more on the terror management function of self-esteem).

Applications of Terror Management Theory

Increasing mortality salience also leads people to work harder at defending their cultural worldview (Arndt, Cook, & Routledge, 2004). For instance, after briefly pondering their mortality, research participants (1) hand out harsher penalties to moral transgressors, (2) respond more negatively to people who criticize their country, (3) give larger rewards to people who uphold cultural standards, and (4) show more respect for cultural icons, such as a flag (Greenberg et al., 1990; Rosenblatt et al., 1989). This need to defend one's cultural worldview may even fuel prejudice and aggression. Reminding subjects of their mortality leads to (1) more negative evaluations of people from different religious or ethnic backgrounds, (2) more stereotypic thinking about minority group members, and (3) more aggressive behavior toward people with opposing political views (McGregor et al., 1998; Schimel et al., 1999).

Terror management theory asserts that much of our behavior is motivated by the overlapping needs to defend our cultural worldview and to preserve our self-esteem. This perspective yields novel hypotheses regarding many phenomena. For instance, Solomon, Greenberg, and Pyszczynski (2004a) explain excessive materialism in terms of the anxiety-buffering function of self-esteem. Specifically, they argue that "conspicuous possession and consumption are thinly veiled efforts to assert that one is special and therefore more than just an animal fated to die and decay" (p. 134). Terror management theory has also been used to explain depressive disorders. According to Arndt et al. (2000), depression occurs when individuals' anxiety buffer fails and they lose faith in the cultural world-view that gave their life meaning. One fascinating study even applied terror management theory to the political process. Cohen et al. (2004) found that mortality salience increases subjects' preference for "charismatic" candidates who articulate a grand vision that makes people feel like they are part of an important movement of lasting significance. Yet another study showed that terror management processes can have an impact on people's reactions to certain types of art (Landau, Greenberg, et al., 2006). When mortality salience is elevated, people's need for a clear, meaningful view of reality is increased, leading them to have more negative reactions to abstract paintings that frustrate their need for meaning.

In another thought-provoking analysis, Jamie Goldenberg (2005, p. 224) argues that "uneasiness surrounding the body stems in part from existential concerns associated with human awareness that the physical body is the vehicle through which life passes unto death." In other words, bodily concerns remind people of their animal nature and hence their ultimate mortality. Based on this analysis, Goldenberg and colleages have predicted and found that mortality salience can increase individuals' ambivalence about the physical aspects of sexuality and lead to the suppression of some sexual urges (Goldenberg et al., 2002; Landau, Goldenberg, et al., 2006). Mortality salience can also inhibit health-protective behaviors, such as breast self-exams by women, when these behaviors highlight the frailty of the human body. Thus, terror management processes may contribute to psychological discomfort about bodily processes, including sexual desires.

Although terror management theory is narrower in scope than psychoanalytic, behavioral, and humanistic theories, it has wide-ranging implications and is being applied to more and more aspects of human behavior. At first glance, a theory that explains everything

Terror management theory has been applied to a remarkably diverse array of phenomena. For example, it has been used to explain conspicuous consumption and to predict people's voting preferences.

from prejudice to sexual ambivalence to compulsive shopping in terms of death anxiety may seem highly implausible. After all, most people do not appear to walk around all day obsessing about the possibility of their death. The architects of terror management theory are well aware of this reality. They explain that the defensive reactions uncovered in their research generally occur when death anxiety surfaces on the fringes of conscious awareness and that these reactions are automatic and subconscious (Pyszczynski, Greenberg, & Solomon, 1999). They also assert that people experi-ence far more reminders of their mortality than most of us appreciate. They point out that people may be reminded of their mortality by a variety of everyday events, such as driving by a cemetery or funeral home, reading about an auto accident, visiting a doctor's office, hearing about a celebrity's heart attack, learning about alarming medical research, skipping over the obituaries in the newspaper, and so forth. Thus, the processes discussed by terror management theory may be more commonplace than one might guess.

Culture and Personality

LEARNING OBJECTIVES
▶ *Discuss whether the five-factor model has any relevance in non-Western cultures.*
▶ *Explain how researchers have found both cross-cultural similarities and disparities in personality.*
▶ *Summarize recent research on the accuracy of perceptions of national character.*

Are there connections between culture and personality? The investigation of this question dates back to the 1930s and 1940s, when researchers set out to identify various cultures' *modal personality* (Kardiner & Linton, 1945) or *national character* (Kluckhohn & Murray, 1948). These investigations sought to describe the *prototype* or *typical* personality in various cultures. For example, Ruth Benedict (1934) concluded that American Pueblo Indians were sober, orderly, conventional, and cooperative. Largely guided by Freud's psychoanalytic theory, this line of research generated interest for a couple decades, but ultimately met with little success (Bock, 2000; LeVine, 2001). Part of the problem may have been the rather culture-bound, Eurocentric nature of Freudian theory, but the crux of the problem was that it was unrealistic to expect to find a single, dominant personality profile in each culture.

Studies of the links between culture and personality dwindled to almost nothing for many decades. However, in recent decades psychology has become more interested in cultural factors, sparking a renaissance in culture-personality research. This research has sought to determine whether Western personality constructs are relevant to other cultures and whether cultural differences can be seen in the strength of specific personality traits. These studies have found evidence of both continuity and variability across cultures.

For the most part, continuity has been apparent in cross-cultural comparisons of the *trait structure* of personality. When English language personality scales have been translated and administered in other cultures, the predicted dimensions of personality have emerged from the factor analyses (Paunonen & Ashton, 1998). For example, when scales that tap the Big Five personality traits have been administered and subjected to factor analysis in other cultures, the usual five traits have typically emerged (Katigbak et al., 2002; McCrae et al., 2005b). Thus, research tentatively suggests that the basic dimensions of personality trait structure may be universal.

On the other hand, some cross-cultural variability is seen when researchers compare the average trait scores of samples from various cultural groups. For example, in a study comparing 51 cultures, McCrae et al. (2005a) found that Brazilians scored relatively high in neuroticism, Australians in extraversion, Germans in openness to experience, Czechs in agreeableness, and Malaysians in conscientiousness, to give but a handful of examples. These findings should be viewed as very preliminary, as more data are needed from larger and more carefully selected samples. Nonetheless, the findings suggest that genuine cultural differences may exist in some personality traits. That said, the observed cultural disparities in average trait scores were modest in size.

The availability of the data from the McCrae et al. (2005a) study allowed Terracciano et al. (2005) to re-visit the concept of *national character*. Terracciano and his colleagues asked subjects from many cultures to describe the *typical* member of *their* culture on rating forms guided by the five-factor model. Generally, subjects displayed substantial agreement on these ratings of what was typical for their culture. The averaged ratings, which served as the measures of each culture's national character, were then correlated with the actual mean trait scores for various cultures compiled in the McCrae et al. (2005a) study. The results were defini-tive—the vast majority of the correlations were extremely low and often even negative. In other words, there was little or no relationship between perceptions of national character and actual trait scores for various cultures (see **Figure 2.20**). People's beliefs about national character, which often fuel cultural prejudices, turned out to be profoundly inaccurate stereotypes (McCrae & Terracciano, 2006).

Figure 2.20

An example of inaccurate perceptions of national character. Terracciano et al. (2005) found that perceptions of national character (the prototype or typical personality for a particular culture) are largely inaccurate. The data shown here for one culture—Canadians—illustrates this inaccuracy. Mean scores on the Big Five traits for a sample of real individuals from Canada are graphed in red. Averaged perceptions of national character for Canadians are graphed in blue. The discrepancy between perception and reality is obvious. Terracciano et al. found similar disparities between views of national character and actual trait scores for a majority of the cultues they studied. (Adapted from McCrae & Terracciano, 2006)

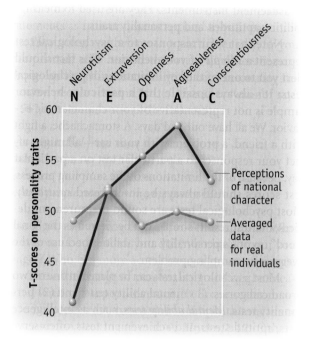

APPLICATION

Assessing Your Personality

LEARNING OBJECTIVES

▶ *Explain the concepts of standardization, test norms, reliability, and validity.*
▶ *Discuss the value and the limitations of self-report inventories.*
▶ *Discuss the value and limitations of projective tests.*

Answer the following "true" or "false."

____ **1.** Responses to personality tests are subject to unconscious distortion.

____ **2.** The results of personality tests are often misunderstood.

____ **3.** Personality test scores should be interpreted with caution.

____ **4.** Personality tests may be quite useful in helping people to learn more about themselves.

If you answered "true" to all four questions, you earned a perfect score. Yes, personality tests are subject to distortion. Admittedly, test results are often misunderstood, and they should be interpreted cautiously. In spite of these problems, however, psychological tests can be very useful.

We all engage in efforts to size up our own personality as well as that of others. When you think to yourself that "this salesman is untrustworthy," or when you remark to a friend that "Howard is too timid and submissive," you are making personality assessments.

In a sense, then, personality assessment is part of daily life. However, psychological tests provide much more systematic assessments than casual observations do.

The value of psychological tests lies in their ability to help people form a realistic picture of their personal qualities. In light of this value, we have included a variety of personality tests in the *Personal Explorations Workbook* that is available to accompany this text, and we have sprinkled a number of short tests throughout the text itself. Most of these questionnaires are widely used personality tests. We hope that you may gain some insights by responding to these scales. But it's important to understand the logic and limitations of such tests. To facilitate your use of these and other tests, this Application discusses some of the basics of psychological testing.

Key Concepts in Psychological Testing

A *psychological test* is a standardized measure of a sample of a person's behavior. Psychological tests are

simultaneously assess a multitude of traits. The Sixteen Personality Factor Questionnaire (16PF), developed by Raymond Cattell and his colleagues (Cattell, Eber, & Tatsuoka, 1970), is a representative example of a multi-trait inventory. The 16PF is a 187-item scale that measures 16 basic dimensions of personality, called source traits, which are shown in **Figure 2.23**.

As we noted earlier, some theorists believe that only five trait dimensions are required to provide a full description of personality. The five-factor model led to the creation of the NEO Personality Inventory. Developed by Paul Costa and Robert McCrae (1985, 1992), the NEO Inventory is designed to measure the Big Five traits: neuroticism, extraversion, openness to experience, agreeableness, and conscientiousness. The NEO Inventory is widely used in research and clinical work.

To appreciate the strengths of self-report inventories, consider how else you might assess your personality. For instance, how assertive are you? You probably have some vague idea, but can you accurately estimate how your assertiveness compares to others? To do that, you need a great deal of comparative information about others' usual behavior—information that all of us lack. In contrast, a self-report inventory inquires about your typical behavior in a wide variety of circumstances requiring assertiveness and generates an exact comparison with the typical behavior reported by many other respondents for the same circumstances. Thus, self-report inventories are much more thorough and precise than casual observations are.

However, these tests are only as accurate as the information that the test-takers provide (Ben-Porath, 2003). Deliberate deception can be a problem with these tests (Rees & Metcalfe, 2003), and some people are unconsciously influenced by the social desirability or acceptability of the statements (Kline, 1995; Paulhus, 1991). Without realizing it, they endorse only those statements that make them look good. This problem provides another reason why personality test results should always be regarded as suggestive rather than definitive.

Projective Tests

Projective tests, which all take a rather indirect approach to the assessment of personality, are used extensively in clinical work. *Projective tests* **ask people to respond to vague, ambiguous stimuli in ways that may reveal the respondents' needs, feelings, and personality traits.** The Rorschach test, for instance, consists of a series of ten inkblots. Respondents are asked to describe what they see in the blots. In the Thematic Apperception Test (TAT), a series of pictures of simple scenes is presented to subjects who are asked to tell stories about what is happening in the scenes and what the characters are feeling (see **Figure 2.24**). For instance, one TAT card shows a young boy contemplating a violin resting on a table in front of him.

The assumption underlying projective testing is that ambiguous materials can serve as a blank screen

Figure 2.23

The Sixteen Personality Factor Questionnaire (16PF). Cattell's 16PF is designed to assess 16 basic dimensions of personality. The pairs of traits listed across from each other in the figure define the 16 factors measured by this self-report inventory. The profile shown is the average profile seen among a group of airline pilots who took the test.

Adapted from Cattell, R. B. (1973, July). Personality pinned down. *Psychology Today*, 40–46. Reprinted by permission of Psychology Today Magazine. Copyright © 1973 Sussex Publishers, Inc.

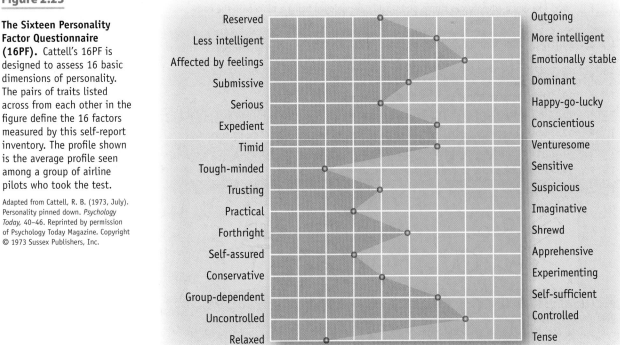

Figure 2.24

The Thematic Apperception Test (TAT). In taking the TAT, a respondent is asked to tell stories about scenes such as this one. The themes apparent in each story can be scored to provide insight about the respondent's personality.

From Murray. H. A. (1971). *Thematic Apperception Test*. Cambridge, MA: Harvard University Press. Copyright © 1943 by The President and Fellows of Harvard College, Copyright © 1971 by Henry A. Murray. Reprinted by permission of the publisher.

onto which people project their characteristic concerns, conflicts, and desires. Thus, a competitive person who is shown the TAT card of the boy at the table with the violin might concoct a story about how the boy is contemplating an upcoming musical competition at which he hopes to excel. The same card shown to a person high in impulsiveness might elicit a story about how the boy is planning to sneak out the door to go dirt-bike riding with friends.

Proponents of projective tests assert that the tests have two unique strengths. First, they are not transparent to subjects. That is, the subject doesn't know how the test provides information to the tester. Hence, it may be difficult for people to engage in intentional deception (Groth-Marnat, 1997). Second, the indirect approach used in these tests may make them especially sensitive to unconscious, latent features of personality.

Unfortunately, the scientific evidence on projective measures is unimpressive (Garb, Florio, & Grove, 1998; Hunsley, Lee, & Wood, 2003). In a thorough review of the relevant research, Lillienfeld, Wood, and Garb (2000) conclude that projective tests tend to be plagued by inconsistent scoring, low reliability, inadequate test norms, cultural bias, and poor validity estimates. They also assert that, contrary to advocates' claims, projective tests are susceptible to some types of intentional deception (primarily, faking poor mental health). Based on their analysis, Lillienfeld and his colleagues argue that projective tests should be referred to as projective "techniques" or "instruments" rather than tests because "most of these techniques as used in daily clinical practice do not fulfill the traditional criteria for psychological tests" (p. 29). In spite of these problems, projective tests continue to be used by many clinicians. Although the questionable scientific status of these techniques is a very real problem, their continued popularity suggests that they yield subjective information that many clinicians find useful (Viglione & Rivera, 2003).

KEY IDEAS

The Nature of Personality

▶ The concept of personality explains the consistency in individuals' behavior over time and situations while also explaining their distinctiveness. Personality traits are dispositions to behave in certain ways. Some theorists suggest that the complexity of personality can be reduced to just five basic traits: extraversion, neuroticism, openness to experience, agreeableness, and conscientiousness.

Psychodynamic Perspectives

▶ Freud's psychoanalytic theory emphasizes the importance of the unconscious. Freud described personality structure in terms of three components (id, ego, and superego), operating at three levels of awareness, that are involved in internal conflicts, which generate anxiety.

▶ According to Freud, people often ward off anxiety and other unpleasant emotions with defense mechanisms, which work through self-deception. Freud believed that the first five years of life are extremely influential in shaping adult personality. He describes five psychosexual stages that children undergo in their personality development.

▶ Jung's analytical psychology stresses the importance of the collective unconscious. Adler's individual psychology emphasizes how people strive for superiority to compensate for feelings of inferiority.

Behavioral Perspectives

▶ Behavioral theories view personality as a collection of response tendencies shaped through learning. Pavlov's classical conditioning can explain how people acquire emotional responses.

▶ Skinner's model of operant conditioning shows how consequences such as reinforcement, extinction, and punishment shape behavior. Bandura's social cognitive theory shows how people can be conditioned indirectly through observation. He views self-efficacy as an especially important personality trait.

Humanistic Perspectives

▶ Humanistic theories take an optimistic view of people's conscious, rational ability to chart their own courses of action. Rogers focused on the self-concept as the critical aspect of personality. He maintained that incongruence between one's self-concept and reality creates anxiety and leads to defensive behavior.

▶ Maslow theorized that needs are arranged hierarchically. He asserted that psychological health depends on fulfilling the need for self-actualization.

Biological Perspectives

▶ Eysenck believes that inherited individual differences in physiological functioning affect conditioning and thus influence personality. Recent twin studies have provided impressive evidence that genetic factors shape personality.

▶ Behavioral genetics research also suggests that the family has surprisingly little influence over personality. Evolutionary psychologists maintain that natural selection has favored the emergence of the Big Five traits as crucial dimensions of personality.

A Contemporary Empirical Approach: Terror Management Theory

▶ Terror management theory proposes that self-esteem and faith in a cultural worldview shield people from the profound anxiety associated with their mortality. Consistent with this analysis, increasing mortality salience leads people to make efforts to bolster their self-esteem and defend their worldviews. These defensive reactions are automatic and subconscious, but they influence many aspects of everyday behavior.

Culture and Personality

▶ Research suggests that the basic trait structure of personality may be much the same across cultures, as the Big Five traits usually emerge in cross-cultural studies. Cultural variations have been found in average trait scores on the Big Five traits, but the differences are modest. People's perceptions of national character appear to be remarkably inaccurate.

Application: Assessing Your Personality

▶ Psychological tests are standardized measures of behavior—usually mental abilities or aspects of personality. Test norms indicate what represents a high or low score. Psychological tests should produce consistent results upon retesting, a quality called reliability. Validity refers to the degree to which a test measures what it was designed to measure.

▶ Self-report inventories, such as the 16PF and NEO Personality Inventory, ask respondents to describe themselves. Self-report inventories can provide a better snapshot of personality than casual observations can, but they are vulnerable to deception and social desirability bias.

▶ Projective tests, such as the Rorschach and TAT, assume that people's responses to ambiguous stimuli reveal something about their personality. Projective tests' reliability and validity appear to be disturbingly low.

KEY TERMS

Archetypes p. 41
Behaviorism p. 43
Classical conditioning p. 44
Collective
    unconscious p. 41
Compensation p. 41
Conditioned response
    (CR) p. 44
Conditioned stimulus
    (CS) p. 44
Conscious pp. 36–37
Defense mechanisms p. 38
Displacement p. 38
Ego p. 36
Evolutionary
    psychology p. 58
Extinction p. 46
Factor analysis p. 33
Fixation p. 39
Heritability ratio p. 56
Hierarchy of needs
    pp. 52–53
Hindsight bias p. 58
Humanism p. 50
Id p. 36
Identification p. 39
Incongruence p. 51
Need for
    self-actualization p. 53
Negative
    reinforcement p. 47
Observational learning p. 48

Oedipal complex p. 40
Operant conditioning p. 46
Personality p. 33
Personality trait p. 33
Positive reinforcement p. 46
Preconscious p. 37
Projection p. 38
Projective tests p. 66
Psychodynamic
    theories p. 35
Psychological test p. 63
Psychosexual stages p. 39
Punishment p. 48
Rationalization p. 38
Reaction formation p. 38
Regression p. 38
Reliability p. 64
Repression p. 38
Self-concept p. 51
Self-efficacy p. 49
Self-report inventories p. 65
Standardization p. 64
Superego p. 36
Test norms p. 64
Twin studies p. 56
Unconditioned response
    (UCR) p. 44
Unconditioned stimulus
    (UCS) p. 44
Unconscious p. 37
Validity p. 64

KEY PEOPLE

Alfred Adler pp. 41–42
Albert Bandura pp. 48–49
Hans Eysenck pp. 55–56
Sigmund Freud pp. 35–41
Carl Jung p. 41

Abraham Maslow pp. 52–54
Ivan Pavlov pp. 43–46
Carl Rogers pp. 50–52
B. F. Skinner pp. 46–48

PRACTICE TEST

1. Which of the following is *not* included in McCrae and Costa's five-factor model of personality?
   a. Neuroticism
   b. Extraversion
   c. Conscientiousness
   d. Authoritarianism

2. You're feeling guilty after your third bowl of ice cream. You tell yourself it's all right because yesterday you skipped lunch. Which defense mechanism is at work?
   a. Conceptualization
   b. Displacement
   c. Rationalization
   d. Identification

3. According to Adler, _____ is a universal drive to adapt, improve oneself, and master life's challenges.
   a. compensation
   b. striving for superiority
   c. avoiding inferiority
   d. social interest

4. The strengthening of a response tendency by virtue of the fact that the response leads to the removal of an unpleasant stimulus is
   a. positive reinforcement.
   b. negative reinforcement.
   c. primary reinforcement.
   d. punishment.

5. Self-efficacy is
   a. the ability to fulfill one's potential.
   b. one's belief about one's ability to perform behaviors that should lead to expected outcomes.
   c. a durable disposition to behave in a particular way in a variety of situations.
   d. a collection of beliefs about one's nature, unique qualities, and typical behavior.

6. According to Rogers, disparity between one's self-concept and actual experience is referred to as
   a. a delusional system.
   b. dissonance.
   c. conflict.
   d. incongruence.

7. According to Maslow, which of the following is *not* characteristic of self-actualizing persons?
   a. Accurate perception of reality
   b. Being open and spontaneous
   c. Being uncomfortable with solitude
   d. Sensitivity to others' needs

8. If identical twins exhibit more personality resemblance than fraternal twins, it's probably due mostly to
   a. similar treatment from parents.
   b. their greater genetic overlap.
   c. their strong identification with each other.
   d. others' expectations that they should be similar.

9. Research on terror management theory has shown that increased mortality salience leads to all of the following except:
   a. increased striving for self-esteem.
   b. more stereotypic thinking about minorities.
   c. more aggressive behavior toward people with opposing views.
   d. reduced respect for cultural icons.

10. In psychological testing, consistency of results over repeated measurements refers to
   a. standardization.
   b. validity.
   c. statistical significance.
   d. reliability.

Book Companion Website

Visit the Book Companion Website at **academic.cengage. com/psychology/weiten**, where you will find tutorial quizzes, flash cards, and web links for every chapter, a final exam, and more! You can also link to the Psychology Resource Center (accessible directly at **academic.cengage.com/login**) for a range of psychology-related resources.

Personal Explorations Workbook

The following exercises in your *Personal Explorations Workbook* may enhance your self-understanding in relation to issues raised in this chapter. **Questionnaire 2.1:** Desirability of Control Scale. **Personal Probe 2.1:** Who Are You? **Personal Probe 2.2:** How You See Personality.

ANSWERS

1. d Pages 33–34
2. c Pages 38–39
3. b Page 41
4. b Page 47
5. b Page 49
6. d Page 51
7. c Page 54
8. b Page 56
9. d Pages 59–61
10. d Page 64

Stress and Its Effects

You're in your car headed home from school with a classmate. Traffic is barely moving. A radio report indicates that the traffic jam is only going to get worse. You groan as you fiddle impatiently with the radio. Another motorist nearly takes your fender off trying to cut into your lane. Your pulse quickens as you shout insults at the driver, who cannot even hear you. You think about the term paper that you have to work on tonight. Your stomach knots up as you recall all the crumpled drafts you tossed into the wastebasket last night. If you don't finish the paper soon, you won't be able to find any time to study for your math test, not to mention your biology quiz. Suddenly you remember that you promised the person you're dating that the two of you would get together tonight. There's no way. Another fight looms on the horizon. Your classmate asks how you feel about the tuition increase the college announced yesterday. You've been trying not to think about it. You're already in debt up to your ears. Your parents are bugging you about changing schools, but you don't want to leave your friends. Your heartbeat quickens as you contemplate the debate you'll have to wage with your parents. You feel wired with tension as you realize that the stress in your life never seems to let up.

As this example shows, many circumstances can create stress in people's lives. Stress comes in all sorts of packages: large and small, pretty and ugly, simple and complex. All too often, the package is a surprise. In this chapter, we try to sort out these packages. We analyze the nature of stress, outline the major types of stress, and discuss how people respond to stressful events at several levels.

In a sense, stress is what a course on adjustment is all about. Recall from Chapter 1 that adjustment essentially deals with how people manage to cope with various demands and pressures. These demands or pressures represent the core of stressful experience. Thus, the central theme in a course such as this is: How do people adjust to stress, and how might they adjust more effectively?

The Nature of Stress

LEARNING OBJECTIVES

▶ Describe the nature of stress and discuss how common it is.

▶ Distinguish between primary and secondary appraisal of stress.

▶ Summarize the evidence on ambient stress.

▶ Explain how culture and ethnicity are related to stress.

Over the years, the term *stress* has been used in different ways by different theorists. Some have viewed stress as a *stimulus* event that presents difficult demands (a divorce, for instance), while others have viewed stress as the *response* of physiological arousal elicited by a troublesome event (Cooper & Dewe, 2004). However, the emerging consensus among contemporary researchers is that stress is neither a stimulus nor a response but a special stimulus-response transaction in which one feels threatened or experiences loss or harm (Carver, 2007; McEwen, 2000). Hence, we will define **stress as any circumstances that threaten or are perceived to threaten one's well-being and thereby tax one's coping abilities.** The threat may be to one's immediate physical safety, long-range security, self-esteem, reputation, or peace of mind. Stress is a complex concept—so let's dig a little deeper.

Stress Is an Everyday Event

The term *stress* tends to spark images of overwhelming, traumatic crises. People think of hijackings, floods, military combat, and nuclear accidents. Undeniably, these are extremely stressful events. Studies conducted in the aftermath of tornadoes, hurricanes, earthquakes, terrorist attacks, and the like typically find elevated rates of psychological problems and physical illness in the communities affected by these disasters (Raphael & Dobson, 2000; van Griensven et al., 2007; Weisler, Barbee, & Townsend, 2007). However, these unusual and infrequent events represent the tip of the iceberg. Many everyday events, such as waiting in line, having car trouble, shopping for Christmas presents, misplacing your checkbook, and staring at bills you can't pay,

are also stressful. Of course, major and minor stressors are not entirely independent. A major stressful event, such as going through a divorce, can trigger a cascade of minor stressors, such as looking for an attorney, taking on new household responsibilities, and so forth (Pillow, Zautra, & Sandler, 1996).

Richard Lazarus

Courtesy of Richard Lazarus

You might guess that minor stressors would produce minor effects, but that isn't necessarily true. Research shows that routine hassles may have significant negative effects on a person's mental and physical health (Delongis, Folkman, & Lazarus, 1988). Richard Lazarus and his colleagues have devised a scale to measure stress in the form of daily hassles. Their scale lists 117 everyday problems, such as misplacing things, struggling with rising prices, dealing with delays, and so forth. When they compared their hassles scale against another scale that assessed stress in the form of major life events, they found that scores on their hassles scale were more strongly related to subjects' mental health than the scores on the other scale were (Kanner et al., 1981). Other investigators, working with different types of samples and different measures of hassles, have also found that everyday hassles are predictive of mental and physical health (Klumb & Baltes, 2004; Sher, 2003).

Why would minor hassles be more strongly related to mental health than major stressful events? The answer isn't entirely clear yet, but many theorists believe that stressful events can have a *cumulative* or *additive* impact (Seta, Seta, & McElroy, 2002). In other words, stress can add up. Routine stresses at home, at school, and at work might be fairly benign individually, but collectively they could create great strain. Whatever the reason, it is evident that daily hassles are distinct and make unique contributions to psychological distress (Serido, Almeida, & Wethington, 2004).

Stress Lies in the Eye of the Beholder

The experience of feeling threatened depends on what events you notice and how you choose to appraise or interpret them (Monroe & Kelley, 1995). Events that are stressful for one person may be "ho-hum" routine for another. For example, many people find flying in an airplane somewhat stressful, but frequent fliers may not even raise an eyebrow. Some people enjoy the excitement of going out on a date with someone new; others find the uncertainty terrifying.

In discussing appraisals of stress, Lazarus and Folkman (1984) distinguish between primary and secondary appraisal (see **Figure 3.1**). *Primary appraisal* **is an initial evaluation of whether an event is (1) irrelevant to you, (2) relevant but not threatening or (3) stressful.** When you view an event as stressful, you are likely to make a *secondary appraisal,* **which is an evaluation of your coping resources and options for dealing with the stress.** Thus, your primary appraisal would determine whether you saw an upcoming job interview as stressful. Your secondary appraisal would determine how stressful the interview appeared, in light of your assessment of your ability to deal with the event.

It should come as no surprise that people's beliefs about stressful events alter the impact of the events themselves (Daniels, Hartley, & Travers, 2006). Recent research has demonstrated that negative interpretations of events are often associated with increased distress surrounding these events (Boelen, van den Bout & van den Hout, 2003). In fact, when studying a sample of children after the 9/11 terrorist attacks, Lengua and her colleagues (2006) found that children's appraisals of the event as threatening predicted their stress symptoms as much as factors such as their coping style or pre-attack stress load.

Interestingly, people are rarely objective in their appraisals of potentially stressful events. A classic study of hospitalized patients awaiting surgery showed only a slight correlation between the objective seriousness of a person's upcoming surgery and the amount of fear the person experienced (Janis, 1958). Clearly, some people are more prone to feel threatened by life's difficulties than others. A number of studies have shown that anxious, neurotic people are more likely to make threat appraisals as well as to report more stress than others (Cooper & Bright, 2001; Schneider, 2004). Thus, stress lies in the eye (actually, the mind) of the beholder, and people's appraisals of stressful events are highly subjective.

Stress May Be Embedded in the Environment

Although the perception of stress is a highly personal matter, many kinds of stress come from the environmental circumstances that individuals share with others. *Ambient stress* **consists of chronic environmental conditions that, although not urgent, are negatively valued and that place adaptive demands on people.** Features of the environment such as excessive noise, traffic, and pollution can threaten well-being and leave their mark on mental and physical health.

For example, investigators have found an association between chronic exposure to high levels of noise and elevated blood pressure among children attending school near Los Angeles International Airport (Cohen et al., 1980). Similarly, studies of children living near Munich International Airport (Evans, Hygge, & Bullinger, 1995; Hygge, Evans, & Bullinger, 2002) have found elevated stress hormones, reading and memory deficits, and poor task persistence in samples of schoolchildren (see **Figure 3.2**).

Crowding is another source of environmental stress. Temporary experiences of crowding, such as being packed into a rock concert venue with thousands of other fans, can be stressful. Even being crowded in a laboratory setting is related to an increase in reported

Figure 3.1

Primary and secondary appraisal of stress. *Primary appraisal* is an initial evaluation of whether an event is (1) irrelevant to you, (2) relevant, but not threatening, or (3) stressful. When you view an event as stressful, you are likely to make a *secondary appraisal,* which is an evaluation of your coping resources and options for dealing with the stress. (Based on Lazarus & Folkman, 1994)

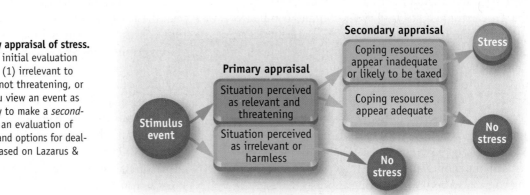

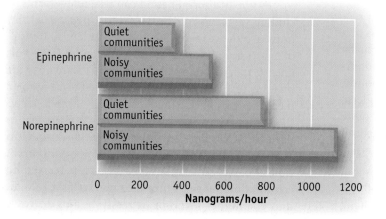

Figure 3.2

Excessive noise and stress hormones. Evans, Hygge, and Bullinger (1995) compared children from noisy areas near Munich International Airport with similar children from quiet neighborhoods in Munich. They found elevated levels of two hormones associated with stress reactions in the children exposed to the high noise of the airport. (Adapted from Evans, Hygge, & Bullinger, 1995)

stress (Martimportugués-Goyenechea & Gomez-Jacinto, 2005). However, most of the research on crowding has focused on the effects of residential density. Generally, studies suggest an association between high density and increased physiological arousal, psychological distress, and social withdrawal (Evans, 2001; Evans, LePore, & Schroeder, 1996). Siddiqui and Pandey (2003) found crowding to be one of the most critical stressors for urban residents in Northern India, indicating that this is an important issue that goes well beyond Western cities.

Psychologists have also explored the repercussions of living in areas that are at risk for disaster. For in-

stance, studies suggest that people who live near nuclear power plants, hazardous waste sites, or polluting industrial facilities experience higher levels of distress (Downey & van Willigen, 2005). Similarly, residents in an area prone to earthquakes or hurricanes may experience increased stress (Carr, 2000; Dougall & Baum, 2000).

Recently, investigators have examined urban poverty and violence as a source of environmental stress. Ewart and Suchday (2002) developed a scale called the City Stress Inventory (CSI) to measure participants' exposure to street crime, gang activity, drug dealing, neighborhood decay, and unruly behavior. They found that scores on the CSI correlated (modestly) with measures of subjects' depressive symptoms, hostility, and irritability. More recently, Suchday and colleagues (2006) found that CSI scores were associated with high blood pressure and negative health habits such as alcohol use. Other studies have found that exposure to community violence, whether as a victim or as a witness, is associated with behavioral problems, anxiety, depression, and anger among urban youth (Foster, Kuperminc, & Price, 2004; Thompson & Massat, 2005).

Stress can be caused by environmental circumstances such as pollution, excessive noise, crowding, traffic jams, and urban decay.

Stress Is Influenced by Culture

Although certain types of events (such as the loss of a loved one) are probably viewed as stressful in virtually all human societies, cultures vary greatly in the predominant forms of stress their people experience. Obviously, the challenges of daily living encountered in modern, Western cities like Montreal or Philadelphia are quite different from the day-to-day difficulties experienced in indigenous societies in Africa or South America. Indeed, culture sets the context in which people experience and appraise stress (Chun, Moos, & Cronkite, 2006). The potential importance of culture is illustrated by the substantial body of evidence which suggests that *cultural change*—such as increased modernization and urbanization and shifting values and customs—has been a major source of stress in many societies around the world (Dessler, 2000). In some cases, a specific cultural group may be exposed to pervasive stress that is unique to that group (Berry & Ataca, 2000). For example, the ethnic cleansing of Albanians in Kosovo in 1999 and the devastating and widespread destruction from the tsunami in Indonesia and regions of Southeast Asia in 2004 were extraordinary forms of stress distinctive to these societies. Our discussion of stress will largely focus on the types of stressors confronted in everyday life in contemporary, Western society, but you should be aware that life in our society is not necessarily representative of life around the world.

Moreover, even within the modern, Western world, disparities can be found in the constellation of stressors experienced by specific cultural groups (Mino, Profit, & Pierce, 2000). In recent years, researchers have shown a new interest in the effects of ethnicity-related sources of stress experienced by African Americans, Hispanic Americans, Asian Americans, and other minority groups (Contrada et al., 2000). Social scientists interested in ethnicity have traditionally focused their attention on the causes of institutional racism, such as discrimination in hiring and in access to health care. But their focus has been shifting to the effects of subtle discrimination in day-to-day living. Although overt racial discrimination in America clearly has declined in recent decades, covert expressions of ethnic prejudice continue to be commonplace (Dovidio & Gaertner, 1999). For example, in one study of 520 African Americans, 96 percent of the respondents reported experiencing some type of racist discrimination in the most recent year—and 95 percent of these subjects indicated that they found this discrimination to be stressful (Klonoff & Landrine, 1999).

Everyday discrimination can take many forms, including verbal insults (ethnic slurs), negative evaluations, avoidance, denial of equal treatment, and threats of aggression. Feldman-Barrett and Swim (1998) emphasize that these acts of discrimination are often ambiguous (examples: "The clerk seemed to be ignoring me," "The teacher seemed disdainful of me"). Hence, theorists assert that minority group members may experience stress not only from explicit discrimination but also from the subjective perception of discrimination in ambiguous situations. In fact, perceived discrimination has been linked to greater psychological distress, higher levels of depression, and decreased well-being for a variety of minority groups, including sexual minorities such as lesbians (Lewis et al., 2006; Moradi & Risco, 2006; Sellers et al., 2006).

In addition to discrimination, members of ethnic minorities experience stress because they are keenly aware of negative racial stereotypes and often worry that others will interpret their behavior in ways that confirm these derogatory stereotypes (Steele, 1997). So the threat of *stereotype confirmation* can become a source of chronic apprehension. At the other extreme, individuals are often chastised by members of their own group for "acting white" or abandoning their cultural heritage (Contrada et al., 2000). Thus, ethnic minorities may be under constant pressure to conform to the expectations and values of their own group. In fact, for immigrants, **acculturation, or changing to adapt to a new culture,** is a major source of stress related to reduced well-being (Moradi & Risco, 2006; Ying & Han, 2006). Lopez (2005) surveyed Latino freshman during their first year at a predominately white college and found that they reported stress from their own Latino community (shown through statements such as "pressures to show loyalty to my race") as well as from experiencing discrimination ("being treated rudely due to race").

It seems likely that the extra layers of stress experienced by minority group members takes its toll on them. Scientists are still exploring the degree to which ethnicity-related stress may have detrimental effects on individuals' mental and physical health.

Web Link 3.1 **Centre for Stress Management**

This British website houses a diverse collection of brief online articles concerned with many aspects of the stress process. It also features links to many other sites around the world that provide information on stress.

Major Types of Stress

- ▶ *Distinguish between acute and chronic stressors.*
- ▶ *Describe frustration as a form of stress.*
- ▶ *Outline the three types of conflict, and discuss typical reactions to conflicts.*

- ▶ *Summarize evidence on life change as a form of stress.*
- ▶ *Discuss evidence on pressure as a form of stress.*

An enormous variety of events can be stressful for one person or another. To achieve a better understanding of stress, theorists have tried to analyze the nature of stressful events and divide them into subtypes. One sensible distinction involves differentiating between *acute stressors* and *chronic stressors* (Dougall & Baum, 2001). **Acute stressors are threatening events that have a relatively short duration and a clear endpoint.** Examples would include having a difficult encounter with a belligerent drunk, waiting for the results of a medical test, or having your home threatened by severe flooding. **Chronic stressors are threatening events that have a relatively long duration and no readily apparent time limit.** Examples would include persistent financial strains produced by huge credit card debts, ongoing pressures from a hostile boss at work, or the demands of caring for a sick family member over a period of years. Of course, this distinction is far from perfect. It is hard to decide where to draw the line between a short-lived versus lengthy stressor, and even brief stressors can have long-lasting effects.

None of the proposed schemes for classifying stressful events has turned out to be altogether satisfactory. Classifying stressful events into nonintersecting categories is virtually impossible. Although this problem presents conceptual headaches for researchers, it need not prevent us from describing four major types of stress: frustration, conflict, change, and pressure. As you read about each of them, you'll surely recognize some familiar situations.

Frustration

"It has been very frustrating to watch the rapid deterioration of my parents' relationship. Over the last year or two they have argued constantly and have refused to seek any professional help. I have tried to talk to them, but they kind of shut me and my brother out of their problem. I feel very helpless and sometimes even very angry, not at them, but at the whole situation."

This scenario illustrates frustration. As psychologists use the term, *frustration* **occurs in any situation in which the pursuit of some goal is thwarted.** In essence, you experience frustration when you want something and you can't have it. Everyone has to deal with frustra-tion virtually every day. Traffic jams, long daily commutes, and annoying drivers, for instance, are a routine source of frustration that can elicit anger and increase levels of stress (Evans & Wener, 2006; Hennessy & Wiesenthal, 1999). Even artificially induced frustration in a laboratory setting leads to increased aggression (Verona & Curtin, 2006). Fortunately, most frustrations are brief and insignificant. You may be quite upset when you go to the auto shop to pick up your car and find that it hasn't been fixed as promised. However, a few days later you'll probably have your precious car back, and all will be forgotten.

Of course, some frustrations can be sources of significant stress. *Failures* and *losses* are two common kinds of frustration that are often very stressful. All people fail in at least some of their endeavors. Some make failure almost inevitable by setting unrealistic goals for themselves. People tend to forget that for every newly appointed vice-president in the business world, there are dozens of middle-level executives who don't get promoted. Losses may be especially frustrating when people are deprived of something they are accustomed to having. For example, there are few things that are more painful and frustrating than losing a dearly loved friend or family member.

More often than not, frustration appears to be the culprit at work when people feel troubled by environmental stress (Graig, 1993). Excessive noise, heat, pollution, and crowding are most likely stressful because they frustrate the desire for quiet, a comfortable body temperature, clean air, and adequate privacy. Interestingly, frustration in the workplace often results in burnout (Lewandowski, 2003), a specific effect of stress that we will discuss later in this chapter.

Conflict

"Should I or shouldn't I? I became engaged at Christmas. My fiancé surprised me with a ring. I knew if I refused the ring he would be terribly hurt and our relationship would suffer. However, I don't really know whether or not I want to marry him. On the other hand, I don't want to lose him either."

Like frustration, conflict is an unavoidable feature of everyday life. That perplexing question "Should I or shouldn't I?" comes up countless times on a daily basis. *Conflict* **occurs when two or more incompatible motivations or behavioral impulses compete for expression.** As we discussed in Chapter 2, Sigmund Freud proposed over a century ago that internal conflicts generate considerable psychological distress. This link between conflict and distress was measured with precision in studies by Laura King and Robert Emmons (1990, 1991). They used an elaborate questionnaire to assess the overall amount of internal conflict experienced by subjects. They found higher levels of conflict to be associated with higher levels of psychological distress.

Conflicts come in three types, which were originally described by Kurt Lewin (1935) and investigated extensively by Neal Miller (1944, 1959). These types—approach-approach, avoidance-avoidance, and approach-avoidance—are diagrammed in **Figure 3.3**.

Neal Miller

In an *approach-approach conflict* **a choice must be made between two attractive goals.** The problem, of course, is that you can choose just one of the two goals. For example, you have a free afternoon; should you play tennis or go to the movies? You're out for a meal; do you want to order the pizza or the spaghetti? You can't afford both; should you buy the blue sweater or the gray jacket? Among the three kinds of conflict, the approach-approach type tends to be the least stressful. People don't usually stagger out of restaurants, exhausted by the stress of choosing which of several appealing entrees to eat. In approach-approach conflicts you typically have a reasonably happy ending, whichever way you decide to go. Nonetheless, approach-approach conflicts centering on important issues may sometimes be troublesome. If you are torn between two appealing college majors or two attractive boyfriends, you may find the decision-making process quite stressful.

In an *avoidance-avoidance conflict* **a choice must be made between two unattractive goals.** Forced to choose between two repelling alternatives, you are, as they say, "caught between a rock and a hard place." For example, let's say you have painful backaches. Should you submit to surgery that you dread, or should you continue to live with the pain? Obviously, avoidance-avoidance conflicts are most unpleasant and highly stressful. Typically, people keep delaying their decision as long as possible, hoping that they will somehow be able to escape the conflict situation. For example, you might delay surgery in the hope that your backaches will disappear on their own.

In an *approach-avoidance conflict* **a choice must be made about whether to pursue a single goal that**

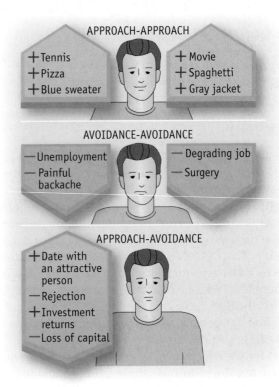

Figure 3.3

Types of conflict. Psychologists have identified three basic types of conflict. In approach-approach and avoidance-avoidance conflicts, the person is torn between two goals. In an approach-avoidance conflict only one goal is under consideration, but it has both positive and negative aspects.

has both attractive and unattractive aspects. For instance, imagine that you're offered a career promotion that will mean a large increase in pay. The catch is that you will have to move to a city that you hate. Approach-avoidance conflicts are common, and they can be highly stressful. Any time you have to take a risk to pursue some desirable outcome, you are likely to find yourself in an approach-avoidance conflict. Should you risk rejection by asking out that attractive person in class? Should you risk your savings by investing in a new business that could fail? Approach-avoidance conflicts often produce *vacillation*. That is, people go back and forth, beset by indecision that can create stress. Fortunately we are equipped to focus on the positive aspects of our decision once it has been made (Brehm, 1956).

Change

"After graduation, I landed my dream job and moved to another state. For the first time, I am living alone, far away from my friends and family. My biggest stress is getting used to my new life. Everything is different. I am learning how to do my new job, trying to make friends, and navigating my way around my new city. I love my job and my

BLONDIE © 2001. Reprinted with special permission of King Features Syndicate.

new location, but I am having difficulties dealing with all these changes at once."

Life changes may represent a key type of stress. **Life changes are any noticeable alterations in one's living circumstances that require readjustment.** Research on life change began when Thomas Holmes, Richard Rahe, and their colleagues set out to explore the relation between stressful life events and physical illness (Holmes & Rahe, 1967; Rahe & Arthur, 1978). They interviewed thousands of tuberculosis patients to find out what kinds of events preceded the onset of their disease. Surprisingly, the frequently cited events were not uniformly negative. The list included plenty of aversive events, as expected, but patients also mentioned many seemingly positive events, such as getting married, having a baby, or getting promoted.

Why would positive events, such as moving to a nicer home, produce stress? According to Holmes and Rahe, it is because they produce *change*. Their thesis is that disruptions of daily routines are stressful. According to their theory, changes in personal relationships, changes at work, changes in finances, and so forth can be stressful even when the changes are welcomed.

Based on this analysis, Holmes and Rahe (1967) developed the Social Readjustment Rating Scale (SRRS) to measure life change as a form of stress. The scale assigns numerical values to 43 major life events that are supposed to reflect the magnitude of the readjustment required by each change (see **Figure 3.4** on the next page). In responding to the scale, respondents are asked to indicate how often they experienced any of these 43 events during a certain time period (typically, the past year). The person then adds up the numbers associated with each event checked. This sum is an index of the amount of change-related stress the person has recently experienced.

The SRRS and similar scales have been used in thousands of studies by researchers all over the world. Overall, these studies have shown that people with higher scores on the SRRS tend to be more vulnerable to many kinds of physical illness—and many types of psychological problems as well (Lynch et al., 2005; Rahe et al., 2000; Scully, Tosi, & Banning, 2000). These results have attracted a great deal of attention, and the SRRS has been reprinted in many newspapers and popular magazines. The attendant publicity has led to the widespread conclusion that life change is inherently stressful.

More recently, however, experts have criticized this research, citing problems with the methods used and raising questions about the meaning of the findings (Hobson & Delunas, 2001; Jones & Kinman, 2001; Monroe & McQuaid, 1994). At this point, it is a key interpretive issue that concerns us. Many critics have argued that the SRRS does not measure *change* exclusively. The list of life changes on the SRRS is dominated by events that are clearly negative or undesirable (marital separation, fired at work, and so on). These negative events probably generate great frustration. So even though the scale contains some positive events, it could be that frustration (generated by negative events), rather than change, creates most of the stress assessed by the scale.

To investigate this possibility, researchers came up with ways to take into account the desirability and undesirability of subjects' life changes. Participants were asked to indicate the desirability of the events that they checked off on the SRRS and similar scales. The findings in these studies clearly indicated that life change is *not* the crucial dimension measured by the SRRS and that in fact undesirable or negative life events cause most of the stress tapped by the scale (McLean & Link, 1994; Turner & Wheaton, 1995).

Should we discard the notion that change is stressful? Not entirely. Other lines of research, independent of work with the SRRS, support the hypothesis that change is an important form of stress. For instance, researchers have found associations between geographic mobility and impaired mental and physical health that

digestion to help the body save and store energy. The fight-or-flight response is mediated by the *sympathetic division* of the autonomic nervous system, which mobilizes bodily resources for emergencies. In one experiment, Cannon studied the fight-or-flight response in cats by confronting them with dogs. Among other things, he noticed an immediate acceleration in breathing and heart rate and a reduction in digestive processes.

Shelley Taylor and her colleagues (2000) have questioned whether the fight-or-flight model applies equally well to both males and females. They note that in most species females have more responsibility for the care of young offspring than males do. Using an evolutionary perspective, they argue that this disparity may make fighting and fleeing less adaptive for females, as both responses may endanger offspring and thus reduce the likelihood of an animal passing on its genes. Taylor and colleagues maintain that evolutionary processes have fostered more of a "tend and befriend" response to stress in females. According to this analysis, in reacting to stress, females allocate more effort to the care of offspring and to seeking help and support. Consistent with this theory, David and Lyons-Ruth (2005) found gender differences in how infants respond to threat. Females infants showed more approach behaviors to frightening mothers (for example, mothers who suddenly loomed over the infant or assumed an attack posture) than male infants did. More research is needed to evaluate this provocative analysis. Even though they hypothesize gender differences in behavioral responses to stress, Taylor and her colleagues are quick to note that the "basic neuroendocrine core of stress responses" is largely the same for males and females.

Imagine, for instance, your reaction if your car were to spin out of control on the highway. Your heart would race, and your blood pressure would surge. You might get "goosebumps" and experience a "knot in your stomach." These reflex responses are part of the fight-or-flight syndrome seen in many species. In a sense, this automatic reaction is a leftover from our evolutionary past. It is clearly an adaptive response for many animals, as the threat of predators often requires a swift response of fighting or fleeing. Likewise, the fight-or-flight response probably was adaptive among ancestral humans who routinely had to deal with acute stressors involving threats to their physical safety. But in our modern world, the fight-or-flight response may be less adaptive for human functioning than it was thousands of generations ago (Neese & Young, 2000). Most modern stressors cannot be handled simply through fight or flight. Work pressures, marital problems, and financial difficulties require far more complex responses. Moreover, these chronic stressors often continue for lengthy periods of time, so that the fight-or-flight response leaves one in a state of enduring physiological arousal. Concern about the effects of prolonged physi-

cal arousal was first voiced by Hans Selye, a Canadian scientist who conducted extensive research on stress.

The General Adaptation Syndrome

The concept of stress was popularized in both scientific and lay circles by Hans Selye (1936, 1956, 1982). Although born in Vienna, Selye spent his entire professional career at McGill University in Montreal, Canada. Beginning in the 1930s, Selye exposed laboratory animals to a diverse array of both physical and psychological stressors (heat, cold, pain, mild shock, restraint, and so on). The patterns of physiological arousal he observed in the animals were largely the same, regardless of the type of stress. Thus, Selye concluded that stress reactions are *nonspecific.* In other words, they do not vary according to the specific type of stress encountered. Initially, Selye wasn't sure what to call this nonspecific response to a variety of noxious agents. In the 1940s, he decided to call it *stress,* and his influential writings gradually helped make the word part of our everyday vocabulary (Cooper & Dewe, 2004).

Hans Selye

Selye (1956, 1974) formulated a seminal theory of stress reactions called the general adaptation syndrome (see **Figure 3.10**). The *general adaptation syndrome* **is a model of the body's stress response, consisting of three stages: alarm, resistance, and exhaustion.** In the first stage of the general adaptation syndrome, an *alarm reaction* occurs when an organism recognizes the existence of a threat. Physiological arousal increases as the body musters its resources to combat the challenge. Selye's alarm reaction is essentially the fight-or-flight response originally described by Cannon.

However, Selye took his investigation of stress a couple of steps further by exposing laboratory animals to *prolonged stress,* similar to the chronic stress often endured by humans. If stress continues, the organism may progress to the second phase of the general adaptation syndrome, called the *stage of resistance.* During this phase, physiological changes stabilize as coping efforts get under way. Typically, physiological arousal continues to be higher than normal, although it may

---

Web Link 3.4 **The American Institute of Stress**

The American Institute of Stress is a nonprofit organization established in 1978 at the request of stress pioneer Hans Selye. Its Board of Trustees reads like a who's who of stress research. The resources available online are a bit limited, as one has to send for the information packets published by the institute. But the site contains an interesting tribute to Selye.

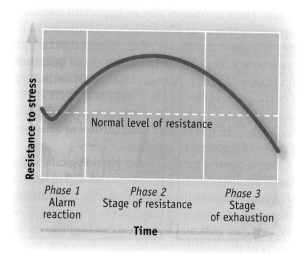

Figure 3.10

The general adaptation syndrome. According to Selye, the physiological response to stress can be broken into three phases. During the first phase, the body mobilizes its resources for resistance after a brief initial shock. In the second phase, resistance levels off and eventually begins to decline. If the third phase of the general adaptation syndrome is reached, resistance is depleted, leading to health problems and exhaustion.

level off somewhat as the organism becomes accustomed to the threat.

If the stress continues over a substantial period of time, the organism may enter the third stage, called the *stage of exhaustion.* According to Selye, the body's resources for fighting stress are limited. If the stress cannot be overcome, the body's resources may be depleted, and physiological arousal will decrease. Eventually, the individual may collapse from exhaustion. During this phase, the organism's resistance declines. This reduced resistance may lead to what Selye called "diseases of adaptation," such as ulcers or high blood pressure.

Selye's theory and research forged a link between stress and physical illness. He showed how prolonged physiological arousal that is meant to be adaptive could lead to diseases. His theory has been criticized because it ignores individual differences in the appraisal of stress (Lazarus & Folkman, 1984), and his belief that stress reactions are nonspecific remains the subject of debate (Kemeny, 2003; McCarty & Pacak, 2000). However, his model provided guidance for generations of researchers who worked out the details of how stress reverberates throughout the body. Let's look at some of those details.

Brain-Body Pathways

When you experience stress, your brain sends signals to the endocrine system along two major pathways (Clow, 2001; Dallman, Bhatnagar, &

Viau, 2000; Felker & Hubbard, 1998). **The *endocrine system* consists of glands that secrete chemicals called hormones into the bloodstream.** The major endocrine glands, such as the pituitary, pineal, thyroid, and adrenal glands, are shown in **Figure 3.11**.

The hypothalamus, a small structure near the base of the brain, appears to initiate action along both pathways. The first pathway (shown on the right in **Figure 3.12** on the next page) is routed through the autonomic nervous system. The hypothalamus activates the sympathetic division of the ANS. A key part of this activation involves stimulating the central part of the adrenal glands (the adrenal medulla) to release large amounts of *catecholamines* into the bloodstream. These hormones radiate throughout your body, producing many important physiological changes. The net result of catecholamine elevation is that your body is mobilized for action (Lundberg, 2000). Heart rate and blood flow increase, pumping more blood to your brain and muscles. Respiration and oxygen consumption

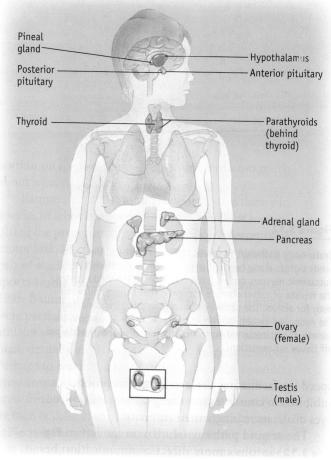

Figure 3.11

The endocrine system. The endocrine glands secrete hormones into the bloodstream. The locations of the principal endocrine glands are shown here. The hormones released by these glands regulate a variety of physical functions and play a key role in the physiological response to stress.

Major disasters, such as Hurricane Katrina, which devastated New Orleans and the Gulf Coast region, are just one of about a half-dozen types of calamitous events that frequently lead to posttraumatic stress disorders.

Afghanistan and Iraq wars. Similar to Vietnam veterans, these U.S. troops are showing elevated rates of PTSD upon returning home (Friedman, 2006).

Although posttraumatic stress disorder is widely associated with the experiences of veterans, it is seen in response to other cases of traumatic stress as well, and it appears to be much more common than originally believed. Research suggests that 7%–8% of people have suffered from PTSD at some point in their lives, with prevalence higher among women (10 percent) than men (5 percent) (Ozer et al., 2003). PTSD is seen in children as well as adults (La Greca, 2000). In some instances, PTSD does not surface until many months or years after a person's exposure to severe stress (Holen, 2000).

What types of stress besides combat are severe enough to produce PTSD? The syndrome is frequently seen after a rape, a serious automobile accident, a robbery or assault, or the witnessing of someone's death

(Koren, Arnon, & Klein, 1999; Stein et al., 1997b). Studies indicate that PTSD is also common in the wake of major disasters, such as floods, hurricanes, earthquakes, fires, and so forth (Koopman, Classen, & Spiegel, 1994; Vernberg et al., 1996). Unfortunately, research by Stein et al. (1997b) suggests that the various types of traumatic events that can cause PTSD are more common than most people realize (see **Figure 3.14**).

Vulnerability to PTSD is not limited to victims, survivors, and witnesses of traumatic events. Rescue workers and cleanup crews who have to grapple with the gruesome carnage of major disasters, dangerous working conditions, and tremendous fatigue also have an elevated risk for PTSD and often are "forgotten victims" of disasters (Ursano et al., 1999). When examining disaster workers who responded to the events of 9/11, researchers found elevated levels of PTSD, depression, and general psychological distress, even over

Figure 3.14

The prevalence of traumatic events. We tend to think that traumatic events are relatively unusual and infrequent, but research by Stein et al. (1997b) suggests otherwise. When they interviewed over 1000 people in Winnipeg, they found that 74.2 percent of the women and 81.3 percent of the men reported having experienced at least one highly traumatic event. The percentage of respondents reporting specific types of traumatic events are summarized in this graph.

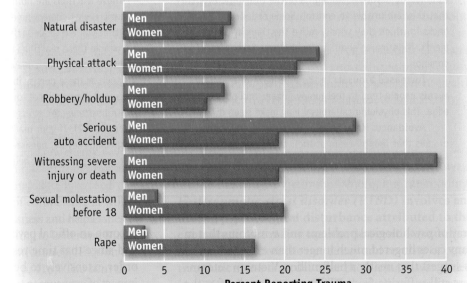

Selected Effects of Trauma

Function	Effect
Cognitive processes	Impaired
Emotional expression	Suppressed
Memory for prior stressors	Increased
Ruminations on trauma	Increased
Vulnerability to gastric ulcers	Increased
Vulnerability to inflammatory bowel disease	Increased

Figure 3.15

The effects of trauma on psychological and physical functioning. Scientists have discovered many negative effects of experiencing extreme stress. This table presents only a limited set of ways that the experience of trauma can affect us psychologically and physically.

Adapted from Overmier, J. B., & Murison, R. (2005). Trauma and resulting sensitization effects are modulated by psychological factors. *Psychoneuroendocrinology, 30*(10), 965–973, Table 2. Copyright © 2005 Elsevier Ltd. All rights reserved. Adapted by permission.

a year later (Alvarez & Hunt, 2005; Fullerton, Ursano, & Wang, 2004). Psychologists have the opportunity to make an important contribution to society by identifying protective and proactive interventions that would make rescue and relief workers less vulnerable to the negative effects of trauma (see **Figure 3.15**).

What are the symptoms of posttraumatic stress disorder? Common symptoms include reexperiencing the traumatic event in the form of nightmares and flashbacks, emotional numbing, alienation, problems in social relations, and elevated arousal, anxiety, and guilt (Flannery, 1999; Shalev, 2001). PTSD is also associated with an elevated risk for substance abuse, depression, and anxiety disorders, as well as a great variety of physical health problems (Brady, Back, & Coffey, 2004; Fairbank, Ebert, & Caddell, 2001). The frequency and severity of posttraumatic symptoms usually decline gradually over time, but in many cases the symptoms never completely disappear.

Although PTSD is fairly common in the wake of traumatic events, the vast majority of people who experience such events do *not* develop PTSD (Bonanno et al., 2006; Ozer & Weiss, 2004). Thus, a current focus of research is to determine what factors make certain people more (or less) susceptible than others to the ravages of severe stress (Bonanno, 2004). According to McKeever and Huff (2003), this vulnerability probably depends on complex interactions among a number of biological and environmental factors. One key predictor that emerged in a recent review of the relevant research is the *intensity of one's reaction at the time of the traumatic event* (Ozer et al., 2003). Individuals who have especially intense emotional reactions during or immediately after the traumatic event go on to show elevated vulnerability to PTSD. Vulnerability seems to be greatest among people whose reactions are so intense that they report *dissociative experiences* (a sense that things are not real, that time is stretching out, that one is watching oneself in a movie). You can consult Chapter 15 for a fuller discussion of PTSD risk factors.

Psychological Problems and Disorders

Posttraumatic stress disorders are caused by an acute episode of extreme stress. Of greater relevance to most of us are the effects of chronic, prolonged, everyday stress. On the basis of clinical impressions, psychologists have long suspected that chronic stress might contribute to many types of psychological problems and mental disorders. Since the late 1960s, advances in the measurement of stress have allowed researchers to verify these suspicions in empirical studies. In the domain of common psychological problems, studies indicate that stress may contribute to poor academic performance (Akgun & Ciarrochi, 2003), insomnia and other sleep disturbances (Vgontzas, Bixler, & Kales, 2000), sexual difficulties (Lemack, Uzzo, & Poppas, 1998), alcohol abuse (Colder, 2001; Edwards et al., 2006), and drug abuse (Goeders, 2004).

Above and beyond these everyday problems, research reveals that stress often contributes to the onset of full-fledged psychological disorders, including depression (Rehm, Wagner, & Ivens-Tyndal, 2001), schizophrenia (McGlashan & Hoffman, 2000), anxiety disorders (Falsetti & Ballenger, 1998), and eating disorders (Cooper, 1995). We'll discuss the complex relations between stress and mental disorders in detail in Chapter 15.

Physical Illness

Stress can also have an impact on one's physical health. The idea that stress can contribute to physical ailments is not entirely new. Evidence that stress can cause physical illness began to accumulate back in the 1930s. By the 1950s, the concept of psychosomatic disease was widely accepted. *Psychosomatic diseases* **were defined as genuine physical ailments thought to be caused in part by stress and other psychological factors.** The classic psychosomatic illnesses were high blood pressure, peptic ulcers, asthma, skin disorders such as eczema and hives, and migraine and tension headaches (Kaplan, 1989; Rogers, Fricchione, & Reich, 1999). Please note, these diseases were not regarded as *imagined* physical ailments. The term *psychosomatic* has often been misused to refer to physical ailments that are "all in one's head," but that is an entirely different syndrome (see Chapter 15). Rather, psychosomatic diseases were viewed as authentic organic maladies that were heavily stress related.

Since the 1970s, the concept of psychosomatic disease has gradually fallen into disuse because research has shown that stress can contribute to the development of a diverse array of other diseases previously believed to be purely physiological in origin. Although there is room for debate on some specific diseases, stress may influence the onset and course of heart disease, stroke, tuberculosis, multiple sclerosis, arthritis, diabetes, leukemia, cancer, various types of infectious disease, and probably many other types of illnesses (Brummett et al., 2004; Critelli & Ee, 1996; Dougall & Baum, 2001; see Chapter 14). Thus, it has become apparent that there is nothing unique about the psychosomatic diseases that requires a special category. Modern evidence continues to demonstrate that the classic psychosomatic diseases are influenced by stress, but so are numerous other diseases (Levenson et al., 1999). Of course, stress is only one of many factors that may contribute to the development of physical illness. Nonetheless, it is sobering to realize that stress can have an impact on one's physical health.

Positive Effects

The effects of stress are not entirely negative. Recent years have brought increased interest in positive aspects of the stress process, including favorable outcomes that follow in the wake of stress (Folkman & Moskowitz, 2000). To some extent, the new focus on the possible benefits of stress reflects a new emphasis on "positive psychology." Some influential theorists have argued that the field of psychology has historically devoted too much attention to pathology, weakness, and damage and how to heal suffering (Seligman, 2003). This approach has yielded valuable insights and progress, but it has also resulted in an unfortunate neglect of the forces that make life worth living. The positive psychology movement seeks to shift the field's focus away from negative experiences. As Martin Seligman and Mihaly

Csikszentmihalyi (2000) put it, "The aim of positive psychology is to begin to catalyze a change in the focus of psychology from preoccupation with only repairing the worst things in life to also building positive qualities" (p. 5). The advocates of positive psychology argue for increased research on well-being, contentment, hope, courage, perseverance, nurturance, tolerance, and other human strengths and virtues (Aspinwall & Staudinger, 2003; Peterson & Seligman, 2004). One of these strengths is resilience in the face of stress. The beneficial effects of stress may prove more difficult to pinpoint than the harmful effects because they may be more subtle. However, there appear to be at least three ways in which stress can have positive effects.

First, stress can promote positive psychological change, or what Tedeschi and Calhoun (1996) call *posttraumatic growth*. Experiences of posttraumatic growth are now well documented, and it appears that this phenomenon is evident in people facing a variety of stressful circumstances, including bereavement, cancer, sexual assault, and combat (Tedeschi & Calhoun, 2004). Stressful events sometimes force people to develop new skills, reevaluate priorities, learn new insights, and acquire new strengths. In other words, the adaptation process initiated by stress may lead to personal changes for the better. Confronting and conquering a stressful challenge may lead to improvements in specific coping abilities and to an enhanced self-concept. For example,

---

Recommended
READING

The End of Stress as We Know It
by Bruce McEwen with Elizabeth Norton Lasley (Joseph Henry Press, 2002)

The title of this book is a bit misleading, as it suggests that the author will provide some stunning new secret that will permit readers to end the stress in their lives. In reality, one of the principal points that McEwen makes is that stress is normal, inevitable, and not necessarily bad. McEwen is a renowned stress researcher whose main focus has been on neuroendocrine responses to stress. In keeping with his background, what he provides in this book is an exceptionally lucid account of how stress affects brain function and cardiovascular and immune system processes. This potentially difficult material is presented in a lively and understandable fashion. The coverage of "how not to be stressed out" is relatively modest. The author's advice is empirically sound but fairly conventional and not overly detailed. In sum, this book provides an outstanding overview of the physiology of stress, but it offers less than you might expect—given its title—on coping with stress.

a breakup with a boyfriend or a girlfriend may lead individuals to change aspects of their behavior that they find unsatisfactory. Moreover, even if people do not conquer stressors, they may be able to learn from their mistakes. In a review of recent research on posttraumatic growth, Helgeson, Reynolds, and Tomich (2006) found that it is related to lower levels of depression and enhanced well-being. In contrast, it is also related to increased intrusive thoughts about the stressful event. They note that these thoughts do not necessarily indicate distress. It could be that people are working through the stressful event and that in this process the growth happens.

Second, stressful events help satisfy the need for stimulation and challenge. Studies suggest that most people prefer an intermediate level of stimulation and challenge in their lives (Sutherland, 2000). Although we think of stress in terms of stimulus overload, underload can be stressful as well (Goldberger, 1993). Thus,

most people would experience a suffocating level of boredom if they lived a stress-free existence. In a sense, then, stress fulfills a basic need of the human organism.

Third, today's stress can inoculate and psychologically prepare individuals so that they are less affected by tomorrow's stress. Some studies suggest that exposure to stress can increase stress tolerance—as long as the stress isn't overwhelming (Meichenbaum, 1993). Further, by dealing with a stressful event people will be better prepared for subsequent stress (Janoff-Bulman, 2004). Thus, a woman who has previously endured business setbacks may be much better prepared than most people to deal with a bank foreclosure on her home. In light of the negative effects that stress can have, improved stress tolerance is a desirable goal. We'll look next at the factors that influence the ability to tolerate stress.

Factors Influencing Stress Tolerance

LEARNING OBJECTIVES

▶ *Explain how social support moderates the impact of stress.*
▶ *Describe the hardiness syndrome and how it influences stress tolerance.*
▶ *Discuss how optimism is related to stress tolerance.*

Some people seem to be able to withstand the ravages of stress better than others (Holahan & Moos, 1990, 1994). Why? Because a number of *moderator variables* can soften the impact of stress on physical and mental health. To shed light on differences in how well people tolerate stress, we'll look at a number of key moderator variables, including social support, hardiness, and optimism. As you'll see, these factors influence people's emotional, physical, and behavioral responses to stress. These complexities are diagrammed in **Figure 3.16** on the next page, which builds on **Figure 3.6** (on page 80) to provide a more complete overview of the factors involved in individual reactions to stress.

Social Support

Friends may be good for your health! This startling conclusion emerges from studies on social support as a moderator of stress. *Social support* **refers to various types of aid and succor provided by members of one's social networks.** In fact, social support is regarded as such an important factor influencing stress tolerance that over 1,100 articles are published on the topic each year (Taylor, 2007). For example, Jemmott and Magloire (1988) examined the effect of social support on

immune response in a group of students going through the stress of final exams. They found that students who reported stronger social support had higher levels of an antibody that plays a key role in warding off respiratory infections. Positive correlations between high social support and greater immunal functioning have been observed in quite a number of studies with diverse samples (Uchino, Cacioppo, & Kiecolt-Glaser, 1996).

Over the last two decades, a vast body of studies have found evidence that social support is favorably related to physical health (Taylor, 2007; Wills & Fegan, 2001). Social support seems to be good medicine for the mind as well as the body, as most studies also find an association between social support and mental health (Davis, Morris, & Kraus, 1998; Sarason, Pierce, & Sarason, 1994). It appears that social support serves as a protective buffer during times of high stress, reducing the negative impact of stressful events—and that social support has its own positive effects on health, which may be apparent even when people aren't under great stress (Peirce et al., 1996; Wills & Fegan, 2001). The stress-buffering effects of social support were apparent in a study that found strong social support to be a key factor reducing the likelihood of posttraumatic stress disorders among Vietnam veterans (King et al., 1998).

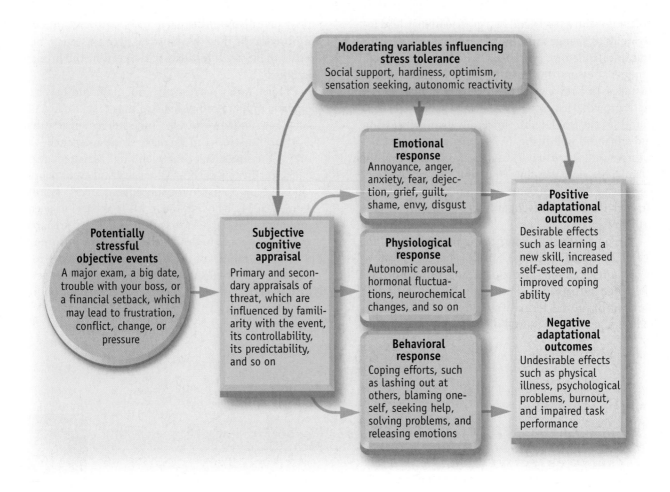

Figure 3.16

Overview of the stress process. This diagram builds on Figure 3.6 (the multidimensional response to stress) to provide a more complete overview of the factors involved in stress. This diagram adds the potential effects of stress (seen on the far right) by listing some of the positive and negative adaptational outcomes that may result from stress. It also completes the picture by showing moderating variables (seen at the top) that can influence the effects of stress (including some variables not covered in the chapter).

The mechanisms underlying the connection between social support and wellness have been the subject of considerable debate (Hobfoll & Vaux, 1993). A variety of mechanisms may be at work. Among other things, social support could promote wellness by making appraisals of stressful events more benign, dampening the intensity of physiological reactions to stress, reducing health-impairing behaviors such as smoking and drinking, encouraging preventive behaviors such as regular exercise and medical checkups, and fostering more constructive coping efforts (Taylor, 2007; Wills & Fegan, 2001).

Interestingly, recent studies suggest that *providing* social support to others can also have both psychological benefits (lower depression and perceived stress) and physical benefits (lower blood pressure) (Brown et al., 2003; Piferi & Lawler, 2006). Another study found that the personality trait of *sociability* (being friendly and agreeable), which certainly helps people build supportive social networks, is independently associ-

ated with reduced susceptibility to infectious disease (Cohen et al., 2003). Yet another study has demonstrated that many pet owners view their pets as sources of support in their lives, with resultant health benefits (Allen, Blascovich, & Mendes, 2002). Thus, it appears that there are many aspects of social support that have some bearing on our wellness.

Hardiness

Another line of research indicates that a syndrome called *hardiness* may moderate the impact of stressful events. Suzanne (Kobasa) Ouellette reasoned that if stress affects some people less than others, some people must be *hardier* than others. Hence, she set out to determine what factors might be the key to these differences in hardiness.

Suzanne Ouellette

The availability of social support is a key factor influencing stress tolerance. Decades of research have shown that social support reduces the negative effects of stress and has positive effects of its own.

Kobasa (1979) used a modified version of the Holmes and Rahe (1967) stress scale (SRRS) to measure the amount of stress experienced by a group of executives. As in most other studies, she found a modest correlation between stress and the incidence of physical illness. However, she carried her investigation one step further than previous studies. She compared the high-stress executives who exhibited the expected high incidence of illness against the high-stress executives who stayed healthy. She administered a battery of psychological tests and found that the hardier executives "were more committed, felt more in control, and had bigger appetites for challenge" (Kobasa, 1984, p. 70). These traits have also shown up in many other studies of hardiness (Maddi, 2002, 2006; Ouellette, 1993).

Thus, **hardiness is a disposition marked by commitment, challenge, and control that is purportedly associated with strong stress resistance.** Hardiness may reduce the effects of stress by altering stress appraisals or fostering more active coping (Crowley, Hayslip, & Hobdy, 2003; Maddi, 2006; Maddi & Hightower, 1999). The benefits of hardiness showed up in a study of Vietnam veterans, which found that higher hardiness was related to a lower likelihood of developing posttraumatic stress disorders (King et al., 1998). Although the research on hardiness is promising, debate continues about how to measure hardiness and about its key elements (Klag & Bradley, 2004; Oullette & DiPlacido, 2001; Younkin & Betz, 1996).

Optimism

Everyone knows someone whose glass is half full, who sees the world through rose-colored glasses, who is an

Recommended **READING**

Why Zebras Don't Get Ulcers: The Acclaimed Guide to Stress, Stress-Related Diseases, and Coping by Robert M. Sapolsky (W. H. Freeman, 2004)

This book provides a superb, wide-ranging discussion of the nature and effects of stress. The author is a neuroscientist at Stanford University whose research focuses on such issues as the relationship between stress and the cellular and molecular events underlying neural decay in the hippocampal area of the brain. That is not the type of résumé that you would normally associate with lively, witty discourse, but the book is written with flair and humor. Sapolsky's basic thesis is that the physiological response to stress is a remnant of evolution that is no longer adaptive for the majority of stressful situations that humans face. He outlines in detail how neuroendocrine responses to stress can cause or worsen a host of physical and psychological afflictions, including cardiovascular disease, ulcers, colitis, diarrhea, infectious diseases, and depression. Sapolsky does an excellent job of making complicated research understandable. Although opinionated, his overviews of research are scientifically sound and thoroughly documented in notes at the back of the book. This is not a coping manual, yet it is probably the most insightful and interesting dissection of the stress response available today and is highly worthwhile reading.

Calvin and Hobbes

optimist. *Optimism* **is a general tendency to expect good outcomes.** Pioneering research in this area by Michael Scheier and Charles Carver (1985) found a correlation between optimism as measured by the Life Orientation Test (see **Figure 3.17**) and relatively good physical health in a sample of college students. In another study that focused on surgical patients, optimism was found to be associated with a faster recovery and a quicker return to normal activities after coronary artery bypass surgery (Scheier et al., 1989). Yet another study found optimism to be associated with more effective immune functioning (Segerstrom et al., 1998). More recently, optimism was inversely related to PTSD symptoms for college students who knew a victim of the 9/11 terrorist attacks (Ai, Santangelo, & Cascio, 2006). Twenty years of research with the Life Orientation Test has consistently shown that optimism is associated with better mental and physical health (Carver & Scheier, 2005; Scheier, Carver, & Bridges, 2001).

In a related line of research, Christopher Peterson and Martin Seligman have studied how people explain bad events (personal setbacks, mishaps, disappointments, and such). These researchers identified a *pessimistic explanatory style,* in which people tend to blame setbacks on their own personal shortcomings, versus an *optimistic explanatory style,* which leads people to attribute setbacks to temporary situational factors. In

two retrospective studies of people born many decades ago, they found an association between this optimistic explanatory style and relatively good health (Peterson,

Figure 3.17

The Life Orientation Test (LOT). The personality trait of optimism, which appears to foster resilience in the face of stress, can be measured by the Life Orientation Test (LOT) developed by Scheier and Carver (1985). Follow the instructions for this scale to obtain an estimate of your own optimism. High and low scores are based on scoring three-fifths of a standard deviation above or below the mean.

Adapted from Scheier, M. F., & Carver, C. S. (1985). Optimism, coping, and health: Assessment and implications of generalized outcome expectancies. *Health Psychology, 4,* 219–247. Copyright © 1985 Lawrence Erlbaum & Associates. Adapted by permission of the publisher and authors.

Measuring Optimism

In the following spaces, mark how much you agree with each of the items, using the following scale:

4 = strongly agree
3 = agree
2 = neutral
1 = disagree
0 = strongly disagree

_____ 1. In uncertain times, I usually expect the best.

_____ 2. It's easy for me to relax.

_____ 3. If something can go wrong for me, it will.

_____ 4. I always look on the bright side of things.

_____ 5. I'm always optimistic about my future.

_____ 6. I enjoy my friends a lot.

_____ 7. It's important for me to keep busy.

_____ 8. I hardly ever expect things to go my way.

_____ 9. Things never work out the way I want them to.

_____ 10. I don't get upset too easily.

_____ 11. I'm a believer in the idea that "every cloud has a silver lining."

_____ 12. I rarely count on good things happening to me.

Scoring
Cross out and ignore the responses you entered for items 2, 6, 7, and 10, which are "filler" items. For items 3, 8, 9, and 12, you need to reverse the numbers you entered. If you entered a 4, change it to 0. If you entered a 3, change it to 1. If you entered a 2, leave it unchanged. If you entered a 1, change it to 3. If you entered a 0, change it to 4. Now add up the numbers for items 1, 3, 4, 5, 8, 9, 11, 12, using the new numbers for the reversed items. This sum is your score on the Life Orientation Test. For college students, approximate norms are as follows: High score (25–32), intermediate score (18–24), low score (0–17).

Seligman, & Vaillant, 1988) and increased longevity (Peterson et al., 1998). Many other studies have linked the optimistic explanatory style to superior physical health (Peterson & Bossio, 2001), as well as higher academic achievement, increased job productivity, enhanced athletic performance, and higher marital satisfaction (Gillham et al., 2001).

Why does optimism promote a host of desirable outcomes? Above all else, research suggests that optimists cope with stress in more adaptive ways than pessimists (Aspinwall, Richter, & Hoffman, 2001; Carver & Scheier, 2002; Chang, 1996). Optimists are more likely to engage in action-oriented, problem-focused, carefully planned coping and are more willing than pessimists to seek social support. In comparison, pessimists are more likely to deal with stress by avoiding it, giving up, or engaging in denial. We will be discussing these specific types of coping styles in the next chapter.

APPLICATION

Monitoring Your Stress

LEARNING OBJECTIVES
▶ *List five problems with the SRRS.*
▶ *Summarize how the LES corrects some of the problems that are characteristic of the SRRS.*
▶ *Explain why one should be cautious in interpreting scores on stress scales.*

Rank the following five events in terms of how stressful they would be for you (1 = most stressful, 5 = least stressful):

___ **1.** Change in residence
___ **2.** Fired at work
___ **3.** Death of a close family member
___ **4.** Pregnancy
___ **5.** Personal injury or illness

All five events appear on the Social Readjustment Rating Scale (SRRS), developed by Holmes and Rahe (1967), which we described earlier (see **Figure 3.4** on page 78). If you ranked them in the same order as Holmes and Rahe's subjects, the rankings would be 5, 3, 1, 4, and 2. If you didn't rank them in that order, don't worry about it. That merely shows that the perception of stress is personal and subjective. Unfortunately, the SRRS fails to take this subjectivity into account. That is just one of a number of basic problems with the SRRS.

The SRRS and the research associated with it have received a great deal of publicity. The scale has been reprinted in many popular newspapers and magazines. In these articles, readers have been encouraged to attribute great significance to their scores. They have sometimes been told that they should reduce or minimize change in their lives if their scores are high (Cohen, 1979). Such bold advice could be counterproductive and needs to be qualified carefully. Therefore, in this application section we'll elaborate on some of the problems with the SRRS as a measurement scale, introduce you to an improved scale for measuring stress, and explain why scores on any stress scale should be interpreted with caution.

Problems with the SRRS

As you learned earlier in this chapter, the SRRS was developed in the early 1960s by Thomas Holmes and Richard Rahe (1967). They designed the scale to measure the amount of change-related stress that people experience. In a host of studies, these scores have been found to be related to the likelihood of developing an intimidating array of physical illnesses and psychological problems (Dougall & Baum, 2001; Lynch et al., 2005; Turner & Wheaton, 1995).

Courtesy, Eleanor Holmes Williams

Thomas Holmes

Before we discuss the shortcomings of the SRRS, we should emphasize that Holmes and Rahe deserve enormous credit for recognizing the potential importance of stress and for developing a scale that would permit its measurement. They pioneered a new area of research that has turned out to be extremely productive. However, their groundbreaking foray into the assessment of stress was not without its flaws, and their scale has been improved on. So, borrowing from the analyses of a number of critics (Derogatis, 1982; Rabkin, 1993; Schroeder & Costa, 1984), let's look at some of the major problems with the SRRS. Although our list is not exhaustive, we highlight the key problems.

First, as already discussed, the assumption that the SRRS measures change exclusively has been shown to be inaccurate. We now have ample evidence that the desirability of events affects adaptational outcomes more than the amount of change that they require (Turner & Wheaton, 1995). Thus, it seems prudent to view the SRRS as a measure of diverse forms of stress, rather than as a measure of change-related stress (McLean & Link, 1994).

Second, the SRRS fails to take into account differences among people in their subjective perception of how stressful an event is. For instance, while divorce may deserve a stress value of 73 for *most* people, a particular person's divorce might generate much less stress and merit a value of only 25.

Third, many of the events listed on the SRRS and similar scales are highly ambiguous, leading people to be inconsistent as to which events they report experiencing (Monroe & McQuaid, 1994). For instance, what qualifies as "trouble with boss"? Should you check that because you're sick and tired of your supervisor? What constitutes a "change in living conditions"? Does your purchase of a great new sound system qualify? As you can see, the SRRS includes many "events" that are described inadequately, producing considerable ambiguity about the meaning of one's response. Problems in recalling events over a period of a year also lead to inconsistent responding on stress scales, thus lowering their reliability (Klein & Rubovits, 1987).

Fourth, the SRRS does not sample from the domain of stressful events very thoroughly. Do the 43 events listed on the SRRS exhaust all the major stresses that people typically experience? Studies designed to explore that question have found many significant omissions (Dohrenwend et al, 1993; Wheaton, 1994).

Fifth, the correlation between SRRS scores and health outcomes may be inflated because subjects' neuroticism affects both their responses to stress scales and their self-reports of health problems. Neurotic individuals have a tendency to recall more stress than others and to recall more symptoms of illness than others (Watson, David, & Suls, 1999). These tendencies mean that some of the correlation between high stress and high illness may simply reflect the effects of subjects' neuroticism (Critelli & Ee, 1996). This is another case of the third variable problem in correlation that we introduced in Chapter 1 (see **Figure 3.18**). The possible contaminating effects of neuroticism obscure the meaning of scores on the SRRS and similar measures of stress.

The Life Experiences Survey

In light of these problems, a number of researchers have attempted to develop improved versions of the SRRS. For example, the Life Experiences Survey (LES), assembled by Irwin Sarason and colleagues (1978), has become a widely used measure of stress in contemporary research (for examples see Ames et al., 2001; Denisoff & Endler, 2000; Malefo, 2000). The LES revises and builds on the SRRS in a variety of ways that correct, at

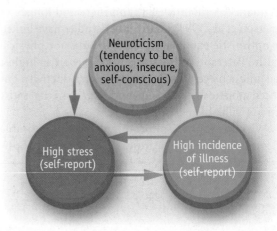

Figure 3.18

Neuroticism as a possible factor underlying the stress-illness correlation. Many studies have found a correlation between subjects' scores on self-report stress scales, such as the SRRS, and their reports of how much illness they have experienced. However, neurotic subjects, who are anxious, insecure, and self-conscious, tend to recall more stress *and* more illness than others. Although there is a great deal of evidence that stress contributes to the causation of illness, some of the stress-illness correlation may be due to neuroticism causing high recall of both stress and illness.

least in part, most of the problems just discussed (see Hobson & Delunas, 2001 and Rahe et al., 2000 for other modernized versions of the SRRS).

Specifically, the LES recognizes that stress involves more than mere change and asks respondents to indicate whether events had a positive or negative impact on them. This strategy permits the computation of positive change, negative change, and total change scores, which helps researchers gain much more insight into which facets of stress are most crucial.

The LES also takes into consideration differences among people in their appraisal of stress, by dropping the normative weights and replacing them with personally assigned weightings of the impact of relevant events. Ambiguity in items is decreased by providing more elaborate descriptions of many items to clarify their meaning. The scale still contains some ambiguity, but there is no complete solution for this problem.

The LES deals with the failure of the SRRS to sample the full domain of stressful events in several ways. First, some significant omissions from the SRRS have been added to the LES. Second, the LES allows the respondent to write in personally important events that are not included on the scale. Third, the LES reprinted here (in **Figure 3.19**) has an extra section just for students. Sarason and colleagues (1978) suggest that special, tailored sections of this sort be added for specific populations whenever it is useful.

Arriving at your scores on the LES is very simple. Respond to the items in **Figure 3.19** and add up all the positive impact ratings on the right side. The total is

Figure 3.19

The Life Experiences Survey (LES). Like the SRRS, the LES is designed to measure change-related stress. However, Sarason, Johnson, and Siegel (1978) corrected many of the problems apparent in the SRRS. Follow the instructions to determine your positive, negative, and total change scores.

The Life Experiences Survey (LES)

Instructions. Listed below are a number of events that sometimes bring about change in the lives of those who experience them and that necessitate social readjustment. Examine each event on the list and if that event has occurred in your life during the past year please indicate the extent to which you viewed the event as having either a positive or negative impact on your life at the time the event occurred. That is, circle a number on the appropriate line to indicate the type and extent of impact that the event had. A rating of −3 would indicate an extremely negative impact. A rating of 0 suggests no impact, either positive or negative. A rating of +3 would indicate an extremely positive impact.

	Extremely negative	Moderately negative	Somewhat negative	No impact	Slightly positive	Moderately positive	Extremely positive
Section 1							
1. Marriage	−3	−2	−1	0	+1	+2	+3
2. Detention in jail or comparable institution	−3	−2	−1	0	+1	+2	+3
3. Death of spouse	−3	−2	−1	0	+1	+2	+3
4. Major change in sleeping habits	−3	−2	−1	0	+1	+2	+3
5. Death of a close family member	−3	−2	−1	0	+1	+2	+3
a. Mother	−3	−2	−1	0	+1	+2	+3
b. Father	−3	−2	−1	0	+1	+2	+3
c. Brother	−3	−2	−1	0	+1	+2	+3
d. Sister	−3	−2	−1	0	+1	+2	+3
e. Grandmother	−3	−2	−1	0	+1	+2	+3
f. Grandfather	−3	−2	−1	0	+1	+2	+3
g. Other (specify)	−3	−2	−1	0	+1	+2	+3
6. Major change in eating habits (much more or much less food intake)	−3	−2	−1	0	+1	+2	+3
7. Foreclosure on mortgage or loan	−3	−2	−1	0	+1	+2	+3
8. Death of a close friend	−3	−2	−1	0	+1	+2	+3
9. Outstanding personal achievement	−3	−2	−1	0	+1	+2	+3
10. Minor law violations	−3	−2	−1	0	+1	+2	+3
11. Male: Wife/girlfriend's pregnancy	−3	−2	−1	0	+1	+2	+3
12. Female: Pregnancy	−3	−2	−1	0	+1	+2	+3
13. Changed work situation (different work responsibility, major change in working conditions, working hours, etc.)	−3	−2	−1	0	+1	+2	+3
14. New job	−3	−2	−1	0	+1	+2	+3
15. Serious illness or injury of close family member:							
a. Mother	−3	−2	−1	0	+1	+2	+3
b. Father	−3	−2	−1	0	+1	+2	+3
c. Brother	−3	−2	−1	0	+1	+2	+3
d. Sister	−3	−2	−1	0	+1	+2	+3
e. Grandmother	−3	−2	−1	0	+1	+2	+3
f. Grandfather	−3	−2	−1	0	+1	+2	+3
g. Spouse	−3	−2	−1	0	+1	+2	+3
h. Other (specify)	−3	−2	−1	0	+1	+2	+3
16. Sexual difficulties	−3	−2	−1	0	+1	+2	+3
17. Trouble with employer (in danger of losing job, being suspended, being demoted, etc.)	−3	−2	−1	0	+1	+2	+3
18. Trouble with in-laws	−3	−2	−1	0	+1	+2	+3
19. Major change in financial status (a lot better off or a lot worse off)	−3	−2	−1	0	+1	+2	+3

(continued)

Adapted from Sarason, I. G., Johnson, J. H., & Siegel, J. M. (1978). Assessing the impact of life changes. *Journal of Consulting and Clinical Psychology, 46*, 932–946. Copyright © 1978 by the American Psychological Association. Reprinted by permission of the publisher and author.

The Life Experiences Survey (LES) *(continued)*

	Extremely negative	Moderately negative	Somewhat negative	No impact	Slightly positive	Moderately positive	Extremely positive
20. Major change in closeness of family members (increased or decreased closeness)	−3	−2	−1	0	+1	+2	+3
21. Gaining a new family member (through birth, adoption, family member moving in, etc.)	−3	−2	−1	0	+1	+2	+3
22. Change in residence	−3	−2	−1	0	+1	+2	+3
23. Marital separation from mate (due to conflict)	−3	−2	−1	0	+1	+2	+3
24. Major change in church activities (increased or decreased attendance)	−3	−2	−1	0	+1	+2	+3
25. Marital reconciliation with mate	−3	−2	−1	0	+1	+2	+3
26. Major change in number of arguments with spouse (a lot more or a lot fewer)	−3	−2	−1	0	+1	+2	+3
27. Married male: Change in wife's work outside the home (beginning work, ceasing work, changing to a new job, etc.)	−3	−2	−1	0	+1	+2	+3
28. Married female: Change in husband's work (loss of job, beginning new job, retirement, etc.)	−3	−2	−1	0	+1	+2	+3
29. Major change in usual type and/or amount of recreation	−3	−2	−1	0	+1	+2	+3
30. Borrowing for a major purchase (buying a home, business, etc.)	−3	−2	−1	0	+1	+2	+3
31. Borrowing for a smaller purchase (buying a car or TV, getting school loan, etc.)	−3	−2	−1	0	+1	+2	+3
32. Being fired from job	−3	−2	−1	0	+1	+2	+3
33. Male: Wife/girlfriend having abortion							
34. Female: Having abortion	−3	−2	−1	0	+1	+2	+3
35. Major personal illness or injury	−3	−2	−1	0	+1	+2	+3
36. Major change in social activities, e.g., parties, movies, visiting (increased or decreased participation)	−3	−2	−1	0	+1	+2	+3
37. Major change in living conditions of family (building new home, remodeling, deterioration of home or neighborhood, etc.)	−3	−2	−1	0	+1	+2	+3
38. Divorce	−3	−2	−1	0	+1	+2	+3
39. Serious injury or illness of close friend	−3	−2	−1	0	+1	+2	+3
40. Retirement from work	−3	−2	−1	0	+1	+2	+3
41. Son or daughter leaving home (due to marriage, college, etc.)	−3	−2	−1	0	+1	+2	+3
42. End of formal schooling	−3	−2	−1	0	+1	+2	+3
43. Separation from spouse (due to work, travel, etc.)	−3	−2	−1	0	+1	+2	+3
44. Engagement	−3	−2	−1	0	+1	+2	+3
45. Breaking up with boyfriend/girlfriend	−3	−2	−1	0	+1	+2	+3
46. Leaving home for the first time	−3	−2	−1	0	+1	+2	+3
47. Reconciliation with boyfriend/girlfriend	−3	−2	−1	0	+1	+2	+3
Other recent experiences that have had an impact on your life. List and rate.							
48. _____	−3	−2	−1	0	+1	+2	+3
49. _____	−3	−2	−1	0	+1	+2	+3
50. _____	−3	−2	−1	0	+1	+2	+3

(continued)

The Life Experiences Survey (LES) *(continued)*

	Extremely negative	Moderately negative	Somewhat negative	No impact	Slightly positive	Moderately positive	Extremely positive
Section 2. Students only							
51. Beginning a new school experience at a higher academic level (college, graduate school, professional school)	−3	−2	−1	0	+1	+2	+3
52. Changing to a new school at the same academic level (undergraduate, graduate, etc.)	−3	−2	−1	0	+1	+2	+3
53. Academic probation	−3	−2	−1	0	+1	+2	+3
54. Being dismissed from dormitory or other residence	−3	−2	−1	0	+1	+2	+3
55. Failing an important exam	−3	−2	−1	0	+1	+2	+3
56. Changing a major	−3	−2	−1	0	+1	+2	+3
57. Failing a course	−3	−2	−1	0	+1	+2	+3
58. Dropping a course	−3	−2	−1	0	+1	+2	+3
59. Joining a fraternity/sorority	−3	−2	−1	0	+1	+2	+3
60. Financial problems concerning school (in danger of not having sufficient money to continue)	−3	−2	−1	0	+1	+2	+3

your positive change score. Your negative change score is the sum of all of the negative impact ratings that you made on the left. Adding these two values yields your total change score. Approximate norms for all three of these scores are listed in **Figure 3.20** so that you can get some idea of what your score means.

Research to date suggests that the negative change score is the crucial one; positive change has not been found to be a good predictor of adaptational outcomes. Thus far, research has shown that negative change scores are related to a variety of negative adaptational outcomes.

Norms for LES

Score category	Negative change	Positive change	Total change
High	14 and above	16 and above	28 and above
Medium	4–13	7–15	12–27
Low	0–3	0–6	0–11

Figure 3.20

Norms for the Life Experiences Survey (LES). Approximate norms for college students taking the LES are shown for negative, positive, and total change scores. These norms are based on 345 undergraduates studied by Sarason, Johnson, and Siegel (1978). Data for males and females were combined, as gender differences were negligible. Negative change scores are the best predictor of adaptational outcomes.

Adapted from Sarason, I. G., Johnson, J. H., & Siegel, J. M. (1978). Assessing the impact of life changes. *Journal of Consulting and Clinical Psychology, 46*, 932–946. Copyright © 1978 by the American Psychological Association. Reprinted by permission of the publisher and author.

A Cautionary Note

There is merit in getting an estimate of how much stress you have experienced lately, but scores on the LES or any measure of stress should be interpreted with caution. You need not panic if you add up your negative change score and find that it falls in the "high" category. Although it is clear that a connection exists between stress and a variety of undesirable adaptational outcomes, a high score shouldn't cause undue concern.

For one thing, the strength of the association between stress and adaptational problems is modest. Most of the correlations observed between stress scores and illness have been low to moderate in magnitude, often less than .30 (Monroe & McQuaid, 1994). For researchers and theorists, it is interesting to find any relationship at all. However, the link between stress and adaptational problems is too weak to permit us to make confident predictions about individuals. Many people endure high levels of stress without developing significant problems.

Second, stress is only one of a multitude of variables that affect susceptibility to various maladies. Stress interacts with many other factors, such as lifestyle, coping skills, social support, hardiness, and genetic inheritance, in influencing one's mental and physical health.

It's important to remember that stress is only one actor on a crowded stage. In light of these considerations, you should evaluate the potential meaning of SRRS or LES scores with caution. A high score should be food for thought, but not reason for alarm.

KEY IDEAS

The Nature of Stress

▶ Stress involves transactions with the environment that are perceived to be threatening. Stress is a common, everyday event, and even routine hassles can be problematic. To a large degree, stress lies in the eye of the beholder. According to Lazarus and Folkman, primary appraisal determines whether events appear threatening, while secondary appraisal assesses whether one has the resources to cope with challenges. How one appraises an event can alter the impact of the event.

▶ Some of the stress that people experience comes from their environment. Examples of environmental stimuli that can be stressful include excessive noise, crowding, community violence, and urban decay. Stress can vary with culture. Within Western culture, ethnicity can be a source of stress in a variety of ways.

Major Types of Stress

▶ Stress can be acute or chronic. Major types of stress include frustration, conflict, change, and pressure. Frustration occurs when an obstacle prevents one from attaining some goal. There are three principal types of conflict: approach-approach, avoidance-avoidance, and approach-avoidance.

▶ A large number of studies with the SRRS suggest that change is stressful. Although that may be true, it is now clear that the SRRS is a measure of general stress rather than just change-related stress.

▶ Pressure (to perform and to conform) also appears to be stressful. Often this pressure is self-imposed.

Responding to Stress

▶ Emotional reactions to stress typically involve anger, fear, or sadness. However, people also experience positive emotions while under stress and these positive emotions may promote resilience. Emotional arousal may interfere with coping. As tasks get more complex, the optimal level of arousal declines.

▶ Physiological arousal in response to stress was originally called the fight-or-flight response by Cannon. Taylor has proposed an alternative response ("tend and befriend") that might be more applicable to females. Selye's general adaptation syndrome describes three stages in the physiological reaction to stress: alarm, resistance, and exhaustion. Diseases of adaptation may appear during the stage of exhaustion.

▶ In response to stress, the brain sends signals along two major pathways to the endocrine system. Actions along these paths release two sets of hormones into the bloodstream, catecholamines and corticosteroids. Stress can also lead to suppression of the immune response. Behavioral responses to stress involve coping, which may be healthy or maladaptive. If people cope effectively with stress, they can short-circuit potentially harmful emotional and physical responses.

The Potential Effects of Stress

▶ Common negative effects of stress include impaired task performance, disruption of attention and other cognitive processes, pervasive emotional exhaustion known as burnout, posttraumatic stress disorder, a host of everyday psychological problems, full-fledged psychological disorders, and varied types of damage to physical health.

▶ However, stress can also have positive effects, including posttraumatic growth. Stress fulfills a basic human need for challenge and can lead to personal growth and self-improvement. Stress can also have an inoculation effect, preparing us for the next stressful event.

Factors Influencing Stress Tolerance

▶ People differ in how much stress they can tolerate without experiencing ill effects. A person's social support can be a key consideration in buffering the effects of stress. The personality factors associated with hardiness—commitment, challenge, and control—may increase stress tolerance. People high in optimism also have advantages in coping with stress.

Application: Monitoring Your Stress

▶ It can be useful to attempt to measure the amount of stress in one's life, but the much-used SRRS is marred by a variety of shortcomings. It does not really measure change exclusively, and it fails to account for the subjective nature of stress. Some of the items on the SRRS are ambiguous, and the scale does not sample the domain of stress thoroughly.

▶ In contrast, the LES is an improved measure of stress that recognizes the subjectivity of stress and the importance of the desirability of life events. The LES also samples the domain of stressful events a little more thoroughly and has less ambiguity than the SRRS. Negative change scores on the LES have been found to be predictive of a variety of adaptational outcomes. Even still, individual results should be interpreted with caution.

KEY TERMS

Acculturation p. 74
Acute stressors p. 75
Ambient stress p. 72
Approach-approach conflict p. 76
Approach-avoidance conflict p. 76
Autonomic nervous system (ANS) p. 83
Avoidance-avoidance conflict p. 76
Burnout p. 88
Chronic stressors pp. 75
Conflict p. 76
Coping pp. 86
Emotions p. 80
Endocrine system p. 85
Fight-or-flight response p. 82
Frustration p. 75
General adaptation syndrome p. 84
Hardiness p. 95
Life changes p. 77
Optimism p. 96
Posttraumatic stress disorder (PTSD) p. 89
Pressure pp. 78–79
Primary appraisal p. 72
Psychosomatic diseases p. 92
Secondary appraisal p. 72
Social support p. 93
Stress p. 71

KEY PEOPLE

Susan Folkman pp. 81–82
Barbara Fredrickson p. 81
Thomas Holmes and Richard Rahe pp. 77, 97
Suzanne (Kobasa) Ouellette pp. 94–95
Richard Lazarus p. 71
Neal Miller p. 76
Hans Selye pp. 84–85
Shelley Taylor p. 84

1. Concerning the nature of stress, which statement is *not* accurate?
   a. Stress is an everyday event.
   b. Stress lies in the eye of the beholder.
   c. Stress may be embedded in the environment.
   d. Stress is always imposed on us by others.

2. Secondary appraisal refers to:
   a. second thoughts about what to do in a stressful situation.
   b. second thoughts about whether an event is genuinely threatening.
   c. initial evaluation of an event's relevance, threat, and stressfulness.
   d. evaluation of coping resources and options for dealing with a stressful event.

3. Kelli is having a hard time deciding whether she should buy a coat. On the one hand, it is a name brand coat on sale for a great price. On the other hand, it is an ugly mold-green color. Kelli is experiencing what type of conflict?
   a. approach-approach
   b. avoidance-avoidance
   c. approach-avoidance
   d. life change

4. José just completed writing an 8-page term paper. When he went to save it, the computer crashed and he lost all his work. What type of stress is José experiencing?
   a. Frustration   c. Life change
   b. Conflict   d. Pressure

5. The optimal level of arousal for a task appears to depend in part on:
   a. one's position on the optimism/pessimism scale.
   b. how much physiological change an event stimulates.
   c. the complexity of the task at hand.
   d. how imminent a stressful event is.

6. The fight-or-flight response is mediated by the:
   a. sympathetic division of the autonomic nervous system.
   b. sympathetic division of the endocrine system.
   c. visceral division of the peripheral nervous system.
   d. parasympathetic division of the autonomic nervous system.

7. Selye exposed lab animals to various stressors and found that:
   a. each type of stress caused a particular physiological response.
   b. each type of animal responded to stress differently.
   c. patterns of physiological arousal were similar, regardless of the type of stress.
   d. patterns of physiological arousal were different, even when stressors were similar.

8. Stress can _____ the functioning of the immune system.
   a. stimulate
   b. destroy
   c. suppress
   d. enhance

9. Salvador works as a security guard at a shopping center. His boss overloads him with responsibility but never gives him any credit for all his hard work. He feels worn down, disillusioned, and helpless at work. Salvador is probably experiencing:
   a. an alarm reaction.
   b. burnout.
   c. posttraumatic stress disorder.
   d. a psychosomatic disorder.

10. A personal disposition marked by commitment, challenge, and control and that appears to be related to stress resistance is called:
    a. hardiness.
    b. optimism.
    c. courage.
    d. conscientiousness.

Book Companion Website

Visit the Book Companion Website at **academic.cengage. com/psychology/weiten**, where you will find tutorial quizzes, flash cards, and web links for every chapter, a final exam, and more! You can also link to the Psychology Resource Center (accessible directly at **academic.cengage.com/login**) for a range of psychology-related resources.

Personal Explorations Workbook

The following exercises in your *Personal Explorations Workbook* may enhance your self-understanding in relation to issues raised in this chapter. **Questionnaire 3.1:** Sensation-Seeking Scale. **Personal Probe 3.1:** Where's the Stress in Your Life? **Personal Probe 3.2:** Stress—How Do You Control It? **Personal Probe 3.3:** Working Through and Assessing the Impact of a Stressful Event.

ANSWERS

1. d Pages 71–73
2. d Page 72
3. c Page 76
4. a Page 75
5. c Page 82
6. a Pages 82–84
7. c Page 84
8. c Page 86
9. b Page 88
10. a Pages 94–95

CHAPTER 4

Coping Processes

"I have begun to believe that I have intellectually and emotionally outgrown my husband. However, I'm not really sure what this means or what I should do. Maybe this feeling is normal and I should ignore it and continue my present relationship. This seems to be the safest route. Maybe I should seek a lover while continuing with my husband. Then again, maybe I should start anew and hope for a beautiful ending with or without a better mate."

The woman quoted above is in the throes of a thorny conflict. Although it is hard to tell just how much emotional turmoil she is experiencing, it's clear that she is under substantial stress. What should she do? Is it psychologically healthy to remain in an emotionally hollow marriage? Is seeking a secret lover a reasonable way to cope with this unfortunate situation? Should she just strike out on her own and let the chips fall where they may? These questions have no simple answers. As you'll soon see, decisions about how to cope with life's difficulties can be incredibly complex.

In the previous chapter we discussed the nature of stress and its effects. We learned that stress can be a challenging, exciting stimulus to personal growth. However, we also saw that stress can prove damaging to people's psychological and physical health because it often triggers physiological responses that may be harmful. These responses to stress tend to be largely automatic. Controlling them depends on the coping responses people make to stressful situations. Thus, a person's mental and physical health depends, in part, on his or her ability to cope effectively with stress.

This chapter focuses on how people cope with stress. We begin with a general discussion of the concept of coping. Then we review some common coping patterns that tend to have relatively little value.

After discussing these ill-advised coping techniques, we offer an overview of what it means to engage in healthier, "constructive" coping. The remainder of the chapter expands on the specifics of constructive coping. We hope our discussion provides you with some new ideas about how to deal with the stresses of modern life.

The Concept of Coping

LEARNING OBJECTIVES
▶ Describe the variety of coping strategies that people use.
▶ Discuss the role of flexibility in coping.

In Chapter 3, you learned that *coping* **refers to efforts to master, reduce, or tolerate the demands created by stress.** Let's take a closer look at this concept and discuss some general points about coping.

People cope with stress in many ways. A number of researchers have attempted to identify and classify the various coping techniques that people use in dealing with stress. Their work reveals quite a variety of coping strategies. For instance, in a review of the literature, Skinner et al. (2003) found over 400 distinct cop-

ing techniques. Carver, Scheier, and Weintraub (1989) found that they could sort their participants' coping tactics into 14 categories, which are listed in **Figure 4.1**. Thus, in grappling with stress, people select their coping tactics from a large and varied menu of options.

It is most adaptive to use a variety of coping strategies. Even with a large menu of coping tactics to choose from, most people come to rely on some strategies more than others (Carver & Scheier, 1994; Shiota, 2006). Of course, an individual's coping strategies are

Types of Coping Strategies	
Coping strategy	**Example**
Active coping	I take additional action to try to get rid of the problem.
Planning	I come up with a strategy about what to do.
Suppression of competing activities	I put aside other activities in order to concentrate on this.
Restraint coping	I force myself to wait for the right time to do something.
Seeking social support for instrumental reasons	I ask people who have had similar experiences what they did.
Seeking social support for emotional reasons	I talk to someone about how I feel.
Positive reinterpretation and growth	I look for the good in what is happening.
Acceptance	I learn to live with it.
Turning to religion	I seek God's help.
Focus on and venting of emotions	I get upset and let my emotions out.
Denial	I refuse to believe that it has happened.
Behavioral disengagement	I give up the attempt to get what I want.
Mental disengagement	I turn to work or other substitute activities to take my mind off things.
Alcohol-drug disengagement	I drink alcohol or take drugs in order to think about it less.

Figure 4.1

Classifying coping strategies. Carver, Scheier, and Weintraub (1989) sorted their subjects' coping responses into 14 categories. The categories are listed here (column 1) with a representative example from each category (column 2). As you can see, people use quite a variety of coping strategies.

From Carver, C. S., Scheier, M. F., & Weintraub, J. K. (1989). Assessing coping strategies: A theoretically based approach. *Journal of Personality and Social Psychology, 56*(2), 267–283. Copyright 1989 by the American Psychological Association. Reprinted by permission of the publisher and author.

also influenced by situational demands, and Cheng (2001, 2003) has argued that flexibility in coping is more desirable than consistently relying on the same strategy. Cheng and Cheung (2005) identified a key difference between individuals with high and low coping flexibility. Flexible copers can differentiate among stressful events in terms of controllability and impact, important information to know when choosing a coping strategy. Indeed, the ability to select a specific coping strategy to meet a specific adversity helps people avoid becoming stuck in a rut with a problematic strategy (Carbonell, Reinherz, & Beardslee, 2005). While everyone has an individual style of coping with life's difficulties, this need for flexibility may explain why people's coping strategies show only moderate stability across varied situations (Schwartz et al., 1999).

Coping strategies vary in their adaptive value. In everyday terms, when we say that someone "coped with her problems," we imply that she handled them effec-tively. In reality, however, all strategies are not created equal. Coping processes range from the helpful to the counterproductive (Carver et al., 1989; Vaillant, 2000). For example, coping with the disappointment of not getting a good grade by plotting to sabotage your professor's computer would be a negative way of coping. Hence, we will distinguish between coping patterns that tend to be helpful and those that tend to be maladaptive. Bear in mind, however, that our generalizations about the adaptive value of various coping strategies are based on trends or tendencies identified by researchers. Unlike what many self-help books and talk show hosts would have you believe, no coping strategy can guarantee a successful outcome. Furthermore, the adaptive value of a coping technique depends on the exact nature of the situation. As you'll see in the next section, even ill-advised coping strategies may have adaptive value in some instances.

Common Coping Patterns of Limited Value

LEARNING OBJECTIVES

▶ Analyze the adaptive value of giving up as a response to stress.

▶ Describe the adaptive value of aggression as a response to stress.

▶ Evaluate the adaptive value of indulging yourself as a response to stress.

▶ Discuss the adaptive value of negative self-talk as a response to stress.

▶ Explain how defense mechanisms work.

▶ Evaluate the adaptive value of defense mechanisms, including recent work on healthy illusions.

"Recently, after an engagement of 22 months, my fiancée told me that she was in love with someone else, and that we were through. I've been a wreck ever since. I can't study because I keep thinking about her. I think constantly about what I did wrong in the relationship and why I wasn't good enough for her. Getting drunk is the only way I can get her off my mind. Lately, I've been getting plastered about five or six nights a week. My grades are really hurting, but I'm not sure that I care."

This young man is going through a difficult time and does not appear to be handling it very well. He's blaming himself for the breakup with his fiancée. He's turning to alcohol to dull the pain that he feels, and it sounds like he may be giving up on school. These coping responses aren't particularly unusual in such situations, but they're only going to make his problems worse.

In this section, we'll examine some relatively common coping patterns that tend to be less than optimal. Specifically, we'll discuss giving up, aggression, self-indulgence, blaming yourself, and defense mechanisms. Some of these coping tactics may be helpful in certain circumstances, but more often than not, they are counterproductive.

Giving Up

When confronted with stress, people sometimes simply give up and withdraw from the battle. This response of apathy and inaction tends to be associated with the emotional reactions of sadness and dejection. Martin Seligman (1974, 1992) has developed a model of this giving-up syndrome that appears to shed light on its causes. In Seligman's original research, animals were subjected to electric shocks they could not escape. The animals were then given an opportunity to learn a response that would allow them to escape the shock. However, many of the animals became so apathetic and listless they didn't even try to learn the escape response. When researchers made similar manipulations with *human* subjects using inescapable noise (rather than shock) as the stressor, they observed parallel results (Hiroto & Seligman, 1975). This syndrome is referred to as learned helplessness. **Learned helplessness is passive behavior produced by exposure to unavoidable aver-**

Martin Seligman

Courtesy of Martin E. P. Seligman

sive events. Unfortunately, this tendency to give up may be transferred to situations in which one is not really helpless. Hence, some people routinely respond to stress with fatalism and resignation, passively accepting setbacks that might be dealt with effectively. Interestingly, Evans and Stecker (2004) argue that environmental stressors, such as excessive noise, crowding, and traffic (see Chapter 3), often produce a syndrome that resembles learned helplessness.

Seligman originally viewed learned helplessness as a product of conditioning. However, research with human participants has led Seligman and his colleagues to revise their theory. Their current model proposes that people's *cognitive interpretation* of aversive events determines whether they develop learned helplessness. Specifically, helplessness seems to occur when individuals come to believe that events are beyond their control. This belief is particularly likely to emerge in people who exhibit a pessimistic explanatory style. Among other things, such people tend to attribute setbacks to personal inadequacies instead of situational factors (Abramson, Seligman, & Teasdale, 1978; Seligman, 1990). As discussed in Chapter 3, this explanatory style is associated with poorer physical health and increased depression and anxiety (Wise & Rosqvist, 2006).

Overall, giving up is not a highly regarded method of coping. Carver and his colleagues (1989, 1993) have studied this coping strategy, which they refer to as *behavioral disengagement,* and found that it is associated with increased rather than decreased distress. A recent study of college students after the September 11 terrorist attacks supports this assertion, finding that behavioral disengagement was associated with increased anxiety shortly after the attack, even for those indirectly affected (see **Figure 4.2**; Liverant, Hafmann, & Litz, 2004). Furthermore, many studies suggest that learned helplessness can contribute to depression (Seligman & Isaacowitz, 2000). However, giving up could be adaptive in some instances. For example, if you were thrown into a job that you were not equipped to handle, it might be better to quit rather than face constant pressure and diminishing self-esteem. There is something to be said for recognizing one's limitations, avoiding unrealistic goals, and minimizing self-imposed stress.

Acting Aggressively

A young man, aged 17, cautiously edged his car into traffic on the Corona Expressway in Los Angeles. His slow speed apparently irritated the men in a pickup truck behind him. Unfortunately, he angered the wrong men—they shot him to death. During that same weekend there were six other roadside shootings in the Los Angeles area; all of them triggered by minor incidents or "fender benders." Frustrated motorists are attacking each other more and

Correlation Between Selected Coping Strategies and Anxiety	
Specific coping strategy	**Correlation with anxiety**
Behavioral disengagement	.28
Mental disengagement	.38
Denial	.37
Focus on distressing emotions	.25

Figure 4.2

The relationship among methods of coping and anxiety. Approximately two months after the 9/11 terrorist attacks, Liverant and colleagues (2004) administered a coping inventory and a measure of anxiety to college students living in Boston who were indirectly affected by the attacks. Just 4 out of 13 coping strategies (those listed here) were significant predictors of participants' anxiety. As you can see, strategies that reflect giving up (such as behavioral and mental disengagement) were among the most maladaptive coping responses for this sample.

Adapted from Liverant, G. I., Hofmann, S. G., & Litz, B. T. (2004). Coping and anxiety in college students after the September 11th terrorist attacks. *Anxiety, Stress, & Coping, 17*(2), 127–139. (Table III). Copyright © 2004 by Routledge. Adapted by permission of Taylor & Francis.

more frequently, especially on the overburdened highways of Los Angeles.

These tragic incidents of highway violence—so-called "road rage"—exemplify maladaptive ways in which drivers cope with the stress, anxiety, and hostility experienced while driving. These incidents have unfortunately become common enough that some professionals are calling for road rage to become an official psychiatric diagnosis (Ayar, 2006). Road rage vividly illustrates that people often respond to stressful events by acting aggressively. **Aggression is any behavior intended to hurt someone, either physically or verbally.** Snarls, curses, and insults are much more common than shootings or fistfights, but aggression of any kind can be problematic.

Many years ago, a team of psychologists (Dollard et al., 1939) proposed the *frustration-aggression hypothesis,* which held that aggression is always due to frustration. Decades of research eventually showed that there isn't an inevitable link between frustration and aggression, but this research also supported the basic idea that frustration *does* frequently elicit aggression (Berkowitz, 1989).

People often lash out aggressively at others who had nothing to do with their frustration, especially when they can't vent their anger at the real source of their frustration. Thus, you'll probably suppress your anger rather than lash out verbally at a police officer who gives you a speeding ticket. Twenty minutes later, however, you might be downright brutal in rebuking a waiter who is slow in serving your lunch. As

Lashing out at others with verbal aggression tends to be an ineffective coping tactic that often backfires, creating additional stress.

we discussed in Chapter 2, this diversion of anger to a substitute target was noticed long ago by Sigmund Freud, who called it *displacement*. Unfortunately, research suggests that when people are provoked, displaced aggression is a common response (Hoobler & Brass, 2006; Marcus-Newhall et al., 2000).

Freud theorized that behaving aggressively could get pent-up emotion out of one's system and thus be adaptive. He coined the term **catharsis to refer to this release of emotional tension.** The Freudian notion that it is a good idea to vent anger has become widely disseminated and accepted in modern society. Books, magazines, and self-appointed experts routinely advise that it is healthy to "blow off steam" and thereby release and reduce anger.

However, experimental research generally has *not* supported the catharsis hypothesis. Indeed, *most studies find just the opposite: behaving in an aggressive manner tends to fuel more anger and aggression* (Bushman, 2002; Bushman, Baumeister, & Stack, 1999). Moreover, Carol Tavris (1982, 1989) points out that aggressive behavior frequently backfires because it elicits aggressive responses from others that generate more anger. She asserts, "Aggressive catharses are almost impossible to find in continuing relationships because parents, children, spouses and bosses usually feel obliged to aggress

back at you" (1982, p. 131). Hurting someone, especially someone irrelevant to the situation, is not likely to alleviate frustration. Moreover, the interpersonal conflicts that often emerge from aggressive behavior may produce additional stress.

Conventional wisdom holds that watching violent media or playing violent video games can be cathartic—that watching a murder on a TV show or killing a fictional character in a game can release pent-up anger and hostility. However, the research evidence strongly suggests that this is simply not true. Craig Anderson and Brad Bushman (2001) conducted a groundbreaking review of the research on violent video games and found that playing these games was related to increased aggression, physiological arousal, and aggressive thoughts, and decreased prosocial behavior. In fact, they found that the relationship between media violence and aggressive behavior was almost as strong as the relationship between smoking and cancer (Bushman & Anderson, 2001; see **Figure 4.3**). Exposure to media violence not only desensitizes people to violent acts, it also encourages aggressive self-views and automatic aggressive responses (Bartholow, Bushman, & Sestir, 2006; Uhlmann & Swanson, 2004). Experimental studies using an array of violent media, diverse laboratory conditions, and many kinds of samples continue to find convergent evidence that video games and other forms of violent media do not provide cathartic effects; rather, they increase aggressive tendencies (Anderson, 2004).

Recommended **READING**

Anger: The Misunderstood Emotion
by Carol Tavris (Simon & Schuster, 1989)

With the possible exception of anxiety, anger is the emotion elicited by stress more than any other. It's a powerful emotion that can be harnessed to achieve admirable goals. The work of some of the world's great reformers and leaders has been fueled by moral outrage. However, anger also lies at the center of many human woes—wrecked friendships, destroyed marriages, murders, and wars. Hence, anger is a profoundly important emotion. Carol Tavris analyzes virtually every facet of anger in her book. She carefully scrutinizes common beliefs about anger and concludes that many of them are inaccurate. For instance, she argues convincingly against the idea that aggression can drain off anger through catharsis and the idea that anger and aggression are overpowering, instinctual responses. Tavris's book is a delight to read. It's witty, lively, practical, thought provoking, and frequently eloquent.

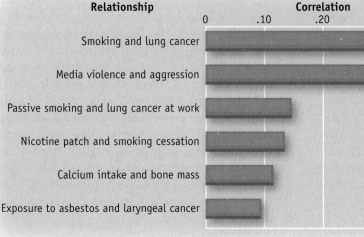

Figure 4.3 area:

Relationship	Correlation

	0	.10	.20	.30	.40
Smoking and lung cancer					
Media violence and aggression					
Passive smoking and lung cancer at work					
Nicotine patch and smoking cessation					
Calcium intake and bone mass					
Exposure to asbestos and laryngeal cancer					

Figure 4.3

Comparison of the relationship between media violence and aggression to other correlations.
Many studies have found a correlation between exposure to media violence and aggression. However, some critics have argued that the correlation is too weak to have any practical significance in the real world. In a rebuttal of this criticism, Bushman and Anderson (2001) note that the average correlation in studies of media violence and aggression is .31. They argue that this association is almost as strong as the correlation between smoking and the probability of developing lung cancer, which is viewed as relevant to real-world issues and notably stronger than a variety of other correlations shown here that are assumed to have practical importance.

Indulging Yourself

Stress sometimes leads to reduced impulse control, or *self-indulgence* (Tice, Bratslavsky, & Baumeister, 2001). For instance, after an exceptionally stressful day, some people head for their kitchen, a grocery store, or a restaurant in pursuit of something chocolate. In a similar vein, others cope with stress by making a beeline for the nearest shopping mall for a spending spree. Still others respond to stress by indulging in injudicious patterns of drinking, smoking, gambling, and drug use.

In their classification of coping responses, Moos and Billings (1982) list *developing alternative rewards* as a common response to stress. It makes sense that when things are going poorly in one area of your life, you may try to compensate by pursuing substitute forms of satisfaction. Thus, it is not surprising that there is evidence relating stress to increases in eating

(Barker, Williams, & Galambos, 2006), smoking (Kassel, Stroud, & Paronis, 2003), and consumption of alcohol and drugs (Goeders, 2004; Spada & Wells, 2006). In fact, Ng and Jeffery (2003) speculate that the general relationship between stress and poor physical health might be due in part to these unhealthy behaviors.

A more recent manifestation of this coping strategy is the tendency to immerse oneself in the online world of the Internet. Kimberly Young (1998) has described a syndrome called **Internet addiction, which consists of spending an inordinate amount of time on the Internet and inability to control online use** (see **Figure 4.4**). People who exhibit this syndrome tend to feel anxious, depressed, or empty when they are not online (Kandell, 1998). Their Internet use is so excessive, it begins to interfere with their functioning at work, at school, or at home, leading victims to start concealing the extent of their dependence on the Internet. Some people exhibit pathological Internet use for one particular purpose, such as online sex or online gambling, whereas others exhibit a general, global pattern of Internet addiction (Davis, 2001). It is difficult to estimate the prevalence of Internet addiction, but the syndrome does *not* appear to be rare (Greenfield, 1999; Morahan-Martin & Schumacher, 2000). Research suggests that Internet addiction is not limited to shy, male computer whizzes, as one might expect (Young, 1998). Although there is active debate about the wis-

---

Internet Addiction Test

To assess your level of addiction, answer the following questions using this scale:

1 = Not at all 2 = Rarely 3 = Occasionally 4 = Often 5 = Always

1. How often do you find that you stay online longer than you intended?	1	2	3	4	5
2. How often do you neglect household chores to spend more time online?	1	2	3	4	5
3. How often do you prefer the excitement of the Internet to intimacy with your partner?	1	2	3	4	5
4. How often do you form new relationships with fellow online users?	1	2	3	4	5
5. How often do others in your life complain to you about the amount of time you spend online?	1	2	3	4	5
6. How often do your grades or school work suffer because of the amount of time you spend online?	1	2	3	4	5
7. How often do you check your e-mail before something else that you need to do?	1	2	3	4	5
8. How often does your job performance or productivity suffer because of the Internet?	1	2	3	4	5
9. How often do you become defensive or secretive when anyone asks you what you do online?	1	2	3	4	5
10. How often do you block out disturbing thoughts about your life with soothing thoughts of the Internet?	1	2	3	4	5
11. How often do you find yourself anticipating when you will go online again?	1	2	3	4	5
12. How often do you fear that life without the Internet would be boring, empty, and joyless?	1	2	3	4	5
13. How often do you snap, yell, or act annoyed if someone bothers you while you are online?	1	2	3	4	5
14. How often do you lose sleep due to late-night log-ins?	1	2	3	4	5
15. How often do you feel preoccupied with the Internet when off-line, or fantasize about being online?	1	2	3	4	5
16. How often do you find yourself saying "just a few more minutes" when online?	1	2	3	4	5
17. How often do you try to cut down the amount of time you spend online and fail?	1	2	3	4	5
18. How often do you try to hide how long you've been online?	1	2	3	4	5
19. How often do you choose to spend more time online over going out with others?	1	2	3	4	5
20. How often do you feel depressed, moody, or nervous when you are off-line, which goes away once you are back online?	1	2	3	4	5

After you've answered all the questions, add the numbers you selected for each response to obtain a final score. The higher your score, the greater your level of addiction and the problems your Internet usage causes. Here's a general scale to help measure your score.

20–39 points: You are an average online user. You may surf the Web a bit too long at times, but you have control over your usage.

40–69 points: You are experiencing frequent problems because of the Internet. You should consider their full impact on your life.

70–100 points: Your Internet usage is causing significant problems in your life. You need to address them now.

Figure 4.4

Measuring addiction to the Internet. The questions on Young's (1998) Internet Addiction Test highlight the traits that make up this syndrome. You can check to see whether you exhibit any signs of Internet addiction by responding to the items and computing your score.

From Young, K. S. (1998). *Caught in the Net: How to recognize the signs of Internet addiction—and a winning strategy for recovery.* New York: John Wiley. Copyright ©1998 John Wiley & Sons, Inc. This material is used by permission of John Wiley & Sons, Inc.

Experts disagree about whether excessive Internet use should be characterized as an addiction, but the inability to control online use appears to be an increasingly common syndrome.

dom of characterizing excessive Internet surfing as an *addiction* (Goldsmith & Shapira, 2006), it is clear that this coping strategy can result in a disruption of time, ultimately increasing one's stress levels (Chou, Condron, & Belland, 2005).

There is nothing inherently maladaptive about indulging oneself as a way of coping with life's stresses. If a hot fudge sundae, some new clothes, or chatting online can calm your nerves after a major setback, who can argue? However, if a person consistently responds to stress with excessive self-indulgence, obvious problems are likely to develop. Excesses in eating may produce obesity. Excesses in drinking and drug use may endanger one's health and affect work quality. Given the risks associated with self-indulgence, it has rather marginal adaptive value.

Blaming Yourself

In a postgame interview after a tough defeat, a prominent football coach was brutally critical of himself. He said that he had been outcoached, that he had made poor decisions, and that his game plan was faulty. He almost eagerly assumed all the blame for the loss himself. In reality, he had taken some reasonable chances that didn't go his way and had suffered the effects of poor execution by his players. Looking at it objectively, the loss was attributable to the collective failures of 50 or so players and coaches. However, the coach's unrealistically negative self-evaluation was a fairly typical response to frustration. When confronted by stress (especially frustration and pressure), people often become highly self-critical.

The tendency to engage in "negative self-talk" in response to stress has been noted by a number of influential theorists. As we will discuss in greater detail later in this chapter, Albert Ellis (1973, 1987) calls this

phenomenon "catastrophic thinking" and focuses on how it is rooted in irrational assumptions. Aaron Beck (1976, 1987) analyzes negative self-talk into specific tendencies. Among other things, he asserts that people often (1) unreasonably attribute their failures to personal shortcomings, (2) focus on negative feedback from others while ignoring favorable feedback, and (3) make unduly pessimistic projections about the future. Thus, if you performed poorly on an exam, you might respond to this stress by blaming it on your woeful stupidity, dismissing a classmate's comment that the test was unfair, and hysterically predicting that you will flunk out of school.

According to Ellis, catastrophic thinking causes, aggravates, and perpetuates emotional reactions to stress that are often problematic. Along even more serious lines, researchers have found that self-blame is associated with increased distress and depression for individuals who have experienced a variety of traumas such as sexual assault, war, and natural disasters (Frazier, Mortensen, & Steward, 2005, Jeney-Gammon et al., 1993; Kraaij & Garnefski, 2006). Although being realistic and recognizing one's weaknesses has value, Ellis and Beck agree that self-blame as a coping strategy can be enormously counterproductive. We cover Ellis's advice on more constructive thinking later in this chapter and we discuss Beck's recommendations for more effective coping in our chapter on psychotherapy (Chapter 16).

Using Defensive Coping

Defensive coping is a common response to stress. We noted in Chapter 2 that the concept of defense mechanisms was originally developed by Sigmund Freud. Though rooted in the psychoanalytic tradition, this concept has gained acceptance from psychologists of most persuasions (Cramer, 2000). Building on Freud's initial insights, modern psychologists have broadened the scope of the concept and added to Freud's list of defense mechanisms.

The Nature of Defense Mechanisms
Defense mechanisms are largely unconscious reactions that protect a person from unpleasant emotions

---

Web Link 4.1 **American Self-Help Clearinghouse Sourcebook**

This online clearinghouse provides contact information for hundreds of self-help groups and organizations across the United States. For individuals trying to cope with specific problems or challenging life situations, one of these groups may be particularly helpful with focused advice and suggestions.

Common Defense Mechanisms

Mechanism	Example
Denial of reality. Protecting oneself from unpleasant reality by refusing to perceive or face it.	A smoker concludes that the evidence linking cigarette use to health problems is scientifically worthless.
Fantasy. Gratifying frustrated desires by imaginary achievements.	A socially inept and inhibited young man imagines himself chosen by a group of women to provide them with sexual satisfaction.
Intellectualization (isolation). Cutting off emotion from hurtful situations or separating incompatible attitudes in logic-tight compartments.	A prisoner on death row awaiting execution resists appeal on his behalf and coldly insists that the letter of the law be followed.
Undoing. Atoning for or trying to magically dispel unacceptable desires or acts.	A woman who feels guilty about insulting her co-worker excessively praises her after each insult.
Overcompensation. Covering up felt weaknesses by emphasizing some desirable characteristic, or making up for frustration in one area by overgratification in another.	A dangerously overweight woman goes on eating binges when she feels neglected by her husband.

Figure 4.5

Additional defense mechanisms. Like the seven defense mechanisms described in our discussion of Freudian theory in Chapter 2 (see **Figure 2.4** on page 39), these five defenses are frequently used in our efforts to cope with stress.

Adapted from Carson, R. C., Butcher, J. N., & Coleman, J. C. (1988). *Abnormal psychology and modern life.* Published by Allyn & Bacon, Boston, MA. Copyright © 1988 by Pearson Education. Adapted by permission of the publisher.

such as anxiety and guilt. A number of coping strategies fit this definition. For example, Laughlin (1979) lists 49 different defenses. In our discussion of Freud's theory in Chapter 2, we described seven common defenses. **Figure 4.5** introduces another five defenses that people use with some regularity. Although widely discussed in the popular press, defense mechanisms are often misunderstood. We will use a question-answer format to elaborate on the nature of defense mechanisms in the hopes of clearing up any misconceptions.

What do defense mechanisms defend against? Above all else, defense mechanisms shield the individual from the *emotional discomfort* elicited by stress. Their main purpose is to ward off unwelcome emotions or to reduce their intensity. Foremost among the emotions guarded against is anxiety. People are especially defensive when the anxiety is the result of some threat to their self-esteem. They also use defenses to prevent dangerous feelings of anger from exploding into acts of aggression. Guilt and dejection are two other emotions that people often try to evade through defensive maneuvers.

How do they work? Defense mechanisms work through *self-deception.* They accomplish their goals by distorting reality so it does not appear so threatening.

Let's say you're doing poorly in school and are in danger of flunking out. Initially, you might use *denial* to block awareness of the possibility that you could flunk out. This tactic might temporarily fend off feelings of anxiety. If it becomes difficult to deny the obvious, you might resort to *fantasy,* daydreaming about how you will salvage adequate grades by getting spectacular scores on the upcoming final exams, when the objective fact is that you are hopelessly behind in your studies. Thus, defense mechanisms work their magic by bending reality in self-serving ways (Bowins, 2004).

Are they conscious or unconscious? Mainstream Freudian theory originally assumed that defenses operate entirely at an unconscious level. However, the concept of defense mechanisms has been broadened to include maneuvers that people may have some awareness of. Thus, defense mechanisms operate at varying levels of awareness and can be conscious or unconscious (Erdelyi, 2001).

Are they normal? Definitely. Everyone uses defense mechanisms on a fairly regular basis. They are entirely normal patterns of coping. The notion that only neurotic people use defense mechanisms is inaccurate.

Can Defense Mechanisms Ever Be Healthy?

The most critical question concerning defense mechanisms is: *Are they healthy?* This is a complicated question. More often than not, the answer is no. Generally, defense mechanisms are poor ways of coping for a number of reasons. First, defensive coping is an avoidance strategy, and avoidance rarely provides a genuine solution to our problems. In fact, Holahan and his colleagues (2005) found that avoidance coping is associated with increased chronic and acute life stressors as well as increased depressive symptoms. Second, defenses such as denial, fantasy, and projection represent "wishful thinking," which is likely to accomplish little. In a study of how students coped with the stress of taking the Medical College Admissions Test (MCAT), Bolger (1990) found that students who engaged in a lot of wishful thinking experienced greater increases in anxiety than other students as the exam approached. Third, a repressive coping style has been related to poor health, in part because repression often leads people to delay facing up to their problems (Weinberger, 1990). For example, if you were to block out obvious warning signs of cancer or diabetes and fail to obtain needed medical care, your defensive behavior could be fatal. Although

illusions may protect us from anxiety in the short term, they can create serious problems in the long term.

Shelley Taylor

Most theorists used to regard accurate contact with reality as the hallmark of sound mental health (Jahoda, 1958; Jourard & Landsman, 1980). However, Shelley Taylor and Jonathon Brown (1988, 1994) have reviewed several lines of evidence suggesting that defensive "illusions" may be adaptive for mental health and well-being. First, they note that "normal" people tend to have overly favorable self-images. In contrast, depressed subjects exhibit less favorable—but more realistic—self-concepts. Second, normal subjects overestimate the degree to which they control chance events. In comparison, depressed participants are less prone to this illusion of control. Third, normal individuals are more likely than depressed subjects to display unrealistic optimism in making projections about the future.

A variety of other studies have also provided support for the hypothesis that positive illusions promote well-being. For example, studies of individuals diagnosed with AIDS show that those with unrealistically optimistic expectations of the likely course of their disease actually experience a less rapid course of illness (Reed et al., 1999). In a laboratory study, Taylor et al. (2003) found that subjects who tended to exhibit positive illusions showed lower cardiovascular responses to stress, quicker cardiovascular recovery from stress, and lower levels of a key stress hormone. Further, a study of retirees found that those who held an exaggerated youthful bias reported higher self-esteem, better perceived health, and less boredom than those who held an accurate perception of their age (Gana, Alaphilippe, & Bailly, 2004).

As you might guess, critics have expressed considerable skepticism about the idea that illusions are adaptive. For example, Colvin and Block (1994) make an eloquent case for the traditional view that accuracy and realism are healthy. Moreover, they report data showing that overly favorable self-ratings are correlated with maladaptive personality traits (Colvin, Block, & Funder, 1995). One possible resolution to this debate is Roy Baumeister's (1989) theory that it's all a matter of degree and that there is an "optimal margin of illusion." According to Baumeister, extreme self-deception is maladaptive, but small illusions may often be beneficial.

The Nature of Constructive Coping

▶ *Describe the nature of constructive coping.*

▶ *Distinguish among the three categories of constructive coping.*

Our discussion thus far has focused on coping strategies that tend to be less than ideal. Of course, people also exhibit many healthful strategies for dealing with stress. We will use the term *constructive coping* **to refer to efforts to deal with stressful events that are judged to be relatively healthful.** No strategy of coping can guarantee a successful outcome. Even the healthiest coping responses may turn out to be ineffective in some cases. Thus, the concept of constructive coping is simply meant to convey a healthy, positive connotation, without promising success.

What makes a coping strategy constructive? Frankly, in labeling certain coping responses constructive or healthy, psychologists are making value judgments. It's a gray area in which opinions will vary to some extent. Nonetheless, some consensus emerges from the burgeoning research on coping and stress management. Key themes in this literature include the following:

1. Constructive coping involves confronting problems directly. It is task relevant and action oriented. It involves a conscious effort to rationally evaluate your options in an effort to solve your problems.

2. Constructive coping is based on reasonably realistic appraisals of your stress and coping resources. A little self-deception may sometimes be adaptive, but excessive self-deception and highly unrealistic negative thinking are not.

3. Constructive coping involves learning to recognize and manage potentially disruptive emotional reactions to stress.

4. Constructive coping involves learning to exert some control over potentially harmful or destructive habitual behaviors. It requires the acquisition of some behavioral self-control.

These points should give you a general idea of what we mean by constructive coping. They will guide our discourse in the remainder of this chapter as we discuss how to cope more effectively with stress. To organize our discussion, we will use a classification scheme proposed by Moos and Billings (1982) to divide constructive coping techniques into three broad categories: *appraisal-focused coping* (aimed at changing one's interpretation of stressful events), *problem-focused coping* (aimed at altering the stressful situation itself), and *emotion-focused coping* (aimed at managing potential emotional distress). **Figure 4.6** shows common coping strategies that fall under each category. It is important to note that many strategies could fall under more than one category. For instance, one could seek social support for practical purposes (problem focused) or emotional purposes (emotion focused).

Figure 4.6

Overview of constructive coping tactics. Coping tactics can be organized in several ways, but we will use the classification scheme shown here, which consists of three categories: appraisal-focused strategies, problem-focused strategies, and emotion-focused strategies. The list of coping tactics in each category is not exhaustive. We will discuss most, but not all, of the listed strategies in our coverage of constructive coping.

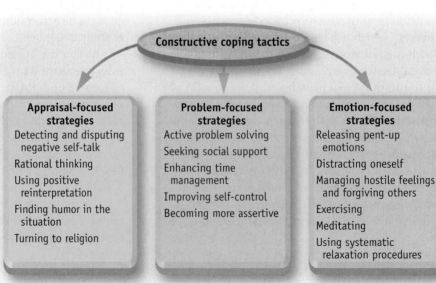

Constructive coping tactics

Appraisal-focused strategies
Detecting and disputing negative self-talk
Rational thinking
Using positive reinterpretation
Finding humor in the situation
Turning to religion

Problem-focused strategies
Active problem solving
Seeking social support
Enhancing time management
Improving self-control
Becoming more assertive

Emotion-focused strategies
Releasing pent-up emotions
Distracting oneself
Managing hostile feelings and forgiving others
Exercising
Meditating
Using systematic relaxation procedures

Sally Forth, Copyright © 1984 News Group Chicago, reprinted by permission of North American Syndicate.

Appraisal-Focused Constructive Coping

LEARNING OBJECTIVES

▶ *Explain Ellis's analysis of the causes of maladaptive emotions.*

▶ *Describe some assumptions that contribute to catastrophic thinking.*

▶ *Describe some ways to reduce catastrophic thinking.*

▶ *Discuss the merits of humor and positive reinterpretation as coping strategies.*

People often underestimate the importance of the appraisal phase in the stress process. They fail to appreciate the highly subjective feelings that color the perception of threat to one's well-being. A useful way to deal with stress is to alter your appraisal of threatening events. In this section, we'll examine Albert Ellis's ideas about reappraisal and discuss the value of using humor and positive reinterpretation to cope with stress.

Ellis's Rational Thinking

Courtesy, Albert Ellis Institute

Albert Ellis

Albert Ellis (1977, 1985, 1996, 2001a, 2001b) is a prominent theorist who believes that people can short-circuit their emotional reactions to stress by altering their appraisals of stressful events. Ellis's insights about stress appraisal are the foundation for his widely used system of therapy. **Rational-emotive behavior therapy is an approach to therapy that focuses on altering clients' patterns of irrational thinking to reduce maladaptive emotions and behavior.**

Ellis maintains that *you feel the way you think.* He argues that problematic emotional reactions are caused by negative self-talk, which, as we mentioned earlier, he calls catastrophic thinking. **Catastrophic thinking involves unrealistic appraisals of stress that exaggerate the magnitude of one's problems.** Ellis uses a simple

A-B-C sequence to explain his ideas (see **Figure 4.7** on the next page):

A. *Activating event.* The A in Ellis's system stands for the activating event that produces the stress. The activating event may be any potentially stressful transaction. Examples might include an automobile accident, the cancellation of a date, a delay while waiting in line at the bank, or a failure to get a promotion you were expecting.

B. *Belief system.* B stands for your belief about the event. This represents your appraisal of the stress. According to Ellis, people often view minor setbacks as disasters, engaging in catastrophic thinking: "How awful this is. I can't stand it!" "Things never turn out fairly for me." "I'll be in this line forever." "I'll never get promoted."

C. *Consequence.* C stands for the consequence of your negative thinking. When your appraisals of stressful events are highly negative, the consequence tends to be emotional distress. Thus, you feel angry, outraged, anxious, panic stricken, disgusted, or dejected.

Ellis asserts that most people do not understand the importance of phase B in this three-stage sequence. They unwittingly believe that the activating event (A) *causes* the consequent emotional turmoil (C). However, Ellis maintains that A does *not* cause C. It only appears to do so. Instead, Ellis asserts that B causes C. Emotional

Figure 4.7

Albert Ellis's A-B-C model of emotional reactions. Most people are prone to attribute their negative emotional reactions (C) directly to stressful events (A). However, Ellis argues that emotional reactions are really caused by the way individuals think about these events (B).

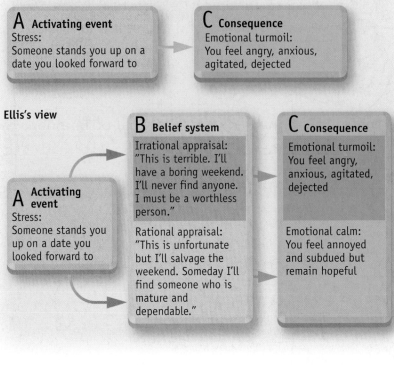

The commonsense view

A Activating event
Stress:
Someone stands you up on a date you looked forward to

C Consequence
Emotional turmoil:
You feel angry, anxious, agitated, dejected

Ellis's view

A Activating event
Stress:
Someone stands you up on a date you looked forward to

B Belief system
Irrational appraisal:
"This is terrible. I'll have a boring weekend. I'll never find anyone. I must be a worthless person."

Rational appraisal:
"This is unfortunate but I'll salvage the weekend. Someday I'll find someone who is mature and dependable."

C Consequence
Emotional turmoil:
You feel angry, anxious, agitated, dejected

Emotional calm:
You feel annoyed and subdued but remain hopeful

distress is actually caused by one's catastrophic thinking in appraising stressful events.

According to Ellis, it is common for people to turn inconvenience into disaster and make "mountains out of molehills." For instance, imagine that someone stands you up on a date that you were eagerly looking forward to. You might think, "Oh, this is terrible. I'm going to have another boring weekend. People always mistreat me. I'll never find anyone to fall in love with. I must be an ugly, worthless person." Ellis would argue that such thoughts are irrational. He would point out that it does not follow logically from being stood up that you (1) must have a lousy weekend, (2) will never fall in love, or (3) are a worthless person. Thinking this way does nothing but increase distress. Indeed, recent research indicates that the tendency toward catastrophic thinking is a risk factor for developing posttraumatic stress disorder (see Chapter 3) (Bryant & Guthrie, 2005).

Web Link 4.2 **The Albert Ellis Institute**

Albert Ellis developed rational-emotive behavior therapy in the mid-1950s as an effective alternative to psychoanalytically inspired treatment approaches. This site demonstrates the growth of Ellis's approach over the subsequent decades.

The Roots of Catastrophic Thinking

Ellis (1994, 1995, 2004) theorizes that unrealistic appraisals of stress are derived from the irrational assumptions that people hold. He maintains that if you scrutinize your catastrophic thinking, you will find that your reasoning is based on an unreasonable premise, such as "I must have approval from everyone" or "I must perform well in all endeavors." These faulty assumptions, which most people hold unconsciously, generate catastrophic thinking and emotional turmoil. To facilitate emotional self-control, it is important to learn to spot irrational assumptions and the unhealthy patterns of thought that they generate. Here are four particularly common irrational assumptions:

1. *I must have love and affection from certain people.* Everyone wants to be liked and loved. There is nothing wrong with that. However, many people foolishly believe that they should be liked by everyone they come into contact with. If you stop to think about it, that's clearly unrealistic. Once individuals fall in love, they tend to believe that their future happiness depends absolutely on the continuation of that one, special relationship. They believe that if their current love relationship were to end, they would never again be able to achieve a comparable one. This is an unrealistic view of the future. Such views make the person anxious during a relationship and severely depressed if it comes to an end.

LIVING IN TODAY'S WORLD

Thinking Rationally About the Threat of Traumatic Events

Some traumatic events, whether natural (such as earthquakes) or human-made (such as war) can provoke psychological instability in an entire population. For instance, the death, destruction, and havoc wreaked by terrorists is not an end in itself, but a means to an end—the creation of widespread anxiety, fear, and alarm (Everly & Mitchell, 2001). Unfortunately, a normal feature of human mental processing makes it much too easy for terrorists to achieve their goal. However, being aware of this cognitive tendency can help people to be more rational about the threat of traumatic events. To introduce you to this cognitive tendency, consider the following problem:

Various causes of death are paired up below. For each pairing, decide which is the more likely cause of death.
  Asthma or tornadoes?
  Syphilis or botulism (food poisoning)?
  Tuberculosis or floods?

Would you believe that the first choice in each pair causes at least 18 times as many deaths as the second choice? If your guesses were wrong, don't feel bad. Most people tend to greatly overestimate the likelihood of dramatic and vivid—but infrequent—events that receive heavy media coverage. Thus, the number of fatalities caused by tornadoes, floods, and food poisonings is usually overestimated (Slovic, Fischhoff, & Lichtenstein, 1982), whereas fatalities caused by asthma and other run-of-the-mill diseases tend to be underestimated. This tendency to overestimate the improbable reflects the operation of the *availability heuristic,* which involves basing the estimated probability of an event on the ease with which relevant instances come to mind.

Relying on the availability heuristic is a normal cognitive tendency. However, to the extent that certain events occur infrequently but are easily available in memory, your estimates will be biased. Instances of hurricanes, tornadoes, and terrorists attacks are readily available in memory because these events receive a great deal of media attention. The result is that people tend to greatly exaggerate the likelihood that they might be a victim of such adverse events, and such overestimates fuel fear. Ironically, experiencing fear results in greater perceptions of being at risk (Keller, Siegrist, & Gutscher, 2006), which then makes one feel more fear—creating a vicious cycle of anxiety and alarm.

Admittedly, no one knows what the future might bring in the way of disasters or terrorist attacks. However, based on what has happened in recent years, your chances of being harmed by a terrorist are microscopic in comparison to your chances of perishing in an automobile accident (Myers, 2001). Since 9/11, many Americans have been reluctant to fly because the airplane hijackings that occurred on 9/11 remain salient in their minds. But think about it: Even if you knew in advance that terrorists planned to blow up a commercial flight next week, your chances of choosing that specific flight would only be about 1 in 173,000.

In sum, it is wise to be mindful of the natural tendency to overestimate the likelihood that you might be affected by a traumatic event. Thinking more rationally about the probability of being victimized can reduce people's collective sense of alarm.

---

2. *I must perform well in all endeavors.* We live in a highly competitive society. We are taught that victory brings happiness. Consequently, we feel that we must always win. For example, many sports enthusiasts are never satisfied unless they perform at their best level. However, by definition, their best level is not their typical level, and they set themselves up for inevitable frustration.

3. *Other people should always behave competently and be considerate of me.* People are often angered by others' stupidity and selfishness. For example, you may become outraged when a mechanic fails to fix your car properly or when a salesperson treats you rudely. It would be nice if others were always competent and considerate, but you know better—they are not! Yet many people go through life unrealistically expecting others' efficiency and kindness in every situation.

4. *Events should always go the way I like.* Some people simply won't tolerate any kind of setback. They assume that things should always go their way. For

achievement motivation, and high distractibility. The type of irrational thinking described by Albert Ellis also seems to foster procrastination (Bridges & Roig, 1997), as do a strong fear of failure (Lay, 1992) and excessive perfectionism (Flett, Hewitt, & Martin, 1995).

Other factors besides personality can affect procrastination. Schraw and colleagues (2007) identified six general principles related to academic procrastination, including these three:

1. *Desire to minimize time on a task.* As you know, the modern student is busy—studying, working, socializing, and maintaining a personal life. Time is at a premium. Sometimes delaying as much academic work as possible seems to be a way to safeguard some personal time. As one student reported, "The truth is, I just don't have time *not* to procrastinate. If I did everything the way it could be done, I wouldn't have a life" (Schraw et al., 2007, p. 21).

2. *Desire to optimize efficiency.* Procrastination can be viewed as allowing one to be optimally efficient, concentrating academic work into focused time frames. Students reported that being pressed for time means that there is less opportunity for busywork, boredom, or false starts.

3. *Close proximity to reward.* Schraw et al. (2007) found that students often procrastinate because they are rewarded for it. By putting off academic work until the last minute, students not only get more immediate feedback (the grade), but they also get a sudden release of stress. In this way, procrastination is similar to other thrill-seeking behaviors.

Although these principles seem reasonable and many people rationalize their delaying tactics by claiming that "I work best under pressure" (Ferrari, 1992; Lay, 1995), the empirical evidence suggests otherwise. Studies show that procrastination tends to have a negative impact on the quality of task performance (Ferrari, Johnson, & McCown, 1995; Tice & Baumeister, 1997). In fact, Britton and Tesser (1991) found that time management was a better predictor of college GPA than SAT scores! Procrastinators may often underestimate how much time will be required to complete a task effectively, or they experience unforeseen delays and then run out of time because they didn't allow any "cushion." Another consideration is that waiting until the last minute may make a task more stressful—and while the release of this built-up stress might be exciting, performance often declines under conditions of high stress (as we saw in Chapter 3).

Moreover, work quality may not be the only thing that suffers when people procrastinate. Studies indicate that as a deadline looms, procrastinators tend to experience elevated anxiety and increased health problems (Lay et al., 1989; Tice & Baumeister, 1997). People

who recognize that they need to alter their eating behavior or start an exercise regimen routinely put off these commitments, promising themselves that they will start tomorrow, or next week, or next month. In a similar vein, many people procrastinate about getting health checkups or even seeking medical treatment for existing maladies (Sirois, Melia-Gordon, & Pychyl, 2003).

People who struggle with procrastination often impose deadlines and penalties on themselves. This practice can be helpful, but self-imposed deadlines are not as effective as externally imposed deadlines (Ariely & Wertenbroch, 2002). Let's discuss some effective ways to manage your time.

Time-Management Techniques

Individuals vary in their time perspectives. Some people are *future oriented,* able to see the consequences of immediate behavior for future goals, whereas others are *present oriented,* focused on immediate events and not worried about consequences. These orientations influence how they manage their time and meet their time-related commitments. Future-oriented individuals, for example, are less likely to procrastinate and are more reliable in meeting their commitments (Harber, Zimbardo, & Boyd, 2003). Regardless of orientation, most people could benefit from more effectively managing their time.

What's the key to better time management? Most people assume that it's increased *efficiency*—that is, learning to perform tasks more quickly. Improved efficiency may help a little, but time-management experts maintain that efficiency is overrated. They emphasize that the key to better time management is increased *effectiveness*—that is, learning to allocate time to your most important tasks. This distinction is captured by a widely quoted slogan in the time-management literature: "Efficiency is doing the job right, while effectiveness is doing the right job." Here are some suggestions for using your time more effectively (based on Lakein, 1996; Mackenzie, 1997; Morgenstern, 2000):

1. *Monitor your use of time.* The first step toward better time management is to monitor your use of time to see where it all goes (Douglass & Douglass, 1993). Doing so requires keeping a written record of your activities, similar to that shown in **Figure 4.11**. At the end of each week, you should analyze how your time was allocated. Based on your personal roles and responsibilities, create categories of time use such as studying, child care, housework, commuting, working at the office, working at home, going online, eating, and sleeping. For each day, add up the hours allocated to each category. Record this information on a summary sheet like that in **Figure 4.12** (on p. 126). Two weeks of recordkeeping should allow you to draw some conclusions about where your time goes. Your records will help you make informed decisions about reallocating your time. When you begin your time-management program, these records will also give you a baseline for comparison, so that you can see whether your program is working.

2. *Clarify your goals.* You can't wisely allocate your time unless you decide what you want to accomplish. Lakein (1996) suggests that you ask yourself, "What are my lifetime goals?" Write down all the goals that you can think of, even relatively frivolous things like going deep-sea fishing or becoming a wine expert. Some of your goals will be in conflict. For instance, you can't

become a vice-president at your company in Wichita and still move to the West Coast. Thus, the tough part comes next. You have to wrestle with your goal conflicts. Figure out which goals are most important to you, and order them in terms of priority. These priorities should guide you as you plan your activities on a daily, weekly, and monthly basis.

3. *Plan your activities using a schedule.* People resist planning because it takes time, but in the long run planning saves time. Thorough planning is essential to effective time management (McGee-Cooper & Trammell, 1994). At the beginning of each week, you should make up a list of short-term goals. This list should be

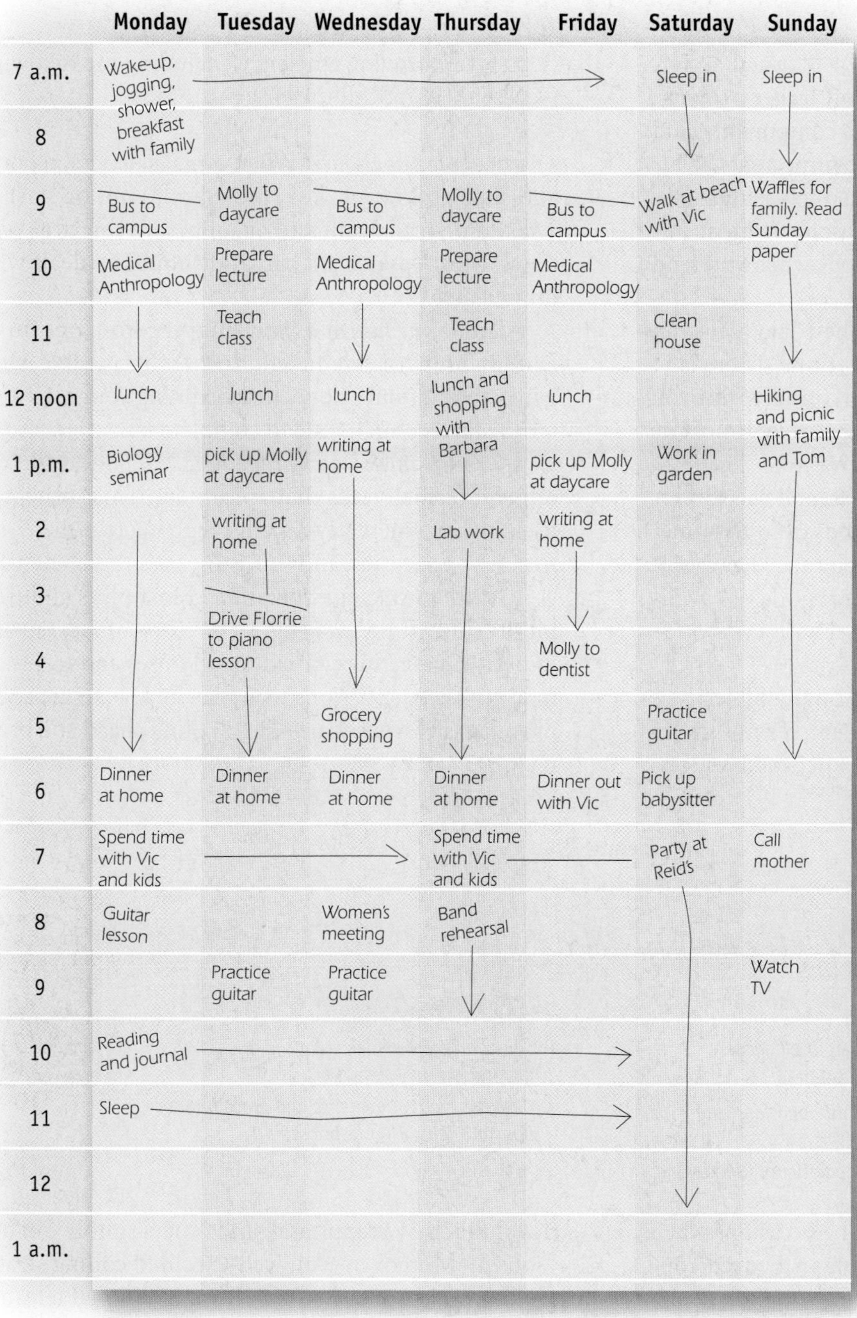

	Monday	Tuesday	Wednesday	Thursday	Friday	Saturday	Sunday
7 a.m.	Wake-up, jogging, shower, breakfast with family					Sleep in	Sleep in
8							
9	Bus to campus	Molly to daycare	Bus to campus	Molly to daycare	Bus to campus	Walk at beach with Vic	Waffles for family. Read Sunday paper
10	Medical Anthropology	Prepare lecture	Medical Anthropology	Prepare lecture	Medical Anthropology		
11		Teach class		Teach class		Clean house	
12 noon	lunch	lunch	lunch	lunch and shopping with Barbara	lunch		Hiking and picnic with family and Tom
1 p.m.	Biology seminar	pick up Molly at daycare	writing at home		pick up Molly at daycare	Work in garden	
2		writing at home		Lab work	writing at home		
3							
4		Drive Florrie to piano lesson			Molly to dentist		
5			Grocery shopping			Practice guitar	
6	Dinner at home	Dinner at home	Dinner at home	Dinner at home	Dinner out with Vic	Pick up babysitter	
7	Spend time with Vic and kids			Spend time with Vic and kids		Party at Reid's	Call mother
8	Guitar lesson		Women's meeting	Band rehearsal			
9		Practice guitar	Practice guitar				Watch TV
10	Reading and journal						
11	Sleep						
12							
1 a.m.							

Figure 4.11

Example of a time log. Experts recommend keeping a detailed record of how you use your time if you are to improve your time management. This example shows the kind of recordkeeping that should be done.

Figure 4.12

Time use summary. To analyze where your time goes, you need to review your time log and create a weekly time use summary, like the one shown here. The exact categories to be listed on the left depend on your circumstances and responsibilities.

Time Use Summary Form

Activity	Mon.	Tues.	Wed.	Thurs.	Fri.	Sat.	Sun.	Total	%
1. Sleeping	8	6	8	6	8	7	9	52	31
2. Eating	2	2	3	2	3	2	3	17	10
3. Commuting	2	2	2	2	2	0	0	10	6
4. Housework	0	1	0	3	0	0	2	6	4
5. In class	4	2	4	2	4	0	0	16	9
6. Part-time job	0	5	0	5	0	3	0	13	8
7. Studying	3	2	4	2	0	4	5	20	12
8. Relaxing	5	4	3	2	7	8	5	34	20
9.									
10.									

translated into daily "to do" lists of planned activities. To avoid the tendency to put off larger projects, break them into smaller, manageable components, and set deadlines for completing the components. Your planned activities should be allocated to various time slots on a written schedule. Schedule your most important activities into the time periods when you tend to be most energetic and productive.

4. *Protect your prime time.* The best-laid plans can quickly go awry because of interruptions. There isn't any foolproof way to eliminate interruptions, but you may be able to shift most of them into certain time slots while protecting your most productive time. The trick is to announce to your family, friends, and co-workers that you're blocking off certain periods of "quiet time" when visitors and phone calls will be turned away. Of course, you also have to block off periods of "available time" when you're ready to deal with everyone's problems.

5. *Increase your efficiency.* Although efficiency is not the key to better time management, it's not irrelevant. Time-management experts do offer some suggestions for improving efficiency, including the following (Klassen, 1987; Schilit, 1987):

▶ *Handle paper once.* When e-mails, letters, reports, and such cross your desk, they should not be stashed away to be read again and again before you deal with them. Most paperwork can and should be dealt with immediately.

▶ *Tackle one task at a time.* Jumping from one problem to another is inefficient. Insofar as possible, stick with a task until it's done. In scheduling your activities, try to allow enough time to complete tasks.

▶ *Group similar tasks together.* It's a good idea to bunch up small tasks that are similar. This strategy is useful when you're paying bills, replying to e-mails, returning phone calls, and so forth.

▶ *Make use of your downtime.* Most of us endure a lot of "downtime," waiting in doctors' offices, sitting in needless meetings, or riding on buses and trains. In many of these situations, you may be able to get some of your easier work done—if you think ahead and bring it along.

Emotion-Focused Constructive Coping

LEARNING OBJECTIVES

▶ *Describe the nature and value of emotional intelligence.*

▶ *Analyze the adaptive value of expressing emotions.*

▶ *Discuss the importance of managing hostility and forgiving others' transgressions.*

▶ *Explain how exercise can foster improved emotional functioning.*

▶ *Summarize the evidence on the effects of meditation.*

▶ *Describe the requirements and procedure for Benson's relaxation response.*

Let's be realistic: There are going to be occasions when appraisal-focused coping and problem-focused coping are not successful in warding off emotional turmoil. Some problems are too serious to be whittled down much by reappraisal, and others simply can't be "solved." Moreover, even well-executed coping strategies may take time to work before emotional tensions begin to subside. Thus, it is helpful to be able to recognize and modulate one's emotions. In this section, we will discuss a variety of coping abilities and strategies that relate mainly to the regulation of emotions.

Enhancing Emotional Intelligence

According to some theorists, *emotional intelligence* is the key to being resilient in the face of stress (Slaski & Cartwright, 2003). The concept of emotional intelligence was originally formulated by Peter Salovey and John Mayer (1990). **Emotional intelligence consists of the ability to perceive and express emotion, assimilate emotion in thought, understand and reason with emotion, and regulate emotion.** Emotional intelligence includes four essential components (Salovey, Mayer, & Caruso, 2002, 2005). First, people need to be able to accurately perceive emotions in themselves and others and have the ability to express their own emotions effectively. Second, people need to be aware of how their emotions shape their thinking, decision making, and coping with stress. Third, people need to be able to understand and analyze their emotions, which may often be complex and contradictory. Fourth, people need to be able to regulate their emotions so that they can dampen negative emotions and make effective use of positive emotions.

Several tests have been developed to measure the concept of emotional intelligence. The test that has the strongest empirical foundation is the Mayer-Salovey-Caruso Emotional Intelligence Test (2002). The authors have strived to make this test a performance-based measure of the ability to deal effectively with emotions rather than a measure of personality or temperament. Preliminary results suggest that they have made considerable progress toward this goal, as evidenced by the scale's ability to predict intelligent management of emotions in real-world situations (Ciarrochi, Dean, & Anderson, 2002; Lam & Kirby, 2002; Mayer et al., 2001). It has been found to reliably predict the quality of subjects' social interactions (Lopes et al., 2004), leadership effectiveness (Antoniou, 2005), and even physical health (Schutte et al., 2007). At present, ways to cultivate emotional intelligence are being explored in classrooms and workplaces. In fact, a recent study found that positive emotional expression can lead to an increase in emotional intelligence (Wing, Schutte, & Byrne, 2006). That leads us to our next topic.

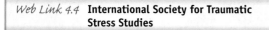

Web Link 4.4 **International Society for Traumatic Stress Studies**

This site offers a vast storehouse of information relating to coping with traumatic events. The resources are divided into those for the general public, for professionals, and for the news media.

Expressing Emotions

Try as you might to redefine or resolve stressful situations, you no doubt still go through times when you feel wired with stress-induced tension. When this happens, there's merit in the commonsense notion that you should try to release the emotions welling up inside. Why? Because the physiological arousal that accompanies emotions can become problematic. For example, research suggests that people who inhibit the expression of anger and other emotions are somewhat more likely than other people to have elevated blood pressure (Jorgensen et al., 1996). Moreover, research suggests that efforts to actively suppress emotions result in increased stress and autonomic arousal (Butler et al., 2003; Gross, 2001). Please note that such findings do not mean you should act aggressively (a coping strategy of limited value discussed earlier in the chapter). Instead, we are focusing on appropriate expression of emotions.

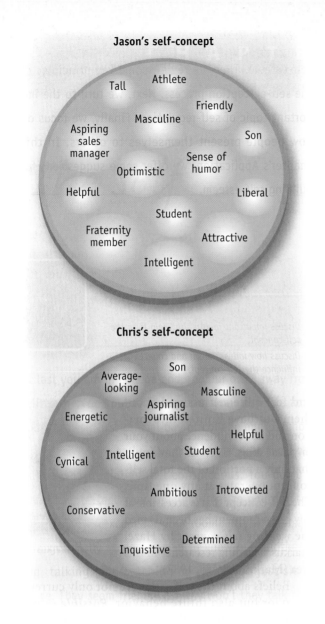

Jason's self-concept

Tall · Athlete · Friendly · Masculine · Aspiring sales manager · Son · Optimistic · Sense of humor · Helpful · Liberal · Student · Fraternity member · Attractive · Intelligent

Chris's self-concept

Son · Average-looking · Masculine · Aspiring journalist · Energetic · Helpful · Cynical · Intelligent · Student · Ambitious · Introverted · Conservative · Determined · Inquisitive

Figure 5.1

The self-concept and self-schemas. The self-concept is composed of various self-schemas, or beliefs about the self. Jason and Chris have different self-concepts, in part, because they have different self-schemas.

as an alcoholic like Uncle George or an adult without an intimate relationship like your next-door neighbor. In these cases, possible selves function as images to be avoided (Norman & Aron, 2003).

Individuals' beliefs about themselves are not set in concrete—but neither are they easily changed. People are strongly motivated to maintain a consistent view of the self across time and situations. Thus, once the self-concept is established, the individual has a tendency to preserve and defend it. In the context of this stability, however, self-beliefs do have a certain dynamic quality (Markus & Wurf, 1987). When coupled with

educational strategies, for example, "academic possible selves" led to positive changes in planning, test scores, grades, and attendance in a sample of low-income minority youth (Oyserman, Bybee, & Terry, 2006). Self-concepts seem to be most susceptible to change when people shift from an important and familiar social setting to an unfamiliar one—for example, when moving off to college or to a new city for one's first "real" job. This flexibility clearly underscores the social foundations of the self-concept.

Self-Discrepancies

Some people perceive themselves pretty much the way they'd like to see themselves. Others experience a gap between what they actually see and what they'd like to see. For example, Nathan describes his actual self as "shy" but his ideal self as "outgoing." According to E. Tory Higgins (1987), individuals have several organized self-perceptions: an *actual self* (qualities you believe you *actually* possess), an *ideal self* (characteristics you would *like* to have), and an *ought self* (traits you believe you *should* possess). The ideal and ought selves serve as personal standards or self-guides that direct behavior. *Self-discrepancy* consists of a mismatch between the self-perceptions that make up the actual self, ideal self, and ought self.

Self-Discrepancies and Their Effects

The differences among one's actual, ideal, and ought selves influence how one feels about oneself and can create some particular emotional vulnerabilities (Higgins, 1999). According to Higgins, when people live up to their personal standards (ideal or ought selves), they experience high self-esteem; when they don't meet their own expectations, their self-esteem suffers (Moretti & Higgins, 1990). In addition, he says, certain types of self-discrepancies are associated with specific emotions (see **Figure 5.2**). One type of self-discrepancy occurs when the *actual* self is at odds with the *ideal* self. Such instances trigger *dejection-related* emotions (sadness, disappointment). As actual-ideal discrepancies outnumber actual-ideal congruencies,

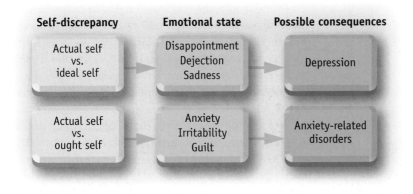

Figure 5.2

Types of self-discrepancies, their effects on emotional states, and possible consequences. According to E. Tory Higgins (1989), discrepancies between actual and ideal selves produce disappointment and sadness, whereas discrepancies between actual and ought selves result in irritability and guilt. Such self-discrepancies can make individuals vulnerable to more serious psychological problems, such as depression and anxiety-related disorders.

sadness increases and cheerfulness decreases (Higgins, Shah, & Friedman, 1997). Consider Tiffany's situation: She knows that she's attractive, but she is also overweight and would like to be thinner. Self-discrepancy theory predicts that she would feel dissatisfied and dejected. Interestingly, research has shown an association between discrepant actual/ideal views of body shape and eating disorders (Strauman et al., 1991).

A second type of discrepancy involves a mismatch between *actual* and *ought* selves. Let's say you don't stay in touch with your grandparents as often as you feel you should. According to Higgins, actual/ought self-discrepancies produce *agitation-related* emotions (irritability, anxiety, and guilt). As actual-ought discrepancies outnumber actual-ought congruencies, anxiety increases and calm emotions decrease (Higgins, Shah, & Friedman, 1997). Extreme discrepancies of this type can result in anxiety-related psychological disorders.

Everyone experiences self-discrepancies, yet most people manage to feel reasonably good about themselves. How is this possible? Three factors seem to be important: the amount of discrepancy you experience, your awareness of the discrepancy, and whether the discrepancy is actually important to you (Higgins, 1999). Thus, a pre-med major who gets a C in calculus will probably feel a lot worse than an English major who gets a C in the course.

Although people use both ideal and ought selves as personal standards, they usually rely on just one of these self-guides. These "preferences" are rooted in parent-child interactions and individual temperament (Higgins, 1987). If Kyle's parents typically communicate with him in terms of what they would *like* him to do, he will probably develop a strong *ideal* self-guide.

If their communications usually take the form of what they think he *ought* to do, Kyle will probably develop a strong *ought* self-guide.

Coping with Self-Discrepancies

Can individuals do anything to blunt the negative emotions and blows to self-esteem associated with self-discrepancies? Yes! For one thing, people can *change their behavior* to bring it more in line with their ideal or ought selves. For instance, if your ideal self is a person who gets above-average grades and your actual self just got a D on a test, you can study more effectively for the next test to improve your grade. But what about the times you can't match your ideal standards? Perhaps you had your heart set on making the varsity tennis team but didn't make the cut. Maybe you had planned to go to medical school but barely managed to eke out C's in your science courses. One way to ease the discomfort associated with such discrepancies is to bring your ideal self a bit more in line with your actual abilities. You may not achieve your ideal self right away, if ever, but by behaving in ways that are consistent with that self, you will get closer to it and be more content (Haidt, 2006; Wilson, 2002). Alternatively, subtle encouragement to consider ways to approach an ideal self (perhaps a constructive, friendly suggestion from a friend or a teacher) is apt to raise your spirits in a positive way (Shah & Higgins, 2001).

Another, less positive, approach is to *blunt your self-awareness,* or how much you focus on what you like or dislike about yourself, your self-perceived strengths and shortcomings, and so on. You can do so by avoiding situations that increase your self-awareness—if you don't want to appear to be shy, don't attend a party where you expect to spend a miserable evening talking to yourself. If your weight is bothering you, you might avoid shopping for new clothes (as well as gazing into full-length mirrors).

Some people use alcohol to blunt self-awareness. In one study, college students were first put into either a high or a low self-awareness group based on test scores (Hull & Young, 1983). Then, both groups were given a brief version of an intelligence test as well as false feedback on their test performance. Half of the high self-awareness group were told that they had done quite well on the test and the other half were told that they had done quite poorly. Next, supposedly as part of a separate study, these participants were asked to taste and evaluate various wines for 15 minutes. The

When people don't live up to their personal standards, self-esteem suffers, and some turn to alcohol to blunt their awareness of the discrepancy.

experimenters predicted that the high self-awareness participants who had been told that they had done poorly on the IQ test would drink more than the other groups, and this is precisely what the study found (see **Figure 5.3**). Those who couldn't escape negative information about themselves drank more alcohol to reduce their self-awareness.

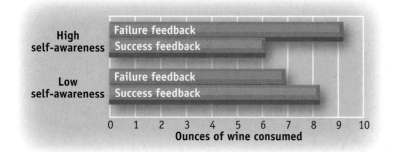

Figure 5.3

Self-awareness and alcohol consumption. Individuals who were high in self-awareness drank significantly more wine in a 15-minute period if they believed that they had performed poorly on an IQ test than did any other group. This finding shows how people sometimes try to blunt self-awareness to cope with self-discrepancies.

From Hull, J. G., & Young, R. D. (1983), Self-consciousness, self-esteem, and success-failure as determinants of alcohol consumption in male social drinkers. *Journal of Personality and Social Psychology, 44,* 1097–1109. Copyright © 1983 American Psychological Association. Reprinted by permission of the publisher and author.

Similarly, in the real world it has been found that alcoholics who have high self-awareness and who experience negative or painful life events relapse more quickly and completely (Hull, Young, & Jouriles, 1986).

Heightened self-awareness doesn't always make people focus on self-discrepancies and negative aspects of the self. If that were true, most people would feel a lot worse about themselves than they actually do. As you recall, self-concepts are made up of numerous self-beliefs—many of them positive, some negative. Because individuals have a need to feel good about themselves, they tend to focus on their positive features rather than their "warts" (Tesser, 2001). In fact, when a person's self-concept is threatened (a job interview doesn't go well), the individual can recover by affirming competence in an unrelated domain (focusing on extraordinary talent as a salsa dancer) (Aronson, Cohen, & Nail, 1999; Steele, 1988).

Factors Shaping the Self-Concept

A variety of sources influence one's self-concept. Chief among them are one's own observations, feedback from others, and cultural values.

One's Own Observations

Individuals begin observing their own behavior and drawing conclusions about themselves early in life. Children will make statements about who is the tallest, who can run fastest, or who can swing the highest. Leon Festinger's (1954) *social comparison theory* **proposes that individuals compare themselves with others in order to assess their abilities and opinions.** People compare themselves to others to determine how attractive they are, how they did on the history exam, how their social skills stack up, and so forth. In short, social comparisons can be ego enhancing (Helgeson & Michelson, 1995).

Although Festinger's original theory claimed that people engage in social comparison for the purpose of accurately assessing their abilities, research suggests that they also engage in social comparison to improve their skills and to maintain their self-image (Wheeler & Suls, 2005; Wood & Wilson, 2003). Sometimes social comparison is self-focused, such as when a successful professional woman compares her "current self" to the passive, withdrawn "past self" of high school (Ross & Wilson, 2002; Wilson & Ross, 2000). Generally, however, people compare themselves against others with particular qualities. A *reference group* **is a set of people who are used as a gauge in making social comparisons.** We choose our reference groups strategically.

For example, if you want to know how you did on your first test in social psychology (ability appraisal), your reference group would likely be the entire class. In terms of acquiring accurate self-knowledge about your performance, this sort of comparison is a good one if you are confident your classmates are similar to you (Wheeler, Koestner, & Driver, 1982).

What happens when people compare themselves to others who are better or worse off than them? For instance, if you want to improve your tennis game (skill development), your reference group should be limited to superior players, whose skills give you a goal to pursue. Such *upward social comparisons* can motivate you and direct your future efforts (Blanton et al., 1999). On the other hand, if your self-esteem needs bolstering, you will probably make a *downward social comparison*, looking to those whom you perceive to be worse off, thereby enabling you to feel better about yourself (Aspinwall & Taylor, 1993; Lockwood, 2002). We have more to say about downward social comparison a little later in the chapter.

People's observations of their own behavior are not entirely objective. The general tendency is to distort reality in a positive direction (see **Figure 5.4**). In other words, most people tend to evaluate themselves in a more positive light than they really merit (Taylor & Brown, 1988, 1994). The strength of this tendency was highlighted in a large survey of high school seniors conducted as part of the Scholastic Aptitude Test (SAT) (Myers, 1980). By definition, 50 percent of students must be "above average" and 50 percent "below average" on specific questions. However, 100 percent of the respondents saw themselves as above average in "ability to get along with others." And 25 percent of the respondents thought that they belonged in the top 1 percent!

As she sees herself: Unchanged since age 22. Sociable, scintillating, sexy.

As the husband sees her: Older than her years. Someone more suited to suburban domesticity and the PTA.

As he sees himself: Stylish haircut, benevolent, generous, powerful. A smooth operator.

As the wife sees him: Somewhat of a slob, moody, not very decisive or strong.

© Pat Bruno/Positive Images

Figure 5.4

Distortions in self-images. How people see themselves may be different from how others see them. These pictures and text illustrate the subjective quality of self-concept and people's perception of others. Generally, self-images tend to be distorted in a positive direction.

Although the general tendency is to distort reality in a positive direction, most people make both positive and negative distortions. For example, you might overrate your social skill, emotional stability, and intellectual ability while underrating your physical attractiveness. Also, a minority of people consistently evaluate themselves in an unrealistically negative way. Thus, the tendency to see oneself in an overly favorable light is strong but not universal.

Feedback from Others

Individuals' self-concept is shaped significantly by the feedback they get from important people in their lives. Early on, parents and other family members play a dominant role. Parents give their children a great deal of direct feedback, saying such things as "We're so proud of you" or "If you just tried harder, you could do a lot better in math." Most people, especially when young, take this sort of feedback to heart. Thus, it comes as no surprise that studies find a link between parents' views of a child and the child's self-concept (Berne & Savary, 1993; Burhans & Dweck, 1995). There is even stronger evidence for a relationship between children's *perceptions* of their parents' attitudes toward them and their own self-views (Felson, 1989, 1992).

Teachers, Little League coaches, Scout leaders, classmates, and friends also provide feedback during childhood. In later childhood and adolescence, parents and classmates are particularly important sources of feedback and support (Harter, 2003). Later in life, feedback from close friends and marriage partners assumes importance. In fact, there is evidence that a close partner's support and affirmation can bring the loved one's actual self-views and behavior more in line with

his or her ideal self (Drigotas et al., 1999). For this situation to happen, the partner needs to hold views of the loved one that match the target person's ideal self and behave in ways to bring out the best in the person. If the target person's behavior can closely match the ideal self, then self-views can move nearer to the ideal self. Researchers have labeled this process the *Michelangelo phenomenon* to reflect the partner's role in "sculpting" into reality the ideal self of a loved one.

Keep in mind that people filter feedback from others through their existing self-perceptions. That is, individuals don't see themselves exactly as others see them but rather as they *believe* others see them (Baumeister & Twenge, 2003; Tice & Wallace, 2003). Thus, feedback from others usually reinforces people's self-views.

Social Context

Receiving feedback from others reveals that the self-concept does not develop in isolation. Of course, it's not only people that matter; so do the social contexts where interactions occur. Think about it: You're much more boisterous (and less self-conscious) when you are out with friends at a dance or a diner than when you are sitting in class. Similarly, attending a funeral encourages you to think about yourself differently and to monitor your actions more carefully than going to a raucous Super Bowl party. Social context affects how people think and feel about others, as well. In office settings, for example, a superior will act and feel like a leader with subordinates but will quickly change demeanor and outlook in the presence of an equal (Moskowitz, 1994). Social contexts can affect self-concept indirectly, too. When a situation triggers a bad mood—you rarely play croquet, don't particularly care about the game, and lose a round to a friend—even those aspects of your self that are not central to who you are can suddenly seem negative (Sedikides, 1995). The resulting thoughts and

Whether positive or negative, feedback from others plays an important role in shaping a youngster's self-concept.

feelings caused by the situation can compel you to engage in more critical self-evaluations than usual.

Cultural Values

Self-concept is also shaped by cultural values. Among other things, the society in which one is reared defines what is desirable and undesirable in personality and behavior. For example, American culture puts a high premium on individuality, competitive success, strength, and skill. When individuals meet cultural expectations, they feel good about themselves and experience increases in self-esteem and vice versa (Cross & Gore, 2003).

Cross-cultural studies suggest that different cultures shape different conceptions of the self (Cross & Markus, 1999; Cross & Gore, 2003). One important way cultures differ is on the dimension of individualism versus collectivism (Hofstede, 1983; Triandis, 1989, 2001). *Individualism* **involves putting personal goals ahead of group goals and defining one's identity in terms of personal attributes rather than group memberships.** In contrast, *collectivism* **involves putting group goals ahead of personal goals and defining one's identity in terms of the groups one belongs to** (such as one's family, tribe, work group, social class, caste, and so on). Although it's tempting to think of these perspectives in either-or terms, it is more appropriate to view them as points along a continuum. Thus, it is more accurate to say that certain cultures are more or less individualistic (or collectivist) than others rather than seeing them as either one or the other.

Here is a clever but telling example illustrating the difference between individualist and collectivist cultures where simple choice is concerned. American students and Indian students selected a pen from a group composed of one blue pen and four red ones. American students consistently picked the singular blue pen, while the Indian students always chose the common

red pen (Nicholson, 2006). In Western culture, we need to remember that "agency," or how people express their sense of power or influence in the social world, is not always found in other cultures or cultural contexts (Markus & Kitayama, 2004). In a follow-up study, once the students made their choice, some were told "Actually, you can't have that pen. Here, take this one instead." All students were then told to try their new pen, either one "chosen" or one "given" to them, and to rate it. The Americans preferred the pens they originally chose, so that those who were "given" a different pen devalued it. How did the Indian students react? They showed no preference for either the pen they freely chose or the one that was given to them. Individualistic cultures promote freedom and choice, and people who live in these cultures do not like to have either threatened.

A variety of factors influence societies' tendencies to cherish individualism or collectivism. Among other things, increases in a culture's affluence, education, urbanization, and social mobility tend to foster more individualism (Triandis, 1994). Many contemporary societies are in transition, but generally speaking North American and Western European cultures tend to be individualistic, whereas Asian, African, and Latin American cultures tend to be collectivist (Hofstede, 1980, 1983).

Individuals reared in individualistic cultures usually have an *independent view of the self,* perceiving themselves as unique, self-contained, and distinct from others. In contrast, individuals reared in collectivist cultures typically have an *interdependent view of the self.* They see themselves as inextricably connected to others and believe that harmonious relationships with others are of utmost importance. Thus, in describing herself, a person living in an individualistic culture might say, "I am kind," whereas someone in a collectivist culture might respond, "My family thinks I am kind" (Triandis, 2001). **Figure 5.5** depicts the self-conceptions of individuals from these contrasting cultures.

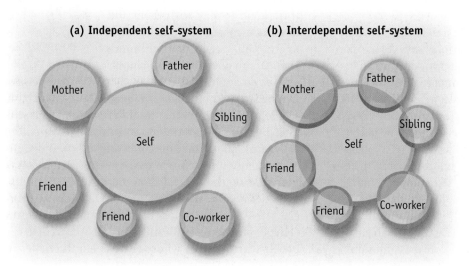

(a) Independent self-system

Father
Mother
Sibling
Self
Friend
Friend
Co-worker

(b) Interdependent self-system

Father
Mother
Sibling
Self
Friend
Friend
Co-worker

Figure 5.5

Independent and interdependent views of the self. (a) Individuals in cultures that support an independent view perceive the self as clearly separated from significant others. (b) Individuals in cultures that support an interdependent view perceive the self as inextricably connected to others.

Adapted from Markus, H. R., & Kitayama, S. (1991). Culture and the self: Implications for cognition, emotion, and motivation. *Psychological Review, 98,* 224–253. Copyright © 1991 American Psychological Association. Adapted by permission of the publisher and author.

Individuals with an independent view of the self are socialized to maintain their sense of self as a separate person—to "look out for number one," claim more than their share of credit for group successes, and disavow responsibility for group failure. Those with an interdependent view of the self are taught to adjust themselves to the needs of the groups to which they belong and to maintain the interdependence among individuals. In this situation, social duties and obligations assume great importance and people are likely to see themselves as responsible for group failures (Cross & Gore, 2003).

Researchers have noted parallels between the self-views promoted by individualistic and collectivist cultures and the self-views of some groups. For example, women usually have more interdependent self-views than men (Cross & Madson, 1997). But don't take this finding to mean that men are less social than women; rather, it means that men and women get their social needs met in different ways (Baumeister & Sommer, 1997). Thus women are usually involved in close relationships involving intimate friends and family members (*relational* interdependence), while men tend to interact in social groups such as clubs and sports teams (*collective* interdependence) (Gabriel & Gardner, 1999). These gender differences in self-views may explain other observed gender differences, such as women being more likely than men to share their feelings and thoughts with others.

Cultural values are also responsible for various stereotypes that can mold people's self-perceptions and behavior. And stereotypes—about gender, ethnicity, class, sexual orientation, and religion—can influence self-conceptions.

Self-Esteem

LEARNING OBJECTIVES

▶ *Describe the implications of self-concept confusion and self-esteem instability.*

▶ *Discuss how high and low self-esteem are related to adjustment.*

▶ *Distinguish between high self-esteem and narcissism, and discuss narcissism and aggression.*

▶ *Discuss some key influences in the development of self-esteem.*

▶ *Summarize the findings on ethnicity and gender regarding self-esteem.*

One of the functions of the self-concept is to evaluate the self; the result of this self-evaluation is termed *self-esteem*. **Self-esteem refers to one's overall assessment of one's worth as a person.** Do you think of yourself in primarily positive or negative terms? Self-esteem is a global self-evaluation that blends many specific evaluations about one's adequacy as a student, an athlete, a worker, a spouse, a parent, or whatever is personally relevant. **Figure 5.6** shows how specific elements of the self-concept may contribute to self-esteem. If you feel basically good about yourself, you probably have high self-esteem.

People with high self-esteem are confident, taking credit for their successes in various ways (Blaine & Crocker 1993) while seeking venues for demonstrating their skills (Baumeister, 1998). Compared to individuals with low self-esteem, they are also relatively sure of who they are (Campbell, 1990). In reality, the self-views of people with low self-esteem are not more negative; rather, they are more confused and tentative (Campbell, 1990; Campbell & Lavallee, 1993). In other words, their self-concepts seem to be less clear, less complete, more self-contradictory, and more susceptible to short-term fluctuations than the self-views of high-self-esteem individuals. According to Roy Baumeister (1998), an eminent researcher on the self, this "self-concept confusion" means that individuals with low self-esteem simply don't know themselves well enough to strongly endorse many personal attributes on self-esteem tests, which results in lower self-esteem scores.

Self-esteem can be construed in two ways: as trait or state. *Trait self-esteem* refers to the ongoing sense of confidence people possess regarding their abilities (athletic, assertive) and characteristics (friendliness, helpfulness). People's traits tend to stay with them and to remain constant; if one has high or low self-esteem in childhood, chances are one will have a similar level as an adult (Block & Robins, 1993; Trzesniewski, Donnellan, & Robins, 2003). **Figure 5.7** presents a basic self-report measure often used in research when self-esteem is studied as a trait. In contrast, *state self-esteem* is dynamic and changeable, referring to how individuals feel about themselves in the moment (Heatherton & Polivy, 1991). Feedback from others, self-observation, one's point in the life span, moods, a temporary financial setback, even the loss of one's alma mater's team (Hirt et al., 1992)—all can lower one's current sense of self-worth. Those whose self-esteem fluctuates in

Roy Baumeister

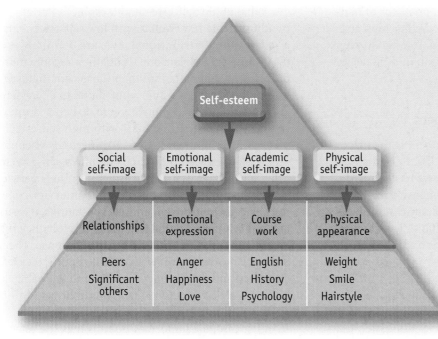

Figure 5.6

The structure of self-esteem. Self-esteem is a global evaluation that combines assessments of various aspects of one's self-concept, each of which is built up from many specific behaviors and experiences. (Adapted from Shavelson, Hubner, & Stanton, 1976)

response to daily experiences are highly sensitive to interactions and events that have potential relevance to their self-worth, and they may even mistakenly view irrelevant events as having significance (Kernis & Goldman, 2002). They always feel their self-worth is on the line. As we will shortly learn, such tendencies have important implications for adjustment.

Investigating self-esteem is challenging for several reasons. For one thing, obtaining accurate measures of self-esteem is difficult. The problem is that researchers tend to rely on self-reports from subjects, which ob-

viously may be biased. As you've seen, most individuals typically hold unrealistically positive views about themselves; moreover, some people may choose not to disclose their actual self-esteem on a questionnaire. (What about you? Did you answer the questions in **Figure 5.7** truthfully and without any self-enhancing biases? How can you be sure?) Second, in probing self-esteem it is often quite difficult to separate cause from effect. Thousands of correlational studies report that high and low self-esteem are associated with various behavioral characteristics. For instance, you saw in

---

The Rosenberg (1965) Self-Esteem Scale

Using the scale below, indicate your agreement with each of the following statements.

1	2	3	4
Strongly disagree	Disagree	Agree	Strongly agree

____ 1. I feel that I am a person of worth, at least on an equal basis with others.

____ 2. I feel that I have a number of good qualities.

____ 3. All in all, I am inclined to feel that I am a failure.

____ 4. I am able to do things as well as most other people.

____ 5. I feel I do not have much to be proud of.

____ 6. I take a positive attitude toward myself.

____ 7. On the whole, I am satisfied with myself.

____ 8. I wish I could have more respect for myself.

____ 9. I certainly feel useless at times.

____ 10. At times I think I am no good at all.

To calculate your score, first reverse the scoring for the five negatively worded items (3, 5, 8, 9, and 10) as follows: 1 = 4, 2 = 3, 3 = 2, 4 = 1. Then, sum your scores across the 10 items. Your total score should fall between 10 and 40. A higher score indicates higher self-esteem.

Figure 5.7

A popular measure of self-esteem: Rosenberg Self-Esteem Scale. The scale shown here is a widely used research instrument that taps respondents' feelings of general self-esteem.

Adapted from Rosenberg, M. (1965). *Society and the adolescent self-image.* Princeton, NJ: Princeton University Press. Copyright © 1965 by Princeton University Press.

Chapter 1 that self-esteem is a good predictor of happiness. However, it is hard to tell whether high self-esteem causes happiness or vice versa. You should keep this problem in pinpointing causation in mind as we zoom in on this fascinating topic.

The Importance of Self-Esteem

Popular wisdom holds that self-esteem is the key to practically all positive outcomes in life. In fact, its actual benefits are much fewer—but, we hasten to add, not unimportant. A recent comprehensive review of research looked at the purported and actual advantages of self-esteem (Baumeister et al., 2003). Let's look at the findings that relate to self-esteem and adjustment.

Self-Esteem and Adjustment

The clearest advantages of self-esteem are in the *emotional sphere.* Namely, self-esteem is strongly and consistently related to happiness. In fact, Baumeister and his colleagues are persuaded that high self-esteem actually leads to greater happiness, although they acknowledge that research has not clearly established the direction of causation. On the other side, low self-esteem is more likely than high self-esteem to lead to depression.

In the area of *achievement,* high self-esteem has not been shown to be a reliable cause of good academic performance. In fact, it may actually be the (weak) result of doing well in school. Baumeister and his colleagues speculate that other factors may underlie both self-esteem and academic performance. Regarding job performance, the results are mixed. Some studies find that high self-esteem is linked to better performance, but others find no difference. And it may be that occupational success leads to high self-esteem.

In the *interpersonal realm,* Baumeister and his colleagues report that people with high self-esteem claim to be more likable and attractive, to have better relationships, and to make better impressions on others than people with low self-esteem. Interestingly, these advantages seem to exist mainly in the minds of the beholders because objective data (ratings of peers) do not support these views. In fact, Mark Leary's *sociometer theory* suggests that self-esteem is actually a subjective measure of one's interpersonal popularity and success (Leary et al., 1995; Leary & Baumeister, 2000). Regarding romantic relationships, those with low self-esteem are more likely to distrust their partners' expressions of love and support and to worry about rejection compared to high-self-esteem individuals. Still there is no evidence that self-esteem (high or low) is related to how quickly relationships end. When it comes to working in groups, high-self-esteem people are more likely to speak up and to criticize the group's approach. And they are perceived as contributing more to groups.

What about self-esteem and *coping,* a key aspect of adjustment? Individuals with low self-esteem *and* a self-blaming attributional style are definitely at a disadvantage here. For one thing, they become more demoralized after a failure than those with high self-esteem do. For them, failure contributes to depression and undermines their motivation to do better the next time. By contrast, individuals with high self-esteem persist longer in the face of failure. Second, as can be seen in **Figure 5.8**, individuals with low self-esteem often have negative expectations about their performance (in a social situation, at a job interview, on a test). Because self-esteem affects expectations, it operates in a self-perpetuating fashion. As a result, they feel anxious and may not prepare for the challenge. Then, if they blame themselves when they do poorly, they feel depressed and deliver one more blow to their already battered self-esteem. Of course, this cycle also works (in the opposite way) for those with high self-esteem. In either case, the important point is that self-esteem can affect not only the present, but also the future.

Finally, all may not be well for all high-self-esteem individuals; some may be more secure in their self-evaluations than others. Some researchers distinguish between people with *secure high self-esteem* and those with *defensive high self-esteem* (Jordan, Spencer, & Zanna, 2003; Jordan et al., 2003; Kernis & Paradise, 2002). Both groups demonstrate similarly high scores

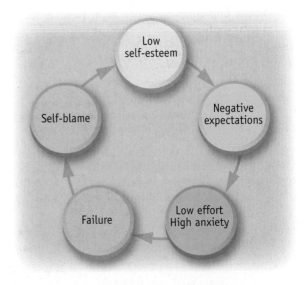

Figure 5.8

The vicious circle of low self-esteem and poor performance. Low self-esteem is associated with low or negative expectations about performance. These low expectations often result in inadequate preparation and high anxiety, which heighten the likelihood of poor performance. Unsuccessful performance triggers self-blame, which feeds back to lower self-esteem.

Adapted from Brehm, S. S., & Kassin, S. M. (1993). *Social psychology.* Boston: Houghton Mifflin. Copyright © 1993 by Houghton Mifflin Company. Adapted with permission.

on self-esteem measures. However, those with secure levels of esteem are quite confident in their positive self-views, neither needing nor seeking reassurance from others. Persons with defensive high self-esteem, on the other hand, have more delicate self-views undergirded by feelings of uncertainty, self-doubt, and insecurity, which can compel them to overreact to any unfavorable evaluation. Unfortunately, these folks need to be coddled and praised all the time, leading them to lash out at virtually any criticism, even when it is mild and intended to be helpful.

High Self-Esteem Versus Narcissism

Although feeling good about oneself is desirable, problems arise when people's self-views are inflated and unrealistic. Indeed, high self-esteem may not be all it's cracked up to be (Crocker & Park, 2004). *Narcissism is the tendency to regard oneself as grandiosely self-important.* Narcissistic individuals passionately want to think well of themselves and are highly sensitive to criticism (Twenge & Campbell, 2003). They are preoccupied with fantasies of success, believe that they deserve special treatment, and react aggressively when they experience threats to their self-views (ego threats). Those with fragile (unstable) self-esteem also respond in this manner (Kernis, 2003a, 2003b). On the other hand, individuals whose positive self-appraisals are secure or realistic are not so susceptible to ego threats and are less likely to resort to hostility and aggression in the face of them. Note that narcissists' aggression must be provoked; without provocation, they are no more likely to aggress than non-narcissists (Baumeister, Bushman, & Campbell, 2000; Twenge & Campbell, 2003).

Baumeister and his colleagues speculate that narcissists who experience ego threats have an elevated propensity to engage in aggression such as partner abuse, rape, gang violence, individual and group hate crimes, and political terrorism (Baumeister, 1999; Baumeister, Smart, & Boden, 1996; Bushman et al., 2003). Is there any evidence to support this idea? In a series of studies,

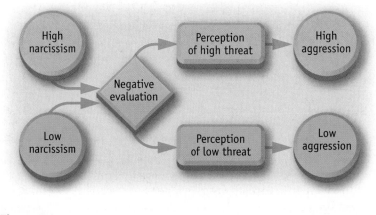

Figure 5.9

The path from narcissism to aggression. Individuals who score high on narcissism perceive negative evaluations by others to be extremely threatening. This experience of ego threat triggers strong hostile feelings and aggressive behavior toward the evaluator in retaliation for the perceived criticism. Low scorers are less likely to perceive negative evaluations as threatening and, therefore, behave much less aggressively toward evaluators. (Adapted from Bushman & Baumeister, 1998).

researchers gave participants the opportunity to aggress against someone who had either insulted or praised an essay they had written (Bushman & Baumeister, 1998). The narcissistic participants reacted to their "insultors" with exceptionally high levels of aggression (see **Figure 5.9**). Another study compared male prisoners and college men on narcissism and self-esteem. Violent offenders scored significantly higher in narcissism, but their self-esteem scores were similar to those of the college men (Bushman & Baumeister, 2002).

These findings have important practical implications (Baumeister et al., 1996). Most rehabilitation programs for spousal abusers, delinquents, and criminals are based on the faulty belief that these individuals suffer from low self-esteem. In opposition to this view, current research suggests that efforts to boost (already inflated) self-esteem are misguided; a better approach is to help such individuals develop more self-control and more realistic views of themselves. Keep in mind, too, that narcissism cannot account for all problems associated with self-esteem. One recent series of studies found that low self-esteem among adolescents, not narcissism, predicted the incidence of aggression and of antisocial and delinquent behavior (Donnellan et al., 2005).

The Development of Self-Esteem

Although people's sense of self-worth emerges in early childhood, individual differences in self-esteem begin to stand out in middle childhood and remain across the lifespan (Harter, 2006). The typical pattern found involves high self-esteem in childhood, an observed fall in adolescence (especially among girls), a gradual return

---

Web Link 5.3 **Self-Esteem vs. Narcissism: Implications for Teachers of Young Children**

Self-esteem in early childhood can be undermined by well-intentioned but ill-informed teachers who misunderstand how self-esteem is developed. Lilian G. Katz explores durable foundations for a child's self-worth in this online book from ERIC, the Education Resources Information Center.

Self-Esteem and Threats to Mortality

One consequence of living in a post–9/11 world is that people experience anxiety about the possibility of terrorist attacks in the United States, as well as elsewhere. As explained in Chapter 2, *terror management theory (TMT)* is an influential new theoretical perspective asserting that self-esteem plays a pivotal role in people's efforts to deal with the threats to mortality posed by modern terrorism (Greenberg, Solomon, & Pyszczynski, 1997). As you may recall, terror management theory notes that human beings are the only creatures that live with the knowledge that they will die. According to TMT, the instinctive desire to live is juxtaposed against the inevitability of death, which produces the potential for paralyzing terror (Pyszczynski, Greenberg, & Goldenberg, 2003). To diminish the existential terror resulting from the awareness of their mortality, people are thought to rely on two defenses: efforts aimed at validating one's cultural worldview and those that bolster self-esteem.

First, belonging to a culture supposedly reduces the fear of death because it provides a sense of meaning beyond oneself and a sense of belonging to a larger entity that will live beyond one's own lifetime. This idea has considerable support. Compared to participants who are not reminded about their own death, those for whom death is made salient are more likely to endorse negative evaluations of outgroup members (Schimel et al., 1999) and to endorse harsh punishments for those who violate cultural values (Greenberg et al., 1990).

More relevant to the current discussion is the second terror management mechanism, which ascribes great importance to self-esteem. Terror management theory proposes that the principal function of self-esteem is to serve as a buffer against death-related anxiety. The idea is that people can reduce or ward off their fear of death by focusing on thoughts and experiences that help them feel good about themselves. This idea was supported in a series of experiments in which people were shown graphic scenes of death aimed at building anxiety about their own mortality (Greenberg et al., 1992). Prior to viewing these scenes, half of the participants were given positive feedback to temporarily increase their self-esteem. Interestingly, the group that got the "self-esteem boost" showed less anxiety and less defensiveness in viewing the gruesome scenes than a control group that didn't receive the prior positive feedback.

A worldview implicit in TMT, that goodness must triumph heroically over evil, poses problems because it focuses on the transient nature of life (Pyszczynski, Solomon, & Greenberg, 2003). Specifically, to transcend death and find self-worth, people on both sides feel they must fight and, if necessary, kill others to eradicate wickedness; people are either saints or demons (Haidt & Algoe, 2004). Terror management theory has some interesting implications for thinking about terrorism and promoting peace. First, TMT theorists argue that the emphasis on mortality must be reduced. Second, fundamentalist belief systems in places like the Middle East must be constructively changed so as not to emphasize that self-worth and meaning can be achieved only by harming or eliminating groups or even nations (Pyszczynski et al., 2003).

People's reactions to terror have also been considered in light of TMT. One study, which focused on how interpersonal communication can reduce existential terror, interviewed young adults on a large Midwest university's campus two weeks after the fall of the World Trade Center Towers (Yum & Schenck-Hamlin, 2005). Participants reported initially feeling shock and disbelief on September 11, 2001. In the hours and days following the event, however, many reported looking for purpose or value in living, engaging in meaningful conversations with others, searching for or giving out information, and (unfortunately) making intolerant or prejudiced comments about Arab Muslims, all acts related to self-esteem. Another study looked at the effects of homegrown terrorism to discern whether existential terror maintains marital ties. Analyzing divorce rates in Oklahoma between 1985 and 2000, Nakonezny and colleagues found a decrease in divorces following the Oklahoma City bombing in April 1995 (Nakonezny, Reddick, & Rodgers, 2004). Perhaps awareness of mortality and the fragility of life encouraged some people to stay together.

Although TMT offers an intriguing perspective on the function of self-esteem, key aspects of the theory have not been tested (Crocker & Nuer, 2004), and alternative explanations can account for existing results (Leary, 2004). That said, there is quite a bit of empirical support for the specific idea that high self-esteem counteracts anxiety (Baumeister et al., 2003). This anxiety-buffering function of high self-esteem seems particularly relevant in these troubled times.

and rise in adulthood, and a precipitous decline once more during old age (Robins & Trzesniewski, 2005). Because the foundations of self-esteem are laid early in life (Harter, 2003), psychologists have focused much of their attention on the role of parenting in self-esteem development. Indeed, there is ample evidence that parental involvement, acceptance, support, and exposure to clearly defined limits have marked influence on children's self-esteem (Felson, 1989; Harter, 1998).

Two major dimensions underlie parenting behavior: acceptance and control (Maccoby & Martin, 1983). Diana Baumrind (1967, 1971, 1978) identified four distinct parenting styles as interactions between these two dimensions (see **Figure 5.10**). *Authoritative parenting* uses high emotional support and firm, but reasonable limits (high acceptance, high control). *Authoritarian parenting* entails low emotional support with rigid limits (low acceptance, high control). *Permissive parenting* uses high emotional support with few limits (high acceptance, low control), and *neglectful parenting* involves low emotional support and few limits (low acceptance, low control). Baumrind and others have found correlations between these parenting styles and

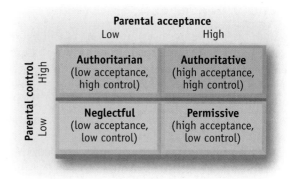

Figure 5.10

Baumrind's four parenting styles. Four parenting styles result from the interactions of parental acceptance and parental control, as theorized by Diana Baumrind.

Adapted from Baumrind, D. (1971). Current patterns of parental authority [Monograph]. *Developmental Psychology, 4*(1, Part 2), 1–103. Copyright © 1971 American Psychological Association. Adapted by permission of the publisher and author.

children's traits and behaviors, including self-esteem (Furnham & Cheng, 2000; Maccoby & Martin, 1983). Authoritative parenting is associated with the highest self-esteem scores, and this finding holds true across different ethnic groups (Wissink, Dekovic, & Meijer, 2006). Authoritarian parenting, permissive parenting, and neglectful parenting are second, third, and fourth in line. These studies were correlational, so keep in mind they don't demonstrate that parenting style *causes* high or low self-esteem.

Of course, parents are not the only significant people in a person's life: teachers, classmates, and close friends also play important roles. As you would expect, children who perceive they have the most support from the key people in their lives have the highest self-esteem, whereas those who have the lowest perceived support have the lowest self-esteem (Harter, 2003). For older children and adolescents, approval from parents and approval from classmates are the two strongest predictors of high self-esteem; by college age, peers have much more impact on self-esteem than parents do (Harter, 1993).

Children (and adults) also make their own judgments about themselves. Perceiving oneself as successful in domains that are highly valued is important in these self-evaluations (Harter, 2003; MacDonald, Saltzman, & Leary, 2003). For instance, if Maria values success in the academic and social areas and sees herself as competent in these arenas, she will have higher self-esteem than Heather, who also values these domains but rates herself low on one or both of them. An important basis for self-judgments is how well one "stacks up" against a selected reference group (recall social comparison theory).

Significant others play a key role in shaping self-esteem.

Ethnicity, Gender, and Self-Esteem

Because prejudice and discrimination are still pervasive in the United States, people commonly assume that members of minority groups have lower self-esteem than members of the majority group. Research both supports and contradicts this assumption. On the one hand, the self-esteem of Asians, Hispanics, and Native Americans is lower than that of whites, although the differences are small (Twenge & Crocker, 2002). On the other hand, the self-esteem of blacks is higher than that of whites (Gray-Little & Hafdahl, 2000; Twenge & Crocker, 2002). Adding gender to the mix complicates the picture even more. White males have higher self-esteem than white females, but minority males have lower self-esteem than minority females (Twenge & Crocker, 2002).

Thus, ethnicity and gender interact in complex ways in self-esteem. The role of cultural differences in the self-concept may provide some insight here. Recall our earlier discussion of individualism and collectivism. Note that differences on this dimension are found not only between nations but also within a given country. And here's another fact: High individualism is associated with high self-esteem. What's interesting here is that the pattern of ethnic differences in individualism closely mirrors the pattern of ethnic differences in self-esteem (Twenge & Crocker, 2002). That is, blacks score higher than whites, whites do not differ significantly from Hispanics, and Hispanics score higher than Asian Americans. Thus, the ethnic differences in self-esteem are likely rooted in how the different groups view themselves, based on cultural messages.

Although females are not a minority group, they resemble ethnic minorities in that they tend to have lower status and less power than males. The popular press abounds with reports of low self-esteem in adolescent girls and women (Orenstein, 1994; Pipher, 1994). Is there any empirical basis for this assertion? In a massive undertaking, researchers examined gender differences in self-esteem by statistically summarizing the results of several hundred studies (with respondents ranging from 7 to 60 years of age) as well as the data from three nationally representative surveys of adolescents and young adults (Kling et al., 1999). In both analyses, males scored higher on self-esteem than females, although the differences were small for the most part. The largest difference occurred in the 15- to 18-year-old age group. Also, white girls have lower self-esteem than minority girls do. The fact that white girls tend to have more negative body images than minority girls may be a factor in their lower self-esteem (Twenge & Crocker, 2002).

Basic Principles of Self-Perception

LEARNING OBJECTIVES

▶ *Distinguish between automatic and controlled processing.*

▶ *Define self-attributions, and identify the key dimensions of attributions.*

▶ *Explain how optimistic and pessimistic explanatory styles are related to adjustment.*

▶ *Discuss four motives that guide self-understanding.*

▶ *Describe four strategies people use to maintain positive feelings about the self.*

Now that you're familiar with some of the major aspects of the self, let's consider how people construct and maintain a coherent and positive view of the self. First we'll look at the basic cognitive processes involved and then at the fascinating area of self-attributions. Then we will move on to discussions of explanatory style and the key motives guiding self-understanding, with a special emphasis on self-enhancement techniques.

Cognitive Processes

People are faced with an inordinate number of decisions on a daily basis. How do they keep from being overwhelmed? The key lies in how people process information. According to Shelley Taylor (1981a), people are "cognitive misers." In this model, cognitive resources (attention, memory, and so forth) are limited, so the mind works to "hoard" them by taking cognitive short-cuts. For example, you probably have the same morning routine—shower, drink coffee, read the paper as you eat breakfast, check e-mail, and so forth. Because you do these things without a lot of thought, you can conserve your attentional, decision-making, and memory capacities for important cognitive tasks. This example illustrates the default mode of handling information: *automatic processing*. On the other hand, when important decisions arise or when you're trying to understand why you didn't get that job you wanted, you spend those precious cognitive resources. This mode is termed *controlled processing*. Ellen Langer (1989) describes these two states as *mindlessness* and *mindfulness,* respectively. Mindfulness promotes cognitive flexibility, which in turn can lead to self-acceptance (Carson & Langer, 2006) and well-being (Langer, 2002). In contrast, mindlessness leads to rigid thinking.

Another way that cognitive resources are protected is through *selective attention,* with high priority given to information pertaining to the self (Bargh, 1997). An example of this tendency is a phenomenon known as the "cocktail party effect"—the ability to pick out the mention of your name in a roomful of chattering people (Moray, 1959; Wood & Cowan, 1995).

Another principle of self-cognition is that people strive to understand themselves. One way they do so, as you saw in our discussion of social comparison theory, is to compare themselves with others (Wood & Wilson, 2003). Yet another is to engage in attributional thinking, our next topic.

Self-Attributions

Let's say that you win a critical match for your school's tennis team. To what do you attribute your success? Is your new practice schedule starting to pay off? Did you have the home court advantage? Perhaps your opponent was playing with a minor injury? This example from everyday life illustrates the nature of the self-attribution process. *Self-attributions* **are inferences that people draw about the causes of their own behavior.** People routinely make attributions to make sense out of their experiences. These attributions involve inferences that ultimately represent guesswork on each person's part.

Fritz Heider (1958) was the first to assert that people tend to locate the cause of a behavior either within a person, attributing it to personal factors, or outside of a person, attributing it to environmental factors. He thus established one of the crucial dimensions along which attributions are made: internal versus external. The other two dimensions are stable—unstable and controllable—uncontrollable. Let's discuss these different types of attributions in greater detail.

Internal or external. Elaborating on Heider's insight, various theorists have agreed that explanations of behavior and events can be categorized as internal or external attributions (Jones & Davis, 1965; Kelley, 1967; Weiner, 1974, 2006). *Internal attributions* **ascribe the causes of behavior to personal dispositions, traits, abilities, and feelings.** *External attributions* **ascribe the causes of behavior to situational demands and environmental constraints.** For example, if you credit your poor statistics grade to your failure to prepare adequately for the test or to getting overly anxious dur-

ing the test, you are making internal attributions. An external attribution could be that the course is simply too hard, that the teacher is unfair, or that the book is incomprehensible.

Whether one's self-attributions are internal or external can have a tremendous impact on one's personal adjustment. Studies suggest that people who attribute their setbacks to internal, personal causes while discounting external, situational explanations may be more prone to depression than people who display opposite tendencies (Riso et al., 2003).

Stable or unstable. A second dimension people use in making causal attributions is the stability of the causes underlying behavior (Weiner, 1986, 1994). A stable cause is one that is more or less permanent and unlikely to change over time. A sense of humor and intelligence are *stable internal* causes of behavior. *Stable external* causes of behavior include such things as laws and rules (speed limits, no smoking areas). Unstable causes of behavior are variable or subject to change. *Unstable internal* causes of behavior include such things as mood (good or bad) and motivation (strong or weak). *Unstable external* causes could be the weather and the presence or absence of other people. According to Bernard Weiner (1986, 1994), the stable-unstable dimension in attribution cuts across the internal-external dimension, creating four types of attributions for success and failure, as shown in **Figure 5.11**.

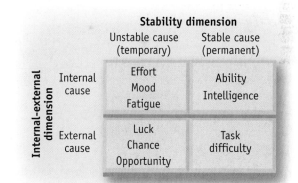

Figure 5.11

Key dimensions of attributional thinking. Weiner's model assumes that people's explanations for success and failure emphasize internal versus external causes and stable versus unstable causes. For example, if you attribute an outcome to great effort or to lack of effort, you are citing causes that lie within the person. Since effort can vary over time, the causal factors at work are unstable. Other examples of causal factors that fit into each of the four cells in Weiner's model are shown in the diagram.

From Weiner, B., Frieze, I., Kukla, A., Reed, L.. & Rosenbaum, R. M. (1972). Perceiving the causes of success and failure. In E. E. Jones, D. E. Kanuouse, H. H. Kelly, R. E. Nisbett, S. Valins, & B. Weiner (Eds.), *Perceiving causes of behavior.* Morristown, NJ: General Learning Press. Reprinted by permission of the author.

Let's apply Weiner's model to a concrete event. Imagine that you are contemplating why you just landed the job you wanted. You might credit your situation to internal factors that are stable (excellent ability) or unstable (hard work on your eye-catching résumé). Or you might attribute the outcome to external factors that are stable (lack of top-flight competition) or unstable (luck). If you didn't get the job, your explanations would fall in the same four categories: internal-stable (lack of ability), internal-unstable (inadequate effort on your résumé), external-stable (too much competition in your field), and external-unstable (bad luck).

Controllable or uncontrollable. A third dimension in the attribution process acknowledges the fact that sometimes events are under one's control and sometimes they are not (Weiner, 1986, 1994). For example, the amount of effort you expend on a task is typically perceived as something under your control, whereas an aptitude for music is viewed as something you are born with (beyond your control). Controllability can vary with each of the other two factors.

These three dimensions appear to be the central ones in the attribution process. Research has documented that self-attributions are motivational, guiding one toward or away from possible courses of action. Thus, one's self-beliefs can influence future expectations (success or failure) and emotions (pride, hopelessness, guilt), and these expectations and emotions can combine to influence subsequent performance (Weiner,

1986, 1994, 2006). Self-attributions, then, play a key role in one's feelings, motivational state, and behavior.

Explanatory Style

Julio and Josh are freshmen who have just struck out trying to get their first college dates. After this disappointment, they reflect on the possible reasons for it. Julio speculates that his approach was too subtle. Looking back, he realizes that he wasn't very direct because he was nervous about asking the woman out. When she didn't reply, he didn't follow up for fear that she didn't really want to go out with him. On further reflection, he reasons that she probably didn't respond because she wasn't sure of his intentions. He vows to be more direct the next time. Josh, on the other hand, mopes, "I'll never have a relationship. I'm a total loser." On the basis of these comments, who do you think is likely to get a date in the future? If you guessed Julio, you are probably correct. Let's see why.

According to Martin Seligman (1991), people tend to exhibit, to varying degrees, an *optimistic explanatory style* or a *pessimistic explanatory style* (see **Figure 5.12**). As we saw in Chapter 3, **explanatory style refers to the tendency to use similar causal attributions for a wide variety of events in one's life.** The person with an optimistic explanatory style usually attributes setbacks to external, unstable, and specific factors. A person who failed to get a desired job, for example, might attribute this misfortune to factors in the interview situation ("The room was really hot," "The questions were

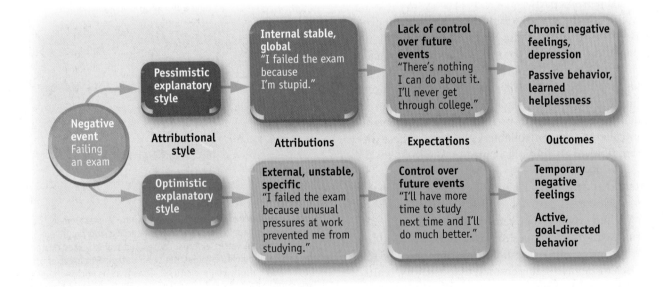

Figure 5.12

The effects of attributional style on expectations, emotions, and behavior. The pessimistic explanatory style is seen in the top row of boxes. This attributional style, which attributes setbacks to internal, stable, and global causes, tends to result in an expectation of lack of control over future events, depressed feelings, and passive behavior. A more adaptive, optimistic attributional style is shown in the bottom row of boxes.

slanted") rather than to personal shortcomings. This style can be psychologically protective (Wise & Rosqvist, 2006), helping people to discount their setbacks and thus maintain a favorable self-image. It also helps people bounce back from failure. One study found that optimistic students had more confidence and performed better than pessimistic students after a sports failure (Martin-Krumm et al., 2003).

In contrast, people with a pessimistic explanatory style tend to attribute their setbacks to internal, stable, and global (or pervasive) factors. These attributions make them feel bad about themselves and pessimistic about their ability to handle challenges in the future. Such a style can foster passive behavior and make people more vulnerable to learned helplessness and depression (Peterson, Maier, & Seligman, 1993), especially when they expect that things won't work out in their favor (Peterson & Vaidya, 2001). Of more concern is some suggestive evidence from a longitudinal sample of people that "catastrophizing"—attributing negative events to global causes—predicted accidental and violent deaths (Peterson et al., 1998). Luckily, cognitive-behavioral therapy appears to be successful in helping depressed individuals change their pessimistic explanatory style (Seligman et al., 1999).

Motives Guiding Self-Understanding

Whether people evaluate themselves by social comparisons, attributional thinking, or other means, they are highly motivated to pursue self-understanding. In seeking self-understanding, people are driven by four major motives: assessment, verification, improvement, and enhancement (Biernat & Billings, 2001; Sedikides & Strube, 1997).

Self-Assessment

The *self-assessment motive* is reflected in people's desire for truthful information about themselves (Trope, 1983, 1986). Unfortunately, many of these self-assessments are quite flawed; the only good news is that the person is typically unaware of this fact (Dunning, Heath, & Suls, 2004). Still, there is some hope. Individuals do seek accurate feedback about many types of information, including their personal qualities, abilities, physical features, and so forth. It's obvious why people look for accurate information. After all, it helps them set realistic goals and behave in appropriate ways (Oettingen & Gollwitzer, 2001). Still, the bald truth is not always welcome. Accordingly, people are also motivated by other concerns.

Self-Verification

The *self-verification motive* drives people toward information that matches what they already believe about themselves, whether it is positive or negative. This tendency to strive for a consistent self-image ensures that individuals' self-concepts are relatively stable. Individuals maintain consistent self-perceptions in a number of subtle ways and are often unaware of doing so (Schlenker & Pontari, 2000). For example, people maintain consistency between their past and present behavior by erasing past memories that conflict with present ones. To illustrate, people who were once shy and who later became outgoing have been shown to recall memories about themselves that indicate that they perceive themselves as always having been outgoing (Ross & Conway, 1986).

Another way people maintain self-consistency is by seeking out feedback and situations that will confirm their existing self-perceptions and avoiding potentially disconfirming situations or feedback. According to William Swann's *self-verification theory,* **people prefer to receive feedback from others that is consistent with their own self-views.** Thus, people with positive self-concepts should prefer positive feedback from others and those with negative self-concepts should prefer negative feedback. Research usually finds this to be the case (Swann, Rentfrow, & Guinn, 2003). In one study, college men were divided into a positive self-concept group or a negative self-concept group based on test scores. They were then asked to choose a partner for a subsequent 2- to 3-hour interaction. Participants were led to believe that one of the prospective partners held views of him that were consistent with his self-view and that the other held views of him that were inconsistent with his self-view. As predicted, subjects with positive self-views preferred partners who viewed them positively, whereas those with negative self-views chose partners who viewed them negatively (Swann, Stein-Seroussi, & Geisler, 1992). Among depressed persons, the persistent self-views predicted by self-verification processes may account for treatment setbacks or ongoing dysphoria (Petit & Joiner, 2006).

Self-Improvement

What is your current self-improvement project? To study more? To get more exercise? When people seek to better themselves, the *self-improvement motive* comes into play. In trying to improve, individuals typically look to successful others for inspiration (Collins, 1996). Advertisers of personal care products (tooth whiteners, exercise machines, and so forth) tap into this motive by showing before-and-after photographs of individuals who have used the products.

Self-Enhancement

Finally, people are motivated by the *self-enhancement motive. Self-enhancement* **is the tendency to maintain positive feelings about oneself.** One example of self-enhancement is the tendency to hold flattering views of one's personal qualities, a tendency termed the *better-than-average effect* (Alicke, 1985; Buckingham & Alicke, 2002). You've already seen an example of this effect in our earlier report that 100 percent of students who took the SAT rated themselves above average in the ability to get along with others—a mathematical impossibility. Students can take perverse pleasure in knowing that faculty also succumb to this bias: 94 percent of them regard their teaching as above average (Cross, 1977)!

A second example of self-enhancement concerns *illusions of control* (Langer, 1975), in which people overestimate their degree of control over outcomes. Thus, individuals who pick their own "lucky" numbers on lottery tickets falsely believe that they can influence the outcome of such random events, an act and inference that makes them feel good (Dunn & Wilson, 1990). A third form of self-enhancement is the tendency to have *unrealistic optimism about future events* (Weinstein, 1980). For example, most people believe that they will have a brighter future and experience fewer negative events than others (Helweg-Larsen & Shepperd, 2001), especially where health and safety are concerned (Weinstein, 1982).

The four self-motives of assessment, verification, improvement, and enhancement permit flexibility in making self-evaluations. Although you would think that accurate information would be the most useful to people, that doesn't seem to be the case. In a series of studies that pitted self-assessment, self-verification, and self-enhancement against each other, the self-enhancement motive was found to be the strongest, the self-verification motive a distant second, and the self-assessment motive an even more distant third (Sedikides, 1993).

Methods of Self-Enhancement

The powerful self-enhancement motive drives individuals to seek positive (and reject negative) information about themselves. Let's examine four cognitive strategies people commonly use in this process.

Downward Comparisons

We've already mentioned that people routinely compare themselves to others as a means of learning more about themselves (social comparison). However, once a threat to self-esteem enters the picture, people often adjust their strategy and choose to compare themselves with those who are worse off than they are (Wood, 1989). *Downward social comparison* **is a defensive tendency to compare oneself with someone whose troubles are more serious than one's own.** Why do people change strategies under threat? Because they need to feel better. Research shows that downward social comparisons are associated with increases in both mood and self-esteem (Reis, Gerrard, & Gibbons, 1993).

A dramatic example of downward comparison can be found in the aftermath of the terrorist attacks on the World Trade Center and the Pentagon in September 2001. Compared to the devastating losses suffered by the victims and families, most people's problems suddenly appeared insignificant. There are also more common examples. If you have ever been in a serious traffic accident in which your car was "totaled," you probably reassured yourself by reflecting on the fact that at least no one was seriously injured. Similarly, people with chronic illnesses may compare themselves with those who have life-threatening diseases.

Self-Serving Bias

Suppose that you and three other individuals apply for a part-time job in the parks and recreation department and you are selected for the position. How do you explain your success? Chances are, you tell yourself that you were hired because you were the most qualified for the job. But how do the other three people interpret their negative outcome? Do they tell themselves that you got the job because you were the most able? Un-

PEANUTS reprinted by permission of United Feature Syndicate, Inc.

likely! Instead, they probably attribute their loss to "bad luck" or to not having had time to prepare for the interview. These different explanations for success and failure reflect **the *self-serving bias,* or the tendency to attribute one's successes to personal factors and one's failures to situational factors** (Miller and Ross, 1975).

For example, in one experiment, two strangers jointly took a test. They then received bogus success or failure feedback about their test performance and were asked to assign responsibility for the test results. Successful participants claimed credit, but those who failed blamed their partners (Campbell et al., 2000). Still, people don't always rush to take credit. In another experiment in the just-cited study, participants were actual friends. In this case, participants shared responsibility for both successful and unsuccessful outcomes. Thus, friendship places limits on the self-serving bias.

Although the self-serving bias has been documented in a variety of cultures (Fletcher & Ward 1988), it seems to be particularly prevalent in individualistic, Western societies, where the emphasis on competition and high self-esteem motivates people to try to impress others, as well as themselves. In contrast, Japanese subjects exhibit a *self-effacing bias* in explaining successes (Akimoto & Sanbonmatsu, 1999; Markus & Kitayama, 1991), as they tend to attribute their successes to the help they receive from others or to the ease of the task, while downplaying the importance of their ability. When they fail, Japanese subjects tend to be more self-critical than subjects from individualistic cultures (Heine & Renshaw, 2002). They are more likely to accept responsibility for their failures and to use their setbacks as an impetus for self-improvement (Heine et al., 2001). When Japanese students' apprehension at being evaluated is reduced, however, one study found they make more internal attributions for success than failure (Kudo, 2003). Studies have also failed to find the usual self-serving bias in Nepalese and Chinese samples (Lee & Seligman, 1997; Smith & Bond, 1999).

Basking in Reflected Glory

When your favorite sports team won the national championship last year, did you make a point of wearing the team cap? And when Ben, your best friend, won that special award, do you remember how often you told others the good news about him? If you played a role in someone's success, it's understandable that you would want to share in the recognition; however, people often want to share recognition even when they are on the

People frequently claim association with others who are successful (basking in reflected glory) to maintain positive feelings about the self.

sidelines of an outstanding achievement. ***Basking in reflected glory* is the tendency to enhance one's image by publicly announcing one's association with those who are successful.**

Robert Cialdini and his colleagues (1976) studied this phenomenon on college campuses with nationally ranked football teams. The researchers predicted that, when asked how their team had fared in a recent football game, students would be more likely to say, "We won" (in other words, to bask in reflected glory, or to "BIRG"—pronounced with a soft "g") when the home team had been successful than to respond "We lost" when it had been defeated. Indeed, the researchers found that students were more likely to BIRG when their team won than when it lost. Also, subjects who believed that they had just failed a bogus test were more likely to use the words "we won" than those who believed they had performed well.

A related self-enhancement strategy is "CORFing," or *cutting off reflected failure.* Because self-esteem is partly tied to an individual's associations with others, people often protect their self-esteem by distancing themselves from those who are unsuccessful (Boen, VanBeselaere, & Feys, 2002; Cialdini et al., 1976). Thus, if your cousin is arrested for drunk driving, you may tell others that you don't really know him very well. Interestingly, BIRGing and CORFing are apparently not limited to the U.S. or only to public settings. Websites of Belgian and Dutch soccer teams receive significantly more "surfers" after the teams win matches (BIRGing) than when they lose (CORFing) (Boen, VanBeselaere, & Feys, 2002).

Self-Handicapping

When people fail at an important task, they need to save face. In such instances, individuals can usually come up with a face-saving excuse ("I had a terrible stomachache"). Curiously, some people actually behave in a way that sets them up to fail so that they have a ready-made excuse for failure, should it occur. *Self-handicapping is the tendency to sabotage one's performance to provide an excuse for possible failure.* For example, when a big test is looming, they put off studying until the last minute or go out drinking the night before the test. If, as is likely, they don't do well on the exam, they explain their poor performance by saying they didn't prepare. (After all, wouldn't you rather have others believe that your poor performance is due to inadequate preparation rather than to lack of ability?) People use a variety of tactics for handicapping their performance: alcohol, drugs, procrastination, a bad mood, a distracting stimulus, anxiety, depression, and being overcommitted (Baumeister, 1998).

Self-handicapping should not be confused with *defensive pessimism,* a trait causing some people to mentally identify the worst possible outcome and to then subsequently work hard to make sure it never occurs (Norem, 1989, 2002; Norem & Smith, 2006). (Take the quiz in **Figure 5.13** to learn whether you are a defensive pessimist.) Although the two constructs appear

The Positive Power of Negative Thinking: Using Defensive Pessimism to Harness Anxiety and Perform at Your Peak
by Julie Norem (Basic Books, 2002)

Can negative thoughts, such as fear of failing or performing poorly, ever be a good thing? Perhaps a little anxiety can help rather than harm. Surprisingly, social-personality psychologist Julie Norem of Wellesley College argues that some negative self-views can actually galvanize one's resolve and lead to success. How so? Imagine the benefits of "defensive pessimism" by envisioning "worst case" scenarios prior to undertaking a difficult or challenging task and then working hard to avoid them. Once you identify the demons and dangers blocking you from your goal, you can plan a strategy for moving forward. Setting expectations at low or even moderate levels can lead to large emotional dividends if you end up outperforming your beginning benchmarks. If nothing else, defensive pessimism is a compelling antidote to overly naïve optimism or maladaptive self-strategies, such as denial, procrastination, or self-handicapping.

similar, defensive pessimists are motivated to avoid bad outcomes, whereas self-handicappers undermine their own efforts (Elliot & Church, 2003; Martin et al., 2003). Imagine working on a huge end-of-term project for a class—one that will make or break your final course

Figure 5.13

The Defensive Pessimism Questionnaire. Think of a situation where you want to do your best. It may be related to work, your social life, or to any of your goals. When you answer the following questions, think about how you prepare for that kind of situation. Rate how true each statement is for you. Directions for determining your score on the scale are provided following the questions.

Adapted from Norem, J. K. (2001). *The positive power of negative thinking: Using defensive pessimism to manage anxiety and perform at your peak.* New York: Basic Books. Copyright © 2001 by Julie K. Norem. Reprinted with permission from Perseus Book Group.

Defensive Pessimism Questionnaire

Using this scale, rate your agreement with the following statements.

1	2	3	4	5	6	7
Not at All True of Me						Very True of Me

___ I often start out expecting the worst, even though I will probably do okay.

___ I worry about how things will turn out.

___ I carefully consider all possible outcomes.

___ I often worry that I won't be able to carry through my intentions.

___ I spend lots of time imagining what could go wrong.

___ I imagine how I would feel if things went badly.

___ I try to picture how I could fix things if something went wrong.

___ I'm careful not to become overconfident in these situations.

___ I spend a lot of time planning when one of these situations is coming up.

___ I imagine how things would feel if things went well.

___ In these situations, sometimes I worry more about looking like a fool than doing really well.

___ Considering what can go wrong helps me to prepare.

To figure out where you stand, add your scores for all the questions. Possible scores range from 12 to 84, and higher scores indicate a stronger tendency to use defensive pessimism. If you score above 50, you would qualify as a defensive pessimist in Norem's studies. Scores falling below 30 indicate optimism (for more on the use of this questionnaire, please see Norem [2001]).

grade. Optimists cope with anxiety by anticipating they will do their best. Defensive pessimists will expect the worst and then get right to work, ending up pleasantly surprised when they do well. People engaging in self-handicapping, however, might procrastinate or do any number of things that, as we will see, can undermine their successful completion of the project.

Self-handicapping seems like a "win-win" strategy: If you fail, you have a face-saving excuse ready, and if you happen to succeed, you can claim that you are unusually gifted! However, it probably has not escaped your attention that self-handicapping is highly risky. By giving yourself an attributional "out" in case of failure, your self-defeating behavior will likely result in poor performance (Zuckerman, Kieffer, & Knee, 1998). Moreover, while self-handicapping may save you from negative self-attributions about your ability, it does not prevent others from making different negative attributions about you. For example, people believe that individuals are less competent when they self-handicap

than when they don't (Rhodewalt et al., 1995). Also, others may perceive you as lazy, inclined to drink too much, or highly anxious, depending on the means you use to self-handicap, perceptions that are sometimes accurate (Zuckerman & Tsai, 2005). Consequently, this self-enhancement tactic has serious drawbacks.

Potentially, anyone can engage in self-handicapping behavior (surely, you have come up with an excuse or two when things did not go your way), but research suggests that high-status individuals, especially men, are prone to do so (Lucas & Lovaglia, 2005). Why? Self-handicapping is likely to occur when self-esteem is threatened. Thus, high-status individuals will be more motivated to preserve their level of self-worth than people of a lower status. Interestingly, when gender is controlled, race and ethnicity matter somewhat: European Americans self-handicap more than non-European Americans (Lucas & Lovaglia, 2005), as do narcissists, who tend to be arrogant or conceited (Rhodelwalt, Tragakis, & Finnerty, 2006).

Self-Regulation

LEARNING OBJECTIVES

▶ *Define self-regulation, and explain the ego-depletion model of self-regulation.*

▶ *Explain why self-efficacy is important to psychological adjustment.*

▶ *Describe how individuals develop self-efficacy.*

▶ *Describe the three categories of self-defeating behavior.*

"Should I have that hot fudge sundae or not?" "I guess I'd better get started on that English paper." People are constantly trying to resist impulses and make themselves do things they don't want to do. *Self-regulation* **is the process of directing and controlling one's behavior.** Clearly, the ability to manage and direct what you think, how you feel, and how you behave is tied to your success at work, your relationships, and your mental and physical health (Baumeister & Vohs, 2003). Being able to forgo immediate gratification (studying instead of partying) and focus one's behavior toward important, longer-range goals (graduating and getting a good job) is of paramount importance if one is to be successful in life.

It's possible that people have a limited amount of self-control resources. So if you tax these resources resisting temptation in a given situation, you may have a hard time resisting the next temptation or persisting at a new task. At least that's the idea behind the *ego-depletion model of self-regulation* (Baumeister et al., 1998). To investigate this hypothesis, researchers asked college students to participate in a study of taste perception (the study was actually on self-control) (Baumeister et al., 1998). Some participants were asked to eat two or three radishes in 5 minutes but not to touch

the chocolate candy and chocolate chip cookies that were nearby. Others were asked to eat some candy or some cookies but were told not to eat any of the nearby radishes. A control group didn't participate in this part of the study. Then all subjects were asked to solve what were, unbeknownst-to-them, unsolvable puzzles while they supposedly waited for another part of the study. Researchers measured the subjects' self-control by the amount of time they persisted at the puzzles and the number of attempts they made. According to the ego-depletion model, the radish-eaters would use more self-control resources (resisting the chocolate) than would the chocolate-eaters (resisting the radishes) or the subjects in the no-food control group. Thus, this group should have the fewest self-control resources to use for persisting at a difficult task. As you can see in **Figure 5.14** on the next page, the radish-eaters gave up sooner and made fewer attempts on the puzzles than the chocolate-eaters or the control group. One of the reasons people rely so often on habit and automatic processing is to conserve these important self-control resources (Baumeister, Muraven, & Tice, 2000).

Self-regulation seems to develop early and remain relatively stable. One study reported that 4-year-olds who were better at delaying gratification did better in

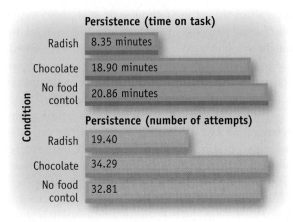

Persistence (time on task)

Condition	
Radish	8.35 minutes
Chocolate	18.90 minutes
No food contol	20.86 minutes

Persistence (number of attempts)

Condition	
Radish	19.40
Chocolate	34.29
No food contol	32.81

Figure 5.14

Persistence on unsolvable puzzles. Participants who were instructed to eat radishes and not to eat chocolate chip cookies or chocolate candy used more self-control resources than participants who were instructed to eat the chocolate and not to touch the radishes or participants in the no-food control group. Because the radish-eaters had relatively few self-control resources to help them persist at a difficult task (unsolvable puzzles), they persisted for the shortest time and made the fewest attempts to solve the puzzles compared to the other two groups. (Adapted from Baumeister et al., 1998)

terms of both academic performance and social competence some ten years later (Mischel, Shoda, & Peake, 1988; Shoda, Mischel, & Peake, 1990). Recent evidence suggests that self-regulation is malleable and can be strengthened like a muscle, which means that with regular "exercise," people can become less vulnerable to ego depletion effects (Baumeister et al., 2006). In this section, we examine self-efficacy, a key aspect of self-regulation, and then discuss self-defeating behavior, a case of self-control failure.

Self-Efficacy

As explained in Chapter 2, *self-efficacy* **refers to one's belief about one's ability to perform behaviors that should lead to expected outcomes.** Self-efficacy represents people's conviction that they can achieve specific goals. According to Albert Bandura (1997, 2000), efficacy beliefs vary according to the person's skills. You may have high self-efficacy when it comes to making friends but low self-efficacy when it comes to speaking in front of a group. However, simply having a skill doesn't guarantee that you will be able to put it into practice. Like the Little Engine That Could, you must also *believe* that you are capable of doing so ("I *think* I can, I *think* I can . . ."). In other words, self-

Courtesy, Albert Bandura

Albert Bandura

efficacy is concerned not with the skills you have, but with your *beliefs about what you can do* with these skills.

Correlates of Self-Efficacy

A number of studies have shown that self-efficacy affects individuals' commitments to goals, their performance on tasks, and their persistence toward goals in the face of obstacles (Maddux & Gosselin, 2003). Self-efficacy is related to health promotion (Bandura, 2004), academic success (Schunk, 2003), career choice (Betz & Klein, 1996), and job performance (Stajkovic & Luthans, 1998). Because of the importance of self-efficacy in psychological adjustment, it is worth keeping in mind that self-efficacy is learned and can be changed. Research shows that increasing self-efficacy is an effective way to improve health (losing weight, stopping smoking) (Maddux & Gosselin, 2003) and to treat a variety of psychological problems, including test anxiety (Smith, 1989), fear of computer use (Wilfong, 2006), phobias (Williams, 1995), fear of sexual assault (Ozer & Bandura, 1990), eating disorders (Goodrick et al., 1999), and substance abuse (DiClemente, Fairhurst, & Piotrowski, 1995), including marijuana dependence (Lozano, Stephens, & Roffman, 2006).

Developing Self-Efficacy

Self-efficacy is obviously a valuable quality. How does one acquire it? Bandura (1997, 2000) identifies four sources of self-efficacy: mastery experiences, vicarious experiences, persuasion/encouragement, and interpretation of emotional arousal.

1. *Mastery experiences.* The most effective path to self-efficacy is through mastering new skills. Sometimes new skills come easily—learning how to use the copy machine in the library, for instance. Some things are harder to master, such as learning how to use a spreadsheet program or how to play the piano. In acquiring more difficult skills, people usually make mistakes. How they handle these failure experiences is the key to learning self-efficacy. If you give up when you make mistakes, your failure instills self-doubts or low self-efficacy. On the other hand, if you persist through failure experiences to eventual success, you learn the lesson of self-efficacy: I *can* do it!

2. *Vicarious experiences.* Another way to improve self-efficacy is by watching others perform a skill you want to learn. It's important that you choose a model who is competent at the task, and it helps if the model is similar to you (in age, gender, and ethnicity). For example, if you're shy about speaking up for yourself, observing someone who is good at doing so can help you develop the confidence to do it yourself. Picking successful role models is important—watching unsuccessful ones can undermine self-efficacy.

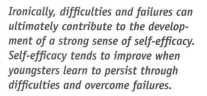

Ironically, difficulties and failures can ultimately contribute to the development of a strong sense of self-efficacy. Self-efficacy tends to improve when youngsters learn to persist through difficulties and overcome failures.

3. *Persuasion and encouragement.* Although it is less effective than the first two approaches, a third way to develop self-efficacy is through the encouragement of others. For example, if you're having a hard time asking someone for a date, a friend's encouragement might give you just the push you need. Of course, persuasion doesn't always work. And, unless encouragement is accompanied by specific and concrete suggestions, this tactic is unlikely to be successful.

4. *Interpretation of emotional arousal.* The physiological responses that accompany feelings and one's interpretations of these responses are another source of self-efficacy. Let's say you're sitting in class waiting for your professor to distribute an exam. You notice that your palms are moist and your heart is pounding. If you attribute these behaviors to fear, you can temporarily dampen your self-efficacy, thus decreasing your chances of doing well. Alternatively, if you attribute your sweaty palms and racing heart to the arousal everyone needs to perform well, you may be able to boost your self-efficacy and increase your chances of doing well. Of course, self-regulation doesn't always succeed. That's the case in self-defeating behavior, our next topic.

Self-Defeating Behavior

People typically act in their own self-interest. But sometimes they knowingly do things that are bad for them—such as smoking, having unprotected sex, and completing important assignments at the last minute. **Self-defeating behaviors are seemingly intentional actions that thwart a person's self-interest.** According to Roy Baumeister (1997; Baumeister & Scher, 1988), there are three categories of intentional self-defeating behaviors: deliberate self-destruction, tradeoffs, and counterproductive strategies. The key difference among these three behaviors lies in how intentional they are. As you can see in **Figure 5.15**, attempts at deliberate self-destruction involve the most intent; counterproductive strategies are the least intentional, and trade-offs fall in between.

In *deliberate self-destruction,* people want to harm themselves and they choose courses of action that will forseeably lead to that result. Although this type of behavior may occur in individuals with psychological disorders, deliberate self-destruction appears to be infrequent in normal populations.

In *tradeoffs,* people foresee the possibility of harming themselves but accept it as a necessary accompaniment to achieving a desirable goal. Overeating, smoking, and drinking to excess are examples that come

Three Categories of Self-Defeating Behavior

Type of self-defeating behavior	Harm foreseen?	Harm desired?
Deliberate self-destruction	Yes	Yes
Tradeoffs	Yes	No
Counterproductive strategies	No	No

Figure 5.15

Three categories of self-defeating behavior. Roy Baumeister and Steven Scher (1988) distinguished three categories of self-defeating behaviors, based on how intentional the behaviors are. Intentionality is determined by two factors: an individual's awareness that a behavior could bring possible harm and an individual's desire to harm himself or herself. Deliberate self-destruction is the most intentional, followed by tradeoffs, then counterproductive strategies. (Based on Baumeister & Scher, 1988)

Self-defeating behaviors come in many forms with many underlying motivations. Overeating is a matter of tradeoffs. People realize that excessive eating may be harmful in the long run, but it is enjoyable at the time.

readily to mind. Other examples include procrastinating (putting off tasks feels good in the short run, but the struggle to meet looming deadlines results in poor performance and increased stress and illness), failing to follow prescribed health care advice (it's easier to slack off now, but doing so leads to future problems), shyness (avoiding social situations protects against anxiety but makes loneliness more likely), and self-handicapping (getting drunk before an exam explains poor performance but increases the chances of failure). People engage in tradeoffs because they bring immediate, positive, and reliable outcomes, not because they want to hurt themselves in the short or the long run.

In *counterproductive strategies,* a person pursues a desirable outcome but misguidedly uses an approach that is bound to fail. Of course, you can't always know in advance if a strategy will pay off. Thus, people must *habitually* use this strategy for it to qualify as self-defeating. For example, some people tend to persist in unproductive endeavors, such as pursuing an unreachable career goal or an unrequited love. People persist in these behaviors because they erroneously believe they'll be successful, not because they are intent on self-defeat.

To conclude, although most people engage in self-defeating behavior at some time, there is little evidence that they deliberately try to harm themselves or to fail at a task. Instead, self-defeating behavior appears to be the result of people's distorted judgments or strong desires to escape from immediate, painful feelings.

Self-Presentation

LEARNING OBJECTIVES
▶ *Explain why and when individuals engage in impression management.*
▶ *Cite some strategies people use to make positive impressions on others.*
▶ *Describe how high self-monitors are different from low self-monitors.*

Whereas your self-concept involves how you see yourself, your public self involves how you want others to see you. **A *public self* is an image presented to others in social interactions.** This presentation of a public self may sound deceitful, but it is perfectly normal, and everyone does it (Schlenker, 2003). Many self-presentations (ritual greetings, for example) take place automatically and without awareness. But when it really counts (job interviews, for example), people consciously strive to make the best possible impression.

Typically, individuals have a number of public selves that are tied to certain situations and certain people. For instance, you may have one public self for your parents and another for your peers. You may have still others for your teachers, your boss, your co-workers, and

so forth. Also, people differ in the degree of overlap or congruence among their various public selves (see **Figure 5.16**). Does it matter whether you perceive yourself to be essentially the same person in different situations? It seems so. People who see themselves as being similar across different social roles (with friends, at work, at school, with parents, with romantic partners) are better adjusted than those who perceive less integration in their self-views across these roles (Donahue et al., 1993; Lutz & Ross, 2003; but see Baird, Le, & Lucas, 2006).

Impression Management

Interestingly, people think others notice and evaluate them more than is the actual case (Gilovich, Kruger, &

Medvec, 2002). This common tendency is aptly termed *the spotlight effect.* People also normally strive to make a positive impression on others to be liked, respected, hired, and so forth (Baumeister & Twenge, 2003). The sociologist Erving Goffman (1959) used the term *face* to describe the idealized image of ourselves we try to create in the minds of others. **Impression management refers to usually conscious efforts by people to influence how others think of them.** To see impression management in operation, let's look at a study of behavior in simulated job interviews (von Baeyer, Sherk, & Zanna, 1981). In this study, female job applicants were led to believe that the man who would interview them held either traditional, chauvinistic views of women or just the opposite. The researchers found that applicants who expected a chauvinist presented themselves in a more traditionally feminine manner than subjects in the other condition. Their self-presentation efforts extended to both their appearance (they wore more makeup) and their communication style (they talked less and gave more traditional answers to a question about marriage and children). In a job interview, people are particularly attentive to making a good impression, but impression management also operates in everyday interactions, although individuals may be less aware of it (Schlenker, 2003). Let's look at some common impression management strategies.

Impression Management Strategies

One reason people engage in impression management is to claim a particular identity (Baumeister, 1998). Thus, you select a type of dress, hairstyle, and manner of speech to present a certain image of yourself. Tattoos and body piercings also create a specific image. A

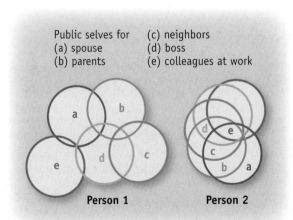

Figure 5.16

Public selves and adjustment. Person 1 has divergent public selves with relatively little overlap among them. Person 2, whose public selves are more congruent with each other, is likely to be better adjusted than Person 1.

second motive for impression management is to gain liking and approval from others—by editing what you say about yourself and by using various nonverbal cues such as smiles, gestures, and eye contact. Because self-presentation is practiced so often, people usually do it automatically. At other times, however, impression management may be used intentionally—to get a job, a date, a promotion, and so forth. Some common self-presentation strategies include ingratiation, self-promotion, exemplification, intimidation, and supplication (Jones, 1990). To this list, we add a rarely recognized strategy, negative acknowledgment.

1. *Ingratiation.* Of all the self-presentation strategies, ingratiation is the most fundamental and most frequently used. **Ingratiation is behaving in ways to make oneself likable to others.** For example, *giving compliments* is effective, as long as you are sincere (people dislike insincerity and can often detect it). *Doing favors for others* is also a common tactic, as long as your gestures aren't so spectacular they leave others feeling indebted (Gordon, 1996). Other ingratiation tactics include *expressing liking for others* and *going along with others* (to get others to like you, it helps to do the things that they want to do).

2. *Self-promotion.* The motive behind self-promotion is earning respect. You do so by playing up your strong points so you will be perceived as competent. For instance, in a job interview, you might find ways to mention that you earned high honors at school and that you were president of the student body and a member of the soccer team. To keep from coming across as a braggart, you shouldn't go overboard with self-promotion. For this reason, false modesty often works well.

3. *Exemplification.* Because most people try to project an honest image, you have to demonstrate exemplary behavior to claim special credit for integrity or character. Occupations fraught with danger, such as those in the military or law enforcement, provide obvious opportunities to exemplify moral virtue. A less dramatic, but still effective, strategy is to behave consistently according to high ethical standards—as long as you don't come across as self-righteous. Also, your words and deeds need to match unless you want to be labeled a hypocrite.

4. *Negative acknowledgment.* Can confessing you've made a relatively minor error motivate people to like you a bit more? Ward and Brenner (2006) found that making negative acknowledgments—candidly admitting to possessing some negative quality—triggered positive responses. In one study, when a hypothetical college student divulged that his high school record was by no means an outstanding one, his grades were judged more favorably than when he did not comment on his academic history. In another study, a speaker from another country was evaluated as having a clearer voice when he pointed out his strong accent than when he failed to do so. Perhaps negative acknowledgment leads people to see one as honest. As long as the quality does not define the person, admitting that one is not perfect, that everyone makes small mistakes, may sometimes be an advantage.

5. *Intimidation.* This strategy sends the message, "Don't mess with me." Intimidation usually works only in nonvoluntary relationships—for instance, when it's hard for workers to find another employer or for an economically dependent spouse to leave a relationship. Obvious intimidation tactics include threats and the withholding of valuable resources (salary increases, promotions, sex). A more subtle tactic is emotional intimidation—holding over a person's head the threat of an aggressive outburst if you don't get your way. The other self-presentation strategies work by creating a favorable impression; intimidation usually generates dislike. Nonetheless, it can work.

6. *Supplication.* This is usually the tactic of last resort. To get favors from others, individuals try to present themselves as weak and dependent—as in the song, "Ain't Too Proud to Beg." Students may plead or break into tears in an instructor's office in an attempt to get a grade changed. Because of the social norm to help those in need, supplication may work; however, unless the supplicator has something to offer the potential benefactor, it's not an effective strategy.

Individuals tailor their use of self-presentation strategies to match the situation. For instance, it's unlikely that you'd try intimidating your boss; you'd be more likely to ingratiate or promote yourself with him or her. As you can see in **Figure 5.17**, all of these strategies carry risks. Thus, to make a good impression, you must use these strategies skillfully.

Perspectives on Impression Management

Curiously, almost all research on self-presentation has been conducted on first meetings between strangers, yet the vast majority of actual social interactions take place between people who already know each other. Noting the gap between reality and research, Dianne Tice and her colleagues (1995) investigated whether self-presentation varied in these two situations. They found that people strive to make positive impressions when they interact with strangers but shift toward modesty and neutral self-presentations when they are with friends. Why the difference? Because strangers don't know you, you want to give them positive information so they'll form a good impression of you. Besides, strangers have no way of knowing whether you are bending the truth. On the other hand, your friends already know your positive qualities. Thus, belaboring them is unnecessary and may make you seem immodest. Likewise, your friends know you well enough to know whether you are grandstanding, so you don't bother. The best approach to managing impressions may be a balanced one. Robinson, Johnson, and Shields (1995) found that people who presented themselves using a mix of self-promoting and self-deprecating comments were viewed as more genuine and likeable than those who relied exclusively on either type of descriptions.

How good are people at discerning the results of their impression management attempts? As we noted earlier, individuals are much better judges of how peo-

Strategic Self-Presentation Strategies

Presentation Strategy	Impression Sought	Emotion to Be Aroused in Target	Negative Impressions Risked
Ingratiation	Likable	Affection	Boot-licker, conformist
Self-promotion	Competent	Respect	Conceited, defensive
Exemplification	Morally superior	Guilt	Hypocrite, sanctimonious
Intimidation	Dangerous	Fear	Blusterer, ineffectual
Supplication	Helpless	Obligation	Undeserving, lazy

Figure 5.17

Strategic self-presentation strategies. Individuals rely on a variety of self-presentation strategies to present a certain image of themselves to others. Five strategies described by Jones (1990) are compared here. A sixth strategy (negative acknowledgment) is also discussed in the text. To avoid the risks associated with the strategies, it's important to use the tactics skillfully. (Based on Jones, 1990)

ple, in general, view them than they are of how specific persons evaluate them.

Self-Monitoring

According to Mark Snyder (1979, 1986; Gangestad & Snyder, 2000), people vary in their awareness of how they are perceived by others. *Self-monitoring* **refers to the degree to which people attend to and control the impressions they make on others.** People who are high self-monitors seem to be very sensitive to their impact on others. Low self-monitors, on the other hand, are less concerned about impression management and behave more spontaneously.

Courtesy, Mark Snyder

Mark Snyder

Compared to low self-monitors, high self-monitors want to make a favorable impression and try to tailor their actions accordingly; they are skilled at deciphering what others want to see. In fact, high self-monitors manage their social relations well, earning status from others by offering them aid while avoiding asking for assistance themselves (Flynn et al., 2006). Because they control their emotions well and deliberately regulate nonverbal signals, they are talented at self-presentation (Gangestad & Snyder, 2000). In contrast, low self-monitors are more likely to express their true beliefs or, possibly, to try to convey the impression that they are sincere and genuine individuals.

As you might infer, these two personality types view themselves differently (Gangestad & Snyder, 2000). Low self-monitors see themselves as having strong principles and behaving in line with them, whereas high self-monitors perceive themselves as flexible and pragmatic. Because high self-monitors don't see a necessary connection between their private beliefs and their public actions, they aren't troubled by discrepancies between beliefs and behavior.

In the upcoming Application, we redirect our attention to the critical issue of self-esteem and outline seven steps for boosting it.

APPLICATION

Building Self-Esteem

LEARNING OBJECTIVES
▶ *Explain when it is inadvisable to increase one's self-esteem and why this is so.*
▶ *List seven ways to build self-esteem.*

Answer the following "yes" or "no."
____ **1.** I worry that others don't like me.
____ **2.** I have very little confidence in my abilities.
____ **3.** I often feel awkward in social situations and just don't know how to take charge.
____ **4.** I have difficulty accepting praise or flattery.
____ **5.** I have a hard time bouncing back from failure experiences.

If you answered "yes" to most of these questions, you may suffer from low self-esteem. As we noted earlier, people with low self-esteem are less happy and more prone to depression, become demoralized after failures, and are anxious in relationships. Moreover, even people with high global self-esteem may have pockets of low self-esteem. For example, you may feel great about your "social self" but not so good about your "academic self." Thus, this Application can be useful to many people.

We have one caveat, however: It is possible for self-esteem to be too high—recall our earlier discussion about narcissism, ego threats, and violence. Better adjustment is associated with realistically high (and stable) self-esteem. Thus, our suggestions are directed to those whose self-esteem could use a legitimate boost, not to those whose self-esteem is inflated. The latter group can benefit from developing more realistic self-views.

As you saw in our discussion of self-efficacy, there is ample evidence that efforts at self-improvement can

Web Link 5.5 **Building Self-Esteem**

The Counseling Center at the University of Florida offers tips on how to build self-esteem and self-confidence at this website.

KEY IDEAS

Self-Concept

▶ The self-concept is composed of a number of beliefs about what one is like, and it is not easily changed. It governs both present and future behavior. Discrepancies between one's ideal self and one's actual or ought self can produce negative emotions and lowered self-esteem. To cope with these negative states, individuals may bring their behavior in line with their ideal selves or blunt their awareness of self-discrepancies.

▶ The self-concept is shaped by several factors, including individuals' observations of their own behavior, which often involve social comparisons with others. Self-observations tend to be biased in a positive direction. In addition, feedback from others shapes the self-concept; this information is also filtered to some extent. Cultural guidelines also affect the way people see themselves. Members of individualistic cultures usually have an independent view of the self, whereas those in collectivist cultures often have an interdependent view of the self.

Self-Esteem

▶ Self-esteem is a person's global evaluation of his or her worth. Like the self-concept, it tends to be stable, but it can fluctuate in response to daily ups and downs.

▶ Compared to those with high self-esteem, individuals with low self-esteem are less happy, are more likely to be depressed, are more prone to giving up after failure, and are less trusting of others.

▶ Narcissistic individuals are prone to aggression when their self-esteem is threatened. Self-esteem develops through interactions with significant others. Self-esteem, ethnicity, and gender interact in complex ways.

Basic Principles of Self-Perception

▶ To avoid being overwhelmed with information, people use automatic processing; for important decisions, they use controlled processing. To explain the causes of their behavior, individuals make self-attributions. Generally, people attribute their behavior to internal or external factors and to stable or unstable factors. Controllability-uncontrollability is another key dimension of self-attributions.

▶ People tend to use either an optimistic explanatory style or a pessimistic explanatory style to understand various events that occur in their lives, and these attributional styles are related to psychological adjustment.

▶ People are guided by four distinct motives in seeking to understand themselves. The self-assessment motive directs people toward accurate feedback about the self. The self-verification motive drives people toward information that matches their current self-views, even though doing so may involve some distortion of reality. The self-improvement motive underlies people's attempts to better themselves. The self-enhancement motive enables people to maintain positive views of themselves.

▶ Common self-enhancement strategies include downward comparisons, the self-serving bias, basking in reflected glory, and self-handicapping.

Self-Regulation

▶ Self-regulation involves setting goals and directing behavior to meet those goals. A key aspect of self-regulation is self-efficacy—an individual's belief that he or she can achieve specific goals. Engaging in self-control can temporarily deplete what appears to be a limited underlying resource. Self-efficacy plays a key role in adjustment and can be learned through mastery experiences, vicarious experiences, persuasion, and positive interpretations of emotional arousal.

▶ Sometimes normal people knowingly do things that are bad for them. These self-defeating actions fall into three categories: deliberate self-destruction, tradeoffs, and counterproductive strategies.

Self-Presentation

▶ Public selves are the various images that individuals project to others. Generally, people try to manage the impressions they make by using a variety of strategies, including ingratiation, self-promotion, negative acknowledgment, exemplification, intimidation, and supplication. High self-monitors seem to be more concerned about making favorable impressions than low self-monitors are.

Application: Building Self-Esteem

▶ The seven building blocks to higher self-esteem are (1) recognize that you control your self-image, (2) learn more about yourself, (3) don't let others set your goals, (4) recognize unrealistic goals, (5) modify negative self-talk, (6) emphasize your strengths, and (7) approach others with a positive outlook.

KEY TERMS

KEY PEOPLE

PRACTICE TEST

1. Which of the following statements about the self-concept is false?
   a. It is composed of one dominant belief about the self.
   b. It is composed of many self-beliefs.
   c. It is relatively stable over time.
   d. It influences present as well as future behavior.

2. Mismatches between one's actual and ought selves result in lower self-esteem and:
   a. dejection-related feelings.
   b. agitation-related feelings.
   c. feelings of self-enhancement.
   d. no particular feelings.

3. A person reared in a collectivist culture is likely to have a(n) _____ self-view, whereas a person reared in an individualistic culture is likely to have a(n) _____ self-view.
   a. self-discrepant; self-consistent
   b. self-consistent; self-discrepant
   c. independent; interdependent
   d. interdependent; independent

4. Low self-esteem is associated with:
   a. happiness.
   b. high trust of others.
   c. self-concept confusion.
   d. recovering after failure experiences.

5. Aggression in response to self-esteem threats is more likely to occur in people who are:
   a. high in self-esteem.
   b. low in self-esteem.
   c. narcissistic.
   d. self-defeating.

6. Which of the following is *not* a basic principle of self-perception?
   a. People are "cognitive spenders."
   b. People's explanatory style is related to adjustment.
   c. People want to receive information that is consistent with their self-views.
   d. People want to maintain positive feelings about the self.

7. Keisha is upset when a textbook is stolen, but she feels better after she hears that a classmate's book bag, including her cell phone, was stolen. This is an example of:
   a. the self-serving bias.
   b. basking in reflected glory.
   c. downward comparison.
   d. self-handicapping.

8. Which of the following statements about self-efficacy is true?
   a. It can be developed by persevering through failure until one achieves success.
   b. It is something that one is born with.
   c. It refers to a person's general self-confidence.
   d. It refers to conscious efforts to make a certain impression on others.

9. The self-presentation strategy of ingratiation involves trying to make others:
   a. respect you.
   b. fear you.
   c. feel sorry for you.
   d. like you.

10. Which of the following will *not* help you build higher self-esteem?
    a. Minimizing negative self-talk
    b. Comparing yourself with those who are the best in a given area
    c. Working to improve yourself
    d. Approaching others with positive expectations

Book Companion Website

Visit the Book Companion Website at **academic.cengage.com/psychology/weiten**, where you will find tutorial quizzes, flash cards, and web links for every chapter, a final exam, and more! You can also link to the Psychology Resource Center (accessible directly at **academic.cengage.com/login**) for a range of psychology-related resources.

Personal Explorations Workbook

The following exercises in your *Personal Explorations Workbook* may enhance your self-understanding in relation to issues raised in this chapter. **Questionnaire 5.1:** Self-Monitoring Scale. **Personal Probe 5.1:** How Does Your Self-Concept Compare to Your Self Ideal? **Personal Probe 5.2:** Examining Your Self Evaluation. **Personal Probe 5.3:** Analyzing Your Emerging Self.

ANSWERS

1. a   Pages 141–142
2. b   Page 143
3. d   Pages 147–148
4. c   Page 148
5. c   Page 151
6. a   Pages 154–158
7. c   Page 158
8. a   Pages 162–163
9. d   Page 165
10. b   Pages 167–169

Social Thinking and Social Influence

You have a new boss at work. Your old boss was let go because of poor performance. The new boss looks very serious. He always wears a white shirt and a conservative tie, and he rarely smiles. Unlike your old boss, who was friendly and joked around a lot, this fellow is very reserved. He rarely even says hello to you when your paths cross in the halls or out in the parking lot. You wonder whether he doesn't like you or just treats everyone that way. Maybe he's just driven by his work. You resolve to ask around the office to see how he acts around your co-workers. You do know that he fired a woman who worked a few doors down the hall. You're not sure why; she seemed nice, always smiling and saying hello. She sure looked like a hard worker. Maybe he thought she was too friendly? The new boss is also not much older than you—in fact, he might be your age. What if he thinks you are not working hard enough? Maybe he feels you should have advanced farther in the company, that you are too nice? Could he be thinking about firing you?

This situation illustrates the process of person perception in everyday life. Everyone asks and answers "why" questions about the people around them. Individuals constantly form impressions to try to make sense of the people they encounter, not only to understand them but also to predict how they will behave. This chapter explores how people form impressions of others, as well as how and why such judgments can be incorrect. Our consideration of social cognition then broadens to examine the problems posed by prejudice. We then look at how others try to influence our beliefs and behavior. To do so, we explore the power of persuasive messages and the social pressures to conform and obey. As you will learn, social thinking and social influence play important roles in personal adjustment.

Forming Impressions of Others

LEARNING OBJECTIVES

▶ Cite the five sources of information people use to form impressions of others.

▶ Describe the key differences between snap judgments and systematic judgments.

▶ Define attributions and explain when people are likely to make them.

▶ Describe two expectancies that can distort observer's perceptions.

▶ Describe four important cognitive distortions and how they operate.

▶ Describe some ways in which the process of creating perceptions of others is efficient, selective, and consistent.

Do you recall the first time you met your roommate? She seemed friendly but a little shy, and perhaps a bit on the neat side, so much so that you wondered whether you two would get along. You like things less structured; not messy, but decidedly lived-in or comfortable. You were worried that you'd have to change your ways, straightening up your space all the time. Happily, once you got to know her better, she warmed up to you and your clutter—now you are close friends. As people interact with others, they constantly engage in *person perception,* **the process of forming impressions of others.** Because impression formation is usually such an easy and automatic process, people are unaware that it is taking place. Nonetheless, the process is a complex one. Let's review some of its essential aspects.

Key Sources of Information

Because you can't read other people's minds, you are dependent on *observations* of others to determine what they are like. In forming impressions of others, people rely on five key sources of observational information: appearance, verbal behavior, actions, nonverbal messages, and situational cues.

1. *Appearance.* Despite the admonition, "You can't judge a book by its cover," people frequently do exactly that. Physical features such as height, weight, skin color, and hair color are some of the cues used to "read" other people. Regardless of their accuracy, beliefs about physical features are used to form impressions of others (Hellström & Tekle, 1994). For example, Americans learn to associate the wearing of eyeglasses with studiousness. Style of dress, clothing or jewelry that designates religious beliefs, body piercings, and tattoos also provide clues about others. Failing to dress appro-

priately for a job interview can reduce the chances of being hired (Turner-Bowker, 2001).

2. *Verbal behavior.* Another obvious source of information about others is what they say. People form impressions based on what and how much others self-disclose, how often they give advice and ask questions, and how judgmental they are (Berry et al., 1997). If Tanisha speaks negatively about most of the people she knows, you will probably conclude that she is a critical person.

3. *Actions.* Because people don't always tell the truth, you have to rely on their behavior to provide insights about them. For instance, when you learn that Jamal volunteers five hours a week at the local homeless shelter, you are likely to infer that he is a caring person. In impression formation, actions speak louder than words.

4. *Nonverbal messages.* Another key source of information about others is nonverbal communication: facial expressions, eye contact, body language, and gestures (DePaulo & Friedman, 1998; Forrest & Feldman, 2000; Frank & Ekman, 1997). These nonverbal cues provide information about people's emotional states and dispositions. For example, in our culture a bright smile and good eye contact signal friendliness and openness. Also, because people know that verbal behavior is easily manipulated, they often rely on nonverbal cues to determine the truth of what others say (Frank & Ekman, 1997).

5. *Situations.* The setting in which behavior occurs provides crucial information about how to interpret a person's behavior (Ross & Nisbett, 1991; Trope & Gaunt, 2003). For instance, without situational cues (such as being at a wedding versus a funeral), it would be hard to know whether a person crying was happy or sad.

In forming impressions of others, people rely on cues such as appearance, actions, and verbal and nonverbal messages, as well as the nature of the situation.

When it comes to drawing inferences about people, one bad piece of information can outweigh or undo a collection of positive characteristics. Social psychological research repeatedly demonstrates that the presence of a trait perceived to be negative (e.g., "untrustworthy") can have more influence on forming people's impressions than several positive qualities ("warm," "open," "friendly," "clever") (Skowronski & Carlston, 1989; Vonk, 1993). When an immoral act is performed, other good or virtuous behaviors cannot undo the damage to people's perceptions of the offender's character (Riskey & Birnbaum, 1974). In fact, a single bad deed can eliminate a good reputation, but one good deed cannot redeem an otherwise bad standing in the eyes of others (Skowronski & Carlston, 1992). Thus, in the realm of person perception *bad tends to be stronger than good.*

Snap Judgments Versus Systematic Judgments

In their interactions with others, people are bombarded with more information than they can possibly handle. To avoid being overwhelmed, they rely on alternative ways to process information. *Snap judgments* about others are those made quickly and based on only a few bits of information and preconceived notions. Thus, they may not be particularly accurate. Nevertheless, people can get by with superficial assessments of others quite often. As Susan Fiske (2004) puts it, "good-enough accuracy in forming impressions allows us to navigate our social seas and not collide or run aground too often" (p. 132). Often, interactions with others are so fleeting or inconsequential that it makes

Susan Fiske

little difference that such judgments are imprecise. Does it really matter that you mistakenly infer that the blonde postal clerk is a fun-loving person, or that your bespectacled restaurant server is an intellectual? You may never interact with them again, and even if you do, your interactions are not likely to be significant to either of you.

On the other hand, when it comes to selecting a friend, a mate, a boss, or an employee, it's essential that your impressions be as accurate as possible. Thus, it's not surprising that people are motivated to take more care in these assessments. In forming impressions of those who can affect their welfare and happiness, people make *systematic judgments* rather than snap decisions (see **Figure 6.1**). That is, they take the time to observe the person in a variety of situations and to compare that person's behavior with that of others in similar situations.

In assessing what a significant individual is like, people are particularly interested in learning why the person behaves in a certain way. This deeper level of understanding is vital if one is to make accurate predictions about the person's future behavior. After all, when you're choosing a partner for an important group project, you want to choose the right person so that you don't end up doing all the work yourself. How do people make such decisions? What information do they consider? To determine the cause of others' behavior, people engage in the process of causal attribution.

Attributions

As we have noted in earlier chapters, **attributions are inferences that people draw about the causes of their own behavior, others' behavior, and events.** In Chapter 5, we focused on self-attributions. Here, we'll apply attribution theory to the behavior of *other people*. For example, suppose that your boss bawls you out for

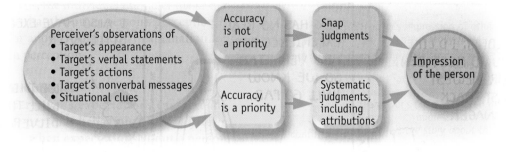

Figure 6.1

The process of person perception. In forming impressions of others, perceivers rely on various sources of observational information. When it's important to form accurate impressions of others, people are motivated to make systematic judgments, including attributions. When accuracy isn't a priority, people make snap judgments about others.

Adapted from Brehm, S. S., & Kassin, S. M. (1993) *Social psychology*. Boston: Houghton Mifflin. Copyright © 1993 by Houghton Mifflin Company. Adapted with permission.

doing a sloppy job on an insignificant project. To what do you attribute this tongue lashing? Was your work really that bad? Is your boss just in a grouchy mood? Is your boss under too much pressure?

In Chapter 5, we noted that attributions have three key dimensions: internal versus external, stable versus unstable, and controllable versus uncontrollable (Jones & Davis, 1965; Kelley, 1950; Weiner, 1974). For this discussion, we focus only on the internal/external dimension (Heider, 1958). When people ascribe the causes of someone's behavior to personal dispositions, traits, abilities, or feelings, they are making *internal* attributions. When they impute the causes of their behavior to situational demands and environmental constraints, they are making *external* attributions. For example, if a friend's business fails, you might attribute the failure to your friend's lack of business skills (an internal factor) or to negative trends in the economy (an external factor).

The types of attributions people make about others can have a tremendous impact on everyday social interactions. For example, blaming a friend's business failure on poor business "smarts" rather than on a poor economy will obviously affect how you view your friend—not to mention whether you'll lend her money! In fact, there is evidence that spouses' attributions for each other's behavior can affect their marital satisfaction (Fletcher & Thomas, 2000; Karney & Bradbury 2000).

Obviously, people don't make attributions about every person they meet. Research suggests that people are relatively selective in this process (Jones, 1990; Malle, 2004; Malle & Knobe, 1997). It seems that people are most likely to make attributions (1) when others behave in unexpected or negative ways, (2) when events are personally relevant, and (3) when they are suspicious about another person's motives. For example, if Serena laughs loudly at the local student hangout, no one bats an eye. But if she does so in the middle of a serious

lecture, it raises eyebrows and generates speculation about why she behaved this way.

Some aspects of the attribution process are logical (Trope & Gaunt, 2003). Nonetheless, research also shows that the process of person perception is sometimes illogical and unsystematic, as in the case of snap judgments. Other sources of error also creep into the process, a topic we take up next.

Perceiver Expectations

Remember Evan, that bully from the fourth grade? He made your life miserable—constantly looking for opportunities to poke fun at you and beat you up. Now when you meet someone named Evan, your initial reaction is negative, and it takes a while to warm up to him (Andersen & Chen, 2002). Why? Your negative past experiences with an Evan have led you to expect the worst, whether or not it's warranted (Andersen, Reznik, & Manzella, 1996). This is just one example of how *perceiver expectations* can influence the perception of others. Let's look at two of the principles governing perceiver expectations: confirmation bias and self-fulfilling prophecy.

Confirmation Bias

Shortly after you begin interacting with someone, you start forming hypotheses about what the person is like. In turn, these hypotheses can influence your behavior toward that person in such a way as to confirm your ex-

---

Web Link 6.1 **Social Psychology Network**

Wesleyan University social psychologist Scott Plous offers a broad collection of more than 5,000 web links related to all aspects of social and general psychology, including how people understand and influence each other interpersonally.

Selectivity

The old saying that "people see what they expect to see" has been confirmed repeatedly by social scientists. In a classic study, Harold Kelley (1950) showed how a person is preceded by his or her reputation. Students in a class at the Massachusetts Institute of Technology were told that a new lecturer would be speaking to them that day. Before the instructor arrived, the students were given a short description of him, with one important variation. Half the students were led to expect a "warm" person, while the other half were led to expect a "cold" one (see **Figure 6.6**). All the participants were exposed to exactly the same 20 minutes of lecture and interaction with the new instructor. However, those who were led to expect a warm person rated the instructor as significantly more considerate, sociable, humorous, good-natured, informal, and humane than those who were led to expect a cold person.

Consistency

How many times did your parents remind you to be on your best behavior when you were meeting someone for the first time? As it turns out, they were onto something! Considerable research supports the idea that first impressions are powerful (Asch, 1956; Belmore, 1987). **A *primacy effect* occurs when initial information carries more weight than subsequent information.** We risk being labeled a hypocrite, for example, if we say one thing and then do another (such as claiming to have an open mind and then make a cutting, judgmental remark about someone) rather than the reverse (Barden, Rucker, & Petty, 2005). Initial negative impressions may be especially hard to change (Mellers, Richards, & Birnbaum, 1992). Thus, getting off on the wrong foot may be particularly damaging. As noted earlier in this chapter, negative information can outweigh positive factors; bad can indeed be stronger than good. Only if people are motivated to form an accurate impression and are not tired will they be less likely to lock in their initial impressions (Webster, Richter, & Kruglanski, 1996).

Mr. Blank is a graduate student in the Department of Economics and Social Science here at M.I.T. He has had three semesters of teaching experience in psychology at another college. This is his first semester teaching Ec. 70. He is 26 years old, a veteran, and married. People who know him consider him to be a rather cold person, industrious, critical, practical, and determined.	Mr. Blank is a graduate student in the Department of Economics and Social Science here at M.I.T. He has had three semesters of teaching experience in psychology at another college. This is his first semester teaching Ec. 70. He is 26 years old, a veteran, and married. People who know him consider him to be a very warm person, industrious, critical, practical, and determined.

Figure 6.6

Descriptions of the guest lecturer in Kelley's (1950) study. These two descriptions, provided to two groups of students before the lecturer spoke, differ by only an adjective. But this seemingly small difference caused the two groups to form altogether different perceptions of the lecturer.

Why are primacy effects so potent? Because people find comfort in cognitive *consistency;* cognitions that contradict each other tend to create tension and discomfort. This principle applies to people's perceptions of others. Hence, once people believe that they have formed an accurate picture of someone, they tend to tune out or discount subsequent information that seems to contradict that picture (Belmore, 1987). It is not impossible to override an initial impression, but the built-in preference for consistency makes it more difficult than most people realize.

To conclude, although the process of person perception is highly subjective, people are relatively accurate perceivers of others (Fiske, 1998). Even when misperceptions occur, they are often harmless. However, there clearly are occasions when such inaccuracies are problematic. This is certainly true in the case of prejudice, which we consider next.

The Problem of Prejudice

LEARNING OBJECTIVES
▶ *Explain how "old-fashioned" and modern discrimination differ.*
▶ *Describe some of the key determinants of prejudice, and explain how they work.*
▶ *Describe the operation of several strategies for reducing prejudice.*

The terrorist attacks of September 11, 2001 were an extreme demonstration of the destructive power of prejudice—hatred of one group by another. Unfortunately, antagonism between groups continues to be a problem, both on the international scene and at home. For example, after the September 11 attacks, hate crimes increased against Americans presumed to be Muslims or Arabs. Why is it so hard for members of different groups to get along?

Let's begin our discussion by clarifying a couple of terms that are often confused. ***Prejudice* is a negative attitude toward members of a group;** *discrimination*

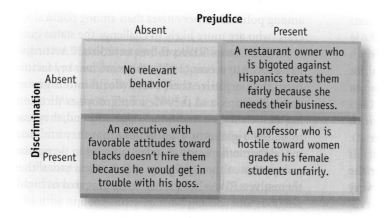

Prejudice

	Absent	Present
Absent	No relevant behavior	A restaurant owner who is bigoted against Hispanics treats them fairly because she needs their business.
Present	An executive with favorable attitudes toward blacks doesn't hire them because he would get in trouble with his boss.	A professor who is hostile toward women grades his female students unfairly.

(Discrimination — rows; Prejudice — columns)

Figure 6.7

Prejudice and discrimination. Prejudice and discrimination are highly correlated, but they don't necessarily go hand in hand. As the examples in the blue cells show, there can be prejudice without discrimination and discrimination without prejudice.

involves behaving differently, usually unfairly, toward the members of a group. Prejudice and discrimination do tend to go together, but that is not always the case (see **Figure 6.7**). One classic social psychology study found almost no discriminatory behavior aimed at a Chinese couple traveling around the country with a white professor in the 1930s. Before making the trips, the professor anticipated that they would encounter some prejudice about where they could stay or dine, but they were only declined service a few times. When the professor wrote to all the establishments they visited months later to ask whether Chinese guests were welcome, however, the majority of the responses were, in fact, prejudiced and rather uninviting, showing that attitudes don't always predict behavior (LaPiere, 1934). Why can people respond in discriminatory ways sometimes but not always? It is possible that a restaurant owner would be prejudiced against Chicanos and yet treat them like anyone else because he needed their business. This is an example of prejudice without discrimination. Although it is probably less common, discrimination without prejudice may also occur. For example, an executive who has favorable attitudes toward blacks may not hire them because he thinks his boss would be upset.

"Old-Fashioned" Versus Modern Discrimination

Over the past 40 years, prejudice and discrimination against minority groups have diminished in the United States. Racial segregation is no longer legal, and discrimination based on race, ethnicity, gender, and religion is much less common than it was in the 1950s and 1960s. Thus, the good news is that overt, or *"old-fashioned," discrimination* against minority groups has

declined. The bad news is that a more subtle form of prejudice and discrimination has emerged (Dovidio & Gaertner, 1996; Gaertner & Dovidio, 1986). That is, people may privately harbor racist or sexist attitudes but express them only when they feel that such views are justified or that it's safe to do so. This new phenomenon has been termed *modern discrimination* (also called "modern racism"). Modern discrimination is also operating when people endorse equality as an abstract principle but oppose concrete programs intended to promote equality on the grounds that discrimination against minority groups no longer exists (Wright & Taylor, 2003). In **Figure 6.8**, you can see the kinds of items used to measure old-fashioned and modern sexism.

While modern racists do not wish to return to the days of segregation, they also feel that minority groups should not push too fast for advancement or receive special treatment by the government. Individuals who endorse statements that favor "modern" discrimination ("Blacks are getting too demanding in their push for equal rights") are much

---

Items Related to Old-Fashioned Sexism

1. Women are generally not as smart as men.
2. It is more important to encourage boys than to encourage girls to participate in athletics.

Items Related to Modern Sexism

1. Discrimination against women is no longer a problem in the United States.
2. Over the past few years, the government and news media have been showing more concern about the treatment of women than is warranted by women's actual experiences.

Scoring: Possible responses to the statements range from "strongly agree" to "strongly disagree." Individuals who moderately or strongly agree with the above items reflect old-fashioned or modern sexism, respectively.

Figure 6.8

Measuring old-fashioned and modern sexism. Research shows similarities between old-fashioned and modern beliefs about both racism and sexism. Janet Swim and colleagues (1995) have developed a scale to measure the presence of both types of sexism. Four items from the 13-item scale are shown here. Old-fashioned sexism is characterized by endorsement of traditional gender roles and acceptance of stereotypes that portray females as less competent than males. In contrast, subtle, modern sexism is characterized by denial of continued discrimination and rejection of policies intended to help women.

From Swim, J. K., Aikin, K. J., Hall, W. S., & Hunter, B. A. (1995). Sexism and racism: Old-fashioned and modern prejudices. *Journal of Personality and Social Psychology, 68*, 199–214. Copyright © 1995 American Psychological Association. Adapted by permission of the publisher and author.

port for intergroup contact that meets these conditions as a means of reducing prejudice (Pettigrew & Tropp, 2000, 2006).

The "jigsaw classroom" uses these principles to reduce prejudice in schoolchildren (Aronson & Patnoe, 1997). In this intervention, six children are first assigned to an "expert group" in which they help each other learn specialized information prepared by the teacher about a study topic. Thus, each child becomes an "expert" on a subtopic. Then the children are assigned to ethnically mixed groups of six where they teach each other their school lessons. This arrangement puts all children on an equal footing (equal-status contact) and reduces competition for the teacher's attention and grades (scarce resources).

Children taught in a jigsaw classroom learn as much as peers taught in a traditional classroom setting. In addition, "jigsaw" children get an important bonus: Prejudice is replaced with positive feelings for ethnically different children, and the self-esteem of minority kids gets a big boost. The jigsaw concept may have broader societal applications, as well. Elliot Aronson, the social psychologist who pioneered the jigsaw classroom, suggests that the concept can be used to prevent violence in schools, even that rising to the horrific level of the Columbine massacre (Aronson, 2001).

To conclude, although prejudice remains a complex and distressing social problem, a number of effective strategies are available to combat it.

The Power of Persuasion

LEARNING OBJECTIVES

▶ Cite the key elements in the persuasion process.
▶ Describe several source factors that influence persuasion.
▶ Discuss the evidence on one-sided versus two-sided messages and the value of arousing fear or positive feelings in persuasion.

▶ Describe several receiver factors that influence persuasion.
▶ Explain how the two cognitive routes to persuasion operate.

Every day you are bombarded by attempts to alter your attitudes through persuasion. You may not even be out of bed before you start hearing radio advertisements that are meant to persuade you to buy specific toothpastes, cell phones, and athletic shoes. When you watch the morning news, you hear statements from numerous government officials, all of which have been carefully crafted to shape your opinions. On your way to school, you see billboards showing attractive models draped over cars in the hopes that they can induce positive feelings that will transfer to the vehicles. Walking to class, a friend tries to get you to vote for his candidate for student body president. "Does it ever let up?" you wonder.

When it comes to persuasion, the answer is "no." As Anthony Pratkanis and Elliot Aronson (2000) note, Americans live in the "age of propaganda." In light of this reality, let's examine some of the factors that determine whether persuasion works.

Persuasion involves the communication of arguments and information intended to change another person's attitudes. What are attitudes? For the purposes of our discussion, we'll define *attitudes* as beliefs and feelings about people, objects, and ideas. Let's look more closely at two of the terms in this definition. We use the term *beliefs* to mean thoughts and judgments about people, objects, and ideas. For example, you may *believe* that equal pay for equal work is a fair policy or that capital punishment is not an effective deterrent to

crime. The "feeling" component of attitudes refers to the positivity and negativity of one's feelings about an issue as well as how strongly one feels about it. For example, you may *strongly favor* equal pay for equal work but only *mildly disagree* with the idea that capital punishment reduces the crime rate. Psychologists assume that attitudes predict behavior—if you are favorably disposed toward some new product, you are likely to buy it; if not, you won't (Eagly & Chaiken, 1998). Of course, there is more to the persuasion side of the attitude-behavior relation: Read on.

The Elements of the Persuasion Process

The process of persuasion includes four basic elements (see **Figure 6.11**). The *source* is the person who sends a communication, and the *receiver* is the person to whom the message is sent. Thus, if you watched a presidential address on TV, the president would be the source, and you and millions of other viewers would be the receivers in this persuasive effort. The *message* is the information transmitted by the source; the *channel* is the medium through which the message is sent. In examining communication channels, investigators have often compared face-to-face interaction against appeals sent via mass media (such as television and radio). Although the research on communication channels is interesting, we'll confine our discussion to source, message, and receiver variables.

Source Factors

Persuasion tends to be more successful when the source has high *credibility* (Petty, Wegener, & Fabrigar, 1997). Two subfactors make a communicator credible: expertise and trustworthiness. People try to convey their *expertise* by mentioning their degrees, their training, and their experience, or by showing an impressive grasp of the issue at hand (Wood & Kallgren, 1988). As to *trustworthiness*, whom would you believe if you were told that your state needs to reduce corporate taxes to stimulate its economy—the president of a huge corporation in your state or an economics professor from out of state? Probably the latter. Trustworthiness is undermined when a source, such as the corporation president, appears to have something to gain. In contrast, trustworthiness is enhanced when people appear to argue against their own interests (Petty et al., 2001). This effect explains why salespeople often make remarks like "Frankly, my snowblower isn't the best and they have a better brand down the street if you're willing to spend a bit more . . ."

Likability is a second major source factor and includes a number of subfactors (Petty et al., 1997). A key consideration is a person's *physical attractiveness* (Petty et al., 1997). For example, one researcher found that attractive students were more successful than less attractive students in obtaining signatures for a petition (Chaiken, 1979). People also respond better to sources who are *similar* to them in ways that are relevant to the issue at hand (Mackie, Worth, & Asuncion, 1990). Thus, politicians stress the values they and their constituents hold in common.

Source variables are used to great effect in advertising. Many companies spend a fortune to obtain a spokesperson such as George Foreman, who combines trustworthiness, likability, and a knack for connecting with the average person. Companies quickly abandon spokespersons whose likability declines. For example, McDonald's and Sprite cancelled advertising contracts with basketball star Kobe Bryant after he was accused of rape. On the other hand, sometimes celebrities whose careers are in trouble can be used: Kevin Federline, who was married to pop-singer Britney Spears, was portrayed in a 2007 Super Bowl commercial as having to deal with his decline in popularity by taking a job in a fast food restaurant. Federline was shown flipping burgers in the ad, which quickly caused a controversy because viewers presumed he was poking fun at the lives and livelihoods of food service workers. Federline apologized,

Figure 6.11

Overview of the persuasion process. The process of persuasion essentially boils down to *who* (the source) communicates *what* (the message) *by what means* (the channel) *to whom* (the receiver). Thus, four sets of variables influence the process of persuasion: source, message, channel, and receiver factors. The diagram lists some of the more important factors in each category (including some that are not discussed in the text due to space limitations).

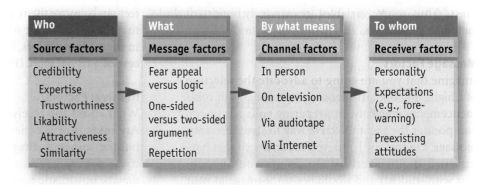

Who	What	By what means	To whom
Source factors	**Message factors**	**Channel factors**	**Receiver factors**
Credibility	Fear appeal versus logic	In person	Personality
Expertise		On television	Expectations (e.g., forewarning)
Trustworthiness	One-sided versus two-sided argument	Via audiotape	
Likability		Via Internet	Preexisting attitudes
Attractiveness	Repetition		
Similarity			

Forming Impressions of Others

▶ In forming impressions of other people, individuals rely on appearance, verbal behavior, actions, nonverbal messages, and situational cues. Individuals usually make snap judgments about others unless accurate impressions are important. To explain the causes of other people's behavior, individuals make attributions (either internal or external).

▶ People often try to confirm their expectations about what others are like, which can result in biased impressions. Self-fulfilling prophecies can actually change a target person's behavior in the direction of a perceiver's expectations. Cognitive distortions are caused by categorizing, stereotyping, the fundamental attribution error, and defensive attributions. The process of person perception is characterized by the themes of efficiency, selectivity, and consistency.

The Problem of Prejudice

▶ Prejudice is a particularly unfortunate outcome of the tendency to view others inaccurately. Blatant ("old-fashioned") discrimination occurs relatively infrequently today, but subtle expressions of prejudice and discrimination ("modern discrimination") have become more common.

▶ Common causes of prejudice include right-wing authoritarianism, cognitive distortions, competition between groups, and threats to social identity. Strategies for reducing prejudice are rooted in social thinking and collaborative intergroup contact.

The Power of Persuasion

▶ The success of persuasive efforts depends on several factors. A source of persuasion who is expert, trustworthy, likable, physically attractive, and similar to the receiver tends to be relatively effective. Although there are some limitations, two-sided arguments, arousal of fear, and generation of positive feelings are effective elements in persuasive messages. Persuasion is undermined when receivers are forewarned or have beliefs that are incompatible with the position being advocated.

▶ Persuasion takes place via two processes. The central route to persuasion requires a receiver to be motivated to process persuasive messages carefully (elaboration). A favorable reaction to such an evaluation will result in positive attitude change. When a receiver is unmotivated or unable to process persuasive messages carefully, persuasion may take place via the peripheral route (on the basis of simple cues such as a catchy tune).

The Power of Social Pressure

▶ Asch found that subjects often conform to the group, even when the group reports inaccurate judgments. Asch's experiments may have produced public compliance while subjects' private beliefs remained unchanged. Both normative and informational influence can produce conformity. Being mindful of social pressures and getting support from others with similar views are ways to resist conformity pressures.

▶ In Milgram's landmark study of obedience to authority, subjects showed a remarkable tendency to follow orders to shock an innocent stranger. Milgram's findings highlight the influence of situational pressures on behavior. Although people often obey authority figures, sometimes they are disobedient, usually because they have social support.

Application: Seeing Through Compliance Tactics

▶ Although they work for different reasons, all compliance tactics have the same goal: getting people to agree to requests. The foot-in-the-door and the lowball technique are based on the principle of consistency, while the door-in-the-face technique and the tactic of offering "giveaway" items rely on the principle of reciprocity. When advertisers suggest that products are in short supply, they are using the scarcity principle. Understanding these strategies can make you less vulnerable to manipulation.

Attitudes   p. 188
Attributions   p. 174
Bystander effect   p. 195
Channel   p. 188
Compliance   p. 194
Confirmation bias   p. 176
Conformity   p. 192
Defensive attribution   p. 180
Discrimination   pp. 182–183
Door-in-the-face
   technique   p. 200
Elaboration likelihood
   model   p. 191
Foot-in-the-door
   technique   p. 198
Fundamental attribution
   error   p. 179

Informational
   influence   p. 194
Lowball technique   p. 199
Message   p. 188
Need for cognition p. 191
Normative influence   p. 194
Obedience   p. 195
Person perception   p. 173
Persuasion   p. 188
Prejudice   p. 182
Primacy effect   p. 182
Receiver   p. 188
Reciprocity principle   p. 199
Self-fulfilling
   prophecy   p. 177
Source   p. 188
Stereotypes   p. 178

Solomon Asch   pp. 192–194
Robert Cialdini   pp. 193,
   198–201
Susan Fiske   p. 174
Stanley Milgram
   pp. 195–197

Richard Petty and
   John Cacioppo
   pp. 191–192
Muzafer Sherif   p. 186

1. Mindfulness operates when people:
   a. make snap judgments.
   b. are on "cognitive automatic pilot."
   c. make systematic judgments.
   d. are not concerned about forming accurate impressions.

2. Which of the following is *not* a type of cognitive distortion in perception?
   a. Categorizing
   b. The bystander effect
   c. Stereotypes
   d. Defensive attribution

3. Which of the following is *not* a theme in person perception?
   a. Efficiency
   b. Selectivity
   c. Consistency
   d. Mindfulness

4. "Old-fashioned" discrimination is _____; modern discrimination is _____.
   a. blatant; subtle
   b. legal; illegal
   c. common; rare
   d. race-based; gender-based

5. Which of the following is a cause of prejudice?
   a. Mindfulness
   b. Right-wing authoritarianism
   c. Jigsaw classrooms
   d. Activities based on superordinate goals

6. Receivers who are forewarned that someone will try to persuade them will most likely
   a. be very open to persuasion.
   b. get up and stomp out of the room.
   c. not be very open to persuasion.
   d. heckle the persuader.

7. Compared to attitudes formed via the peripheral route, those formed via the central route
   a. operate subliminally.
   b. are hard to change.
   c. last only a short time.
   d. are poor predictors of behavior.

8. When people change their outward behavior but not their private beliefs, _____ is operating.
   a. conformity
   b. persuasion
   c. obedience
   d. compliance

9. The results of Milgram's (1963) study imply that:
   a. situational factors can exert tremendous influence over behavior.
   b. in the real world, most people resist pressures to act in harmful ways.
   c. most people are willing to give obviously wrong answers on rigged perceptual tasks.
   d. disobedience is far more common than obedience.

10. When charities send prospective donors free address labels and the like, which of the following social influence principles are they using?
    a. The consistency principle
    b. The scarcity principle
    c. The reciprocity principle
    d. The foot-in-the-door principle

Book Companion Website

Visit the Book Companion Website at **academic.cengage.com/psychology/weiten**, where you will find tutorial quizzes, flash cards, and web links for every chapter, a final exam, and more! You can also link to the Psychology Resource Center (accessible directly at **academic.cengage.com/login**) for a range of psychology-related resources.

Personal Explorations Workbook

The following exercises in your *Personal Explorations Workbook* may enhance your self-understanding in relation to issues raised in this chapter. **Questionnaire 6.1:** Argumentativeness Scale. **Personal Probe 6.1:** Can You Identify Your Prejudicial Stereotypes? **Personal Probe 6.2:** How Do You Operate in a Group?

ANSWERS

1. c Page 174
2. b Pages 177–180
3. d Pages 181–182
4. a Pages 183–184
5. b Page 184
6. c Page 191
7. b Page 192
8. d Page 194
9. a Page 197
10. c Page 199

CHAPTER 7

Interpersonal Communication

"Why don't you wear your new tie?" Robin suggests to Brian, as they are dressing to go out. "There you go again, telling me what to wear!" Brian retorts. To which Robin zings back with, "Oh, wear whatever you want. I don't care if you want to look like you're colorblind!" Could this couple have side-stepped the bad feelings and fight that are brewing? You bet! The keys to managing such encounters are recognizing the pitfalls of interpersonal communication and honing one's skills to deal effectively with them—two things you'll learn about in this chapter.

Communication skills are highly relevant to adjustment because they can be critical to happiness and success in life. In this chapter, we begin with an overview of the communication process and then turn to the important topic of nonverbal communication. Next, we discuss ways to communicate more effectively and examine common communication problems. Finally, we look at interpersonal conflict, including constructive ways to deal with it. In the Application, we consider ways to develop an assertive communication style.

The Process of Interpersonal Communication

LEARNING OBJECTIVES

▶ *List and explain the six components of the communication process.*

▶ *List several important differences between face-to-face and electronically mediated communication.*

▶ *Discuss how interpersonal communication is important to adjustment.*

Communication can be defined as the process of sending and receiving messages that have meaning. Your personal thoughts have meaning, of course, but when you "talk to yourself," you are engaging in *intra*personal communication. In this chapter, we will focus on *inter*personal communication—the transmission of meaning between two or more people. For the most part, we'll concentrate on two-person interactions.

We define **interpersonal communication as an interactional process in which one person sends a message to another.** Note several points about this definition. First, for communication to qualify as *interpersonal,* at least two people must be involved. Second, interpersonal communication is a *process.* By this, we simply mean that it usually involves a series of actions: Kelli talks/Jason listens, Jason responds/Kelli listens, and so on. Third, this process is *interactional.* Communication is generally not a one-way street: Both participants send as well as receive information when they're interacting. A key implication of this fact is that you need to pay attention to both *speaking* and *listening* if you want to be an effective communicator.

Components of the Communication Process

Let's take a look at the essential components of the interpersonal communication process. The key elements are (1) the sender, (2) the receiver, (3) the message, (4) the channel through which the message is sent, (5) noise or interference, and (6) the context in which the message is communicated. As we describe these components, refer to **Figure 7.1** to see how they work together.

The *sender* is the person who initiates the message. In a typical two-way conversation, both people serve as senders (as well as receivers). Keep in mind that each person brings a unique set of expectations and understandings to each communication situation. The *receiver* is the person to whom the message is targeted.

The *message* refers to the information or meaning that is transmitted from the sender to the receiver. The message is the *content* of the communication—that is, the ideas and feelings conveyed to another person. Two important cognitive processes

underlie the transmission of messages: Speakers *encode* or transform their ideas and feelings into symbols and organize them into a message; receivers *decode* or translate a speaker's message into their own ideas and feelings (see **Figure 7.1**). Generally, fluent speakers of a language are unaware of these processes. If you've ever learned a new language, however, you have consciously experienced encoding (groping for the right word to express an idea) and decoding (trying to discover a word's meaning by how it is used).

The primary means of sending messages is language, but people also communicate to others nonverbally, through the facial expressions, gestures, and vocal inflections used to supplement (and sometimes entirely change) the meaning of verbal messages. For example, when you say, "Thanks a lot," your inflection can convey either sincere gratitude or heavy sarcasm.

The *channel* refers to the sensory channel through which the message reaches the receiver. Typically, people receive information from multiple channels simultaneously. They not only hear what the other person says, they also see the person's facial expressions, observe his or her gestures, experience eye contact, and sometimes feel the person's touch. Note that the messages in the various channels may be consistent or

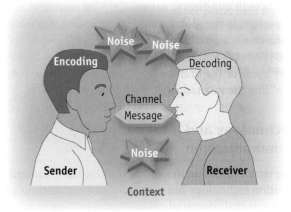

Figure 7.1

A model of interpersonal communication. Interpersonal communication involves six elements: the sender, the receiver, the message, the channel through which the message is transmitted, distorting noise, and the context in which the message is sent. In conversations, both participants function as sender and receiver.

After you've learned a little about another person, you may want to move the relationship to a deeper level. This is where self-disclosure comes into play, the topic we'll address next.

Self-Disclosure

Self-disclosure **is the act of sharing information about yourself with another person.** In other words, self-disclosure involves opening up about yourself to others. The information you share doesn't have to be a deep, dark secret, but it may be. Conversations with strangers and acquaintances typically start with superficial self-disclosure—your opinion of the TV show you saw last night or your views on who will win the World Series. Typically, only when people have come to like and trust each other do they begin to share private information—such as self-consciousness about one's weight, or jealousy of one's brother (Greene, Derlega, & Mathews, 2006). **Figure 7.10** illustrates how self-disclosure varies according to type of relationship.

In discussing self-disclosure, we will focus on verbal communication. But keep in mind that *non*verbal communication plays an equally important role in self-disclosure (Laurenceau & Kleinman, 2006). For example, you have already seen how nonverbal cues can support or completely change the meaning of the words they accompany. Also, nonverbal behaviors can determine whether interactions have positive, neutral, or negative outcomes. Thus, if you tell a friend about a very distressing experience and she signals her concern via sympathtic nonverbal cues (eye contact, leaning forward, intent facial expression), your feelings about the interaction will be positive. But if she conveys a lack of interest (looking around the room, bored facial expression), you will walk away with negative feelings.

Self-disclosure is critically important to adjustment for several reasons. First, sharing fears and problems (as well as good news) with others who are trustworthy and supportive plays a key role in mental health

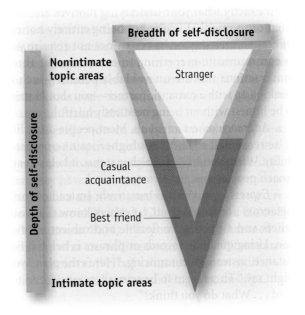

Figure 7.10

Breadth and depth of self-disclosure. Breadth of self-disclosure refers to how many topics one opens up about; depth refers to how far one goes in revealing private information. Both the breadth and depth of one's disclosures are greater with best friends as opposed to casual acquaintances or strangers. (Adapted from Altman & Taylor, 1973)

(Greene et al., 2006). Recall from Chapter 4 that sharing your feelings can reduce stress. And after mutual self-disclosures, people experience a boost in positive feelings (Vittengl & Holt, 2000). Second, emotional (but not factual) self-disclosures lead to feelings of closeness, as long as disclosers feel that listeners are understanding and accepting (Laurenceau & Kleinman 2006; Reis & Shaver, 1988). And, as you saw in Chapter 1, having close relationships is an important ingredient of happiness.

Third, self-disclosure in romantic relationships correlates positively with relationship satisfaction (Greene

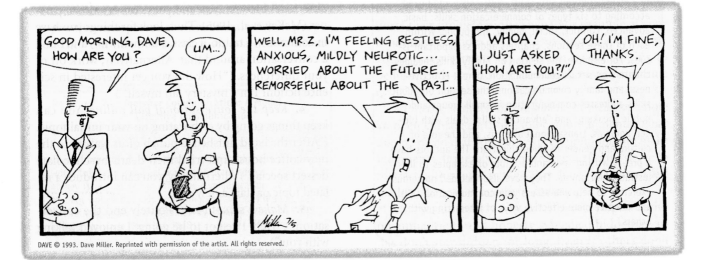

Self-disclosure can be a risky business. In many instances self-disclosure can lead to increased intimacy, but that depends on the nature of the relationship and the disclosure. Hence, when making disclosures it is important to pay attention to others' nonverbal reactions.

© Mary Kate Denny/PhotoEdit

et al., 2006). More specifically, *equity* in self-disclosure, rather than high self-disclosure, may be the critical factor that helps couples avoid stress (Bowers, Metts, & Duncanson, 1985).

Reducing the Risks of Self-Disclosure

Let's face it: Disclosing private information to others is a risky business. When you reveal private things about yourself to others, they might reject you or divulge your confidences to someone else. A study of European college students reported that they revealed others' personal emotional disclosures to third parties in 66%–78% of the cases (Christophe & Rime, 1997). Although the researchers did not ask the students if they had been sworn to secrecy, in 85 percent of the cases the students were intimates (versus acquaintances) of the self-disclosers. Moreover, more emotionally intense disclosures were more likely to be shared—and with more people—than less emotionally intense revelations. Thus, if you have a secret you cannot risk others knowing but that is troubling you, it is probably safer to share it with a trained counselor. Alternatively, writing about an issue, such as in a journal, can help you feel better (Pennebaker, 1997; Sloan & Marx, 2004). Lab studies have also shown that written disclosures in e-mail form can have beneficial effects (Sheese, Brown, & Graziano, 2004).

While it pays to be discriminating about sharing private business, limiting your conversations to superficial topics won't deepen a relationship. To safely steer the conversation toward more intimate topics, we advise using the strategy of *gradual* self-disclosure. Moving gradually gives you the chance to observe how the other person responds to your self-disclosures. Of course, the principle of gradual self-disclosure doesn't always hold. Many people can tell, early on, which relationships they want to remain relatively superficial and which they would like to become more intimate. But, for most situations, we advise gradual self-disclosure as the optimal route to close relationships because it entails less risk and stress.

How can you gauge whether it's safe to share personal information with someone? It should reassure you to know that self-disclosure is *usually* reciprocated in depth and topic (Collins & Miller, 1994). Thus, a good strategy is to monitor your partners' verbal and nonverbal cues for their reactions to your disclosures. If you make a personal disclosure and the other person reciprocates with a parallel disclosure, this reciprocity ordinarily signals comfort with more intimacy. Of course, some people who aren't comfortable engaging in self-disclosure themselves are sincerely willing to listen to you anyway. Thus, you can't depend on reciprocity alone as an indicator of another's interest.

That's why tuning in to nonverbal signals is of crucial importance (Laurenceau & Kleinman, 2006). When people are uncomfortable, they will usually send you a nonverbal message to that effect to avoid the awkwardness of an obvious verbal warning. "Stop" cues include reduced eye contact and a puzzled, apprehensive, or pained facial expression. Your partner may angle his or her body away from you, increase the distance between you, or shuffle his or her feet impatiently. In contrast, when listeners lean forward, appear relaxed, and maintain good eye contact, they are likely interested in your self-disclosure.

What about the risk of self-disclosure in computer-mediated communication? Because of the relative anonymity of the Internet, self-disclosure in e-mail and chat rooms involves less face-to-face risk (Bargh & McKenna, 2004). Still, electronically mediated communication has risks of its own, including your e-mail messages being passed on without your knowledge and predators taking adavantage of you. We'll explore the implications of electronically mediated communication for relationship development in Chapter 8.

Self-Disclosure and Relationship Development

Earlier, we noted that self-disclosure leads to feelings of intimacy. Actually, the process is a little more complicated than that. Research suggests that only certain types of disclosures lead to feelings of closeness (Laurenceau, Barrett, & Rovine, 2005). For instance, emotional-evaluative self-disclosures (how you feel about your sister, for instance) do, but factual-descriptive self-disclosures (that you have three siblings, for example) do not. Moreover, for intimacy to develop in a relationship, a discloser must feel understood and cared for (Reis & Patrick, 1996; Lin & Huang, 2006). In other words, self-disclosure alone doesn't lead to intimacy.

Self-disclosure varies over the course of relationships. At the beginning of a relationship, high levels of mutual disclosure prevail (Taylor & Altman, 1987). Once a relationship is well established, the level of disclosure tapers off, although responsiveness remains high (Reis & Patrick, 1996). Also, in established relationships, people are less likely to reciprocate disclosures in the same conversation. Thus, when a lover or a good friend reveals private information, you frequently respond with words of sympathy and understanding rather than a like disclosure. This movement away from equal exchanges of self-disclosure appears to be based on twin needs that emerge as intimate relationships develop: (1) the need for connection (via openness) and (2) the need for autonomy (via privacy) (Planalp, Fitness, & Fehr, 2006). By reciprocating support (versus information), individuals can strengthen relationships while maintaining a sense of privacy. In fact, successfully balancing these contradictory needs seems to be an important factor in relationship satisfaction (Finkenauer & Hazam, 2000).

When relationships are in distress, self-disclosure patterns change. For example, one or both individuals may decrease the breadth and depth of their self-disclosures, indicating that they are emotionally withdrawing (Baxter, 1988).

Culture, Gender, and Self-Disclosure

Americans generally assume that personal sharing is essential to close friendships and happy romantic partnerships. This view is consistent with an individualistic culture that emphasizes the individual and the expression of each person's unique feelings and experiences. In collectivist cultures such as China and Japan, people are open about their group memberships and status because these factors guide social interactions; however, sharing personal information is reserved for established relationships (Samovar et al., 2007).

Web Link 7.4 **Cross-Cultural Communication Strategies**

Citizens of the 21st century are challenged to communicate sensitively with individuals from other cultural groups both within the United States and around the world. This site, maintained by the Conflict Research Consortium at the University of Colorado, provides commentaries by experts on a variety of intercultural communication settings.

In the United States, it has been found that females tend to be more openly self-disclosing than males, although the disparity seems smaller than once believed (Fehr, 2004). This gender difference is strongest in *same-gender* friendships, with female friends sharing more personal information than male friends (Reis, 1998; Wright, 2006). In *other-gender* relationships, self-disclosure is more equal, although men with traditional gender-role attitudes are less likely to self-disclose, because they view sharing personal information as a sign of weakness. Also, women share more personal information and feelings, whereas men share more nonpersonal information, both in conversations and e-mail messages (Boneva, Kraut, & Frohlich, 2001; Kilmartin, 2007).

Gender disparities in self-disclosure are attributed to socialization. In American culture, most men are taught to conceal tender emotions and feelings of vulnerability, especially from other men (Athenstaedt, Haas, & Schwab, 2004; Kilmartin, 2007). But different gender patterns are found in other countries (Reis & Wheeler, 1991). For example, in Jordan and Japan, where early intimacy between male and female friends is discouraged, close contacts between same-gender friends is encouraged.

And, in the early stages of other-gender relationships, American men often disclose more than women (Derlega et al., 1985). This finding is consistent with the traditional expectations that males should initiate relationships and females should encourage males to talk. Thus, it is an oversimplification to say that American women are always more open than men. We will take up other aspects of gender and communication in the Chapter 10 Application.

Effective Listening

Effective listening is a vastly underappreciated skill. There's a lot of truth in the old saying, "We have two ears and only one mouth, so we should listen more than we speak." Because listeners process speech much more rapidly than people speak (between 500 and 1,000 words per minute versus 125–175 words per minute), it's easy for them to become bored, distracted, and inattentive (Hanna, Suggett, & Radtke, 2008). Fatigue and preoccupation with one's own thoughts are other factors that interfere with effective listening.

To be a good listener, you need to keep four points in mind. First, *signal your interest in the speaker by using nonverbal cues.* Face the speaker squarely and lean toward him or her (rather than slouching or leaning back in a chair). This posture shows that you are interested in what the other person has to say. Try not to cross your arms and legs, as this posture can signal defensiveness. Maintaining eye contact with the speaker also conveys your attentiveness. (You know how annoy-

Being a good listener is an essential skill that contributes to success in relationships and on the job.

ing it is to talk with someone whose eyes are roaming around the room.) Communicate your feelings about what the speaker is saying by nodding your head or raising your eyebrows.

Second, *hear the other person out before you respond.* Listeners often tune out or interrupt a conversational partner when (1) they know someone well (because they believe that they already know what the speaker will say), (2) a speaker has mannerisms listeners find frustrating (stuttering, mumbling, speaking in a monotone), and (3) a speaker discusses ideas (abortion, politics) that generate strong feelings or uses terms (*welfare cheat, redneck*) that push "hot buttons." Although it is challenging not to tune out a speaker or lob an insult in these situations, you'll be better able to formulate an appropriate response if you allow the speaker to complete his or her thought.

Third, *engage in active listening* (Verderber et al., , 2008). Pay attention to what the speaker is saying and mindfully process the information. Active listening also involves the skills of clarifying and paraphrasing. In-

evitably, a speaker will skip over an essential point or say something that is confusing. When this happens, you need to ask for clarification. "Was Bill her boyfriend or her brother?" Clarifying ensures that you have an accurate picture of the message and also tells the speaker that you are interested. Paraphrasing takes clarifying another step. To paraphrase means to state concisely what you believe the speaker said. You might say, "Let me see if I've got this right . . ." or "Do you mean . . .?" It's obviously silly to paraphrase every single thing the speaker says; you need to paraphrase only when the speaker says something important. Paraphrasing has a number of benefits: It reassures the speaker that you are "with" him or her, it derails misinterpretations, and it keeps you focused on the conversation.

Paraphrasing can take several forms (Verderber et al., , 2008). In *content paraphrasing,* you focus on the literal meaning of the message. In *feelings paraphrasing,* you focus on the emotions connected to the content of the message. If your friend declares, "I just can't believe he showed up at the party with his old girlfriend!," a feelings paraphrase is obviously in order ("You were really hurt by that").

To develop your skill at paraphrasing, try practicing it with a friend. Have the friend tell you about something; your job is to paraphrase from time to time to be sure that you really understand what your friend is trying to communicate. After each paraphrase, your friend can tell you whether he or she agrees with your interpretation. Don't be surprised if you have to reparaphrase several times. Keep trying until you get it right. You may discover that paraphrasing is harder than you think!

Finally, *pay attention to the other person's nonverbal signals.* Listeners use a speaker's words to get the "objective" meaning of a message, but they rely on nonverbal cues for the emotional and interpersonal meanings of a message. Your knowledge of body language, tone of voice, and other nonverbal cues can give you deeper understanding of what others are communicating. Remember that these cues are available not only

DILBERT © 2004 Scott Adams. Distributed by permission of United Feature Syndicate, Inc.

when the other person is speaking but also when you are talking. If you often get signals that your listener is drifting away, you might be going overboard on irrelevant details or, perhaps, hogging the conversation. The antidote is active listening.

Most people are inadequate listeners because they are unaware of the elements of effective listening—information you now have. Also, effective listening hinges largely on your attitude. If you're willing to work at it, you can become a good listener fairly quickly.

Communication Problems

LEARNING OBJECTIVES
▶ *Discuss four responses to communication apprehension.*
▶ *Describe four barriers to effective communication.*

In this section, we focus on two problems that can interfere with effective communication: anxiety and communication barriers.

Communication Apprehension

It's the first day of your child psychology class and you have just learned that 30-minute oral presentations are a course requirement. Do you welcome this requirement as an opportunity to polish your public speaking skills or, panic-stricken, do you race to the nearest computer station to drop the class? If you opted for the latter, you may suffer from **communication apprehension, or anxiety caused by having to talk with others.** Some people experience communication apprehension in all speaking situations (including one-on-one encounters), but most people who have the problem notice it only when they have to speak before groups.

Bodily experiences associated with communication apprehension can range from "butterflies" in the stomach to cold hands, dry mouth, and a racing heart rate. These physiological effects are stress-induced "fight or flight" responses of the autonomic nervous system (see Chapter 3). The physiological responses themselves aren't the root of communication apprehension; rather, the problem lies in the speaker's *interpretation* of these bodily responses. That is, high scorers on measures of communication apprehension frequently interpret the bodily changes they experience in public speaking situations as indications of fear. In contrast, low scorers often chalk up these reactions to

Web Link 7.5 **Effective Presentations**

Students often tell teachers that they are terrified of making a presentation in front of a class. Professor Jeff Radel (University of Kansas Medical Center) has crafted an excellent set of guides to show the best ways of communicating by means of oral presentations, visual materials, and posters.

the normal excitement in such a situation (Richmond & McCroskey, 1995).

Researchers have identified four responses to communication apprehension (Richmond & McCroskey, 1995). The most common is *avoidance,* or choosing not to participate when confronted with a voluntary communication opportunity. If people believe that speaking will make them uncomfortable, they will typically avoid the experience. *Withdrawal* occurs when people unexpectedly find themselves trapped in a communication situation they can't escape. Here they may clam up entirely or say as little as possible. *Disruption* refers to the inability to make fluent oral presentations or to engage in appropriate verbal or nonverbal behavior. Of course, inadequate communication skills can produce this same behavioral effect, and it isn't always possible for the average person to identify the actual cause of the problem. *Overcommunication* is a relatively unusual response to high communication apprehension, but it does occur. An example would be someone who attempts to dominate social situations by talking nonstop. Although such individuals are seen as poor communicators, they are not usually perceived as having communication apprehension. That's because we expect to see this problem only in those who talk very little. Of course, overcommunication may be caused by other factors as well.

Obviously, avoidance and withdrawal tactics are merely short-term strategies for coping with communication apprehension (Richmond & McCroskey, 1995). Because it is unlikely that you can go though life without having to speak in front of a group, it is important to learn to cope with this stressful event rather than avoid it time and again. Allowing the problem to get out of hand can result in self-limiting behavior, such as refusing a job promotion that entails public speaking. People with high communication apprehension are likely to have difficulties in relationships, at work, and at school (Richmond & McCroskey, 1995).

Happily, there are effective ways to reduce speech anxiety. With the technique of visualization, for ex-

Being able to speak effectively before a group is a highly useful skill, so it is important to overcome communication apprehension.

ample, you picture yourself successfully going through all of the steps involved in preparing for and making a presentation. Research shows that people who practice visualization have less anxiety and fewer negative thoughts when they actually speak compared to previsualization levels (Ayres, Hopf, & Ayres, 1994). Both *cognitive restructuring* (Chapter 4) and *systematic desensitization* (Chapter 16) are also highly effective methods for dealing with this problem.

Barriers to Effective Communication

Earlier in the chapter, we discussed noise and its disruptive effects on interpersonal communication. Now we want to check out some psychological factors that contribute to noise. These barriers to effective communication can reside in the sender, in the receiver, or sometimes in both. Common obstacles include defensiveness, motivational distortion, self-preoccupation, and game playing.

Defensiveness

Perhaps the most basic barrier to effective communication is *defensiveness*—**an excessive concern with protecting oneself from being hurt.** People usually react defensively when they feel threatened, such as when they believe that others are evaluating them or trying to control or manipulate them. Defensiveness is also triggered when others act in a superior manner. Thus, those who flaunt their status, wealth, bril-

liance, or power often put receivers on the defensive. Dogmatic people who project "I'm always right" also breed defensiveness. A threat need not be real to elicit defensive behavior. If you persuade yourself that Brandon won't like you, your interactions with him will probably not be very positive. And, if the self-fulfilling prophecy kicks in, you may produce the negative reaction you fear. Strive to cultivate a communication style that minimizes defensiveness in others. At the same time, keep in mind that you don't have complete control over others' perceptions and reactions.

Motivational Distortion

In Chapter 6, we discussed distortions and expectancies in person perception. These same processes operate in communication. That is, motivational distortion occurs when people hear what they want to hear instead of what is actually being said. Each person has a unique frame of reference—certain attitudes, values, and expectations—that can influence what he or she hears. Information that contradicts an individual's own views often produces emotional distress. One way people avoid such unpleasant feelings is to engage in *selective attention,* or actively choosing to attend to information that supports their beliefs and ignoring information that contradicts them. Similarly, an individual may read unintended meanings into statements or jump to erroneous conclusions. This tendency to distort information occurs most often when people are discussing issues they feel strongly about, such as politics, racism, sexism, homosexuality, or abortion.

Self-Preoccupation

Who hasn't experienced the frustration of trying to communicate with someone who is so self-focused as to make two-way conversation impossible? These annoying individuals seem to talk to hear themselves talk. If you try to slip in a word about *your* problems, they cut you off by proclaiming, "That's nothing. Listen to what happened to me!" Further, self-preoccupied people are poor listeners. When someone else is talking, they're mentally rehearsing their next comments. Because they are self-focused, these individuals are usually oblivious to their negative impact on others. Self-preoccupied people arouse negative reactions in others for several reasons. First, their remarks are usually so self-serving (seeking to impress, to gain unwarranted sympathy, and so on) that others find it offensive. Another problem is that they consistently take up more than their fair share of conversation time. After a "conversation" with such a person, listeners feel ignored. No wonder people try to avoid these individuals if they can. If they can't, they usually respond only minimally to end the conversation quickly. Needless to say, you risk alienating others if you ignore the norm that conversations should involve a mutual sharing of information.

Game Playing

"Game playing" is another barrier to effective communication. Game playing was first described by Eric Berne (1964), who originated *transactional analysis*, a theory of personality and interpersonal relations that emphasizes patterns of communication. In Berne's scheme, *games* **are manipulative interactions with predictable outcomes, in which people conceal their real motives.** For instance, Yvonne knows that Carlos gets upset when she mentions her former boyfriend. So when they're out with others, she "innocently" inquires, "Say, has anyone seen Rodrigo lately?" Here, the hidden agenda is to make Carlos feel bad. If Yvonne's behavior produces the desired response, she "wins." In the broadest sense, game playing can include the deliberate (or sometimes unintentional) use of ambiguous, indirect, or deceptive statements. Some game playing involves "verbal fencing" to avoid having to make clear one's meaning or intent. Particularly problematic are repetitive games that result in bad feelings and that erode the trust and respect that are essential to good relationships.

Interpersonal Conflict

LEARNING OBJECTIVES

▶ Cite some positive outcomes associated with constructive interpersonal conflict.

▶ Describe five types of conflicts.

▶ Describe five personal styles of dealing with interpersonal conflict.

▶ List seven tips for coping effectively with interpersonal conflict.

People do not have to be enemies to be in conflict, and being in conflict does not make people enemies. ***Interpersonal conflict* exists whenever two or more people disagree.** By this definition, conflict occurs between friends and lovers as well as between competitors and enemies. The discord may be caused by a simple misunderstanding, or it may be a product of incompatible goals, values, attitudes, or beliefs. Because conflict is an unavoidable aspect of interactions, knowing how to deal constructively with it is essential. Many studies report associations between effective conflict management and relationship satisfaction (Gill, Christensen, & Fincham, 1999; Kline et al., 2006).

Beliefs About Conflict

Many people assume that any kind of conflict is bad and that it should be suppressed if at all possible. In reality, conflict is neither inherently bad nor inherently good. It is a natural phenomenon that may lead to either good or bad outcomes, depending on how people deal with it. When people see conflict as negative, they tend to avoid dealing with it. Of course, sometimes avoiding conflict can be good. If a relationship or an issue is of little importance to you, or if you believe that the costs of confrontation are too high (your boss might fire you), avoidance might be the best way to handle a conflict. Also, cultures differ in how conflict should be handled. Collectivist cultures (such as China and Japan) often avoid conflict, whereas individualistic cultures tend to encourage direct confrontations (Samovar et al., 2007). In individualistic cultures, the consequences of avoiding conflict depend on the nature of the relationship. When relationships and issues are important to you, avoiding conflict is generally counterproductive. For one thing, it can lead to a self-perpetuating cycle (see **Figure 7.11**).

When dealt with openly and constructively, interpersonal conflict can lead to a variety of valuable outcomes (Clark & Grote, 2003). Among other things, constructive confrontation may (1) bring problems out into the open where they can be solved, (2) put an

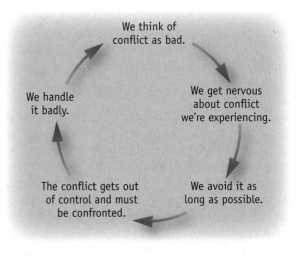

Figure 7.11

The conflict avoidance cycle. Avoiding conflict can lead to a self-perpetuating cycle: (1) People think of conflict as bad, (2) they get nervous about a conflict they are experiencing, (3) they avoid the conflict as long as possible, (4) the conflict gets out of control and must be confronted, and (5) they handle the confrontation badly. In turn, this negative experience sets the stage for avoiding conflict the next time—usually with the same negative outcome. (Adapted from Lulofs, 1994)

Disagreements are a fact of everyday life, so effective communicators need to learn how to deal with them constructively.

end to chronic sources of discontent in a relationship, and (3) lead to new insights through the airing of divergent views.

Types of Conflict

To manage conflict effectively, you need to know what you're dealing with. A useful scheme categorizes conflicts into five types: pseudoconflicts, factual conflicts, policy conflicts, value conflicts, and ego conflicts (Verderber, Verderber, & Berryman-Fink, 2007).

A *pseudoconflict* is just what it says: a false conflict. The game playing between Yvonne and Carlos is one type of pseudoconflict. The goal of the game is to "hook" the other person so that an unresolved issue comes out. The "fight" between Brian and Robin that introduced the chapter is another example of a pseudoconflict. Brian's retort, "There you go again, telling me what to wear," was intended to draw Robin into a fight about power issues in their relationship. Robin's comeback that Brian looked like he was colorblind was an acceptance of Brian's invitation to fight. Had Robin been able to identify the interchange as a pseudoconflict, she could have declined his invitation using a nondefensive tone of voice ("I was just making a suggestion. Wear what you like"). The key to managing such encounters is being able to recognize the game and not allowing yourself to be drawn in.

A second type of conflict occurs when people disagree about issues of a factual nature. For instance, Keisha and DeWayne disagree about whether they are supposed to meet another couple at the restaurant or be picked up so they can all drive in one car. The way to deal with such *fact-based conflicts* is to check the facts and then not dwell on who was right and who was wrong. But, note that either party can escalate the disagreement into an argument with insulting comments ("Can't you ever get anything straight?").

Recommended READING

The Argument Culture: Moving from Debate to Dialogue
by Deborah Tannen (Random House, 1998)

In this thought-provoking work, Tannen claims that public interchanges in America are increasingly framed as battles or games. Hence, the focus has become trying to win arguments rather than trying to understand what is being said. While acknowledging that opposition can be useful and necessary, Tannen is concerned with what she sees as a trend for Americans to use an adversarial approach to the exclusion of other ways of communicating in public. And living in "the argument culture" is having negative effects on Americans and the larger society. With an easygoing style, Tannen brings in research and wide-ranging examples from politics, the media, the legal profession, the classroom, and the Internet to bolster her thesis.

To halt the growth of the argument culture, Tannen advocates using nonadversarial ways to negotiate disagreements and mediate conflicts. For instance, she urges people to start looking for ways that both sides can win disagreements (as opposed to thinking in terms of one side "winning" and the other "losing"). In addition, she urges people to get out of the "dualism trap." Instead of asking, "What is the other *side*?" individuals can ask, "What are the other *sides*?" Tannen recommends setting up discussions with three or more people rather than using the debate-prone two-person format. She also suggests reducing the use of war metaphors (the battle of the sexes, the war on drugs, "annihilating" the other team, and so forth) and replacing them with less combative figures of speech.

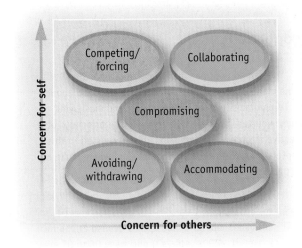

Figure 7.12

Five styles of handling interpersonal conflict. In dealing with discord, individuals typically prefer one of five styles. The two dimensions of *concern for self* and *concern for others* underlie each of the five styles.

repeatedly to discuss a problem and Tony refuses to do so, relationship difficulties can arise. A particular problem occurs when an avoider has greater power in a relationship (parent, supervisor, romantic partner). This situation prevents the less powerful person from airing his or her concerns and breeds frustration and resentment. Of course, in some cases it is good to postpone a discussion, especially if one or both individuals are tired or rushed or need time to cool off. Postponing qualifies as avoiding only if the promised discussion never takes place.

▶ *Accommodating* (low concern for self, high concern for others). Like the avoider, the accommodator feels uncomfortable with conflict. However, instead of ignoring the disagreement, this person brings the conflict to a quick end by giving in easily. People who are overly concerned about acceptance and approval from others commonly use this strategy of surrender. Habitual accommodating is a poor way of dealing with conflict because it does not generate creative thinking and effective solutions. Moreover, feelings of resentment (on both sides) may develop because the accommodator often likes to play the role of a martyr. Of course, when you don't have strong preferences (for instance, where to eat out), occasional accommodating is perfectly appropriate. Also, in some cultures (such as Japan), it is the preferred style of dealing with conflict (Samovar et al., 2007).

▶ *Competing/forcing* (high concern for self, low concern for others). The competitor turns every conflict into a black-and-white, win-or-lose situation. Competitors will do virtually anything to emerge victorious

from confrontations; thus, they can be deceitful and aggressive—including using verbal attacks and physical threats. They rigidly adhere to one position and will use threats and coercion to force the other party to submit. This style is undesirable because, like accommodation, it fails to generate creative solutions to problems. Moreover, this approach is especially likely to lead to postconflict tension, resentment, and hostility.

▶ *Compromising* (moderate concern for self and others). Compromising is a pragmatic approach to conflict that acknowledges the divergent needs of both parties. Compromisers are willing to negotiate and to meet the other person halfway. With this approach, each person gives up something so both can have partial satisfaction. Because both parties gain some satisfaction, compromising is a fairly constructive approach to conflict, especially when the issue is moderately important.

▶ *Collaborating* (high concern for self and others). Whereas compromising simply entails "splitting the difference" between positions, collaborating involves a sincere effort to find a solution that will optimally satisfy both parties. In this approach, conflict is viewed as a mutual problem to be solved as effectively as possible. Collaborating thus encourages openness and honesty. It also stresses the importance of criticizing the other person's *ideas* in a disagreement rather than the other *person.* To collaborate, you have to work on clarifying differences and similarities in positions so that you can build on the similarities. Generally, this is the most productive approach for dealing with conflict. Instead of resulting in a postconflict residue of tension and resentment, collaborating tends to produce a climate of trust.

Dealing Constructively with Conflict

As you have seen, the most effective approach to conflict management is collaborating. To help you implement such an approach, we will offer some specific suggestions. But, before we get down to specifics, there are a few principles to keep in mind (Alberti & Emmons, 2001; Verderber et al., 2007). First, in a conflict situation, try to give the other person the benefit of the doubt; don't automatically assume that those who disagree with you are ignorant or mean-spirited. Show respect for their position, and do your best to empathize with, and fully understand, their frame of reference. Second, approach the other person as an equal. If you have a higher status or more power (parent, supervisor), try to set this difference aside. Third, define the conflict as a mutual problem to be solved cooperatively, rather than as a win-lose proposition. Fourth, choose a mutually acceptable time to sit down and work on resolving the conflict. It is not always best to tackle the conflict when and where it first arises. Finally, communicate your flexibility and willingness to modify your position.

Here are some explicit guidelines for dealing effectively with interpersonal conflict (Alberti & Emmons, 2001; Verderber et al., 2007):

▶ *Make communication honest and open.* Don't withhold information or misrepresent your position. Avoid deceit and manipulation.

▶ *Use specific behaviors to describe another person's annoying habits rather than general statements about their personality.* You'll probably get further with your roommate if you say something like, "Please throw your clothes in the hamper" rather than "You're such an inconsiderate slob." Remarks about specific actions are less threatening and are less likely to be taken personally. They also clarify what you hope will change.

▶ *Avoid "loaded" words.* Certain words are "loaded" in the sense that they tend to trigger negative emotional reactions in listeners. For example, you can discuss politics without using terms such as "right-winger" and "knee-jerk liberal."

▶ *Use a positive approach and help the other person save face.* Saying "I love it when we cook dinner together" will go over better than "You never help with dinner, and I resent it." Similarly, you can increase your chances of having a request accepted if you say, "I realize that you are very busy, but I'd really appreciate it if you would look at my paper again. I've marked the places I'd like you to reconsider."

▶ *Limit complaints to recent behavior and to the current situation.* Dredging up past grievances only rekindles old resentments and distracts you from the current problem. And avoid saying things like "You

Web Link 7.6 The Conflict Resolution Information Source

This excellent resource on conflict management is provided by the University of Colorado's Conflict Research Consortium. The site is actually a gateway to a huge variety of resources on conflict management and is easy to navigate.

always say you're too busy" or "You *never* do your fair share of the housework." Such categorical statements are bound to put the other person on the defensive.

▶ *Assume responsibility for your own feelings and preferences.* Rather than "*You* make me mad," say "*I* am angry." Or, try "I'd appreciate it if you'd water the garden" instead of "Do you think the garden needs watering?"

▶ *Use an assertive (as opposed to submissive or aggressive) communication style.* This approach will make it easier to head off and deal constructively with conflict situations. In our upcoming Application, we elaborate on *assertive communication* and its usefulness in a wide variety of interpersonal communication situations—for example, making acquaintances, developing relationships, and resolving conflicts.

We'll close this section with some food for thought. Think of relationships as having a "bank account" (Notarius & Markman, 1993). People make both deposits to (kindnesses, compliments) and withdrawals from (negative interactions, hostile comments) these accounts. Happy couples know that to avoid being overdrawn, it's important to make frequent deposits to offset the unavoidable withdrawals (Kline, et al., 2006).

APPLICATION

Developing an Assertive Communication Style

LEARNING OBJECTIVES
▶ *Differentiate assertive communication from submissive and aggressive communication.*
▶ *List five steps that lead to more assertive communication.*

Answer the following questions "yes" or "no."

____ **1.** When someone asks you for an unreasonable favor, is it difficult to say no?

____ **2.** Do you feel timid about returning flawed merchandise?

____ **3.** Do you have a hard time requesting even small favors from others?

____ **4.** When a group is hotly debating an issue, are you shy about speaking up?

____ **5.** When a salesperson pressures you to buy something you don't want, is it hard for you to resist?

If you answered "yes" to several of these questions, you may need to increase your assertiveness. Many people

about sports, work, vehicles, and computers than personal concerns. E-mail communications also reflect this gender difference (Colley & Todd, 2002). Whose friendships are more intimate, men's or women's? Currently, there is controversy over this question. The most widely accepted view is that women's friendships are closer and more satisfying—because they involve more self-disclosure (Fehr, 2004; Reis, 1998).

In some countries, men's same-gender friendships are more intimate (Reis, 1998). What short-circuits intimate connections between American men? Several factors stand out (Kilmartin, 2007; Bank & Hansford, 2000). First, men are socialized to be self-sufficient, which inhibits self-disclosure. Second, fear of homosexuality, which is stronger in males than females, is a barrier to intimacy between male friends. Third, traditional gender-role expectations encourage men to see each other as competitors. Why reveal weaknesses to someone who might take advantage of you?

The boundaries between the friendship and romantic or sexual relationships of gay men and lesbians appear to be more complex than those of heterosexuals (Peplau & Fingerhut, 2007; Diamond & Dubé, 2002). Many intimate relationships among lesbians begin as friendships and progress to romance and then to a sexual relationship (Peplau & Spaulding, 2003). Obviously, discerning and negotiating these shifts can be difficult. Also, both lesbians and gay men are much more likely than heterosexuals to maintain social contacts with former sexual partners (Solomon, Rothblum, & Balsam, 2004). One possible explanation for this phenomenon is the small size of some gay and lesbian social networks (Peplau & Fingerhut, 2007). Also, compared to heterosexual couples, gay and lesbian couples have less support from families and societal institutions (Kurdek, 2005). So, maintaining close connections with friends is especially important.

Romantic Love

LEARNING OBJECTIVES

▶ Summarize the research findings on the experience of love in gay and straight couples.

▶ Discuss some gender differences regarding love.

▶ Define passion, intimacy, and commitment, and describe Sternberg's eight types of love.

▶ Discuss adult attachment styles, including their correlates and stability.

▶ Discuss the course of romantic love over time.

▶ Explain why relationships end and what couples can do to help relationships last.

Wander through a bookstore and you'll see an overwhelming array of titles such as *Men Who Can't Love, Women Who Love Too Much,* and *How to Survive the Loss of a Love.* Turn up your radio and you'll hear the refrains of "This Love," "Like I Love You," and "I Will Always Love You." Although there are other forms of love, such as parental love and platonic love, these books and songs are all about *romantic love,* a subject of consuming interest for almost everyone.

Love is difficult to define, difficult to measure, and frequently difficult to understand. Nonetheless, psychologists have conducted thousands of studies and developed a number of interesting theories on love and romantic relationships.

Sexual Orientation and Love

Sexual orientation **refers to a person's preference for emotional and sexual relationships with individuals of the same gender, the other gender, or either gender.** *Heterosexuals* seek emotional-sexual relationships with members of the other gender. *Homosexuals* seek emotional-sexual relationships with members of the same gender. *Bisexuals* seek emotional-sexual relationships with members of both genders. In recent years,

the terms *gay* and *straight* have become widely used to refer to homosexuals and heterosexuals, respectively. *Gay* can refer to homosexuals of either gender, but most homosexual women prefer to call themselves *lesbians.*

Most studies of romantic love and relationships suffer from **heterosexism, or the assumption that all individuals and relationships are heterosexual.** For instance, most questionnaires on romantic love and romantic relationships fail to ask participants about their sexual orientation. Thus, when data are analyzed, there is no way to know whether subjects are referring to same- or other-gender romantic partners. Assuming that their subjects are all heterosexuals, researchers proceed to describe their findings without any mention of homosexuals. Because most people identify themselves as heterosexual, heterosexism in research isn't likely to distort conclusions about heterosexuals; however, it renders homosexual relationships invisible. Consequently, psychologists don't know as much about homosexual relationships as they would like to. Researchers are now devoting much more attention to this issue.

We discuss gay and lesbian relationships more in Chapter 9, so we will just touch on the basics here. We *do* know that homosexual romances and relationships

The experience of romantic love seems to be the same regardless of a person's sexual orientation.

are essentially the same as those of heterosexuals. Both groups experience romantic and passionate love and make commitments to relationships (Diamond, 2006; Kurdek, 1994, 1998). Both heterosexual and homosexual couples say they want their partners to have characteristics similar to theirs, hold similar values about relationships, report similar levels of relationship satisfaction, and perceive their relationships to be loving and satisfying (Peplau & Fingerhut, 2007). When relationship differences are found, they are much more likely to be rooted in gender than in sexual orientation, as we'll see next.

Gender Differences

The stereotype holds that women are more romantic than men. Nonetheless, much of the research evidence suggests just the opposite—that men are the more romantic gender (Dion & Dion, 1988). For example, men hold more romantic beliefs ("Love lasts forever" or "There is one perfect love in the world for everyone") (Peplau, Hill, & Rubin, 1993). In addition, men fall in love more easily than women, whereas women fall out of love more easily than men (Hill, Rubin, & Peplau, 1976; Rubin, Peplau, & Hill, 1981). Also, women are more likely than men to say that they would marry someone they didn't love (Peplau & Gordon, 1985).

Thus, much of the evidence—which admittedly is limited—suggests that men are more romantic than women. However, there are some ways in which women

seem more romantic. For one thing, women are more likely to report physical symptoms associated with being in love—for instance, feeling like they are "floating on a cloud" (Peplau & Gordon, 1985). Second, women are somewhat more likely to verbalize and display tender emotions (Dindia & Allen, 1992).

Research also supports the view that women are more selective in choosing a partner than men are (Kenrick et al., 1990). Evolutionary social psychologists would explain women's tendency to be more "picky" in terms of the parental investment model we discussed earlier. The sociocultural explanation is based on the fact that heterosexual women are still more economically dependent on their partners than vice versa. This means that choosing a potential partner solely for romantic reasons may be a luxury that men (gay or straight) can more easily afford than heterosexual women. Support for this perspective comes from a previously mentioned study showing that women who prefer men with high incomes are those in countries with limited opportunities for females (Eagly & Wood, 1999).

Theories of Love

Can the experience of love be broken down into certain key components? How are romantic love relationships similar to other types of close relationships? These are the kinds of questions that two current theories of love address.

Triangular Theory of Love

Robert Sternberg's (1986, 1988) *triangular theory of love* posits that all love experiences are made up of three components: intimacy, passion, and commitment. Each of the components is represented as a point of a triangle, from which the theory derives its name (see **Figure 8.12** on the next page).

Robert Sternberg

Intimacy **refers to warmth, closeness, and sharing in a relationship.** Signs of intimacy include giving and receiving emotional support, valuing the loved one, wanting to promote the welfare of the loved one, and sharing one's self and one's possessions with another. As we've already discussed, self-disclosure is necessary to achieve and maintain feelings of intimacy in a relationship, whether platonic or romantic.

Passion **refers to the intense feelings (both positive and negative) experienced in love relationships, including sexual desire.** Passion is related to drives that lead to romance, physical attraction, and sexual consummation. Although sexual needs may be dominant in many close relationships, other needs also figure

KEY IDEAS

Perspectives on Close Relationships

▶ Close relationships are those that are important, interdependent, and long-lasting. They include friendships as well as work, family, and romantic relationships. People in individualistic cultures believe that romantic love is a prerequisite for marriage, whereas those in collectivist cultures are accustomed to arranged marriages.

▶ The Internet offers many new vehicles for meeting others and developing relationships. The differences between Internet and face-to-face communication have important implications for established psychological theories and principles of relationship development.

Initial Attraction and Relationship Development

▶ People are initially drawn to others who are nearby, who are seen often, and who are physically attractive. Although physical attractiveness plays a key role in initial attraction, people also seek other desirable characteristics, such as kindness, intelligence, dependable character, and maturity. Couples often match up on looks, but sometimes men trade status for physical attractiveness in women, and vice versa.

▶ As people get acquainted, they prefer others who like them and those who have desirable personality characteristics. Similarity is a key factor in relationship development. Couples tend to be similar in age, race, religion, education, and attitudes.

▶ Once relationships are established, people engage in various maintenance behaviors and actions to sustain them. Interdependence (social exchange) theory uses principles of reinforcement to predict relationship satisfaction and commitment. How individuals apply social exchange principles depends on whether they are in exchange or communal relationships.

Friendship

▶ The key ingredients of friendship are loyalty, emotional support, and letting friends be themselves. Women's same-gender friendships are usually characterized by self-disclosure and intimacy, whereas men's same-gender friendships typically involve doing things together. Some friendship issues are more complex for homosexuals than heterosexuals.

Romantic Love

▶ Research indicates that the experience of romantic love is the same for heterosexual and homosexual individuals. Contrary to stereotypes, men may be more romantic than women. In choosing a partner, women are more selective than men.

▶ Sternberg's triangular theory of love proposes that passion, intimacy, and commitment combine into eight types of love. Hazan and Shaver theorize that love relationships follow the form of attachments in infancy. Researchers subsequently expanded the number of attachment styles from three to four: secure, preoccupied, avoidant-dismissing, and avoidant-fearful. Each style has a characteristic profile. Although attachment styles show stability over time, it is possible for them to change.

▶ Initially, romantic love is usually characterized by passion, but strong passion appears to fade over time for a number of reasons. In relationships that continue, passionate love evolves into a less intense, more mature form of love.

▶ The chief causes of relationship failure are the tendency to make premature commitments, ineffective conflict management skills, boredom with the relationship, and the availability of a more attractive relationship. To help relationships last, couples should take the time to know each other very well, emphasize the positive qualities in their partner and relationship, engage in novel activities together, and develop effective conflict management skills.

Application: Overcoming Loneliness

▶ Loneliness involves discontent with the extent and quality of one's interpersonal network. A surprisingly large number of people in our society are troubled by loneliness. The age groups most affected by loneliness contradict stereotypes.

▶ The origins of chronic loneliness can often be traced to early negative behavior that triggers rejection by peers and teachers. Social trends may also promote loneliness. Loneliness is associated with shyness, poor social skills, and self-defeating attributions.

▶ The keys to overcoming loneliness include resisting the temptation to withdraw from social situations, avoiding self-defeating attributions, and working on one's social skills.

KEY TERMS

Actor-observer effect   p. 259
Attachment styles   p. 255
Close relationships   p. 237
Commitment   p. 254
Comparison level   p. 249
Comparison level for
    alternatives   p. 249
Heterosexism   p. 253
Interdependence
    theory   p. 248
Intimacy   p. 253
Investments   p. 249
Loneliness   p. 261

Matching hypothesis   p. 243
Mere exposure effect   p. 241
Parental investment
    theory   p. 244
Passion   p. 253
Proximity   p. 241
Reciprocal liking   p. 246
Relationship
    maintenance   p. 247
Sexual orientation   p. 252
Shyness   p. 263
Social exchange
    theory   p. 248

KEY PEOPLE

David Buss   pp. 244–245
Cindy Hazan and
    Philip Shaver
    pp. 254–256

Harold Kelley and
    John Thibaut
    pp. 248–250
Robert Sternberg
    pp. 253–254

PRACTICE TEST

1. Arranged marriages are most common in:
   a. individualistic cultures.
   b. collectivist cultures.
   c. unrequited cultures.
   d. both individualistic and collectivist cultures.

2. Which of the following is a relationship issue that operates differently in online versus face-to-face interactions?
   a. Physical proximity
   b. Physical attractiveness
   c. Self-disclosure
   d. All of the above

3. The mere exposure effect refers to an increase in positive feelings due to:
   a. seeing someone often.
   b. interacting with someone often.
   c. communicating via e-mail often.
   d. seeing someone only once.

4. The matching hypothesis suggests that people match up on the basis of:
   a. religion.
   b. personality.
   c. socioeconomic status.
   d. looks.

5. An individual's personal standard of what constitutes an acceptable balance of rewards and costs in a relationship is termed:
   a. social exchange.
   b. comparison level.
   c. proximity level.
   d. relationship satisfaction.

6. Women's same-gender friendships are typically based on _____; men's are typically based on _____.
   a. shopping together; hunting together
   b. attending sports events; attending sports events
   c. shared activities; intimacy and self-disclosure
   d. intimacy and self-disclosure; shared activities

7. If a researcher fails to determine the sexual orientation of her research participants and reports her findings without any mention of homosexuals, her study suffers from:
   a. homosexism.
   b. social exchange.
   c. heterosexism.
   d. romantic bias.

8. A sociocultural explanation for the finding that women are more selective than men in choosing partners is that women:
   a. have better vision than men.
   b. have less economic power than men.
   c. are less superficial than men.
   d. have to compensate for being more romantic than men.

9. Adults who tend to keep their distance from others and who are unconcerned about social rejection would be classified in which of the following attachment styles?
   a. Secure
   b. Preoccupied
   c. Avoidant-dismissing
   d. Avoidant-fearful

10. A self-defeating attributional style associated with loneliness involves attributing loneliness to:
    a. internal, stable factors.
    b. internal, unstable factors.
    c. external, stable factors.
    d. external, unstable factors.

Book Companion Website

Visit the Book Companion Website at **academic.cengage.com/psychology/weiten**, where you will find tutorial quizzes, flash cards, and web links for every chapter, a final exam, and more! You can also link to the Psychology Resource Center (accessible directly at **academic.cengage.com/login**) for a range of psychology-related resources.

Personal Explorations Workbook

The following exercises in your *Personal Explorations Workbook* may enhance your self-understanding in relation to issues raised in this chapter. **Questionnaire 8.1:** Social Avoidance and Distress Scale. **Personal Probe 8.1:** How Do You Relate to Friends? **Personal Probe 8.2:** Analyzing Your Views of Social Connectedness.

ANSWERS

1. b Pages 237–238
2. d Pages 239–240
3. a Page 241
4. d Pages 243–244
5. b Page 249
6. d Pages 251–252
7. c Page 252
8. b Page 253
9. c Page 256
10. a Pages 263–264

of the research in this area has focused on the effects of mothers' employment outside the home. In 2006, the U.S. Department of Labor reported that 70.9% of mothers with children under the age of 18 were employed. What does the research on maternal employment show? Although most Americans seem to believe that maternal employment is detrimental to children's development, the vast majority of empirical studies have found little evidence that a mother's working is harmful to her children (Bianchi, 2000; Haas, 1999; Perry-Jenkins et al., 2001). For instance, studies generally have not found a link between mothers' employment status and the quality of infant-mother emotional attachment (Etaugh, 1993; NICHD Early Child Care Research Network, 1997). Some studies have found that maternal employment in the first year after a child's birth may have negative effects on youngster's cognitive skills during early and middle childhood (Han, Waldfogel, & Brooks-Gunn, 2001; Hill et al., 2005), but these effects are modest and are inconsistent across ethnic groups (Han et al., 2001; Harvey, 1999).

Maternal employment has also been shown to have positive associations on children's development. Recent data from the Canadian National Longitudinal Survey of Children and Youth indicate that maternal employment is related to decreased hyperactivity, lower levels of anxiety, and increased prosocial behavior at age 4 (Nomaguchi, 2006). High-quality child care is also related to advanced language functioning (Belsky, 2006). Further, while maternal employment doesn't eliminate poverty, it does mean that fewer children are raised in poverty (Esping-Anderson, 2007; Lichter & Crowley, 2004). Children brought up in poverty exhibit poorer physical health, reduced mental health, lower academic performance, and increased delinquency in comparison to other children (Seccombe, 2001). However, experts are careful to note that any benefits of maternal employment also come at the cost of fewer positive interactions between the mother and child (Nomaguchi, 2006).

Financial Difficulties

How do couples' financial resources affect marital adjustment and family functioning? Neither financial stability nor wealth can ensure marital satisfaction. However, poverty can produce daunting challenges and serious problems for married couples (Rank, 2004). Without money, families live in constant dread of financial drains such as illness, layoffs, or broken appliances. Spontaneity in communication may be impaired by an understandable reluctance to talk about financial concerns. Thus, it is not surprising that serious financial worries among couples are associated with increased hostility in husbands, increased depression in wives, and lower marital happiness in both husbands and wives

(White & Rogers, 2001). Similarly, husbands' job insecurity is predictive of wives' reports of marital conflict and their thoughts of divorce (Fox & Chancey, 1998). Moreover, evidence consistently demonstrates that the risk of separation and divorce increases as husbands' income declines (Ono, 1998; South & Lloyd, 1995).

Even when financial resources are plentiful, money can be a source of marital strain. Quarrels about how to spend money are common and are potentially damaging at all income levels. For instance, studies have found that perceptions of financial problems (regardless of a

Recommended
READING

Why Marriages Succeed or Fail . . . and How You Can Make Yours Last
by John Gottman (with Nan Silver)
(Simon & Schuster, 1995)

This book is about communication in intimate relationships—a subject that Gottman has studied intensively for over 20 years. A psychology professor at the University of Washington, Gottman is justifiably famous for his landmark research on the prediction of divorce. He has demonstrated that he can predict which couples will divorce with remarkable accuracy, based on careful examination of the couples' communication patterns. According to Gottman, the marriages that last are not those that appear to be free of conflict but those in which couples are able to resolve the conflicts that inevitably arise in intimate relationships. Gottman categorizes couples into three types based on their style of conflict resolution. In *validating marriages,* couples compromise often and work out their disagreements calmly. In *conflict-avoiding marriages,* couples rarely confront their disagreements openly. In *volatile marriages,* couples have frequent and passionate disputes. For all three types, the crucial consideration, according to Gottman, is the relative balance of positive versus negative interactions.

In this practical, readable analysis of marital communication, the author provides plenty of case histories to make ideas come alive. The book also includes many thought-provoking scales that readers can take to evaluate their own communication styles and tendencies. For example, there are scales to measure stonewalling, defensiveness, and the other communication tendencies Gottman characterizes as the "Four Horsemen of the Apocalypse." *Why Marriages Succeed or Fail* is an outstanding book loaded with exercises, quizzes, and tips that should help readers improve their marital communication. Gottman has written two other highly practical books on marriage that are worth consulting: *10 Lessons to Transform Your Marriage* (2006) and a more elaborate and detailed analysis titled *The Relationship Cure* (2001).

family's actual income) are associated with decreased marital satisfaction (Dean, Carroll, & Yang, 2007). In a study that examined how happily married couples handled their money in comparison to couples that eventually divorced, Schaninger & Buss (1986) found that the happy couples engaged in more joint decision making on finances. Thus, the best way to avoid troublesome battles over money is probably to engage in extensive planning of expenditures together.

Inadequate Communication

Effective communication is crucial to the success of a marriage and is consistently associated with increased marital satisfaction (Litzinger & Gordon, 2005; Rogge et al., 2006). The damaging role that poor communication can play in marital relations was clearly demonstrated in a study of couples getting a divorce (Cleek & Pearson, 1985). In this study, communication difficulties were the most frequently cited problem among both husbands and wives (see **Figure 9.7**). Spouses' strategies for resolving conflicts may be particularly crucial to marital satisfaction (Crohan, 1992). Many partners respond to conflict by withdrawing and refusing to communicate—a pattern associated with deteriorating marital satisfaction over time (Heavey, Christensen, & Malamuth, 1995; Roberts, 2000). Couples need to feel safe discussing conflict; the ability to communicate emotions is associated with better marital adjustment (Cordova, Gee, & Warren, 2005).

A number of studies have compared communication patterns in happy and unhappy marriages. This research indicates that unhappily married couples (1) find it difficult to convey positive messages, (2) misunderstand each other more often, (3) are less likely to recognize that they have been misunderstood, (4) use more frequent, and more intense, negative messages, and (5) often differ in the amount of self-disclosure they prefer in the relationship (Noller & Fitzpatrick, 1990; Noller & Gallois, 1988; Sher & Baucom, 1993). Above all else, unhappy couples tend to get caught up in escalating cycles of conflict from which they cannot escape, whereas happy couples find ways to exit the cycles (Fincham, 2003).

The importance of marital communication was underscored in a widely cited study by John Gottman and his colleagues that attempted to predict the likelihood of divorce in a sample of 52 married couples (Buehlman, Gottman, & Katz, 1992). Each couple provided an oral history of their relationship and a 15-minute sam-

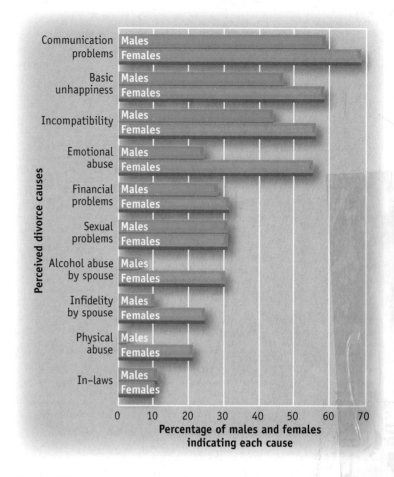

Figure 9.7

Causes of divorce. When Cleek and Pearson (1985) asked divorcing couples about their perceptions regarding the causes of their divorce, both men and women cited communication difficulties more than any other cause.

ple of their interaction style, during which they discussed two problem areas in their marriage. The investigators rated the spouses on a variety of factors that mostly reflected the subjects' ways of relating to each other. Based on these ratings, they were able to predict which couples would divorce within three years with 94% accuracy! Follow-up research has demonstrated that marital adjustment depends not on whether there is conflict (conflict is virtually inevitable) but rather on how conflict is handled when it occurs (Driver et al., 2003).

John Gottman

John Gottman, who is probably the world's foremost authority on marital communication, asserts that conflict and anger are normal in marital interactions and that they are not, in and of themselves, predictive of marital dissolution. Instead, Gottman (1994) identifies four other communication patterns, which he calls the "Four Horsemen of the Apocalypse," that are risk factors for divorce: contempt, criticism, defensiveness,

and stonewalling. *Contempt* involves communicating insulting feelings that one's spouse is inferior. *Criticism* involves constantly expressing negative evaluations of one's partner. *Defensiveness* involves responding to contempt and criticism with obstructive communication that escalates marital conflict. *Stonewalling* involves refusing to listen to one's partner, especially the partner's complaints. Gottman eventually added a fifth trouble-some communication pattern, *belligerence*, which involves provocative, combative challenges to partners' power and authority (Gottman et al., 1998; Gottman, Gottman, & DeClaire, 2006). Given the importance of good communication, many approaches to marital therapy emphasize the development of better communication skills in partners (Gottman et al., 2002).

Divorce

LEARNING OBJECTIVES

▶ *Describe the evidence on changing divorce rates.*
▶ *Discuss how men and women tend to adjust to divorce.*
▶ *Analyze the evidence on the effects of divorce on children.*
▶ *Summarize data on the frequency and success of remarriage and its impact on children.*

"*In the ten years that we were married I went from twenty-four to thirty-four and they were a very significant ten years. I started a career, started to succeed, bought my first house, had a child, you know, very significant years. And then all of a sudden, every goddamn thing, I'm back to zero. I have no house. I don't have a child. I don't have a wife. I don't have the same family. My economic po-sition has been shattered. And nothing recoverable. All these goals which I had struggled for, every goddamn one of them, is gone.*"—A recently divorced man quoted in Marital Separation (*Weiss, 1975, p. 75*)

The dissolution of a marriage tends to be a bone-jarring event for most people, as this bitter quote illustrates.

Any of the problems discussed in the previous section might lead a couple to consider divorce. However, people appear to vary in their threshold for divorce, just as they do in their threshold for marriage. Some couples will tolerate a great deal of disappointment and bickering without seriously considering divorce. Other couples are ready to call their attorney as soon as it becomes apparent that their expectations for marital bliss were somewhat unrealistic. Typically, however, divorce is the culmination of a gradual disintegration of the relationship brought about by an accumulation of interrelated problems, which often date back to the beginning of couples' relationships (Huston, Niehuis, & Smith, 2001).

Divorce Rates

Although relatively accurate statistics are available on divorce rates, it is still difficult to estimate the percentage of marriages that end in divorce. It is clear that divorce rates increased dramatically between the 1950s and 1980s, but they appear to have stabilized and even declined slightly since the 1980s (Amato et al., 2003). When divorce rates were at their peak, the most widely cited estimates of future divorce risk were around 50% (Bumpass, Raley, & Sweet, 1995). However, the modest reductions in divorce rates in recent years appear to have lowered the risk of divorce to 40%–45% for today's couples (Bramlett & Mosher, 2001; Whitehead & Popenoe, 2001). The decline in divorce rates is encouraging, but the chances of marital dissolution remain quite high. In 2001, about one in five adults had

been divorced (Kreider, 2005). Although most people realize that divorce rates are high, they have a curious tendency to underestimate the likelihood that they will personally experience a divorce. On the average, people peg their probability of divorce at about 10%–11%, which is far below the actual probability for the population as a whole (Fowers et al., 2001).

Divorce rates are higher among blacks than whites or Hispanics, among lower-income couples, among couples who cohabitated, among couples who do not have children, among people who marry at a relatively young age, and among those whose parents divorced (Faust & McKibben, 1999; Rodrigues et al., 2006). As **Figure 9.8** shows, the vast majority of divorces occur during the first decade of a marriage (Hiedemann, Suhomlinova, & O'Rand, 1998). What types of marital problems are predictive of divorce? The most frequently cited problems include communication difficulties (not talking; being moody, critical, and easy to anger), infidelity, jealousy, growing apart, foolish spending behavior, and substance abuse problems (Amato & Previti, 2003; Amato & Rogers, 1997).

A wide variety of social trends have probably contributed to increasing divorce rates (Amato et al., 2003; Giddens, 2001; Sabatelli & Ripoll, 2004). The stigma attached to divorce has gradually eroded. Many religious denominations are becoming more tolerant of divorce, and marriage has thus lost some of its sacred quality. The shrinking of families probably make divorce a more viable possibility. The entry of more women into the workforce has made many wives less

The high divorce rate has led to some novel ways of dealing with its worrisome legal aspects. Attorney Robert Nordyke discovered that the drive-up window at his new office—a former savings and loan branch in Salem, Oregon—was perfect for serving legal papers on his clients' spouses.

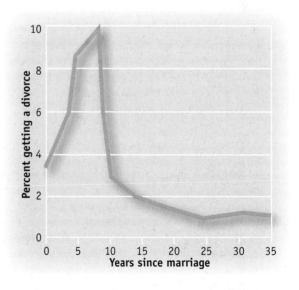

Figure 9.8

Divorce rate as a function of years married. This graph shows the distribution of divorces in relation to how long couples have been married. As you can see, the vast majority of divorces occur in the early years, with divorce rates peaking between the fifth and tenth years of marriage. (Data from National Center for Health Statistics)

Should the Government Promote Marriage?

As noted in the main body of the chapter, research evidence suggests that marriage is good for one's health and happiness (Hawkins & Booth, 2005; Waite & Gallagher, 2000). And studies show that children whose parents divorce exhibit an increased risk for quite a variety of negative outcomes (Amato, 2003; Barber & Demo, 2006). These findings suggest that both adults and children are most likely to flourish in stable, loving families, but social trends are clearly moving in just the opposite direction. Marriage rates are down and divorce rates are up, cohabitation rates are skyrocketing, and more and more children are being born out of wedlock (Bianchi & Casper, 2000). Concerns about these trends have led some religious leaders and public officials to argue that government entities ought to do more to promote a culture of marriage (Hackstaff, 1999; Popenoe, 1999; Wagner, 1998). At first glance, this sounds like a sensible, enlightened policy that everyone ought to be able to agree on, but in reality this issue turns out to be surprisingly complex and controversial.

The pro-marriage movement has been gathering momentum since the early 1990s. The advocates of this movement argue that people today are overly focused on their personal happiness and are unwilling to endure hardship and show loyalty when the going gets rough in a marriage (Fowers, 2000). They also assert that the emergence of no-fault divorce laws since the 1970s has made it too easy to get a divorce. Hence, the pro-marriage advocates campaign for policies that would make divorces more difficult to obtain. For example, several states have enacted *covenant marriage* laws (Rosier & Feld, 2000). Couples who choose to enter into a covenant marriage agree to complete premarital education programs and pledge to divorce only in response to severe problems (such as spouse abuse or a lengthy prison term), and only after seeking extensive marriage counseling (Hawkins et al., 2002). Other advocated reforms have included waiting periods for divorces of up to five years and more demanding legal proceedings for divorces involving children. More proactive proposals have included mandating high school education programs touting the value of marriage, providing government subsidies for marriage counseling, and requiring couples to complete premarital relationship skills training (Amato, 2004b). Some pro-marriage proponents have also suggested giving married couples preferential treatment (over single, divorced, and cohabiting individuals) in regard to government benefits, such as welfare payments and housing subsidies (Murray, 2001).

Critics of the pro-marriage movement raise a variety of objections. First, they question the meaning of the research findings that serve as the rationale for this movement. Although they acknowledge that married people are somewhat healthier and happier than nonmarried adults, they point out that the data are correlational and that there is no solid evidence that being married *causes* this difference (Huston & Melz, 2004). They argue that causation probably runs the other way—that being healthy and happy causes people to have better marital opportunities and greater marital success. Indeed, there is empirical support for this notion (Lyubomirsky, King, & Diener, 2005). In a similar vein, they admit that experiencing divorce can be harmful for children but suggest that remaining in a home filled with bitter discord can be just as harmful (Booth & Amato, 2001).

Second, the critics express concern that restricting access to divorce could leave some spouses and children stranded in homes riddled with alcoholism, drug abuse, or domestic violence (Gelles, 1996). Third, critics point out that making divorces harder to get just may not be a realistic option in today's society (Coontz, 1997). Although a majority of adults agree—in the abstract—that divorce laws should be tougher, they do not want *their own* personal freedom in this area to be impeded. Consistent with this finding, only 3 percent of couples have chosen covenant marriage in the state (Louisiana) that first offered this option (Licata, 2002). Further, preliminary data suggest that choosing a convenant marriage might not reduce marital instability (Brown et al., 2006).

Fourth, critics argue that if the government wants to promote marital success, it should focus more on making it *easier to stay married,* as opposed to harder to get a divorce. In particular, they note that divorce rates tend to be high in lower social classes where families could be better strengthened by improving social services (such as child care and job training). Finally, critics maintain that the pro-marriage movement treats the traditional nuclear family as the only legitimate family form and that pro-marriage programs will unfairly discriminate against single parents, divorced persons, cohabiting couples, and gay and lesbian partners (Coltrane, 2001; Scanzoni, 2004).

financially dependent on the continuation of their marriage. New attitudes emphasizing individual fulfillment seem to have counterbalanced older attitudes that encouraged dissatisfied spouses to suffer in silence. Reflecting all these trends, the legal barriers to divorce have also diminished.

Deciding on a Divorce

Divorces are often postponed repeatedly, and they are rarely executed without a great deal of agonizing forethought (Ahrons, 1999). Indecision is common, as roughly two out of five divorce petitions are eventually withdrawn (Donovan & Jackson, 1990). The decision to divorce is usually the outcome of a long series of smaller decisions or relationship stages that may take years to unfold, so divorce should be viewed as a process rather than a discrete event (Morrison & Cherlin, 1995; Rollie & Duck, 2006). Wives' judgments about the likelihood of their marriages ending in divorce tend to be more accurate than husbands' judgments (South, Bose, & Trent, 2004). This finding may be related to the fact that wives initiate two-thirds of divorce actions (Hetherington, 2003).

It is difficult to generalize about the relative merits of divorce as opposed to remaining in an unsatisfactory marriage. Extensive research clearly shows that people who are currently divorced suffer a higher incidence of both physical and psychological maladies and are less happy than those who are currently married (Amato, 2001; Waite & Gallagher, 2000). Furthermore, the process of getting divorced is stressful for both spouses. We might guess that as divorce becomes more commonplace, it should also become less traumatic, but available evidence does not support this supposition (Kitson, 1992). As painful as marital dissolution may be, remaining in an unhappy marriage is also potentially detrimental. Research has shown that in comparison to divorced individuals, unhappily married people tend to show poorer physical health, lower levels of happiness, less life satisfaction, and lower self-esteem (Hawkins & Booth, 2005; Wickrama et al., 1997). Moreover, like other stressful life events, divorce can lead to personal growth and positive changes in the self (Tashiro, Frazier, & Berman, 2006), so the picture is not entirely negative.

Adjusting to Divorce

Objectively speaking, divorce appears to be more difficult and disruptive for women than for men, especially in terms of finances (Clarke-Stewart & Bailey, 1989; Sayer, 2006). Women are more likely to assume the responsibility of raising the children, whereas men tend to reduce their contact with their children. Within

Web Link 9.4 **Divorce Central**

Divorce Central is one of a number of excellent sites that provide information and advice on legal, emotional, and financial issues for individuals contemplating or going through a divorce. Annotated links to the other outstanding divorce-related sites can also be found here.

the first year after divorce, half of fathers basically lose contact with their kids (Carter & McGoldrick, 1999). Another key consideration is that divorced women are less likely than their ex-husbands to have adequate income or a satisfying job (Smock, Manning, & Gupta, 1999). For example, one well-designed study found that custodial mothers experienced a 36% percent decrease in their standard of living, whereas noncustodial fathers experienced a 28% *increase* (Bianchi, Subaiya, & Kahn, 1999). The economic consequences of divorce clearly are more severe for women than for men, but in this era of two-income families, many men also experience a noticeable decline in their standard of living after going through a divorce (McManus & DiPrete, 2001).

Although divorce appears to impose greater stress on women than men, researchers do *not* find consistent gender differences in postdivorce adjustment (Amato, 2001). In the aggregate, the magnitude of the negative effects of divorce on individuals' psychological and physical well-being seems to be pretty similar for husbands and wives. Among both men and women, high preoccupation with one's ex-spouse is associated with poorer adjustment to divorce (Masheter, 1997). Factors associated with favorable postdivorce adjustment include having higher income, getting remarried, having more positive attitudes about divorce, and being the partner who initiated the divorce (Wang & Amato,

"That's right, Phil. A separation will mean—among other things—watching your own cholesterol."

2000). Forgiveness of the ex-spouse is also associated with increased well-being and lowered depression (Rye et al., 2004). Interestingly, research shows that the relationship between divorce and adjustment is also influenced by preexisting factors. That is, even before getting married, people who eventually divorce are less happy than people who remain married (Lucas, 2005).

Effects of Divorce on Children

Roughly half of all divorces involve children. When couples have children, decisions about divorce must take into account the potential impact on their offspring. Widely publicized research by Judith Wallerstein and her colleagues has painted a rather bleak picture of how divorce affects youngsters (Wallerstein & Kelly, 1980; Wallerstein & Blakeslee, 1989; Wallerstein, Lewis, & Blakeslee, 2000). This research has followed a sample of 60 divorced couples and their 131 children since 1971. At the 10-year follow-up, almost half of the participants were characterized as "worried, underachieving, self-deprecating, and sometimes angry young men and women" (Wallerstein & Blakeslee, 1989, p. 299). Even *25 years* after their parents' divorce, a majority of subjects were viewed as troubled adults who found it difficult to maintain stable and satisfying intimate relationships (Wallerstein, 2005). The enduring, long-term effects of divorce reported by Wallerstein were particularly disturbing and generated great interest from the media, resulting in an abundance of TV interviews, magazine articles, and so forth.

Although the lengthy follow-up in Wallerstein's research is commendable, critics point out that her study suffers from a variety of flaws (Amato, 2003; Cherlin, 1999; Kelly & Emery, 2003). It was based on a small sample of children from a wealthy area in California that clearly was not representative of the population at large. There was no comparison group, and conclusions were based on impressions from clinical interviews, in which it is easy for interviewers to see what they want to see. Further, critics caution against drawing causal conclusions from corrlelational data (Gordon, 2005). Coltrane and Adams (2003) also note that Wallerstein is part of a conservative political-religious movement that favors traditional family arrangements and reforms that would make divorces more difficult to obtain. Hence, her conclusions may be shaped in part by a political agenda.

Are Wallerstein's findings consistent with other research? Yes and no. The results of another long-running study by E. Mavis Hetherington (1993, 1999, 2003), which used a larger and more representative sample, a control group, and conventional statistical comparisons, suggest that Wallerstein's conclusions are unduly pessimistic. According to Hetherington, di-

vorce can be traumatic for children, but a substantial majority adjust reasonably well after two to three years, and only about 25% show serious psychological or emotional problems in adulthood (versus 10% in the control group).

E. Mavis Hetherington

Another complicated issue in assessing the effects of divorce is the choice of whom should be used as a baseline for comparison. One can argue that children of divorce should be compared to children from intact homes characterized by persistent marital discord, a group that also shows elevated rates of many types of adjustment problems (Morrison & Coiro, 1999; Papp, Cummings, & Schermerhorn, 2004).

Although Wallerstein's conclusions appear overly negative, *they differ from the results of other research only in degree* (Amato, 2003). After a divorce, many children exhibit depression, anxiety, nightmares, dependency, aggression, withdrawal, distractibility, lowered academic performance, reduced physical health, precocious sexual behavior and substance abuse (Barber & Demo, 2006; Kelly & Emery, 2003; Knox, 2000). Although these problems dissipate in most children after a few years, divorce can have a lasting impact that extends into adulthood. Experiencing divorce during childhood is a risk factor for many subsequent problems in one's adult years, including maladjustment, marital instability, and reduced occupational attainments (Amato, 1999). Children have more adjustment problems when their parents have a history of particularly bitter, acrimonious conflict (Amato, 2001).

So what can we conclude about the effects of divorce on children? *Overall, the weight of evidence suggests that divorce tends to have harmful effects on many children but can have beneficial effects for children if their parents' relationship is dominated by conflict* (Booth & Amato, 2001). However, the latter assertion is based on the assumption that the parents' divorce brings their bickering to an end. Unfortunately, the conflicts between divorcing spouses often continue for many years after they part ways (Hopper, 2001). This pattern has led to a recent interest in divorce education and intervention programs to ease the transition for families; such efforts still need to be scientifically evaluated (Blaisure & Geasler, 2006). It is also reasonable to conclude that *divorces have highly varied effects on children that depend on a complex constellation of interacting factors.* As Furstenberg and Kiernan (2001) put it, "Many researchers have become increasingly wary about public discussions of divorce that treat it as an undifferentiated and uniform occurrence resulting in similar outcomes for all children" (p. 446).

Remarriage

Evidence that adequate courtship opportunities exist for the divorced is provided by the statistics on remarriage: Roughly three-quarters of divorced people eventually remarry (Bramlett & Mosher, 2001). The mean length of time between divorce and remarriage is within three to four years (Kreider, 2005).

How successful are second marriages? The answer depends on your standard of comparison. Divorce rates *are* higher for second than for first marriages (of divorced people), though the average duration for second marriages is about the same as for first, about eight to nine years (Kreider, 2005; Mason, 1998). However, this statistic may simply indicate that this group of people see divorce as a reasonable alternative to an unsatisfactory marriage. Nonetheless, studies of marital adjustment suggest that second marriages are slightly less successful than first marriages (Brown & Booth, 1996). Of course, if you consider that in this pool of people *all* the first marriages ran into serious trouble, then the second marriages look rather good by comparison. As with first marriages, communica-

tion plays a major role in marital satisfaction for both spouses (Beaudry et al., 2004).

Another major issue related to remarriage is its effect on children. Adaptation to remarriage can be difficult for children. Evidence suggests that on the average, interaction in stepfamilies appears to be somewhat less cohesive and warm than interaction in first-marriage families, and stepparent-stepchild relations tend to be more negative and distant than parent-child relations in first marriages (Pasley & Moorefield, 2004). Stepfamily formation can be a negative experience for children who feel powerless or who undergo dramatic changes in living spaces, rules, and expectations (Stoll et al., 2005).

Taken as a whole, the evidence suggests that children in stepfamilies are a little less well adjusted than children in first marriages and are roughly similar in adjustment to children in single-parent homes (Coleman, Ganong, & Fine, 2001). In an analysis of 61 studies, Jeynes (2006) found that children in stepfamilies tend to show lower academic achievement and psychological well-being than those from intact or single-parent families. However, the differences between stepfamilies and other types of families in the adjustment of their children tend to be modest. For example, **Figure 9.9** highlights some representative results from one large-scale study (Acock & Demo, 1994).

Although remarried couples tend to have more open communication, the evidence suggests that second marriages are slightly less successful than first marriages, on the average.

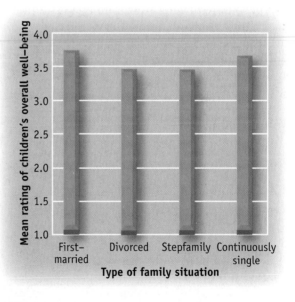

Figure 9.9

Children's adjustment in four types of families. Acock and Demo (1994) assessed children's adjustment in four types of family structures: first marriages, divorced single-parent homes, stepfamilies, and families in which the mother never married. The comparisons of 2,457 families did turn up some statistically significant differences, as children's overall well-being was highest in intact first marriages. However, as you can see, the differences were rather small, and the authors concluded that "family structure has a modest effect on children's well-being."

Alternatives to Marriage

▶ *Describe stereotypes of single life, and summarize evidence on the adjustment of single people.*

▶ *Discuss the prevalence of cohabitation and whether it improves the probability of marital success.*

▶ *Discuss the stability and dynamics of intimate relationships among homosexual couples.*

▶ *Outline some misconceptions about gay couples.*

So far we have been discussing the traditional model of marriage, which, as we noted at the beginning of the chapter, has been challenged by a variety of social trends. More and more people are choosing alternatives to marriage. In this section we examine some of these alternatives, including remaining single, cohabitation, and gay relationships.

Remaining Single

The pressure to marry is substantial in our society (Berliner, Jacob, & Schwartzberg, 1999). People are socialized to believe that they are not complete until they have found their "other half" and have entered into a partnership for life. And reference is often made to people's "failure" to marry. In spite of this pressure, an increasing proportion of young adults are remaining single (Teachman, Tedrow, & Crowder, 2001), as **Figure 9.10** shows.

Does the increased number of single adults mean that people are turning away from the institution of marriage? Perhaps a little, but for the most part, no. A variety of factors have contributed to the growth of the single population. Much of this growth is a result of

the increase in the median age at which people marry and the increased rate of divorce. The vast majority of single, never-married people *do* hope to marry eventually. In one study of never-married men and women (South, 1993), 87.4% of the 926 respondents ages 19 to 25 agreed with the statement "I would like to get married someday," and in a recent study of unmarried parents, most expected to marry (Waller & McLanahan, 2005).

Singles continue to be stigmatized and plagued by two disparate stereotypes (Byrne & Carr, 2005; De-Frain & Olson, 1999). On the one hand, single people are sometimes portrayed as carefree swingers who are too busy enjoying the fruits of promiscuity to shoulder marital responsibilities. On the other hand, they are seen as losers who have not succeeded in snaring a mate, and they may be portrayed as socially inept, maladjusted, frustrated, lonely, and bitter. These stereotypes do a great injustice to the diversity that exists among those who are single. In fact, the negative stereotypes of singles have led some researchers to coin the term *singlism* to capture how single people can be victims of prejudice and discrimination (DePaulo & Morris, 2005, 2006).

Moving beyond stereotypes, what do scientists know about singlehood? It is true that single people exhibit poorer mental and physical health than married people (Joung et al., 1997; Waite, 1995), and they rate themselves as less happy than their married counterparts (Stack & Eshleman, 1998; Waite, 2000). However, the differences are modest, and the happiness gap has shrunk, especially among women. The physical health benefits of being married appear to be greater for men than for women (Waite, 2000; Wu & Hart, 2002). But most studies find that single women are more satisfied with their lives and less distressed than comparable single men, and various lines of evidence suggest that women get along without men better than men get along without women (Davies, 1995; Marker, 1996).

Why is being married associated with greater health and happiness? The *health benefits* of marriage may result because spouses provide emotional and social support that buffers the negative effects of

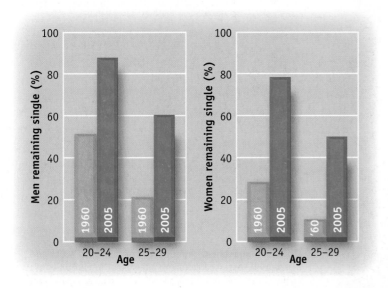

Figure 9.10

The proportion of young people who remain single. This graph shows the percentage of single men and women, ages 20–24 or 25–29, in 2005 as compared to 1960 (based on U.S. Census data). The proportion of people remaining single has increased substantially for both sexes, in both age brackets. Single men continue to outnumber single women in these age brackets.

stress and because they discourage their partners' unhealthy habits (Joung et al., 1997; Murphy, Glaser, & Grundy, 1997). Another consideration is that married people tend to have higher incomes (Hirschl, Altobelli, & Rank, 2003), and affluence is associated with better health (Adler & Snibbe, 2003). The *greater happiness* of married people has been attributed to the advantages they enjoy in social support, financial well-being, and physical health (Stack & Eshleman, 1998). However, when interviewing life-long single women between the ages of 65 and 77, Baumbusch (2004) found that these women expressed satisfaction with their decision to remain single and emphasized the importance of their independence.

Cohabitation

As we noted earlier in the chapter, *cohabitation* refers to living together in a sexually intimate relationship outside of marriage. Recent years have witnessed a tremendous increase in the number of cohabiting couples (see **Figure 9.11**). Although cohabitation is still illegal in six states (Florida, Michigan, Mississippi, North Carolina, Virginia, and West Virginia), over 55.2 million couples are living together unmarried in the United States (Roberts, 2006). Increasing rates of cohabitation are not unique to the United States and are even higher in many European countries (Kiernan, 2004). However, the percentage of couples living together at any one time does not accurately convey how widespread this phenomenon has become, because cohabiting unions tend to be short (Seltzer, 2004).

Cohabitation tends to conjure up images of college students or other well-educated young couples without children, but these images are misleading. In reality, cohabitation rates have always been higher in the less-educated and lower-income segments of the population (Bumpass & Lu, 2000). Moreover, many cohabitating couples have children: About half of previously married cohabitants and 35% of never-married cohabitants have children in their household (Smock, 2000).

Although many people see cohabitation as a threat to the institution of marriage, many theorists see it as a new stage in the courtship process—a sort of trial marriage. Consistent with this view, about three-quarters of female cohabitants expect to marry their current partner (Lichter, Batson, & Brown, 2004). In spite of these expectations, however, cohabitants report that they are less satisfied with their relationships than married couples (Brown & Booth, 1996; Nock, 1995). Moreover, cohabitating relationships are notably less durable than marital relationships (Seltzer, 2004). Conceiving a child during cohabitation tends to increase couples' chances of staying together (Manning, 2004).

As a prelude to marriage, cohabitation should allow people to experiment with marital-like responsibilities and reduce the likelihood of entering marriage with unrealistic expectations, suggesting that couples who cohabit before they marry should go on to more successful marriages than those who do not. Although this analysis sounds plausible, researchers have *not* found that premarital cohabitation increases the likelihood of subsequent marital success. In fact, studies have consistently found an association between premarital cohabitation and *increased* marital discord and divorce rates (Bumpass & Lu, 2000; Cohan & Kleinbaum, 2002; Teachman, 2003).

What accounts for this finding? Many theorists argue that this nontraditional lifestyle has historically attracted a more liberal and less conventional segment of the population with a weak commitment to the institution of marriage and relatively few qualms about getting divorced. This explanation has considerable empirical support (Hall, 1996; Smock, 2000; Stanley, Whitton, & Markman, 2004), but some support also exists for the alternative explanation—that the experience of cohabitation changes people's attitudes, values, or habits in ways that somehow increase their vulnerability to divorce (Kamp Dush, Cohan, & Amato, 2003; Seltzer, 2001).

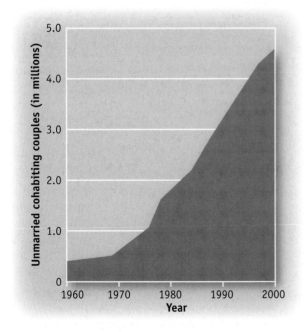

Figure 9.11

Cohabitation in the United States. The number of unmarried couples living together has been increasing rapidly since 1970 (based on U.S. Census data). This increase shows no signs of leveling off.

Gay Relationships

Up until this point, we have, for purposes of simplicity, focused our attention on *heterosexuals,* those who seek

Despite the common stereotype that homosexuals rarely form long-term relationships, the fact is that they are similar to heterosexual couples in their attitudes and behaviors, and many enjoy long-term commitments in marriage-like arrangements.

© Ron Chapple/Thinkstock/Alamy

emotional-sexual relationships with members of the other gender. However, we have been ignoring a significant minority group: *homosexual* men and women, who seek emotional-sexual relationships with members of the same gender. (In everyday language, the term *gay* is used to refer to homosexuals of both genders, although many homosexual women prefer the term *lesbian* for themselves.)

How large is this minority group? No one knows for sure. Part of the problem is that this question is vastly more complex than it appears at first glance (LeVay, 1996; Gates & Sell, 2007). Sexual orientation is best represented as a continuum (as we will discuss in Chapter 13), so where do you draw the lines between heterosexuality, bisexuality, and homosexuality? Researchers distinguish among three components of sexual orientation: sexual attraction, overt behavior, and sexual identity (Savin-Williams, 2006). So where, for instance, do you put a person who is married and has never engaged in homosexual behavior but who reports homosexual fantasies and acknowledges being strongly drawn to members of the same sex? The other part of the problem is that many people have prejudicial attitudes about homosexuality, which makes gays cautious and reluctant to give candid information about their sexuality (Smith & Gates, 2001). Small wonder then that estimates of the portion of the population that is homosexual vary widely (Gonsiorek & Weinrich, 1991; Savin-

Williams, 2006). A frequently cited statistic is 10%, but recent surveys suggest that this percentage may be an overestimate. Michaels (1996) has combined data from two of the better large-scale surveys to arrive at the estimates seen in **Figure 9.12**. As you can see, the numbers are open to varying interpretations, but as a

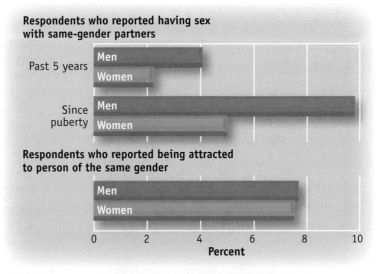

Figure 9.12

How common is homosexuality? The answer to this question is both complex and controversial. Michaels (1996) brought together data from large-scale surveys to arrive at the estimates shown here. If you look at how many people have actually had a same-sex partner in the last five years, the figures are relatively low, but if you count those who have had a same-sex partner since puberty, the figures more than double. Still another way to look at it is to ask people whether they are attracted to people of the same sex (regardless of their actual behavior). This approach suggests that about 8 percent of the population could be characterized as homosexual.

whole they suggest that about 5%–8% of the population could reasonably be characterized as homosexual.

Attitudes about gay relationships have become more favorable in recent years, but over half of Americans still condemn homosexual relations as morally wrong and oppose gay marriage and gays' right to adopt children (Herek, 2002). **Homophobia, a type of prejudice and discrimination against homosexuals,** is common, and gay men and lesbians continue to be victims of employment and housing discrimination, not to mention verbal and physical abuse and hate crimes (Herek, 2000; Herek, Cogan, & Gillis, 2002). African Americans, especially men, hold more negative attitudes toward gays than their white counterparts (Lemelle & Battle, 2004). With rare exceptions, gay couples cannot legally formalize their unions by getting married, and in fact, during the past decade many states passed laws prohibiting same-gender marriages. Gay couples are also denied many economic benefits available to married couples. For example, they can't file joint tax returns, and gay individuals often can't obtain employer-provided health insurance for their partner.

Comparisons to Heterosexual Couples

Devoting a separate section to gay couples may seem to imply that the dynamics of their close relationships are different from those seen in heterosexual couples. Actually, this assumption appears to be much less true than is widely thought. It is true that gays' close relationships unfold in a vastly different social context than heterosexuals' marital or cohabitating relationships. As Garnets and Kimmel (1991) point out, gay relationships "develop within a social context of societal disapproval with an absence of social legitimization and support; families and other social institutions often stigmatize such relationships and there are no prescribed roles and behaviors to structure such relationships" (p. 170).

Although gay relationships evolve in a different social context, research has documented that close relationships, gay or heterosexual, function in similar ways (Herek, 2006; Kurdek, 2006). Both types of couples report similar levels of love and commitment in their relationships, similar levels of overall satisfaction with their relationships, and similar levels of sexual satisfaction (Kurdek, 1998; Peplau, 1991). Resemblance is also apparent when researchers study what gays and heterosexuals want out of their relationships (Peplau, 1988; see **Figure 9.13**). Futhermore, homosexual and heterosexual couples are similar in terms of the factors that predict relationship satisfaction, the sources of conflict in their relationships, and their patterns of conflict resolution (Kurdek, 2004).

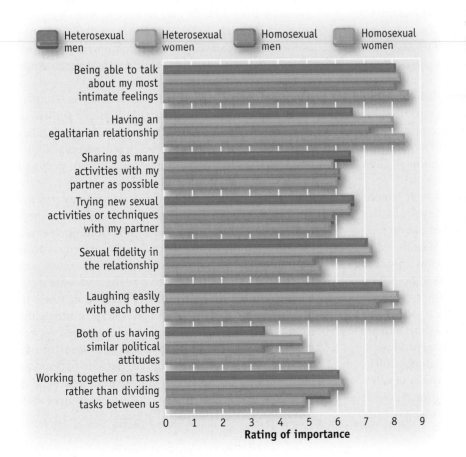

Figure 9.13

Comparing priorities in intimate relationships. Peplau (1981) asked heterosexual men and women and homosexual men and women to rate the significance (9 = high importance) of various aspects of their intimate relationships. As you can see, all four groups returned fairly similar ratings. Peplau concluded that gays and heterosexuals largely want the same things out of their relationships.

From Peplau, L. A. (1981, March). What homosexuals want. *Psychology Today, 3*, 28–38. Reprinted with permission from Psychology Today Magazine. Copyright © 1981 Sussex Publishers, Inc.

Given the lack of moral, social, legal, and economic supports for gay relationships, are gay unions less stable than marital unions? Researchers have not yet been able to collect adequate data on this question, but the limited data available suggest that gay couples' relationships *are* somewhat briefer and more prone to breakups than heterosexual marriages (Kurdek, 1998; Peplau, 1991). If that's the case, it's probably because gay relationships face fewer barriers to dissolution— that is, fewer practical problems that make breakups difficult or costly (Kurdek, 1998; Peplau & Cochran, 1990). Interestingly, Herek (2006) argues that (1) because gay and heterosexual relationships are similar on psychosocial dimensions, (2) because sexual orientation is unrelated to an individual's ability to provide a healthy family environment, and (3) given that marriage is associated with improved psychological and physical health, perhaps gay couples and their children could benefit from recognized legal partnerships. Of course, this topic is currently the subject of much national debate, one that psychologists will no doubt follow closely.

Misconceptions About Gay Relationships

Although research indicates striking similarities between homosexual and heterosexual relationships, basic misconceptions about the nature of gay relationships remain widespread. Let's look at some of these inaccurate stereotypes.

First, many people assume that most gay couples adopt traditional masculine and feminine roles in their relationships, with one partner behaving in a cross-gendered manner. This appears to be true in only a small minority of cases. In fact, on the whole, gay couples appear to be more flexible about role expectations than heterosexuals (Reimann, 1997). In comparison to married couples, gay couples display a more equitable balance of power in their relationships and are less likely to adhere to traditional gender roles (Rosenbluth, 1997; Solomon, Rothblum, & Balsam, 2004). As with heterosexual relationships, there is a negative association between adherence to traditional gender roles and relationship satisfaction among gay male couples (Wester, Pionke, & Vogel, 2005).

Second, popular stereotypes suggest that gays only rarely get involved in long-term intimate relationships. In reality, most homosexual men, and nearly all homosexual women, prefer stable, long-term relationships, and at any one time roughly 40%–60% of gay males and 45%–80% of lesbians are involved in committed relationships (Kurdek, 2004). Lesbian relationships are generally sexually exclusive. About half of committed male couples have "open" relationships, allowing for the possibility of sexual activity (but not affection) with outsiders. While intimate relationships among gays appear to be less stable than marriages among straights, they may compare favorably with heterosexual cohabitation, which would be a more appropriate baseline for comparison. Both gays and heterosexual cohabitants may face opposition to their relationship from their families and from society in general, and neither enjoys the legal and social sanctions of marriage.

Third, lesbians and gay men tend to be thought of as individuals rather than as members of families. This thinking reflects a bias that homosexuality and family just don't mesh (Allen & Demo, 1995). In reality, gays are very much involved in families as sons and daughters, as parents and stepparents, as aunts, uncles, and grandparents (Johnson & Colluci, 1999). Although exact data are not available, far more are parents than most people realize. Many of these parental responsibilities are left over from previous marriages, as about 20%–30% of gays have been heterosexually married (Kurdek, 2004). But an increasing number of homosexuals are opting to have children in the context of their gay relationships (Falk, 1994; Gartrell et al., 1999).

What do we know about gays and lesbians as parents? The evidence suggests that gays are similar to their heterosexual counterparts in their approaches to parenting and that their children are similar to the children of heterosexual parents in terms of personal development and peer relations (Patterson, 2001, 2006). The overall adjustment of children with gay parents appears similar in quality to that of children of heterosexual parents (Chan et al., 1998; Golombok et al., 2003; Tasker, 2005). Moreover, the vast majority of children of gay parents grow up to identify themselves as heterosexual (Bailey & Dawood, 1998), and some studies suggest that they are no more likely than others to become homosexual (Flaks et al., 1995). In sum, children reared by gay and lesbian parents do not appear to suffer any special ill effects and do not seem noticeably different from other children. Decades of research indicates that the quality of child-parent interactions is much more important to a child's development than parental sexual orientation (Patterson, 2006).

Understanding Intimate Violence

LEARNING OBJECTIVES

▶ *Discuss the incidence of partner abuse and the characteristics of batterers.*
▶ *Discuss why women stay in abusive relationships.*
▶ *Discuss the incidence and consequences of date rape.*
▶ *Explain the factors that contribute to date rape.*

Answer the following statements "true" or "false."

___ **1.** Most rapes are committed by strangers.

___ **2.** Research indicates that aggressive pornography does *not* contribute to sexual coercion.

___ **3.** Most women in abusive relationships are attracted to violent men.

___ **4.** Most men who have witnessed domestic violence as children will batter their intimate partners.

All of the above statements are false, as you will see in this Application, which examines the darker side of intimate relationships. Most of us assume that we will be safe with those whom we love and trust. Unfortunately, some people are betrayed by individuals to whom they feel closest. ***Intimate violence* is aggression toward those who are in close relationship to the aggressor.** Intimate violence takes many forms: psychological, physical, and sexual abuse. Tragically, this violence sometimes ends in homicide. In this Application, we'll focus on two serious social problems: partner abuse and date rape.

Partner Abuse

Cases such as the O. J. Simpson trial and the disappearance and murder of Laci Peterson have dramatically heightened public awareness of partner violence, particularly wife battering and homicide. ***Battering encompasses physical abuse, emotional abuse, and sexual abuse*** (Lundberg-Love & Wilkerson, 2006). *Physical abuse* can include kicking, biting, punching, choking, pushing, slapping, hitting with an object, and threatening with or using a weapon. Examples of *emotional abuse* include humiliation, name calling, controlling what the partner does and with whom the partner socializes, refusing to communicate, unreasonable withholding of money, and questioning of the partner's sanity. *Sexual abuse* is characterized as using sexual behavior to control, manipulate, or demean the other person (Nichols, 2006). We will focus primarily on physical abuse of partners.

Incidence and Consequences

As with other taboo topics, obtaining accurate estimates of physical abuse is difficult. Research suggests that about 25% of women and 7% of men have been physically assaulted by an intimate partner at some point in their lives (Tjaden & Thoennes, 2000). Wives attack their husbands more than most people realize (P. Pearson, 1998), but much of wives' aggression appears to be retaliation for abuse and women tend to inflict less physical damage than men (Johnson, 2000; Swan &

© AP Images/Ben Margot

The disappearance and murder of Californian Laci Peterson focused international attention on the problem of violence in intimate relationships. Laci's husband, Scott, was eventually convicted of murdering his wife and unborn child.

Snow, 2006). Thus, women are the principal victims of severe, dangerous abuse. A woman is the victim in 85% of nonfatal violent crimes committed by intimate partners and in 75% of murders by spouses (Rennison & Welchans, 2000). That said, women commit one-quarter of spousal murders, so it is an oversimplification to assume that partner abuse involves only male aggression against women. It is also inaccurate to assume that intimate violence is seen only in marital relationships. Partner abuse is also a significant problem for cohabiting heterosexual couples (DeMaris et al., 2003) and for gay and lesbian couples (Greenwood et al., 2002; Renzetti, 1995).

The effects of battering reverberate beyond the obvious physical injuries. Victims of partner abuse tend to suffer from severe anxiety, depression, feelings of helplessness and humiliation, stress-induced physical illness, symptoms of posttraumatic stress disorder, and increased vulnerability to suicide (Brewster, 2002; Lundberg-Love & Wilkerson, 2006). Children who witness marital violence also experience ill effects, such as anxiety, depression, reduced self-esteem, and increased delinquency (Johnson & Ferraro, 2001).

Characteristics of Batterers

Men who batter women are a diverse group, so a single profile has not emerged (Dixon & Browne, 2003. Some factors associated with an elevated risk for domestic violence include unemployment, drinking and drug problems, a tendency to anger easily, attitudes that condone aggression, and high stress (Stith et al., 2004). Males who were beaten as children or who witnessed their mothers being beaten are more likely to abuse their wives than other men are, although most men who grow up in these difficult circumstances do not become batterers (Stith et al., 2000). Battering appears to be somewhat more common in families of lower socioeconomic status, but no social class is immune (Roberts, 2002). Batterers tend to be jealous in relationships, have unrealistic expectations of their partners, blame others for their own problems, and have their feelings hurt easily (Lundberg-Love & Wilkerson, 2006). In many instances, the motivation for battering is to use it as a tool to exert control over women

Web Link 9.6 **Office on Violence Against Women**

This U.S. Department of Justice office was created in 1995 after federal legislation mandated national efforts to reduce domestic violence, sexual assault, and stalking. This site provides a wide variety of legal and social scientific resources in support of this mission.

(Johnson & Ferraro, 2001). Other relationship factors that are associated with domestic violence include having frequent disagreements, exhibiting a heated style of dealing with disagreements, and pairing a man holding traditional gender role attitudes with a woman who has nontraditional views of gender roles (DeMaris et al., 2003).

Why Do Women Stay in Abusive Relationships?

Women leave abusive partners more often than popular stereotypes suggest (Johnson & Ferraro, 2001), but people are still perplexed by the fact that many women remain in abusive relationships that seem horrible and degrading. However, research shows that this phenomenon is not really that perplexing. A number of seemingly compelling reasons explain why many women feel that leaving is not a realistic option, and many of the reasons revolve around fear. Many fear economic hardship and believe that they won't be able to survive financially without their husband (Choice & Lamke, 1997). Many simply have no place to go and fear becoming homeless (Browne, 1993a). Many feel guilty and ashamed about their failing relationship and don't want to face disapproval from family and friends, who are likely to fall into the trap of blaming the victim (Barnett & La Violette, 1993). Above all else, many fear that if they try to leave, they may precipitate more brutal violence and even murder (DeMaris & Swinford, 1996; Grothues & Marmion, 2006). Unfortunately, this fear is not an unrealistic one, in that many men have shown remarkable persistence in tracking down, stalking, threatening, beating, and killing their ex-partners. Despite the many difficulties of leaving abusive relationships (see **Figure 9.14**), attention is still focused on why women stay rather than on why men batter and on what interventions can prevent women from being brutalized or killed when they do leave (Koss et al., 1994). Treatment programs for men who batter their wives can be helpful in decreasing further violence, but the effectiveness of these programs is rather modest (Babcock, Green, & Robie, 2004; Roberts, 2002).

Date Rape

Unfortunately, intimate violence is not limited to marital relations. **Date rape refers to forced and unwanted intercourse in the context of dating.** Date rape can occur on a first date, with someone you've dated for a while, or with someone to whom you're engaged. Many people confuse date rape with seduction. The latter occurs when a woman is persuaded *and agrees* to have sex. Date rape often occurs when seduction fails and the man goes on to have sex with the woman without her consent. The force used in date rape is typically

Perceived Reasons for Returning to Abusive Relationships

Reasons	Mean rating
Give the abuser one more chance	10.0
Lack of financial resources	9.1
Emotional dependency on the abuser	9.0
Lack of housing resources	8.7
Lack of job opportunities	7.7
Denial of cycle of violence	7.6
Lack of support or follow-through by the legal system	7.6
Lack of child-care resources	7.1
Lack of transportation	6.7
Fear that the abuser will find her and do her harm	6.7
Lack of support from other family members	6.6
Fear that the abuser will get custody of the children	5.8
Fear that the abuser will kidnap the children	5.8
Children miss the absent parent	5.6
Lack of professional counseling	5.1
Fear that the abuser will harm the children	4.6

Figure 9.14

Perceived reasons for returning to abusive relationships. Shelters for battered wives generally report that the majority of their clients return to their partners. In one study (Johnson, Crowley, & Sigler, 1992), workers at ten shelters in Alabama were asked to rate the reasons that women returned to abusive relationships. The most frequently cited reasons are listed here in order of rated importance. As you can see, a variety of factors appear to propel women back into abusive relationships.

From Johnson, I. M., Crowley, J., & Sigler, R. T. (1992). Agency response to domestic violence: Services provided to battered women. In E. C. Viano (Ed.), *Intimate violence: Interdisciplinary perspectives* (pp. 191–202, Table on p. 199). Philadelphia: Taylor & Francis. Copyright © 1992 Hemisphere Publishing. Reprinted with permission of Taylor & Francis, Inc.

The rape allegations against basketball star Kobe Bryant focused a great deal of attention on the problem of date rape, which is far more common than most people realize.

verbal or physical coercion, but sometimes it involves a weapon.

Incidence and Consequences

How common is date rape? It's much more common than widely realized. Research suggests that 13%–30% of women are likely to be victimized by date rape or attempted sexual coercion at some point in their lives (Abbey et al., 2004; Koss & Cook, 1993; Spitzberg, 1999). Most people naively assume that the vast majority of rapes are committed by strangers who leap from bushes or dark alleys to surprise their victims. In reality, research indicates that strangers are responsible for only a small minority of rapes and that over half of all rapes occur in the context of dating relationships (see

Figure 9.15 on the next page). Most rape victims are between the ages of 16 and 24 (Sampson, 2003).

How are women affected by date rape? All rape is traumatic, but it is particularly shattering for a woman to be raped by someone she has trusted. In the aftermath of date rape, women typically experience a variety of emotional reactions, including fear, anger, anxiety, self-blame, and guilt (Kahn & Andrioli Mathie, 1999). Many rape victims suffer from depression, symptoms of posttraumatic stress disorder, and increased risk for suicide (Foa, 1998; Slashinski, Coker, & Davis, 2003; Ullman, 2004). Negative reactions can be exacerbated if the woman's family and friends are not supportive—particularly if family or friends blame the victim for the attack. In addition to the trauma of the rape, women also have to cope with the possibilities of pregnancy and sexually transmitted disease (Golding, 1996). Moreover, if the rape survivor presses charges against her attacker, she may have to deal with difficult legal proceedings, negative publicity, and social stigma.

KEY IDEAS

Challenges to the Traditional Model of Marriage

▶ The traditional model of marriage is being challenged by the increasing acceptability of singlehood, the increasing popularity of cohabitation, the reduced premium on permanence, changes in gender roles, the increasing prevalence of voluntary childlessness, and the decline of the traditional nuclear family. Nonetheless, marriage remains quite popular.

Moving Toward Marriage

▶ A multitude of factors influence an individual's motivation to marry. The norm for our society is to select a mate and engage in a monogamous marriage. Mate selection is influenced by endogamy, homogamy, and gender. Women place more emphasis on potential partners' ambition and financial prospects, whereas men are more interested in a partner's youthfulness and physical attractiveness.

▶ According to Murstein, the process of mate selection goes through three stages, which emphasize the stimulus value of the potential partner, value compatibility, and adequacy of role enactments. There are some premarital predictors of marital success, such as family background, age, length of courtship, and personality, but the relations are weak. The nature of a couple's premarital interactions is a better predictor of marital adjustment.

Marital Adjustment Across the Family Life Cycle

▶ The family life cycle is an orderly sequence of developmental stages that families tend to progress through. Newly married couples tend to be very happy before the arrival of children. Today more couples are struggling with the decision about whether to have children. The arrival of children is a major transition that is handled best by parents who have realistic expectations about the difficulties inherent in raising a family.

▶ As children reach adolescence, parents should expect more conflict as their influence declines. They must learn to relate to their children as adults and help launch them into the adult world. Most parents no longer struggle with the empty nest syndrome. Adult children returning home may be more of a problem.

Vulnerable Areas in Marital Adjustment

▶ Gaps in expectations about marital roles may create marital stress. Disparities in expectations about gender roles and the distribution of housework may be especially common and problematic. Work concerns can clearly spill over to influence marital functioning, but the links between parents' employment and marital adjustment are complex.

▶ Wealth does not ensure marital happiness, but a lack of money can produce marital problems. Inadequate communication is a commonly reported marital problem, which is predictive of divorce.

Divorce

▶ Divorce rates have increased dramatically in recent decades, but they appear to be stabilizing. Deciding on a divorce tends to be a gradual process marred by indecision. Unpleasant as divorce may be, the evidence suggests that toughing it out in an unhappy marriage can often be worse.

▶ Wallerstein's research suggests that divorce tends to have extremely negative effects on children. Hetherington's research suggests that most children recover from divorce after a few years. The effects of divorce on children vary, but negative effects can be long-lasting.

▶ A substantial majority of divorced people remarry. These second marriages have a somewhat lower probability of success than first marriages.

Alternatives to Marriage

▶ An increasing proportion of the young population are remaining single, but this fact does not mean that people are turning away from marriage. Although singles generally have the same adjustment problems as married couples, evidence suggests that singles tend to be somewhat less happy and less healthy.

▶ The prevalence of cohabitation has increased dramatically. Logically, one might expect cohabitation to facilitate marital success, but research has consistently found an association between cohabitation and marital instability.

▶ Gay relationships develop in a starkly different social context than marital relationships. Nonetheless, studies have found that heterosexual and homosexual couples are similar in many ways. Gay relationships are characterized by great diversity. It is not true that gay couples usually assume traditional masculine and feminine roles, nor is it true that gays rarely get involved in long-term intimate relationships or family relations.

Application: Understanding Intimate Violence

▶ Research suggests that about 25% of women and 7% of men have been victims of partner abuse. Women are the principal victims of serious, dangerous abuse. Men who batter their partners are diverse, but control is often the central issue. Women stay in abusive relationships for a variety of compelling, practical reasons, including economic realities.

▶ Over half of rapes are committed in the context of dating. Estimates suggest that the chances of a woman being victimized by date rape at some time in her life range from 13% to 30%. Rape is a traumatic experience that has many serious consequences. Alcohol, drug use, and gender-based sexual standards all contribute to date rape. Miscommunication revolving around token resistance is particularly problematic.

KEY TERMS

Battering p. 295	Homophobia p. 293
Cohabitation p. 269	Intimate violence p. 295
Date rape p. 296	Marriage p. 269
Endogamy p. 272	Monogamy p. 271
Family life cycle p. 275	Polygamy p. 271
Homogamy p. 272	

KEY PEOPLE

John Gottman pp. 283–284	Bernard Murstein p. 273
E. Mavis Hetherington p. 288	Judith Wallerstein p. 288

PRACTICE TEST

1. Which of the following is *not* one of the social trends that are undermining the traditional model of marriage?
   a. Increased acceptance of singlehood
   b. Increased voluntary childlessness
   c. Increased acceptance of cohabitation
   d. Increased premium on permanence in marriage

2. Endogamy refers to:
   a. the tendency to marry within one's social group.
   b. the tendency to marry someone with similar characteristics.
   c. the final marriage in serial monogamy.
   d. norms that promote marriage outside one's social unit.

3. Based on trends in the data, which of the following couples has the greatest likelihood of marital success?
   a. Stephanie and Barry whose parents are divorced.
   b. Jessica and Carlos who are both perfectionists.
   c. Gwen and Aaron who had a long courtship.
   d. Carla and Turk who married at a very young age.

4. The transition to parenthood tends to be easier when:
   a. the newborn child was planned for.
   b. the parents have realistic expectations.
   c. the new parents are relatively young.
   d. the father is not heavily involved in child care.

5. Which of the following characteristics in young children is related to maternal employment?
   a. increased hyperactivity
   b. higher anxiety
   c. decreased cognitive skills
   d. increased prosocial behavior

6. When financial resources are plentiful in a marriage, arguments about money:
   a. may still be a problem.
   b. don't occur.
   c. are a big problem only if the wife earns more than her husband.
   d. are unrelated to marital satisfaction.

7. The evidence suggests that the negative effects of divorce on former spouses' *psychological* adjustment are:
   a. exaggerated for both sexes.
   b. greater for men than women.
   c. greater for women than men.
   d. about the same for men and women.

8. What is the most probable reason for the increase in the proportion of young people who are single?
   a. Loss of faith in the institution of marriage
   b. Increased individualism and declining collectivism
   c. The median age at which people get married has increased
   d. An increase in the number of young people unwilling to undertake the financial burdens of marriage and family

9. Research on cohabitation indicates that:
   a. most cohabitants are just not interested in marriage.
   b. most cohabitants would eventually like to marry.
   c. cohabitation is declining.
   d. cohabitation experience improves the chances that one's marriage will be successful.

10. Which of the following has been supported by research on intimate relationships among gay men and lesbians?
    a. Gay couples adopt traditional male/female gender roles.
    b. Gays rarely become involved in long-term relationships.
    c. Gays have impoverished family relations.
    d. Gays want the same things out of intimate relationships that heterosexuals want.

Book Companion Website

Visit the Book Companion Website at **academic.cengage. com/psychology/weiten,** where you will find tutorial quizzes, flash cards, and web links for every chapter, a final exam, and more! You can also link to the Psychology Resource Center (accessible directly at **academic.cengage.com/login**) for a range of psychology-related resources.

Personal Explorations Workbook

The following exercises in your *Personal Explorations Workbook* may enhance your self-understanding in relation to issues raised in this chapter. **Questionnaire 9.1:** Self-Report Jeaelousy Scale. **Personal Probe 9.1:** How Do Behave in Intimate Relationships? **Personal Probe 9.2:** Thinking About Your Attitudes About Marriage and Cohabitations.

ANSWERS

1. d Pages 269–270
2. a Page 272
3. c Pages 273–274
4. b Pages 276–277
5. d Page 282
6. a Pages 282–283
7. d Page 287
8. c Page 290
9. b Page 291
10. d Pages 293–294

Gender and Behavior

On January 14, 2005, Harvard University President Lawrence H. Summers spoke at a conference of the National Bureau of Economic Research about Harvard's policies regarding diversity. Dr. Summers focused his remarks on the issue of women's underrepresentation in tenured positions in science and engineering at top universities. He offered three broad hypotheses about this gender disparity. The one that attracted the most media attention was what he called "different availability of aptitude at the high end." While he acknowledged that there are differences in socialization and patterns of discrimination between men and women, he ranked innate gender differences in mathematical and scientific ability as having greater "importance" in explaining the disparity. Dr. Summers based much of his argument on standardized tests, even though, in his own words, "These tests are not a very good measure and are not highly predictive with respect to people's ability." He went on to say, "Because if my reading of the data is right—it's something people can argue about—that there are some systematic differences in variability in different popula-tions. . . . So my sense is that the unfortunate truth—I would far prefer to believe something else, because it would be easier to address what is surely a serious social problem if something else were true—is that the combination of the [expectations for high-powered jobs] and the differing variances probably explains a fair amount of this problem" (Harvard Crimson, 2005).

As you may recall, Lawrence Summers' remarks on this issue sparked a contentious debate among academics, scientists, and the public. The war of words lingered for months and eventually led to Summers' resignation as President of Harvard. This scenario demonstrates in a highly compelling way that gender research is relevant, important, and frequently controversial. Obviously, psychologists have a lot to offer in this area, and gender has been examined for many decades and from various perspectives. In this chapter, we explore some intriguing and controversial questions: Are there genuine behavioral and cognitive differences between males and females? If so, what are their origins? Are traditional gender-role expectations healthy or unhealthy? Why are gender roles in our society changing, and what does the future hold? After addressing those questions, in the Application we explore gender and communication styles.

Gender Stereotypes

LEARNING OBJECTIVES

▶ *Distinguish between sex and gender.*
▶ *Explain the nature of gender stereotypes and their connection with instrumentality and expressiveness.*
▶ *Discuss four important points about gender stereotypes.*
▶ *Describe androcentrism.*

Let's begin by clarifying some terms. Some scholars prefer to use the term *gender* to refer to male-female differences that are learned and *sex* to designate biologically based differences between males and females. However, as respected authority Janet Shibley Hyde (2004) points out, making this sharp distinction between sex and gender fails to recognize that biology and culture

Courtesy, Janet Shibley Hyde

Janet Shibley Hyde

interact. Following this reasoning, we'll use **gender to mean the state of being male or female.** (When we use the term *sex,* we're referring to sexual behavior.) It's important to note that, as *we* use the term, *gender* says nothing about the *causes* of behavior. In other words, if we say that there are gender differences in aggressive behavior, we are simply stating that males and females differ in this area. This behavioral disparity might be caused by biological factors, by environmental factors, or by both. **Figure 10.1** sorts out a number of gender-related terms that we will use in our discussions.

Gender-Related Concepts

Term	Definition
Gender	The state of being male or female
Gender identity	An individual's perception of himself or herself as male or female
Gender stereotypes	Widely held and often inaccurate beliefs about males' and females' abilities, personality traits, and social behavior
Gender differences	Actual disparities in behavior between males and females, based on research observations
Gender roles	Culturally defined expectations about appropriate behavior for males and females
Gender-role identity	A person's identification with the traits regarded as masculine or feminine (one's sense of being masculine or feminine)
Sexual orientation	A person's preference for sexual partners of the other gender (heterosexual), the same gender (homosexual), or both genders (bisexual)

Figure 10.1

Terminology related to gender. The topic of gender involves many closely related ideas that are easily confused. The gender-related concepts introduced in this chapter are summarized here for easy comparison.

(Lippa, 2005). As you may know, the human brain is divided into two halves. **The *cerebral hemispheres* are the right and left halves of the cerebrum, which is the convoluted outer layer of the brain.** The largest and most complicated part of the human brain, the cerebrum is responsible for most complex mental activities.

Some evidence suggests that the right and left cerebral hemispheres are specialized to handle different cognitive tasks (Sperry, 1982; Springer & Deutsch, 1998). For example, it appears that the *left hemisphere* is more actively involved in *verbal and mathematical processing*, while the *right hemisphere* is specialized to handle *visual-spatial and other nonverbal processing*. This pattern is generally seen in both right-handed and left-handed people, although it is less consistent among those who are left-handed.

After these findings on hemispheric specialization surfaced, some researchers began looking for disparities between male and female brain organization as a way to explain the then-observed gender differences in verbal and spatial skills. Some thought-provoking findings have been reported. For instance, males exhibit more cerebral specialization than females (Bryden, 1988; Hines, 1990). In other words, males tend to depend more heavily than females on the left hemisphere in verbal processing and on the right hemisphere in spatial processing. Gender differences have also been found in the size of the *corpus callosum*, **the band of fibers connecting the two hemispheres of the brain** (Steinmetz et al., 1995). More specifically, some studies suggest that females tend to have a larger corpus callosum. This greater size might allow for better interhemispheric transfer of information, which in turn might underlie the more bilateral organization of female brains (Innocenti, 1994, Lippa, 2005). Thus, some theorists have argued that these differences in brain organization are responsible for gender differences in verbal and spatial ability (Clements et al. 2006; Kimura & Hampson, 1993).

Although this idea is intriguing, there are some important limitations in this line of reasoning. First, studies have not consistently found that males have more specialized brain organization than females (Fausto-Sterling, 1992; Kaiser et al., 2007), and the finding of a larger corpus callosum in females does not always show up (Hines, 1990). Second, because a significant amount of brain development occurs over the first five to ten years after birth, during which time males and females are socialized differently, it is possible that different life experiences may accumulate to produce slight differences in brain organization (Hood et al., 1987). In other words, the biological factors that supposedly cause gender differences in cognitive functioning may actually reflect the influence of environmental factors. Third, gender accounts for only a small amount of the variance in lateralization and is depen-

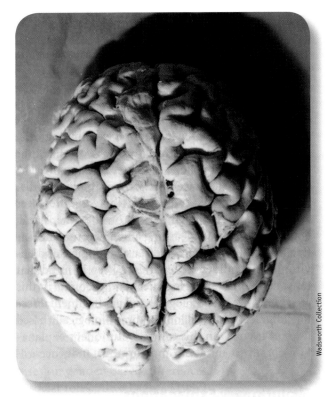

Studies have shown that the brain's cerebral hemispheres, shown here, are somewhat specialized in the kinds of cognitive tasks they handle and that such specialization is more pronounced in males than in females. Whether this difference bears any relation to gender differences in behavior is yet to be determined.

dent on the type of task (Boles, 2005). Finally, it's important to remember that male and female brains are much more similar than they are different.

Consequently, even though the popular press has often touted the idea that there are "male brains" and "female brains" that are fundamentally different (Bleier, 1984), the notion that cerebral specialization is linked to gender differences in mental abilities is still under debate. As brain imaging techniques such as MRIs become more sophisticated, the research in this area will no doubt advance.

Hormonal Influences

Biological explanations of gender differences have also focused on the possible role of hormones. As we discussed in Chapter 3, **hormones are chemical substances released into the bloodstream by the endocrine glands.** In this section we'll examine the effect of hormones on prenatal sexual differentiation and on sexual and aggressive behavior.

Prenatal Gender Differentiation

Hormones play a key role in gender differentiation during prenatal development. Biological gender is determined by sex chromosomes: An XX pairing produces a female, and an XY pairing produces a male. However, both male and female embryos are essentially the same until about 8 to 12 weeks after conception. Around this time, male and female gonads (sex glands) begin to produce different hormonal secretions. The high level of *androgens* (male hormones) in males and the low level of androgens in females lead to the differentiation of male and female genital organs.

The influence of prenatal hormones on genitalia is clear; however, their influence on behavioral gender differentiation is harder to establish and becomes apparent only when something interferes with normal prenatal hormonal secretions (Hines, 2004). Scientists have studied children born to mothers given an androgen-like drug to prevent miscarriage. Two trends have been noted in this research (Collaer & Hines, 1995). First, females exposed prenatally to abnormally high levels of androgens exhibit more male-typical behavior than other females do. Second, males exposed prenatally to abnormally low levels of androgens exhibit more female-typical behavior than other males. For example, girls with *congenital adrenal hyperplasia* (elevated levels of androgens) tend to show increased interest in "male" toys, regardless of parental encouragement to play with "female" toys (Pasterski et al., 2005; Servin et al., 2003).

These findings suggest that prenatal hormones shape gender differences in humans. But there are a number of problems with this evidence (Basow, 1992; Fausto-Sterling, 1992). First, there is much more and much stronger evidence for females than for males. Second, behavior is always subject to social factors after birth. Third, it's always dangerous to draw conclusions about the general population based on small samples of people who have abnormal conditions. Fourth, most of the endocrine disorders studied have multiple effects (besides altering hormone level) that make it difficult to isolate actual causes. Finally, most of the research is necessarily correlational, and it is always risky to draw causal conclusions from correlational data.

Sexual and Aggressive Behavior

The hormone testosterone plays an important role in *sexual desire* for both men and women (Bancroft, 2002a). That is, when testosterone is reduced or eliminated, both men and women show decreases in sexual drive. A handful of studies have also reported associations between levels of male and female hormones and specific traits, but the results of these studies are inconsistent (Fausto-Sterling, 1992; Hines, 1982). For instance, testosterone has been linked with higher levels of *aggression* (impulsive and antisocial behavior) in humans, but the picture is complicated because aggressive behavior can produce increases in testosterone (Dabbs, 2000). In fact, a recent study demonstrated that simply interacting with a gun increased testosterone levels in males (Klinesmith, Kasser, & McAndrew, 2006).

The nature of the connection between hormones and gender-specific behaviors is not well understood. Hormones have less influence on human behavior than they do on animal behavior, because humans are more susceptible to environmental influences. We still have much to learn about the complicated ways in which hormones interact with social and psychological factors.

The overall evidence suggests that, aside from obvious physical differences, biological factors play a relatively minor role in gender differences. In contrast, efforts to link gender differences to disparities in the way males and females are socialized have proved more fruitful. We consider this perspective next.

Environmental Origins of Gender Differences

LEARNING OBJECTIVES

▶ *Define socialization and gender roles, and describe Margaret Mead's findings on the variability of gender roles and their implications.*

▶ *Explain how reinforcement and punishment, observational learning, and self-socialization operate in gender-role socialization.*

▶ *Describe how parents and peers influence gender-role socialization.*

▶ *Describe how schools and the media influence gender-role socialization.*

Socialization **is the acquisition of the norms and roles expected of people in a particular society.** This process includes all the efforts made by a society to ensure that its members learn to behave in a manner that's considered appropriate. Teaching children about gender roles is an important aspect of the socialization process. *Gender roles* **are cultural expectations about what is appropriate behavior for each gender.** For example,

in our culture women have been expected to rear children, cook meals, clean house, and do laundry. On the other hand, men have been expected to be the family breadwinner, do yardwork, and tinker with cars.

Are gender roles in other cultures similar to those seen in our society? Generally, yes—but not necessarily. Despite a fair amount of cross-cultural consistency in gender roles, some dramatic variability occurs as well (Gibbons, 2000). For instance, anthropologist Margaret Mead (1950) conducted a now-classic study of three tribes in New Guinea. In one tribe, *both* genders followed our masculine role expectations (the Mundugumor); in another, *both* genders approximated our feminine role (the Arapesh). In a third tribe, the male and female roles were roughly the *reverse* of our own (the Tchambuli). Such remarkable discrepancies between cultures existing within 100 miles of one another demonstrate that gender roles are not a matter of biological destiny. Instead, like other roles, gender roles are acquired through socialization.

Keep in mind that gender roles and gender stereotypes are intertwined, each fueling the other. As we noted earlier, Eagly's social role theory suggests that gender differences often occur (and seem bigger than they actually are) because males and females are guided by different role expectations. In the next section, we'll discuss how society teaches individuals about gender roles.

Processes in Gender-Role Socialization

How do people acquire gender roles? Several key learning processes come into play, including reinforcement and punishment, observational learning, and self-socialization.

Reinforcement and Punishment
In part, gender roles are shaped by the power of rewards and punishment—the key processes in operant conditioning (see Chapter 2). Parents, teachers, peers, and others often reinforce (usually with tacit approval) "gender-appropriate" behavior (Fagot & Hagan, 1991; Lippa, 2005). For example, a young boy who has hurt himself may be told that "big boys don't cry." If he succeeds in inhibiting his crying, he may get a pat on the back or a warm smile—both powerful reinforcers. Over time, a consistent pattern of such reinforcement will strengthen the boy's tendency to "act like a man" and suppress emotional displays.

Most parents take gender-appropriate behavior for granted and don't go out of their way to reward it. On the other hand, parents are much less tolerant of gender-inappropriate behavior, especially in their sons (Lytton & Romney, 1991; Sandnabba & Ahlberg, 1999). For instance, a 10-year-old boy who enjoys playing with dollhouses will probably elicit strong disapproval. Reactions usually involve ridicule or verbal reprimands rather than physical punishment.

Observational Learning
Younger children commonly imitate the behavior of a parent or an older sibling. This imitation, or *observational learning,* occurs when a child's behavior is influenced by observing others, who are called *models.* Parents serve as models for children, as do siblings,

Parents typically reward "gender-appropriate" behavior in their children.

teachers, relatives, and others who are important in children's lives. Models are not limited to real people; television, movie, and cartoon characters can also serve as models.

According to *social cognitive theory* (see Chapter 2), young children are more likely to imitate people who are nurturant, powerful, and similar to them (Bussey & Bandura, 1984, 1999, 2004). Children imitate both genders, but most children are prone to imitate same-gender models. Thus, observational learning often leads young girls to play with dolls, dollhouses, and toy stoves. By contrast, young boys are more likely to tinker with toy trucks, miniature gas stations, and tool kits. Interestingly, same-gender peers may be even more influential models than parents are (Maccoby, 2002).

Self-Socialization
Children are not merely passive recipients of gender-role socialization. Rather, they play an active role in this process, beginning early in life (Lippa, 2005; Martin, Ruble, & Szkrybalo, 2002). Because society labels people, characteristics, behavior, and activities by gender, children learn that gender is an important social category. For example, they learn that females wear dresses and males don't. Around 2 to 3 years of age,

Children learn behaviors appropriate to their gender roles very early in life. According to social learning theory, girls tend to do the sorts of things their mothers do, while boys tend to follow in their fathers' footsteps.

children begin to identify themselves as male or female (Martin et al., 2002). In addition, they begin to organize the various pieces of gender-relevant information into gender schemas. **Gender schemas are cognitive structures that guide the processing of gender-relevant information.** Basically, gender schemas work like lenses that cause people to view and organize the world in terms of gender (Bem, 1993).

Self-socialization begins when children link the gender schema for their own gender to their self-concept. Once this connection is made, children are motivated to selectively attend to activities and information that are consistent with the schema for their own gender. For example, Terrance knows that he is a boy and also has a "boy" schema that he attaches to himself. Now his self-esteem is dependent on how well he lives up to his boy schema. In this way, children get involved in their own socialization. They are "gender detectives," working diligently to discover the rules that are supposed to govern their behavior (Martin & Ruble, 2004).

Sources of Gender-Role Socialization

Four major sources of gender-role messages are parents, peers, schools, and the media. Keep in mind that gender-role socialization varies depending on one's culture (Best & Thomas, 2004). For example, black families

typically make fewer distinctions between girls and boys when compared to white families (Hill, 2002). By contrast, gender roles are relatively rigidly defined in Asian and Hispanic families (Chia et al., 1994; Comas-Diaz, 1987). Also, gender roles are changing, so the generalizations that follow may say more about how *you* were socialized than about how your children will be.

Parents

Although a meta-analysis of 172 studies of parental socialization practices suggests that parents don't treat girls and boys as differently as one might expect (Lytton & Romney, 1991), there are some important disparities. For one thing, there is a strong tendency for both mothers and fathers to emphasize and encourage *play activities* that are "gender appropriate." For example, studies show that parents encourage boys and girls to play with different types of toys (Wood, Desmarais, & Gugula, 2002). As **Figure 10.8** indicates, gender differences are found in toy preferences. Even in private child-care settings, the toys that are available for children are often gender stereotypic (Chick, Heilman-Houser, & Hunter, 2002). Generally, boys have less leeway to play with "feminine" toys than girls do with "masculine" toys. As children grow older, their leisure activities often vary by gender: Jaime plays in Little League and Alexis gets dancing lessons.

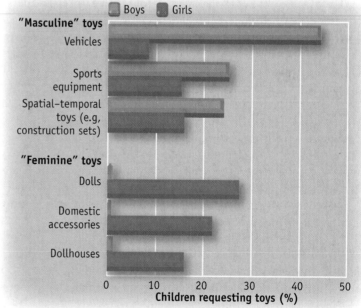

Figure 10.8

Toy preferences and gender. This graph depicts the percentage of boys and girls asking for various types of toys in letters to Santa Claus (adapted from Richardson & Simpson, 1982). Boys and girls differed substantially in their toy preferences, which probably reflects the effects of gender-role socialization.

Adapted from Richardson, J. G., & Simpson, C. H. (1982). Children, gender and social structure: An analysis of the contents of letters to Santa Claus. *Child Development, 53,* 429–436. Copyright © 1982 by the Society for Research in Child Development, Inc. Adapted by permission.

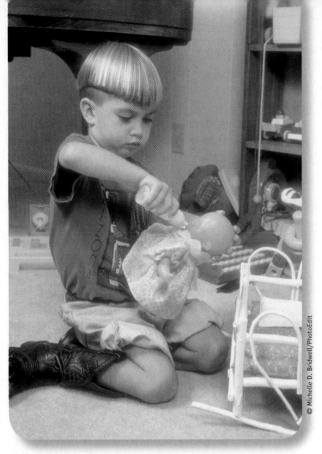

Boys are under more pressure than girls to behave in gender-appropriate ways. Little boys who show an interest in dolls are likely to be chastised by both parents and peers.

Too, the picture books parents buy for their children typically depict characters engaging in gender stereotypic activities (Gooden & Gooden, 2001). Even books that parents and teachers rate as "nonsexist" portray female characters with stereotypic personalities, chores, and leisure activities (Diekman & Murnen, 2004). Interestingly, this gender bias holds for representations of parents in these books as well. In a content analysis of 200 prominent children's picture books, Anderson and Hamilton (2005) found that fathers were underrepresented and, when they did appear, were withdrawn and ineffectual.

Another way parents emphasize gender is in the assignment of *household chores* (Lytton & Romney, 1991; Cunningham, 2001). Tasks are doled out on the basis of gender stereotypes: Girls usually do laundry and dishes, whereas boys mow the lawn and sweep the garage.

Finally, parents' attitudes about gender roles have been shown to influence the gender roles their children acquire (Fiese & Skillman, 2000). Gender expectations vary by ethnicity and socioeconomic status. African American families seem to place less emphasis on traditional gender roles than white American families do (Hill, 2002). By contrast, Hispanic families usually encourage traditional gender-role behavior, and Asian American families typically encourage subservience in their daughters (Tsai & Uemera, 1988). Also, middle-class parents may allow their children to deviate more from traditional gender roles than lower-class parents do (Reid & Paludi, 1993). Because social class cuts across ethnicity with regard to gender-role attitudes, the findings in this area are complex (Flannagan & Perese, 1998).

Peers

Children's' preferences for play activities are also highly influenced by peers (Lippa, 2005). Peers form an important network for learning about gender-appropriate and gender-inappropriate behavior. Between the ages of 4 and 6, children tend to separate into same-gender groups. From then to about age 12, boys and girls spend much more time with same-gender than other-gender peers. Moreover, according to Eleanor Maccoby (1998, 2002), over time boys' and girls' groups develop different "subcultures" (shared understandings and interests) that strongly shape youngsters' gender-role socialization (Maccoby, 1998, 2002).

Play among same-gender peers takes different forms for boys and girls (Maccoby, 1998, 2002). Boys play in larger groups and roam farther away from home, whereas girls prefer smaller groups and stay near the house. In addition, high status in boys' groups tends to be achieved by engaging in dominant behavior (telling others what to do and enforcing orders). In contrast, girls usually express their wishes as suggestions rather than demands. Also, boys engage in rough-and-tumble play much more frequently than girls do (Lippa, 2005).

Because both boys and girls are critical of peers who violate traditional gender norms, they perpetuate stereotypical behavior. Among children ages 3–11, boys are devalued more than girls for dressing like the other gender, whereas girls are evaluated more negatively than boys for playing like the other gender—for instance, loudly and roughly versus quietly and gently (Blakemore, 2003). Further, "gender atypical boys" more often report being a victim of bullying, more loneliness, and greater distress than their "typical" peers (Young & Sweeting, 2004).

Schools

The school environment figures importantly in socializing gender roles (Meece & Scantlebury, 2006; Sadker & Sadker, 1994). Children's grade-school *textbooks* have often ignored or stereotyped girls and women (AAUW Educational Foundation, 1992). Traditionally, these books have portrayed males as clever, heroic, and adventurous, whereas females have been shown performing domestic chores. Although the depiction of stereotypical gender roles has declined considerably since the 1970s, researchers still find significant differences in how males and females are portrayed, even in supposedly nonsexist books (Diekman & Murnen, 2004). Many high school and college textbooks also contain gender bias. The most common problems are using generic masculine language ("policeman" versus "police officer" and so forth) and portraying males and females in stereotypic roles. In addition, subtle word choices can reinforce stereotypes, such as passivity in females (for example, women were *given* the right to vote; Meece & Scantlebury, 2006).

Gender bias in schools also shows up in *teachers' treatment of boys and girls*. Preschool and grade-school teachers often reward gender-appropriate behavior in their pupils (Fagot et al., 1985). Teachers also tend to pay greater attention to boys—helping them, praising them, and scolding them more than females (Sadker & Sadker, 1994). By contrast, girls tend to be less visible in the classroom and to receive less encouragement for academic achievement from teachers. These findings have been replicated in other cultures as well (Best & Thomas, 2004). Overall, these teacher-student interactions reinforce the gender stereotype of male competence and dominance (Meece & Scantlebury, 2006). With regard to teacher training, many teacher education textbooks still give little attention to gender equity (Zittleman & Sadker, 2002).

Gender bias also shows up in *academic and career counseling*. Despite the fact that females obtain higher grades than males (on the average) in all subjects from elementary school through college (Halpern, 2004, 2006), many counselors continue to encourage male students to pursue high-status careers in medicine or engineering while guiding female students toward less prestigious careers (Read, 1991). Differential treatment by counselors and teachers can facilitate barriers to women's career choices (Betz, 2006; Halpern, 2006).

The Media

Television is yet another source of gender-role socialization (Luecke-Aleksa et al., 1995). American youngsters spend a lot of time watching TV (see **Figure 10.9**). A recent Nielsen Media Research report (2006) found that TV viewing is at an all-time high, with the average household watching 8 hours, 14 minutes of TV per day! A systematic review of the literature indicates that contemporary youth view an average of 1.8–2.8 hours of TV a day, with 28% watching more than 4 hours per day (Marshall, Gorely, & Biddle, 2006). Approximately 35% of children are raised in homes where the TV is on "always" or "most of the time," and these children have lower reading ability than their peers (Vandewater et al., 2005). African American children and adolescents spend more time in front of the tube than their white peers (Roberts et al., 1999).

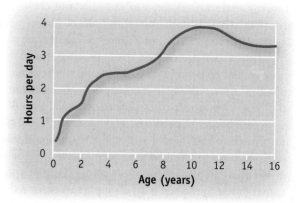

Figure 10.9

Television viewing habits. As children grow up, they spend more and more time watching TV until viewing time begins to decline slightly around age 12. Research shows that children's conceptions of gender roles are influenced to a considerable degree by what they watch on television.

Adapted from Liebert, R. M., & Sprafkin, J. (1988). *The early window: Effects of television on children and youth,* 3rd ed. Boston: Allyn & Bacon. Copyright © 1988 by Pearson Education. Adapted by permission of the publisher.

An analysis of male and female characters on prime-time *television programs* showed that the number and variety of roles of female TV characters have increased over the past 30 years but that these shifts lag behind the actual changes in women's lives (Glascock, 2001; Signorielli & Bacue, 1999). Compared to males, females appear less often, are less likely to be employed (especially in prestigious positions), are more likely to be younger, and are more likely to appear in secondary and comedy roles. As compared to female characters, males are still more likely to demonstrate competence-related behaviors such as reaching a goal, showing ingenuity, and answering questions (Aubrey & Harrison, 2004). In traditional children's adventure *cartoons* (as opposed to educational cartoons), male characters appear more often and engage in more physical aggression, whereas female characters are much more likely to show fear, act romantic, be polite, and act supportive (Leaper et al., 2002).

Television commercials are even more gender-stereotyped than TV programs (Furnham & Mak, 1999; Lippa 2005). Women are frequently shown worrying about trivial matters such as laundry and cleaning products, whereas men appear as bold outdoorsmen or energetic sports fans. In a study of gender stereotyping in TV commercials on five continents, researchers reported that, in all the countries studied, men appeared more often than women in both on- and off-screen announcer roles (Furnham & Mak, 1999). In a recent content analysis of 1,337 prime-time commercials from the three major networks, Ganahl and colleagues (2003) found that women were underrepresented in commercials (except for beauty products) and that they often played support roles for men.

Another manifestation of gender bias is television's inordinate *emphasis on women's physical appearance* (Lauzen & Dozier, 2002). Males on television may or may not be good-looking, but the vast majority of females are young, attractive, and sexy (Signorielli & Bacue, 1999). Overweight female characters are much more likely than male characters to receive negative comments about their weight (Fouts & Burggraf, 1999; Fouts & Vaughan, 2002). As you'll see in the Chapter 15 Application, these cultural expectations have been cited as a cause of the disproportionately high incidence of eating disorders in females and are related to the development of unhealthy body images (Smolak, 2006).

A meta-analysis reported a link between the number and type of television programs children watch and the acquisition of gender-stereotyped beliefs. Children who watched a lot of television held more stereotyped beliefs about gender than children who watched less

TV (Herrett-Skjellum & Allen, 1996). Still, this research is correlational, so it is quite likely that other factors—such as parental values—come into play as well. Nonetheless, once gender stereotypes are learned, they are difficult to change.

TV is not the only medium that perpetuates gender stereotypes; gender-role socialization is a multimedia event. Most *video games* push a hypermasculine stereotype featuring search-and-destroy missions, fighter pilot battles, and male sports (Lippa, 2005). Of the few video games directed at girls, the great majority of them are highly stereotypic (shopping and Barbie games). Also, *music videos* frequently portray women as sex objects and men as dominating and aggressive (Sommers-Flanagan, Sommers-Flanagan, & Davis, 1993), and these portrayals appear to influence viewers' sexual attitudes (Kalof, 1999). As demonstrated in a content analysis of *educational software* for young children, most software programs had more male than female characters, portrayed males in more stereotypical ways, and focused more on gender-stereotypical appearance for females (Sheldon, 2004).

Gender-Role Expectations

LEARNING OBJECTIVES

▶ List five elements of the traditional male role, and contrast it with the modern male role.

▶ Describe three common problems associated with the traditional male role.

▶ List three major expectations of the female role.

▶ Describe three common problems associated with the female role.

▶ Describe two ways in which women are victimized by sexism.

Traditional gender roles are based on several unspoken assumptions: that all members of the same gender have basically the same traits, that the traits of one gender are very different from the traits of the other gender, and that masculine traits are more highly valued. In recent decades, many social critics and theorists in psychology and other fields have scrutinized gender roles, identifying the essential features and the ramifications of traditional roles. In this section, we review the research and theory in this area and note changes in gender roles over the past 30 to 40 years. We begin with the male role.

Role Expectations for Males

A number of psychologists have sought to pinpoint the essence of the traditional male role (Brannon, 1976; Levant, 1996, 2003; Pleck, 1995). Many consider *antifemininity* to be the central theme that runs through the male gender role. That is, "real men" shouldn't act in any way that might be perceived as feminine. For example, men should not publicly display vulnerable emotions, should avoid feminine occupations, and should not show obvious interest in relationships—especially homosexual ones. Five key attributes constitute the traditional male role (Brannon, 1976; Jansz, 2000):

1. *Achievement.* To prove their masculinity, men need to beat out other men at work and at sports. Having a high-status job, driving an expensive car, and making lots of money are aspects of this element.

2. *Aggression.* Men should be tough and fight for what they believe is right. They should aggressively defend themselves and those they love against threats.

3. *Autonomy.* Men should be self-reliant and not admit to being dependent on others.

4. *Sexuality.* Real men are heterosexual and are highly motivated to pursue sexual activities and conquests.

5. *Stoicism.* Men should not share their pain or express their "soft" feelings. They should be cool and calm under pressure.

Gender-role expectations for males have remained relatively stable for years. However, the male role may be undergoing some changes. According to Joseph Pleck (1995), who has written extensively on this issue, in the *traditional male role,* masculinity is validated by individual physical strength, aggressiveness, and emotional inexpressiveness. In the *modern male role,* masculinity is validated by economic achievement, organizational power, emotional control (even over anger), and emotional sensitivity and self-expression, but only with women.

Thus, in modern societies, the traditional male role coexists with some new expectations. Some theorists use the plural "masculinities" to describe these variations in the male gender role (Smiler, 2004). This flux in expectations means that males are experiencing role inconsistencies and pressures to behave in ways that conflict with traditional masculinity: to communicate personal feelings, to nurture children and share

in housework, to integrate sexuality with love, and to curb aggression (Levant, 1996, 2003). Some psychologists believe that these pressures have shaken traditional masculine norms sufficiently that many men are experiencing a masculinity crisis and diminished pride in being a man (Levant, 1996, 2003). Indeed, college men who experience gender-role conflict report higher levels of internalized shame (Thompkins & Rando, 2003). The rise in popularity of men's groups and organizations such as the Promise Keepers may reflect this confusion. The good news is that boys and men are beginning to get more attention from psychological theorists, researchers, and clinicians.

Problems with the Male Role

It is often assumed that only females suffer from the constricting binds of traditional gender roles. Not so. Increasingly, the costs of the male role are a cause for concern (Levant, 1996; Pleck, 1995). As we examine the relevant research, keep in mind that many variables besides gender factor into problems related to male roles. For instance, many researchers are calling for a closer examination of the influence of culture on gender-role stress (Carter et al., 2005; Wester et al. 2006).

Pressure to Succeed

Most men are socialized to be highly competitive and are taught that a man's masculinity is measured by the size of his paycheck and job status. As Christopher Kilmartin (2000) notes, "There is always another man who has more money, higher status, a more attractive partner, or a bigger house. The traditional man . . . must constantly work harder and faster" (p. 13). Small wonder, then, that so many men pursue success with a fervor that is sometimes dangerous to their health. The extent of this danger is illustrated by men's life expectancy, which is about six years shorter than women's (of course, factors besides gender roles contribute to this difference).

The majority of men who have internalized the success ethic are unable to fully realize their dreams. This is a particular problem for African American and Hispanic men, who experience more barriers to financial success than European American men do (Biernat & Kobrynowicz, 1997). How does this "failure" affect men? Although many are able to adjust to it, many are not. The men in this latter group are likely to suffer

"Norman won't collaborate."

from shame and poor self-esteem (Kilmartin, 2000). Men's emphasis on success also makes it more likely that they will spend long hours on the job. This pattern in turn decreases the amount of time families can spend together and increases the amount of time partners spend on housework and child care.

Interestingly, younger men seem less inclined to embrace the success ethic than older men. A significantly smaller proportion of men between the ages of 18 and 37 are work focused (they want to spend more time with their families) compared to men age 38 and older (Families and Work Institute, 2004).

Gender differences in pressure to succeed might be more perceived than real. When asked about *perceptions*, college students rated the typical man as worrying about achievement more that the typical woman. However, when asked about their *own* worry, females reported more worry about achievement than male students did (Wood et al. 2005). Perhaps this finding reflects men's not wanting to express that they are worrying about anything.

The Emotional Realm

Most young boys are trained to believe that men should be strong, tough, cool, and detached (Brody, 2000; Jansz, 2000). Thus, they learn early to hide vulnerable emotions such as love, joy, and sadness because they believe that such feelings are feminine and imply weakness. Over time, some men become strangers to their own emotional lives (Levant, 1996). It seems that men with traditional views of masculinity are more likely to suppress outward emotions and to fear emotions, supposedly because such feelings may lead to a loss of composure (Jakupcak et al., 2003). Keep in mind, however, that this view is challenged by some researchers (Wong & Rochlen, 2005). As with many gender gaps, differences in emotionality tend to be small, inconsistent, and dependent on the situation. For instance, Robertson and colleagues (2001) found that males who were more traditionally masculine were more emotionally expressive in a structured exercise than when they were simply asked to talk about their emotions.

Males' difficulty with "tender" emotions has serious consequences. First, as we saw in Chapter 3, suppressed emotions can contribute to stress-related disorders. And worse, men are less likely than women to seek help from health professionals (Addis & Mahalik, 2003; Berger et al., 2005). Second, men's emotional inexpressiveness can cause problems in their relationships with partners and children. For example, men who endorse traditional masculine norms report lower relationship satisfaction, as do their female partners (Burn & Ward, 2005). Further, children whose fathers are warm, loving, and accepting toward them have higher self-esteem and lower rates of aggression and behavior

Recommended
READING

The Masculine Self
by Christopher T. Kilmartin
(McGraw-Hill, 2000)

This small paperback, written for college courses on gender, is highly readable. Kilmartin's major purpose in writing the book was to help readers "understand the difference between being male and being a 'generic human being'" (p. xiv). The implication is that androcentrism may render invisible the uniqueness of the male experience.

Kilmartin, a psychologist, does an excellent job of blending classic and contemporary research findings to shed light on important questions. About half of the book is devoted to a thorough and research-based discussion of current problem areas for men: emotions, physical health, work, sexuality, violence, relationships, and mental health. He also addresses the important issues of race, ethnicity, sexual orientation, and age. In addition, he integrates male gender-role theory into the major perspectives on personality—psychoanalytic, social learning, humanistic, and biological. There is also a chapter on cultural influences.

The book closes with an enlightening discussion of contemporary men's movements, including the mythopoetic movement (Robert Bly and Sam Keen), profeminism, the men's rights movement (Robert Farrell), and Promise Keepers. Also included is an interesting discussion of men's studies, an emerging area of scholarly work.

Two other books, also written by psychologists, focus on helping *boys* deal with gender-role pressures: *Real Boys: Rescuing Our Sons from the Myths of Boyhood,* by William Pollack (1998), and *Raising Cain: Protecting the Emotional Life of Boys,* by Dan Kindlon and Michael Thompson (1999). Although Pollack's book could better address relationships between boys and their fathers, both books offer insightful first-person accounts of the challenges boys face, especially from male peers and in the school setting.

problems (Rohner & Veneziano, 2001). On a positive note, fathers are increasingly involving themselves with their children. And 30% of fathers report that they take equal or greater responsibility for their children than their working wives do (Bond et al., 2003).

One emotion males are allowed to express is anger. Sometimes this anger translates into physical aggression or violence. Men commit nearly 90% of violent crimes in the United States and almost all sexual assaults (U.S. Department of Justice, 2003).

Sexual Problems

Men often experience sexual problems that derive partly from their gender-role socialization, which gives them a "macho" sexual image to live up to. There are few things that men fear more than a sexual encounter in which they are unable to achieve an erection (Doyle, 1989). Unfortunately, these very fears often *cause* the dysfunction that men dread (see Chapter 13). The upshot is that men's obsession with sexual performance can produce anxiety that may interfere with their sexual responsiveness.

Another problem is that many men learn to confuse feelings of intimacy and sex. In other words, if a man experiences strong feelings of connectedness, he is likely to interpret them as sexual feelings. This confusion has a number of consequences (Kilmartin, 2000). For one thing, sex may be the only way some men can allow themselves to feel intimately connected to another. Thus, men's keen interest in sex may be driven, in part, by strong needs for emotional intimacy that don't get satisfied in other ways. The confusion of intimacy and sex may underlie the tendency for men (compared to women) to perceive eye contact, a compliment, an innocent smile, a friendly remark, or a brush against the arm as a sexual invitation (Kowalski, 1993). Finally, the sexualization of intimate feelings causes inappropriate anxiety when men feel affection for another man, thus promoting homophobia.

As we discussed in Chapter 9, **homophobia is the intense fear and intolerance of homosexuality.** Because homosexuality still has a social stigma attached to it, fear of being labeled homosexual keeps many people, who might otherwise be more flexible, adhering to traditional gender roles. This situation is particularly true for males. Indeed, endorsement of traditional gender roles and hypermasculinity are both related to negative attitudes toward homosexuality (Whitley, 2001). One reason that homophobia is more prevalent among males is that the male role is rooted in the fear of appearing feminine—and feminine characteristics are mistakenly associated with gay males (Maurer, 1999). Second, homophobia is much more common in men than in women because males feel more pressure to avoid any behavior characteristic of the other gender (Herek, 2003). Although they will tolerate "tomboyism" in girls, parents (especially fathers) are highly intolerant of any "sissy" behavior exhibited by their sons. This intense pressure against appearing feminine contributes not only to homophobia among heterosexual males but also to negative attitudes toward females (Friedman, 1989).

Role Expectations for Females

In the past 30 years, the role expectations for American women have undergone dramatic changes, especially with regard to work. Prior to the 1970s, a woman was expected to be a wife and a stay-at-home mother. Today, there are three major expectations:

1. *The marriage mandate.* Even though more women are choosing to remain single, there is still a stigma attached to singlehood in a society where marriage is the norm (Gordon, 2003). Most women are socialized to feel incomplete until they find a mate. Women attain adult status when they get married. In the context of marriage, women are expected to be responsible for cooking, cleaning, and other housework.

2. *The motherhood mandate.* The imperative of the female role is to have children. This expectation has been termed the "motherhood mandate" (Rice & Else-Quest, 2006; Russo, 1979). The prevailing ideology of today's motherhood mandate is that of "intensive mothering"—mothering should be wholly child-centered, and mothers should be self-sacrificing rather than persons who also have needs and interests (Arendell, 2000).

3. *Work outside the home.* Most of today's young women, especially those who are college educated, expect to work outside the home, and they also want a satisfying family life (Family and Work Institute, 2004; Konrad, 2003). As you can see in **Figure 10.10**, the percentage of women in the labor force has been steadily rising over the last 30 years.

The marriage and motherhood mandates fuel women's focus on *heterosexual success*—learning how

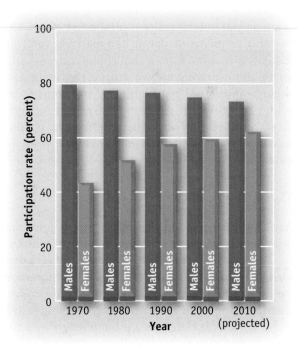

Figure 10.10

Increases in women's workforce participation. The percentage of women who work outside the home has increased steadily over the past century, especially since 1970. In 2010, close to two-thirds of women are projected to be in the labor force, about 10% fewer than men. (Data from U.S. Bureau of the Census, 2000, 2003, 2004a)

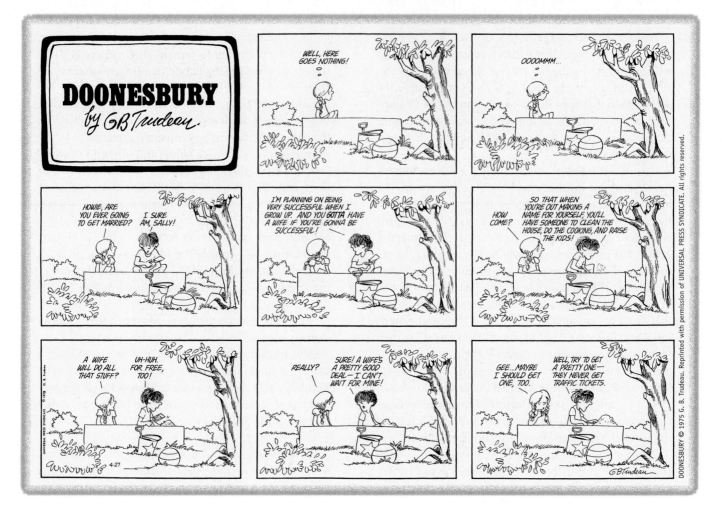

to attract and interest males as prospective mates. The resulting emphasis on dating and marriage can lead some women away from a challenging career—they worry about driving away a prospective mate who might be threatened by a high-achieving woman (Arnold, 1995). Because younger men are more supportive of their wives' working than older men, this conflict should ease for younger women (Family and Work Institute, 2004).

Problems with the Female Role

Writers in the feminist movement generated some compelling analyses of the problems associated with the pre-1970s traditional role of wife and mother (Friedan, 1964; Millett, 1970). Many criticized the assumption that women, unlike men, did not need an independent identity; it should be sufficient to be Jim Smith's wife and Jason and Robin's mother. Increasingly over the past 40 years, girls and women have been encouraged

Web Link 10.7 **Feminist Majority Foundation**

This site brings together a massive set of resources dealing with issues from a feminist perspective.

to develop and use their talents, and work opportunities for women have greatly expanded. Still, there are problems with the female role.

Diminished Career Aspirations

Despite recent efforts to increase women's opportunities for achievement, young women continue to have lower career aspirations than young men with comparable backgrounds and abilities (Wilgosh, 2001). Also, they are more likely to underestimate their achievement than boys (who overestimate theirs) (Eccles, 2001). This thinking is especially likely when estimating performance on "masculine" tasks such as science and math versus "feminine" (social skills, language) or gender-neutral tasks. This is a problem because science and math are the foundations for many high-paying, high-status careers, and it is often the lack of math background (as opposed to ability) that contributes to the inferior performance for some women (Betz, 2006). Higher intelligence and good grades are generally associated with higher career aspirations, but this trend is less likely to hold true for girls than for boys (Kelly & Cobb, 1991).

The discrepancy between women's abilities and their level of achievement has been termed the *ability-achievement gap* (Hyde, 1996). The roots of this gap seem to lie in the conflict between achievement and

Gender Stereotypes and "Appearance Pressure"

Currently in the United States, the ideal physique for women is an hourglass shape with medium-sized breasts packaged in a relatively thin body. For men, the ideal physique includes broad shoulders, narrow hips, narrow waist, and muscularity. Images of these gender ideals pervade "women's" and "men's" magazines as well as those that focus on fitness (Vartanian, Giant, & Passino, 2001). To make matters worse, many of the images are computer-enhanced and unrealistic. Physically attractive men and women dominate television programs and commercials. In an ironic use of the term, "reality" television shows such as *Extreme Makeover* and *Dr. 90210* depict real men and women undergoing extensive plastic surgery to improve their lives. The media message for today's women: thin is "in"; for men: you need "six-pack abs" to be attractive.

Weight is particularly important for women because men generally prefer thinner women to those who are heavier. For many years, this concern with thinness has existed among white and Asian Americans, but it has been a lesser concern among Hispanics and black Americans (Polivy & Herman, 2002). Unfortunately, some recent evidence suggests that the thin female ideal may be spreading to these two groups as well (Barnett, Keel, & Conoscenti, 2001; Bay-Cheng et al., 2002, but also see Schooler et al. 2004). Failure to live up to these ideals can create body dissatisfaction and lead to eating disorders (Smolak, 2006)

Today, males also seem to be experiencing "appearance pressure." Recent studies show that adolescent boys, college men, and adult males all prefer to be more muscular (Morrison, Morrison, & Hopkins, 2003; Olivardia, Pope, & Phillips, 2000). Pressure on males also appears to be coming from women, who prefer a large torso with narrow waist and hips (Maisey et al., 1999). More men are dieting, working out, and seeking surgery than has been true in the past (Olivardia et al., 2000).

Do televised images of body ideals have any impact on viewers? Unfortunately, it seems that they do—negative ones. For example, in one study, college men and women were exposed to either sexist ads, nonsexist ads, or no ads (Lavine, Sweeney, & Wager, 1999). (The sexist ads portrayed both men and women as sex objects as part of a bogus marketing research study.) The results showed that both the men and women who were exposed to sexist ads had greater body dissatisfaction than students in the other two conditions. In a correlational study, the amount of exposure to ideal body images of women on television (based on viewing habits) was measured. Women with a lot of exposure to these ideal images were more likely to prefer a smaller waist and hips and a medium-sized bust for themselves (Harrison, 2003). Further, both women and men who viewed ideal body images of women were more likely to approve of cosmetic surgery for women.

The current social pressures to attain an ideal body shape push many individuals into unhealthy eating behaviors. Experts say that eating disorders are at an all-time high (Gleaves et al., 2000). And some males may turn to dangerous anabolic steroids to build up their muscle mass (Courtenay, 2000). Another response to "attractiveness pressure" is the increased rate of cosmetic surgeries. Between 2003 and 2004, a 48 percent increase occurred in the number of cosmetic surgeries performed on Americans who were 18 and younger (Springen, 2004). Thus, the pressure to live up to an unrealistic, and sometimes unhealthy, ideal body shape is a significant adjustment challenge facing both males and females today.

femininity that is built into the traditional female role. Many women worry that they will be seen as unfeminine if they boldly strive for success. Of course, this is not a concern for all women. Still, gender discrimination remains a barrier for those who aim for prestigious careers.

Juggling Multiple Roles

Another problem with the female role is that societal institutions have not kept pace with the reality of women's lives. Women are able to successfully manage marriage and a career. But when children enter the picture, the emotional and time demands on women increase dramatically (Hoffnung, 2004).

Today 60% of married women with children under the age of 6 work outside the home (U.S. Bureau of the Census, 2004b). Yet the workplace (and many husbands and fathers) still operate as if women were stay-at-home moms and as if there were no single-parent families. This gap between policies based on outdated assumptions about women's lives and reality means that women who "want it all" experience burdens and conflicts that most men do not. That's because most men typically have *major* day-to-day responsibilities in only *one* role: worker. But most women have major day-to-day responsibilities in *three* roles: spouse, parent, and worker.

Although more men, and especially younger men, are giving additional time to household chores and child care, women still do most of this work (Family & Work Institute, 2004; Shapira-Berman, 2004). One way today's college-educated women deal with these conflicts is to postpone marriage and motherhood (and to have small families) to pursue more education or to launch their careers (Hoffnung, 2004). Women are more likely than men to expect childrearing to disrupt their careers (Singer, Cassin, & Dobson, 2005). Once women in high-powered careers are established, some are temporarily "stopping out" of the workforce to focus on childbearing and rearing their young children (Wallis, 2004). Given the three-role reality of their lives, they trade off the worker role and income for a slower pace and less stress to rear young children, although they miss the stimulation and recognition from their work. (But keep in mind that these women have husbands who can support the family.) Their strategy: "You can have it all, just not all at the same time" (Wallis, 2004, p. 53).

Of course multiple roles, in themselves, are not inherently problematic. In fact, there is some evidence that multiple roles can be beneficial for mental health, as you'll see in Chapter 12. Rather, the problem stems from the tensions among these roles and the unequal sharing of role responsibilities. Greater participation in household tasks and child-care by husbands or others as well as family-friendly workplaces and subsidized quality child-care programs would alleviate women's stress in this area. However, this issue is not clear cut. Goldberg and Perry-Jenkins (2004) note that women with traditional gender roles whose husbands did *more* child care after the birth of their first child experienced greater distress. Of course, this tendency can also be interpreted as women who did *less* child care than they expected, experiencing greater distress perhaps because they were not living up to their own gender-role expectations.

Ambivalence About Sexuality

Like men, women may have sexual problems that stem, in part, from their gender-role socialization. For many women, the problem is difficulty in enjoying sex. Why? For one thing, many girls are still taught to suppress or deny their sexual feelings (Hyde & DeLamater, 2003). For another, they are told that a woman's role in sex is a passive one. In addition, girls are encouraged to focus on romance rather than on gaining sexual experience. As a result, many women feel uncomfortable (guilty, ashamed) with their sexual urges. The experience of menstruation (and its association with blood and pain) and the fear of pregnancy add another dimension of negativity to sex. And females' concerns about sexual exploitation and rape also foster negative emotions. Thus, when it comes to sexuality, women are likely to have ambivalent feelings instead of the largely positive feelings that men have (Tolman, 2002; Hyde, 2004). Unfortunately, this ambivalence is often viewed as sexual "dysfunction" for women, as opposed to an attitude resulting from narrow gender roles and beliefs (Drew, 2003).

Sexism: A Special Problem for Females

Intimately intertwined with the topic of gender roles is the issue of sexism. **Sexism is discrimination against people on the basis of their gender.** (Using our terminology, the term should be "genderism," but we'll stick with standard terminology for the sake of clarity.) Sexism usually refers to discrimination by men against women. However, sometimes *women* discriminate against other women and sometimes *men* are the victims of gender-based discrimination. In this section, we'll discuss two specific problems: economic discrimination and aggression toward women.

Economic Discrimination

Women are victimized by two forms of economic discrimination: differential access to jobs and differential treatment once on the job. Concerning *job access*, the

Recommended
READING

The Mismeasure of Woman
by Carol Tavris (Touchstone, 1993)

The title and thesis of this book refer to Protagoras's statement that "Man is the measure of all things." Tavris, a social psychologist, has written this book for the nonprofessional audience and uses her natural wit and humor to excellent advantage. She points out the fallacy of using a male-centered standard for evaluating "what is normal" for both men and women. Using research findings, she exposes numerous myths about males and females that are the source of misunderstanding and frustration for many. Tavris is not interested in replacing a male-centered view with a female-dominant view but rather in expanding our view of what it means to be human. She urges people to move away from the tendency to think in "us versus them" terms about gender issues. Instead, she suggests that men and women need to work together and rethink how they need to be to have the kind of relationships and work that are life enhancing.

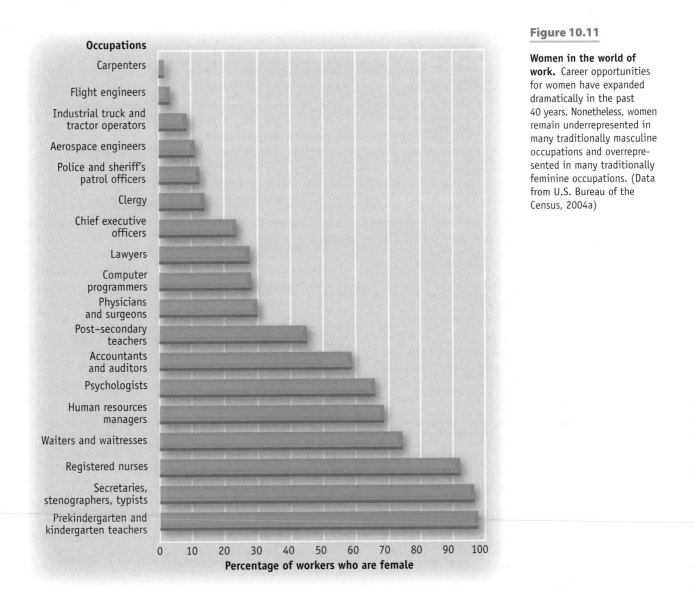

Figure 10.11

Women in the world of work. Career opportunities for women have expanded dramatically in the past 40 years. Nonetheless, women remain underrepresented in many traditionally masculine occupations and overrepresented in many traditionally feminine occupations. (Data from U.S. Bureau of the Census, 2004a)

Occupations

Carpenters
Flight engineers
Industrial truck and tractor operators
Aerospace engineers
Police and sheriff's patrol officers
Clergy
Chief executive officers
Lawyers
Computer programmers
Physicians and surgeons
Post–secondary teachers
Accountants and auditors
Psychologists
Human resources managers
Waiters and waitresses
Registered nurses
Secretaries, stenographers, typists
Prekindergarten and kindergarten teachers

0 10 20 30 40 50 60 70 80 90 100
Percentage of workers who are female

problem is that women still lack the same employment opportunities as men. For example, in 2003, only 6% of mechanical engineers were women and only 30% of physicians and 14% of Congresspersons were women (U.S. Bureau of the Census, 2004a). Further, women hold only 27.5% of all computer and mathematical related jobs (U.S. Bureau of the Census, 2005). Ethnic minority women are even less likely than white women to work in these occupations. On the other hand, women are overrepresented in "pink-collar ghetto" occupations, such as secretary and preschool and kindergarten teacher (see **Figure 10.11**).

The second aspect of economic discrimination is *differential treatment* on the job. For example, women typically earn lower salaries than men in the same jobs (see **Figure 10.12** on the next page). And occupations that are male dominated typically pay more than those that are female dominated (Pratto & Walker, 2004). Further, when women demonstrate leadership qualities such as confidence, ambitiousness, and assertiveness,

they are evaluated less favorably than men because this behavior contradicts the female gender stereotype (Eagly & Karau, 2002; Lyness & Heilman, 2006). There appears to be a *glass ceiling* that prevents most women and ethnic minorities from being advanced to top-level professional positions (Reid, Miller, & Kerr, 2004). For example, as of February 2005 there were only eight female CEOs of Fortune 500 companies (Inskeep, 2005). Ironically, men employed in traditionally female fields are promoted more quickly than their female counterparts, a phenomenon dubbed the *glass escalator* (Hultin, 2003; Williams, 1998).

Aggression Toward Females

Forms of aggression toward girls and women include rape, intimate violence, sexual harassment, sexual abuse, incest, and violent pornography. We've discussed a number of these problems elsewhere (in particular, consult the Application for Chapter 9), so we'll focus here on sexual harassment. *Sexual harassment* has be-

Figure 10.12

The gender gap in annual wages. Women continue to earn less than men in all occupational categories, as these 2005 data for selected occupations make clear. Many factors can contribute to this gender gap in earned income, but economic discrimination is probably a major consideration. (Data from U.S. Bureau of Labor Statistics, 2005)

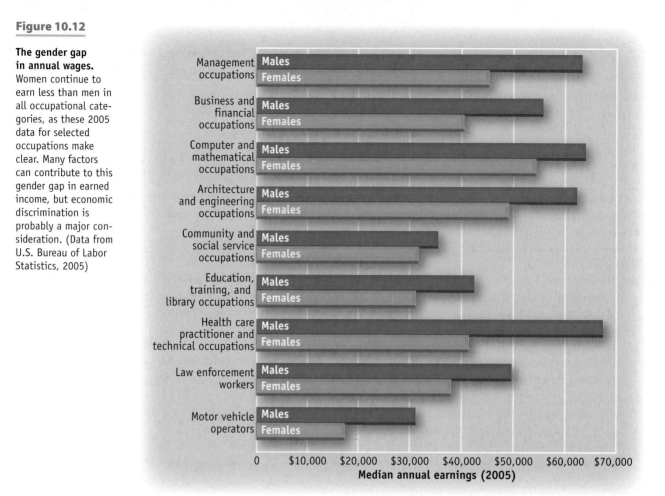

come recognized as a widespread problem that occurs not only on the job but also at home (obscene telephone calls), while walking outside (catcalls and whistles), and in medical and psychotherapy settings. It also takes place in schools and colleges (see **Figure 10.13**). Teachers and professors who pressure students for sexual favors in exchange for grades have been singled out for strong criticism.

Recent research shows that minority women experience a form of "double jeopardy" when it comes to workplace harassment. Berdahl and Moore (2006) surveyed employees from five ethnically diverse organizations and found that women experience more harassment than men, that minorities experience more harassment than whites, and that minority women experience more harassment than any other group. Betz (2006) distinguishes between two categories of sexual harassment in the workplace. In *quid pro quo harassment* employees are expected to give in to sexual demands in exchange for employment, raises, promotions, and so forth. In *hostile environment harassment* employees are exposed to sexist or sexually oriented comments, cartoons, posters, and so forth. Given that harassment continues to be a major problem in the workplace and is related to poorer job outcomes (Settles et al., 2006), future researchers will no doubt

continue to examine the relationship between ethnicity and gender in this area.

Sexual Harassment in the Schools	
Type of harassment	**Percentage reporting**
Received suggestive gestures, looks, comments, or jokes	89
Touched, pinched, or grabbed	83
Leaned over or cornered	47
Received sexual notes or pictures	28
Pressured to do something sexual	27
Forced to do something sexual	10
Other form of harassment	7

Note: Percentages do not add to 100 because readers could indicate more than one type of harassment.

Figure 10.13

Reported incidence of sexual harassment in the schools. This figure depicts common forms of sexual harassment in grades 2 through 12 and the percentage of girls reporting them. (Adapted from Stein, Marshall, & Tropp, 1993)

Adapted from Stein, N., Marshall, N. L., & Tropp, L.R. (1993). *Secrets in public: Sexual harassment in our schools*, p. 4. Copyright © 1993 Center for Research on Women at Wellesley College and the NOW Legal Defense and Education Fund. Adapted by permission.

Gender in the Past and in the Future

LEARNING OBJECTIVES

▶ *Explain the basis for traditional gender roles and why they are changing.*

▶ *Define gender-role identity and discuss two alternatives to traditional gender roles.*

In Western society, gender roles are in a state of transition. As we have noted, sweeping changes in the female role have already occurred. It's hard to imagine today, but less than 100 years ago, women were not allowed to vote or to manage their own finances. Only a few decades ago, it was virtually unheard of for a woman to initiate a date, manage a corporation, or run for public office. In this section, we'll discuss why gender roles are changing and what the future might bring.

Why Are Gender Roles Changing?

Many people are baffled as to why gender roles are changing. They can't understand why age-old traditions are being flouted and discarded. A number of theories attempt to explain why gender roles are in transition. Basically, these theories look at the past to explain the present and the future. A key consideration is that gender roles have always constituted a division of labor. In earlier societies, the division of labor according to gender was a natural outgrowth of some simple realities. In most hunting-and-gathering societies, as well as most herding societies, an economic premium was put on physical strength. Men tend to be stronger than women, so they were better equipped to handle such jobs as hunting and farming. In most societies they got those assignments, whereas women were responsible for gathering, home maintenance, and childrearing (Nielsen, 1990). Another consider-

ation was that women had to assume responsibility for nursing young children. Thus, although people might have worked out other ways of doing things (and some cultures did), there were some basic reasons for dividing labor according to gender in premodern societies.

Traditional gender roles are a carryover from the past. Once traditions are established, they have a way of perpetuating themselves. Over the past century or so in Western society, these divisions of labor have become increasingly antiquated. Therein lies the prime reason for changes in gender roles. *Traditional gender roles no longer make economic sense.* The widespread use of machines to do work has rendered physical strength relatively unimportant. Furthermore, as we move toward a service economy, physical strength will become even less relevant.

The future is likely to bring even more dramatic shifts in gender roles. We can see the beginnings of these changes now. For example, although women still bear children, nursing responsibilities are now optional. Moreover, as women become more economically independent, they will have less need to get married solely for economic reasons. The possibility of developing a fetus outside the uterus may seem farfetched now, but some experts predict that it is only a matter of time. If so, both men and women could be "mothers." In light of these and other changes in modern society, it is safe to say that gender roles are likely to remain in flux for some time to come.

A division of labor based on gender no longer makes economic sense in our society. Relatively few jobs require great physical strength; the rest call for skills possessed by both men and women.

© Paul Wood/Alamy

economic, political and psychological ones. The psychology of gender is well established, and researchers will continue to examine this concept and its changes well into the future. Next, in the Application we'll take a look at how gender affects communication styles.

Bridging the Gender Gap in Communication

LEARNING OBJECTIVES

▶ *Describe how the different socialization experiences of males and females contribute to communication problems between men and women.*

▶ *Describe expressive and instrumental styles of communication.*

▶ *Describe some common mixed-gender communication problems.*

Answer the following questions "true" or "false."

___ **1.** Men talk much more than women in mixed-gender groups.

___ **2.** Women are more likely to ask for help than men.

___ **3.** Women are more willing to initiate confrontations in relationships than men.

___ **4.** Men talk more about nonpersonal issues with their friends than women do.

If you answered true to all of these statements, you were correct. They are just some of the observed differences in communication styles between males and females. While not characteristic of all men and women or of all mixed-gender conversations, these style differences appear to be the source of many misunderstandings between males and females.

When people experience frustrating communication situations in their personal or work relationships, they often attribute them to the other person's quirks or failings. Instead, it seems that some of these frustrating experiences may result from gender differences in communication style. That is, many men and women learn to speak different "languages" in social interactions but don't realize it. Before we go any further, it is important to remember that scholars who advocate the "gender similarity hypothesis" (see Hyde, 2005), argue that gender differences in many areas including communication are exaggerated and that males and females are similar on most psychological variables. As with many of the gender differences we have discussed in this chapter, differences in communication are often small and inconsistent (MacGeorge et al., 2004).

The Clash of Two "Cultures"

According to sociolinguist Deborah Tannen (1990), males and females are typically socialized in different

Photo by Sara Barrett, courtesy of Random House

Deborah Tannen

"cultures." That is, males are likely to learn a language of "status and independence," while females learn a language of "connection and intimacy" (p. 42). Tannen likens male/female communications to other "cross-cultural" communications—full of opportunities for misunderstandings to develop.

These differences in communication styles develop in childhood and are fostered by traditional gender stereotypes and the socializing influences of parents, teachers, media, and childhood social interactions—usually with same-gender peers. As we noted earlier, boys typically play in larger groups, usually outdoors, and farther away from home than girls (Feiring & Lewis, 1987). Thus, boys are less under the scrutiny of adults and are therefore more likely to engage in activities that encourage exploration and independence. Also, boys' groups are often structured in terms of high- and low-status roles. Boys achieve high status in their groups by engaging in dominant behavior (telling others what to do and enforcing compliance). The games that boys play often result in winners and losers, and boys frequently bid for dominance by interrupting each other, calling each

---

Web Link 10.8 **Deborah Tannen's Homepage**

Georgetown University Professor Deborah Tannen has won considerable recognition for her work on communication differences between men and women in diverse settings such as the home and office. Visitors to her homepage will find a complete bibliography of professional and general interest publications by Tannen that explain her sociolinguistic theories.

other names, boasting to each other about their abilities, and refusing to cooperate with each other (Maccoby, 1998, 2002; Maltz & Borker, 1998).

In contrast, girls usually play in small groups or in pairs, often indoors, and gain high status through popularity—the key to which is intimacy with peers. Many of the games girls play do not have winners or losers. And, while it is true that girls vary in abilities and skills, to call attention to oneself as better than others is frowned upon. Girls are likely to express their wishes as suggestions rather than as demands or orders (Maccoby, 1998, 2002; Maltz & Borker, 1998). Dominance tends to be gained by verbal persuasion rather than by the direct bids for power characteristic of boys' social interactions (Charlesworth & Dzur, 1987). These two cultures shape the functions of speech in different ways. According to Eleanor Maccoby (1990), among boys, "speech serves largely egoistic functions and is used to establish and protect an individual's turf. Among girls, conversation is a more socially binding process" (p. 516).

Tannen contends that these different styles carry over into adult social interactions. Many males learn to see the social world as hierarchical. To maintain independence and avoid failure they have to jockey for high status. Hence, she says, men tend to approach conversations as "negotiations in which people try to achieve and maintain the upper hand if they can and protect themselves from others' attempts to put them down and push them around" (p. 25). Females, on the other hand, learn to see the social order as a community in which individuals are connected to others and one where the task is to preserve these connections. Consequently, women tend to approach conversations as "negotiations for closeness in which people try to seek and give confirmation and support, and to reach consensus. They try to protect themselves from others' attempts to push them away" (p. 25).

The idea that there are two cultures founded on gender-based communication styles has intuitive appeal because it confirms people's stereotypes and reduces complex issues to simple explanations. But there's an important caveat here. As we have noted, status, power, and gender role differences can lurk behind what seem to be gender differences. Many of Tannen's assertions are based on observation, and when put to the empirical test, the findings are mixed (Basow & Rubenfeld, 2003; Edwards & Hamilton, 2004; Michaud & Warner, 1997; MacGeorge et al., 2004). Also, there are individual differences in preferred styles: Some women use the "male style" and some men use the "female style." As we have noted, the social context is a much stronger influence on behavior than gender, which means that many people use either style, depending on the situation. Therefore, we caution you not to reduce *all* communication problems between males and females

You Just Don't Understand: Women and Men in Conversation
by Deborah Tannen (Morrow, 1990)

This paperback, a one-time bestseller, addresses the "communication gap" that Tannen believes exists between males and females. Tannen, a sociolinguist, asserts that boys and girls learn different styles of communication through same-gender social interactions in childhood. Because men and women often approach social interactions from different (and sometimes conflict-producing) perspectives, other-gender interactions can be problematic and frustrating. The author describes a wide variety of such interactions and provides numerous examples. In addition, she "translates" many conversations between men and women to illustrate how the different styles operate. Thus, readers can see the difference between what they think they are saying and how their messages may actually be interpreted. Tannen believes that many frustrations caused by gender differences in styles of communication could be alleviated if men and women learned to understand one another's perspectives. Tannen's other recent books, which are also worth reading, include *You're Wearing That? Mothers and Daughters in Conversation* (Random House, 2006) and *Talking from 9 to 5: Women and Men at Work* (Quill, 2001).

to gender-based style differences. It is simply not true that men and women come from different planets! In fact, MacGeorge et al. (2004) suggests that the idea of "different cultures is myth that should be discarded" (p. 143).

Instrumental and Expressive Styles

Because of the differences in their socialization experiences, men are more likely to use an "instrumental" style of communication and women, an "expressive" style, according to many researchers (Block, 1973; Tannen, 1990). An *instrumental style* focuses on reaching practical goals and finding solutions to problems; an *expressive style* is characterized by being able to express tender emotions easily and being sensitive to the feelings of others. Of course, many individuals use both styles, depending on the situation.

In conflict situations, men's instrumental style means that they are more likely to stay calm and problem oriented and to make more efforts to find compromise solutions to problems. However, an instrumental style can have a darker side. When the instrumental behavior of calmness changes to coldness and unresponsiveness, it becomes negative. Research has shown

that this emotional unresponsiveness is characteristic of many men and that it seems to figure importantly in marital dissatisfaction (Larson & Pleck, 1998).

Many studies indicate that women are more skilled than men in nonverbal communication—a key component of the expressive style. For example, they are better at reading and sending nonverbal messages (Hall, 1998; Hall & Matsumoto, 2004). And women tend to be better listeners (Miller, Berg, & Archer, 1983). But women engage in some "negative" expressive behaviors as well (Brehm, 1992). For example, during relationship conflicts, women are more likely to (1) display strong negative emotions (Noller, 1985, 1987); (2) use psychologically coercive tactics, such as guilt manipulations, verbal attacks, and power plays (Barnes & Buss, 1985); and (3) reject attempts at reconciliation (Barnes & Buss, 1985).

Common Mixed-Gender Communication Problems

Let's explore some common mixed-gender communication problems noted by Tannen. To keep things simple, we use "she" and "he" to illustrate various scenarios, but you should interpret these labels loosely for the reasons we have mentioned.

Cross-Purpose Communication
People expect their friends and partners to support and reassure them. When a mismatch occurs between their expectations and reality, they become confused, frustrated, and possibly hurt or angry. Consider a woman who tells her partner about a recurring problem she is having at work—not because she wants help with the problem but because she wants some sympathy. However, thinking that she is seeking a solution to the problem, he gives her advice. She is frustrated because

she did not receive the consolation she sought. He is frustrated about her repeated complaining, because he has offered her the same advice in the past. Although neither wants to frustrate the other, that's exactly what happens because they are talking at cross-purposes. She wants him to commiserate with her, but he thinks she wants him to help her solve a problem. Each assumes the other knows what each wants, and neither does. Cross-purpose communication can crop up quite frequently in intimate relationships.

Talking About People Versus Things
Women's conversations frequently involve sharing the details of their personal lives or talking *about* people. Talking about people isn't necessarily destructive, although it can be if it turns into talking *against* people. As they did in childhood, women share secrets with one another as a way of being close. Men are interested in details, too, but those of a different kind: politics, news, and sports. Women fear being left out by not knowing what is going on in friends' lives; men fear being left out by not knowing what is going on in the world (Tannen, 1990).

Tannen suggests that both women and men need to extend their communication strategies by adding aspects of the other style to their own. Thus, some men may need to learn to be more comfortable talking about their personal lives, whereas some women could benefit by talking more about impersonal topics and talking in a more assertive manner.

Lecturing and Listening
In many mixed-gender conversations, particularly those in public settings, women often end up playing the listener to the man's "lecture." Are men self-centered big-mouths? Are women meek, passive creatures? Instead of these interpretations, Tannen suggests that

men and women are playing different games that are rooted in their childhood experiences. Men are playing "Do you respect me?" and women, "Do you like me?"

As we noted, males use conversation to jockey for status and challenge the authority of others—both men and women. A woman who lacks experience defending herself against these challenges can easily misinterpret an assertive man's style as an attack on her credibility. Similarly, women have been taught to hand off the conversational ball and expect that others will do the same. While most women reciprocate, many men don't. When this happens, some women may feel awkward drawing the focus of the conversation back to themselves, because this style was frowned on during their childhood play with other girls.

To improve this kind of mixed-gender communication problem, Tannen suggests that women who tire of listening need to be more assertive and take some control of the conversation. Also, some men might be relieved to learn that they don't always have to talk. As we noted in Chapter 7, effective listening is a much-underrated communication skill.

Toward a "Shared Language"

Tannen asserts that many frustrations in personal and work relationships could be avoided if men and women were more aware of gender differences in communication styles. Many people misperceive style differences as the other's personal failings. Individuals who are able to see the style differences for what they are can eliminate a lot of negative feelings. As Tannen (1990) says, "Nothing hurts more than being told your intentions are bad when you know they are good, or being told that you are doing something wrong when you know you're just doing it your way" (pp. 297–298). People need to understand that there are different ways of listening, talking, and having conversations, not just their own way. For some hints on how to improve gender-based communication, see **Figure 10.15**.

Hints to Improve Communication

Hints for men

1. Notice whether or not you have a tendency to interrupt women. If you do, work on breaking this habit. When you catch yourself interrupting, say, "I'm sorry, I interrupted you. Go ahead with what you were saying."

2. Avoid responding to a woman's questions in monosyllables ("Yep," "Nope," "Uh-huh"). Give her more details about what you did and explain why.

3. Learn the art of conversational give and take. Ask women questions about themselves. And listen carefully when they respond.

4. Don't order women around. For example, don't say, "Get me the newspaper." First, notice whether it might be an inconvenience for her to do something for you. If it isn't, say, "Would you mind giving me the newspaper?" or "Would you please give me the newspaper?"

5. Don't be a space hog. Be more aware of the space you take up when you sit with others (especially women). Watch that you don't make women feel crowded out.

6. Learn to open up about personal issues. Talk about your feelings, interests, hopes, and relationships. Talking about personal things helps others know who you are (and probably helps you clarify your self-perceptions, too).

7. Learn to convey enthusiasm about things in addition to the victories of your favorite sports teams.

8. Don't be afraid to ask for help if you need it.

Hints for women

1. When others interrupt you, politely but firmly redirect the conversation back to you. You can say, for example, "Excuse me. I haven't finished my point."

2. Look the person you're talking with directly in the eye.

3. A lower-pitched voice gets more attention and respect than a higher-pitched one, which is associated with little girls. Keeping your abdominal muscles firm as you speak will help keep your voice low.

4. Learn to be comfortable claiming more space (without becoming a space hog). If you want your presence to be noted, don't fold yourself up into an unobtrusive object.

5. Talk more about yourself and your accomplishments. This isn't offensive as long as others are doing the same and the circumstances are appropriate. If the conversation turns to photography and you know a lot about the topic, it's perfectly OK to share your expertise.

6. Make a point of being aware of current events so you'll be knowledgeable about what others are discussing and have an opinion to contribute.

7. Resist the impulse to be overly apologetic. Although many women say "I'm sorry" to convey sympathy or concern (not apology), these words are likely to be interpreted as an apology. Because apologizing puts one in a lower-power position, women who use apologetic words inappropriately put themselves at a disadvantage.

Figure 10.15

Hints to improve communication between women and men. To have productive personal and work relationships in today's world demands that people be knowledgeable about gender and communication styles. Men and women may be able to benefit from the suggestions listed here. (Compiled by the authors based on insights from Tannen, 1990)

KEY IDEAS

Gender Stereotypes
▶ Many stereotypes have developed around behavioral differences between the genders, although the distinctions between the male and female stereotypes are less rigid than they used to be. Gender stereotypes may vary depending on ethnicity, and they typically favor males.

Gender Similarities and Differences
▶ Some contemporary researchers have adopted the gender similarity hypothesis, emphasizing the fact that males and females are similar on most psychological variables.

▶ There are no gender differences in general intelligence. When it comes to verbal abilities, gender differences are small, and they generally favor females. Gender differences in mathematical abilities are typically small as well, and they favor males. Males perform much better than females on the spatial ability of mental rotation.

▶ Research shows that males typically are somewhat higher in self-esteem and more physically aggressive than females. Females are higher in relational aggression. Males and females are similar in the experience of emotions, but females are more likely to outwardly display emotions. Males have more permissive attitudes about casual sex and are more sexually active than females. The genders are similar in overall mental health, but they differ in prevalence rates for specific psychological disorders.

▶ The gender differences that do exist are quite small. Moreover, they are group differences that tell us little about individuals. Nonetheless, some people still believe that psychological differences between the genders are substantial. Social role theory and social constructionism provide two explanations for this phenomenon.

Biological Origins of Gender Differences
▶ Biological explanations of gender differences include those based on evolution, brain organization, and hormones. Evolutionary psychologists explain gender differences on the basis of their purported adaptive value in ancestral environments. These analyses are speculative and difficult to test empirically.

▶ Regarding brain organization, some studies suggest that males exhibit more cerebral specialization than females. However, linking this finding to gender differences in cognitive abilities is questionable for a number of reasons.

▶ Efforts to tie hormone levels to gender differences have also been troubled by interpretive problems. Nonetheless, there probably is some hormonal basis for gender differences in aggression and in some aspects of sexual behavior.

Environmental Origins of Gender Differences
▶ The socialization of gender roles appears to take place through the processes of reinforcement and punishment, observational learning, and self-socialization. These processes operate through many social institutions, but parents, peers, schools, and the media are the primary sources of gender-role socialization.

Gender Role Expectations
▶ Five key attributes of the traditional male role include achievement, aggression, autonomy, sexuality, and stoicism. The theme of anti-femininity cuts across these dimensions. Problems associated with the traditional male role include excessive pressure to succeed, difficulty dealing with emotions, and sexual problems. Homophobia is a particular problem for men.

▶ Role expectations for females include the marriage mandate, the motherhood mandate, and working outside the home. Among the principal costs of the female role are diminished aspirations, juggling of multiple roles, and ambivalence about sexuality. In addition to these psychological problems, women also face sexist hurdles in the economic domain and may be victims of aggression.

Gender in the Past and in the Future
▶ Gender roles have always represented a division of labor. They are changing today, and they seem likely to continue changing because they no longer mesh with economic reality. Consequently, an important question is how to move beyond traditional gender roles. The perspectives of androgyny and gender-role transcendence provide two possible answers to this question.

Application: Bridging the Gender Gap in Communication
▶ Because of different socialization experiences, many males and females learn different communication styles. These differences in experience and style seem to underlie a number of mixed-gender communication problems. Men and women need to understand these style differences to reduce interpersonal conflicts and the frustrations they cause.

▶ Men are more likely to use an instrumental style of communication, whereas women tend toward an expressive style. Common mixed-gender communication problems include cross-purposes communication, differences in the tendency to talk about people versus things, and falling into the lecture and listen trap.

KEY TERMS

Aggression   p. 308
Androcentrism   p. 305
Androgyny   p. 328
Cerebral
   hemispheres   p. 312
Corpus callosum   p. 312
Expressiveness   p. 304
Gender   p. 303
Gender-role identity   p. 328
Gender-role transcendence
   perspective   p. 329
Gender roles   p. 313

Gender schemas   p. 315
Gender stereotypes   p. 304
Homophobia   p. 321
Hormones   p. 312
Instrumentality   p. 304
Meta-analysis   p. 306
Sexism   p. 324
Social
   constructionism   p. 310
Social role theory   p. 310
Socialization   p. 313

KEY PEOPLE

Sandra Bem   pp. 328–329
Alice Eagly   p. 310
Janet Shibley Hyde   p. 303

Joseph Pleck   p. 319
Deborah Tannen
   pp. 330–333

1. Taken as a whole, gender differences in verbal abilities are:
   a. small and favor females.
   b. large and favor females.
   c. nonexistent.
   d. small and favor males.

2. Among the following traits, the largest gender differences are found in:
   a. verbal abilities.
   b. mathematical abilities.
   c. physical aggression.
   d. conformity.

3. Which of the following statements about gender differences is false?
   a. Males have higher self-esteem than females.
   b. Males are more physically aggressive than females.
   c. Males have more permissive attitudes about sex than females.
   d. Women talk more than men.

4. The finding that males exhibit more cerebral specialization than females supports which of the following biologically based explanations for gender differences?
   a. Evolutionary theory
   b. Brain organization
   c. Hormones
   d. Social constructionism

5. Four-year-old Rachel seems to pay particular attention to what her mother and her older sister do, and she often imitates them. What is taking place?
   a. Sexism
   b. Observational learning
   c. Operant conditioning
   d. Androcentric bias

6. Parents tend to respond more negatively to _____ behavior, especially in _____.
   a. gender appropriate; boys
   b. gender appropriate; girls
   c. gender inappropriate; boys
   d. gender inappropriate; girls

7. Which of the following statements about peer socialization is true?
   a. Peer groups appear to influence gender-role socialization more in boys than girls.
   b. Girls play in smaller groups and boys in larger groups.
   c. High status in boys' groups is achieved by making suggestions to others.
   d. Peers have relatively little impact on gender-role socialization.

8. Which of the following is *not* a problem with the male role?
   a. Pressure to succeed
   b. Emotional inexpressiveness
   c. Sexual problems
   d. Androgyny

9. Which of the following is *not* a problem with the female role?
   a. Poor nonverbal communication skills
   b. Diminished aspirations
   c. Juggling multiple roles
   d. Ambivalence about sexuality

10. According to Deborah Tannen, men tend to use an _____ communication style, and women tend to use an _____ communication style.
    a. expressive; expressive
    b. expressive; instrumental
    c. instrumental; instrumental
    d. instrumental; expressive

Book Companion Website

 Visit the Book Companion Website at **academic.cengage.com/psychology/weiten,** where you will find tutorial quizzes, flash cards, and web links for every chapter, a final exam, and more! You can also link to the Psychology Resource Center (accessible directly at **academic.cengage.com/login**) for a range of psychology-related resources.

Personal Explorations Workbook

The following exercises in your *Personal Explorations Workbook* may enhance your self-understanding in relation to issues raised in this chapter. **Questionnaire 10.1:** Personal Attributes Questionnaire. **Personal Probe 10.1:** How Do You Feel about Gender Roles? **Personal Probe 10.2:** Reflecting on the Power of Gender Roles.

ANSWERS

1. a Page 306
2. c Pages 306–308
3. d Page 309
4. b Pages 311–312
5. b Page 314
6. c Page 314
7. b Page 316
8. d Pages 319–321
9. a Pages 322–324
10. d Page 331

Development in Adolescence and Adulthood

Teenage son or daughter: "All my parents ever ask me is whether my homework is done or how I'm doing in school. Am I studying hard enough? Do I know how hard it is to get into a good college? As if I don't know all that! Oh, sure, when I'm out with my friends they ask about where I'm going to be and who else is going to be there . . . but they don't see how important my social life is, that what I'm learning from my friends is just as important for life as the stuff I learn about in school. What they don't realize is that homework and school isn't really as important as who I'm with and what we're doing. The parties I go to, the teams I'm on, who my friends are matter as much or more than all those tests and quizzes. They have no idea how complicated my life is!"

Teen's mother or father: "Life is more complicated now than ever. I just want my child to realize how much I've sacrificed and saved and worked to make our lives as carefree as possible. I don't ask a lot, really, but grades really matter today—I wish I knew when I was a teen what I know now! I would have made many different decisions, let me tell you, and I don't want my child to have to learn the hard way or to make the same mistakes. What you do now, the habits you form, will help you in the long run. I know friends are important—I had a lot of friends at that age—but friends will be there. What you learn or don't learn now can affect you in the future. I hope my child understands that I am just trying to help."

Do these scripts sound a little familiar? Have you ever been frustrated by your parents' or your child's unwillingness to see things from your perspective, to understand life as you see it? What the teen and the teen's parents say in this scenario nicely illustrate different levels of cognitive and personality development responding to the same situation. They both see the same world, but they are experiencing that world in different ways because they are in different places in the arcs of their lives.

Until the 1970s, researchers assumed that psychological development slowed to a crawl as people reached adulthood. Now, however, psychologists realize that important developmental changes continue across adulthood, even up until the end of life. As a result, researchers are examining these changes in order to portray the crucial patterns and trends that occur. In this chapter, we review the major changes that take place during adolescence and adulthood. We also examine the topics of dying and death. Finally, this chapter's Application offers some suggestions for being an effective parent.

The Transition of Adolescence

LEARNING OBJECTIVES

▶ *Define and discuss pubescence and secondary sex characteristics.*
▶ *Define and discuss puberty and primary sex characteristics.*
▶ *Summarize the findings on early and late maturation in boys and girls.*
▶ *Describe the cognitive changes that occur during adolescence.*

▶ *Explain Erikson's psychosocial crisis of adolescence and Marcia's four identity statuses.*
▶ *Discuss whether adolescence is a period of emotional turmoil and describe recent trends in adolescent suicide.*

Adolescence is a transitional period between childhood and adulthood. Its age boundaries are not exact, but in our society adolescence begins at around age 13 and ends at about age 22. In some ways, adolescents resemble the children they were, yet the many changes they undergo during this stage ensure that they will be different from children in many respects. Similarly, we see glimpses of the adults that adolescents will become, but more often we observe that they don't behave much like adults. As adolescents mature, we see fewer resemblances to children and more similarities to adults.

Although most societies have at least a brief period of adolescence, this phenomenon is not universal across cultures (Schlegel & Barry, 1991). In some cultures, young people move almost directly from childhood to adulthood. A protracted period of adolescence is seen primarily in industrialized nations. In these societies, rapid technological progress has made lengthy education, and therefore prolonged economic dependence, the norm. Thus, in our own culture, middle school, high school, and college students often have a "marginal" status. They are capable of reproduction and are physiologically mature, yet they have not achieved the emotional and economic independence from their parents that are the hallmarks of adulthood. Globalization, immigration, and the emergence of new technologies, among other influences in daily life may alter our current conceptions of adolescence in the future (Larson, 2002). Let's begin our discussion of adolescent development with its most visible aspect: the physical changes that transform the body of a child into that of an adult.

Physical Changes

Do you remember your middle school days when your body grew so fast that your clothes just couldn't "keep up"? This phase of rapid growth in height and weight is called the *adolescent growth spurt*—"spurt" because of the relatively sudden increases in body height and weight. Brought on by hormonal changes, it typically starts at about age 11 in girls and about two years later in boys (Malina, 1990).

Psychologists use the term *pubescence* **to describe the two-year span preceding puberty during which the changes leading to physical and sexual maturity take place.** Besides growing taller and heavier during pubescence, children begin to take on the physical features that characterize adults of their respective genders. These bodily changes are termed *secondary sex characteristics*—**physical features that distinguish one gender from the other but that are not essential for reproduction.** For example, boys go through a voice change, develop facial hair, and experience greater skeletal and muscle growth in the upper torso, leading to broader shoulders and enhanced upper-body strength. Females experience breast growth and a widening of the pelvic bones, plus increased fat deposits in this area, resulting in wider hips (Dick et al., 2001; Susman, Dorn, & Schiefelbein, 2003). **Figure 11.1** details these physical changes in boys and girls.

The physical changes we've been describing are triggered by the pituitary gland. This "master gland" of the endocrine system sends signals to the adrenal glands (on top of the kidneys) and gonads (ovaries and testes), which in turn secrete the hormones responsible for the changes in physical characteristics that differentiate males and females.

Note that the capacity to reproduce is not attained in pubescence. This ability develops during *puberty,* **the stage that marks the beginning of adolescence and during which sexual functions reach maturity.** During puberty, the *primary sex characteristics*— **the structures necessary for reproduction**—develop fully. In the male, these structures include the testes, penis, and related internal structures; in females, they include the ovaries, vagina, uterus, and other internal reproductive structures (see **Figure 11.1**).

In females, the onset of puberty is typically signaled by *menarche*—**the first occurrence of menstruation.** American girls typically reach menarche between ages 12 and 13, with further sexual maturation continuing until approximately age 16 (Susman et al.,

2003). Most girls are sterile for 12 to 18 months following menarche. (Nevertheless, pregnancy is a possibility for some girls at this age, so any girl who has begun to menstruate should assume that she can become pregnant.) Breast development and the presence of pubic hair serve as important social criteria of adolescence for girls.

In males, there is no clear-cut marker of the onset of sexual maturity, although the capacity to ejaculate is used as an index of puberty (the onset of sperm production not being a visible event). *Spermarche,* **or the first ejaculation,** usually occurs through masturbation, rather than nocturnal emissions (Hyde, 1994a). Experts note that ejaculation may not be a valid index of actual maturity, as early ejaculations may contain seminal fluid but not active sperm. The average age of spermarche in American boys is around age 13 (Halpern et al., 2000), with complete sexual maturation occurring at about 18 (Susman et al., 2003).

As we have noted, puberty arrives about two years later in boys than in girls. In fact, the major reason that adult males are taller than adult females is that males typically experience two additional years of development before the onset of the growth spurt (Graber, Petersen, & Brooks-Gunn, 1996). Generational changes have occurred in the timing of puberty, at least for girls in industrialized countries (Anderson, Dallal, & Must, 2003). (To date, no valid method has been found for establishing the existence of a comparable trend among boys.) Today's girls begin puberty earlier, and complete it more rapidly, than their counterparts in earlier generations. This trend apparently reflects improvements in nutrition and medical care (Brooks-Gunn, 1991). In the United States and some other industrialized countries, this trend appears to have leveled off, probably

Figure 11.1

Physical development during pubescence and puberty. During pubescence, the two years prior to puberty, a growth spurt occurs and secondary sex characteristics develop. During puberty, the primary sex characteristics mature. These various physical changes are caused by hormonal secretions.

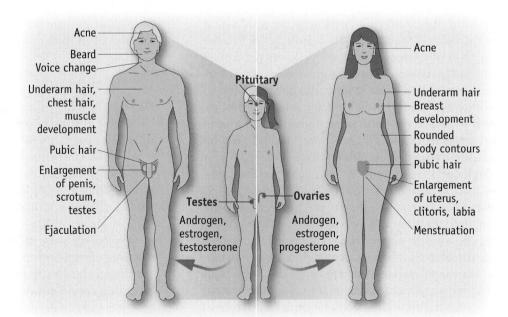

For Better or For Worse®

PUBERTY and YOU

IF MY BODY IS UNDER-GOING A MASSIVE PHYSICAL AND HORMONAL CHANGE RIGHT NOW....

WHY DOES IT TAKE SO LONG TO SHOW?!

because of the high standard of living (Tanner, 1990). Thus, the onset of sexual maturation may have a genetically predetermined age "floor."

Puberty also brings important changes in other body organs. For instance, the heart and lungs increase considerably in size, and the heart rate drops. These changes are more marked for boys than for girls and are responsible, in part, for the superior performance of males in certain physical activities relative to females. Before about age 12, boys and girls are similar in physical strength, speed, and endurance. After puberty, boys have clear advantage in all three areas (Smoll & Schutz, 1990). After sexual maturation has been attained, adolescents continue to mature physically until their secondary sex characteristics are fully developed and their body has reached adult height and proportions. In girls, such growth continues until about 17 years of age; in boys, it goes on until about age 20.

Variation in the onset of pubescence and puberty is normal. Still, the timing of these physical changes figures importantly in adjustment. More specifically, research suggests that girls who mature early and boys who mature late seem to feel particularly anxious and self-conscious about their changing bodies (Graber et al., 1997; Sinkkonen, Anttila, & Siimes, 1998). The early-maturing girl is taller and heavier than most of the girls and nearly all of the boys her age. The late-maturing boy is shorter and slighter than most of the boys and nearly all of the girls his age. To make matters worse, both groups have body types that are at odds with the cultural ideals of extreme slenderness for females and muscular physique for males.

Compared to other girls, those who mature early fare more poorly in school, are less popular, have lower self-confidence, and have earlier sexual experiences and more unwanted pregnancies (Ge, Conger, & Elder, 1996; Stattin & Magnusson, 1990). They are also more likely to have tried alcohol, cigarettes, and marijuana (Lanza & Collins, 2002), to have more negative body

images (Striegel-Moore et al., 2001), and to be depressed (Rierdan & Koff, 1991). Girls who mature early are often socially isolated from their peers who are maturing "on time," which propels the former to seek out older adolescent friends, thereby compounding their emotional distress (Ge et al., 2003). At age 24, early-maturing women have had more self-reported psychological disorders and current psychosocial symptoms compared to on-time maturers (Graber et al., 2004). Late-maturing boys have been found to feel more inadequate, to feel more insecure, and to think less of themselves than other boys do (Siegel, 1982). Still, early-maturing boys who were perceived by others to be well adjusted reported more emotional distress and hostile feelings than their less-developed peers (Ge, Conger, & Elder, 2001). At age 24, late-maturing males had engaged in significantly more deviant behavior and substance abuse than other men (Graber et al.,

As they mature, adolescents look increasingly like adults, although boys typically lag two years behind girls in physical development.

2004). Optimal adjustment for girls is associated with puberty coming "on time," whereas optimal adjustment for boys is most often related to early puberty. Girls' and boys' *perceptions* of the timing of their puberty and their feelings of attractiveness follow this same pattern (see **Figure 11.2**).

Cognitive Changes

Around the time of early adolescence, major changes take place in thinking and problem solving (Eccles, Wigfield, & Byrnes, 2003). Compared to those who are younger, adolescents can think more abstractly and more efficiently. They also become more self-aware and self-reflective and can view problems from several perspectives rather than only one. Thus, the thinking of adolescents is qualitatively different from that of younger children (Fischer & Bidell, 1998; Flavell, Miller, & Miller, 2001). Whereas children go about solving problems on a trial-and-error basis, most adolescents are capable of solving problems by generating a number of possible hypotheses and systematically testing them. These sudden intellectual advances in early adolescence can have a down side: Teens sometimes miss obvious answers through overanalysis, making a reasoning task (such as organizing a potluck

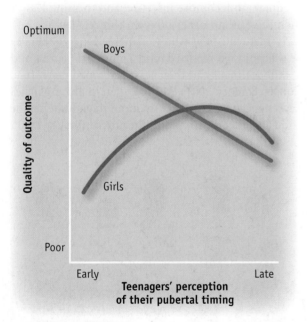

Figure 11.2

Perceived timing of puberty and optimal adjustment. For girls, feelings of attractiveness and a positive body image are associated with the perception that puberty arrives "on time"; for boys, these feelings are associated with the perception that puberty arrives early.

Adapted from Tobin-Richards, M. H., Boxer, A. A., & Petersen, A. C. (1983). The psychological significance of pubertal change: Sex differences in perceptions of self during early adolescence. In J. Brooks-Gunn & A. C. Petersen (Eds.), *Girls at puberty: Biological and psychosocial perspectives.* New York: Plenum Publishing. Copyright © 1983 Plenum Publishing Co. Adapted by permission of Springer Science and Business Media and the authors.

Web Link 11.1 **Adolescent Health and Mental Health**

Visitors at this website will find links to resources about adolescence that cover many of the pressing health and mental health issues important to this phase of development. The site is edited by Michael Fenichel, a prominent psychologist in the use of the Internet to distribute quality professional information to the public.

party and deciding who brings what type of dish) more complicated than it needs to be. Elkind (1978) refers to the resulting "Why didn't I think of that?" moments as *pseudostupidity.*

As would be expected, adolescents show increases across several spheres of knowledge compared to children. For example, as individuals age, they know more facts (declarative knowledge), have more skills (procedural knowledge), and have a greater understanding of why one problem-solving approach works better than another (conceptual knowledge) (Byrnes, 2001; Eccles et al., 2003).

Adolescents are also more skilled than children in deductive reasoning skills (Eccles et al., 2003). These skills involve the ability to reach logical conclusions when given certain information (including that which is contrary to fact). Age-related increases have also been found in mathematical, spatial, and scientific reasoning ability, as well as in some memory processes (Byrnes, 2001; Eccles et al., 2003).

Another facet of cognitive functioning involves decision making about taking risks . Numerous studies have looked at age differences in the tendency to engage in physically harmful risky behavior: smoking, drinking, and unprotected sex (Byrnes, Miller, & Schafer, 1999). Most research shows that older adolescents are more likely than younger adolescents and children to engage in such behavior (DiClemente, Hansen, & Ponton, 1995; Eccles et al., 2003). When researchers examine risky behavior by ethnic groups, they find that white teens are more likely to smoke or drink alcohol than Hispanics or blacks, while the latter group is more likely to have had sexual intercourse than either of the other two groups (Blum et al., 2000). Because "risky" adolescents are as knowledgeable about the possible negative outcomes of their behavior as "nonrisky" adolescents, psychologists speculate that the causes of risk-taking behavior are not cognitively rooted (Eccles et al., 2003). Instead, they probably involve other aspects of decision making, such as self-regulation (see Chapter 5).

Personality Changes

Adolescents are faced with a number of challenges in the realm of personality, including greater autonomy

(Noom, Dekovic, & Meeus, 2001) and "individuation," determining which attitudes, feelings, and beliefs are truly their own (Josselson, 1988). They must grapple with identity questions and deal with the stresses of moving from childhood to adulthood.

The Search for Identity

As adulthood looms closer, adolescents turn their attention to their place in the larger social order. Erik Erikson (1968), an influential psychoanalyst who followed in Sigmund Freud's footsteps, devised an elaborate theory of development over the lifespan that has been enormously influential in understanding how youngsters cope with identity issues in adolescence. Erikson's theory partitioned the life span into eight stages, each of which brings a *psychosocial crisis* involving transitions in important social relationships. **Figure 11.3** depicts all eight of Erikson's stages. We'll discuss the fifth stage in this section and subsequent stages in our upcoming coverage of adult development. According to Erikson, *identity* **refers to having a relatively clear and stable sense of who one is in the larger society.** Developing a sense of identity involves wrestling with such important issues as "Who am I?" "What do I stand for?" and "What kind of work do I want to do?" Gender, ethnicity, and sexual orientation are also important aspects of identity development.

Erik Erikson

© Ted Streshinsky/Corbis

According to Erikson, identity emerges out of an "identity crisis," or a period of personal questioning during which individuals reflect on and experiment with various occupational possibilities and value choices (political, religious, sexual, and so forth). For most people, an identity crisis is not a sudden or agonizing experience but rather the gradual evolution of a sense of who one is. An identity crisis usually ends with a commitment to a specific career and personal value system. According to James Marcia (1980), these two factors of crisis and commitment combine in various ways to produce four identity statuses (see **Figure 11.4** on the next page) instead of just the two outcomes shown in **Figure 11.3**. Note that these are not stages that people pass through, but rather statuses that characterize a person's identity orientation at any particular time. Thus, a person may never experience some of the statuses, including identity achievement. The point is that in the midst of all the biological, psychological, and social changes, adolescents try to maintain a connection to their past selves as they develop into their future selves (Chandler, et al., 2003).

The status of *identity foreclosure* is a premature commitment to visions, values, and roles prescribed by one's parents. *Moratorium* involves delaying commit-

---

Erikson's Stages of Psychosocial Development

Stage	Psychosocial crisis	Significant social relationships	Favorable outcome
1. First year of life	Trust versus mistrust	Mother or mother substitute	Trust and optimism
2. Second and third years	Autonomy versus doubt	Parents	A sense of self-control and adequacy
3. Fourth through sixth years	Initiative versus guilt	Basic family	Purpose and direction; ability to initiate one's own activities
4. Age 6 through puberty	Industry versus inferiority	Neighborhood, school	Competence in intellectual, social, and physical skills
5. Adolescence	Identity versus diffusion	Peer groups and outgroups; models of leadership	An integrated image of oneself as a unique person
6. Early adulthood	Intimacy versus isolation	Partners in friendship and sex; competition, cooperation	An ability to form close and lasting relationships, to make career commitments
7. Middle adulthood	Generativity versus stagnation	Divided labor and shared household	Concern for family, society, and future generations
8. The aging years	Integrity versus despair	"Humankind," "my kind"	A sense of fulfillment and satisfaction with one's life; willingness to face death

Figure 11.3

Overview of Erikson's stages. Building on earlier work by Sigmund Freud (see Chapter 2), Erik Erikson (1963) divided the life span into eight stages. Each stage involves a psychosocial crisis (column 2) that is played out in certain social relationships (column 3). If a crisis is handled effectively, a favorable outcome results (column 4).

Adapted from Erikson, E. H. (1963). *Childhood and society* (2nd ed.). New York: W. W. Norton. Copyright © 1950, 1963 by W. W. Norton & Co. Inc. Copyright renewed 1978, 1991 by Erik H. Erikson. Used by permission of W. W. Norton & Company, Inc. Futher permission from Hogarth Press (UK). Reprinted by permission of The Random House Group Ltd.

Marcia's Four Identity Statuses		
	Crisis present	**Crisis absent**
Commitment present	*Identity achievement* (successful achievement of a sense of identity)	*Identity foreclosure* (unquestioning adoption of parental or societal values)
Commitment absent	*Identity moratorium* (active struggling for a sense of identity)	*Identity diffusion* (absence of struggle for identity, with no obvious concern about this)

Figure 11.4

Marcia's four identity statuses. According to James Marcia, the experience of an identity crisis and the development of personal commitments can combine into four possible identity statuses, as shown in this diagram.

Adapted from Marcia, J. E. (1980). Identity in adolescence. In J. Adelson (Ed.), *Handbook of adolescent psychology* (pp. 159–210). New York: Wiley. Copyright © 1980 by John Wiley & Sons. Inc. Adapted by permission of John Wiley & Sons, Inc.

ment for a while to experiment with alternative ideologies. *Identity achievement* is arriving at a sense of self and direction after some consideration of alternative possibilities. Finally, *identity diffusion* is an inability to make identity commitments. In both identity achieve-

Recommended READING

The Hurried Child: Growing Up Too Fast, Too Soon
by David Elkind (Perseus Publishing, 2006)

In this eye-opening book, psychologist David Elkind shows how recent changes in the structure of family life have altered views of children and their needs. Earlier generations saw children as needing adult protection and guidance, a view consistent with the "traditional" family structure, in which at least one parent was available to the children at all times. Today, in many stepfamilies, single-parent households, and dual-earner families, such nurturing is impossible for parents to provide. Many of these parents have alleviated their anxiety about parenthood by adopting a new conception of children as "superkids" who can take care of themselves.

This new view of children as "miniature adults" is mirrored in every facet of children's culture: education, television, movies, and music. Computer software for infants, video games for children, and the Internet also encourage the hurrying of intellectual and social development. Thus, society as a whole conspires with the parents to "hurry" children to outgrow their need for nurturance as quickly as possible.

According to Elkind, pressuring children to grow up fast can produce negative outcomes ranging from academic failure to psychosomatic illness to teenage suicide. Nevertheless, he maintains an attitude of optimism and hope that, with awareness of the pressures today's children face, parents can and will seek to alleviate their children's stress. Reading this book can help a concerned parent to do just that.

ment and foreclosure, the identity crisis is resolved because a sense of commitment is present. Of course, in foreclosure, the commitment is not an independently developed one, as is desirable. Individuals in both the moratorium and diffusion statuses have not resolved the identity crisis. While those experiencing identity diffusion have given up the search for identity, "moratoriums" are still pursuing it. As they move into their 20s, adolescents typically shift from the foreclosure and diffusion statuses to the moratorium or achievement statuses (Kroger, 1997; Meeus, 1996).

Considerable research has been done on identity statuses and their characteristics (Marcia, 1980, 1991; Marcia et al., 1993). Compared to those in other statuses, adolescents in identity foreclosure are strongly connected to their families, cognitively rigid, conventional, and conservative in their values. Those going through a moratorium are conflicted between conforming and rebelling, have ambivalent feelings toward their parents, and are perceived by others to be intense. The identity-diffused feel alienated from their parents, exhibit lower levels of moral reasoning, and show less emotional intimacy than those in the other statuses. Those who experience identity achievement are more cognitively flexible, function at higher levels of moral reasoning, and have more emotionally intimate relationships.

Time of Turmoil?

Is adolescence a period of emotional upheaval and turmoil? G. Stanley Hall (1904), the first psychologist

Web Link 11.2 **Erik Erikson Tutorial Homepage**

Margaret Anderson, who teaches at Cortland College in New York, has developed a set of tutorials on major figures of importance to educational psychology. Her Erik Erikson tutorial includes a summary of his eight stages of development, biographical details, some controversies regarding his theories, and links to other online sources.

to study adolescence, thought so. In fact, he specifically characterized adolescence as a period of "storm and stress." Hall attributed this turmoil to the conflicts between the physical changes of puberty and society's demands for social and emotional maturity.

Does research support Hall's idea? To answer this question, Jeffrey Arnett (1999) looked at the research on three relevant issues. First, there is evidence that *parent-adolescent conflicts* increase during (early) adolescence (Laursen, Coy, and Collins, 1998). Adolescents also experience more *volatile emotions and extremes of mood* than preadolescents or adults do (Larson & Richards, 1994). Finally, adolescents engage in more *risky behaviors:* delinquent and antisocial behavior, alcohol and substance abuse, careless sexual practices, and school failure (Perkins & Borden, 2003).

Increases in these areas are not found in more traditional (preindustrial) cultures (Suarez-Orozco & Suarez-Orozco, 1995). Thus, Arnett argues that there is support for a modified storm-and-stress view that takes into account individual differences and cultural variations. Studies focused on the experience of normal adolescents in Western culture, however, indicate that even when conflicts arise, most teens continue to enjoy close relationships with their parents (Larson et al., 1996; van Wel, Linssen, & Abma, 2000). In fact, those adolescents who behave most autonomously and display some independence are also likely to claim a close connection to their parents, who continue to be asked for advice and guidance about life (Fuligni & Eccles, 1993). So, where positive regard for parents is concerned, there is some calm and continuity in the eye of the adolescent storm (Offer, Ostrov, & Howard, 1981; van Wel et al., 2000). Still, even for adolescents who do experience turmoil, it is important not to exaggerate the phenomenon. Based on her extensive studies of adolescents, Anne Petersen (1987) has concluded, "The adolescent's journey toward adulthood is inherently marked by change and upheaval, but need not be fraught with chaos or deep pain" (p. 34).

As young people progress through adolescence, the differences between the vast majority who can cope with the transition to adulthood and the small minority who cannot become increasingly obvious. Emotionally, for example, the general trend between the ages of 6 to 18 is a downward one, such that children feel less competent on various dimensions each year (Jacobs et al., 2002). Those adolescents who have trouble coping are prone to depression, suicidal behavior, drug and alcohol abuse, and chronic delinquency (Petersen, 1988; Takanishi, 1993).

Adolescent Suicide

Adolescent suicide rates have risen alarmingly in recent decades. Suicide among 15- to 24-year-olds increased dramatically after 1960, while it rose only slightly in the general population during this time. Despite these increases, only a small minority of adolescents commit suicide (Meehan et al., 1992). Also, even with the increased rate in the 15–24 age group, the incidence of suicide in this group is about the same as or lower than that for any older age group.

Actually, the suicide crisis among teenagers involves *attempted suicide* more than *completed suicide.* Attempted suicides are technically called **parasuicides, a term referring to self-destructive behavior that is not fatal nor entirely intentional.** In other words, adolescents who act out in this manner are not consciously trying to end their lives (De Leo et al., 2004; Diekstra, Kienhorst, & de Wilde, 1996). Parasuicides can range from minor (e.g., inflicting small cuts or wounds on the wrist) to potentially deadly acts (e.g., jumping from a high ledge, ingesting a bottle of pills). Consistent themes accompanying parasucide, however, are excessive emotional turmoil, bewilderment, and nervous distress.

Experts estimate that when all age groups are lumped together, suicide attempts outnumber actual suicidal deaths by a ratio of about 8 to 1 (Cross & Hirschfeld, 1986). However, the ratio of attempted to completed suicides among adolescents is much higher than that for any other age group—anywhere from 100:1 to 200:1 (Maris, Berman, & Silverman, 2000). Suicide attempts by adolescents tend to be desperate cries for attention, help, and support. Gay and lesbian youth are much more likely to attempt suicide than their hetero-

Most adolescents who attempt suicide have a long history of stress and personal problems and are socially isolated. A perceived failure at school or a perceived social slight can be the "final straw" that triggers a suicide attempt in such teens.

Recommended READING

Emerging Adulthood: The Winding Road from the Late Teens Through the Twenties
by Jeffrey Jensen Arnett
(Oxford University Press, 2006)

Is adolescence expanding so that young people are taking longer and longer to make mature decisions or to plan their lives? When do adults become adults? How do they do so? These sorts of questions are representative of the new stage, time of life, and research topic known as "emerging adulthood." According to Arnett, the years between 18 and 29 are radically different for the current generation than in generations past—the social clock seems to stop for a bit, allowing for self-focused exploration of possibilities relating to work, family, and future.

What makes the argument interesting is the experience and behavior of the people in this age group. At the same time they are exploring new horizons involving, for example, love and sex, they feel at sea, uncertain about what to do and what is to come. And yet, according to Arnett, emerging adults are quite able to reach a balance among their conflicting thoughts, feelings, and longings. Adolescents, parents, and emerging adults themselves (to which group do you belong?) will want to consider the thought-provoking possibilities for the twentysomething generation of Americans.

The positive outcome of Erikson's sixth stage is intimacy, or the capacity to relate openly to others and to make emotional commitments. Isolation, the negative outcome, is characterized by difficulties in forming relationships with others.

Arnett (2000, 2004) made the radical claim for "emerging adulthood," a period of time running from the late teen years through the 20s. Young adults are not necessarily marrying or having children as early as in past generations, for example, and their dependence on their own parents for emotional as well as financial support seems different from that of previous generations. Arnett suggests that young people are using this new time of growth to discover their identities more fully where career and family is concerned. The question for psychological research is whether emerging adulthood represents a real and new stage of development or whether its demographic reality is more historical (and potentially short term) than evolutionary. Research, too, needs to definitively determine whether emerging adulthood is limited to fast-paced, industrialized Western countries or whether the same pattern of development can be discerned in other cultures, as well.

Erikson's Theory: Intimacy Versus Isolation

In Erikson's sixth stage, the psychosocial crisis centers on whether a person can develop the capacity to share *intimacy* with others (refer back to **Figure 11.3**). Erik-son was not concerned simply with the young adult's need to find a marriage partner. Rather, he was concerned with more subtle issues, such as whether one can learn to open up to others, truly commit to others, and give of oneself unselfishly. The person who can experience genuine intimacy is thought to be more likely to develop a mature and successful long-term relationship. Failure to favorably resolve this psychosocial crisis leads to difficulties in relating to others in an authentic fashion. The resulting sense of isolation can foster competitive interactions with friends and troublesome intimate relationships.

Jacob Orlofsky and his colleagues (1973) found support for five intimacy statuses, based on the quality of a person's relationships with others.

1. *Intimate.* Individuals in this status are capable of forming open and close relationships with both male and female friends and are involved in a committed relationship.

2. *Preintimate.* Although people in this category are capable of mature, reciprocal relationships, they haven't yet experienced a committed relationship because they are ambivalent about making commitments.

3. *Stereotyped.* Men and women in this status have relationships that are superficial and not very close. They often see others as objects to manipulate rather than to share with.

4. *Pseudointimate.* These individuals are typically involved in a relatively permanent relationship, but it resembles the stereotyped relationship in quality.

5. *Isolate.* Isolates avoid social situations and appear to be loners whose social interactions consist of casual conversations with a few acquaintances.

According to Erikson, the ability to establish and maintain intimate relationships depends on having successfully weathered the identity crisis of adolescence. The rationale here is that without a clear sense of yourself before you enter into an intimate relationship, you risk becoming overly dependent on someone else for your identity. Researchers typically find that college males and females in the more advanced identity statuses (achievement and moratorium) are most likely to be in the more advanced intimacy statuses (intimate and preintimate) (Fitch & Adams, 1983). Similarly, those experiencing identity foreclosure or diffusion predominate in the less advanced intimacy statuses (stereotyped, pseudointimate, and isolate). A similar pattern has been found in adults up to 35 years of age (Raskin, 1986; Tesch & Whitbourne, 1982).

Going beyond Erikson's theory, two specific developmental tasks of early adulthood are adjusting to full-time work and adjusting to marriage and family life. After all, Sigmund Freud (1935) famously claimed that the healthy adult individual is one who can "love and work."

Adjusting to the World of Work

Young adults are confronted with several major challenges in their work lives (Super, 1957, 1985, 1988). To start, they need to complete their schooling and secure their first job. At this point in career development, many people are still only tentatively committed to their chosen occupational area. If their first experiences are not rewarding, they may shift to another area, where they continue to explore their work options.

Web Link 11.3 **Adult Development and Aging (APA Division 20)**

Psychological researchers interested in adulthood and aging form a distinct division within the American Psychological Association—Division 20. The division's homepage contains a wide range of educational, instructional, and clinical resources and references for this area of concern.

People in their twenties change jobs on the average of every two years (Peterson & Gonzales, 2005).

Once men begin working full-time, they tend to stay in the workforce until they retire (a continuous pattern). Women's work lives often have a discontinuous pattern—typically because women have greater child-care responsibilities. Thus, they may move in and out of the workforce at different points in their lives (Betz, 1993). Those women who maintain full-time careers nonetheless often end up working a veritable "second shift" by managing the household responsibilities and children (Hochschild, 1989). Equality and opportunity for women in the workplace does not necessarily mean equality on the home front. Although many couples share domestic duties, a large part of the traditional ones (e.g., child care, food preparation, housekeeping) seem to fall to women.

Adjusting to Marriage and Family Life

Although an increasing proportion of the population under 35 are remaining single (Teachman, Polonko, & Scanzoni, 1999), most people marry or become involved in committed relationships during early adulthood. Today, the average age of first marriage for women is about 25; for men, it is about 27 (U.S. Bureau, of the Census 2004a). As noted in Chapter 9, the first few years of married life tend to be very happy. The early years of committed gay and lesbian relationships also follow this pattern (Peplau & Spalding, 2003).

Compared to earlier generations, more of today's married couples are choosing not to have children (Bulcroft & Teachman, 2004), but the vast majority plan to do so. The arrival of the first child represents a major transition. Among other things, it triggers a shift toward traditional roles for husband and wife (Cowan & Cowan, 1997). This shift is significant because greater discrepancies between the responsibilities of husband and wife after childbirth are associated with more marital conflict as well as declines in marital satisfaction and mental health, particularly for women (Perry-Jenkins, Repetti, & Crouter, 2001).

As already noted, even in dual-earner families, women typically bear greater responsibilities in the realms of child care and housework (Bond et al., 2003). Thus, mothers experience more work-family conflicts than fathers do. After the first few years of married life, marital satisfaction typically declines and continues at a lower level until middle adulthood, when it rises again (Glenn, 1998).

Like heterosexual married couples, most gay and lesbian couples are in dual-worker relationships. Unlike married couples, however, committed homosexual couples are more likely to have a flexible division of labor, where the workload is shared and tasks are completed based on personal preference (Peplau & Spalding, 2003).

Middle Adulthood
(From About Age 40 to 65)

Compared to early adulthood, which requires learning so many new roles, middle adulthood is an easier period.

Erikson's Theory: Generativity Versus Stagnation

The challenge of middle adulthood is acquiring *generativity,* or a concern for the welfare of future generations (refer to **Figure 11.3**). According to Erikson and researchers who have used the construct (e.g., McAdams, 1997), generativity is a desire to "give back" to the people one loves or knows, or even to help the community where one resides. Such giving can take the form of sharing a talent or a skill, leading a youth group, organizing a charity event, or simply spending time doing activities that can promote the greater good, such as volunteer work. The important point is that being a "generative" person helps the self by establishing meaning and purpose at the same time it helps others in direct and literal ways. The desire to be generative motivates people to leave something behind that can represent the best of themselves while establishing connections to others.

Adults demonstrate generativity when they provide unselfish guidance to younger people. The recipients of this guidance are often their own children, but not necessarily. Generativity can often occur as a result of one's work (Wethington, 2002). For example, a middle-aged college professor may gain great satisfaction from working with students. Or a 50-year-old attorney might mentor a younger woman in her law firm. Thus, generativity and its opposite, stagnation, do not hinge on a person's having children. Stagnation is characterized by self-absorption and self-indulgent preoccupation with one's own needs.

A number of studies support Erikson's views on generativity and middle adulthood. For example, researchers have found that generativity increases between young adulthood and middle age (de St. Aubin, McAdams, & Kim, 2004; Stewart, Ostrove, & Helson, 2001). Studies also report that highly generative individuals are well adjusted (low levels of anxiety and depression) and high in life satisfaction (Ackerman, Zuroff, & Moskowitz, 2000; Grossbaum & Bates, 2002). More specific challenges of middle age include confronting the aging process and making transitions in work and family roles. Let's look at these issues.

Confronting the Aging Process

What does it mean to be "middle aged"? How do we know whether we are still a young adult or in our mid-years? The middle years can begin around age 40 and continue to the mid-60s. But what happens if a 70-year-old feels and acts like someone who is 50? Is she no longer middle-aged? The conceptual and experiential difficulty people face is that the whole idea of middle age as a stage of life is a relatively new one. Prior to the 20th century, there was no "midlife" per se (Moen & Wethington, 1999). Great strides in health, wealth, and social well-being have expanded the life span dramatically over the last century (see **Figure 11.7**). As a result, the nature and fabric of middle age has changed (Willis & Reid, 1999). Around 1900, the outer

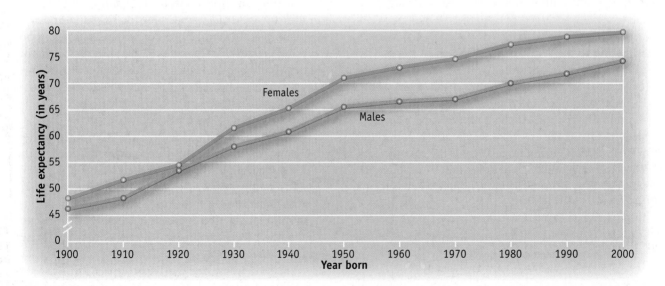

Figure 11.7

Trends in life expectancy. Average life expectancy at birth in the United States has increased dramatically since 1900, as this graph shows. Today, on average, people live about 30 years longer than their ancestors from a century ago. This increase in longevity has changed people's typical developmental trajectories and has altered the concept of aging. (Data from National Center for Health Statistics, 2006)

ZITS © Jerry Scott and Jim Borgman. Reprinted by permission of King Features Syndicate.

rim of people's life span was 50 years. Can you imagine being considered an elderly person at age 50? In our time, some might argue that 50 is an age where things are just getting interesting, where many adults are just hitting their strides (e.g., career is presumably on track, children are grown and soon to be out on their own). Of course, modern or not, midlife presents several challenges.

Chief among these challenges is coming to terms with the aging process. Middle-aged adults notice a number of physical transformations: changes in vision that often require glasses or bifocals for reading, the onset of wrinkles and sagging skin, weight gain, tooth and gum problems, and more bodily aches and pains and general "creakiness" (Lachman, 2004; Whitbourne, 2001). Even people's height decreases (around an inch on average) as the vertebrae in their spines compresses a bit (Merrill & Verbrugge, 1999). In addition, people are forced to acknowledge their mortality as they witness the deaths of parents, colleagues, and friends.

Actual chronological aging does affect everyone, but for many people, the perception of aging does not (Staudinger & Bluck, 2001). After early adulthood, people perceive themselves to be younger than they actually are (Montepare & Lachman, 1989). In **Figure 11.8**, you can see that the gap between actual and subjective age widens over time, especially among women, suggesting that women find it harder to accept growing older. This attitude no doubt reflects the "double standard of aging"—the perception that women's attractiveness declines more with age than men's does (Zebrowitz & Montepare, 2000). On a positive note, feeling younger than one's actual age is correlated with greater psychological adjustment and health (Lachman, 2004).

Transitions in the Parenting Role
As children grow up, parental influence tends to decline, and the early years of parenting—which once seemed so difficult—are often recalled with fondness. When children reach adolescence and seek to establish their

own identities, gradual realignment occurs in parent-child relationships. As a result, conflicts over values are common, and power struggles frequently ensue (Arnett, 1999). Parents overwhelmingly rate adolescence as the most difficult stage of childrearing (Steinberg, 2001). Still, on balance, most parents have little regret about their decision to have children and rate parenthood as a positive experience (Demo, 1992).

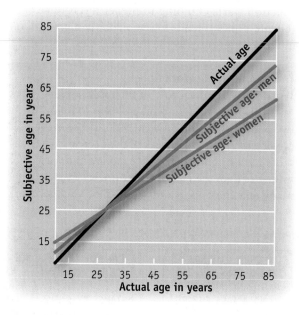

Figure 11.8

Discrepancies between actual and subjective age. After early adulthood, people see themselves as younger than they really are. This gap between reality and perception increases with age, especially among women. This graph also shows that adolescents perceive themselves to be older than they really are, while the age perceptions of young adults match reality fairly closely.

Adapted from Montepare, J., & Lachman, M. E. (1989). You're only as old as you feel: Self-perceptions of age, fears of aging, and life satisfaction. *Psychology and Aging, 4,* 73–78. Copyright © 1989 American Psychological Association. Adapted by permission of the publisher and author.

Although "emptying of the nest" is widely believed to be a traumatic event for parents, especially mothers, only about 25 percent of mothers and fathers report being very sad or unhappy when the last child leaves home (Lewis & Lin, 1996). Although its impact may be relatively minor, the "empty nest syndrome" may not be limited exclusively to parents. Interestingly, younger siblings who remain at home after their brothers or sisters leave report some sadness as a result (Rosen, Ackerman, & Zosky, 2002). For most women who are parents, the "empty nest" is associated with improved mood and well-being; however, when their young adult children return home for a time (as "emerging adults" often do), mothers' moods and the sexual relationships of the parents can suffer (Dennerstein, Dudley, & Guthrie, 2002). An interesting phenomenon is that in recent decades, the percentage of young adults who return home to live with their parents has increased. Returning home is due to a number of factors: inability to find a job, marital separation, divorce, or job loss. To date, research indicates that young adults living with their parents has a small negative impact on parent-child relationships (White & Rogers, 1997).

The postparental period often provides couples with more freedom and time to devote to each other, to travel, and to pursue new leisure interests. As offspring strike out on their own, couples' marital satisfaction starts climbing to higher levels once again (Glenn, 1998). It tends to remain fairly high until one of the spouses (usually the husband) dies.

Transitions in the Work Role

Work plays a central role in the midlife years (Lachman, 2004). At midlife, workers seem to follow one of two patterns (Papalia & Olds, 1995). Those in the *stable career pattern* are at the peak of their careers. They have more responsibility, earn more money, and wield more influence than their younger co-workers. As we noted, many take the opportunity to mentor younger work-ers, an expression of generativity. Some workers in this group continue to work at a frantic pace, struggling to accomplish their goals as they hear their social clocks ticking. Others seem content with their work achievements and begin to shift some of their attention and energy to family and leisure activities.

Workers in the *changing careers pattern* make up a more varied group. Whereas all are seeking to begin a different type of work, their reasons for doing so are quite varied. Some are looking for a new line of work because they have been forced out of a job by cutbacks. Others are seeking new careers because they want new challenges at this time in their lives. A third group is composed of women who are entering or reentering the workforce because family concerns now occupy less of their time and energy.

Is There a Midlife Crisis?

How well do people adjust to middle age? One important factor in people's midlife adjustment is whether they feel in control (Lachman & Firth, 2004; Wrosch, Heckhausen, & Lachman, 2006). Life areas in which such control can matter a great deal include psychological and social well-being, interpersonal relationships, and physical health. Having a sense or perception of control in midlife allows a person to constructively react to the challenges and demands of midlife, as well as the inevitable physical declines, such as being able to cope well with memory loss (Lachman, 2006). Perhaps perceiving such control even allows people to consider their own mortality and positive responses they can make (leading to generativity, for instance).

What happens if individuals feel out of control? Much has been made about whether most people go through a **midlife crisis—a turbulent period of doubts and reappraisal of one's life.** Two influential studies of adult development in the 1970s both concluded that a midlife crisis is a normal transition experienced by a majority of people. Daniel Levinson and his colleagues

CATHY © Cathy Guisewite. Reprinted with permission of UNIVERSAL PRESS SYNDICATE. All rights reserved.

Do most adults go through a midlife crisis in their 40s? The research on this question is contradictory, but overall, the evidence suggests that only a minority of people in their 40s struggle with a midlife crisis.

(1978) found that most of their subjects (all men) went through a midlife crisis around the ages of 40 to 45. This transition was marked by life reevaluation and emotional turmoil. Roger Gould (1978) found that people tended to go through a midlife crisis between the ages of 35 and 45. His subjects reported feeling pressed by time. They heard their social clocks ticking loudly as they struggled to achieve their life goals.

Since the landmark studies of Levinson and Gould, many other researchers have questioned whether the midlife crisis is a normal developmental transition. A number of studies have failed to detect an increase in emotional turbulence at midlife (Baruch, 1984; Eisler & Ragsdale, 1992; Roberts & Newton, 1987). How can we explain this discrepancy? Levinson and Gould both depended primarily on interview and case study methods to gather their data. However, when knitting together impressionistic case studies, it is easy for investigators to see what they expect to see. Given that the midlife crisis has long been a part of developmental folklore, Levinson and Gould may have interpreted their case study data in this light (McCrae & Costa, 1984). In any case, investigators relying on more objective measures of emotional stability have found signs of midlife crises in only a tiny minority (2%–5%) of subjects (Chiriboga, 1989; McCrae & Costa, 1990). Typically, these are individuals whose circumstances

in early adulthood (family pressures, poverty, and so forth) severely limited their chances to achieve life satisfaction (McAdams, 1988). To summarize, midlife may bring a period of increased reflection as people contemplate the remainder of their lives, but it's clear that the fabled midlife crisis is not typical (Lemme, 1999).

The original research on "midlife crisis" was skewed toward the experience of men. What about women? How do they react to this stage of life? Instead of being a time of crisis, midlife can be a time of promise or rebirth for women (Heckhausen, 2001). What we might call "midcourse corrections"—new adventures, new relationships, new purpose—can occur (Stewart & Ostrove, 1998). If there is a "crisis" in the lives of women, it may be actually a constructive one. As one author put it, "It may be that part of the resilience of the midlife crisis [myth] lies in its benefit: to anticipate the worst at midlife and be pleasantly surprised by one's own comparatively smooth sail" (Heckhausen, 2001, p. 378). Of course, researchers find that such "turning points" are more often caused by unexpected events (divorce, job transfers, serious illness), which can occur at any time in adulthood (Lachman & Bertrand, 2001; Wethington, Kessler, & Pixley, 2004). In fact, some evidence exists for a "quarter-life" crisis (mid-20s and early 30s) involving the search for meaningful work and relationships (Lachman, 2004; Robbins & Wilner, 2001).

Late Adulthood (After Age 65)

Late adulthood also has its share of developmental transitions. These challenges include adjusting to retirement, adapting to changes in one's support network, coping with health problems, and confronting death. Let's begin by discussing Erikson's views of late adulthood.

Erikson's Theory: Integrity Versus Despair

The challenge of Erikson's last stage is to achieve *ego integrity* (refer to **Figure 11.3**). People who achieve integrity are able to look back on their lives with a sense of satisfaction and to find meaning and purpose there. The opposite, despair, is the tendency to dwell on the mistakes of the past, bemoan paths not chosen, and contemplate the approach of death with bitterness. Erikson asserts that it is better to face the future in a spirit of acceptance than to wallow in regret and resentment. In a test of Erikson's theory, researchers studied male and female adults over a 20-year span (Whitbourne et al., 1992). Among other things, they found that favorable resolutions of earlier stages lead to favorable resolutions of later stages. Another study of participants ages 17 to 82 reported that subjective well-being was correlated with increasing age and psychological maturity and that the factors of generativity

Figure 11.14

Parenting styles, school performance, and school misconduct. Lamborn and colleagues (1991) classified the families of over 4,000 14- to 18-year-olds into four parenting styles, based on adolescents' ratings of their parents. They then compared the youths on a number of outcomes, including high school grade point average and frequency of school misconduct. Adolescents from authoritative families showed the highest competence and adjustment (higher grades, less misconduct), while those from neglectful families showed the lowest.

Data from Lamborn, S. D., Mounts, N. S., Steinberg, L., & Dornbusch, S. M. (1991). Patterns of competence and adjustment among adolescents from authoritative, authoritarian, indulgent, and neglectful families. *Child Development, 62,* 1049–1065. Copyright © 1991 by the Society for Research in Child Development. Used with permission of SRCD.

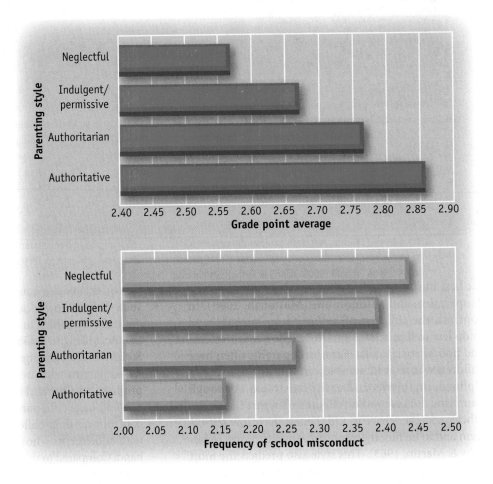

1. *Set high, but reasonable standards.* Children should be expected to behave in a socially appropriate manner for their age and to do as well as they can in school and in other activities. Parents who don't expect much from their children are teaching them not to expect much from themselves.

2. *Stay alert for "good" behavior and reward it.* Most parents pay attention to children when they are misbehaving and ignore them when they're being good. This approach is backward! Develop the habit of praising good behavior so a child knows what you want.

3. *Explain your reasons when you ask a child to do something.* Don't assume that a child can read your mind. Explaining the purpose of a request can transform what might appear to be an arbitrary request into a reasonable one. It also encourages self-control in a child.

4. *Encourage children to take the perspective of others.* Talk to children about the effects of their behavior on others ("How would you feel if Keisha did that to you?"). This role-playing approach fosters moral development and empathy in children.

5. *Enforce rules consistently.* Children need to have a clear idea about what is expected of them and to know that there will be consequences when they fail to meet your standards. This practice also fosters self-control in children.

Using Punishment Effectively

To use punishment effectively, most parents probably should use it less often. That's because punishment often has unintended, negative side effects. A recent meta-analysis of 88 studies on corporal punishment reported that it *is* associated with stopping the punished behavior (Gershoff, 2002). Still, the bad news is that punishment is also associated with a host of problematic outcomes: reduced quality of parent-child relationships, poorer mental health in childhood and adulthood, increased delinquency and aggression in childhood, and increased aggression and criminal behavior in adulthood.

Many professionals decry the use of physical punishment for these reasons. Others assert that occasional, mild spankings should not be conflated with harsher punishment (which was the case in Gershoff's meta-analysis). Advocates of this position argue that infrequent, mild spankings can reduce disobedience and fighting and are not associated with negative out-

The 10 Basic Principles of Good Parenting
by Laurence Steinberg
(Simon & Schuster, 2004)

Laurence Steinberg, a respected researcher in developmental psychology, has consolidated the voluminous findings on child development and parenting into ten basic principles of effective parenting. Steinberg asserts that these principles can be universally applied—regardless of a family's income, race, or parental status (two-parent or single-parent). His principles are designed to foster competence, responsibility, security, and kindness in children and to help adults be happier and more confident parents.

Steinberg's ten principles are: "What You Do Matters," "You Cannot Be Too Loving," "Be Involved in Your Child's Life," "Adapt Your Parenting to Fit Your Child," "Establish Rules and Set Limits," "Help Foster Your Child's Independence," "Be Consistent," "Avoid Harsh Discipline," "Explain Your Rules and Decisions," and "Treat Your Child with Respect." For each principle, Steinberg elaborates on the concept, explains how the principle applies to children of different ages, and offers "dos and don'ts."

comes (Baumrind, Larzelere, & Cowan, 2002; Larzelere, 2000). The following guidelines summarize research evidence on how to make punishment effective while minimizing its side effects (Berkowitz, 1993):

1. *Punishment should not damage the child's self-esteem.* To be effective, punishment should get across the message that it is the behavior that is undesirable, not the child. Unduly harsh physical punishment, derogatory accusations, and other hurtful words erode the child's self-esteem.

2. *Punishment should be swift.* A delay in delivering punishment undermines its impact. A parent who says, "Wait until your father (or mother) gets home..." is making a fundamental mistake. (He or she is also unfairly setting up the other parent as the "heavy.") Quick punishment highlights the connection between the prohibited behavior and its negative outcome.

3. *Punishment should be consistent.* If you want to eliminate an undesirable behavior, you should punish it every time it occurs. When parents are inconsistent about punishing a particular behavior, they only create confusion in the child.

4. *Punishment should be explained.* When children are punished, the reason for their punishment should be explained as fully as possible, given the constraints of their age. The more children understand the reason they are punished, the more effective the punishment tends to be. These explanations, characteristic of the authoritative style, also foster the development of self-control.

5. *Point out alternative, positive ways for your child to behave and reinforce these actions.* One shortcoming of punishment is that it only tells a child what not to do. A better strategy is to punish an undesirable response and reward a positive alternative behavior. Children usually engage in undesirable behavior for a reason. Suggest another response that serves the same purpose and reward a child for doing it. For example, many troublesome behaviors exhibited by children are primarily attention-seeking devices. Punishment of these responses will be more effective if you can provide a child with more acceptable ways to gain attention.

The Transition of Adolescence

▶ During pubescence, the adolescent growth spurt takes place and secondary sex characteristics develop. During puberty, which begins a few years later, the primary sex characteristics mature. The onset of puberty marks the beginning of adolescence. Girls typically mature two years earlier than boys. Boys who mature late and girls who mature early may find puberty particularly stressful.

▶ During adolescence, cognitive changes also occur, including development of the ability to apply logic to hypothetical situations, increases in knowledge, and greater skills in deductive reasoning. Despite greater cognitive sophistication, older adolescents are more likely to engage in physically harmful risky behavior, suggesting that this behavior is governed by noncognitive factors.

▶ In the realm of personality, adolescents must develop a clear sense of identity. Some theorists assert that adolescence is a period of turmoil, and there is research support for a modified storm-and-stress view that recognizes cultural and individual differences. Attention should be paid to youths who display symptoms of serious problems such as depression, suicidal behavior, drug and alcohol abuse, and chronic delinquency. Suicide among adolescents has greatly increased since 1960, but very few young people actually succeed in taking their lives.

The Expanse of Adulthood

▶ During early adulthood, individuals make more major role changes than in any other developmental stage. In Erikson's theory, the key psychosocial crisis for young adults is intimacy versus isolation. Specific developmental tasks of young adulthood include leaving one's family, entering the workplace and developing a career, finding a mate, having and rearing children, and adjusting to family life.

▶ In middle adulthood, the major psychosocial crisis is generativity versus stagnation, according to Erikson. Additional tasks for this group include confronting the aging process and dealing with transitions in the parental role as children mature and leave home. Midlife adults also experience changes in their work roles. Typically, they follow either the stable career pattern or the changing careers pattern. Few individuals seem to experience a midlife crisis.

▶ The key psychosocial crisis for older adults, according to Erikson, is integrity versus despair. Older adults must adjust to retirement, adapt to changes in their social networks, cope with health problems, and confront their own death.

Aging: a Gradual Process

▶ Physical development during adulthood leads to many obvious changes in physical appearance and sensory acuity. After age 30 there is a steady loss of active brain cells; however, this loss does not appear to underlie reductions in cognitive functioning. Similarly, hormonal changes appear to be only modestly related to midlife distress or declining sexual activity. Unfortunately, health does tend to decline with increasing age for a variety of reasons.

▶ Intelligence seems to remain fairly stable during most of adulthood. Attentional capacity, speed of learning, and success in problem solving all tend to decline slightly during old age. Memory processes also deteriorate but can be exacerbated by self-fulfilling prophecies. However, most people remain capable of sound intellectual functioning in their later years. The adult personality seems to be characterized by both stability and change.

Death and Dying

▶ Attitudes about death vary from one culture to another. Attitudes in this culture are characterized by negativism, avoidance, and fear. Kübler-Ross's research on the process of dying indicated that individuals progress through a sequence of five stages. Later research has called into question the idea that people's reactions to dying follow such a straightforward path.

▶ A wide variation exists between and within cultures regarding how death is acknowledged. Research has revealed a variety of patterns of grieving, calling into question traditional views of the process of mourning. The loss of a child is the most difficult type of death adults must cope with. In dealing with bereavement, people need the support of family and friends. Support groups can also be helpful.

Application: Becoming an Effective Parent

▶ According to Diana Baumrind, parenting styles can be classified as authoritative, authoritarian, permissive, and neglectful. Of Baumrind's four parenting styles, authoritative parenting is associated with the most positive outcomes in children.

▶ Intergenerational conflicts typically increase during adolescence, and parents seem to find these conflicts more difficult to deal with than adolescents do. Effective parenting involves following five key principles, as well as knowing how to use punishment effectively.

Bereavement p. 361
Death anxiety p. 360
Death system p. 359
Dementia p. 354
Identity p. 341
Menarche p. 338
Menopause p. 355
Midlife crisis p. 350
Mourning p. 361
Neurons p. 354

Parasuicide p. 343
Primary sex
   characteristics p. 338
Puberty p. 338
Pubescence p. 337
Secondary sex
   characteristics p. 338
Social clock p. 345
Spermarche p. 338
Working memory p. 358

Diana
   Baumrind pp. 364–367
Erik Erikson p. 341
Elisabeth
   Kübler-Ross pp. 360–361

Laurence
   Steinberg pp. 367–368
Susan Krauss
   Whitbourne p. 353

PRACTICE TEST

1. Primary sex characteristics develop during _____; secondary sex characteristics develop during _____.
   a. menarche, menopause
   b. puberty, pubescence
   c. the sexual stage; the physical stage
   d. adulthood; adolescence

2. Optimal adjustment is associated with puberty arriving _____ for girls and _____ for boys.
   a. late; on time
   b. early; on time
   c. on time; early
   d. late; early

3. Compared to those who are younger, adolescents:
   a. can think more abstractly.
   b. have greater knowledge.
   c. show greater self-awareness.
   d. do all of the above.

4. Which of the following statements about storm and stress in adolescence is false?
   a. Conflicts with parents increase during adolescence.
   b. Adolescents experience more volatile emotions than younger or older individuals do.
   c. Adolescents engage in more risky behaviors than children do.
   d. Heightened emotional turmoil in adolescence is found in all cultures.

5. The life stage that involves more role changes than any other is:
   a. adolescence.
   b. early adulthood.
   c. middle adulthood.
   d. later adulthood.

6. According to Erikson, the psychosocial conflict of middle adulthood is:
   a. identity versus identity diffusion.
   b. intimacy versus isolation.
   c. generativity versus stagnation.
   d. integrity versus despair.

7. Which of the following is a false statement about retirement?
   a. Retirement typically has a negative impact on overall health and life satisfaction.
   b. The best-adjusted retirees have an adequate income, good health, and a social network.
   c. Most older adults maintain their ties to their children.
   d. Retirement is typically a gradual process of cutting back on work hours over a period of years.

8. With regard to whether personality changes with age, it can be concluded that:
   a. a pattern of change is most typical.
   b. a pattern of stability is most typical.
   c. personality is characterized by both stability and change.
   d. no pattern can be discerned.

9. Less anxiety about death is found among those who:
   a. feel they haven't accomplished all that they had hoped.
   b. have a particular religious affiliation.
   c. have ambivalent religious views.
   d. have a well-formulated philosophy of death.

10. Baumrind's authoritative parenting style is characterized by:
    a. high acceptance and high control.
    b. low acceptance and high control.
    c. high acceptance and low control.
    d. low acceptance and low control.

Book Companion Website

 Visit the Book Companion Website at **academic.cengage. com/psychology/weiten**, where you will find tutorial quizzes, flash cards, and web links for every chapter, a final exam, and more! You can also link to the Psychology Resource Center (accessible directly at **academic.cengage.com/login**) for a range of psychology-related resources.

Personal Explorations Workbook

The following exercises in your *Personal Explorations Workbook* may enhance your self-understanding in relation to issues raised in this chapter. **Questionnaire 11.1:** Death Anxiety Scale. **Personal Probe 11.1:** How Do You Feel about Age Roles? **Personal Probe 11.2:** How Flexible Is Development?

ANSWERS

1. b Pages 337–338
2. c Pages 339–340
3. d Page 340
4. d Pages 342–343
5. b Page 345
6. c Page 348
7. a Page 352
8. c Page 359
9. d Page 360
10. a Page 364

CHAPTER 12

Careers and Work

Ben and Sarah, both in their mid-twenties, meet at a party hosted by mutual friends. After exchanging names and describing their connections to the hosts, the next question is, "What do you do for a living?" Their replies to this crucial question will reveal information not only about each other's occupation but also about their social status, lifestyle, personality, interests, and aptitudes. Their responses might also influence whether Ben and Sarah see each other again. In other words, work plays a pivotal role in adult life. According to a recent Gallup poll, 73% Americans rated work as either "extremely" or "very important" in their life (Moore, 2003). In **Figure 12.1**, you can see that how people view their jobs is strongly correlated with their income.

Because work is such a significant aspect of life, psychologists take a great interest in it. *Industrial/organizational (I/O) psychology* **is the study of human behavior in the workplace.** Among other issues, I/O psychologists study worker motivation and satisfaction, job performance, leadership, personnel selection, and diversity in organizations. A recent concern is how individuals balance work and family life (Borman, Klimoski, & Ilgen, 2003).

We begin this chapter by reviewing some important considerations in choosing a career. Then we explore two models of career development and discuss women's career issues. Next, we examine how the workplace and workforce are changing and look at some occupational hazards such as job stress, sexual harassment, and unemployment. Finally, we address the important issues of balancing work, relationships, and

leisure. In the Application, we offer some concrete suggestions for enhancing your chances of landing a desirable job.

Choosing a Career

LEARNING OBJECTIVES

- ▶ *Describe personal and family influences on job choice.*
- ▶ *Cite several helpful sources of career information.*
- ▶ *List some aspects of potential occupations that are important to know about.*

- ▶ *Explain the role of occupational interest inventories in career decisions.*
- ▶ *List five important considerations in choosing an occupation.*

One of your biggest decisions in life is choosing a career. The importance of this decision is enormous. It may determine whether you are employed or unemployed, financially secure or insecure, happy or unhappy. Rapidly advancing technology and the increased training and education required to break into most fields make it more important than ever to choose thoughtfully. In theory, what's involved in making a successful career choice is pretty straightforward. First, you need to have

a clear grasp of your personal characteristics. Second, you need realistic information about potential careers. From there, it's just a matter of selecting an occupation that is a good match with your personal characteristics. In reality, the process is a lot more complicated. Let's take a closer look.

Examining Personal Characteristics and Family Influences

People with limited job skills and qualifications have limited job options. As a result, they must usually take whatever job is available rather than a job that is well suited for them. In fact, *choosing* a career is a luxury usually afforded to the middle and upper classes. For those who *are* able to select a career, personal qualities and family influences come into play.

Personal Characteristics

Making career decisions can be scary. Individuals who exhibit *secure attachment* (see Chapter 8) and who have a sense of *self-efficacy* about career-relevant abilities (see Chapter 5) thus find it easier to make career choices (Fouad, 2007; Wolfe & Betz, 2004).

What other personal characteristics affect career choice? Although *intelligence* does not necessarily predict occupational success, it does predict the likelihood of entering particular occupations. That's because intelligence is related to academic success—the ticket required to enter certain fields. Professions such as law, medicine, and engineering are open only to those who can meet increasingly selective criteria as they advance from high school to college to graduate education and professional training. This relationship between intelligence and occupational level generally holds well for men, but an ability-achievement gap exists for women, as we noted in Chapter 10.

In many occupations, special talents are more important than general intelligence. *Specific aptitudes*

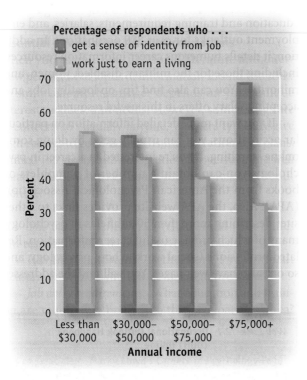

Figure 12.1

How workers view their jobs. The way workers view their jobs is strongly related to their income. Those who earn higher salaries are more likely to obtain a sense of identity from their work, whereas those who earn lower salaries typically see their jobs merely as a way to make a living. (Data from Moore, 2001)

Decline Stage

Deceleration involves a decline in work activity in the years prior to retirement. People redirect their energy and attention toward planning for this major transition. Super's original formulation, which was based on research in the 1950s, projected that deceleration ought to begin at around age 65. Since the 1970s, however, the large baby boom cohort has created an oversupply of skilled labor and professional talent. This social change has created pressures that promote early retirement. Because of these conditions, deceleration often begins earlier than Super initially indicated.

Retirement brings work activity to a halt. People approach this transition with highly varied attitudes. Many individuals look forward to it eagerly. Others approach it with apprehension, unsure about how they will occupy themselves and worried about their financial viability. Still others approach retirement with a combination of hopeful enthusiasm and anxious concern. Although retirement may mean less income, it can also mean more time to spend with friends and on hobbies, travel, and meaningful volunteer work.

As a stage theorist, Super deserves credit for recognizing that people follow different patterns in their career development. For example, he identified several patterns for both men and women that do not coincide with the conventional pattern we have described. In support of Super's model, it has been found that career maturity is correlated with self-esteem and self-efficacy (Creed, Prideaux, & Patton, 2005; Kornspan & Etzel, 2001). A more serious problem with Super's theory is that it assumes that people will remain in the same careers all of their working lives. But today's American workers will have many career changes, a reality that is incompatible with the assumptions of long-term models like Super's. The current thinking about career stages or cycles is that they are shorter and recur periodically over the course of a person's career (Greenhaus, 2003). To be useful, stage models must reflect today's workplace realities.

Women's Career Development

It is currently estimated that 59% of adult women (versus 73% of men) are in the labor force (U.S. Census Bureau, 2006b). Moreover, the odds that a woman will work outside the home during her adult life are greater than 90% (U.S. Department of Labor, 2003). Although women's labor force participation is approaching that of men's, important gender differences remain when it comes to career choice and development. For one thing, most women still subordinate their career goals to their husband's (Betz, 2005). This is even the case with academically gifted women (Arnold, 1995). If a married man wants or needs to move to another job, his wife typically follows him and takes the best job she can find in the new location. Hence, married women usually have less control over their careers than married men do. Also, the high divorce rate (45%) means that many women will have to provide for themselves and their children (Betz, 2006). One study reported that after a divorce, the woman's standard of living drops 27% (Weitzman, 1996). Today's women need to take these factors into account as they consider their career options.

Another gender difference concerns career paths. Men's career paths are usually *continuous,* whereas women's tend to be *discontinuous* (Betz, 1993). In other words, once men start working full-time, they usually continue to work. Women are more likely to interrupt their careers to concentrate on childrearing or family crises (Hynes & Clarkberg, 2005). Because women are having fewer children and are returning to work sooner, the amount of time they are out of the labor force is decreasing. Although labor force discontinuity is a factor in women's lower salaries and status, there is also evidence that women are simply paid less than men (Dey & Hill, 2007; U.S. General Accounting Office, 2003). Women who do not have children usually remain in the labor force and tend to have a pattern of career advancement similar to men's (Blair-Loy & DeHart, 2003).

The Changing World of Work

LEARNING OBJECTIVES

▶ *List six work-related trends.*

▶ *Describe the relationship between education and salary.*

▶ *Summarize important demographic changes that are transforming the workforce.*

▶ *Cite some problems that women and minorities face in today's workplace.*

▶ *Describe some challenges presented by workforce diversity to organizations and workers.*

Before you enter the working world, it's important to get your bearings. In this section we look at several important background issues: contemporary trends in the workplace, the relationship between education and earnings, and diversity in the workforce.

Workplace Trends

Work is an activity that produces something of value for others. For some people, work is just a way to earn a living; for others, work is a way of life. For both types

The growth of technology is significantly changing the nature of work, with both positive and negative effects.

of workers, the nature of work is undergoing dramatic changes. Because such changes can affect your future job prospects, you need to be aware of six important trends:

1. *Technology is changing the nature of work.* Computers and electronic equipment have dramatically transformed the workplace. From the worker's point of view, these changes have both down sides and up sides. On the negative side, computers automate many jobs that people perform, eliminating jobs. The digital workplace also demands that employees have more education and skills than were previously required (Cetron & Davies, 2003). And workers have to keep upgrading their technology skills, which can be stressful. On the positive side, technological advances allow employees to work at home and to communicate with others in distant offices and while traveling. Another "plus" is that computer-driven machines require workers to design, manufacture, sell, and service them.

2. *New work attitudes are required.* Yesterday's workers could usually count on job security. Thus, many could afford a somewhat passive attitude in shaping their careers. But today's workers have job security only as long as they can add value to a company. This situation means that workers must take a more active role in shaping their careers (Smith, 2000). In addition, they must develop a variety of valuable skills, be productive workers, and skillfully market themselves to prospective employers. In the new work environment, the keys to job success are self-direction, self-management, up-to-date knowledge and skills, flexibility, and mobility (Smith, 2000).

3. *Lifelong learning is a necessity.* Experts predict that today's jobs are changing so rapidly that in many cases, work skills will become obsolete over a 10- to 15-year period (Lock, 2005a). Thus, lifelong learning and training will become essential for employees. Every year, nearly one-third of American workers take courses to improve their job skills (American Council on Education, 1997). In some cases, retraining occurs on the job; in others, community colleges and technical institutes provide continuing education. Distance learning courses and programs are also available, although you have to watch out for bogus programs (Mariani, 2001). For suggestions on how to evaluate the quality and accreditation claims of distance education programs, see Web Link 12.3. Workers who know "how to learn" will be able to keep pace with the rapidly changing workplace and will be highly valued. Those who cannot may be left behind.

4. *Independent workers are increasing.* Corporations are downsizing and restructuring to cope with the changing economy and to be competitive globally. In doing so, they are slashing thousands of permanent jobs and doling out the work to temporary employees or to workers in other countries, a practice termed "outsourcing." By reducing the number of regular workers, companies can chop their expenditures on payroll, health insurance, and pension plans, as temporary employees don't typically receive such benefits. A leaner workforce also enables organizations to respond quickly to fast-changing markets. According to Daniel Pink (2001), one way to survive in this new environment is to become a "free agent" and hire out

Web Link 12.3 **DegreeInfo.com**

If you need assistance evaluating distance learning programs, this site can help you. Its purpose is to disseminate accurate information about quality distance-based higher education programs. None of the writers for this site is currently affiliated with any school, although some of them are alumni of regionally accredited distance learning programs.

your skills to one or more organizations on a contract basis. To characterize the "free agent" work pattern, Pink suggests the metaphor of the "LEGO career" instead of the "career ladder." Just as you can construct a variety of structures by assembling LEGO blocks, "free agents" assemble and reassemble the building blocks of their work life (values, interests, aptitudes, and skills) in various combinations to match career opportunities that emerge over time. Many professionals thrive on contract work; they have freedom, flexibility, and high incomes. But for those who are short on skills and entrepreneurial spirit, this work can be stressful and risky. About a third of independent employees would prefer to work for someone else than to work for themselves (Bond et al., 2003).

5. *The boundaries between work and home are breaking down.* Today's technological advances allow people to work at home and stay in touch with the office via high-speed Internet, telephones, and fax machines. Working at home is convenient—workers save time (no commuting) and money (on gas, parking, clothes). Still, family members and friends may interrupt home-workers, necessitating setting rules to protect work time. With the advent of cell phones, pagers, and wireless modems, employees can be contacted any time and any place, making some workers feel as though they are on an "electronic leash." Looking at the flip side, the availability of onsite day care in some large companies means that a traditional home function has moved to the office (Drago, 2007). This development is largely a response to increases in the number of single-parent families and *dual-earner households,* **in which both partners are employed.** Quality onsite day care is a big draw to workers because it allows parents to interact with their children during the day.

6. *The highest job growth will occur in the professional and service occupations.* The United States, like

Web Link 12.4 **U.S. Department of Labor**

With primary responsibility for many job- and work-related matters in the U. S. government, the Labor Department offers a site that can serve as a base to explore a variety of topics, including wages and compensation, worker productivity, and the legal rights of workers (such as protection from sexual harassment).

many other industrialized nations, continues to shift from a manufacturing, or "goods-producing," economy to a service-producing one (U.S. Bureau of Labor Statistics, 2006). Whereas the bulk of yesterday's jobs were in manufacturing, construction, agriculture, and mining, the jobs of the next decade will be in the professional (and related technical) occupations and service occupations. Among the professional occupations, jobs in the computer and health care industries are expected to expand dramatically. In psychology, jobs in health, clinical, counseling, and school psychology are expected to show strong growth. In the service occupations, strong job growth should occur in education, health services, social services, professional services, and business services. **Figure 12.4** depicts 20 occupations expected to grow the most and pay the most between now and 2014.

Education and Earnings

Although many jobs exist for individuals without a college degree, these jobs usually offer the lowest pay and benefits. In fact, all but 1 of the 50 highest-paying occupations require a college degree or higher (U.S. Bureau of Labor Statistics, 2004). (By the way, the high-paying job that doesn't require a college degree is air traffic controller.) In **Figure 12.5**, you can see that the more you

Figure 12.4

High-growth, high-salary occupations. According to the U.S. Department of Labor (2006), between 2004 and 2014 these 20 occupations will have the largest number of job openings and will provide the highest pay. Median annual salaries range from $145,600 (physicians and surgeons) to $30,710 (general maintenance and repair workers). (Adapted from *Occupational Outlook Quarterly,* Spring 2006)

"Best Bet" Occupations, 2004–2014	
Registered nurses	Secondary school teachers, except vocational education
Postsecondary teachers	Carpenters
General and operations managers	First-line supervisors or managers of retail sales workers
Elementary school teachers	
Sales representatives, wholesale and manufacturing, except technical and scientific products	Automotive service technicians and mechanics
Truck drivers, heavy and tractor-trailer	Licensed practical and licensed vocational nurses
Executive secretaries and administrative assistants	Computer software engineers
Accountants and auditors	Police and sheriff's patrol officers
General maintenance and repair workers	Middle-school teachers
First-line supervisors or managers of office and administration support workers	Physicians and surgeons
	First-line supervisors/managers of construction workers

CATHY © Cathy Guisewite. Reprinted with permission of UNIVE

(such as rotating shifts), the press
of control over one's work, inade
a job, and perceived inequities at
Warn, 2003). Fears of being "down:
health care benefits (losing them c
higher premiums), and worries a
plans also dog workers in today's c
tics and conflict with supervisor
co-workers also make the list of j
to adapt to changing technology
fices is another source of work st:
miners face frequent threats to t
High-pressure jobs such as air traff
geon demand virtually perfect pe
can have disastrous consequence:
work" (boring, repetitive tasks) c

learn, the more you earn. This relationship holds for both males and females, although, as you can see, men are paid approximately $12,000 to $35,000 more than women with the same educational credentials.

On the other hand, a college diploma is no guarantee of a great job. In fact, many college graduates are underemployed. **Underemployment is settling for a job that does not fully utilize one's skills, abilities, and training.** About 18% of college graduates take jobs that don't usually require a college degree, and experts predict that this situation is unlikely to change in the near future (Lock, 2005a). And while it's true that the jobs you can obtain with a college degree pay more than those requiring less education, the higher-paying jobs go to college graduates with *college-level* reading, writing, and quantitative skills. College graduates without these skills more often end up in high-school-level jobs (Pryor & Schaffer, 1997).

Current employers are not very happy with the academic skills of many of their employees. According to a survey by the College Board's National Commission on Writing, a majority of U.S. employers say that

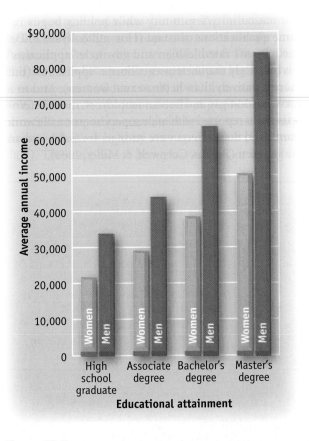

Figure 12.5

Education and income. This graph shows the average incomes of year-round, full-time workers age 18 and over, by gender and educational attainment. As you can see, the more education people have, the higher their income tends to be. However, at all levels women earn less than men with comparable education. (Data from U.S. Bureau of the Census, 2006)

about a third of their workers do not meet the writing requirements of their positions (College Entrance Examination Board, 2004). As new jobs develop, they will require more education and higher skill levels. International competition and technology are the two driving forces here (U.S. Department of Labor, 2000). Thus, computer literacy is an essential complement to a good basic education.

The Changing Workforce

The *labor force* consists of all those who are employed as well as those who are currently unemployed but are looking for work. In this section, we look at some of the changes affecting the workforce and consider how women and other minorities fare in the workplace.

Demographic Changes

The workforce is becoming increasingly diverse, with regard to both gender and ethnicity. In 2005, 61% of married women worked, compared to 41% in 1970 (U.S. Bureau of the Census, 2006b). This increase holds even for women with very young children. For instance, in 1975 only 33% of women with children under the age of 3 worked outside the home. By 2005,

Another way the world of work i
women, ethnic, and gay and lesbian mi
they have *less access to same-gender or s*
models and mentors (Murrell & James,
sexual harassment, a topic we'll take up
more likely to be a problem for workin
for working men. In sum, women and
viduals must contend with discriminat
in a number of forms.

The Challenges of Change

The increasingly diverse workforce pres
to both organizations and workers. Imp
differences exist in managing time and p
tifying with work, and in making decis
2005). These differences can contribu
Another challenge is that some indivi
they are personally paying the price o
the workplace, and this perception caus
Recognizing the problem, some corpora
versity training programs for their emp
cally, these programs can make the p
if they take a blaming stance toward wh
they stir up workers' feelings but provid
support for dealing with them. Thus, it i
such programs be carefully designed (
The strong support of top management
to their success.

Coping with Occupa

LEARNING OBJECTIVES

▶ *List some important sources of job stress.*
▶ *Summarize the effects of job stress on physica
  health.*
▶ *Describe actions that organizations are taking
  job stress.*

Work can bring people deep satisfacti
also be a source of frustration and confli
tion, we explore three challenges to to
job stress, sexual harassment, and unemp

Job Stress

You saw in Chapter 3 that stress can em
corner of your life. However, many the
that the workplace is the primary sour
modern society. Let's examine job stress
ployers and workers can do about it.

Sources of Stress on the Job

Between 2001 and 2004, the number
claiming to feel overworked rose from

---

filled by promotions within organizations. Nonetheless, many organizations do have openings that are not accessible through traditional channels. If you have targeted companies that haven't advertised any vacancies, you may want to initiate the contact yourself. Richard Bolles, author of *Parachute*, suggests the following strategy. First, identify a specific problem that the organization has, then devise a strategy to solve it. Next, find out who has the power to hire and fire (either through library research or a network of personal contacts). Finally, approach this person directly to convince him or her of your unique capability to help.

Landing an Interview

No one is going to hire you without first "checking out the goods." This inspection process typically involves one or more formal interviews. So, how do you get invited for an interview? If you are applying for an advertised vacancy, the traditional approach is to send a résumé with a cover letter to the hiring organization. If your letter and résumé stand out from the crowd, you may be invited for an interview. A good way to increase your chances is to persuade the prospective employer that you are interested enough in the company to have

Recommended READING

Getting from College to Career: 90 Things to Do Before You Join the Real World
by Lindsey Pollack (HarperCollins, 2007)

Pollack, a relatively recent college graduate, has become an expert on career advice for young professionals. In this book she shares 90 things college students need to do to make a successful transition from college to career. She devotes two to four pages to each tip and organizes them into ten chapters such as "Stop Being a Student and Start Being a Professional" (for example, "Clean Up Your Internet Image") and "Give Yourself an Edge" (for example, "Minor in Something Majorly Helpful"). In the "Gain Real World Experience" chapter, she provides great tips on internships (their benefits, how to find them, and how to make the most of them). The author makes excellent use of two unique assets: Her closeness in age to the college students she is advising and her additional years of life and work experience. Her writing style is interesting and informal, and she helpfully illustrates her points by sharing her own experiences (both successes and failures) and those of others. The book also provides a list of useful organizations and websites.

---

done some research on the organization (Pollak, 2007). By taking the time to learn something about a company, you should be able to make a convincing case about the ways in which your expertise will be particularly useful to the organization.

If you are approaching an organization in the absence of a known opening, your strategy may be somewhat different. You may still opt to send a résumé, along with a more detailed cover letter explaining why you have selected this particular company. Another option, suggested by Bolles (2007), is to introduce yourself (by phone or in person) directly to the person in charge of hiring and request an interview. You can increase your chances of success by using your network of personal contacts to identify some acquaintance that you and the person in charge have in common. Then, you can use this person's name to facilitate your approach. After you have an interview, you should follow up with a thank-you note and a résumé that will jog the prospective employer's memory about your training and talents.

Polishing Your Interview Technique

The final, and most crucial, step in the process of securing a job is the face-to-face interview. If you've gotten this far, the employer already knows that you have the necessary training and experience to do the job. Your challenge is to convince the employer that you're the kind of person who would fit well in the organization. Your interviewer will attempt to verify that you have the intangible qualities that will make you a good team player. Even more important, he or she will try to identify any "red flag" behaviors, attitudes, or traits that mark you as an unacceptable risk.

Because interviews are so important, you would think that interviewers' ratings of job applicants are heavily based on job-relevant considerations. Unfortunately, research shows that this is not usually the case. For one thing, confirmation bias (Chapter 6) can operate in interview situations. That is, interviewers who have formed expectations about a job candidate (based on the résumé, letters of recommendation, and the like) often treat the applicant in ways that tend to confirm these expectations, whether positive or negative (Dougherty, Turban, & Callender, 1994).

In addition, researchers find that more attractive candidates are usually rated higher than less attractive ones, as are those who dress in a manner consistent with the dress norms in an organization. If you're in doubt, contact the human resources department and ask about the dress code (Raines, 2006). Also, visible tattoos or body piercings can create a negative impression at a job interview (Swanger, 2006). And remem-

To be successful on a job interview, candidates need to dress appropriately and convey confidence, enthusiasm, and interest in the job.

ber to go easy on the aftershave lotion or perfume—a strong scent can be a real turnoff. Researchers also find that job candidates who are overweight are rated lower than those of average weight (Kutcher & Bragger, 2004). Finally, it has been found that interviewees who emit positive nonverbal cues—leaning forward, smiling, and nodding—are rated higher than those who do not (DeGroot & Motowidlo, 1999). Thus, to do your best in an interview, you should brush up on your nonverbal communication skills (see Chapter 7) and your impression management tactics (see Chapter 5). And remember, because of primacy effects (discussed in Chapter 6), the first few minutes of the interview are crucial.

To create the right impression, you must come across as confident, enthusiastic, and ambitious. By the way, a firm (not wishy-washy or bone-crushing) handshake helps create a positive first impression, especially for women (Chaplin et al., 2000). Your demeanor should be somewhat formal and reserved, and you should avoid any attempts at humor—you never know what might offend your interviewer. Above all, never give more information than the interviewer requests, especially negative information. If asked directly what your weaknesses are—a common ploy—respond with a "flaw" that is really a positive, as in "I tend to work too hard at times." And don't interrupt or contradict your interviewer. Finally, don't ever blame or criticize anyone, especially previous employers, even if you feel that the criticism is justified (Lock, 2005b).

Developing an effective interview technique requires practice. Many experts suggest that you never turn down an interview, because you can always benefit from the practice even if you don't want the job. Advance preparation is also crucial. Never go into an interview cold. Find out all you can about the company before you go. Try to anticipate the questions that will be asked and have some answers ready. You can review commonly asked interview questions on websites and in career books (Yate, 2006). In general, you will not be asked simply to reiterate information from your résumé. Remember, it is your personal qualities that are being assessed at this point. A final word of advice: If possible, avoid any discussion of salary in an initial interview. The appropriate time for salary negotiation is *after* a firm offer of employment has been extended. By the way, you can scope out salary information for many jobs by visiting Web Link 12.8. And you can find additional tips on interviewing at some of the other Web Links in this chapter.

Web Link 12.8 **Salary.com**

This useful site allows you to determine median salaries for numerous occupations at different experience levels and in different geographical areas and compare them to national averages. You can probably get all the information you need for free, but you can also pay (a lot) for a customized salary report.

Because of gender differences in sexual socialization, females tend to begin seeing themselves as sexual persons at a later age than males.

attractiveness and catching a mate. Unlike males, they are not encouraged to experiment with sex or to have numerous sexual partners. It isn't until women actually begin having sexual experiences that they start to see themselves as sexual persons.

Sexual socialization usually takes longer for females than for males because women usually have more emotional baggage connected with sex than men do. One factor is the *fear of pregnancy*. Concerns about becoming pregnant inhibit a woman's enthusiasm for sex. Second, girls hear *negative messages about sex and men* ("Men only want one thing") from their mothers, siblings, and female peers. They are also aware of rape and incest. Third, women typically develop *negative associations about their genitals and sex* that males don't experience: blood and pain associated with menstruation and fears of penetration. A fourth factor is *sexual guilt*. Whereas social norms encourage males to be sexually active, these norms discourage such behavior in females—sexually active women may be looked on as "loose." All these negative associations with sex are combined with the positive rewards of dating and emotional intimacy. Hence, it's no surprise that many women feel ambivalent about sex (Hyde, 2004). These feelings can tilt in the negative direction if early sexual partners are unskilled, impatient, or selfish.

With differing views of sexuality and relationships, males and females can be out of sync with each other—particularly in adolescence and early adulthood. In adulthood, women become more comfortable with themselves as sexual persons, while males become more comfortable with emotional intimacy and commitment. These gender differences mean that communication is essential for mutually satisfying sexual relationships.

Because both members of *same-gender couples* have been socialized similarly, they are less likely than straight couples to have compatibility problems. Like heterosexual women, lesbians typically experience

emotional attraction to their partners before experiencing sexual feelings (Peplau & Fingerhut, 2007). By contrast, gay men (like heterosexual men) tend to place much more importance on physical appearance and sexual compatibility in selecting partners and to then develop emotional relationships out of sexual ones (Diamond, 2006).

Sexual Orientation

Gay, straight, or in between? In this section, we'll explore the intriguing and controversial topic of sexual orientation.

Key Considerations

Most people view heterosexuality and homosexuality as two distinct categories: you're either one or the other. However, many individuals who define themselves as heterosexuals have had homosexual experiences, and vice versa (Kinsey et al., 1948, 1953; Laumann et al., 1994). Thus, it is more accurate to view heterosexuality and homosexuality as end points on a continuum. In-

Alfred Kinsey

deed, Alfred Kinsey devised a seven-point scale, shown in **Figure 13.3**, to characterize sexual orientation.

How are people distributed on this scale? No one knows for sure, because it's hard to get accurate data. Furthermore, there's some debate about where to draw the lines between heterosexuality, bisexuality, and homosexuality on the Kinsey scale. A frequently cited estimate of the number of people who are predominantly homosexual is 10%; however, several influential surveys have reported lower estimates (ACFS Investigators, 1992; Johnson et al., 1992; Laumann et al., 1994). The overall evidence suggests that about 5%–8% of the population could reasonably be characterized as homosexual (Michaels, 1996; see Chapter 9).

Now let's complicate things a little more. Using Kinsey's model, where would you place a person who was married for 10 years, has children, is divorced, and is now involved in a committed homosexual relationship? And what about a person who is married but who has homosexual fantasies and engages in same-gender sex talk on the Internet? Clearly, we need more complex paradigms. One such model portrays sexual orientation as a cluster of seven factors that can be rated along Kinsey's seven-point scale: sexual behavior; emotional preference; sexual fantasies; sexual attraction; social preference; lifestyle, social world, and community; and self-identification (Klein, Sepekoff, & Wolf, 1986). In this view, individuals' ratings on the seven factors may or may not be congruent, and ratings may change over time to match shifts in people's understanding

0	1	2	3	4	5	6
Exclusively heterosexual	Predominantly heterosexual only incidentally homosexual	Predominantly heterosexual more than incidentally homosexual	Equally heterosexual and homosexual	Predominantly homosexual more than incidentally heterosexual	Predominantly homosexual only incidentally heterosexual	Exclusively homosexual

Figure 13.3

Heterosexuality and homosexuality as end points on a continuum. Kinsey and other sex researchers view heterosexuality and homosexuality as ends of a continuum rather than as all-or-none distinctions. Kinsey created this seven-point scale (from 0 to 6) for describing sexual orientation.

of their sexual orientation. Thus, research supports a complex and malleable view of sexual orientation (Diamond, 2003).

Origins

Why do some people become straight and others, gay? A number of *environmental explanations* have been suggested as causes of homosexuality. Freud believed that homosexuality originates from an unresolved Oedipus complex (see Chapter 2). That is, instead of coming to identify with the parent of the same gender, the child continues to identify with the parent of the other gender. Learning theorists assert that homosexuality results from early negative heterosexual encounters or early positive homosexual experiences. Sociologists propose that homosexuality develops because of poor relationships with same-gender peers or because being labeled a homosexual sets up a self-fulfilling prophecy. Surprisingly, a comprehensive review of the causes of sexual orientation found no compelling support for *any* of these explanations of homosexuality (Bell, Weinberg, & Hammersmith, 1981).

Similarly, there is no evidence that parents' sexual orientation is linked to that of their children (Patterson, 2003). That is, heterosexual parents are as likely to produce homosexual (or heterosexual) offspring as homosexual parents are. Children who grow up in gay or lesbian families are predominantly heterosexual.

Researchers have found that extremely feminine behavior in young boys and masculine behavior in young girls is correlated with subsequent homosexuality (Bailey, 2003; Bem, 2000). Consistent with this finding, many gay men and some gay women say they can trace their homosexual leanings back to their early childhood (Bailey, 2003). This connection is less strong in lesbians than it is in gay males, supporting the emerging view that female sexuality is more fluid than that of males (Diamond, 2003; Impett & Peplau, 2006).

Some theorists speculate that *biological factors* are involved in the development of homosexuality, because many gay men and some lesbians can recall having homosexual feelings in their childhood years (Bell, Weinberg, & Hammersmith, 1981; Garnets & Kimmel, 1991). Several lines of research suggest that hormonal secretions during prenatal development may shape sexual development, organize the brain in a lasting manner, and influence subsequent sexual orientation (Cohen-Bendahan, van de Beek, & Berenbaum, 2005; Rahman, 2005). To date, however, the research is inconclusive, so this theory must be viewed with caution. Other researchers have explored the relationship between circulating hormone levels in adults and sexual orientation, but there is no convincing evidence of an association (Bailey, 2003; Banks & Gartrell, 1995).

Genetic factors are also of interest. In an important study, investigators identified gay and bisexual men who had a twin brother or an adopted brother (Bailey & Pillard, 1991). They found that 52% of the subjects' identical twins were gay, that 22% of their fraternal twins were gay, and that 11% of their adoptive brothers were gay. A companion study of lesbian women with twin or adopted sisters reported a similar pattern of results (Bailey et al., 1993; see **Figure 13.4** on the next page). More recent twin studies, with larger and more representative samples, have provided further support for the conclusion that heredity influences sexual orientation, although these studies have yielded smaller estimates of genetic influence (Bailey, Dunne, & Martin, 2000; Kendler et al., 2000). Thus, there may be genetic links to homosexuality.

The bottom line is that it isn't yet clear what determines sexual orientation. Moreover, it appears that complex paradigms are needed to explain male and female homosexuality (Peplau & Garnets, 2000). It is likely that there are a variety of types of homosexuality—and heterosexuality—that will require a variety of explanations rather than a single account (Hyde &

Figure 13.4

Genetics and sexual orientation. A concordance rate indicates the percentage of twin pairs or other pairs of relatives that exhibit the same characteristic. If relatives who share more genetic relatedness show higher concordance rates than relatives who share less genetic overlap, this evidence suggests a genetic predisposition to the characteristic. Recent studies of both gay men and lesbian women have found higher concordance rates among identical twins than fraternal twins, who, in turn, exhibit more concordance than adoptive siblings. These findings are consistent with the hypothesis that genetic factors influence sexual orientation. If *only* genetic factors were responsible for sexual orientation, the identical twin concordance rates would push 100%; because they are much lower, environmental factors must also play a role. (Data from Bailey & Pillard, 1991; Bailey et. al., 1993)

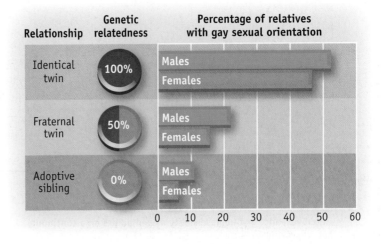

DeLamater, 2003). This issue is exceedingly complex and research is still in its infancy. The most we can conclude is that the explanations must lie in some complex interaction of biological and environmental factors.

Attitudes Toward Homosexuality

The legalization of same-gender marriage in Massachusetts and the legal recognition of civil unions and domestic partnerships in seven other states have set off contentious public debates in the last few years. Fueling the controversy, constitutional amendments banning gay marriage have been introduced in the U.S. Congress and in many state legislatures. Although the public discussion of gay marriage can be divisive, some believe that it has value (Garnets & Kimmel, 2003a). First, it has allowed the gay community to educate straight citizens about the realities and diversity of same-gender couples and their family relationships. Second, it has helped raise the nation's awareness about the facets of discrimination against gays. Although many Americans are opposed to gay marriage, they are much more accepting of other issues related to homosexuality (see **Figure 13.5**). Greater acceptance is due, in part, to the increasing visibility of lesbians and gays in society, including likable gay characters (*Will and Grace*) and individuals (*Queer Eye for the Straight Guy*) on television (Schiappa, Gregg, & Hewes, 2006).

Homophobia is the intense fear and intolerance of homosexuals. Because few people with negative attitudes toward homosexuals have the psychopathology that "phobia" implies, some psychologists believe that *sexual prejudice* is a more appropriate term (Herek, 2003). The lowest levels of sexual prejudice are associated with individuals who personally know someone who is gay (Herek & Capitanio, 1996). Higher levels of sexual prejudice are associated with being older, male, less educated, and living in the South or Midwest and in rural areas (Herek & Capitanio, 1996). Sexual prejudice is also correlated with such psychological factors as authoritarianism (see Chapter 6), traditional

Attitudes about homosexuality are gradually shifting towards greater acceptance of gays. For example, when comedian Ellen DeGeneres first came out of the closet in 1997, there was quite a bit of negative reaction from the general public. Today, however, she has a popular TV talk show and little was said when she was selected to host the movie industry's Academy Awards.

Attitudes Toward Homosexuals

Poll question*	Percent endorsing
1. Homosexuals should have equal rights in terms of job opportunities.	89
2. Gay partners should have the same inheritance rights as married couples.	60
3. Gay partners should have the same health insurance and other employee benefits as married couples.	60
4. Gay partners should have the same social security benefits as married couples.	55
5. Gay and lesbian partners should have the same adoption rights as married couples.	45
6. Which of the following do you support for gay couples?	
a. Marriage rights	28
b. Civil unions	23
c. No legal recognition	43
d. Don't know	6

*Item 1 is based on a May 2–4, 2004 Gallup survey. Items 2–5 are based on a February 5–6, 2004 *Newsweek* survey. Item 6 is based on a May 13–14, 2004 *Newsweek* survey. All surveys are based on randomly selected national samples.

Figure 13.5

Attitudes toward homosexuals. Americans' attitudes toward gays are highly variable, depending on the specific issue. Women generally have more accepting attitudes than men.

gender-role attitudes, and conservative religious and political beliefs (Altemeyer, 1996; Herek & Capitanio, 1996; Whitley, 2001). Unfortunately, negative attitudes sometimes translate into hate crimes. Around a third of gay men and lesbians have been victims of hate crimes (Parrott & Zeichner, 2006).

Sexual Identity Development

Linda Garnets

Douglas C. Kimmel

Developing one's sexual identity is complicated and difficult when it must take place in a climate of sexual prejudice. In discussing that process, we draw heavily on the work of psychologists Linda Garnets and Douglas Kimmel (1991, 2003b). For gays, lesbians, and bisexuals, sexual identity development involves acknowledging, recognizing, and labeling one's sexual orientation; conceptualizing it in positive terms; and disclosing it to others. Compared with earlier generations, recent generations are becoming aware of and are disclosing gay, lesbian, or bisexual identities earlier in life (Floyd & Bakeman, 2006).

Popular television programs like Queer Eye for the Straight Guy *have contributed to the increased acceptance of gays and lesbians.*

Coming to terms with one's homosexuality in a hostile environment is difficult. And LGB people from some minority groups must contend with the additional stress of negative reactions to their sexual orientation in their cultural communities (Harper, Jernewall, & Zea, 2004). Some parents throw their gay children out of the house, and some teachers and peers harass and assault gay and lesbian youth. The quality of a parent-child relationship prior to disclosure may be the best predictor of how parents will initially react and adjust to their child's coming out (Savin-Williams, 2001). At least half of gay and lesbian teenagers reported that they had lost at least one friend because of their sexual orientation (Ryan & Futterman, 1997). High schools and colleges increasingly support groups for LGBT students. And the Internet offers a wealth of resources for LGBT people (see Web Link 13.2).

In deciding to disclose one's sexual orientation to others, people must balance the psychological and social benefits against the costs (losing friends, being fired, falling victim to hate crimes, and losing custody of children). A pragmatic solution to this conflict is *rational outness*—being "as open as possible, because it feels healthy to be honest, and as closed as necessary to protect against discrimination" (Bradford & Ryan, 1987, p. 77). People are more likely to disclose their sexual orientation to close heterosexual friends and siblings than to parents, co-workers, or employers.

Web Link 13.2 **Parents, Families, and Friends of Lesbians and Gays**

The mission of this national organization is to promote the health and well-being of gay, lesbian, bisexual, and transgendered people as well as that of their families and friends. The organization is involved in support, education, and advocacy efforts and has more than 500 chapters in every state and many cities.

Figure 13.7

What men and women want more of during sex. Dating and married couples were asked which sexual activities they wanted more of in their relationships. Men and women all agreed that they wanted more instructions from their partners. They also generally agreed that they wanted warmer, more involved sexual relationships and more experimentation. In terms of gender differences, men wanted their partners to take the initiative and to be wilder and sexier; women wanted more emotional reassurance.

From Hatfield, E., & Rapson, R. L. (1997). *Love, sex, and intimacy: Their psychology, biology, and history.* Boston: Allyn & Bacon. Copyright © 1997 by Pearson Education. Reprinted by permission of the publisher.

What Men and Women Want More of During Sex	
Dating couples	
Men	**Women**
Wish their partners would:	
Be more experimental	Talk more lovingly
Initiate sex more often	Be more seductive
Try more oral-genital sex	Be warmer and more involved
Give more instructions	Give more instructions
Be warmer and more involved	Be more complimentary
Married couples	
Men	**Women**
Wish their partners would:	
Be more seductive	Talk more lovingly
Initiate sex more often	Be more seductive
Be more experimental	Be more complimentary
Be wilder and sexier	Be more experimental
Give more instructions	Give more instructions
	Be warmer and more involved

ignorant or inconsiderate sexual partners, subsequent positive sexual interactions will usually resolve the problem over time. If earlier sexual experiences have been traumatic, as in the case of rape or incest, counseling may be required to help a person view sex positively and enjoy it.

To communicate more easily and effectively about sex, you may want to review Chapter 7. Most of the advice on how to improve verbal and nonverbal communication can be applied to sexual relationships. Assertive communication and constructive conflict-resolution strategies can keep sexual negotiations

healthy. A basic rule is to accentuate the positive ("I like it when you . . .") rather than the negative ("I don't like it when you . . .").

The Human Sexual Response

LEARNING OBJECTIVES

▶ Describe the four phases of the human sexual response cycle.
▶ Discuss gender differences in patterns of orgasm and some reasons for them.

When people engage in sexual activity, exactly how does the body respond? Surprisingly, until William Masters and Virginia Johnson conducted their groundbreaking research in the 1960s, little was known about the physiology of the human sexual response. Masters and Johnson used physiological recording devices to monitor the bodily changes of volunteers engaging in sex. Their observations and interviews with their subjects yielded a detailed description of the human sexual response that won them widespread acclaim.

The Sexual Response Cycle

Masters and Johnson's (1966, 1970) description of the sexual response cycle is a general one, outlining typical rather than inevitable patterns—people vary considerably. **Figure 13.8** shows how the intensity of sexual arousal changes as women and men progress through the four phases of the sexual response cycle.

Excitement Phase

During the initial phase of excitement, the level of arousal usually escalates rapidly. In both sexes, muscle tension, respiration rate, heart rate, and blood pressure increase quickly. In males *vasocongestion*—**engorgement of blood vessels**—produces penile erection, swollen testes, and the movement of the scrotum (the sac containing the testes) closer to the body. In females, vasocongestion leads to a swelling of the clitoris and vaginal lips, vaginal lubrication, and enlargement of the uterus. Most women also experience nipple erection and a swelling of the breasts.

Plateau Phase

The name given to the "plateau" stage is misleading because physiological arousal does not level off. Instead, it continues to build, but at a much slower pace. In women, further vasocongestion produces a tightening of the lower third of the vagina and a "ballooning" of

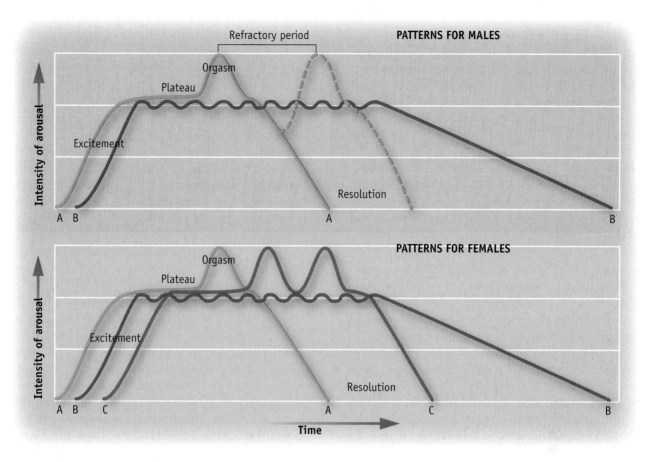

Figure 13.8

The human sexual response cycle. There are similarities and differences between men and women in patterns of sexual arousal. Pattern A, which culminates in orgasm and resolution, is the most typical sequence for both sexes. Pattern B, which involves sexual arousal without orgasm followed by a slow resolution, is also seen in both genders, but it is more common among women. Pattern C, which involves multiple orgasms, is seen almost exclusively in women, as men go through a refractory period before they are capable of another orgasm. (Based on Masters & Johnson, 1966)

the upper two-thirds, which lifts the uterus and cervix away from the end of the vagina. In men, the head of the penis may swell, and the testicles typically enlarge and move closer to the body. Many men secrete a bit of pre-ejaculatory fluid from the tip of the penis that may contain sperm.

Distractions during the plateau phase can delay or stop movement to the next stage. These include ill-timed interruptions like a telephone or doorbell ringing, or a child's knocking—or not!—on the bedroom door. Equally distracting can be such things as physical discomfort, pain, guilt, frightening thoughts, feelings of insecurity or anger toward one's partner, and anxiety about not having an orgasm.

Orgasm Phase

Orgasm occurs when sexual arousal reaches its peak intensity and is discharged in a series of muscular contractions that pulsate through the pelvic area. Heart rate, respiration rate, and blood pressure increase sharply during this exceedingly pleasant spas-

modic response. The male orgasm is usually accompanied by ejaculation of seminal fluid. Some women report that they ejaculate some kind of fluid at orgasm. The prevalence of female ejaculation and the source and nature of the fluid are matters still under debate (Alzate, 1990; Whipple, 2000). The subjective experience of orgasm appears to be essentially the same for men and women.

Resolution Phase

During the resolution phase, the physiological changes produced by sexual arousal subside. If one has not had an orgasm, the reduction in sexual tension may be relatively slow and sometimes unpleasant. After orgasm, men generally experience a *refractory period, a time following male orgasm during which males are largely unresponsive to further stimulation.* The refractory period varies from a few minutes to a few hours and increases with age.

Critics note that the Masters and Johnson model focuses entirely on genital changes during sex and ignores cognitive factors. An alternative is the three-stage model of noted sex therapist Helen Singer Kaplan (1979), which begins with desire, followed by excitement and then orgasm. Since people's thoughts and views about sex underlie many sexual problems, it is helpful to keep in mind that the sexual response involves more than just physical factors.

Gender Differences in Patterns of Orgasm

As a whole, the sexual responses of women and men parallel each other fairly closely. Nonetheless, there are some interesting differences between the genders in their patterns of experiencing orgasm. During *intercourse,* women are less likely than men to reach orgasm (that is, they are more likely to follow pattern B in **Figure 13.8**). According to one survey of American sexual behavior (Laumann et al., 1994), about 29% of women reported that they *always* reached orgasm in their primary sexual relationships, compared to 75% of men (see **Figure 13.9**). Apparently, about 10% of American women have never had an orgasm by any means (Spector & Carey, 1990).

In their laboratory, Masters and Johnson found that the men they studied took about 4 minutes to reach a climax with their partners. Women took about 10–20 minutes to reach orgasm with their partners, but they reached orgasm in about 4 minutes when they masturbated. Clearly, then, women are capable of reaching orgasm more quickly than they typically do. Our point here is not that men and women should race each other to the finish line but that physiological factors are not the likely cause of gender differences related to orgasm.

How do we account for these disparities? First, although most women report that they enjoy intercourse, it is not the optimal mode of stimulation for them. This is because intercourse provides rather indirect stimulation to the clitoris, the most sexually sensitive genital area in most women. Thus, more lengthy *foreplay,* including manual or oral stimulation of the clitoris, is usually the key to enhancing women's sexual pleasure. Many men mistakenly assume that women experience the same degree of pleasurable sensations that they do during sexual intercourse. But this is not the case, as the upper two-thirds of the vagina has relatively few nerve endings—a good thing, since the vagina serves as the birth canal! Manual or oral stimulation of the clitoris is more effective in producing female orgasm than sexual intercourse alone (Bancroft, 2002b). Unfortunately, many couples are locked into the idea that orgasms should be achieved only through intercourse. Even the word *foreplay* suggests that any other form of sexual stimulation is merely preparation for the "main event." Also, most women associate sex with affection, so they want to hear some tender words during a sexual encounter. Men who verbally express their love and affection usually find their partners more responsive.

Research suggests that lesbians have orgasms more often and more easily in sexual interactions than heterosexual women do (Diamond, 2006; Peplau et al., 2004). Kinsey (1953) attributed this difference to female partners' knowing more about women's sexuality and how to optimize women's sexual satisfaction than male partners do. Also, female partners are more likely to emphasize the emotional aspects of lovemaking than male partners (Peplau et al., 2004). Taken together, these facts support a socialization-based explanation of gender differences in orgasmic consistency.

Because women reach orgasm through intercourse less consistently than men, they are more likely than men to fake an orgasm. Surveys reveal that more than half of all adult women (straight and lesbian) have faked an orgasm (Elliott & Brantley, 1997). Men (straight and gay) also fake them, but much less frequently. People typically do so to make their partner feel better or to bring sexual activity to an end when they're tired. Frequent faking is not a good idea, because it can become a vicious cycle and undermine communication about sex (Crooks & Bauer, 2008).

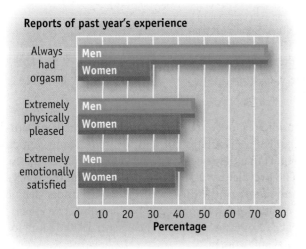

Figure 13.9

Sexual satisfaction with primary partner. A major survey of American sexual behavior showed large gender differences in the consistency of orgasm, a physical measure of sexual satisfaction. Men's and women's subjective evaluations of physical and emotional sexual satisfaction are much more similar. These data indicate that not everyone who has an orgasm every time has a blissful sex life and that factors other than orgasm contribute to a satisfying sex life.

From Laumann, E. O., Gagnon, J. H., Michael, R. T., & Michaels, S. (1994). *The social organization of sexuality: Sexual practices in the United States.* Chicago: University of Chicago Press. Copyright © 1994 by University of Chicago Press. Reprinted by permission.

Sexual Expression

LEARNING OBJECTIVES

▶ *Discuss fantasy as well as kissing and touching as aspects of sexual expression.*

▶ *Discuss the prevalence of self-stimulation and attitudes about it.*

▶ *Discuss oral and anal sex as forms of sexual expression.*

▶ *Discuss intercourse and the preferred sexual activities of gay males and lesbians.*

People experience and express sexuality in myriad ways. *Erogenous zones* **are areas of the body that are sexually sensitive or responsive.** The genitals and breasts usually come to mind when people think of erogenous zones, as these areas are particularly sensitive for most people. But it's worth noting that many individuals fail to appreciate the potential that lies in other areas of the body. Virtually any area of the body can function as an erogenous zone.

Indeed, the ultimate erogenous zone may be the mind. That is, an individual's mental set is extremely important to sexual arousal. Skillful genital stimulation by a partner may have absolutely no impact if a person is not in the mood. Yet fantasy in the absence of any other stimulation can produce great arousal. In this section, we'll consider the most common forms of sexual expression.

Fantasy

Have you ever fantasized about having sex with someone other than your partner? If so, you've had one of the most commonly reported fantasies (see **Figure 13.10**). In fact, a study of university students and employees reported that 98% of men and 80% of women had sexual fantasies involving someone other than their current partner (Hicks & Leitenberg, 2001). As you might expect, women's fantasies tend to be more romantic, while men's tend to contain more explicit imagery (Impett & Peplau, 2006). Most sex therapists view sexual fantasies as harmless ways to enhance sexual excitement and achieve orgasm either during masturbation or with a partner.

Recommended READING

Sexuality Now: Embracing Diversity
by Janell L. Carroll (Thomson Wadsworth, 2007)

Today, almost all colleges offer courses on sexuality. But if you can't enroll in a sexuality course, you may want to read one of the better textbooks. If so, *Sexuality Now* by Janell Carroll is an excellent candidate. Carroll's text is accurate, thorough, up to date, well organized, and written in an engaging, highly readable manner. In addition, the text is sprinkled with first-person accounts, useful questions and answers based on her students' questions, and fascinating multicultural and cross-cultural perspectives on sexuality. Moreover, the book is a paperback and thus more manageable than most heavy, hardcover texts on the topic.

Other sexuality texts of similar quality are *Our Sexuality* by Robert Crooks and Karla Baur (Thomson Wadsworth, 2008) and *Human Sexuality Today* by Bruce M. King (Pearson Prentice Hall, 2005). Any of these books can provide you with an excellent introduction to the realities of human sexual expression.

Fantasies During Intercourse		
Theme	**Subjects reporting fantasy (%)**	
	Males	**Females**
A former lover	42.9	41.0
An imaginary lover	44.3	24.3
Oral-genital sex	61.2	51.4
Group sex	19.3	14.1
Being forced or overpowered into a sexual relationship	21.0	36.4
Others observing you engage in sexual intercourse	15.4	20.0
Others finding you sexually irresistible	55.2	52.8
Being rejected or sexually abused	10.5	13.2
Forcing others to have sexual relations with you	23.5	15.8
Others giving in to you after resisting you at first	36.8	24.3
Observing others engaging in sex	17.9	13.2
A member of the same sex	2.8	9.4
Animals	0.9	3.7

Note: For comparison, the responses of "frequently" and "sometimes" were combined for both males and females to obtain these percentages. The number of respondents answering for a specific fantasy ranged from 103 to 106 for males and from 105 to 107 for females.

Figure 13.10

Common sexual fantasies. The percentage of men and women reporting various sexual fantasies during intercourse is shown here. Sue (1979) concluded that people fantasize about experiences they wouldn't seek out in real life.

Adapted from Sue, D. (1979). The erotic fantasies of college students during coitus. *Journal of Sex Research, 15*(4), 299–305. Copyright © 1979 for the Society for the Scientific Study of Sexuality. Reprinted by permission.

As you saw in **Figure 13.10**, dominance and submission fantasies are not uncommon. Still, just because you fantasize about a particular encounter, such as forced sex, doesn't mean that you really want to have such an experience. Only one-tenth of 1% of women say that they enjoy forced sex, and only one-third of 1% of men say that they enjoy forcing a partner to have sex (Laumann et al., 1994).

Kissing and Touching

Most two-person sexual activities begin with kissing. Kissing usually starts at the lips but may be extended to almost any area of the partner's body. Mutual caressing is also an integral element of sexual stimulation for most couples. Like kissing, this tactile stimulation may be applied to any area of the body. Manual and oral stimulation of the other partner's genitals are related sexual practices.

Men often underestimate the importance of kissing and touching (including clitoral stimulation). It is not surprising, therefore, that heterosexual women commonly complain that their partners are in too much of a hurry (King, 2005). Partners who seek to learn about each other's preferences and who try to accommodate each other are much more likely to have mutually satisfying sexual experiences than those who don't.

Self-Stimulation

Masturbation, or the stimulation of one's own genitals, has traditionally been condemned as immoral because it is nonreproductive. Disapproval and suppression of masturbation were truly intense in the 19th and early 20th centuries, when people believed that the practice was harmful to physical and mental health. Because the term *masturbation* has acquired negative connotations, the preferred terminology is *self-stimulation* or *autoeroticism.* Sometimes people, more often women, use vibrators or other "sex toys" for self-stimulation.

Kinsey discovered over four decades ago that most people masturbate with no ill effects. Sexologists now recognize that self-stimulation is normal and healthy. In fact, sex therapists often prescribe masturbation to treat both male and female sexual problems (see this Chapter's Application). Nonetheless, nearly half of those who engage in the practice feel guilty about it (Laumann et al., 1994).

Self-stimulation is common in our society: By adulthood, nine out of ten males and eight out of ten females report having masturbated at least once (Atwood & Gagnon, 1987). African American males masturbate less than Asian, white, and Hispanic men. Also, masturbation is less common among those with less education (Laumann et al., 1994).

Among married couples, 57% of husbands and 37% of wives report engaging in self-stimulation (Laumann et al., 1994). In fact, masturbation in marriage is often associated with a greater degree of marital and sexual satisfaction (Leitenberg, Detzer, & Srebnik, 1993). Still, couples usually don't talk about it, probably for fear that it will be viewed as a sign of sexual discontent.

Oral and Anal Sex

Oral sex refers to oral stimulation of the genitals. ***Cunnilingus* is oral stimulation of the female genitals; *fellatio* is oral stimulation of the penis.** Partners may stimulate each other simultaneously, or one partner may stimulate the other without immediate reciprocation. Oral-genital sex may be one of several activities in a sexual encounter, or it may be the main event. Oral sex is a major source of orgasms for many heterosexual couples, and it plays a central role in homosexual relationships. A positive aspect of oral sex is that it does not result in pregnancy. This fact partly accounts for the finding that younger teens are more likely to engage in oral sex than in sexual intercourse (Halpern-Felsher et al., 2005). However, some sexually transmitted diseases (human immunodeficiency virus or HIV, for example) can be contracted through mouth-genital stimulation, especially if there are small cracks in the mouth or if the mouth is exposed to semen (Guest, 2004). And a person with a cold sore can pass along the herpes virus during oral sex (or kissing) (Carroll, 2007).

Negative attitudes persist about oral sex, particularly among African Americans, Hispanics, religious conservatives, and those with less education (Laumann et al., 1994). About 80% of men and 70% of women (both gay and straight) report that they have either given or received oral sex at least once (Laumann et al., 1994). Oral sex is now a component in most couples' sexual relationships.

***Anal intercourse* involves insertion of the penis into a partner's anus and rectum.** Legally, it is termed *sodomy* (and is still considered illegal in some states). About 25% of men and women report that they have practiced anal sex at least once (Laumann et al., 1994). Anal intercourse is more popular among homosexual male couples than among heterosexual couples. However, even among gay men it ranks behind oral sex and mutual masturbation in prevalence. Anal sex is risky, as rectal tissues are easily torn, facilitating HIV transmission.

Intercourse

Vaginal intercourse, known more technically as *coitus,* **involves inserting the penis into the vagina and (typically) pelvic thrusting.** It is the most widely endorsed and widely practiced sexual act in our society. In the American sex survey, 95% of heterosexual respondents said that they had practiced vaginal sex the last time they had sex (Laumann et al., 1994). Inserting the penis generally requires adequate vaginal lubrication, or intercourse may be difficult and painful for the woman. This is another good reason for couples to spend plenty of time on mutual kissing and touching, since sexual excitement causes vaginal lubrication: In the absence of adequate lubrication, partners may choose to use artificial lubricants.

Couples use a variety of positions in intercourse and may use more than one position in a single encounter. The man-above, or "missionary," position is the most common, but the woman-above, side-by-side, and rear-entry positions are also popular. Each position has its advantages and disadvantages. Although people are fascinated by the relative merits of various positions, specific positions may not be as important as the tempo, depth, and angle of movements in intercourse. As with other aspects of sexual relations, the crucial consideration is that partners talk to each other about their preferences.

What kinds of sexual activities do homosexuals prefer in the absence of coitus (which is, by definition, a heterosexual act)? As is true with heterosexual couples, the preliminary activities of gay and lesbian couples include kissing, hugging, and petting. Gay men also engage in fellatio, mutual masturbation, and anal intercourse, in that order (Lever, 1994). Lesbians engage in cunnilingus, mutual masturbation, and *tribadism,* in which one partner lies on top of the other and makes thrusting movements so that both receive genital stimulation at the same time.

Patterns of Sexual Behavior

LEARNING OBJECTIVES

▸ Describe how the fear of contracting AIDS has influenced sexual attitudes and practices.

▸ Summarize attitudes toward and prevalence of early sexual experiences.

▸ Summarize the findings on sex patterns in dating couples and married couples.

▸ Compare and contrast sexual behavior in married couples versus committed homosexual couples.

▸ Summarize the evidence on infidelity in committed relationships.

In this section we consider whether fears of contracting acquired immune deficiency syndrome (AIDS) have influenced sexual attitudes and behaviors. Then we'll see how age and type of relationship are related to sexual behavior and then explore the issue of infidelity.

Sex in the Age of AIDS

Over the past 40 years, American sexual attitudes and behaviors have become much more liberal, although this trend has slowed since the 1990s (Christopher & Sprecher, 2000). While heralded by some, the liberal trends have had several serious drawbacks. Two troublesome problems are escalating teenage pregnancy rates and increases in sexually transmitted diseases (Trussell, Brown, & Hogue, 2004). The spread of HIV infection that leads to AIDS remains a special concern. (For a discussion of AIDS, see Chapter 14.) Has public awareness of AIDS put the brakes on the liberalizing trends?

For both pregnancy rates and sexually transmitted diseases, the news is mixed. Although in the United States the teenage birth rate declined 26% between 1991 and 2001, the rate remains one of the highest in the world (Trussell et al, 2004; U.S. Department of Health and Human Services, 2002). Regarding sexually transmitted diseases, rates of genital infections among adolescents remain at high levels. One-fourth of all cases of sexually transmitted diseases occur among teenagers and two-thirds are among people under 25 years of age (Trussell et al., 2004). The good news is that most young people are knowledgeable about HIV and AIDS. Also, between 1991 and 2005, the percentage of high school students who had ever had sexual intercourse decreased, the average number of sex partners decreased, and the incidence of condom use increased, as you can see in **Figure 13.11** (on the next page). Unfortunately, these positive patterns do not hold for all teens. Thus, in the age of AIDS, there is both good and bad news about patterns of sexual behavior.

Figure 13.11

Sexual risk behavior in high school students. In national surveys over a 14-year period, high school students reported on their sexual behavior: whether they had ever had sexual intercourse, the number of sex partners they had had, and whether they had used a condom during their last intercourse. Between 1991 and 2005, sexual risk behavior declined: Fewer students had sex, fewer had four or more sex partners, and more had used a condom during their last sexual encounter. Still, risky behavior increased as students progressed in school.

From Centers for Disease Control. (2006). Trends in sexual risk behaviors among high school students—United States, 1991–2005. *Morbidity and Mortality Weekly Report, 55*(31), 851-854. (Figure based on data in table on pp. 853–854)

Sexual Risk Behavior in High School Students

Grade	Survey year	Ever had intercourse (%)	Four or more sexual partners in lifetime (%)	Condom use during last sexual intercourse (%)
9	1991	39	13	53
	2005	34	9	75
10	1991	48	15	46
	2005	43	12	65
11	1991	62	22	49
	2005	51	16	62
12	1991	67	25	41
	2005	63	21	55

Note: Percentages are rounded to the nearest whole number.

Early Sexual Experiences

By age 22, 90% of Americans have had sexual intercourse. With the average age for marriage being 27 for men and 25 for women, it is obvious that most people are not virgins when they enter committed relationships. Thus, the term *premarital sex* is losing relevance. Another problem is that the term doesn't apply to homosexuals, who aren't permitted to marry under the law (except in Massachusetts as of 2007). Thus, we have chosen to characterize youthful sexual encounters as "early sexual experiences" instead of "premarital sex."

Attitudes

Compared to a generation ago, more people believe that sex before marriage is acceptable, especially if the two people are emotionally committed to each other. Nonetheless, a sexual double standard still exists (Crawford

Sexual encounters with casual acquaintances are common in today's society. Nonetheless, casual sex can be risky for a variety of reasons.

& Popp, 2003). Both men and women are less approving of sexual activity for women than men, especially in the early stages of relationships (Willets, Sprecher, & Beck, 2004).

Prevalence

In **Figure 13.11**, you can see that the percentage of high school students who have had intercourse increases with age—from 34% in grade 9 to 63% in grade 12 (U.S. Department of Health and Human Services, 2006a). Early sexual activity is correlated with parents' lack of education, poor academic performance, and low educational expectations (Lammers et al., 2000). Also, surveys report that African American teenagers, on average, are likely to engage in sex earlier than their Hispanic or European American peers (U.S. Department of Health and Human Services, 2006b), but it is likely that these apparent ethnic differences are actually differences in socioeconomic status (Lammers et al., 2000).

"Hooking up," a phenomenon that has arisen since the late 1990s, involves two strangers or briefly acquainted people having a single sexual encounter. "Friends with benefits" is a related term that refers to friends who engage in sex but who don't have romantic feelings for each other . Unlike a one-night stand, hookups don't always involve intercourse (petting below the waist and oral sex are common). According to one study, 78% of college students have had at least one hookup (Paul, McManus, & Hayes, 2000). It seems that college students wrongly believe that their peers are significantly more comfortable with hooking up than they, themselves, are (Lambert, Kahn, & Apple, 2003). The researchers speculate that these false perceptions might influence students to override their own comfort level and engage in sexual behavior to be in step with the perceived peer norm. **Figure 13.12** depicts men's and women's comfort level with various hooking-up behaviors. Casual sex is risky: People don't always

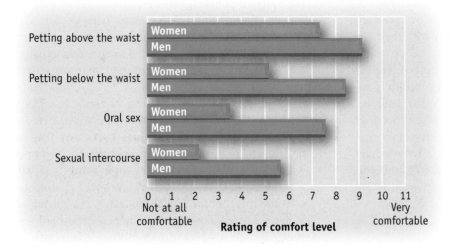

Figure 13.12

Gender differences in comfort level with hooking-up behaviors. College men and women were asked to rate their comfort level with four hooking-up behaviors. The ratings were made on an 11-point scale (11 = *Very comfortable*; 1 = *Not at all comfortable*). As you can see from the mean ratings shown here, men's comfort level significantly exceeded women's for all four behaviors.

From Lambert, T.A., Kahn, A. S., & Apple,,K. J. (2003). Pluralistic ignorance and hooking up. *The Journal of Sex Research, 40*(2) 129-133. Copyright © 2003 Society for the Scientific Study of Sexuality. Reprinted by permission.

practice safer sex, and the risk of contracting sexually transmitted diseases increases with multiple partners.

Sex in Committed Relationships

Sex is a key aspect of most committed, romantic relationships. In this section, we examine patterns of sexual activity in dating couples, married couples, and gay couples.

Sex Between Dating Partners

At some point, couples confront the question of whether or when they should have sex. Some worry that sex might adversely affect the relationship; others fear that not having sex will cause trouble. Is there evidence to support either view? As it turns out, sexual intimacy is a positive predictor of relationship stability (Sprecher & Cate, 2004). However, gender and sexual and relationship satisfaction are also part of this equation. For men, sexual (but not relationship) satisfaction is significantly correlated with relationship stability; for women, relationship (but not sexual) satisfaction is significantly associated with relationship stability (Sprecher, 2002).

Marital Sex

Couples' overall marital satisfaction is strongly related to their satisfaction with their sexual relationship (Sprecher et al., 2006). Of course, it is difficult to know whether good sex promotes good marriages or good marriages promote good sex. In all probability, it's a two-way street. Relationship satisfaction is also correlated with satisfaction in other areas of a relationship (fairness in distribution of household labor, for example) (Impett & Peplau, 2006).

Married couples vary greatly in how often they have sex (see **Figure 13.13**). *On the average,* couples in their 20s and 30s engage in sex about two or three times a week. The frequency of sex among married couples tends to decrease as the years pass (Sprecher et al., 2006). Biological changes play some role in this trend, but

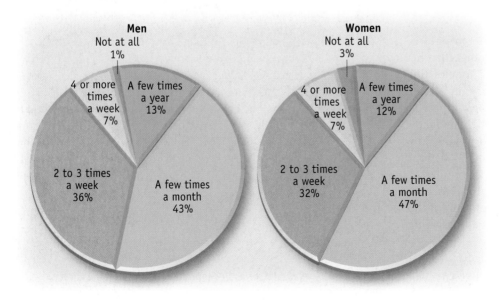

Figure 13.13

Frequency of sex among married men and women. A well-sampled survey asked Americans, "How often have you had sex in the past 12 months?" Married individuals' responses to the question were wide ranging. The most frequent response was "a few times per month" followed by "2 to 3 times a week."

From Michael, R. T., Gagnon, J. H., Laumann, E. O., & Kolata, G. (1994). *Sex in America: A definitive survey.* Boston: Little, Brown. Copyright © 1994 by CSG Enterprises, Inc. Edward O. Lauman, Robert T. Michael, and Gina Kolata. By permission of Little, Brown and Company, Inc., and Brockman, Inc.

social factors seem more compelling. Most couples attribute this decline to increasing fatigue from work and childrearing and to growing familiarity with their sexual routine.

As men and women age, sexual arousal tends to build more slowly and orgasms tend to diminish in frequency and intensity. Males' refractory periods lengthen, and females' vaginal lubrication and elasticity decrease. Nevertheless, older people remain capable of rewarding sexual encounters (Burgess, 2004). A national survey of couples reported that those in the 75 and older age group had sex slightly less than once a month (Call, Sprecher, & Schwartz, 1995).

Sex in Homosexual Relationships

What about the frequency of sex among lesbian, gay, and heterosexual couples? Peplau and her colleagues (2004) report three patterns. First, there is a general decline in the frequency of sexual behavior over time. Second, in the early stages of a relationship, gay males engage in sex more frequently than the other couples. For example, among couples who had been together for two years or less, 67% of gay men reported having sex three or more times a week, compared to 45% of married couples and 33% of lesbian couples (Blumstein & Schwartz, 1983). Third, lesbian couples have sex less often than the other couples.

Like heterosexual women, most lesbians believe that sex and love are intertwined. In contrast (and like straight males), gay men find casual sex more acceptable (Sanders, 2000). Comparative studies find comparable levels of sexual satisfaction in gay, lesbian, and heterosexual couples (Kurdek, 2005). And for both lesbians and gay men, sexual satisfaction is correlated with overall relationship satisfaction.

Infidelity in Committed Relationships

Sexual infidelity occurs when a person who is in a committed relationship engages in erotic activity with someone other than his or her partner. Among married couples, this behavior is also called "adultery" or "extramarital sex." Infidelity among couples in committed relationships (straight and gay) is termed "extradyadic sex." The vast majority of people (91%) in our society believe that extramarital sex is "always" or "almost always wrong" (Saad, 2007). Nonetheless, Americans are fascinated by infidelity, if the popularity of such TV series as *Desperate Housewives* is any gauge!

Although it's not common, extramarital sex can be consensual. Two examples include "swinging" and "open marriage." Swingers are married couples who agree to exchange partners for sex (Rubin, 2001). In "open marriage," both partners agree that it is okay for each to have sex with others (O'Neill & O'Neill, 1972). As we noted, gay male couples are more likely to have "open 'marriages'" than are lesbian or married couples.

Precisely what kind of erotic activity qualifies as "cheating" is debatable, especially between men and women, as you can see in **Figure 13.14**. Are you unfaithful if you develop a deep emotional involvement without sex? No doubt many people would say "yes." Is it "cheating" if a person in a committed relationship uses the Internet for sexual arousal or masturbation? What about exchanging sexually explicit e-mail with someone you've never met face to face? Therapists are seeing more couples for problems related to cyber affairs (Cooper & Griffin-Shelley, 2002).

Prevalence

Despite the fact that most people disapprove of infidelity, a number of people get involved in it. Because of the associated stigma and secrecy, accurate estimates of infidelity are difficult to come by. Surveys report that about 25% of married men and about 10% of married women had engaged in an extramarital affair at least once (Laumann et al., 1994; Wiederman, 1997).

In straight cohabiting relationships, about a third of men and women have engaged in extradyadic sex (Blumstein & Schwartz, 1983). As we noted, sexual openness is more common in committed gay male relationships, and the rates of extradyadic sex for this group are higher than for all other groups (Peplau & Fingerhut, 2007). Committed lesbian relationships are much

The popularity of the TV series Desperate Housewives *suggests that Americans are fascinated by infidelity.*

What Constitutes Infidelity?

Does this constitute cheating in a marriage?	Answered "yes"	
	Married men	Married women
Kissing someone else	59%	75%
Having a sexually explicit conversation on the phone	64%	74%
Having a sexually explicit conversation on the Internet	62%	72%
Holding hands with someone else	40%	49%
Fantasizing about having sex with someone else	39%	43%
Casually flirting with someone else	32%	38%

Figure 13.14

What constitutes infidelity? A 1998 Time/CNN poll asked 397 married men and 431 married women whether various actions constituted cheating in a marriage. Men's responses were more liberal than women's, especially regarding "kissing someone else."

From Handy, B. (1998, August 3). How we really feel about infidelity. *Time*, pp. 52–53. Copyright © 1998 by Time Inc. Reprinted by permission.

more exclusive, in principle and in practice, than gay male relationships (Peplau & Fingerhut, 2007). Rates of lesbian extradyadic sex are also lower than those for married women.

Motivations

Why do people pursue extramarital sexual encounters? Common reasons include dissatisfaction with a relationship, anger toward a partner, and boredom (Willets et al., 2004). Sometimes people need to confirm that they are still desirable, or they want to trigger the end of an unsatisfying relationship. Then again, extramarital sexual activity can occur simply because two people are attracted to each other. Erotic reactions to people other than one's partner do not cease when one makes a permanent commitment. Most people suppress these sexual desires because they disapprove of adultery.

The gender differences in motivations for infidelity parallel the gender differences in sexual socialization. Men tend to engage in extradyadic affairs to obtain sexual variety or more frequent sex, while women usually seek an emotional connection (Buunk & Dijkstra, 2006). Age is also a factor. People between the ages of 18 and 30 are twice as likely to engage in sex outside a committed relationship than people over 50 (Treas & Giesen, 2000). Too, there is some evidence that insecure attachment styles are positively correlated with infidelity (Buunk & Dijkstra, 2006).

Impact

The impact of extramarital sexual activity on marriages has not been investigated extensively. Experts speculate that approximately 20% of all divorces are caused by infidelity (Reinisch, 1990). Still, it's hard to know in these cases whether extramarital sex is a symptom of a disintegrating relationship or its cause. Occasionally, extramarital affairs can have a positive effect on a marriage if they motivate a couple to resolve relationship problems. Participants in extramarital affairs, whether or not they are discovered, may experience loss of self-respect, guilt, stress, and complications of sexually transmitted diseases. Sexual fidelity is positively correlated with relationship satisfaction for lesbian and heterosexual couples, but not for gay male couples (Kurdek, 1991).

Practical Issues in Sexual Activity

LEARNING OBJECTIVES

▶ *Describe constraints on effective contraception and discuss the merits of hormone-based contraceptives and condoms.*

▶ *Describe the various types of STDs, and discuss their prevalence and means of transmission.*

▶ *List some suggestions for safer sexual practices.*

Regardless of the context of sexual activity, two practical issues are often matters of concern: contraception and sexually transmitted diseases. These topics are more properly in the domain of medicine than of psychology, but birth control and sex-related infections certainly do have their behavioral aspects.

Contraception

Most people want to control whether and when they will conceive a child, so they need reliable contraception. Despite the availability of effective contraceptive methods, however, many people fail to exercise much control.

Constraints on Effective Contraception

Effective contraception requires that intimate couples negotiate their way through a complex sequence of steps. First, both people must define themselves as sexually active. Second, both must have accurate knowledge about fertility and conception. Third, their chosen method of contraception must be readily accessible. Finally, both must have the motivation and skill to use the method correctly and consistently. Failure to meet even one of these conditions can result in an unintended pregnancy.

Given the difficulties surrounding effective contraception, it is extremely encouraging that teenage pregnancy rates declined dramatically between 1991 and 2003 (Santelli et al., 2006). The main reasons for this steep decline are improved use of contraceptives and delays in beginning sexual intercourse. Although these changes are heartening, many high school students (23% of girls and 16% of boys) use either withdrawal or no contraception at all (Santelli et al. 2006). These individuals are at high risk for pregnancy and sexually transmitted diseases. In addition, any couple who do not use condoms (even if they use another contraceptive method) can contract sexually transmitted diseases unless both partners have tested negatively for such infections.

Why do some individuals and couples engage in risky sexual behavior? Of course, one cause is ignorance about preventing pregnancy and sexually transmitted diseases. Another factor is conflicting norms about gender and sexual behavior. Men are socialized to be the initiators of sexual activity, but when it comes to birth control, they often rely on women to take charge. It is hard for a woman to maintain an image of sexual naïveté and also be responsible for contraception. Telling her partner that she is "on the pill" or whipping out a condom conveys quite a different image. Unfortunately, a woman's decision to use a condom may be influenced more by concerns about how her partner might perceive her than her perceived susceptibility to infections and attitudes about condom use (Bryan, Aiken, & West, 1999). Finally, alcohol can undermine condom use, although this is not always the case (Cooper, 2006). Some individuals drink as a socially acceptable way to avoid potentially embarrassing discussions about sex.

Selecting a Contraceptive Method

If a couple is motivated to control their fertility, how should they go about selecting a technique? A rational choice requires accurate knowledge of the effectiveness, benefits, costs, and risks of the various methods. **Figure 13.15** summarizes information on most of the methods currently available. The *ideal failure rate* estimates the probability of conception when the technique is used correctly and consistently. The *actual failure rate* is what occurs in the real world, when users' negligence is factored in.

Besides being informed about contraceptive methods, couples must also put this information to use. Contraception is a joint responsibility. Hence, it's essential for partners to discuss their preferences, to decide what method(s) they are going to use, and to *act* on their decision. Let's look in more detail at the two most widely used birth control methods in the Western world: hormone-based contraceptives and condoms.

Hormone-based contraceptives contain synthetic forms of estrogen and progesterone (or progesterone only, in the minipill), which inhibit ovulation in women. Types of hormone-based contraceptives include "the pill," hormonal injectables (Depo-Provera), the transdermal patch (worn on the skin), the vaginal ring (inserted once a month), and contraceptive implants. Many couples prefer these birth control options because contraceptive use is not tied to the sex act. Only the intrauterine device (IUD) permits a similar degree of sexual spontaneity. But these contraceptives do not protect against sexually transmitted diseases.

Except for Depo-Provera, use of hormone-based contraceptives does not appear to increase a woman's overall risk for cancer (Trussell, 2004). Depo-Provera may increase the risk of cervical, liver, and/or breast cancers (Carroll, 2007). In fact, the likelihood of certain forms of cancer (such as uterine and ovarian cancer) is reduced in women who use low-dosage *oral* contra-

Web Link 13.5 **Sexual Health Network**

The health professionals who staff this Connecticut-based site have assembled a comprehensive set of resources related to all aspects of human sexual health. Especially notable are materials discussing sexual functioning for persons with physical injuries or disabilities.

Contraceptive Methods

Method	Ideal failure rate (%)	Actual failure rate (%)	Advantages	Disadvantages
Birth control pills (combination)	0.3	8	Highly reliable; coitus-independent; has some health benefits	Side effects; daily use; continual cost; health risks for some women; no protection against STDs
Minipill (progestin only)	0.3	8	Thought to have low risk of side effects; coitus-independent; has some health benefits	Breakthrough bleeding; daily use; continual cost; health risks for some women; no protection against STDs
Hormonal injectables (Depo-Provera)	0.3	3	Highly reliable; coitus independent; no memory or motivation required for use; reduces risk of endometrial and ovarian cancer	Side effects; use may increase risk of certain cancers; continual cost; injection every 3 months; no protection against STDs
Hormonal ring (NuvaRing)	0.3	8	Highly reliable; coitus independent; no memory or motivation required for use; may offer protection against endometrial and ovarian cancer	Side effects; no data on extended use; no protection against STDs
Subdermal implants (Implanon)	0.1	0.1	Highly reliable; coitus independent; no memory or motivation required for use	Side effects; painful removal; possible scarring at site; no protection from STDs
Transdermal patch	.03	8	No memory or motivation required to use; coitus-independent; very reliable; has some health benefits	Continual cost; skin irritation for some women; no protection against STDs
IUD	0.6	0.8	No memory or motivation required for use; very reliable; some health benefits	Cramping, bleeding, expulsion; risk of pelvic inflammatory disease; no protection against STDs
Diaphragm with spermicidal cream or jelly	6	16	No major health risks; inexpensive	Aesthetic objections; initial cost
Condom (male)	2	15	Protects against STDs; simple to use; male responsibility; no health risks; no prescriptions required	Unaesthetic to some; requires interruption of sexual activity; continual cost
Sponge	9	16	24-hour protection; simple to use; no taste or odor; inexpensive; effective with several acts of intercourse	Aesthetic objections; continual cost; no protection against STDs
Cervical cap with spermicidal cream or jelly	9	16	48-hour protection; no major health risks	May be difficult to insert; may irritate cervix; initial cost
Spermicides	18	29	No major health risks; no prescription required	Unaesthetic to some; must be properly inserted; continual cost; no protection against STDs
Fertility awareness (rhythm)	1–9	25	No cost; acceptable to Catholic church	Requires high motivation and periods of abstinence; unreliable; no protection against STDs
Withdrawal	4	27	No cost or health risks	Reduces sexual pleasure; unreliable; requires high motivation; no protection against STDs
No contraception	85	85	No immediate monetary cost	High risk of pregnancy and STDs

Note: STDs = Sexually transmitted diseases

Figure 13.15

A comparison of widely used contraceptive techniques. Couples can choose from a variety of contraceptive methods. This chart summarizes the advantages and disadvantages of each method. Note that the typical failure rate is much higher than the ideal failure rate for all methods, because couples do not use contraceptive techniques consistently and correctly. (Based on Carroll, 2007; Crooks & Baur, 2008; Hatcher et al., 2004)

ceptives. These methods do slightly increase the risk of certain cardiovascular disorders, such as heart disease and stroke. Thus, alternative methods of contraception should be considered by women who smoke, are over age 35, have any suspicion of cardiovascular disease, have liver disease, or have breast or uterine cancer.

A *condom* is a sheath worn over the penis during intercourse to collect ejaculated semen. The condom is the only widely available contraceptive device for use by males. A condom slightly reduces a man's sensitivity, but many men see this dulling as a plus because it can make sex last longer. Condoms can be purchased in any drugstore without a prescription. If used correctly, the condom is highly effective in preventing pregnancy (Warner, Hatcher, & Steiner, 2004). It must be placed over the penis after erection but before any contact with the vagina, and space must be left at the tip to collect the ejaculate. The man should withdraw before completely losing his erection and firmly hold the rim of the condom during withdrawal to prevent any semen from spilling into the vagina.

Condoms are made of polyurethane, latex rubber, and animal membranes ("skin"). Polyurethane condoms are thinner than latex condoms; however, they are more likely to break and to slip off than latex condoms. Using latex condoms definitely reduces the chances of contracting or passing on various sexually transmitted diseases. However, oil-based creams and lotions (petroleum jelly, massage oil, baby oil, and hand and body lotions, for example) should never be used with *latex* condoms (or diaphragms) (Warner et al., 2004). Within 60 seconds, these products can make microscopic holes in the rubber membrane that are large enough to allow passage of HIV and organisms produced by other sexually transmitted diseases. Water-based lubricants such as Astroglide or K-Y Warming Liquid do not cause this problem. Polyurethane condoms are impervious to oils. Skin condoms do *not* offer protection against sexually transmitted diseases.

In closing, we should mention emergency contraception. Women may seek emergency contraception in cases of sexual assault, contraceptive failure, or unprotected sex. Progestin pills (Plan B) are available from pharmacies without a prescription for women aged 18 and older (younger women must have a prescription) (Alan Guttmacher Institute, 2006). Plan B pills are 95% effective in preventing pregnancy if they are taken within 24 hours after intercourse (75% effective within 72 hours). The drug works like birth control pills, by preventing ovulation or fertilization and implantation of the fertilized egg into the uterine wall ("Condoms—Extra Protection," 2005). If the fertilized egg is already implanted into the wall of the uterus, progestin will not harm it. By contrast, mifepristone (RU 486) is a drug that can induce a miscarriage in the first seven weeks of a pregnancy (Stewart, Ellertson, & Cates, 2004). Prescribed by a physician, mifepristone is typically administered in the form of two pills taken several days apart. Although no substitute for regular birth control, the drug can be used after unprotected sex and is particularly helpful in cases of rape.

Sexually Transmitted Diseases

A *sexually transmitted disease* (STD) is a disease or infection that is transmitted primarily through sexual contact. When people think of STDs, they typically think of syphilis and gonorrhea, but these diseases are only the tip of the iceberg. There are actually around 25 sexually transmitted diseases. Some of them—for instance, pubic lice—are minor nuisances that can readily be treated. Others, however, are severe afflictions that are difficult to treat. For instance, if it isn't detected early, syphilis can cause heart failure, blindness, and brain damage, and AIDS is eventually fatal.

Prevalence and Transmission

No one is immune to sexually transmitted diseases. Even monogamous partners can develop some STDs (yeast infections, for instance). Health authorities estimate that about 19 million new cases occur in the United States each year (Alan Guttmacher Institute, 2006). The highest incidence of STDs occurs in the under-25 age group (Cates, 2004). About one person in four contracts an STD by age 21 (Feroli & Burstein, 2003).

The United States has seen a recent surge of HIV infections stemming from heterosexual transmission (Kaiser Family Foundation, 2007). And an estimated half of all new HIV infections occur in people under age 25. AIDS is increasing more rapidly among women than among men, especially among blacks and Latinas (Kaiser Family Foundation, 2007). Women whose sexual partners have multiple sex partners or who inject drugs are especially at risk. An increasing concern is that a woman's partner may be secretly having sex with other men and may deny that he is gay or bisexual (Kalb & Murr, 2006). Infected women are more likely to be poor and less likely to get treatment (Cowley & Murr, 2004). The rate of HIV infections is also up among young gay and bisexual men, especially blacks and Latinos (Kaiser Family Foundation, 2007).

Women suffer more severe long-term consequences of STDs than men, including chronic pelvic pain, infertility, and cervical cancer (Cates, 2004). Because of the transmission dynamics of sexual intercourse, they are also more likely to acquire an STD from any single sexual encounter. But women are less likely to seek treatment because more of their STDs are asymp-

---

Web Link 13.6 **AIDS HIV AEGIS**

This is the largest and probably most important web-based resource dealing with the human immunodeficiency virus (HIV) and acquired immune deficiency syndrome (AIDS). A simply extraordinary collection of information sources can be found here.

tomatic or not perceived to be serious. Human papillomavirus (HPV) infections cause about half of STDs diagnosed among 15- to 24-year-olds (Alan Guttmacher Institute, 2006). Certain types of HPV can lead to cervical cancer. In 2006, the U.S. Food and Drug Administration approved a vaccine (Gardisil) for use by females aged 9 to 26. It will prevent infection with the types of HPV that lead to cervical cancer.

The principal types of sexually transmitted diseases are listed in **Figure 13.16** on the next page, along with their symptoms and modes of transmission. Most of these infections are spread from one person to another through intercourse, oral-genital contact, or anal-genital contact. Concerning the transmission of STDs, seven points are worth emphasizing:

1. You should consider *any* activity that exposes you to blood (including menstrual blood), semen, vaginal secretions, urine, feces, or saliva as high-risk behavior *unless* you and your partner are in a mutual, sexually exclusive relationship and neither of you is infected.

2. The more sexual partners you have, the higher your chances of exposure to a sexually transmitted infection.

3. Having sexual contact with a male or female sex worker puts you at high risk for contracting an HIV infection.

4. Don't assume that the labels people attach to themselves (heterosexual or homosexual) accurately describe their actual sexual behavior. According to a government study based on a nationally representative sample of individuals aged 15 to 44, 6% of males and 11% of females reported that they had had at least one same-gender sexual experience in their lives (Mosher, Chandra, & Jones, 2005).

5. People can be carriers of sexually transmitted diseases without knowing it. For instance, in its early stages gonorrhea may cause no readily apparent symptoms in women, who may unknowingly transmit the infection to their partners.

6. Even when people know they have a sexually transmitted infection, they may fail to refrain from sex or inform their partners. Guilt and embarrassment cause many people to ignore symptoms of sexually transmitted diseases and continue their normal sexual activities. Many people will lie about homosexual activity, sex with prostitutes, drug use, and the number of sexual partners they have had. So don't assume that sexual partners will warn you that they may be contagious.

7. Engaging in anal intercourse (especially being the receiving partner) puts one at high risk for AIDS. Rectal tissues are delicate and easily torn, thus letting the virus pass through the membrane. Always use a condom during anal sex. Oral-genital sex may also transmit HIV, particularly if semen is swallowed.

Prevention

Abstinence is obviously the best way to avoid acquiring STDs. Of course, this is not an appealing or realistic option for most people. Short of abstinence, the best strategy is to engage in sexual activity only in the context of a long-term relationship, where partners have an opportunity to know each other reasonably well. Casual sex greatly increases the risk for STDs, including HIV.

We offer the following suggestions for safer sex (Crooks & Baur, 2008; King, 2005):

▶ Don't have sex with lots of people. You increase your risk of contracting STDs.

▶ Don't have sex with someone who has had lots of previous partners. People won't always be honest about their sexual history, so it's important to know whether you can trust a prospective partner's word.

▶ If you are not involved in a sexually exclusive relationship, always use latex condoms with spermicides. They have a good track record of preventing STDs and offer effective protection against the AIDS virus. (And never use oil-based lubricants with latex condoms; use water-based lubricants instead.)

▶ If there is any possibility that you or your partner has an STD, abstain from sex, always use condoms, or use other types of sexual expression such as hand-genital stimulation.

▶ Wash your genitals with soap and warm water before and after sexual contact.

▶ Urinate shortly after intercourse.

▶ Because HIV is easily transmitted through anal intercourse, it's a good idea to avoid this type of sex.

▶ Watch for sores, rashes, or discharge around the vulva or penis, or elsewhere on your body, especially the mouth. If you have cold sores, avoid kissing or oral sex.

Along with being judicious about sexual relations, you need to talk openly about safer sexual practices with your partner. But if you don't carry the process one step further and practice what you preach, you remain at risk. As we noted, many people engage in risky sexual behavior—a practice they can ill afford while we are in the grip of the deadly AIDS epidemic.

Unfortunately, the availability of new drug treatments for HIV seems to have increased risk taking among gay and bisexual men (Peterson & Bakeman, 2006). Although these new drugs are welcome news, they cost over $10,000 per year—well out of the reach of those without health insurance (Freedberg et al., 2001).

If you have any reason to suspect that you have an STD, find a good health clinic and get tested *as soon as possible*. It's normal to be embarrassed or afraid of getting bad news, but don't delay. Health professionals are in the business of helping people, not judging them. To be really sure, get tested twice. If both tests are negative,

Sexually Transmitted Diseases (STDs)

STD	Transmission	Symptoms
Acquired immune deficiency syndrome (AIDS)	The AIDS virus is spread by coitus or anal intercourse. There is a chance the virus may also be spread by oral-genital sex, particularly if semen is swallowed. (AIDS can also be spread by non-sexual means: contaminated blood, contaminated hypodermic needles, and transmission from an infected woman to her baby during pregnancy or childbirth.)	Most people infected with the virus show no immediate symptoms; antibodies usually develop in the blood 2-8 weeks after infection. People with the virus may remain symptom-free for 5 years or more. No cure for the disease has yet been found. Common symptoms include fevers, night sweats, weight loss, chronic fatigue, swollen lymph nodes, diarrhea and/or bloody stools, atypical bruising or bleeding, skin rashes, headache, chronic cough, and a whitish coating on the tongue or throat.
Chlamydia infection	The *Chlamydia trichomatis* bacterium is transmitted primarily through sexual contact. It may also be spread by fingers from one body site to another.	In men, chlamydial infection of the urethra may cause a discharge and burning during urination. Chlamydia-caused epididimitis may produce a sense of heaviness in the affected testicle(s), inflammation of the scrotal skin, and painful swelling at the bottom of the testicle. In women, pelvic inflammatory disease caused by chlamydia may disrupt menstrual periods, temperature, and cause abdominal pain, nausea, vomiting, headache, infertility, and ectopic pregnancy.
Human papillomavirus (HPV)	Virus is often on genital skin areas not covered by a condom (vulva, scrotum, etc.); virus is spread primarily through penile-vaginal, oral-genital, oral-anal, or genital-anal contact; transmission most often occurs by asymptomatic individuals.	Often asymptomatic; 10% of infections lead to contagious genital warts, which may appear 3 to 8 months after contact with infected person; HPV is associated with various cancers.
Gonorrhea ("clap")	The *Neisseria gonorrhoeae* bacterium (gonococcus) is spread through penile-vaginal, oral-genital, or genital-anal contact.	Most common symptoms in men are a cloudy discharge from the penis and burning sensations during urination. If the disease is untreated, complications may include inflammation of the scrotal skin and swelling at the base of the testicle. In women, some green or yellowish discharge is produced, but the disease commonly remains undetected. At a later stage, pelvic inflammatory disease may develop.
Herpes	The genital herpes virus (HSV-2) appears to be transmitted primarily by penile-vaginal, oral-genital, or genital-anal contact. The oral herpes virus (HSV-1) is transmitted primarily by kissing, or oral-genital contact.	Small red, painful bumps (papules) appear in the region of the genitals (genital herpes) or mouth (oral herpes). The papules become painful blisters that eventually rupture to form wet, open sores.
Pubic lice ("crabs")	*Phthirus pubis*, the pubic louse, is spread easily through body contact or through shared clothing or bedding.	Persistent itching. Lice are visible and may often be located in pubic hair or other body hair.
Syphilis	The *Treponema pallidum* bacterium (spirochete) is transmitted from open lesions during penile-vaginal, oral-genital, oral-anal, or genital-anal contact.	*Primary stage:* A painless chancre (sore) appears at the site where the spirochetes entered the body. *Secondary stage:* The chancre disappears and a generalized skin rash develops. *Latent stage:* There may be no observable symptoms. *Tertiary stage:* Heart failure, blindness, mental disturbance, and many other symptoms may occur. Death may result.
Trichomoniasis	The protozoan parasite *Trichomonas vaginalis* is passed through genital sexual contact or less frequently by towels, toilet seats, or bathtubs used by an infected person.	In women, white or yellow vaginal discharge with an unpleasant odor; vulva is sore and irritated. Men are usually asymptomatic.
Viral hepatitis	The hepatitis B virus may be transmitted by blood, semen, vaginal secretions, and saliva. Manual, oral, or penile stimulation of the anus is strongly associated with the spread of this virus. Hepatitis A seems to be spread primarily via the fecal-oral route. Oral-anal sexual contact is a common mode of sexual transmission for hepatitis A.	Vary from nonexistent to mild, flulike symptoms to an incapacitating illness characterized by high fever, vomiting, and severe abdominal pain.

Figure 13.16

Overview of common sexually transmitted diseases (STDs). This chart summarizes the symptoms and modes of transmission of nine STDs. Note that intercourse is not required to transmit all STDs—many can be contracted through oral-genital contact or other forms of physical intimacy. (Adapted from Carroll, 2007; Crooks & Baur, 2008; Hatcher et al., 2004)

you can stop worrying. If you have several sexual partners in a year, you should have regular STD checkups. You will have to ask for them, as most doctors and health clinics won't perform them otherwise.

Remember that the symptoms of some STDs disappear as the infection progresses. If your test results are positive, it's essential to get the proper treatment *right away.* Notify your sexual partner(s) so they can be tested immediately, too. And avoid sexual intercourse and oral sex until you and your partner are fully treated and a physician or clinic says you are no longer infectious.

In the Application, we focus on enhancing sexual satisfaction and treating common sexual problems.

APPLICATION

Enhancing Sexual Relationships

LEARNING OBJECTIVES

▶ *List six general suggestions for enhancing sexual relationships.*

▶ *Discuss the nature, prevalence, and causes of common sexual dysfunctions.*

▶ *Describe the strategies for coping with erectile difficulties, premature ejaculation, orgasmic difficulties, and hypoactive sexual desire.*

Answer the following statements "true" or "false."

___ **1.** Sexual problems are unusual.

___ **2.** Sexual problems belong to couples rather than individuals.

___ **3.** Sexual problems are highly resistant to treatment.

___ **4.** Sex therapists sometimes recommend masturbation as a treatment for certain types of problems.

The answers are (1) false, (2) true, (3) false, and (4) true. If you missed several of these questions, you are by no means unusual. Misconceptions about sexuality are the norm rather than the exception. Fortunately, there is plenty of useful information on how to improve sexual relationships.

For the sake of simplicity, our advice is directed to heterosexual couples, but much of what we have to say is also relevant to same-gender couples. For advice aimed specifically at same-gender couples, we recommend *Permanent Partners: Building Gay and Lesbian Relationships That Last* by Betty Berzon (2004).

General Suggestions

Let's begin with some general ideas about how to enhance sexual relationships, drawn from several excellent books on sexuality (Carroll, 2007; Crooks & Baur, 2008; King, 2005). Even if you are satisfied with your sex life, these suggestions may be useful as "preventive medicine."

1. *Pursue adequate sex education.* A surprising number of people are ignorant about the realities of sexual functioning. So the first step in promoting sexual satisfaction is to acquire accurate information about sex. The shelves of most bookstores are bulging with popular books on sex, but many of them are loaded with inaccuracies. A good bet is to pick up a college textbook on human sexuality. The Recommended Readings in this chapter describe books that we think are excellent. Enrolling in a course on human sexuality is also a good idea. Most colleges offer such courses today.

2. *Review your sexual values system.* Many sexual problems stem from a negative sexual values system that associates sex with immorality. The guilt feelings caused by such an orientation can interfere with sexual functioning. Thus, sex therapists often encourage adults to examine the sources and implications of their sexual values.

3. *Communicate about sex.* As children, people often learn that they shouldn't talk about sex. Many people carry this edict into adulthood and have great difficulty discussing sex, even with their partner. Good communication is essential in a sexual relationship. **Figure 13.17** on the next page lists common problems in sexual relations. Many of these problems—such as choosing an inconvenient time, too little erotic activity before intercourse, and too little tenderness afterward—are traceable largely to poor communication. Your partner is not a mind-reader! You have to share your thoughts and feelings. Remember that both men and women say they want more instructions from their partner (refer back to **Figure 13.7**). If you are unsure about your partner's preferences, ask. And provide candid (but diplomatic) feedback when your partner asks for your reactions.

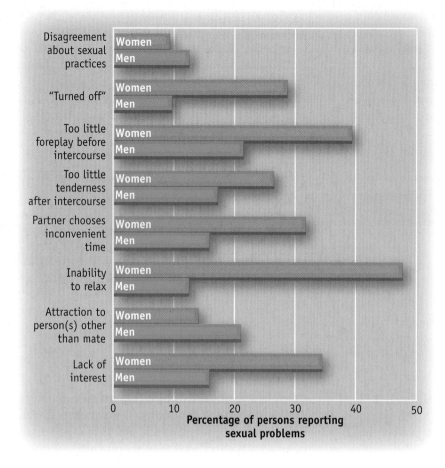

Figure 13.17

Common problems in sexual relations. The percentage of men and women reporting various types of problems in their sexual relationships is shown here, based on a sample of 100 couples. (Adapted from Frank, Anderson, & Rubenstein, 1978.)

4. *Avoid goal setting.* Sexual encounters are not tests or races. Sexual experiences are usually best when people relax and enjoy themselves. People get overly concerned about orgasms or about both partners reaching orgasm simultaneously. A grim determination to climax typically makes it harder to do so. This mental set can lead to disruptive habits like *spectatoring,* or stepping outside the sexual act to judge one's performance. It's better to adopt the philosophy that getting there is at least half the fun.

5. *Enjoy your sexual fantasies.* As we noted earlier, the mind is the ultimate erogenous zone. Although Freudian theory originally saw sexual fantasy as an unhealthy by-product of sexual frustration and immaturity, research shows that sexual fantasies are most common among those who have the fewest sexual problems (Leitenberg & Henning, 1995; Renaud & Byers, 2001). Men and women both report that their sexual fantasies increase their excitement. So don't be afraid to use fantasy to enhance your sexual arousal.

6. *Be selective about sex.* Sexual encounters generally work out better when you have privacy and a relaxed atmosphere, when you are well rested, and when you are enthusiastic. Of course, you can't count on (or insist on) having ideal situations all the time, but you should be aware of the value of being selective. If your heart just isn't in it, it may be wise to wait. Partners often differ about when, where, and how often they like to have sex. Such differences are normal and should not be a source of resentment. Couples simply need to work toward reasonable compromises— through open communication.

Understanding Sexual Dysfunction

Many people struggle with *sexual dysfunctions*—impairments in sexual functioning that cause subjective distress. **Figure 13.18** shows the prevalence of some of the most common sexual problems (Laumann et al., 1994).

Physical, psychological, and interpersonal factors can contribute to sexual problems. *Physical factors* include chronic illness, disabilities, some medications, alcohol, and drugs. *Individual psychological factors* include performance anxiety, negative attitudes about sexuality learned during childhood, spectatoring, fears of pregnancy and STDs, life stresses such as unemployment, and prior sexual abuse. *Interpersonal factors* include ineffective communication about sexual matters and unresolved relationship issues that fuel anger and resentment.

People commonly assume that a sexual problem resides in just one partner (physical or individual psychological factors). While this is sometimes the case, most sexual problems emerge out of partners' unique ways of relating to each other (interpersonal factors). Moreover, even in those cases where a problem may lie more with one partner than another, the couple needs to work together for an acceptable solution. In other words, sexual problems belong to couples rather than to individuals.

Now let's examine the symptoms and causes of four common sexual dysfunctions: erectile difficulties, premature ejaculation, orgasmic difficulties, and low sexual desire.

Erectile difficulties occur when a man is persistently unable to achieve or maintain an erection adequate for intercourse. The traditional name for this problem is *impotence,* but sex therapists have discarded the term because of its demeaning connotation. A man who has never had an erection sufficient for intercourse is said to have *lifelong erectile difficulties.* A man who has had intercourse in the past but who is currently having problems achieving erections is said to have *acquired erectile difficulties.* The latter problem is more common and easier to overcome.

Some 30 million American men are estimated to suffer from erectile difficulties if a broad criterion (the inability to get an erection adequate for satisfactory sexual performance) is used (Levine, 2003). Erectile difficulties affect about 1 in 20 men age 40 and over, and about 1 in 4 over age 65.

Physical factors can play a role in erectile dysfunction. For example, experts estimate that as many as 25% of all cases may be the result of side effects from medication (Miller, 2000). A host of common diseases (such as diabetes) can produce erectile problems as a side effect. Many temporary conditions, such as fatigue, worry about work, an argument with one's partner, a depressed mood, or too much alcohol can cause such incidents. The most common psychological cause of erectile difficulties is anxiety about sexual performance. Anxiety may stem from doubts about

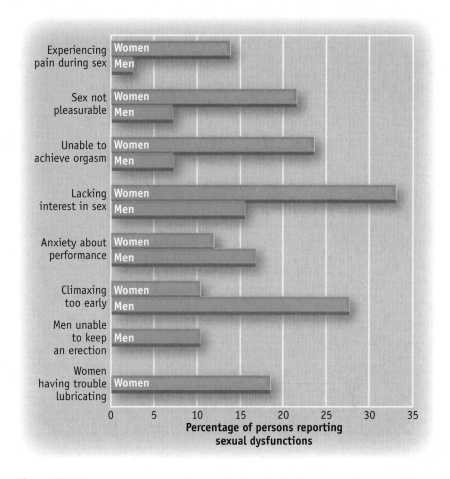

Figure 13.18

Sexual dysfunction in normal couples. This graph shows the prevalence of various sexual dysfunctions during a year in a probability sample of American men and women. The most common problems among men are premature ejaculation and anxiety about performance; in women, they are lack of interest in sex and orgasmic difficulties.

From Laumann, E. O., Gagnon, J. H., Michael, R. T., & Michaels, S. (1994). *The social organization of sexuality: Sexual practices in the United States.* Chicago: University of Chicago Press. Copyright © 1994 by University of Chicago Press. Reprinted by permission.

virility or conflict about the morality of sexual desires. Interpersonal factors can enter in if one's partner turns an incident into a major catastrophe. If the man allows himself to get unduly concerned about his sexual response, the seeds of anxiety may be sown.

Premature ejaculation **occurs when sexual relations are impaired because a man consistently reaches orgasm too quickly.** What is "too quickly"? Obviously, any time estimate is hopelessly arbitrary. The critical consideration is the subjective feelings of the partners. If either partner feels that the ejaculation is persistently too fast for sexual gratification, they have a problem. Approximately 29% of men repeatedly experience premature ejaculation (Laumann et al, 1994).

What causes premature ejaculation? Some men who have a lifelong history of quick ejaculation may have a neurophysiological predisposition to this condition (Metz & Pryor, 2000). But psychological factors are the typical cause. Some men simply don't exert much effort to prolong intercourse. Most of these men

Unresolved sexual problems can be a source of tension and frustration in relationships. Physical, psychological, and interpersonal factors can contribute to sexual difficulties.

do not view their ejaculations as premature, even if their partners do. Other causes can include stress, depression, or anger at one's partner. Some therapists believe that early sexual experiences in which a rapid climax was advantageous can establish a habit of rapid ejaculation.

Orgasmic difficulties occur when people experience sexual arousal but have persistent problems in achieving orgasm. When this problem occurs in men, it is often called *male orgasmic disorder.* The traditional name for this problem in women, *frigidity,* is no longer used because of its derogatory implications. Since this problem is much more common among women, we'll limit our discussion to them. A woman who has never experienced an orgasm through any kind of stimulation is said to have *generalized lifelong orgasmic difficulties.* Women who experience orgasms in some situations or only rarely are said to have *situational orgasmic difficulties.* This category includes women who experience orgasm only through noncoital techniques (oral, manual, and self-stimulation). Although lifelong orgasmic difficulties would seem to be the more severe problem, they are actually more responsive to treatment than situational orgasmic difficulties.

Physical causes of orgasmic difficulties are rare (medications can be a problem). One of the leading psychological causes is a negative attitude toward sex. Women who have been taught that sex is dirty or sinful are likely to approach it with shame and guilt. These feelings can undermine arousal, inhibit sexual expression, and impair orgasmic responsiveness. Arousal may also be inhibited by fear of pregnancy or excessive concern about achieving orgasm.

Some women have orgasmic difficulties because intercourse is too brief. Others fail to experience orgasms because their partners are unconcerned about their needs and preferences. But many couples simply need to explore sexual activities such as manual or oral stimulation of the clitoris that are more effective in producing female orgasm than sexual intercourse, alone (Bancroft, 2002b).

Hypoactive sexual desire, or the lack of interest in sexual activity, seems to be on the rise. Individuals with this problem rarely initiate sex or tend to avoid sexual activities with their partner (Aubin & Heiman, 2004). It occurs in both men and women, but it is more common among women (see **Figure 13.18**). Many attribute the recent increases in this problem to the fast pace of contemporary life and to couples' heavy workloads both at home and the office. In men, low sexual desire is often related to embarrassment about erectile dysfunction (McCarthy, Bodnar, & Handal, 2004). In women, it is most often associated with relationship difficulties (Aubin & Heiman, 2004). Sometimes the problem arises when a person is trying to sort out his or her sexual orientation.

Coping with Specific Problems

William Masters and Virginia Johnson

With the advent of modern sex therapy, sexual problems no longer have to be chronic sources of frustration and shame. *Sex therapy involves the professional treatment of sexual dysfunctions.* Masters and Johnson reported high success rates for their treatments of specific problems, as **Figure 13.19** shows. Although some critics argue that the cure rates reported by Masters and Johnson are overly optimistic, there is a consensus that sexual dysfunctions can be overcome with regularity (McCarthy et al., 2004). The advent of medications to treat sexual problems (Viagra) has resulted in an increased emphasis on medical and individual treatments over relationship interventions (Aubin & Heiman, 2004; McHugh, 2006). Nonetheless, couple-based treatment approaches definitely have their place and are effective (O'Sullivan, McCrudden, & Tolman, 2006). If you're looking for a sex therapist, be sure to get someone who is qualified to work in this specialized field. One professional credential to look for is that provided by the American Association of Sex Educators, Counselors, and Therapists (AASECT).

Erectile Difficulties

Viagra, the much-touted pill for treating erectile disorders, is about 80% effective (Handy, 1998a). Still, it is not without its drawbacks—some of them life threatening. Cialis and Levitra are two similar pills that enhance erections over a longer time period (24 to 36 hours) than Viagra. To work effectively, these pills must be incorporated into the couple's lovemaking style (Rosen, 2000). The expectation that a pill alone will solve sexual problems that stem from relationship or psychological issues can set men up for additional sexual dysfunction (McCarthy et al., 2004).

To overcome psychologically-based erectile difficulties, the key is to decrease the man's performance anxiety. It is a good idea for a couple to discuss the problem openly. The woman should be reassured that the difficulty does not reflect lack of affection by her partner. Obviously, it is crucial for her to be emotionally supportive rather than hostile and demanding.

Masters and Johnson introduced an effective procedure for the treatment of erectile difficulties and other dysfunctions. *Sensate focus is an exercise in which partners take turns pleasuring each other while giving guided verbal feedback and in which certain kinds of stimulation are temporarily forbidden.* One partner stimulates the other, who simply lies back and enjoys it while giving instructions and feedback about what feels good. Initially, the partners are

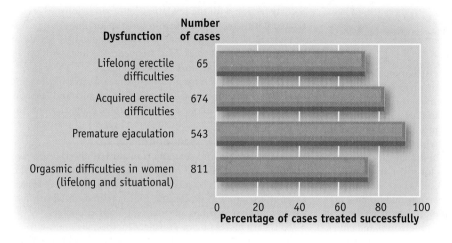

Figure 13.19

Success rates reported by Masters and Johnson in their treatment of sexual dysfunctions. This figure shows the success rates for cases treated between 1959 and 1985. Treatment was categorized as successful only if the change in sexual function was clear and enduring. The minimum follow-up period was two years, and in many cases follow-up was five years later.

Adapted from Masters, W. H., Johnson, V. E., & Kolodny, R. C. (1988). *Human sexuality* (3rd ed.). Boston: Allyn & Bacon. Copyright © 1988 by Pearson Education. Adapted by permission of the publisher.

not allowed to touch each other's genitals or to attempt intercourse. This prohibition should free the man from feelings of pressure to perform. Over a number of sessions, the couple gradually includes genital stimulation in their sensate focus, but intercourse is still banned. With the pressure to perform removed, many men spontaneously get erections. Repeated arousals should begin to restore the man's confidence in his sexual response. As his confidence returns, the couple can move on gradually to attempts at intercourse.

Premature Ejaculation

Men troubled by premature ejaculation range from those who climax almost instantly to those who cannot last the time that their partner requires. In the latter case, simply slowing down the tempo of intercourse may help. Sometimes the problem can be solved indirectly by discarding the traditional assumption that orgasms should come through intercourse. If the female partner enjoys oral or manual stimulation, these techniques can be used to provide her with an orgasm either before or after intercourse. This strategy can reduce the performance pressure for the male partner, and couples may find that intercourse starts to last longer.

For the problem of instant ejaculation, two treatments are very effective: the *stop-start method* (Semans, 1956) and the *squeeze technique* (Masters & Johnson, 1970). With both, the woman brings the man to the verge of orgasm through manual stimulation. Then, she either stops stimulating him (stop-start technique) or squeezes the base or the end of his penis firmly for 3–5 seconds (squeeze technique) until he calms down. She repeats this procedure three or four times before bringing him to

orgasm. These exercises can help a man recognize preorgasmic sensations and teach him that he can delay ejaculation. Medication may also help (Renshaw, 2005).

Orgasmic Difficulties

Negative attitudes and embarrassment about sex are often at the root of women's orgasmic difficulties. Thus, therapeutic discussions are usually geared toward helping nonorgasmic women reduce their ambivalence about sexual expression, become more clear about their sexual needs, and become more assertive about them. Sex therapists often suggest that women who have never had an orgasm try to have one by first using a vibrator and then shifting to masturbation, as the latter more closely approximates stimulation by a partner (Crooks & Baur, 2008). Many women achieve orgasms in intercourse after an initial breakthrough with self-stimulation. To make this transition, it is essential that the woman express her sexual wishes to her partner. Sensate focus is also an effective technique for treating orgasmic difficulties (Heiman & Meston, 1997).

When a woman's orgasmic difficulties stem from not feeling close to her partner, treatment usually focuses on couples' relationship problems more than on sexual functioning per se. Therapists also focus on helping couples improve their communication skills.

Hypoactive Sexual Desire

Therapists consider reduced sexual desire the most challenging sexual problem to treat (Aubin & Heiman, 2004). This is because the problem usually has multiple causes, which can also be difficult to identify. If the problem is a result of fatigue from overwork, couples may be encouraged to allot more time to personal and relationship needs. Sometimes hypoactive sexual desire reflects relationship problems. Treatment for reduced sexual desire is usually more intensive than that for more specific sexual disorders, and it is usually multifaceted to deal with the multiple aspects of the problem.

Medications can be used for low sexual desire. For instance, some older men take supplemental testosterone to offset the age-related decline in this hormone (Crooks & Baur, 2008). And the medical and financial success of Viagra has stimulated pharmaceutical companies to work on developing drugs that will boost women's sexual desire (Diamond et al., 2006; Marshall, 2005). Still, drugs will not solve relationship problems. For these, couples therapy is needed.

KEY IDEAS

Becoming a Sexual Person

▶ One's sexual identity is made up of sexual orientation, body image, sexual values and ethics, and erotic preferences. Physiological factors such as hormones influence sexual differentiation, maturation, and anatomy more than they do sexual activity. Psychosocial factors appear to have more impact on sexual behavior. Sexual identity is shaped by families, peers, schools, and the media. Because of differences in sexual socialization, sexuality usually has different meanings for males and females.

▶ Experts believe that sexual orientation is best viewed as a continuum, with end points of heterosexuality and homosexuality. The determinants of sexual orientation are not yet known but appear to be a complex interaction of biological and environmental factors. Attitudes toward homosexuals are negative, but moving in a positive direction. Coming to terms with a homosexual orientation is a process. Recent evidence suggests that homosexuals are at greater risk for depression and suicide attempts than are heterosexuals, a phenomenon linked to their membership in a stigmatized group.

Interaction in Sexual Relationships

▶ Sexual motives can be grouped into approach and avoidance motives. One's motives for sex are linked to personal and relationship well-being. Men tend to be motivated more by physical gratification, whereas women are more likely to have emotional motives.

▶ Disparities between partners in sexual interest and erotic preferences lead to disagreements that require negotiation. Effective communication plays an important role in sexual and relationship satisfaction.

The Human Sexual Response

▶ The physiology of the human sexual response was described by Masters and Johnson. They analyzed the sexual response cycle into four phases: excitement, plateau, orgasm, and resolution. For a more complete view of this process, individuals' subjective experiences during sexual encounters also need to be factored in.

▶ Women reach orgasm in intercourse less consistently than men, usually because foreplay and intercourse are too brief and because of gender differences in sexual socialization.

Sexual Expression

▶ Sexual fantasies are normal and are an important aspect of sexual expression. Kissing and touching are important erotic activities, but their importance is often underestimated by heterosexual males. Despite the strongly negative attitudes about masturbation that are traditional in our society, this practice is quite common, even among married people. Oral-genital sex has become a common element in most couples' sexual repertoires.

▶ Coitus is the most widely practiced sexual act in our society. Four coital positions are commonly used, each with its advantages and disadvantages. Sexual activities between gay males include mutual masturbation, fellatio, and, less often, anal intercourse. Lesbians engage in mutual masturbation, cunnilingus, and tribadism.

Patterns of Sexual Behavior

▶ American sexual attitudes and behavior have become more liberal over the past 40 years, although this trend slowed in the 1990s. Teen pregnancy rates have declined recently, but they still remain high. STD rates are highest among young people. The incidence of sexually risky behavior among teens has declined sharply in recent years.

▶ Satisfaction with the sexual aspect of a relationship is correlated with overall relationship satisfaction in both gay and straight couples. Younger married couples tend to have sex about two or three times a week. This frequency declines with age in both heterosexual and same-gender couples.

▶ Most Americans strongly disapprove of extramarital sex. Infidelity is uncommon among married couples and lesbians and more common among gay male couples. People become involved in extradyadic relationships for a variety of reasons.

Practical Issues in Sexual Activity

▶ Contraception and sexually transmitted diseases are two practical issues that concern many couples. Many people who do not want to conceive a child fail to use contraceptive procedures effectively, if at all. Contraceptive methods differ in effectiveness and have various advantages and disadvantages.

▶ STDs are increasing in prevalence, especially among those under 25. The danger of contracting STDs is higher among those who have had more sexual partners. In the United States, the rates of HIV infections stemming from heterosexual sex are on the rise, particularly among women. HIV rates are also up among young gay and bisexual men. Using condoms decreases the risk of contracting STDs. Early treatment of STDs is important.

Application: Enhancing Sexual Relationships

▶ To enhance their sexual relationships, individuals need to have adequate sex education and positive values about sex. They also need to be able to communicate with their partners about sex and avoid goal setting in sexual encounters. Enjoying sexual fantasies and being selective about their sexual encounters are also important.

▶ Common sexual dysfunctions include erectile difficulties, premature ejaculation, orgasmic difficulties, and hypoactive sexual desire. Treatments for low sexual desire are less effective than those for more specific sexual problems.

KEY TERMS

Anal intercourse   p. 422
Androgens   p. 408
Bisexuals   p. 407
Coitus   p. 423
Cunnilingus   p. 422
Erectile difficulties   p. 434
Erogenous zones   p. 421
Estrogens   p. 408
Fellatio   p. 422
Gonads   p. 408
Heterosexuals   p. 407
Homophobia   p. 414
Homosexuals   p. 407
Hypoactive sexual
  desire   p. 436
Orgasm   p. 419
Orgasmic difficulties   p. 436
Premature
  ejaculation   p. 435
Refractory period   p. 419
Sensate focus   p. 436
Sex therapy   p. 436
Sexual dysfunction   p. 434
Sexual identity   p. 407
Sexually transmitted disease
  (STD)   p. 430
Vasocongestion   p. 418

KEY PEOPLE

Linda Garnets and
  Douglas Kimmel   p. 415
Alfred Kinsey   pp. 412–413

William Masters and
  Virginia Johnson
  pp. 418–419, 438–439
Letitia Anne Peplau   p. 410

PRACTICE TEST

1. Young men typically feel _____ about sex; young women typically feel _____ about sex.
   a. positive; positive
   b. positive; negative
   c. ambivalent; ambivalent
   d. positive; ambivalent

2. Which of the following statements about sexual orientation is true?
   a. Heterosexuality and homosexuality are best viewed as two distinct categories.
   b. Heterosexuality and homosexuality are best viewed as end points on a continuum.
   c. Biological factors alone probably determine sexual orientation.
   d. Environmental factors alone probably determine sexual orientation.

3. Which of the following describes the correct order of the four phases of Masters and Johnson's sexual response cycle?
   a. Resolution, plateau, excitement, orgasm
   b. Plateau, excitement, orgasm, resolution
   c. Excitement, plateau, orgasm, resolution
   d. Excitement, orgasm, plateau, resolution

4. Sexual fantasies:
   a. are signs of abnormality.
   b. are quite normal.
   c. rarely include having sex with someone other than one's partner.
   d. are an excellent indication of what people want to experience in reality.

5. Which of the following characterizes teen sexual behavior in the "age of AIDS"?
   a. Fewer teens are engaging in risky sexual behavior now than 10 years ago.
   b. The teen pregnancy rate has increased since the early 90s.
   c. About 80 percent of sexually active teens use condoms regularly.
   d. The teen pregnancy rate in America is among the lowest in the world.

6. Regarding overall marital satisfaction and sexual satisfaction, research indicates there is:
   a. a strong relationship.
   b. a weak relationship.
   c. no relationship.
   d. a strong relationship, but only in the first year of marriage.

7. About what percent of Americans strongly disapprove of sexual infidelity?
   a. 10%   c. 60%
   b. 30%   d. 90%

8. Which of the following statements about condom use is false?
   a. It's okay to use oil-based lubricants with polyurethane condoms.
   b. It's okay to use oil-based lubricants with rubber condoms.
   c. Skin condoms do not protect against STDs.
   d. It's okay to use water-based lubricants with rubber or polyurethane condoms.

9. Sexually transmitted diseases:
   a. are all very serious.
   b. always cause symptoms right away.
   c. are most common among people under age 25.
   d. are most common among people between 26 and 40.

10. Which of the following is *not* one of the text's suggestions for enhancing your sexual relationships?
    a. Pursue adequate sex education.
    b. Review your sexual values system.
    c. Communicate about sex.
    d. Set clear goals for each sexual encounter.

Book Companion Website

Visit the Book Companion Website at **academic.cengage.com/psychology/weiten**, where you will find tutorial quizzes, flash cards, and web links for every chapter, a final exam, and more! You can also link to the Psychology Resource Center (accessible directly at **academic.cengage.com/login**) for a range of psychology-related resources.

Personal Explorations Workbook

The following exercises in your *Personal Explorations Workbook* may enhance your self-understanding in relation to issues raised in this chapter. **Questionnaire 13.1:** Sexuality Scale. **Personal Probe 13.1:** How Did You Acquire Your Attitudes About Sex? **Personal Probe 13.2:** Reflecting on the Place of Sexuality Throughout Your Life.

ANSWERS

1. d Pages 410, 412
2. b Pages 412–413
3. c Pages 418–419
4. b Pages 421–422
5. a Pages 423–424
6. a Pages 425–426
7. d Page 426
8. b Page 430
9. c Pages 430–431
10. d Pages 433–434

Psychology and Physical Health

Janet is a fairly typical student. She carries a full course load, works a part-time job, and plans to pursue a challenging career in nursing. She hopes to work in a hospital for a few years until she enrolls in graduate school. Right now, however, her life is regulated by work: homework, her job, and more school-related work in the wards of the teaching hospital where she learns the science and practice of nursing. In a typical semester, Janet feels under control for the first few weeks, but then her work piles up: tests, papers, reading, appointments, labs, and so on. She feels anxious and stressed. Instead of getting eight full hours of sleep, she often does with much less. Fast food becomes a familiar and necessary comfort—she doesn't have time to prepare, let alone eat, healthy and well-balanced meals. Her regular exercise routine often gives way to other time commitments; she can't jog or get to the gym as much as she'd like. By the end of the term, she is anxious, stressed, tired, and run down. In fact, she usually celebrates the end of the semester by getting sick and ending up in bed for a few days instead of having some relaxing times with her friends and family.

Are you at all like Janet? How often do you become ill in a typical semester? Do you begin strong and healthy but feel worn out and frayed by the end? If you are like many students, your lifestyle has a close connection to your health and well-being. In the past few decades, research has demonstrateed quite clearly that health is affected by social and psychological factors as well as biological ones. In other words, health is affected not just by germs or viruses but also by the choices people make and the lives they lead.

This chapter focuses on the fact that more than any other time in history, people's health is more likely to be compromised by *chronic diseases*—conditions that develop across many years—rather than by *contagious diseases*, those caused by specific infectious agents (such as polio, smallpox, or malaria—see **Figure 14.1**). Moreover, lifestyle and stress play a much larger role in the development of chronic diseases than they do in contagious diseases. Today, the three leading chronic diseases (heart disease, cancer, and stroke) account for almost 60% of all deaths in the United States, and these mortality statistics reveal only the tip of the iceberg. Psychological and social factors also contribute to many other, less serious illnesses, such as headaches, backaches, skin disorders, asthma, and ulcers.

In light of these trends, it is not surprising that the way we think about illness is changing. Traditionally,

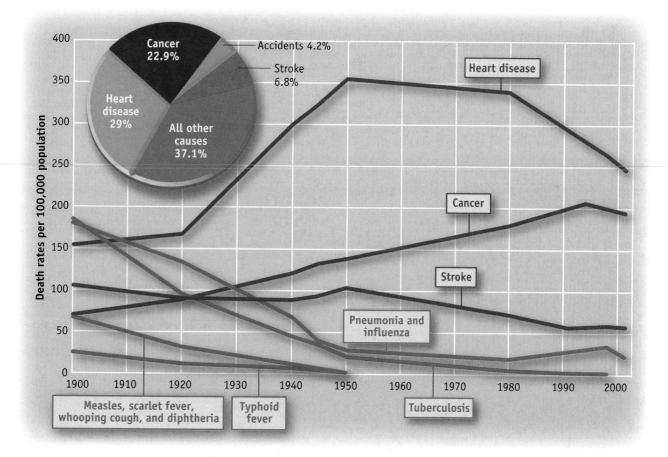

Figure 14.1

Changing patterns of illness. Trends in the death rates for various diseases during the 20th century reveal that contagious diseases (shown in blue) have declined as a threat to health. However, the death rates for stress-related chronic diseases (shown in red) have remained quite high. The pie chart (inset), which depicts the percentage of deaths caused by most of the leading killers today, shows the results of these trends: Three chronic diseases (heart disease, cancer, and stroke) account for almost 60% of all deaths.

illness has been thought of as a purely biological phenomenon produced by an infectious agent or some internal physical breakdown. However, the shifting patterns of disease and new findings relating stress to physical illness have rocked the foundation of this biological model. In its place a new model has gradually emerged (Suls & Rothman, 2004). The *biopsychosocial model* **holds that physical illness is caused by a complex interaction of biological, psychological, and sociocultural factors.** This model does not suggest that biological factors are unimportant. Rather, it simply asserts that biological factors operate in a psychosocial context that can also be highly influential. Medical and psychological professionals who adhere to the biopsychosocial model attend to additional factors, including cultural values, that can affect the ways individuals think about and deal with chronic illness, especially where interactions with health care providers and adherence to treatments are concerned (Sperry, 2006). Similarly, the reactions of family members introduce another level of concern, as illness not only affects the dynamics of how family members respond but also how they relate to the patient and to one another. **Figure 14.2** illustrates how the three factors in the biopsychosocial model affect one another and, in turn, health.

The growing recognition that psychological factors influence physical health led to the development of a new specialty within psychology (Baum, Revenson, & Singer, 2001; Friedman & Adler, 2007). *Health psychology* **is concerned with how psychosocial factors relate to the promotion and maintenance of health and with the causation, prevention, and treatment of illness.** This specialty is relatively young, having emerged in the late 1970s. In this chapter we focus

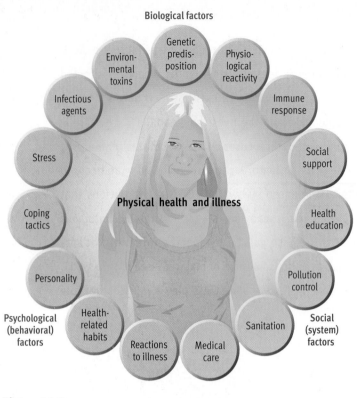

Figure 14.2

The biopsychosocial model. Whether one's health is good or bad, the biopsychosocial model assumes that health is not just attributable to biological processes. According to this increasingly influential view, one's physical health depends on interactions between biolgical factors, psychological factors, and social system factors. Some key factors in each category are depicted here.

on the rapidly growing domain of health psychology. The chapter's first section analyzes the link between stress and illness. The second section examines common health-impairing habits, such as smoking and overeating. The third section discusses how people's reactions to illness can affect their health. The Application expands on one particular type of health-impairing habit: the use of recreational drugs.

Web Link 14.1 **healthfinder**

Through the U.S. Department of Health and Human Services, the government has opened an ambitious online gateway to consumer-oriented information about health in all its aspects. Annotated descriptions are available for all resources identified in no-cost searches of this database.

Stress, Personality, and Illness

LEARNING OBJECTIVES

▶ Describe the Type A personality and evidence regarding its most toxic element.

▶ Discuss possible explanations for the link between hostility and heart disease.

▶ Summarize evidence relating emotional reactions and depression to heart disease.

▶ Describe the evidence linking stress and personality to cancer.

▶ Summarize evidence linking stress to a variety of diseases and immune functioning.

▶ Evaluate the strength of the relationship between stress and illness.

As we noted in Chapter 3, during the 1970s health researchers began to uncover new links between stress and a variety of diseases previously believed to be purely physiological in origin. In this section, we'll look at the evidence on the apparent link between stress and physical illness and discuss how personality factors contribute to this relationship. What does it mean to say that personality can affect wellness? A guiding assumption is that a person's characteristic demeanor can influence his or her physical health. As noted in Chapter 2, personality is made up of the unique grouping of behavioral traits that a person exhibits consistently. Thus, an individual who is chronically grumpy, hostile toward others, and routinely frustrated is more likely to develop an illness and perhaps even to die earlier than someone who is emotionally open, who is friendly, and who leads a balanced life (Friedman, 2007). Of course, the link between personality and disease is somewhat more complex but nonetheless real. We begin with a look at heart disease, far and away the leading cause of death in North America.

Personality, Emotions, and Heart Disease

Heart disease accounts for nearly 30% of the deaths in the United States every year. *Coronary heart disease* **results from a reduction in blood flow through the coronary arteries, which supply the heart with blood.** This type of heart disease causes about 90% of heart-related deaths. Atherosclerosis is the principal cause of coronary disease. *Atherosclerosis* **is a gradual narrowing of the coronary arteries,** usually caused by a buildup of fatty deposits and other debris on the inner walls (see **Figure 14.3**). Atherosclerosis progresses slowly over many years. Narrowed coronary arteries may eventually lead to situations in which the heart is temporarily deprived of adequate blood flow, causing a condition known as *myocardial ischemia.* This ischemia may be accompanied by brief chest pain, called *angina.* If a coronary artery is blocked completely (by a blood clot, for instance), the abrupt interruption of blood flow can produce a full-fledged heart attack, or *myocardial infarction.* Atherosclerosis is more prevalent in men than women and tends to increase with age.

Other established risk factors for coronary disease include smoking, diabetes, high cholesterol levels, and high blood pressure (Greenland et al., 2003; Khot et al., 2003). Smoking and diabetes are somewhat stronger risk factors for women than for men (Stoney, 2003). Contrary to public perception, cardiovascular diseases kill women just as much as men, but these diseases tend to emerge in women about 10 years later than in men (Stoney, 2003).

Recently, attention has shifted to the possibility that inflammation may contribute to atherosclerosis and elevated coronary risk (Hackam & Anand, 2003). Evidence is mounting that inflammation plays a key role in the initiation and progression of atherosclerosis, as well as the acute complications that trigger heart attacks (Albert et al., 2002; Libby, Ridker, & Maseri, 2002). Fortunately, researchers have found a marker—levels of C-reactive protein (CRP) in the blood—that may help physicians estimate individuals' coronary risk more accurately than was possible previously (Ridker, 2001). **Figure 14.4** (on the next page) shows how combined levels of CRP and cholesterol appear to be related to coronary risk. CRP levels are also predictive of the development of high blood pressure, which suggests that hypertension may be part of an inflammatory syndrome (Sesso et al., 2003).

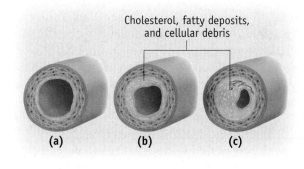

Cholesterol, fatty deposits, and cellular debris

(a)   (b)   (c)

Figure 14.3

Atherosclerosis. Atherosclerosis, a narrowing of the coronary arteries, is the principal cause of coronary disease. **(a)** A normal artery. **(b)** Fatty deposits, cholesterol, and cellular debris on the walls of the artery have narrowed the path for blood flow. **(c)** Advanced atherosclerosis. In this situation, a blood clot might suddenly block the flow of blood through the artery.

Figure 14.4

The relationship of cholesterol and inflammation to coronary risk. Levels of C-reactive protein (CRP) in the blood appear to be a useful index of the inflammation that contributes to atherosclerosis (Ridker, 2001). This graph shows how increasing CRP levels and increasing cholesterol levels combine to elevate cardiovascular risk (for a heart attack or stroke). The relative risks shown are for successive quintiles on each measure (each quintile represents one-fifth of the sample, ordered from those who scored lowest to those who scored highest). The relative risks are in relation to those who fall in the lowest quintile on both measures.

Adapted from Ridker, P. M. (2001). High sensitivity C-reactive protein: Potential adjunct for global risk assessment in primary prevention of cardiovascular disease. *Circulation, 103,* 1813–1818. Copyright © 2001 American Heart Association. Adapted by permission of the publisher Lippincott Williams & Wilkins and the author.

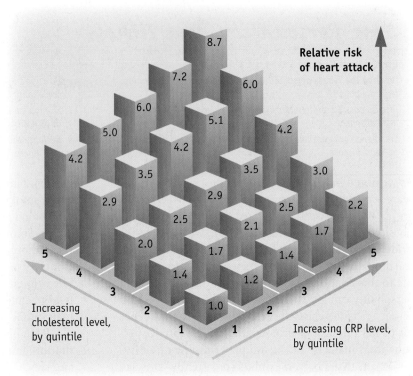

Hostility and Coronary Risk

In the 1960s and 1970s a pair of cardiologists, Meyer Friedman and Ray Rosenman (1974), were investigating the causes of coronary disease. Originally, they were interested in the usual factors thought to produce a high risk of heart attack: smoking, obesity, physical inactivity, and so forth. Although they found these factors to be important, they eventually recognized that a piece of the puzzle was missing. Many people who smoked constantly, got little exercise, and were severely overweight still managed to avoid the ravages of heart disease. Meanwhile, others who seemed to be in much better shape with regard to these risk factors experienced the misfortune of a heart attack. What was their explanation for these perplexing findings? Stress! Specifically, they identified an apparent connection between coronary risk and a pattern of behavior they called the *Type A personality,* which involves self-imposed stress and intense reactions to stress.

Friedman and Rosenman divided people into two basic types (Friedman, 1996; Rosenman, 1993). The *Type A personality* **includes three elements: (1) a strong competitive orientation, (2) impatience and time urgency, and (3) anger and hostility.** In contrast, the *Type B personality* **is marked by relatively relaxed, patient, easygoing, amicable behavior.** Type A's are ambitious, hard-driving perfectionists who are exceedingly time conscious. They routinely try to do several things at once. They fidget frantically over the briefest delays. They tend to be highly competitive, achievement-oriented workaholics who drive themselves with many deadlines. They are easily aggravated and get angry quickly. Type B's are less hurried, less competitive, and less easily angered than Type A's.

Decades of research uncovered a tantalizingly modest correlation between Type A behavior and increased coronary risk. More often than not, studies found an association between Type A personality and an elevated incidence of heart disease, but the findings were not as strong or as consistent as expected (Ragland & Brand, 1988; Smith & Gallo, 2001). However, in recent years, researchers have found a stronger link between personality and coronary risk by focusing on a specific component of the Type A personality: anger and hostility (Myrtek, 2007; Rozanski, Blumenthal, & Kaplan, 1999). *Hostility* **refers to a persistent negative attitude marked by cynical, mistrusting thoughts, feelings of anger, and overtly aggressive actions.** For example, in one study of almost 13,000 men and women who had no prior history of heart disease (Williams et al., 2000), investigators found an elevated incidence of heart attacks among participants who exhibited an angry temperament. The participants, who were followed for a median period of 4.5 years, were classified as being low (37.1%), moderate (55.2%), or high (7.7%) in anger. Among participants with normal blood pressure, the high-anger subjects experienced almost three times as many coronary events as the low-anger subjects (see **Figure 14.5**). In another study, CT scans were used to look for signs of atherosclerosis in a sample of 374

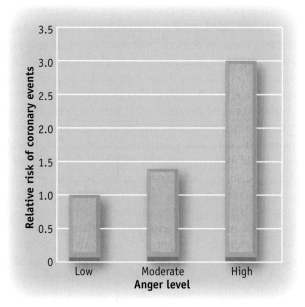

Figure 14.5

Anger and coronary risk. Working with a large sample of healthy men and women who were followed for a median of 4.5 years, Williams et al. (2000) found an association between trait anger and the likelihood of a coronary event. Among subjects who manifested normal blood pressure at the beginning of the study, a moderate anger level was associated with a 36% increase in coronary attacks, and a high level of anger nearly tripled participants' risk for coronary disease. (Based on data in Williams et al., 2000)

men and women whose cynical hostility had been assessed a decade earlier when they were 18 to 30 years old (Irabarren et al., 2000). Participants with above-average hostility scores were twice as likely to exhibit atherosclerosis as participants with below-average hostility scores.

Many other studies have also found an association between hostility and various aspects of cardiovascular disease (Eaker et al., 2004; Nelson, Franks, & Brose, 2005; Niaura et al, 2002), including CRP levels (Suarez, 2004). Thus, recent research trends suggest that hostility may be the crucial toxic element that accounts for the correlation between Type A behavior and heart disease. Interestingly, there is some evidence that hostility plays a greater role in cardiovascular risk for blacks than for whites. One recent study using a sample of healthy participants found that younger African Americans who exhibited high hostility showed a greater elevation in cardiovascular risk factors than a similar group of young white adults (Cooper & Waldstein, 2004). Another study found that African American men are at greater risk than African American women or white men (Scherwitz et al. 1991).

Why are anger and hostility associated with coronary risk? Research has uncovered a number of possible explanations (see **Figure 14.6**). First, anger-prone individuals appear to exhibit greater physiological reactivity than those who are lower in hostility (Smith & Gallo, 1999; Suarez et al., 1998). The frequent ups and downs in heart rate and blood pressure may create wear and tear in their cardiovascular systems.

Second, hostile people probably create additional stress for themselves (Smith, 2006; Smith & Gallo, 2001; Smith, Glazer, & Ruiz, 2004). For example, their quick anger may provoke many arguments and conflicts with others. Consistent with this line of thinking, Smith and colleagues (1988) found that subjects high in hostility reported more hassles, more negative life events, more marital conflict, and more work-related stress than subjects who were lower in hostility.

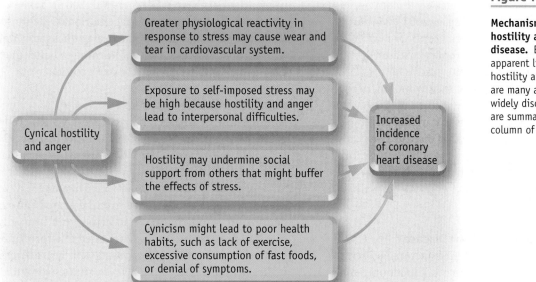

Figure 14.6

Mechanisms that may link hostility and anger to heart disease. Explanations for the apparent link between cynical hostility and heart disease are many and varied. Four widely discussed possibilities are summarized in the middle column of this diagram.

Research suggests that excessive anger and hostility are associated with an increased risk for various types of heart disease.

Third, thanks to their antagonistic ways of relating to others, hostile individuals tend to have less social support than others (Brummett et al., 2001; Chen, Gilligan, & Coups, 2005; Smith, 2003). Women who perceive little or no social support at home or at work are at greater risk for mortality due to a heart attack than other women (Kawachi et al., 1994). Living alone following a cardiac event actually increases a person's risk for a subsequent heart attack. Williams (1996), for example, found that single people or those who had no close friend with whom they could disclose private thoughts and concerns were three times more likely to die in a five-year period than those who had either a spouse or a close friend. As we noted in Chapter 3, research suggests that social support may be an important coping resource that promotes health and buffers the effects of stress (Wills & Fegan, 2001). Moreover, research indicates that low social support may be an independent risk factor for coronary disease (Rozanski, Blumenthal, & Kaplan, 1999).

Fourth, perhaps because of their cynicism, people high in anger and hostility seem to exhibit a higher prevalence of poor health habits that may contribute to the development of cardiovascular disease. For example, people high in hostility are more likely to smoke, drink alcohol and coffee, and be overweight than others (Everson et al., 1997; Siegler et al., 1992; Watkins, Ward, & Southard, 1992).

Emotional Reactions and Heart Disease

Although work on personality risk factors has dominated research on how psychological functioning contributes to heart disease, recent studies suggest that emotional reactions may also be critical. *One line of research has supported the hypothesis that transient mental stress and the resulting emotions that people experience can tax the heart.* Based on anecdotal evidence, cardiologists and laypersons have long voiced suspicions that strong emotional reactions might trigger heart attacks in individuals with coronary disease, but it has been difficult to document this connection. However, advances in cardiac monitoring have facilitated investigation of the issue. As suspected, laboratory experiments with cardiology patients have shown that brief periods of mental stress can trigger acute symptoms of heart disease, such as myocardial ischemia and angina (Gottdiener et al., 1994). Overall, the evidence suggests that mental stress can elicit ischemia in about 30%–70% of patients with ongoing heart problems (Kop, Gottdiener, & Krantz, 2001). Moreover, research indicates that these patients have a higher risk for heart attack than the cardiology patients who do not manifest ischemia in response to mental stress (Krantz et al., 2000).

Researchers have also examined the importance of emotional reactions by having patients keep a diary of their emotions while their cardiac functioning is monitored continuously as they go about their business. For example, Gullette and colleagues (1997) found that the likelihood of ischemia increased two- or threefold when people reported negative emotions, such as tension, frustration, and sadness. In another study, 660 patients who experienced a nonfatal myocardial infarction were subsequently interviewed about events that occurred in the 6 hours prior to the onset of their heart attack (Möller et al., 1999). The interviews suggested that episodes of anger were a frequent trigger for the participants' heart attacks. Consistent with this evidence, studies that have provided stress management training for coronary patients have shown promising results in efforts to reduce the likelihood of additional heart attacks (Claar & Blumenthal, 2003). Taken together, these studies suggest that emotional reactions to stressful events may precipitate heart attacks in people with coronary disease and that learning to better manage one's emotions may reduce one's coronary risk.

Depression and Heart Disease

Another line of research has recently implicated depression as a major risk factor for heart disease. *Depressive disorders,* which are characterized by persistent feelings of sadness and despair, are a fairly common form of psychological disorder (see Chapter 15). Over the years, many studies have found elevated rates of depression among patients suffering from heart disease, but most theorists have explained this correlation by asserting that being diagnosed with heart disease makes people depressed. However, studies conducted in the last decade or so have suggested that the causal relations may also flow in the opposite direction—*that the emotional dysfunction of depression may cause heart*

LIVING IN TODAY'S WORLD

Coping with Traumatic Events

A principal theme of this chapter is that stress can affect one's physical health. In today's world, a major new source of stress is living with the ominous threat of further terrorist attacks and the emotional fallout that results. Aware of these problems, a variety of health organizations have consulted their top experts and posted advice on the Internet about how to cope with terrorism-related anxiety and emotional reactions to traumatic events. The advice on these sites is fairly similar, with a great deal of overlap in content. The best overall list of suggested coping strategies, found at the website of the National Center for PTSD, is provided here. These strategies may be helpful in dealing with this new form of stress:

- Spend time with other people. Coping with stressful events is easier when people support each other.
- If it helps, talk about how you are feeling. Be willing to listen to others who need to talk about how they feel.
- Get back to your everyday routines. Familiar habits can be comforting.

- Take time to grieve and cry if you need to. To feel better in the long run, you need to let these feelings out instead of pushing them away or hiding them.
- Ask for support and help from your family, friends, church, or other community resources. Join or develop support groups.
- Eat healthy food and take time to walk, stretch, exercise, and relax, even if just for a few minutes at a time.
- Make sure you get enough rest and sleep. You may need more sleep than usual when you are highly stressed.
- Do something that just feels good to you, such as taking a warm bath, taking a walk, sitting in the sun, or petting your cat or dog.
- If you are trying to do too much, cut back by putting off or giving up a few things that are not absolutely necessary.
- If TV news reports get too distressing, turn them off and distract yourself by doing something you enjoy.

disease (Thomas, Kalaria, & O'Brien, 2004). For example, Pratt and colleagues (1996) examined a large sample of people 13 years after they were screened for depression. They found that participants who had been depressed at the time of the original study were four times more likely than others to experience a heart attack during the intervening 13 years. Because the participants' depressive disorders preceded their heart attacks, one cannot argue that their heart disease caused their depression. Overall, studies have found that depression roughly doubles one's chances of developing heart disease (Lett et al., 2004; Rudisch & Nemeroff, 2003). Moreover, depression also appears to influence how heart disease progresses, as it is associated with a worse prognosis among cardiology patients (Glassman et al., 2003). Although the new emphasis is on how depression contributes to heart disease, experts caution that the relationship between the two conditions is surely bidirectional and that heart disease also increases vulnerability to depression (Sayers, 2004).

Recent research suggests that the connection of depression to heart disease is more complex than previously realized. Anger, anxiety, and depression are all

cited as predictors of cardiovascular disease, yet different researchers find different results. One explanation for the mixed findings involving these three emotional states is that how they are defined and measured involves considerable conceptual overlap. In other words, what looks like an effect attributable to anxiety in one study might be labeled anger or depression in another, and so on. A solution to this conceptual dilemma might be to explore how a general disposition towards negative emotions could be a better predictor of heart disease than any of the three variables alone (Suls & Bunde, 2005).

Stress and Cancer

If one single word can strike terror into most people's hearts, it is probably *cancer.* People generally view cancer as the most sinister, tragic, loathsome, and unbearable of diseases. In reality, cancer is actually a *collection* of over 200 related diseases that vary in their characteristics and amenability to treatment (Nezu et al., 2003). **Cancer refers to malignant cell growth, which may occur in many organ systems in the body.** The core problem in cancer is that cells begin to reproduce in a rapid, disorganized fashion. As this reproduction process lurches out of control, the teeming new cells clump together to form tumors. If this wild growth continues unabated, the spreading tumors cause tissue damage and begin to interfere with normal functioning in the affected organ systems.

It is widely believed by the general public that stress and personality play major roles in the development of cancer (McKenna et al., 1999). However, the research linking psychological factors to the *onset* of cancer is extremely weak. A few retrospective studies have found evidence that high stress precedes the development of cancer (Cohen, Kunkel, & Levenson, 1998; Katz & Epstein, 2005), but many others have failed to find any connection, and there is no convincing evidence that stress contributes to the causation of cancer (Newell, 1991; Petticrew, Fraser, & Regan, 1999).

Investigators have also attempted to determine whether there is a *cancer-prone personality* that might reflect unsuccessful patterns of coping with stress. The cancer-prone or "Type C" personality is described as someone who is very passive and rarely complains. Type C people are presumed to hold in their emotions to a great degree. This forced emotional inhibition is thought to be one reason such individuals are more likely to develop cancer than people who freely express their thoughts and feelings to others. Indeed, oncologists—physicians who specialize in the treatment of cancer—and other medical professionals have long observed that cancer patients tend to be "nice people"; perhaps their friendly or placid exteriors cover up considerable repressed emotion (Holland & Lewis, 1996). These studies have yielded some intriguing threads of consistency, but they must be viewed with great caution, given the possibility that someone's personality may change after discovering that he or she has cancer.

Although efforts to link psychological factors to the onset of cancer have largely failed, more convincing evidence has shown that stress and personality influence the *course* of the disease. The onset of cancer frequently sets off a chain reaction of stressful events (Andersen, Golden-Kreutz, & DiLillo, 2001). Patients typically have to grapple with fear of the unknown; difficult and aversive treatment regimens; nausea, fatigue, and other treatment side effects; dislocations in intimate relationships; career disruptions; job discrimination; and financial worries. Such stressors may often contribute to the progress of the disease, perhaps by impairing certain aspects of immune system functioning (Andersen, Kiecolt-Glaser, & Glaser, 1994). The impact of all this stress may depend in part on one's personality. Research suggests that mortality rates are somewhat higher among patients who respond with depression, repressive coping, and other negative emo-

tions (Friedman, 1991). In contrast, prospects appear to be better for patients who can maintain their emotional stability and enthusiasm.

Stress and Other Diseases

The development of questionnaires to measure life stress has allowed researchers to look for correlations between stress and a variety of diseases. For example, Zautra and Smith (2001) found an association between life stress and the course of rheumatoid arthritis. Another study found an association between stressful life events and the emergence of lower back pain (Lampe et al., 1998). Other researchers have connected stress to the occurrence of asthmatic reactions (Ritz et al., 2000) and periodontal disease (Marcenes & Sheiham, 1992). Studies have also found an association between high stress and flareups of irritable bowel syndrome (Blanchard & Keefer, 2003) and peptic ulcers (Levenstein, 2002).

These are just a handful of representative examples of research relating stress to physical diseases. **Figure 14.7** provides a longer list of health problems that have been linked to stress. Many of these stress-illness connections are based on tentative or inconsistent findings, but the sheer length and diversity of the list is remarkable. Why should stress increase the risk for so many kinds of illness? A partial answer may lie in immune functioning.

Stress and Immune Functioning

The apparent link between stress and many types of illness probably reflects the fact that stress can undermine the body's immune functioning. **The *immune response* is the body's defensive reaction to invasion by bacteria, viral agents, or other foreign substances.** The human immune response works to protect the body from many forms of disease. Immune reactions are remarkably complex and multifaceted (Chiappelli & Liu, 2000). Hence, there are a great many ways to measure immune function in an organism, and these multiple measures can sometimes produce conflicting, confusing results in research.

Nonetheless, a wealth of studies indicate that experimentally induced stress can impair immune functioning *in animals* (Moynihan & Ader, 1996). That is, stressors such as crowding, shock, food restriction, and restraint reduce various aspects of immune reactivity in laboratory animals (Chiappelli & Hodgson, 2000). Of course, stress can affect animal immune function in natural settings, as well (Nelson & Demas, 2004).

Studies by Janice Kiecolt-Glaser and her colleagues have also related stress to suppressed immune activity *in humans* (Kiecolt-Glaser & Glaser, 1995). In one study, medical students provided researchers with

Health Problems That May Be Linked to Stress

Health Problem	Representative evidence
Common cold	Mohren et al. (2001)
Ulcers	Levenstein (2002)
Asthma	Lehrer et al. (2002)
Migraine headaches	Ramadan (2000)
Premenstrual distress	Stanton et al. (2002)
Vaginal infections	Williams & Deffenbacher (1983)
Herpes virus	Padgett & Sheridan (2000)
Skin disorders	Arnold (2000)
Rheumatoid arthritis	Keefe et al. (2002)
Chronic back pain	Lampe et al. (1998)
Diabetes	Landel-Graham, Yount, & Rudnicki (2003)
Complications of pregnancy	Dunkel-Schetter et al. (2001)
Hyperthyroidism	Yang, Liu, & Zang (2000)
Hemophilia	Buxton et al. (1981)
Stroke	Harmsen et al. (1990)
Appendicitis	Creed (1989)
Multiple sclerosis	Grant et al. (1989)
Periodontal disease	Marcenes & Sheiham (1992)
Hypertension	O'Callahan, Andrews, & Krantz (2003)
Cancer	Holland & Lewis (1993)
Coronary heart disease	Orth-Gomer et al. (2000)
AIDS	Ironson et al. (2000)
Inflammatory bowel disease	Searle & Bennett (2001)
Epileptic seizures	Kelly & Schramke (2000)

Figure 14.7

Stress and health problems. The onset or progress of the health problems listed here *may* be affected by stress. Although the evidence is fragmentary in many instances, it's alarming to see the number and diversity of problems on this list.

blood samples so that their immune response could be assessed at various points (Kiecolt-Glaser et al., 1984). The students provided the baseline sample a month before final exams and contributed the "high-stress" sample on the first day of their finals. The subjects also responded to the Social Readjustment Rating Scale (SRRS; see Chapter 3) as a measure of recent stress. Reduced levels of immune activity were found during the extremely stressful finals week. Reduced immune activity was also correlated with higher scores on the SRRS. In another study, investigators exposed quaran-

Courtesy, Janice Kiecolt-Glaser

Janice Kiecolt-Glaser

tined volunteers to respiratory viruses that cause the common cold and found that those under high stress were more likely to be infected by the viruses (Cohen, Tyrell, & Smith, 1993).

In a thorough review of 30 years of research on stress and immunity, Segerstrom and Miller (2004) conclude that chronic stress can reduce both *cellular immune responses* (which attack intracellular pathogens, such as viruses) and *humoral immune responses* (which attack extracellular pathogens, such as bacteria). They also report that the *duration* of a stressful event is a key factor determining its impact on immune function. Long-lasting stressors, such as caring for a seriously ill spouse or enduring unemployment for months, are associated with greater immune suppression than relatively brief stressors. Underscoring the importance of the link between stress and immune function, a recent study found evidence that chronic stress may produce *premature aging of immune system cells* (Epel et al., 2004). The study revealed that women who were dealing with heavy, long-term stress (caring for a child with a serious, chronic illness, such as cerebral palsy) had immune system cells that appeared to be a decade older than their chronological age, perhaps shedding light for the first time on why people under severe stress often look old and haggard. Unfortunately, evidence suggests that in the face of stress, people's immune systems do not fight off illness as well as they grow older (Graham, Christian, & Kiecolt-Glaser, 2006; Kiecolt-Glaser & Glaser, 2001). To summarize, scientists have assembled impressive evidence that stress can temporarily suppress human immune functioning, which can make people more vulnerable to infectious disease agents.

Conclusions

A wealth of evidence suggests that stress influences physical health. However, virtually all of the relevant research is correlational, so it cannot demonstrate conclusively that stress *causes* illness (Smith & Gallo, 2001; Watson & Pennebaker, 1989). The association between stress and illness could be due to a third variable. Perhaps some aspect of personality or some type of physiological predisposition makes people overly prone to

Web Link 14.2 **Centers for Disease Control and Prevention (CDC)**

The CDC is the federal agency charged with monitoring and responding to serious threats to the nation's health as well as taking steps to prevent illness. This site's "Health Information from A to Z" offers the public in-depth medical explanations of many health problems both common (flu, allergies) and unusual (fetal alcohol syndrome, meningitis).

Figure 14.8

The stress/illness correlation. Based on the evidence as a whole, most health psychologists would probably accept the assertion that stress often contributes to the causation of illness. However, some critics argue that the stress-illness correlation could reflect other causal processes. One or more aspects of personality, physiology, or memory might contribute to the correlation between high stress and a high incidence of illness (see Chapter 3 for additional discussion of this complex issue).

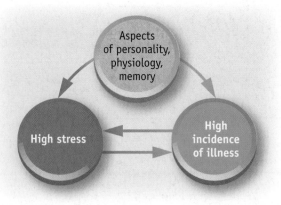

interpret events as stressful *and* overly prone to interpret unpleasant physical sensations as symptoms of illness (see **Figure 14.8**). For instance, in the Chapter 3 Application we discussed how neuroticism might increase individuals' sensitivity to both stress and illness. Moreover, critics of this research note that many of the studies used research designs that may have inflated the apparent link between stress and illness (Schwarzer & Schulz, 2003; Turner & Wheaton, 1995).

Despite methodological problems favoring inflated correlations, the research in this area consistently indicates that the *strength* of the relationship between stress and health is modest. The correlations typically fall in the .20s and .30s (Cohen, Kessler, & Gordon, 1995). Clearly, stress is not an irresistible force

that produces inevitable effects on health. Actually, this fact should come as no surprise. As we saw in Chapter 3, some people handle stress better than others. Furthermore, stress is only one actor on a crowded stage. A complex network of biopsychosocial factors influence health, including genetic endowment, exposure to infectious agents and environmental toxins, nutrition, exercise, alcohol and drug use, smoking, use of medical care, and cooperation with medical advice. In the next section we look at some of these factors as we examine health-impairing habits and lifestyles.

Habits, Lifestyles, and Health

LEARNING OBJECTIVES

▶ *Give some reasons for why people develop health-impairing habits.*

▶ *Discuss the health effects of smoking and the dynamics of giving up smoking.*

▶ *Summarize data on patterns of alcohol use and the short-term risks of drinking.*

▶ *Describe the major long-term health risks and social costs of drinking.*

▶ *Discuss the health risks and determinants of obesity.*

▶ *Outline the key elements in effective weight loss efforts.*

▶ *Provide examples of links between nutrition and health and discuss the basis for poor nutrition.*

▶ *List three general goals intended to foster sound nutrition.*

▶ *Summarize evidence on the benefits and risks of exercise.*

▶ *List four guidelines for embarking on an effective exercise program.*

▶ *Describe AIDS and summarize evidence on the transmission of the HIV virus.*

▶ *Identify some common misconceptions about AIDS and discuss the prevention of AIDS.*

Some people seem determined to dig an early grave for themselves. They do precisely those things they have been warned are particularly bad for their health. For example, some people drink heavily even though they know they're corroding their liver. Others eat all the wrong foods even though they know they're increasing their risk for a heart attack. Unfortunately, health-impairing habits contribute to far more deaths than most people realize. In a recent analysis of the causes of death in the United States, Mokdad and colleagues (2004) estimate that unhealthy behaviors are responsible for about half of all deaths each year. The habits that account for the most premature mortality, by far, are smoking and poor diet/physical inactivity (see **Fig-**

ure 14.9). Other leading behavioral causes of death include alcohol consumption, unsafe driving, contracted sexually transmitted diseases, and illicit drug use.

It may seem puzzling that people behave in self-destructive ways. Why do they do it? Several factors are involved. First, many health-impairing habits creep up on people slowly. For instance, drug use may grow imperceptibly over years, or exercise habits may decline ever so gradually. Second, many health-impairing habits involve activities that are quite pleasant at the time. Actions such as eating favorite foods, smoking cigarettes, and getting "high" are potent reinforcing events. Third, the risks associated with most health-impairing habits are chronic diseases such as cancer that usually

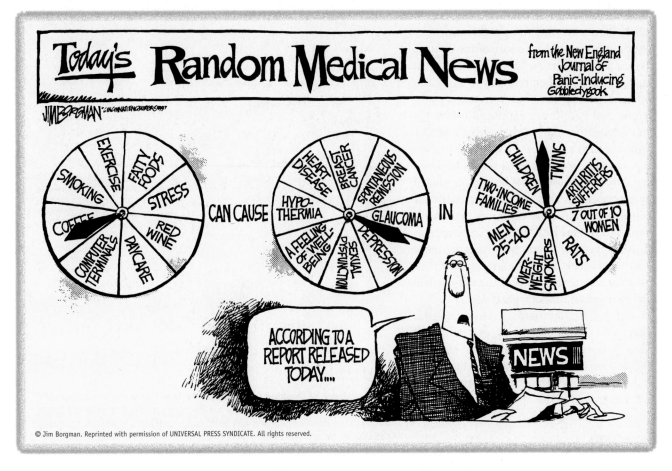

 (from the New England Journal of Panic-Inducing Gobbledygook)

take 10, 20, or 30 years to develop. It is relatively easy to ignore risks that lie in the distant future. Fourth, it appears that *people have a tendency to underestimate the* *risks associated with their own health-impairing habits* while viewing the risks associated with others' self-destructive behaviors much more accurately (Weinstein,

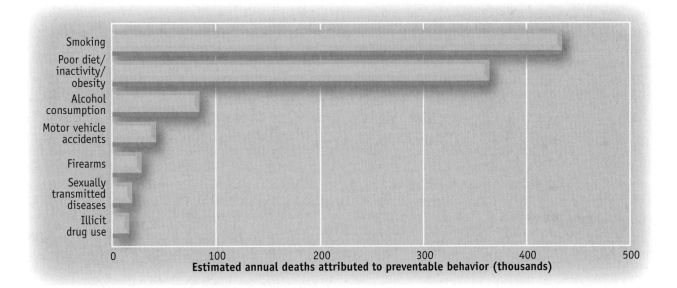

Figure 14.9

Mortality due to health-impairing behaviors. Synthesizing data from many sources, Mokdad and colleagues (2004) estimated the number of annual deaths in the United States attributable to various health-impairing behaviors in an article published in *The Journal of the American Medical Association*. As you can see, their calculations suggest that smoking and obesity are the leading causes of preventable mortality. However, their mortality estimate for obesity has proven controversial and is the subject of some debate (some experts argue that their estimate is too high). (Data from Mokdad et al., 2004)

2003; Weinstein & Klein, 1996). In other words, most people are aware of the dangers associated with certain habits, but they often engage in *denial* when it is time to apply this information to themselves. Yet another problem is that people are exposed to so much conflicting information about what's healthy and what isn't. It seems like every week a report in the media claims that yesterday's standard health advice has been contradicted by new research. This apparent inconsistency confuses people and undermines their motivation to pursue healthy habits. Sometimes it seems that health and happiness are more a matter of luck than anything else. In reality, the actions we take and the self-control we exercise can matter a great deal.

In this section we discuss how health is affected by smoking, drinking, overeating and obesity, poor nutrition, and lack of exercise. We also look at behavioral factors that relate to AIDS. The health risks of recreational drug use are covered in the Application.

Smoking

The percentage of people who smoke has declined noticeably since the mid-1960s (see **Figure 14.10**). Nonetheless, about 25.7% of adult men and 21% of adult women in the United States continue to smoke regularly. Unfortunately, these percentages are slightly higher (28% for both sexes) among college students (Rigotti, Lee, & Wechsler, 2000). Moreover, smoking is even more common in many other societies.

Health Effects

Suspicions about the health risks associated with tobacco use were voiced in some quarters early in the 20th century. However, the risks of smoking were not widely appreciated until the mid-1960s. Since then, accumulating evidence has clearly shown that smokers face a much greater risk of premature death than nonsmokers. For example, the average smoker has an estimated life expectancy *13–14 years shorter* than that of a similar nonsmoker (Schmitz & Delaune, 2005). The overall risk is positively correlated with the number of

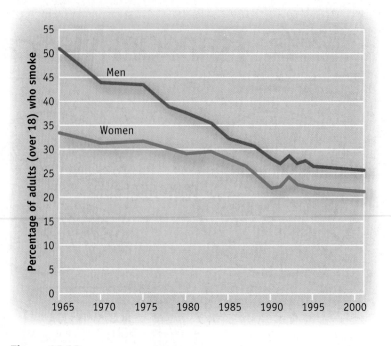

Figure 14.10

The prevalence of smoking in the United States. This graph shows how the percentage of U.S. adults who smoke has declined steadily since the mid-1960s. Although considerable progress has been made, smoking still accounts for about 435,000 premature deaths each year. (Data from Centers for Disease Control)

cigarettes smoked and their tar and nicotine content. Cigar smoking, which has increased dramatically in recent years, elevates health risks almost as much as cigarette smoking (Baker et al., 2000).

Why are mortality rates higher for smokers? Smoking increases the likelihood of developing a surprisingly large range of diseases, as you can see in **Figure 14.11** (Schmitz & Delaune, 2005; Woloshin, Schwartz, & Welch, 2002). Lung cancer and heart disease kill the largest number of smokers. However, smokers also have an elevated risk for oral, bladder, and kidney cancer, as well as cancers of the larynx, esophagus, and pancreas; for atherosclerosis, hypertension, stroke, and other cardiovascular diseases; and for bronchitis, emphysema, and other pulmonary diseases. Most smokers know about the risks associated with tobacco use, but they tend to underestimate the actual risks as applied to themselves (Ayanian & Cleary, 1999) at the same time they overestimate the likelihood they can quit smoking when they want to (Weinstein, Slovic, & Gibson, 2004).

Giving Up Smoking

Studies show that if people can give up smoking, their health risks decline reasonably quickly (Williams et al., 2002). Five years after people stop smoking, their health risk is already noticeably lower than that for people who continue to smoke. The health risks for people who give up tobacco continue to decline until they reach a normal level after about 15 years (see

Web Link 14.3 **The QuitNet Community**

The Boston University School of Public Health sponsors an online community of individuals who seek to quit smoking and tobacco use. A range of excellent resources, including an online support "community" available 24 hours a day, can help make this behavioral health change a reality.

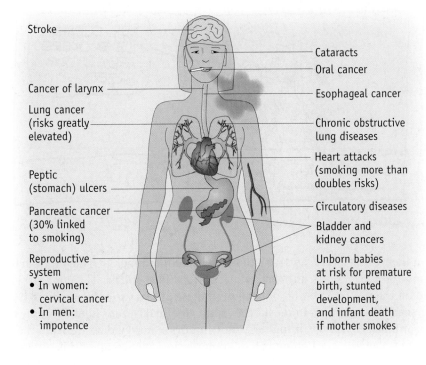

Stroke

Cancer of larynx

Lung cancer
(risks greatly
elevated)

Peptic
(stomach) ulcers

Pancreatic cancer
(30% linked
to smoking)

Reproductive
system
• In women:
  cervical cancer
• In men:
  impotence

Cataracts
Oral cancer
Esophageal cancer
Chronic obstructive
lung diseases
Heart attacks
(smoking more than
doubles risks)
Circulatory diseases
Bladder and
kidney cancers
Unborn babies
at risk for premature
birth, stunted
development,
and infant death
if mother smokes

Figure 14.11

Health risks associated with smoking. This figure provides an overview of the various diseases that are more common among smokers than nonsmokers. As you can see, tobacco elevates one's vulnerability to a remarkably diverse array of diseases, including the three leading causes of death in the modern world—heart attack, cancer, and stroke.

Figure 14.12). Evidence suggests that 70% of smokers would like to quit, but they are reluctant to give up a major source of pleasure and they worry about craving cigarettes, gaining weight, becoming anxious and irritable, and feeling less able to cope with stress (Grunberg, Faraday, & Rahman, 2001).

There are nearly 40 million ex-smokers in the United States. Collectively, they clearly demonstrate that it is possible to give up smoking successfully. But many didn't succeed until their third, fourth, or fifth attempt, and most would testify that quitting isn't easy. Research shows that long-term success rates for efforts to quit smoking are in the vicinity of only 25% (Cohen et al., 1989). Light smokers are somewhat more successful at quitting than heavy smokers. Discouragingly, people who enroll in formal smoking cessation programs are only slightly more successful than people who try to quit on their own (Swan, Hudman, & Khroyan, 2003). In fact, it is estimated that the vast majority of people

Recommended
READING

The Stop Smoking Workbook: The Definitive Step-by-Step Guide to Healthy Quitting
by Lori Stevic-Rust & Anita Maximin
(MJF Books, 1996)

The title says it all—this highly practical book is intended to help smokers through the challenging process of giving up tobacco. Written by two health psychologists, the book begins with a review of facts and myths about smoking, including a detailed review of the habit's physiological effects. Then the authors take the reader through a series of self-assessments intended to help them better understand when and why they smoke. The authors go on to outline strategies for setting a quit date and getting through the first few weeks. They also discuss how to deal with the urge to smoke and how to reduce the likelihood of relapse. The book is loaded with exercises and questionnaires that really make it something of a "workbook." The information is scientifically sound and the coverage of smoking-related issues is thorough.

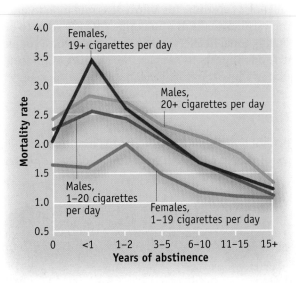

Figure 14.12

Quiting smoking and mortality. Research suggests that various types of health risks associated with smoking decline gradually after people give up tobacco. The data shown here, from the 1990 U.S. Surgeon General's report on smoking, illustrate the overall effects on mortality rates. The mortality rates on the vertical axis show how much death rates are elevated among smokers and ex-smokers in comparison to nonsmokers. For example, a mortality rate of 3.0 would mean that smokers' death rate was triple that of nonsmokers. (Data from U.S. Department of Health and Human Services, 1990)

who successfully give up smoking quit on their own, without professional help (Niaura & Abrams, 2002).

In recent years attention has focused on the potential value of *nicotine substitutes,* which can be delivered via gum, skin patches, nasal sprays, or inhalers. The rationale for nicotine substitutes is that insofar as nicotine is addictive, using a substitute might be helpful during the period when the person is trying to give up cigarettes. Do these substitutes work? They do help. Controlled studies have demonstrated that nicotine substitutes increase long-term rates of quitting in comparison to placebos (Swan et al., 2003). However, the increases are modest and the success rates are still discouragingly low. Nicotine substitutes are not a magic bullet or a substitute for a firm determination to quit. The various methods of nicotine delivery seem to be roughly equal in effectiveness, but combining a couple methods appears to increase the chances of quitting successfully (Schmitz & Delaune, 2005).

Drinking

Alcohol rivals tobacco as one of the leading causes of health problems in Americans. Alcohol encompasses

Overindulging in alcohol is particularly widespread among college students.

a variety of beverages containing ethyl alcohol, such as beers, wines, and distilled spirits. The concentration of alcohol in these drinks varies from about 4% in most beers up to 40% in 80-proof liquor (or more in higher-proof liquors). Survey data indicate that about half of adults in the United States drink. As **Figure 14.13** shows, per capita consumption of alcohol in the United States declined in the 1980s and 1990s, but this decrease followed decades of steady growth, and alcohol consumption remains relatively high, although certainly not the highest in the world.

Drinking is particularly prevalent on college campuses. When researchers from the Harvard School of Public Health (Wechsler et al., 2002) surveyed nearly 11,000 undergraduates at 119 schools, they found that 81% of the students drank. Moreover, 49% of the men and 41% of the women reported that they engage in binge drinking with the intention of getting drunk. Perhaps most telling, college students spend far more money on alcohol ($5.5 billion annually) than they do on their books.

Why Do People Drink?

The effects of alcohol are influenced by the user's experience, relative size and weight, gender, motivation, and mood, as well as by the presence of food in the stomach, the proof of the beverage, and the rate of drinking. Thus, we see great variability in how alcohol affects different people on different occasions. Nonetheless, the central effect is a "Who cares?" brand of euphoria that temporarily boosts self-esteem as one's problems melt away. Negative emotions such as tension, worry, anxiety, and depression are dulled, and inhibitions may be loosened (Johnson & Ait-Daoud, 2005). Thus, when first-year college students are asked why they drink, they say it's to relax, to feel less tense in social situations, to keep friends company, and to forget their problems. Of course, many other factors are also at work (Wood, Vinson, & Sher, 2001). Families and peer groups often encourage alcohol use. Drinking is a widely endorsed and encouraged social ritual

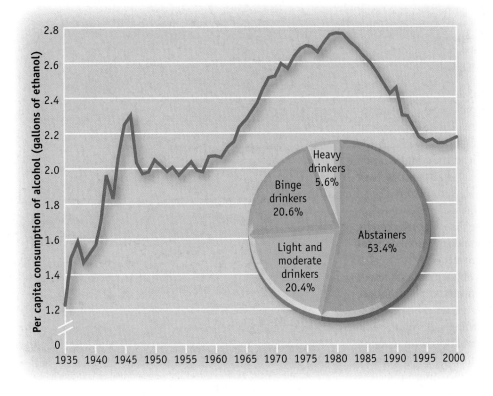

Figure 14.13

Drinking in America. Drinking in the United States, as indexed by per capita consumption (average consumed per person per year) of ethanol in gallons, rose steadily through most of the 20th century, although notable declines occurred during the 1980s and 1990s. The inset shows the percentage of American adults who are abstainers, light drinkers (one or two drinks on the same occasion in the past month), binge drinkers (people who have consumed five or more drinks on the same occasion at least once in the past month), and heavy drinkers (people who have consumed five or more drinks on the same occasion at least five times in the past month). The highest rates of binge drinking and heavy drinking are seen among young adults. (Data from National Institute on Alcohol Abuse and Alcoholism and U.S. Department of Health and Human Services)

in our culture. Its central role is readily apparent if you think about all the alcohol consumed at weddings, sports events, holiday parties, and so forth. Moreover, the alcohol industry spends hundreds of millions of dollars on advertising to convince us that drinking is cool, sexy, sophisticated, and harmless.

Short-Term Risks and Problems

Alcohol has a variety of side effects, including some that can be very problematic. To begin with, we have that infamous source of regret, the "hangover," which may include headaches, dizziness, nausea, and vomiting. In the constellation of alcohol's risks, however, hangovers are downright trivial. For instance, life-threatening overdoses are more common than most people realize. Although it's possible to overdose with alcohol alone, a more common problem is overdosing on combinations of alcohol and sedative or narcotic drugs.

In substantial amounts, alcohol has a decidedly negative effect on intellectual functioning and perceptual-motor coordination. The resulting combination of tainted judgment, slowed reaction time, and reduced coordination can be deadly when people attempt to drive after drinking. Depending on one's body weight, it may take only a few drinks for driving to be impaired. It's estimated that alcohol contributes to 30% of all automobile fatalities in the United States (Yi et al., 1999). Drunk driving is a major social problem and the leading cause of death in young adults. Alcohol is also implicated in many other types of accidents. Victims

test positive for alcohol in 38% of fire fatalities, 49% of drownings, and 63% of fatal falls (Smith, Branas, & Miller, 1999).

With their inhibitions released, some drinkers become argumentative and prone to aggression. In the Harvard survey of undergraduates from 119 schools, 29% of the students who did *not* engage in binge drinking reported that they had been insulted or humiliated by a drunken student, 19% had experienced serious arguments, 9% had been pushed, hit, or assaulted, and 19.5% had been the target of unwanted sexual advances (Wechsler et al., 2002). Worse yet, alcohol appears to contribute to about 90% of student rapes and 95% of violent crime on campus. In society at large, alcohol is associated with a variety of violent crimes, including murder, assault, rape, child abuse, and intimate partner violence (Wood et al., 2001). The phrase "associated with" can also be interpreted literally: A recent study suggests that people become more aggressive when primed to think about alcohol and aggression in the absence of actual consumption (Bartholow & Heinze, 2006). In other words, people's perceptions about alcohol can matter as much as their consumption. Controlled research demonstrates alcohol can serve as a potential cue for aggression, especially among those people who subscribe to the cultural belief that drinking is linked to hostile behavior. Finally, alcohol can also contribute to reckless sexual behavior, which may have ramifications for one's health. In the Harvard survey, 21% of students who drank reported that they had unplanned sex as a result of drinking, and 10% indicated that their drinking had led to unprotected sex.

Long-Term Health Effects

Alcohol's long-term health risks are mostly (but not exclusively) associated with chronic, heavy consumption of alcohol. Estimates of the number of people at risk vary considerably. According to Schuckit (2000) approximately 5–10% of American men and women engage in chronic alcohol abuse and another 10% of men and 3–5% of women probably suffer from *alcohol dependence,* or *alcoholism.* **Alcohol dependence (alcoholism) is a chronic, progressive disorder marked by a growing compulsion to drink and impaired control over drinking that eventually interferes with health and social behavior.** Whether alcoholism is best viewed as a disease or as a self-control problem is the source of considerable debate, but experts have reached a reasonable consensus about the warning signs of alcoholism. These signs include preoccupation with alcohol, drinking to relieve uncomfortable feelings, gulping drinks, clandestine drinking, and the other indicators listed in **Figure 14.14**.

Alcoholism and problem drinking are associated with an elevated risk for a wide range of serious health problems, which are summarized in **Figure 14.15** (Mack, Franklin, & Frances, 2003; Moak & Anton, 1999). Although there is some thought-provoking evidence that moderate drinking may reduce one's risk for coronary disease (Chick, 1998; Mukamal et al., 2003), it is clear

that heavy drinking increases the risk for heart disease, hypertension, and stroke. Excessive drinking is also correlated with an elevated risk for various types of cancer, including oral, stomach, pancreatic, colon, and

Warning Signs of Problem Drinking or Alcoholism

1. Gulping drinks.
2. Drinking to modify uncomfortable feelings.
3. Personality or behavioral changes after drinking.
4. Getting drunk frequently.
5. Experiencing "blackouts"—not being able to remember what happened while drinking.
6. Frequent accidents or illness as a result of drinking.
7. Priming—preparing yourself with alcohol before a social gathering at which alcohol is going to be served.
8. Not wanting to talk about the negative consequences of drinking (avoidance).
9. Preoccupation with alcohol.
10. Focusing social situations around alcohol.
11. Sneaking drinks or clandestine drinking.

Figure 14.14

Detecting a drinking problem. Facing the reality that one has a problem with alcohol is always difficult. This list of the chief warning signs associated with problem drinking is intended to help with this process.

Adapted from Edlin, G., & Golanty, E. (1992). *Health and wellness.* Boston: Jones & Bartlett. Copyright © 1992 Jones & Bartlett Publishers, Inc. Reprinted with permission.

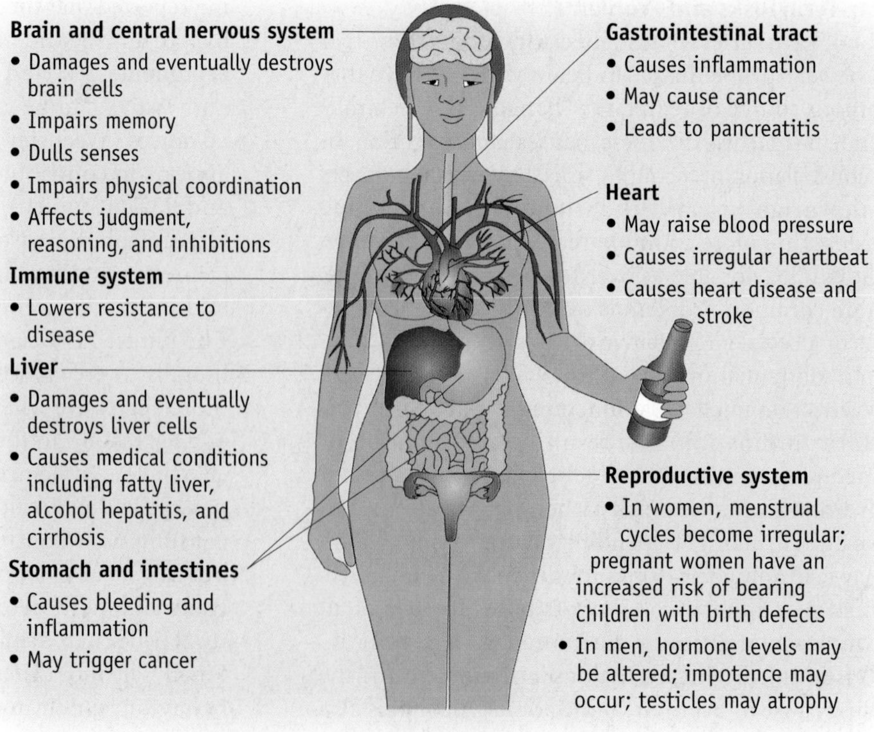

Figure 14.15

Health risks associated with drinking. This figure provides an overview of the various diseases that are more common among drinkers than abstainers. As you can see, alcohol elevates one's vulnerability to a remarkably diverse array of diseases.

Brain and central nervous system
- Damages and eventually destroys brain cells
- Impairs memory
- Dulls senses
- Impairs physical coordination
- Affects judgment, reasoning, and inhibitions

Immune system
- Lowers resistance to disease

Liver
- Damages and eventually destroys liver cells
- Causes medical conditions including fatty liver, alcohol hepatitis, and cirrhosis

Stomach and intestines
- Causes bleeding and inflammation
- May trigger cancer

Gastrointestinal tract
- Causes inflammation
- May cause cancer
- Leads to pancreatitis

Heart
- May raise blood pressure
- Causes irregular heartbeat
- Causes heart disease and stroke

Reproductive system
- In women, menstrual cycles become irregular; pregnant women have an increased risk of bearing children with birth defects
- In men, hormone levels may be altered; impotence may occur; testicles may atrophy

rectal cancer. Moreover, serious drinking problems can lead to cirrhosis of the liver, malnutrition, pregnancy complications, brain damage, and neurological disorders. Finally, alcoholism can produce severe psychotic states, characterized by delirium, disorientation, and hallucinations.

Overeating

Obesity is a common health problem. The criteria for obesity vary considerably. One simple, intermediate criterion is to classify people as obese if their weight exceeds their ideal body weight by 20%. If this criterion is used, 31% of men and 35% of women in the United States qualify as obese (Brownell & Wadden, 2000). Many experts prefer to assess obesity in terms of *body mass index (BMI)*—weight (in kilograms) divided by height (in meters) squared (kg/m2). This increasingly used index of weight controls for variations in height. A BMI of 25.0–29.9 is typically regarded as overweight, and a BMI over 30 is considered obese (Björntorp, 2002). Although American culture seems to be obsessed with slimness, recent surveys show surprisingly sharp increases in the incidence of obesity (Corsica & Perri, 2003). If a BMI over 25 is used as the cutoff, almost two-thirds of American adults are struggling with weight problems (Sarwer, Foster, & Wadden, 2004). Moreover, they have plenty of company from their children, as weight problems among children and adolescents have increased 15%–22% in recent decades (West et al., 2004).

Obesity is similar to smoking in that it exerts a relatively subtle impact on health that is easy for many people to ignore. Nevertheless, the long-range effects can be quite dangerous; obesity is a significant health problem that elevates one's mortality risk (Allison et al., 1999; Bender et al., 1999). In fact, obesity is probably responsible for the early deaths of well over a quarter of a million people in North America each year (De-Angelis, 2004). Overweight people are more vulnerable than others to heart disease, diabetes, hypertension, respiratory problems, gallbladder disease, stroke, arthritis, some cancers, muscle and joint pain, and back problems (Manson, Skerrett, & Willet, 2002; Pi-Sunyer, 2002). For example, **Figure 14.16** shows how the preva-

lence of diabetes, hypertension, coronary disease, and musculoskeletal pain are elevated as BMI increases.

Evolution-oriented researchers have a plausible explanation for the dramatic increase in the prevalence of obesity (Pinel, Assanand, & Lehman, 2000). They point out that over the course of history, most animals and humans have lived in environments in which there was fierce competition for limited, unreliable food resources and starvation was a very real threat. As a result, warm-blooded, foraging animals evolved a propensity to consume more food than immediately necessary when the opportunity presented itself because food might not be available later. Excess calories were stored in the body to prepare for food shortages. This approach to eating remains adaptive for most species of animals that continue to struggle with the ebb and flow of unpredictable food supplies. However, in today's modern, industrialized societies, the vast majority of humans live in environments that provide an abundant, reliable supply of tasty, high-calorie food. In these environments, humans' evolved tendency to overeat when food is plentiful leads most people down a pathway of chronic, excessive food consumption. According to this line of thinking, most people in food-replete environments tend to overeat in relation to their physiological needs, but because of variations in genetics, metabolism, and other factors only some become overweight.

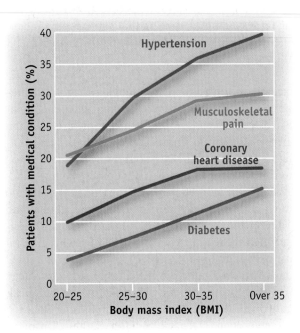

Figure 14.16

Weight and the prevalence of various diseases. This graph shows how obesity, as indexed by BMI, is related to the prevalence of four common types of illness. The prevalence of diabetes, heart disease, muscle pain, and hypertension increases as BMI goes up. Clearly, obesity is a significant health risk. (Data from Brownell & Wadden, 2000)

Determinants of Obesity

A few decades ago it was widely believed that obesity was a function of personality. Obesity was thought to occur mostly in depressed, anxious, compulsive people who overeat to deal with their negative emotions or in individuals who are lazy and undisciplined. However, research eventually showed that there is no such thing as an "obese personality" (Rodin, Schank, & Striegel-Moore, 1989). Instead, research showed that a complex network of interacting factors determine whether people develop weight problems.

Heredity. Chief among the factors contributing to obesity is *genetic predisposition* (Bouchard, 2002). In one influential study, adults raised by foster parents were compared with their biological and foster parents in regard to body mass index (Stunkard et al., 1986). The investigators found that the adoptees resembled their biological parents much more than their adoptive parents. In a subsequent *twin study,* Stunkard and associates (1990) found that identical twins reared apart were far more similar in body mass index than fraternal twins reared together (see Chapter 2 for a discussion of the logic underlying twin studies). Based on a study of over 4000 twins, Allison and colleagues (1994) estimate that genetic factors account for 61% of the variation in weight among men and 73% of the variation among women. These genetic factors probably explain why some people can eat constantly without gaining weight whereas other people grow chubby eating far less. Thus, it appears that some people inherit a genetic vulnerability to obesity (Cope, Fernandez, & Allison, 2004).

Excessive eating and inadequate exercise. The bottom line for overweight people is that their energy intake from food consumption chronically exceeds their energy expenditure from physical activities and resting metabolic processes. In other words, they eat too much in relation to their level of exercise (Wing & Polley, 2001). In modern America, the tendency to eat too much and to exercise too little is easy to understand (Henderson & Brownell, 2004). Tasty, caloric, high-fat foods are readily available nearly everywhere, not just in restaurants and grocery stores but in shopping malls, airports, gas stations, schools, and workplaces. And when people eat out, they tend to eat larger meals and consume more high-fat food than they would at home (French, Harnack, & Jeffery, 2000). Unfortunately, the increased availability of highly caloric food in America has been paralleled by declining physical activity. Modern conveniences, such as cars and elevators, and changes in the world of work, such as the shift to more desk jobs, have conspired to make American lifestyles more sedentary then ever before. Consider how much time the average person, child or adult,

spends watching television, surfing the Internet, playing video games, or even chatting on the phone. Our private lives as well as our work lives promote sedentary comfort, so that many of the activities we engage in each day are more mental or physical. We work and play less with our bodies than past generations and a number of labor-saving devices improve our quality of life while they reduce the rate at which we obtain "natural" exercise that burns off calories.

Set point. People who lose weight on a diet have a rather strong (and depressing) tendency to gain back all the weight they lose. The reverse is also true: People who have to work to put weight on often have trouble keeping it on (Leibel, Rosenbaum, & Hirsch, 1995). According to Richard Keesey (1995), these observations suggest that each body may have a *set point,* or a natural point of stability in body weight. **Set-point theory proposes that the body monitors fat-cell levels to keep them (and weight) fairly stable.** When fat stores slip below a crucial set point, the body supposedly begins to compensate for this change (Keesey, 1993). This compensation apparently leads to increased hunger and decreased metabolism. Studies have raised some doubts about various details of set-point theory, leading some researchers to propose an alternative called *settling-point theory* (Pinel et al., 2000). **Settling-point theory proposes that weight tends to drift around the level at which the constellation of factors that determine food consumption and energy expenditure achieve an equilibrium.** According to this view, weight tends to remain stable as long as there are no durable changes in any of the factors that influence it (e.g., diet, exercise or the lack thereof, stress, sleep). Settling-point theory casts a much wider net than set-point theory, which attributes weight stability to specific physiological processes. Another difference is that set-point theory asserts that an obese person's body will initiate processes that actively defend an excessive weight, whereas settling-point theory suggests that if an obese person makes long-term changes in eating or exercise, that person's settling point will drift downward without active resistance. Thus, settling-point theory is a little more encouraging to those who hope to lose weight.

Socioeconomic factors. Obesity is caused by a combination of genetics, eating behavior, lifestyle issues, and a lack of exercise. What are the effects of social and economic factors, such as family characteristics, marital status, and education, on body weight? Regarding family factors separate from heredity, having obese relatives heightens one's risk for being overweight,. So does being married: single people, including those who were divorced or widowed, are less likely to have a weight problem (Kilicarslan et al., 2006). More years of education is associated with a lower incidence of obesity, while unemployment appears to be predictive of weight increases.

Losing Weight

Whether out of concern about their health or just old-fashioned vanity, an ever-increasing number of people are trying to lose weight. At any given time, about 21% of men and 39% of women are dieting (Hill, 2002). Research has provided some good news for those who need to lose weight. Studies have demonstrated that relatively modest weight reductions can significantly diminish many of the health risks associated with obesity. For example, a 10% weight loss is associated with reduced medical risks (Jeffery et al., 2000). Thus, the traditional objective of obesity treatment—reducing to one's ideal weight—has been replaced by more modest and realistic goals (Sarwer et al., 2004).

While many factors may contribute to obesity, there is only one way to lose weight. Individuals must change their ratio of energy intake (food consumption) to energy output (physical activities). To be quite specific, to lose one pound a person needs to burn up 3,500 more calories than he or she consumes. Those wanting to shed pounds have three options in trying to change their ratio of energy input to energy output: (1) sharply reduce food consumption, (2) sharply increase exercise output, or (3) simultaneously decrease food intake and step up exercise output in more moderate ways. Dieting alone is unlikely to be sufficient to lose weight and to maintain the loss (Jeffery et al., 2004). Virtually all experts recommend the third option. Brownell (1995) emphasizes that exercise is an essential ingredient of an effective weight-loss regimen. Exercise seems especially important for *maintaining* reduced weight, as it is the single best predictor of long-term weight loss (Curioni & Lourenco, 2005; Wing & Polley, 2001). Moreover, exercise can yield many other benefits, which we will discuss momentarily.

Self-modification techniques (see the Chapter 4 Application) can be helpful in achieving gradual weight loss. Indeed, behavior modification procedures represent the cornerstone of most reputable, professional weight-loss programs. Overall, the evidence on weight-loss programs suggests that they are moderately successful in the short term (the first 6 months), but in the long run the vast majority of people regain most of the weight that they lose (Jeffery et al., 2000).

CATHY Copyright © 1982 Cathy Guisewite. Reprinted with permission of UNIVERSAL PRESS SYNDICATE. All rights reserved.

Poor Nutrition

Nutrition is a collection of processes (mainly food consumption) through which an organism utilizes the materials (nutrients) required for survival and growth. The term also refers to the *study* of these processes. Unfortunately, most of us don't study nutrition very much. Moreover, the cunning mass marketing of nutritionally worthless foods makes maintaining sound nutritional habits more and more difficult.

Nutrition and Health

Whether we like it or not, we are very much what we eat. Evidence is accumulating that patterns of nutrition influence susceptibility to a variety of diseases and health problems. For example, in a study of over 42,000 women, investigators found an association between a measure of overall diet quality and mortality. Women who reported poorer quality diets had elevated mortality rates (Kant et al., 2000). What are the specific links between diet and health? In addition to the problems associated with obesity, which we have already discussed, other possible connections between eating patterns and health include the following:

1. Heavy consumption of foods that elevate serum cholesterol level (eggs, cheeses, butter, shellfish, sausage, and the like) appears to increase the risk of cardiovascular disease (Stamler et al., 2000; see **Figure 14.17**). Eating habits are only one of several factors that influence serum cholesterol level, but they do make an important contribution.

2. Vulnerability to cardiovascular diseases may also be influenced by other dietary factors. For example, low-fiber diets may increase the likelihood of coronary disease (Ludwig et al., 1999; Wolk et al., 1999) and high intake of red and processed meats, sweets, potatoes, and refined grains is associated with increased cardiovascular risk (Hu & Willett, 2002). Recent research indicates that the omega 3 fatty acids found in fish and fish oils offer some protection against coronary disease (Din, Newby, & Flapan, 2004).

3. High salt intake is thought to be a contributing factor in the development of hypertension (Vollmer et al., 2001), although there is still some debate about its exact role.

4. High caffeine consumption may elevate one's risk for hypertension (James, 2004) and for coronary disease (Happonen, Voutilainen, Salonen, 2004), although the negative effects of caffeine appear relatively modest.

5. High-fat diets have been implicated as possible contributors to some forms of cancer, especially prostate cancer (Rose, 1997), colon and rectal cancer (Shike, 1999), and breast cancer (Wynder et al., 1997). Some studies also suggest that high-fiber diets may

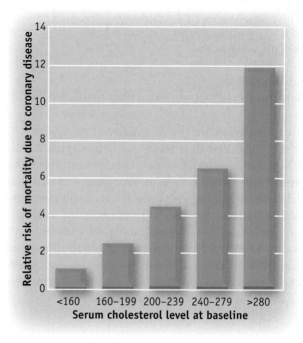

Figure 14.17

The link between cholesterol and coronary risk. In a review of several major studies, Stamler et al. (2000) summarize crucial evidence on the association between cholesterol levels and the prevalence of cardiovascular disease. This graph is based on a sample of over 11,000 men who were 18 to 39 at the beginning of the study (1967–1973) when their serum cholesterol level was measured. The data shown here depict participants' relative risk for coronary heart disease during the ensuing 25 years, as a function of their initial cholesterol level. (Data from Stamler et al., 2000)

reduce one's risk for colon and rectal cancer (Reddy, 1999), but the evidence is not conclusive.

6. Vulnerability to osteoporosis, an abnormal loss of bone mass observed most commonly in postmenopausal women, appears to be elevated by a lifelong pattern of inadequate calcium intake (Kalwarf, Khoury, Lanphear, 2003).

Of course, nutritional habits interact with other factors—genetics, exercise, environment, and so on—to determine whether someone will develop a particular disease. Nonetheless, the examples just described indicate that eating habits can influence physical health.

Web Link 14.5 **Go Ask Alice!**

One of the longest standing and most popular sources of frank information on the Net has been *Alice!* from Columbia University's Health Education Program. Geared especially to the needs of undergraduate students, *Alice!* offers direct answers to questions about relationships, sexuality and sexual health, fitness and nutrition, alcohol and drug consumption, emotional health, and general health.

The Basis for Poor Nutrition

Nutritional deficiencies are more widespread in the United States than most people realize. One study found that 70% of men and 80% of women consumed a diet deficient in at least one of 15 essential nutrients (Murphy et al., 1992). Another study found that young people from over 20 countries routinely ignore nutritional advice by consuming foods that are unhealthy (Wardle et al., 2004). For the most part, these deficiencies are not a result of low income or an inability to afford appropriate foods. Instead, most malnutrition in America is attributable to lack of knowledge about nutrition and lack of effort to ensure good nutrition (West et al., 2004).

In other words, our nutritional shortcomings are the result of ignorance and poor motivation. Americans are remarkably naive about the basic principles of nutrition. Schools tend to provide little education in this area, and most people are not highly motivated to make sure their food consumption is nutritionally sound. Instead, people approach eating very casually, guided not by nutritional needs but by convenience, palatability, and clever advertising.

For most people, then, the first steps toward improved nutrition involve changing attitudes and acquiring information. First and foremost, people need to recognize the importance of nutrition and commit themselves to making a real effort to regulate their eating patterns. Second, people should try to acquire a basic education in nutritional principles.

Nutritional Goals

The most healthful approach to nutrition is to follow well-moderated patterns of food consumption that ensure nutritional adequacy while limiting the intake of certain substances that can be counterproductive. Here are some general guidelines for achieving these goals:

1. *Consume a balanced variety of foods.* Food is made up of a variety of components, six of which are essential to your physical well-being. These six *essential nutrients* are proteins, fats, carbohydrates, vitamins, minerals, and fiber. Proteins, fats, and carbohydrates supply the body with its energy. Vitamins and minerals help release that energy and serve other important functions as well. Fiber provides roughage that facilitates digestion. Educational efforts to promote adequate intake of all essential nutrients have generally suggested that people should be guided by the classic food pyramid published by the U.S. Department of Agriculture (see **Figure 14.18**). Although the food pyramid remains a useful benchmark, it has been subjected to considerable criticism, and hotly debated revisions are under way (Norton, 2004). The principal

Figure 14.18

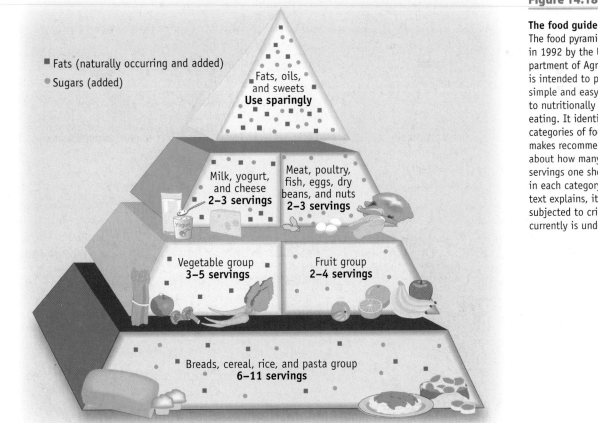

The food guide pyramid. The food pyramid, endorsed in 1992 by the U.S. Department of Agriculture, is intended to provide a simple and easy guide to nutritionally balanced eating. It identifies key categories of food and makes recommendations about how many daily servings one should have in each category. As your text explains, it has been subjected to criticism and currently is under revision.

Eat, Drink, and Be Healthy: The Harvard Medical School Guide to Healthy Eating
by Walter C. Willett (Free Press, 2005)

Harvard Medical School professor Walter Willett is a renowned nutrition researcher who has written a superb book on healthy eating. Willett has been one of the more vocal critics of the food pyramid released by the U.S. Department of Agriculture in 1992. He asserts that "It was built on shaky scientific ground back in 1992. Since then it has been steadily eroded by new research from all parts of the globe" (pp. 15–16). Willett explains that the food pyramid was the product of extensive wrangling between scientists, bureaucrats, and special-interest lobbies, such as the meat, dairy, and sugar industries. Given all the compromises that were struck, it was never an optimal guide for healthy eating. Moreover, the food pyramid does not reflect many important, recent scientific findings on nutrition. Willett reviews these findings and their practical implications in an easy-to-understand, readable style. He sifts through the often contradictory evidence on nutrition and health and makes sense of it all. He describes an alternative healthy eating pyramid and then provides extensive advice on how to eat in a sensible manner.

problem with the food pyramid is its failure to distinguish between different types of fat, different forms of carbohydrates, and different sources of protein (Willett & Stampfer, 2003). For example, the current thinking is that monounsaturated and polyunsaturated fats are healthy, whereas saturated fats should be consumed sparingly. A revised food pyramid, which takes distinctions such as these into consideration, is shown in **Figure 14.19**.

2. *Avoid excessive consumption of saturated fats, cholesterol, refined-grain carbohydrates, sugar, and salt.* These commodities are all overrepresented in the typical American diet. It is particularly prudent to limit the intake of saturated fats by eating less beef, pork, ham, hot dogs, sausage, lunch meats, whole milk, and fried foods. Consumption of many of these foods should also be limited to reduce cholesterol intake, which influences vulnerability to heart disease. In particular, beef, pork, lamb, sausage, cheese, butter, and eggs are high in cholesterol. Refined-grain carbohydrates, such as white bread, pasta, and white rice, are problematic because they increase glucose levels in the blood too quickly. Refined (processed) sugar is believed to be grossly overconsumed. Hence, people should limit their dependence on soft drinks, chocolate, candy, pastries, and high-sugar cereals. Finally, many people should cut down on their salt intake. Doing so may require more than simply ignoring the salt shaker or passing

Figure 14.19

The healthy eating pyramid. This alternative food pyramid was developed by Walter Willett and colleagues at the Harvard Medical School. It corrects a variety of flaws that were apparent in the USDA food pyramid and incorporates recent scientific findings on healthy versus unhealthy fats and carbohydrates.

Adapted from Willett, W. C. (2001). *Eat, drink, and be healthy: The Harvard Medical School guide to healthy eating.* New York: Free Press. Copyright © 2001 by the President and Fellows at Harvard College. Adapted with permission of Simon & Schuster Adult Publishing Group.

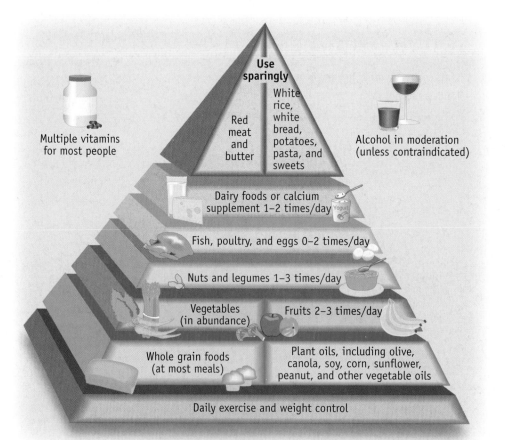

up the potato chips, since many prepackaged foods are loaded with salt.

3. *Increase consumption of polyunsaturated fats, whole-grain carbohydrates, natural sugars, and foods with fiber.* To substitute polyunsaturated fats for saturated ones, people can eat more fish, chicken, turkey, and veal; trim meats of fat more thoroughly; use skim (nonfat) milk; and switch to vegetable oils that are high in polyunsaturated fats. Healthy carbohydrates include whole-grain foods such as whole wheat bread, oatmeal, and brown rice, which are digested more slowly than refined-grain carbohydrates. Fruits and vegetables tend to provide natural sugars and ample fiber. Healthy sources of protein include fish, poultry, eggs, and nuts.

Lack of Exercise

A great deal of evidence suggests that there is a link between exercise and health. Research indicates that regular exercise is associated with increased longevity (Lee & Skerrett, 2001). Moreover, you don't have to be a dedicated athlete to benefit from exercise. Even a moderate level of reasonably regular physical activity is associated with lower mortality rates (Richardson et al., 2004; see **Figure 14.20**). Unfortunately, physical fitness appears to be declining in the United States. Only 25% of American adults get an adequate amount of regular exercise (Dubbert et al., 2004).

Benefits and Risks of Exercise

Exercise is correlated with greater longevity because it promotes a diverse array of specific benefits. First, an appropriate exercise program can enhance cardiovascular fitness and thereby reduce one's susceptibility to cardiovascular problems (Caspersen et al., 1991). Fitness is associated with reduced risk for coronary disease, stroke, and hypertension (Blair, Cheng, & Holder, 2001; Lee et al., 2001). Second, regular physical activity can contribute to the avoidance of obesity (Corsica &

Perri, 2003). Hence, fitness may indirectly reduce one's risk for a variety of obesity-related health problems, including diabetes, respiratory difficulties, arthritis, and back pain. Third, some recent studies suggest that physical fitness is also associated with a decreased risk for colon cancer and for breast and reproductive cancer in women (Thune & Furberg, 2001). The apparent link between exercise and reduced cancer risk has been a pleasant surprise for scientists, who are now scrambling to replicate the findings and figure out the physiological mechanisms underlying this association.

Fourth, exercise may serve as a buffer that reduces the potentially damaging effects of stress (Plante, Caputo, & Chizmar, 2000). This buffering effect may occur because people high in fitness show less physiological reactivity to stress than those who are less fit. Fifth, exercise may have a favorable impact on mental health, which in turn may have positive effects on physical health. Studies have found a consistent association between regular exercise over a period of at least eight weeks and reduced depression (Phillips, Kiernan, & King, 2001), which is important given the evidence that depression is correlated with increased vulnerability to heart disease. Sixth, successful participation in an exercise program can produce desirable personality changes that may promote physical wellness. Research suggests that fitness training can lead to improvements in one's mood, self-esteem, and work efficiency, as well as reductions in tension and anxiety (Dunn, Trivedi, & O'Neal, 2001; Hays, 1999; Sonstroem, 1997).

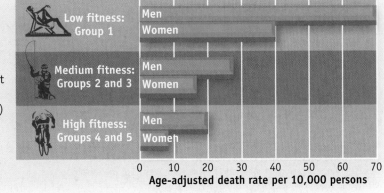

Fitness category
Participants were divided into five categories based on their fitness, ranging from least fit (group 1) to most fit (group 5)

Figure 14.20

Physical fitness and mortality. Blair et al. (1989) studied death rates among men and women who exhibited low, medium, or high fitness. Even medium fitness was associated with lower mortality rates in both genders. The investigators note that one could achieve this level of fitness by taking a brisk half-hour walk each day. (Data from Blair et al., 1989)

Regular exercise has many physical and psychological benefits that promote increased longevity.

Devising an Exercise Program

Putting together a good exercise program is difficult for many people. Exercise is time consuming, and if you're out of shape, your initial attempts may be painful, aversive, and discouraging. People who do not get enough exercise cite lack of time, lack of convenience, and lack of enjoyment as the reasons (Jakicic & Gallagher, 2002). To circumvent these problems, it is wise to heed the following advice (Greenberg, 2002; Jakicic & Gallagher, 2002; Phillips et al., 2001):

1. *Look for an activity that you will find enjoyable.* You have a great many physical activities to choose from (see **Figure 14.21**). Shop around for one that you find intrinsically enjoyable. Doing so will make it much easier for you to follow through and exercise regularly.

2. *Increase your participation gradually.* Don't try to do too much too quickly. An overzealous approach can lead to frustration, not to mention injury. An exercise regimen should build gradually. If you experience injuries, avoid the common tendency to ignore them. Consult your physician to see whether continuing your exercise program is advisable.

3. *Exercise regularly without overdoing it.* Sporadic exercise will not improve your fitness. A widely cited rule of thumb is that you should plan on exercising for a minimum of 30 minutes three to five times a week, or you will gain little benefit from your efforts. At the other extreme, don't try to become fit overnight by

How Beneficial Is Your Favorite Sport?

Physical fitness	Jogging	Bicycling	Swimming	Skating (ice or roller)	Handball/ Squash	Skiing— Nordic	Skiing— Alpine	Basketball	Tennis	Calis- thenics	Walking	Golf	Softball	Bowling
Cardiorespiratory endurance (stamina)	21	19	21	18	19	19	16	19	16	10	13	8	6	5
Muscular endurance	20	18	20	17	18	19	18	17	16	13	14	8	8	5
Muscular strength	17	16	14	15	15	15	15	15	14	16	11	9	7	5
Flexibility	9	9	15	13	16	14	14	13	14	19	7	9	9	7
Balance	17	18	12	20	17	16	21	16	16	15	8	8	7	6
General well-being														
Weight control	21	20	15	17	19	17	15	19	16	12	13	6	7	5
Muscle definition	14	15	14	14	11	12	14	13	13	18	11	6	5	5
Digestion	13	12	13	11	13	12	9	10	12	11	11	7	8	7
Sleep	16	15	16	15	12	15	12	12	11	12	14	6	7	6
Total	**148**	**142**	**140**	**140**	**140**	**139**	**134**	**134**	**128**	**126**	**102**	**67**	**64**	**51**

Figure 14.21

A scorecard on the benefits of 14 sports and exercises. Here is a summary of how seven experts rated the value of 14 sports activities (the highest rating possible on any one item was 21). The ratings were based on vigorous participation four times per week.

Adapted from Conrad, C. C. (1976, May). How different sports rate in promoting physical fitness. *Medical Times,* pp. 45. Copyright 1976 by Romaine Pierson Publishers. Reprinted by permission.

working out too vigorously. One recent study found that people are more likely to stick to an exercise regimen consisting of more frequent workouts of moderate intensity than a regimen of less frequent but more intense workouts (Perri et al., 2002).

4. *Reinforce yourself for your participation.* To offset the inconvenience or pain that may be associated with exercise, it is a good idea to reinforce yourself for your participation. The behavior modification procedures discussed in Chapter 4 can be helpful in devising a viable exercise program.

5. *It's never too late to begin an exercise regimen.* Be forewarned: The number of people who engage in regular exercise declines with age (Phillips et al., 2001). Yet even modest regular exercise has pronounced health benefits, as has been shown in studies with participants well into their 70s, 80s, and 90s (Fiatrone et al., 1993; Raloff, 1996). As they age, people may believe that health declines are not only natural but inevitable (O'Brien & Vertinsky, 1991). A better and more apt belief is this one: Use it or lose it.

Behavior and AIDS

At present, some of the most problematic links between behavior and health may be those related to AIDS, a pandemic, or worldwide epidemic. AIDS stands for *acquired immune deficiency syndrome,* **a disorder in which the immune system is gradually weakened and eventually disabled by the human immunodeficiency virus (HIV).** Being infected with the HIV virus is *not* equivalent to having AIDS. AIDS is the final stage of the HIV infection process, typically manifested about 7–10 years after the original infection (Carey & Vanable, 2003). With the onset of AIDS, one is left virtually defenseless against a host of opportunistic infectious agents. The symptoms of AIDS vary widely depending on the specific constellation of diseases that one develops (Cunningham & Selwyn, 2005). Unfortunately, the worldwide prevalence of this deadly disease continues to increase at an alarming rate, especially in certain regions of Africa (De Cock & Janssen, 2002).

Prior to 1996–1997, the average length of survival for people after the onset of the AIDS syndrome was about 18 to 24 months. Encouraging advances in the treatment of AIDS with drug regimens referred to as *highly active antiretroviral therapy* hold out promise for *substantially* longer survival (Sande & Ronald, 2004). But these drugs are being rushed into service and their long-term efficacy is yet to be determined. Medical experts are concerned that the general public has gotten the impression that these treatments have transformed AIDS from a fatal disease to a manageable one, which is a premature conclusion. HIV strains are evolving, and many have developed resistance to the currently available antiretroviral drugs (Trachtenberg & Sande,

2002). Moreover, many patients do not respond well to the new drugs, and many who are responsive have difficulty sticking to the complicated drug administration regimens that often require people to take 20–30 pills daily and that often have adverse side effects (Catz & Kelly, 2001; Sorenson, Haug, & Batki, 2005). Another daunting problem is that these expensive new drugs remain largely unavailable in developing nations, which have not seen progress in treatment. In some African nations the impact of AIDS has reduced life expectancy to levels not seen for hundreds of years. In Botswana, for instance, projections suggest that life expectancy has declined from 66 to 33 years (Carey & Vanable, 2003).

Transmission

As mentioned in Chapter 13, the HIV virus is transmitted through person-to-person contact involving the exchange of bodily fluids, primarily semen and blood. The two principal modes of transmission in the United States have been sexual contact and the sharing of needles by intravenous (IV) drug users. In the United States, sexual transmission has occurred primarily among gay and bisexual men, but heterosexual transmission has increased in recent years (Catania et al., 2001). In the world as a whole, infection through heterosexual relations has been more common from the beginning. In heterosexual relations, male-to-female transmission is estimated to be about eight times more likely than female-to-male transmission (Ickovics, Thayaparan, & Ethier, 2001). The HIV virus can be found in the tears and saliva of infected individuals, but the concentrations are low, and there is no evidence that the infection can be spread through casual contact. Even most forms of noncasual contact, including kissing, hugging, and sharing food with infected individuals, appear safe (Kalichman, 1995).

Misconceptions

Misconceptions about AIDS are widespread. Ironically, the people who hold these misconceptions fall into two polarized camps. On the one hand, a great many people have unrealistic fears that AIDS can be readily transmitted through casual contact with infected individuals. These people worry unnecessarily about contracting AIDS from a handshake, a sneeze, or an eating utensil. They tend to be paranoid about interacting with homosexuals, thus fueling discrimination against gays. Some people also believe that it is dangerous to donate blood when, in fact, blood donors are at no risk whatsoever.

On the other hand, many young heterosexuals who are sexually active with a variety of partners foolishly downplay their risk for HIV, naively assuming that they are safe as long as they avoid IV drug use and sexual relations with gay or bisexual men. They greatly underestimate the probability that their sexual partners may have previously used IV drugs or had unprotected sex with an infected individual. They don't understand, for instance, that most bisexual men do not disclose their bisexuality to their female partners (Kalichman et al., 1998). Also, because AIDS is usually accompanied by discernible symptoms, many young people believe that prospective sexual partners who carry the HIV virus will exhibit telltale signs of illness. However, as we have already noted, having AIDS and being infected with HIV are not the same thing, and HIV carriers often remain healthy and symptom-free for many years after they are infected. In sum, many myths about AIDS persist, despite extensive efforts to educate the public about this complex and controversial disease. **Figure 14.22** contains a short quiz to test your knowledge of the facts about AIDS.

Prevention

The behavioral changes that minimize the risk of developing AIDS are fairly straightforward, although making the changes is often much easier said than done (Coates & Collins, 1998). In all groups, the more sexual partners a person has, the higher the risk that he or she will be exposed to the HIV virus. Thus, people can reduce their risk by having sexual contacts with fewer partners and by using condoms to control the exchange of semen. It is also important to curtail certain sexual practices (in particular, anal sex) that increase the probability of semen/blood mixing. The 1980s and early 1990s saw considerable progress toward wider use of safe sex practices and the evolution of prevention strategies (Wolitski, Henny, & Lyles, 2006), but new cohorts of young people appear to be much less concerned about the risk of HIV infection than the generation that witnessed the original emergence of AIDS (Catania et al., 2001). In particular, experts are concerned that recent advances in treatment may lead to more casual attitudes about risky sexual practices, a development that would not bode well for public health efforts to slow the spread of AIDS (Cabaj, 2006; Crepaz, Hart, & Marks, 2004). This false sense of security among young adults may have dire consequences in the long run unless they adopt prevention practices and an attitude of vigilance. Indeed, by the year 2015, fully half of all cases of HIV/AIDS in the United States are projected to be among adults who are 50 and older (Centers for Disease Control, 2006).

Figure 14.22

A quiz on knowledge of AIDS. Because misconceptions about AIDS abound, it may be wise to take this brief quiz to test your knowledge.

Adapted from Kalichman, S. C. (1995). *Understanding AIDS: A guide for mental health professionals.* Washington, DC: American Psychological Association. Copyright © 1995 by the American Psychological Association. Adapted with permission of the publisher and author.

AIDS Risk Knowledge Test

Answer the following "true" or "false."

T F	**1.**	The AIDS virus cannot be spread through kissing.
T F	**2.**	A person can get the AIDS virus by sharing kitchens and bathrooms with someone who has AIDS.
T F	**3.**	Men can give the AIDS virus to women.
T F	**4.**	The AIDS virus attacks the body's ability to fight off diseases.
T F	**5.**	You can get the AIDS virus by someone sneezing, like a cold or the flu.
T F	**6.**	You can get AIDS by touching a person with AIDS.
T F	**7.**	Women can give the AIDS virus to men.
T F	**8.**	A person who got the AIDS virus from shooting up drugs cannot give the virus to someone by having sex.
T F	**9.**	A pregnant woman can give the AIDS virus to her unborn baby.
T F	**10.**	Most types of birth control also protect against getting the AIDS virus.
T F	**11.**	Condoms make intercourse completely safe.
T F	**12.**	Oral sex is safe if partners "do not swallow."
T F	**13.**	A person must have many different sexual partners to be at risk for AIDS.
T F	**14.**	It is more important to take precautions against AIDS in large cities than in small cities.
T F	**15.**	A positive result on the AIDS virus antibody test often occurs for people who do not even have the virus.
T F	**16.**	Only receptive (passive) anal intercourse transmits the AIDS virus.
T F	**17.**	Donating blood carries no AIDS risk for the donor.
T F	**18.**	Most people who have the AIDS virus look quite ill.

Answers: 1. T 2. F 3. T 4. T 5. F 6. F 7. T 8. F 9. T 10. F 11. F 12. F 13. F 14. F 15. F 16. F 17. T 18. F

Reactions to Illness

LEARNING OBJECTIVES

▶ *Summarize evidence on patterns of treatment-seeking behavior.*

▶ *Explain the appeal of the "sick role."*

▶ *Identify the factors that tend to undermine doctor-patient communication and how to improve it.*

▶ *Discuss the prevalence of nonadherence to medical advice and its causes.*

So far we have emphasized the psychosocial aspects of maintaining health and minimizing the risk of illness. Health is also affected by how individuals respond to physical symptoms and illnesses. Some people engage in denial and ignore early-warning signs of developing diseases. Others engage in active coping efforts to conquer their diseases. In this section, we discuss the decision to seek medical treatment, the sick role, communication with health providers, and compliance with medical advice.

The Decision to Seek Treatment

Have you ever experienced nausea, diarrhea, stiffness, headaches, cramps, chest pains, or sinus problems? Of course you have; everyone experiences some of these problems periodically. However, whether you view these sensations as *symptoms* is a matter of individual interpretation. When two persons experience the same unpleasant sensations, one may shrug them off as a nuisance, while the other may rush to a physician (Leventhal, Cameron, & Leventhal, 2005; Martin & Leventhal, 2004). Studies suggest that those who are relatively high in anxiety and neuroticism tend to report more symptoms of illness than others do (Feldman et al., 1999). Those who are extremely attentive to bodily sensations and health concerns also report more symptoms than the average person (Barsky, 1988).

Variations in the perception of symptoms help explain why people vary so much in their readiness to seek medical treatment (Cameron, Leventhal, & Leventhal, 1993). Generally, people are more likely to seek medical care when their symptoms are unfamiliar, appear to be serious, last longer than expected, or disrupt their work or social activities (Bernard & Krupat, 1994; Martin et al., 2003). Another key consideration is how friends and family react to the symptoms. Medical consultation is much more likely when friends and family view symptoms as serious and encourage the person to seek medical care, although nagging a person about seeking care can sometimes backfire (Martin et al., 2003). Gender also influences decisions to seek treatment, as women are much more likely than men to utilize medical services (Bertakis et al., 2000). Finally, age matters: Young children (age 5 and under) and older adults (late middle age and beyond) are more likely to utilize health services (U.S. Department of Health and Human Services,

1995). These facts should not be surprising, especially in the case of young children, who often experience frequent illnesses and vaccinations and have parents or caregivers who take them for frequent checkups. As we already know, older folks seek medical attention for chronic health issues (see Chapter 11).

The process of seeking medical treatment can be divided into three stages of active, complex problem solving (Martin et al., 2003). First, people have to decide that their physical sensations *are* symptoms—that they are indicative of illness. Second, they have to decide that their apparent illness warrants medical attention. Third, they have to go to the trouble to make the actual arrangements for medical care, which can be complicated and time consuming. The task of checking insurance coverage, finding an appropriate doctor, negotiating an appointment, arranging to get off work or take care of children, and so forth can be a huge series of hassles.

Robin DiMatteo

Small wonder then, that the biggest problem in regard to treatment seeking is the tendency of many people to delay the pursuit of needed professional consultation. Delays can be important, because early diagnosis and quick intervention can facilitate more effective treatment of many health problems. Unfortunately, procrastination is the norm even when people are faced with a medical emergency, such as a heart attack (Martin & Leventhal, 2004). Why do people dawdle in the midst of a crisis? Robin DiMatteo (1991) mentions a number of reasons, noting that people delay because they often (1) misinterpret and downplay the significance of their symptoms, (2) fret about looking silly if the problem turns out to be nothing, (3) worry about "bothering" their physician, (4) are reluctant to disrupt their plans (to go out to dinner, see a movie, and so forth), and (5) waste time on trivial matters (such as taking a shower, gathering personal items, or packing clothes) before going to a hospital emergency room. In short, people must recognize that the symptoms are serious and then they must exert considerable effort to get medical attention. Regrettably, even minor events or distractions can impede their progress (Anderson, Cacioppo, & Roberts, 1995).

The Sick Role

Although many people tend to delay medical consultations, some people are actually eager to seek medical care. Given this reality, it is not surprising that up to 60% of patients' visits to their primary care physicians appear to have little medical basis (Ellington & Wiebe, 1999). Many of the people who are quick to solicit medical assistance probably have learned that there are potential benefits in adopting the "sick role" (Hamilton, Deemer, & Janata, 2003; Lubkin, 1990). For instance, the sick role absolves people from responsibility for their incapacity and can be used to exempt them from many of their normal duties and obligations (Segall, 1997). Fewer demands are placed on sick people, who can often be selective in deciding which demands to ignore. Illness can provide a convenient, face-saving excuse for one's failures (Wolinksky, 1988). Sick people may also find themselves receiving lots of attention (affection, concern, sympathy) from friends and relatives. This positive attention can be rewarding and can encourage the maintenance of symptoms (Walker, Claar, & Garber, 2002).

Thus, some people grow to *like* the sick role, although they may not be aware of it. Such people readily seek professional care, but they tend to behave in subtle ways that prolong their illness (Kinsman, Dirks, & Jones, 1982). For example, they may only pretend to go along with medical advice, a common problem that we discuss momentarily.

Communicating with Health Providers

When people seek help from physicians and other health care providers, many factors can undermine effective communication. A large portion of medical patients leave their doctors' offices not understanding what they have been told and what they are supposed to do (Johnson & Carlson, 2004). This situation is unfortunate, because good communication is a crucial requirement for sound medical decisions, informed choices about treatment, and appropriate follow-through by patients (Buckman, 2002; Gambone, Reiter, & DiMatteo, 1994).

There are many barriers to effective provider-patient communication (Beisecker, 1990; DiMatteo,

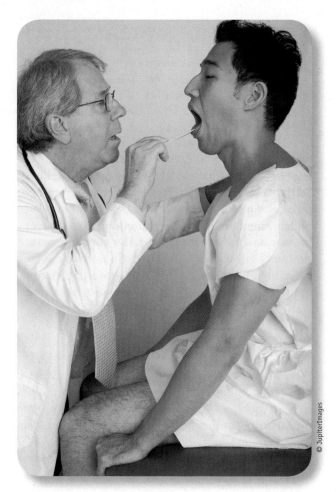

Communication between health care providers and patients tends to be far from optimal for a variety of reasons.

1997). Economic realities dictate that medical visits be generally quite brief, allowing little time for discussion. Illness and pain are subjective matters that may be difficult to describe. Many providers use too much medical jargon and overestimate their patients' understanding of technical terms. Some providers are uncomfortable being questioned and discourage their patients' information seeking. Patients who are upset and worried about their illness may simply forget to report some symptoms or to ask questions they meant to ask. Other patients are evasive about their real concerns because they fear a serious diagnosis. Many patients are reluctant to challenge doctors' authority and are too passive in their interactions with providers. Doctors and nurses often believe their explanations are clear; however, patient misunderstanding can be a common phenomenon, one posing particular problems for individuals whose instructions regarding diagnosis, treatment, and medication are complex (Parker, 2000).

Adherence to Medical Advice

Many patients fail to adhere to the instructions they receive from physicians and other health care profes-

Web Link 14.7 **MedFriendly**

Do you ever wonder what complicated medical terms really mean? Have you tried to read a medical report from a doctor and found yourself not knowing what the doctor was talking about? The MedFriendly site may be your answer in its often humorous, but always clear and helpful definitions of many terms, concepts, and abbreviations used in medicine and health care generally.

sionals. The evidence suggests that noncompliance with medical advice may occur 30% of the time when short-term treatments are prescribed for acute conditions and 50% of the time when long-term treatments are needed for chronic illness (Johnson & Carlson, 2004). Nonadherence takes many forms. Patients may fail to begin a treatment regimen, stop the regimen early, reduce or increase the levels of treatment that were prescribed, or be inconsistent and unreliable in following treatment procedures (Dunbar-Jacob & Schlenk, 2001). Nonadherence is a major problem that has been linked to increased sickness, treatment failures, and higher mortality (Christensen & Johnson, 2002; DiMatteo et al., 2002). Moreover, nonadherence wastes expensive medical visits and medications and increases hospital admissions, leading to enormous economic costs. Robin DiMatteo (2004b) speculates that in the United States alone, nonadherence may be a $300 billion a year drain on the health care system.

Why don't people comply with the advice that they've sought out from highly regarded health care professionals? Physicians tend to attribute noncompliance to patients' personal characteristics, but research indicates that personality traits and demographic factors are surprisingly unrelated to adherence rates (DiMatteo, 2004b). One factor that *is* related to adherence is patients' *social support*. Adherence is improved when patients have family members, friends, or co-workers who remind them and help them to comply with treatment requirements (DiMatteo, 2004a). Another factor is a sense of self-efficacy—patients will adhere to recommendations they believe in and believe they are capable of performing (DiMatteo, 1994). Here are some

other considerations that influence the likelihood of adherence (Dunbar-Jacob & Schlenk, 2001; Johnson & Carlson, 2004):

1. *Frequently, noncompliance is due to patients simply forgetting instructions or failing to understand the instructions as given.* Highly trained professionals often forget that what seems obvious and simple to them may be obscure and complicated to many of their patients.

2. *Another key factor is how aversive or difficult the treatments are.* If the prescribed regimen is unpleasant, compliance will tend to decrease. For example, adherence is reduced when prescribed medications have many severe side effects. And the more that following instructions interferes with routine behavior, the less likely it is that the patient will cooperate successfully.

3. *If a patient has a negative attitude toward a physician, the probability of noncompliance will increase.* When patients are unhappy with their interactions with the doctor, they're more likely to ignore the medical advice provided.

In response to the noncompliance problem, researchers have investigated many methods of increasing patients' adherence to medical advice. Interventions have included simplifying instructions, providing more rationale for instructions, reducing the complexity of treatment regimens, helping patients with emotional distress that undermines adherence, and training patients in the use of behavior modification strategies. All of these interventions can improve adherence, although their effects tend to be modest (Christensen & Johnson, 2002; Roter et al., 1998).

APPLICATION

Understanding the Effects of Drugs

LEARNING OBJECTIVES

▶ *Explain the concepts of drug tolerance, physical and psychological dependence, and overdose.*

▶ *Summarize the main effects and risks of narcotics and sedatives.*

▶ *Summarize the main effects and risks of stimulant drugs and hallucinogens.*

▶ *Summarize the main effects and risks of marijuana and ecstasy (MDMA).*

Answer the following "true" or "false."

___ **1.** Smoking marijuana can make men impotent and sterile.

___ **2.** Overdoses caused by cocaine are relatively rare.

___ **3.** It is well documented that LSD causes chromosome damage.

___ **4.** Hallucinogens are addictive.

___ **5.** Ecstasy is a relatively harmless drug.

As you will learn in this Application, all of these statements are false. If you answered all of them accurately, you may already be well informed about drugs. If not, you *should* be. Intelligent decisions about drugs require an understanding of their effects and risks.

This Application focuses on the use of drugs for their pleasurable effects, commonly referred to as *drug abuse* or *recreational drug use*. Drug abuse reaches into every corner of our society and is a problematic health-impairing habit. Although small declines appear to have occurred in the overall abuse of drugs in recent years, survey data show that illicit drug use has mostly been increasing since the 1960s (Winick & Norman, 2005).

Like other controversial social problems, recreational drug use often inspires more rhetoric than reason. For instance, a former president of the American Medical Association made headlines when he declared that marijuana "makes a man of 35 sexually like a man of 70." In reality, the research findings do not support this assertion. This influential physician later retracted his statement, admitting that he had made it simply to campaign against marijuana use (Leavitt, 1995). Unfortunately, such scare tactics can backfire by undermining the credibility of drug education efforts.

Recreational drug use involves personal, moral, political, and legal issues that are not matters for science to resolve. However, the more knowledgeable you are about drugs, the more informed your decisions and opinions about them will be. Accordingly, this Application is intended to provide you with nonjudgmental, realistic coverage of issues related to recreational drug use. We begin by reviewing key drug-related concepts. Then we examine the effects and risks of five types of widely abused drugs: narcotics, sedatives, stimulants, hallucinogens, and marijuana. We wrap up our coverage with a brief discussion of ecstasy (MDMA), which has stirred up controversy in recent years.

Drug-Related Concepts

The principal types of recreational drugs are described in **Figure 14.23**. This table lists representative drugs in each of the five categories and indicates how the drugs are taken, their principal medical uses, their desired effects, and their common side effects.

Most drugs produce tolerance effects. *Tolerance is a progressive decrease in a person's responsiveness to a drug with continued use.* Tolerance effects usually lead people to consume larger and larger doses of a drug to attain the effects they desire. Tolerance builds more rapidly to some drugs than to others. The first column in **Figure 14.24** indicates whether various categories of drugs tend to produce rapid or gradual tolerance.

In evaluating the potential problems associated with the use of specific drugs, a key consideration is the likelihood of either physical or psychological dependence. Although both forms of drug dependence have a physiological basis (Di Chiara, 1999; Self, 1998), important differences exist between the two syndromes. *Physical dependence exists when a person must continue to take a drug to avoid withdrawal ill-*

Recreational drug users come from all ages and all walks of life.

Comparison of Major Categories of Abused Drugs

Drugs	Methods of administration	Principal medical uses	Desired effects	Short-term side effects
Narcotics (opiates) Morphine Heroin	Injected, smoked, oral	Pain relief	Euphoria, relaxation, anxiety reduction, pain relief	Lethargy, drowsiness, nausea, impaired coordination, impaired mental functioning, constipation
Sedatives Barbiturates (e.g., Seconal) Nonbarbiturates (e.g., Quaalude)	Oral, injected	Sleeping pill, anticonvulsant	Euphoria, relaxation, anxiety reduction, reduced inhibitions	Lethargy, drowsiness, severely impaired coordination, impaired mental functioning, emotional swings, dejection
Stimulants Amphetamines Cocaine	Oral, sniffed, injected, freebased, smoked	Treatment of hyperactivity and narcolepsy; local anesthetic (cocaine only)	Elation, excitement, increased alertness, increased energy, reduced fatigue	Increased blood pressure and heart rate, increased talkativeness, restlessness, irritability, insomnia, reduced appetite, increased sweating and urination, anxiety, paranoia, increased aggressiveness, panic
Hallucinogens LSD Mescaline Psilocybin	Oral		Increased sensory awareness, euphoria, altered perceptions, hallucinations, insightful experiences	Dilated pupils, nausea, emotional swings, paranoia, jumbled thought processes, impaired judgment, anxiety, panic reaction
Cannabis Marijuana Hashish THC	Smoked, oral	Treatment of glaucoma; other uses under study	Mild euphoria, relaxation, altered perceptions, enhanced awareness	Bloodshot eyes, dry mouth, reduced memory, sluggish motor coordination, sluggish mental functioning, anxiety

Figure 14.23

Major categories of abused drugs. This chart summarizes the methods of ingestion, chief medical uses, and principal effects of five major types of recreational drugs. Alcohol is covered in the main body of the chapter. (Based on Julien, 2001; Levinthal, 2002; Lowinson, et al., 2005)

ness (which occurs when drug use is terminated). The symptoms of withdrawal illness (also called abstinence syndrome) vary depending on the drug. Withdrawal from heroin and barbiturates can produce fever, chills, tremors, convulsions, seizures, vomiting, cramps, diarrhea, and severe aches and pains. The agony of withdrawal from these drugs virtually compels addicts to continue using them. Withdrawal from stimulants leads to a different and somewhat milder syndrome dominated by fatigue, apathy, irritability, depression, and disorientation.

Psychological dependence exists when a person must continue to take a drug to satisfy intense men-

tal and emotional craving for it. Psychological dependence is more subtle than physical dependence, as it is not marked by a clear withdrawal reaction. However, psychological dependence can create a powerful, overwhelming need for a drug. The two types of dependence often coexist—that is, many people manifest both psychological and physical dependence on a specific drug. Both types of dependence are established gradually with repeated use of a drug. However, specific drugs vary greatly in their potential for creating dependence. The second and third columns in **Figure 14.24** provide estimates of the risk of each kind of dependence for the drugs covered in our discussion.

Risks Associated with Major Categories of Abused Drugs

Drugs	Tolerance	Risk of physical dependence	Risk of psychological dependence	Fatal overdose potential
Narcotics (opiates)	Rapid	High	High	High
Sedatives	Rapid	High	High	High
Stimulants	Rapid	Moderate	High	Moderate to high
Hallucinogens	Gradual	None	Very low	Very low
Cannabis	Gradual	None	Low to moderate	Very low

Figure 14.24

Specific risks for various categories of drugs. This chart shows estimates of the risk potential for tolerance, dependence, and overdose for the five major categories of drugs discussed in this Application.

An *overdose* is an excessive dose of a drug that can seriously threaten one's life. Any drug can be fatal if a person takes enough of it, but some drugs carry more risk of overdose than others. In **Figure 14.24**, column 4 estimates the risk of accidentally consuming a lethal overdose of various drugs. Drugs that are central nervous system (CNS) depressants—narcotics and sedatives—carry the greatest risk of overdose. It's important to understand that the effects of these drugs are additive. Many overdoses involve lethal *combinations* of CNS depressants. What happens when people overdose on these drugs? Their respiratory system usually grinds to a halt, producing coma, brain damage, and death within a brief period. In contrast, fatal overdoses with CNS stimulants (cocaine and amphetamines) usually involve a heart attack, stroke, or cortical seizure.

Now that our basic vocabulary is spelled out, we can begin to examine the effects and risks of major recreational drugs. Of course, we'll be describing the *typical* effects of each drug. Please bear in mind that the effects of any drug depend on the user's age, body weight, physiology, personality, mood, expectations, and previous experience with the drug. The dose and potency of the drug, the method of administration, and the setting in which the drug is taken also influence its effects (Leavitt, 1995). Our coverage is based largely on comprehensive books by Julien (2001), Levinthal (2002), and Lowinson and colleagues (2005), but we cite additional sources when discussing specific studies or controversial points.

Narcotics

Narcotics (or opiates) are drugs derived from opium that are capable of relieving pain. In government regulations, the term *narcotic* is used in a haphazard way to refer to a variety of drugs besides opiates. The most widely abused opiates are heroin, morphine, and a relatively new painkiller called Oxycontin. However, less potent opiates, such as codeine, Demerol, and Vicodin, are also subject to misuse.

Effects
The most significant narcotics problem in modern, Western society is the use of heroin. Most users inject this drug intravenously with a hypodermic needle. The main effect is an overwhelming sense of euphoria. This "Who cares?" feeling makes the heroin high an attractive escape from reality. Common side effects include nausea, lethargy, drowsiness, constipation, and slowed respiration.

Risks
Narcotics carry a high risk for both *psychological and physical dependence* (Knapp, Ciraulo, & Jaffe, 2005). It

is estimated that there are about 600,000 heroin addicts in the United States (Winick & Norman, 2005). Although heroin withdrawal usually isn't life threatening, it can be terribly unpleasant, so that "junkies" have a desperate need to continue their drug use. Once dependence is entrenched, users tend to develop a *drug-centered lifestyle* that revolves around the need to procure more heroin. This lifestyle occurs because the drug is expensive and available only through highly undependable black market channels. Obviously, it is difficult to lead a productive life if one's existence is dominated by a desperate need to "score" heroin. The inordinate cost of the drug forces many junkies to resort to criminal activities to support their habit.

Heroin is blamed for over 4,000 deaths annually in the United States, so *overdose* is a very real danger. Opiates are additive with other CNS depressants, and most narcotic overdoses occur in combination with the use of sedatives or alcohol. Junkies also risk *contracting infectious disease* because they often share hypodermic needles and tend to be sloppy about sterilizing them. The most common of these diseases used to be hepatitis, but in recent years AIDS has been transmitted at an alarming rate through the population of intravenous drug users (Des Jarlais, Hagan, & Friedman, 2005).

Sedatives

Sedatives are sleep-inducing drugs that tend to decrease central nervous system and behavioral activity. In street jargon, they are often called "downers." Over the years, the most widely abused sedatives have been the barbiturates, which are compounds derived from barbituric acid. However, barbiturates have gradually become medically obsolete and diminished in availability, so sedative abusers have had to turn to drugs in the benzodiazepine family, such as Valium (Wesson et al., 2005).

Effects
People abusing sedatives generally consume larger doses than are prescribed for medical purposes. These overly large doses have a euphoric effect similar to that produced by drinking large amounts of alcohol (Wesson et al., 2005). Feelings of tension, anxiety, and depression are temporarily replaced by a relaxed, pleasant state of intoxication, in which inhibitions may be loosened. Sedatives carry a truckload of dangerous side effects. Motor coordination suffers badly, producing slurred speech and a staggering walk, among other things. Intellectual functioning also becomes sluggish, and judgment is impaired. One's emotional tone may become unstable, with feelings of dejection often intruding on the intended euphoric mood.

Risks

Sedatives have the potential to produce *both psychological and physical dependence.* They are also among the leading causes of *overdoses* in the United States because of their additive interactions with other CNS depressants (especially alcohol) and because of the degree to which they impair judgment. In their drug-induced haze, sedative abusers are likely to take doses they would ordinarily recognize as dangerous. Sedative users also elevate their risk for *accidental injuries* because these drugs can have significant effects on motor coordination. Many users trip down stairs, fall off bar stools, get into automobile accidents, and so forth.

Stimulants

Stimulants **are drugs that tend to increase central nervous system and behavioral activity.** They range from mild, widely available forms, such as caffeine and nicotine, to stronger, carefully regulated stimulants, such as cocaine and amphetamines ("speed"). Here we focus on the latter two drugs.

Cocaine is an organic substance extracted from the coca shrub, which grows most prominently in South America. It is usually consumed as a crystalline powder that is snorted through the nasal cavities, although it can be consumed orally or intravenously. "Crack" is a processed variant of cocaine, consisting of little chips of cocaine that are usually smoked. Smoking crack tends to be more dangerous than snorting cocaine powder because smoking leads to a more rapid absorption of the drug into the bloodstream and more concentrated delivery of cocaine to the brain. That said, all the forms of cocaine and all the routes of administration can deliver highly toxic amounts of the drug to the brain (Repetto & Gold, 2005).

Synthesized in a pharmaceutical laboratory, amphetamines are usually consumed orally. However, speed is also sold as a crystalline powder (called "crank" or "crystal meth") that may be snorted or injected intravenously. A smokable form of methamphetamine, called "ice," is seen in some regions.

Effects

Amphetamines and cocaine have almost indistinguishable effects, except that cocaine produces a very brief high (20–30 minutes unless more is taken), while a speed high can last many hours (Gold, Miller, & Jonas, 1992). Stimulants produce a euphoria very different from that created by narcotics or sedatives. They produce a buoyant, elated, enthusiastic, energetic, "I can conquer the world!" feeling accompanied by increased alertness. Common side effects include increased blood pressure, muscle tension, sweating, and restlessness. Some users

experience unpleasant feelings of irritability, anxiety, and paranoia.

Risks

Stimulants can cause physical dependence, but the physical distress caused by stimulant withdrawal is mild compared to that caused by narcotic or sedative withdrawal. Psychological dependence on stimulants is a more common problem. Cocaine can create an exceptionally *powerful psychological dependence* that compels the user to pursue the drug with a fervor normally seen only when physical dependence exists (Gold & Jacobs, 2005).

Both cocaine and amphetamines can suppress appetite and disrupt sleep. Thus, heavy use of stimulants may lead to poor eating, poor sleeping, and ultimately, a *deterioration in physical health.* Furthermore, stimulant use increases one's risk for stroke, heart attack, and other forms of cardiovascular disease, and crack smoking is associated with a host of respiratory problems (Gourevitch & Arnsten, 2005; Weaver & Schnoll, 1999).

Heavy stimulant use occasionally leads to the onset of a severe psychological disorder called *amphetamine* or *cocaine psychosis* (depending on the drug involved), which is dominated by intense paranoia (King & Ellinwood, 2005). All of the risks associated with stimulant use increase when more potent forms of the drugs (crack and ice) are used. Overdoses on stimulants used to be relatively infrequent (Kalant & Kalant, 1979). However, in recent years, *cocaine overdoses have increased sharply* as more people experiment with more dangerous modes of ingestion. In 2001, cocaine was the leading cause of drug-related emergency room visits (Gold & Jacobs, 2005).

Hallucinogens

Hallucinogens **are a diverse group of drugs that have powerful effects on mental and emotional functioning, marked most prominently by distortions in sensory and perceptual experience.** The principal hallucinogens are LSD, mescaline, and psilocybin, which have similar effects, although they vary in potency. Mescaline comes from the peyote plant, psilocybin comes from a particular type of mushroom, and LSD is a synthetic drug. Common street names for hallucinogens include "acid," "mushrooms," "fry," and "blotter."

Effects

Hallucinogens intensify and distort perception in ways that are difficult to describe, and they temporarily impair intellectual functioning as thought processes become meteoric and jumbled. These drugs can produce awesome feelings of euphoria that sometimes include an almost mystical sense of "oneness" with the human race. This is why they have been used in religious ceremonies in various cultures. Unfortunately, at the other end of the emotional spectrum, they can also produce nightmarish feelings of anxiety, fear, and paranoia, commonly called a "bad trip."

Risks

There is no potential for physical dependence on hallucinogens, and no deaths attributable to overdose are known to have occurred. Psychological dependence has been reported but appears to be rare. Research reports that LSD increases chromosome breakage were based on poor methodology (Dishotsky et al., 1971). However, like most drugs, hallucinogens may be harmful to a fetus if taken by a pregnant woman.

Although the dangers of hallucinogens have probably been exaggerated in the popular press, there are some significant risks (Pechnick & Ungerleider, 2005). Emotion is highly volatile with these drugs, so users can never be sure that they won't experience *acute panic* from a terrifying bad trip. Generally, this disorientation subsides within a few hours, leaving no permanent emotional scars. However, in such a severe state of disorientation, *accidents and suicide* are possible. *Flashbacks* are vivid hallucinogenic experiences occurring months after the original drug ingestion. They do not appear to be a common problem, but repetitious flashbacks have proved troublesome for some individuals. In a small minority of users, hallucinogens may contribute to the emergence of a *variety of psychological disorders* (psychoses, depressive reactions, paranoid states) that may be partially attributable to the drug (Pechnick & Ungerleider, 2005).

Marijuana

Cannabis is the hemp plant from which marijuana, hashish, and THC are derived. Marijuana (often called "pot," "weed," "reefer," or "grass") is a mixture of dried leaves, flowers, stems, and seeds taken from the plant, while hashish comes from the plant's resin. THC, the active chemical ingredient in cannabis, can be synthesized for research purposes (for example, to give to animals).

Effects

When smoked, cannabis has an almost immediate impact that may last several hours. The effects of the drug vary greatly, depending on the user's expectations and experience with it, the drug's potency, and the amount smoked. The drug has subtle effects on emotion, perception, and cognition (Grinspoon, Bakalar, & Russo, 2005). Emotionally, the drug tends to create a mild, re-laxed state of euphoria. Perceptually, it enhances the impact of incoming stimulation, thus making music sound better, food taste better, and so on. Cannabis tends to produce a slight impairment in cognitive functioning (especially short-term memory) and perceptual-motor coordination while the user is high. However, there are huge variations among users.

Risks

Overdose and physical dependence are not problems with marijuana, but as with any other drug that produces pleasant feelings, it has the potential to produce *psychological dependence* (Grinspoon, Bakalar, & Russo, 2005). There is no solid evidence that cannabis causes psychological disorders. However, marijuana can cause *transient problems with anxiety and depression* in some people. Studies also suggest that cannabis may have a more *negative effect on driving* than has been widely believed (Ramaekers, Robbe, & O'Hanlon, 2000). Like tobacco smoke, marijuana smoke carries carcinogens and impurities into the lungs, thus increasing one's chances for *respiratory and pulmonary diseases, and probably lung cancer* (Stephens, 1999). However, the evidence on other widely publicized risks remains controversial. Here is a brief overview of the evidence on some of these controversies:

▶ *Does marijuana reduce one's immune response?* Research with animals clearly demonstrates that cannabis can suppress various aspects of immune system responding (Cabral & Pettit, 1998). However, infectious diseases do not *appear* to be more common among marijuana smokers than among nonsmokers. Hence, it is unclear whether marijuana increases susceptibility to infectious diseases in humans (Bredt et al., 2002; Klein, Friedman, & Specter, 1998).

▶ *Does marijuana lead to impotence and sterility in men?* In animal research, cannabis temporarily decreases testosterone levels and sperm production (Brown & Dobs, 2002). Citing these findings, the popular media have frequently implied that marijuana is likely to make men sterile and impotent. However, research with humans has yielded weak, inconsistent, and reversible effects on testosterone and sperm levels (Brown & Dobs, 2002). At present, the evidence suggests that marijuana has little lasting impact on male smokers' fertility or sexual functioning (Grinspoon, Bakalar, & Russo, 2005).

▶ *Does marijuana have long-term negative effects on cognitive functioning?* It has long been known that marijuana has a negative impact on attention and memory while users are high, but until recently studies had failed to find any permanent cognitive deficits attributable to cannabis use. However, a spate of recent studies using more elaborate and precise assessments of cognitive functioning *have* found an association between chronic, heavy marijuana use and measureable impairments in attention and memory (see **Figure 14.25**) that show up when users are not high (Ehrenreich et al., 1999; Solowij et al., 2002). That said, the cognitive deficits that have been observed are modest and certainly not disabling, and one study found that the deficits vanished after a month of marijuana abstinence (Pope, Gruber, & Yurgelun-Todd, 2001; Pope et al., 2001).

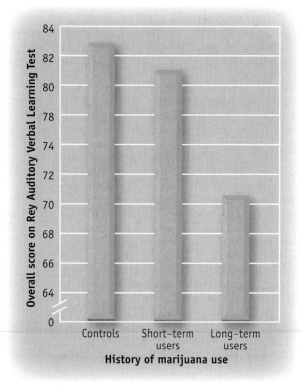

Figure 14.25

Chronic cannabis use and cognitive performance. Solowij and associates (2002) administered a battery of neuropsychological tests to 51 long-term cannabis users, who had smoked marijuana regularly for an average of 24 years; 51 short-term cannabis users, who had smoked marijuana regularly for an average of 10 years; and 33 control subjects who had little or no history of cannabis use. The cannabis users were required to abstain from smoking marijuana for a minimum of 12 hours prior to their testing. The study found evidence suggestive of subtle cognitive impairments among the long-term cannabis users on many of the tests. The graph shown here depicts the results observed for overall performance on the Rey Auditory Verbal Learning Test, which measures several aspects of memory functioning.

Ecstasy (MDMA)

The newest drug controversy in Western society centers on MDMA, better known as "ecstasy." MDMA was originally formulated in 1912 but was not widely used in the United States until the 1990s, when it became popular in the context of "raves" and dance clubs (Millman & Beeder, 1994). This compound is related to both amphetamines and hallucinogens, especially mescaline. It produces a high that typically lasts a few hours or more. Users report that they feel warm, friendly, euphoric, sensual, insightful, and empathetic, yet alert and energetic. Problematic side effects include increased blood pressure, muscle tension, sweating, blurred vision, insomnia, and transient anxiety.

Empirical research on ecstasy is still in its infancy, so assertions about its risks and dangers must be tentative and provisional. Data on adverse effects are also complicated by the fact that the vast majority of MDMA users ingest it in conjunction with many other drugs (Hammersley et al., 1999; Pedersen & Skrondal, 1999). Yet another complicating factor is that MDMA often contains potentially harmful impurities, contaminants, and toxic by-products introduced during its illicit manufacture (Grob & Poland, 2005).

MDMA does not appear to be especially addictive, but psychological dependence can clearly become a problem for some people. MDMA has been implicated in cases of stroke and heart attack, seizures, heat stroke, and liver damage, but its exact contribution is hard to gauge given all the other drugs that MDMA users typically consume (Burgess, O'Donohoe, & Gill, 2000; Grob & Poland, 2005). Chronic, heavy use of ecstasy appears to be associated with sleep disorders, depression, and elevated anxiety and hostility (Morgan, 2000). Moreover, studies of former MDMA users suggest that ecstasy may have subtle, long-term effects on cognitive functioning (Medina et al., 2005; Parrott, 2000). Quite a few studies have found memory deficits in former users (Bhattachary & Powell, 2001; Zakzanis & Young, 2001). Other studies have found decreased performance on laboratory tasks requiring attention and learning (Gouzoulis-Mayfrank et al., 2000). Thus, although more research is needed, there are many reasons to be concerned about the possible effects of ecstasy.

KEY IDEAS

Stress, Personality, and Illness

▶ The biopsychosocial model holds that physical health is influenced by a complex network of biological, psychological, and sociocultural factors. Stress is one of the psychological factors that can affect physical health. In particular, cynical hostility has been implicated as a contributing cause of coronary heart disease. A number of mechanisms may contribute to this connection.

▶ Emotional reactions may also influence susceptibility to heart disease. Recent research has suggested that transient mental stress and the negative emotions that result may tax the heart. Yet another line of research has identified the emotional dysfunction of depression as a risk factor for heart disease.

▶ The connection between psychological factors and the onset of cancer is not well documented, but stress and personality may influence the course of the disease. Researchers have found associations between stress and the onset of a variety of other diseases. Stress may play a role in a variety of diseases because it can temporarily suppress immune functioning. While there's little doubt that stress can contribute to the development of physical illness, the link between stress and illness is modest.

Habits, Lifestyles and Health

▶ People commonly engage in health-impairing habits and lifestyles. These habits creep up slowly, and their risks are easy to ignore because the dangers often lie in the distant future.

▶ Smokers have much higher mortality rates than nonsmokers because they are more vulnerable to a variety of diseases. Giving up smoking can reduce one's health risks, but doing so is difficult and relapse rates are high.

▶ Drinking rivals smoking as a source of health problems. In the short term, drinking can impair driving, cause various types of accidents, and increase the likelihood of aggressive interactions or reckless sexual behavior. In the long term, chronic, excessive alcohol consumption increases one's risk for numerous health problems, including cirrhosis of the liver, heart disease, hypertension, stroke, and cancer.

▶ Obesity elevates one's risk for many health problems. Body weight is influenced by genetic endowment, eating and exercise habits, and perhaps set point or settling point. Weight loss is best accomplished by decreasing caloric consumption while increasing exercise.

▶ Poor nutritional habits have been linked to many health problems, including cardiovascular diseases and some types of cancer, although some of the links are tentative. One's health can best be served by following balanced food consumption patterns while limiting the intake of saturated fats, cholesterol, refined carbohydrates, sugar, and salt.

▶ Lack of exercise is associated with elevated mortality rates. Regular exercise can reduce one's risk for cardiovascular disease, cancer, and obesity-related diseases; buffer the effects of stress; and lead to desirable personality changes.

▶ Although misconceptions abound, HIV is transmitted almost exclusively by sexual contact and the sharing of needles by intravenous drug users. One's risk for HIV infection can be reduced by avoiding IV drug use, having fewer sexual partners, using condoms, and curtailing certain sexual practices.

Reactions to Illness

▶ Variations in seeking treatment are influenced by the severity, duration, and disruptiveness of one's symptoms and by the reactions of friends and family. The biggest problem is the tendency of many people to delay needed medical treatment. At the other extreme, a minority of people learn to like the sick role because it earns them attention and allows them to avoid stress.

▶ Good communication is crucial to effective health services, but many factors undermine communication between patients and health providers, such as short visits, overuse of medical jargon, and patients' reluctance to ask questions.

▶ Noncompliance with medical advice is a major problem, which appears to occur 30%–50% of the time. The likelihood of nonadherence is greater when instructions are difficult to understand, when recommendations are difficult to follow, and when patients are unhappy with their doctor.

Application: Understanding the Effects of Drugs

▶ Recreational drugs vary in their potential for tolerance effects, psychological dependence, physical dependence, and overdose. The risks associated with narcotics use include both types of dependence, overdose, and the acquisition of infectious diseases.

▶ Sedatives can also produce both types of dependence, are subject to overdoses, and elevate the user's risk for accidental injuries. Stimulant use can lead to psychological dependence, overdose, psychosis, and a deterioration in physical health. Cocaine overdoses have increased greatly in recent years.

▶ Hallucinogens can in some cases contribute to accidents, suicides, and psychological disorders, and they can cause flashbacks. The risks of marijuana use include psychological dependence, impaired driving, transient problems with anxiety and depression, and respiratory and pulmonary diseases. Recent studies suggest that marijuana use may have some long-term negative effects on cognitive processes.

▶ More research is needed, but it appears that the use of ecstasy (MDMA) may contribute to a variety of acute and chronic physical maladies. MDMA may also have subtle, negative effects on cognitive functioning.

KEY TERMS

KEY PEOPLE

1. The greatest threats to health in our society today are:
   a. environmental toxins.
   b. accidents.
   c. chronic diseases.
   d. contagious diseases caused by specific infectious agents.

2. Which of the following is *not* associated with elevated coronary risk?
   a. Cynical hostility
   b. Strong emotional reactions to transient mental stress
   c. Obsessive-compulsive disorder
   d. Depression

3. Why do people tend to act in self-destructive ways?
   a. Because many health-impairing habits creep up on them
   b. Because many health-impairing habits involve activities that are quite pleasant at the time
   c. Because the risks tend to lie in the distant future
   d. All of the above

4. Some short-term risks of alcohol consumption include all but which of the following?
   a. Hangovers and life-threatening overdoses in combination with other drugs
   b. Poor perceptual coordination and driving drunk
   c. Increased aggressiveness and argumentativeness
   d. Transient anxiety from endorphin-induced flashbacks

5. Twin studies and other behavioral genetics research suggest that:
   a. genetic factors have little impact on people's weight.
   b. heredity has scant influence on BMI but does influence weight.
   c. heredity accounts for 60% or more of the variation in weight.
   d. heredity is responsible for severe, morbid obesity but has little influence over the weight of normal people.

6. Which of the following has *not* been found to be a mode of transmission for AIDS?
   a. Sexual contact among homosexual men
   b. The sharing of needles by intravenous drug users
   c. Sexual contact among heterosexuals
   d. Sharing food

7. Regarding the seeking of medical treatment, the biggest problem is:
   a. the tendency of many people to delay seeking treatment.
   b. the tendency of many people to rush too quickly for medical care for minor problems.

   c. not having enough doctors to cover peoples' needs.
   d. the tendency of people in higher socioeconomic categories to exaggerate their symptoms.

8. In which of the following cases are people most likely to follow the instructions they receive from health care professionals?
   a. When the instructions are complex and punctuated with impressive medical jargon
   b. When they do not fully understand the instructions but still feel the need to do something
   c. When they like and understand the health care professional
   d. All of the above

9. Which of the following risks is *not* typically associated with narcotics use?
   a. Overdose   c. Physical dependence
   b. Infectious disease   d. Flashbacks

10. The use of sedatives may result in personal injury because they:
    a. cause motor coordination to deteriorate.
    b. enhance motor coordination too much, making people overconfident about their abilities.
    c. suppress pain warnings of physical harm.
    d. trigger hallucinations such as flying.

Book Companion Website

Visit the Book Companion Website at **academic.cengage. com/psychology/weiten**, where you will find tutorial quizzes, flash cards, and web links for every chapter, a final exam, and more! You can also link to the Psychology Resource Center (accessible directly at **academic.cengage.com/login**) for a range of psychology-related resources.

Personal Explorations Workbook

The following exercises in your *Personal Explorations Workbook* may enhance your self-understanding in relation to issues raised in this chapter. **Questionnaire 14.1:** Chronic Self-Destructiveness Scale. **Personal Probe 14.1:** How Do Your Health Habits Rate? **Personal Probe 14.2:** Examining Specific Health Habits.

ANSWERS

1. c Page 441
2. c Pages 443–447
3. d Pages 450–451
4. d Pages 455–456
5. c Page 458
6. d Page 465
7. a Page 467
8. c Pages 468–469
9. d Page 472
10. a Page 473

CHAPTER 15

Psychological Disorders

"The government of the United States was overthrown more than a year ago! I'm the president of the United States of America and Bob Dylan is vice president!" So said Ed, the author of a prominent book on journalism, who was speaking to a college journalism class, as a guest lecturer. Ed also informed the class that he had killed both John and Robert Kennedy, as well as Charles de Gaulle, the former president of France. He went on to tell the class that all rock music songs were written about him, that he was the greatest karate expert in the universe, and that he had been fighting "space wars" for 2000 years. The students in the class were mystified by Ed's bizarre, disjointed "lecture," but they assumed that he was putting on a show that would eventually lead to a sensible conclusion. However, their perplexed but expectant calm was shattered when Ed pulled a hatchet from the props he had brought with him and hurled the hatchet at the class! Fortunately, he didn't hit anyone, as the hatchet sailed over the students' heads. At that point, the professor for the class realized that Ed's irrational behavior was not a pretense. The professor evacuated the class quickly while Ed continued to rant and rave about his presidential administration, space wars, vampires, his romances with female rock stars, and his personal harem of 38 "chicks." *(Adapted from Pearce, 1974)*

Clearly, Ed's behavior was abnormal. Even *he* recognized that when he agreed later to be admitted to a mental hospital, signing himself in as the "President of the United States of America." What causes such abnormal behavior? Does Ed have a mental illness, or does he just behave strangely? What is the basis for judging behavior as normal versus abnormal? How common are such disorders? These are just a few of the questions we address in this chapter as we discuss psychological disorders and their complex causes.

Abnormal Behavior: Concepts and Controversies

Misconceptions about abnormal behavior are common. We therefore need to clear up some preliminary issues before we describe the various types of psychological disorders. In this section, we discuss (1) the medical model of abnormal behavior, (2) the criteria of abnormal behavior, (3) the classification of psychological disorders, and (4) the prevalence of such disorders.

The Medical Model Applied to Abnormal Behavior

In Ed's case, there's no question that his behavior was abnormal. But does it make sense to view his unusual and irrational behavior as an *illness*? This is a controversial question. **The *medical model* proposes that it is useful to think of abnormal behavior as a disease.** This point of view is the basis for many of the terms used to refer to abnormal behavior, including mental *illness*, psychological *disorder*, and psycho*pathology* (*pathology* refers to manifestations of disease). The medical model gradually became the dominant way of thinking about abnormal behavior during the 19th and 20th centuries, and its influence remains strong today.

The medical model clearly represented progress over earlier models of abnormal behavior. Prior to the 18th century, most conceptions of abnormal behavior were based on superstition. People who behaved strangely were thought to be possessed by demons, to be witches in league with the devil, or to be victims of God's punishment. Their disorders were "treated" with chants, rituals, exorcisms, and such. If the people's behavior was seen as threatening, they were candidates for chains, dungeons, torture, and death (see **Figure 15.1**).

The rise of the medical model brought improvements in the treatment of those who exhibited abnormal behavior. As victims of an illness, they were viewed with more sympathy and less hatred and fear. Although living conditions in early asylums were often deplorable, gradual progress was made toward more humane

Figure 15.1

Historical conceptions of mental illness. Throughout most of history, psychological disorders were thought to be caused by demonic possession, and the mentally ill were candidates for chains and torture.

care of the mentally ill. It took time, but ineffectual approaches to treatment eventually gave way to scientific investigation of the causes and cures of psychological disorders.

© David Lees/Corbis

Thomas Szasz

However, in recent decades, some critics have suggested that the medical model may have outlived its usefulness (Kiesler, 1999). A particularly vocal critic has been Thomas Szasz (1974, 1993). He asserts that "strictly speaking, disease or illness can affect only the body; hence there can be no mental illness. . . . Minds can be 'sick' only in the sense that jokes are 'sick' or economies are 'sick'" (1974, p. 267). He further argues that abnormal behavior usually involves a deviation from social norms rather than an illness. He contends that such deviations are "problems in living" rather than medical problems. According to Szasz, the medical model's disease analogy converts moral and social questions about what is acceptable behavior into medical questions.

Although Szasz's criticism has some merit, we'll take the position that the disease analogy continues to be useful, although you should keep in mind that it is *only* an analogy. Medical concepts such as *diagnosis, etiology,* and *prognosis* have proven valuable in the treatment and study of abnormality. **Diagnosis involves distinguishing one illness from another. Etiology refers to the apparent causation and developmental history of an illness. A prognosis is a forecast about the probable course of an illness.** These medically based concepts have widely shared meanings that permit clinicians, researchers, and the public to communicate more effectively in their discussions of abnormal behavior.

Criteria of Abnormal Behavior

If your next-door neighbor scrubs his front porch twice every day and spends virtually all his time cleaning and recleaning his house, is he normal? If your sister-in-law goes to one physician after another seeking treatment for ailments that appear imaginary, is she psychologically healthy? How are we to judge what's normal and what's abnormal? More important, who's to do the judging?

These are complex questions. In a sense, *all* people make judgments about normality in that they all express opinions about others' (and perhaps their own) mental health. Of course, formal diagnoses of psychological disorders are made by mental health professionals. In making these diagnoses, clinicians rely on a variety of criteria, the foremost of which are the following:

1. *Deviance.* As Szasz has pointed out, people are often said to have a disorder because their behavior deviates from what their society considers acceptable. What constitutes normality varies somewhat from one culture to another, but all cultures have such norms. When people ignore these standards and expectations, they may be labeled mentally ill. For example, *transvestic fetishism* is a sexual disorder in which a man achieves sexual arousal by dressing in women's clothing. This behavior is regarded as disordered because a man who wears a dress, brassiere, and nylons is deviating from our culture's norms. This example illustrates the arbitrary nature of cultural standards regarding normality, as the same overt behavior (cross-gender dressing) is acceptable for women yet deviant for men.

2. *Maladaptive behavior.* In many cases, people are judged to have a psychological disorder because their everyday adaptive behavior is impaired. This is the key criterion in the diagnosis of substance use (drug) disorders. In and of itself, alcohol and drug use is not terribly unusual or deviant. However, when the use of cocaine, for instance, begins to interfere with a person's social or occupational functioning, a substance use disorder exists. In such cases, it is the maladaptive quality of the behavior that makes it disordered.

3. *Personal distress.* Frequently, the diagnosis of a psychological disorder is based on an individual's re-

© AP Images/David Davies/PA

This man clearly exhibits a certain type of deviance, but does that mean that he has a psychological disorder? The criteria of mental illness are more subjective and complicated than most people realize, and to some extent, judgments of mental health represent value judgments.

port of great personal distress. This is usually the criterion met by people who are troubled by depression or anxiety disorders. Depressed people, for instance, may or may not exhibit deviant or maladaptive behavior. Such people are usually labeled as having a disorder when they describe their subjective pain and suffering to friends, relatives, and mental health professionals.

Although two or three criteria may apply in a particular case, people are often viewed as disordered when only one criterion is met. As you may have already noticed, diagnoses of psychological disorders involve *value judgments* about what represents normal or abnormal behavior (Sadler, 2005; Widiger & Sankis, 2000). The criteria of mental illness are not nearly as value-free as the criteria of physical illness. In evaluating physical diseases, people can usually agree that a weak heart or a malfunctioning kidney is pathological, regardless of their personal values. However, judgments about mental illness reflect prevailing cultural values, social trends, and political forces, as well as scientific knowledge (Kutchins & Kirk, 1997; Mechanic, 1999).

These realities are readily apparent if you consider how psychiatric views of homosexuality have changed over time. Homosexuality used to be listed as a sexual disorder in the American Psychiatric Association's diagnostic system (which we will discuss shortly). Because homosexuality was viewed as pathological, many gays were coaxed or coerced into therapeutic treatments for their "disorder" that often proved demeaning or harmful (Smith, Bartlett, & King, 2004). However, in 1973 a committee appointed by the American Psychiatric Association voted to delete homosexuality from the official list of psychological disorders. This action occurred for several reasons (Bayer, 1987; Forstein, 2004; Rothblum, Solomon, & Albee, 1986). First, attitudes toward homosexuality in our society had become more tolerant. Second, gay rights activists campaigned vigorously for the change. Third, research showed that gays and heterosexuals were indistinguishable on measures of psychological health. Although this long-overdue decision was informed by scientific findings, it was also influenced by political lobbying and shifts in social values.

Antonyms such as *normal* versus *abnormal* and *mental health* versus *mental illness* imply that people can be divided neatly into two distinct groups: those who are normal and those who are not. In reality, it is often difficult to draw a line that clearly separates normality from abnormality. On occasion, everyone experiences personal distress. Everybody acts in deviant ways once in a while. And

Web Link 15.1 **Psych Central**

The work of John Grohol, Psych Central is arguably the premier site on the web for all aspects of mental health, including psychological disorders and treatment, professional issues, and information for mental health care consumers. This site offers nearly 2,000 annotated listings to information sources.

everyone displays some maladaptive behavior. People are judged to have psychological disorders only when their behavior becomes *extremely* deviant, maladaptive, or distressing. Thus, normality and abnormality exist on a continuum. It's a matter of degree, not an either-or proposition (see **Figure 15.2**).

Psychodiagnosis: The Classification of Disorders

Obviously, we cannot lump all psychological disorders together without giving up all hope of understanding them better. A sound taxonomy of mental disorders can facilitate empirical research and enhance communication among scientists and clinicians (First, 2003; Zimmerman & Spitzer, 2005). Hence, a great deal of effort has been invested in devising an elaborate system for classifying psychological disorders.

Guidelines for psychodiagnosis were extremely vague and informal prior to 1952, when the American Psychiatric Association unveiled its *Diagnostic and Statistical Manual of Mental Disorders* (Nathan & Langenbucher, 2003). This classification scheme described about 100 disorders. Revisions intended to improve the system were incorporated into the second edition (DSM-II) published in 1968, but the diagnostic guidelines were still pretty sketchy. However, the third edition (DSM-III), published in 1980, represented a

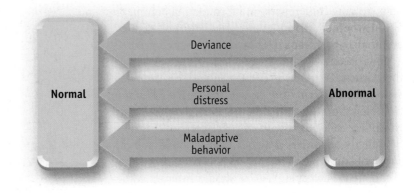

Figure 15.2

Normality and abnormality as a continuum. No sharp boundary divides normal and abnormal behavior. Behavior is normal or abnormal in degree, depending on the extent to which it is deviant, personally distressing, or maladaptive.

major advance, as the diagnostic criteria were made much more explicit, concrete, and detailed to facilitate more consistent diagnoses across clinicians (Blacker & Tsuang, 1999). The current, fourth edition (DSM-IV), released in 1994 and revised slightly in 2000, made use of intervening research to refine the criteria introduced in DSM-III. Each revision of the DSM system has expanded the list of disorders covered. The current version describes about three times as many types of psychological disorders as the original DSM (Houts, 2002).

The publication of DSM-III in 1980 introduced a new multiaxial system of classification, which asks for judgments about individuals on five separate dimensions, or "axes." **Figure 15.3** provides an overview of the entire system and the five axes. The diagnoses of disorders are made on Axes I and II. Clinicians record most types of disorders on Axis I. They use Axis II to list long-running personality disorders or mental retardation. People may receive diagnoses on both Axes I and II.

The remaining axes are used to record supplemental information. A patient's physical disorders are listed on Axis III (General Medical Conditions). On Axis IV (Psychosocial and Environmental Problems), the clinician makes notations regarding the types of stress experienced by the individual in the past year. On Axis V (Global Assessment of Functioning), estimates are made of the individual's current level of adaptive functioning (in social and occupational behavior, viewed as a whole) and of the individual's highest level of functioning in the past year. Most theorists agree that the multiaxial system is a step in the right direction because it recognizes the importance of information besides a traditional diagnostic label.

Work is currently underway to formulate the next edition (DSM-V) of the diagnostic system (e.g., Banzato, 2004; Spitzer, First, & Wakefield, 2007; Widiger & Simonsen, 2005), which is tentatively scheduled for publication in 2011. Clinical researchers are collecting data, holding conferences, and formulating arguments about whether various syndromes should be added, eliminated, or renamed. Should complicated grief reactions become a standard diagnostic option (Lichtenthal, Cruess, & Prigerson, 2004)? Should the diagnostic system use the term drug *dependence* or drug *addiction* (O'Brien, Volkow, & Li, 2006)? Should pathological gambling be lumped with impulse-control disorders or addictive disorders (Potenza, 2006)? Should the category of somatoform disorders (see pp. 489–491) be eliminated (Fava et al., 2007)? Should Internet addiction be added to the official list of disorders (Sandoz, 2004)? Vigorous debates about issues such as these will occupy clinical researchers in the upcoming years, and DSM-V may look somewhat different from its predecessors.

The Prevalence of Psychological Disorders

How common are psychological disorders? What percentage of the population is afflicted with mental illness? Is it 10%? Perhaps 25%? Could the figure range as high as 40% or 50%?

Such estimates fall in the domain of *epidemiology—the study of the distribution of mental or physical disorders in a population.* In epidemiology, *prevalence refers to the percentage of a population that exhibits a disorder during a specified time period.* In the case of mental disorders, the most interesting data are the estimates of *lifetime prevalence,* the percentage of people having a specific disorder at any time in their lives.

Studies published in the 1980s and early 1990s found psychological disorders in roughly *one-third* of the population (Regier & Kaelber, 1995; Robins, Locke, & Regier, 1991). Subsequent research, which focused on a somewhat younger sample (ages 18–54 instead of over age 18), suggested that about 44% of the adult population will struggle with some sort of psychological disorder at some point in their lives (Kessler & Zhao, 1999; Regier & Burke, 2000). The most recent large-scale epidemiological study estimated the lifetime risk of a psychiatric disorder to be 51% (Kessler et al., 2005a). Obviously, all these figures are *estimates* that depend to some extent on the sampling methods and assessment techniques used (Wakefield, 1999).

The progressively higher estimates in recent years have begun to generate some controversy in the field. Some experts believe that recent estimates are implausibly high and that they may trivialize psychiatric diagnoses (Wakefield & Spitzer, 2002). Characterizing someone as mentally ill doesn't mean much if the label is applicable to half of the population. The debate centers on where to draw the line between normal difficulties in functioning and full-fledged mental illness—that is, when do symptoms qualify as a disease (Regier, Narrow, & Rae, 2004)? Critics of the recent high estimates argue that they include many people whose problems have little clinical significance—in other words, their problems don't require treatment (Narrow et al., 2002). Those who defend the recent research argue that it

---

Web Link 15.2 **NAMI: The National Alliance for the Mentally Ill**

Professional and lay evaluators have consistently found NAMI among the most helpful and informative organizations dealing with the entire spectrum of mental disorders, including schizophrenia and depression. The NAMI site offers a particularly rich array of information on specific mental disorders and on how patients and their families can find support.

Axis I
Clinical Syndromes

1. *Disorders usually first diagnosed in infancy, childhood, or adolescence*
   This category includes disorders that arise before adolescence, such as attention deficit disorders, autism, mental retardation, enuresis, and stuttering.

2. *Organic mental disorders*
   These disorders are temporary or permanent dysfunctions of brain tissue caused by diseases or chemicals. Examples are delirium, dementia, and amnesia.

3. *Substance-related disorders*
   This category refers to the maladaptive use of drugs and alcohol. Mere consumption and recreational use of such substances are not disorders. This category requires a maladaptive pattern of use, as with alcohol abuse and cocaine dependence.

4. *Schizophrenia and other psychotic disorders*
   The schizophrenias are characterized by psychotic symptoms (for example, grossly disorganized behavior, delusions, and hallucinations) and by over 6 months of behavioral deterioration. This category also includes delusional disorder and schizoaffective disorder.

5. *Mood disorders*
   The cardinal feature is emotional disturbance. Patients may, or may not, have psychotic symptoms. These disorders include major depression, bipolar disorder, dysthymic disorder, and cyclothymic disorder.

6. *Anxiety disorders*
   These disorders are characterized by physiological signs of anxiety (for example, palpitations) and subjective feelings of tension, apprehension, or fear. Anxiety may be acute and focused (panic disorder) or continual and diffuse (generalized anxiety disorder).

7. *Somatoform disorders*
   These disorders are dominated by somatic symptoms that resemble physical illnesses. These symptoms cannot be accounted for by organic damage. There must also be strong evidence that these symptoms are produced by psychological factors or conflicts. This category includes somatization, conversion disorder, and hypochondriasis.

8. *Dissociative disorders*
   These disorders all feature a sudden, temporary alteration or dysfunction of memory, consciousness, identity, and behavior, as in dissociative amnesia and multiple personality.

9. *Sexual and gender-identity disorders*
   There are three basic types of disorders in this category: gender identity disorders (discomfort with identity as male or female), paraphilias (preference for unusual acts to achieve sexual arousal), and sexual dysfunctions (impairments in sexual functioning).

Axis II
Personality Disorders

These disorders are patterns of personality traits that are longstanding, maladaptive, and inflexible and involve impaired functioning or subjective distress. Examples include borderline, schizoid, and antisocial personality disorders.

Axis III
General Medical Conditions

Physical disorders or conditions are recorded on this axis. Examples include diabetes, arthritis, and hemophilia.

Axis IV
Psychosocial and Environmental Problems

Axis IV is for reporting psychosocial and environmental problems that may affect the diagnosis, treatment, and prognosis of mental disorders (Axes I and II). A psychosocial or environmental problem may be a negative life event, an environmental difficulty or deficiency, a familial or other interpersonal stress, an inadequacy of social support or personal resources, or another problem that describes the context in which a person's difficulties have developed.

Axis V
Global Assessment of Functioning (GAF) Scale

Code	Symptoms
100	Superior functioning in a wide range of activities
90	Absent or minimal symptoms, good functioning in all areas
80	Symptoms transient and expectable reactions to psychosocial stressors
70	Some mild symptoms or some difficulty in social, occupational, or school functioning, but generally functioning pretty well
60	Moderate symptoms or difficulty in social, occupational, or school functioning
50	Serious symptoms or impairment in social, occupational, or school functioning
40	Some impairment in reality testing or communication or major impairment in family relations, judgment, thinking, or mood
30	Behavior considerably influenced by delusions or hallucinations, serious impairment in communication or judgment, or inability to function in almost all areas
20	Some danger of hurting self or others, occasional failure to maintain minimal personal hygiene, or gross impairment in communication
10	Persistent danger of severely hurting self or others
1	

Figure 15.3

Overview of the DSM diagnostic system. Published by the American Psychiatric Association, the *Diagnostic and Statistical Manual of Mental Disorders* is the formal classification system used in the diagnosis of psychological disorders. It is a *multiaxial* system, which means that information is recorded on the five axes described here.

Adapted with permission from the *Diagnostic and Statistical Manual of Mental Disorders,* 4th ed. *Text revision.* Copyright © 2000 American Psychiatric Association.

makes sense to count people with mild disorders because mild disorders often progress into more severe disorders and this progression might be prevented by early diagnosis and intervention (Kessler et al., 2003). The outcome of this debate is difficult to predict, as both points of view have merit.

In any event, whether one goes with conservative or liberal estimates, the prevalence of psychological disorders is quite a bit higher than most people assume. The data that yielded the 44% estimate of total lifetime prevalence are summarized in **Figure 15.4**, which shows prevalence estimates for the most common classes of disorders. As you can see, the most common types of psychological disorders are (1) substance (alcohol and drugs) use disorders, (2) anxiety disorders, and (3) mood disorders.

We are now ready to start examining the specific types of psychological disorders. Obviously, we cannot cover all of the diverse disorders listed in DSM-IV. However, we will introduce most of the major categories of disorders to give you an overview of the many forms abnormal behavior takes. In discussing each set of disorders, we begin with brief descriptions of the specific syndromes or subtypes that fall in the category. Then we focus on the *etiology* of the disorders in that category. Although many paths can lead to specific disorders, some are more common than others. We highlight some of the common paths in order to enhance your understanding of the roots of abnormal behavior.

Recommended
READING

The Burden of Sympathy: How Families Cope with Mental Illness
by David A. Karp
(Oxford University Press, 2001)

Although psychological disorders are quite common, they remain shrouded in mystery. Mental illness is not a topic that people want to talk about, and little advice is available for the families of people suffering from psychological disorders. Nevertheless, millions of people are troubled by severe disorders such as schizophrenia and bipolar disorder, so millions of families must struggle with these trying and difficult afflictions. This book thus fills an important need. Based on extensive interviews, Karp, a sociologist, discusses the devastating effects that mental illness can have on patients' families and how they deal with these effects. Although this is not a "how to" manual, it includes many useful insights about the mental health system and a good deal of concrete, realistic advice. Other worthwhile books intended for families of psychiatric patients include *How to Cope with Mental Illness in Your Family: A Self-Care Guide for Offspring and Parents* (Marsh & Dickens, 1997) and *When Someone You Love Has a Mental Illness: A Handbook for Family, Friends, and Caregivers* (Woolis, 1992).

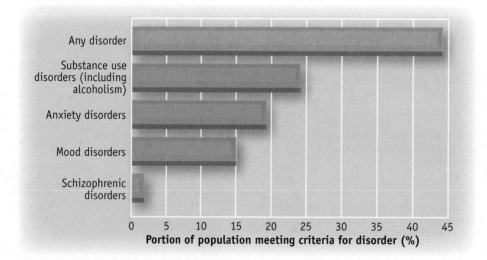

Figure 15.4

Lifetime prevalence of psychological disorders. The estimated percentage of people who have, at any time in their life, suffered from one of four types of psychological disorders or from a disorder of any kind (top bar) is shown here. Prevalence estimates vary somewhat from one study to the next, depending on the exact methods used in sampling and assessment. The estimates shown here are based on pooling data from Waves 1 and 2 of the Epidemiological Catchment Area studies and the National Comorbidity Study, as summarized by Regier and Burke (2000) and Dew, Bromet, and Switzer (2000). These studies, which collectively evaluated over 28,000 subjects, provide the best data to date on the prevalence of mental illness in the United States.

Anxiety Disorders

LEARNING OBJECTIVES
▶ List and describe four types of anxiety disorders.
▶ Discuss the contribution of biological factors and conditioning to the etiology of anxiety disorders.
▶ Explain the contribution of cognitive factors and stress to the etiology of anxiety disorders.

Everyone experiences anxiety from time to time. It is a natural and common reaction to many of life's difficulties. For some people, however, anxiety becomes a chronic problem. These people experience high levels of anxiety with disturbing regularity. ***Anxiety disorders are a class of disorders marked by feelings of excessive apprehension and anxiety.*** There are four principal types of anxiety disorders: generalized anxiety disorder, phobic disorder, obsessive-compulsive disorder, and panic disorder. They are not mutually exclusive, as many people who develop one anxiety syndrome often suffer from another at some point in their lives (Merikangas, 2005).

Generalized Anxiety Disorder

The *generalized anxiety disorder* is marked by a chronic, high level of anxiety that is not tied to any specific threat. People with this disorder worry constantly about yesterday's mistakes and tomorrow's problems. They worry excessively about minor matters related to family, finances, work, and personal illness (Sanderson & Barlow, 1990). In particular, they worry about how much they worry (Barlow et al., 2003). Their anxiety is frequently accompanied by physical symptoms, such as muscle tension, diarrhea, dizziness, faintness, sweating, and heart palpitations. Generalized anxiety disorder tends to have a gradual onset, has a lifetime prevalence of about 5%, and is seen more frequently in females than males (Brown, 1999; Merikangas, 2005).

Phobic Disorder

In a phobic disorder, an individual's troublesome anxiety has a specific focus. **A *phobic disorder* is marked by a persistent and irrational fear of an object or situation that presents no realistic danger.** Although mild phobias are extremely common, people are said to have a phobic disorder only when their fears seriously interfere with their everyday behavior. Phobic reactions tend to be accompanied by physical symptoms of anxiety, such as trembling and palpitations (Rapee & Barlow, 2001). The following case provides an example of a phobic disorder:

Hilda is 32 years of age and has a rather unusual fear. She is terrified of snow. She cannot go outside in the snow.

She cannot even stand to see snow or hear about it on the weather report. Her phobia severely constricts her day-to-day behavior. Probing in therapy revealed that her phobia was caused by a traumatic experience at age 11. Playing at a ski lodge, she was buried briefly by a small avalanche of snow. She had no recollection of this experience until it was recovered in therapy. (Adapted from Laughlin, 1967, p. 227)

As Hilda's unusual snow phobia illustrates, people can develop phobic responses to virtually anything. Nonetheless, certain types of phobias are relatively common, as the data in **Figure 15.5** (on the next page) show. Particularly common are acrophobia (fear of heights), claustrophobia (fear of small, enclosed places), brontophobia (fear of storms), hydrophobia (fear of water), and various animal and insect phobias (Antony & McCabe, 2003). People troubled by phobias typically realize that their fears are irrational, but they still are unable to calm themselves when they encounter a phobic object.

Panic Disorder and Agoraphobia

A *panic disorder* is characterized by recurrent attacks of overwhelming anxiety that usually occur suddenly and unexpectedly. These paralyzing attacks are accompanied by physical symptoms of anxiety. After a number of anxiety attacks, victims often become apprehensive, wondering when their next panic attack will occur. Their concern about exhibiting panic in public sometimes escalates to the point where they are afraid to leave home. This creates a condition called *agoraphobia.*

***Agoraphobia* is a fear of going out to public places** (its literal meaning is "fear of the marketplace or open places"). Because of this fear, some people become prisoners confined to their homes, although many can venture out if accompanied by a trusted companion (Hollander & Simeon, 2003). As its name suggests, agoraphobia has traditionally been viewed as a phobic disorder. However, more recent evidence suggests that agoraphobia is mainly a complication of panic disorder. About two-thirds of people who suffer from panic disorder are female (Horwath & Weissman, 2000). The onset of panic disorder typically occurs during late adolescence or early adulthood (Pine & McClure, 2005a).

Figure 15.5

Common phobias. Frequently reported phobias are listed here, along with their typical age of onset and information on gender differences in phobias.

From Marks, I. M. (1969). *Fears and phobias.* San Diego: Academic Press. Copyright 1969 by Isaac Marks. Reprinted by permission.

Common Phobias

	Percent of all phobias	Gender difference	Typical age of onset
Agoraphobia (fear of places of assembly, crowds, open spaces)	10%–50%	Large majority are women	Early adulthood
Social phobia (fear of being observed doing something humiliating)	10%	Majority are women	Adolescence
Specific phobias *Animals* Cats (ailurophobia) Dogs (cynophobia) Insects (insectophobia) Spiders (arachnophobia) Birds (avisophobia) Horses (equinophobia) Snakes (ophidiophobia) Rodents (rodentophobia)	5%–15%	Vast majority are women	Childhood
Inanimate objects Dirt (mysophobia) Storms (brontophobia) Heights (acrophobia) Darkness (nyctophobia) Closed spaces (claustrophobia)	20%	None	Any age
Illness-injury (nosophobia) Death (thanatophobia) Cancer (cancerophobia) Venereal disease (venerophobia)	15%–25%	None	Middle age

Cartoon by Harris © 1990. Reprinted by permission of ScienceCartoonsPlus.com.

Obsessive-Compulsive Disorder

Obsessions are *thoughts* that repeatedly intrude on one's consciousness in a distressing way. Compulsions are *actions* that one feels forced to carry out. Thus, **an obsessive-compulsive disorder (OCD) is marked by persistent, uncontrollable intrusions of unwanted thoughts (obsessions) and urges to engage in senseless rituals (compulsions).** To illustrate, let's examine the bizarre behavior of a man once reputed to be the wealthiest person in the world:

The famous industrialist Howard Hughes was obsessed with the possibility of being contaminated by germs. This led him to devise extraordinary rituals to minimize the possibility of such contamination. He would spend hours methodically cleaning a single telephone. He once wrote a three-page memo instructing assistants on exactly how to open cans of fruit for him. The following is just a small portion of the instructions that Hughes provided for a driver who delivered films to his bungalow. "Get out of the car on the traffic side. Do not at any time be on the side of the car between the car and the curb. . . . Carry only one can of film at a time. Step over the gutter opposite the place where the sidewalk dead-ends into the curb from a point as far out into the center of the road as possible. Do not ever walk on the grass at all, also do not step into the gutter at all. Walk to the bungalow keeping as near to the center of the sidewalk as possible." (Adapted from Barlett & Steele, 1979, pp. 227–237)

Obsessions often center on fear of contamination, inflicting harm on others, suicide, or sexual acts. Compulsions usually involve stereotyped rituals that temporarily relieve anxiety. Common examples include constant handwashing; repetitive cleaning of things that are already clean; endless rechecking of locks, faucets, and such; and excessive arranging, counting, and hoarding of things (Pato, Eisen, & Phillips, 2003). Specific types of obsessions tend to be associated with specific types of compulsions. For example, obsessions about contamination tend to be paired with cleaning compulsions, and obsessions about symmetry tend to be paired with ordering and arranging compulsions (Leckman et al., 1997). Although many of us can be compulsive at times, full-fledged obsessive-compulsive disorders occur in roughly 2.5% of the population

Repetitive handwashing is an example of a common compulsive behavior.

(Turner et al., 2001). The typical age of onset for OCD is late adolescence, with most cases (75%) emerging before the age of 30 (Kessler et al., 2005a). OCD can be a particularly debilitating disorder, as it is often associated with severe social and occupational impairments (Torres et al., 2006).

Etiology of Anxiety Disorders

Like most psychological disorders, anxiety disorders develop out of complicated interactions among a variety of factors. Conditioning and learning appear especially important, but biological factors may also contribute to anxiety disorders.

Biological Factors

Recent studies suggest that there may be a weak to moderate genetic predisposition to anxiety disorders, depending on the specific type of disorder (Hettema, Neale, & Kendler, 2001; McMahon & Kassem, 2005). These findings are consistent with the idea that inherited differences in temperament might make some people more vulnerable than others to anxiety disorders. Kagan and his colleagues (1992) have found that about 15%–20% of infants display an *inhibited temperament*, characterized by shyness, timidity, and wariness, which appears to have a strong genetic basis. Research suggests that this temperament is a risk factor for the

development of anxiety disorders (Coles, Schofield, & Pietrefesa, 2006).

One influential theory holds that *anxiety sensitivity* may make people vulnerable to anxiety disorders (McWilliams et al., 2007; Reiss, 1991; Schmidt, Zvolensky, & Maner, 2006). According to this notion, some people are very sensitive to internal physiological symptoms of anxiety and are prone to overreact with fear when they experience these symptoms. Anxiety sensitivity may fuel an inflationary spiral in which anxiety breeds more anxiety, which eventually spins out of control in the form of an anxiety disorder.

Recent evidence suggests that a link may exist between anxiety disorders and neurochemical activity in the brain. **Neurotransmitters are chemicals that carry signals from one neuron to another.** Therapeutic drugs (such as Valium) that reduce excessive anxiety appear to alter activity at synapses for a neurotransmitter called GABA. This finding and other lines of evidence suggest that disturbances in the neural circuits using GABA may play a role in some types of anxiety disorders (Skolnick, 2003). Abnormalities in other neural circuits using the transmitter serotonin have been implicated in panic and obsessive-compulsive disorders (Sullivan & Coplan, 2000). Thus, scientists are beginning to unravel the neurochemical bases for anxiety disorders.

Conditioning and Learning

Many anxiety responses may be *acquired through classical conditioning* and *maintained through operant conditioning* (see Chapter 2). According to Mowrer (1947), an originally neutral stimulus (the snow in Hilda's case, for instance) may be paired with a frightening event (the avalanche) so that it becomes a conditioned stimulus eliciting anxiety (see **Figure 15.6** on the next page). Once a fear is acquired through classical conditioning, the person may start avoiding the anxiety-producing stimulus. The avoidance response is negatively reinforced because it is followed by a reduction in anxiety. This process involves operant conditioning (also shown in **Figure 15.6**). Thus, separate conditioning processes may create and then sustain specific anxiety responses (Levis, 1989). Consistent with this view, studies find that a substantial portion of people suffering from phobias can identify a traumatic conditioning experience that probably contributed to their anxiety disorder (Antony & McCabe, 2003; King, Eleonora, & Ollendick, 1998).

The tendency to develop phobias of certain types of objects and situations may be explained by Martin Seligman's (1971) concept of *preparedness*. Like many theorists, Seligman believes that classical conditioning creates most phobic responses. *However, he suggests that people are biologically prepared by their evolutionary history to acquire some fears much more easily than*

Figure 15.6

Conditioning as an explanation for phobias. (1) Many phobias appear to be acquired through classical conditioning when a neutral stimulus is paired with an anxiety-arousing stimulus. (2) Once acquired, a phobia may be maintained through operant conditioning, because avoidance of the phobic stimulus leads to a reduction in anxiety, resulting in negative reinforcement.

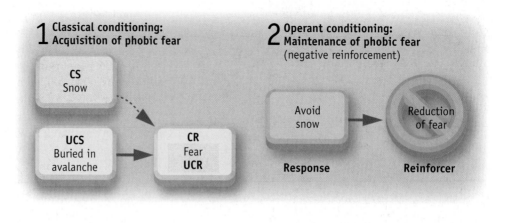

1 Classical conditioning: Acquisition of phobic fear

CS — Snow

UCS — Buried in avalanche

CR — Fear UCR

2 Operant conditioning: Maintenance of phobic fear (negative reinforcement)

Avoid snow — **Response**

Reduction of fear — **Reinforcer**

---

others. His theory would explain why people develop phobias of ancient sources of threat (such as snakes and spiders) much more readily than modern sources of threat (such as electrical outlets or hot irons). Some laboratory studies have yielded evidence consistent with the idea that we are wired by evolution to readily develop certain conditioned fears, but the evidence is inconsistent (Ohman & Mineka, 2003; Rapee & Barlow, 2001).

There are a number of problems with conditioning models of phobias (Rachman, 1990). For instance, many people with phobias cannot recall or identify a traumatic conditioning experience that led to their phobia. Conversely, many people endure extremely traumatic experiences that should create a phobia but do not. To provide better explanations for these complexities, conditioning models of anxiety disorders are currently being revised to include a larger role for cognitive factors (de Jong & Merckelbach, 2000).

Cognitive Factors

Cognitive theorists maintain that certain styles of thinking make some people particularly vulnerable to anxiety disorders. According to these theorists, some people are prone to suffer from problems with anxiety because they tend to (a) misinterpret harmless situations as threatening, (b) focus excessive attention on perceived threats, and (c) selectively recall information that seems threatening (Beck, 1997; McNally, 1994, 1996). In one intriguing test of the cognitive view, anxious and nonanxious subjects were asked to read 32 sentences that could be interpreted in either a threatening or a nonthreatening manner (Eysenck et al., 1991). For instance, one such sentence was "The doctor examined little Emma's growth," which could mean that the doctor checked her height or the growth of a tumor. As **Figure 15.7** shows, the anx-

Web Link 15.3 **National Institute of Mental Health: For the Public**

A wealth of information on psychological disorders is available at this subpage of the U.S. National Institute of Mental Health's massive website. Visitors will find detailed online booklets on generalized anxiety disorder, obsessive-compulsive disorder, panic disorder, depression, bipolar disorder, and so forth. Brief fact sheets, dense technical reports, and many other resources are also available.

ious subjects interpreted the sentences in a threatening way more often than the nonanxious subjects did. Thus, the cognitive view holds that some people are prone to anxiety disorders because they see threat in every corner of their lives (Aikens & Craske, 2001; Riskind, 2005).

Figure 15.7

Cognitive factors in anxiety disorders. Eysenck and his colleagues (1991) compared how subjects with anxiety disorders and nonanxious subjects tended to interpret sentences that could be viewed as threatening or nonthreatening. Consistent with cognitive models of anxiety disorders, anxious subjects were more likely to interpret the sentences in a threatening light.

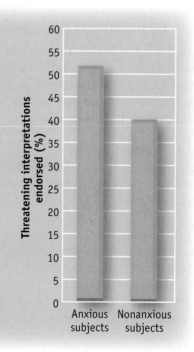

Threatening interpretations endorsed (%)

Anxious subjects — Nonanxious subjects

Stress

Finally, studies have supported the long-held suspicion that anxiety disorders are stress related (Sandin et al., 2004; Venturello et al., 2002). For instance, Faravelli and Pallanti (1989) found that patients with panic disorder had experienced a dramatic increase in stress in the month prior to the onset of their disorder. In another study, Brown et al. (1998) found an association between stress and the development of social phobia. Thus, there is reason to believe that high stress often helps precipitate the onset of anxiety disorders.

Somatoform Disorders

LEARNING OBJECTIVES

▶ Describe three types of somatoform disorders.
▶ Summarize what is known about the causes of somatoform disorders.

Chances are, you have met people who always seem to be complaining about aches, pains, and physical maladies of doubtful authenticity. When physical illness appears *largely* psychological in origin, people are said to suffer from somatoform disorders. *Somatoform disorders* **are physical ailments that cannot be fully explained by organic conditions and are largely due to psychological factors.** Although their symptoms are more imaginary than real, victims of somatoform disorders are *not* simply faking illness. Deliberate feigning of illness for personal gain is another matter altogether, called *malingering*.

People with somatoform disorders typically seek treatment from physicians practicing neurology, internal medicine, or family medicine, instead of from psychologists or psychiatrists. Making accurate diagnoses of somatoform disorders can be difficult, because the causes of physical ailments are sometimes hard to identify. In some cases, a problem is misdiagnosed as a somatoform disorder when a genuine organic cause for a person's physical symptoms goes undetected despite medical examinations and tests (Yutzy, 2003). Diagnostic ambiguities such as these have led some theorists to argue that the category of somatoform disorders should be eliminated in DSM-V (Mayou et al., 2005), but other theorists have expressed vigorous disagreement (Rief, Henningsen, & Hiller, 2006). In this section, we will look at three specific types of somatoform disorders: somatization disorder, conversion disorder, and hypochondriasis.

Somatization Disorder

Individuals with somatization disorders are often said to "cling to ill health." A *somatization disorder* **is marked by a history of diverse physical complaints that appear to be psychological in origin.** Somatization disorder occurs mostly in women (Guggenheim, 2000) and often coexists with depression or anxiety disorders (Gureje et al., 1997). Victims report an endless succession of minor physical ailments that seem to wax and wane in response to the stress in their lives (Servan-Schreiber, Kolb, & Tabas, 1999). They usually have a long and complicated history of medical treatment from many doctors. The distinguishing feature of this disorder is the diversity of victims' physical complaints. Over the years, they report a mixed bag of cardiovascular, gastrointestinal, pulmonary, neurological, and genitourinary symptoms. The unlikely nature of such a mixture of symptoms occurring together often alerts a physician to the possible psychological basis for the patient's problems. However, somatization patients are typically resistant to the suggestion that their symptoms might be the result of psychological distress (Hollifield, 2005).

Conversion Disorder

Conversion disorder **is characterized by a significant loss of physical function with no apparent organic basis, usually in a single organ system.** Common symptoms include partial or complete loss of vision, partial or complete loss of hearing, partial paralysis, severe laryngitis or mutism, seizures, vomiting, and loss of feeling or function in limbs, such as that seen in the following case:

Mildred was a rancher's daughter who lost the use of both of her legs during adolescence. Mildred was at home alone one afternoon when a male relative attempted to assault her. She screamed for help, and her legs gave way as she slipped to the floor. She was found on the floor a few minutes later when her mother returned home. She could not get up, so she was carried to her bed. Her legs buckled when she made subsequent attempts to walk on her own. Due to her illness, she was waited on hand and foot by her family and friends. Neighbors brought her homemade things to eat or to wear. She became the center of attention in the household. (Adapted from Cameron, 1963, pp. 312–313)

People with conversion disorder are usually troubled by more severe ailments than people with somatization disorder. In some cases of conversion disorder, there are telltale clues about the psychological origins of the illness because the patient's symptoms are not consistent with medical knowledge about their apparent disease. For instance, the loss of feeling in one hand that is seen in "glove anesthesia" is inconsistent with the known facts of neurological organization (see **Figure 15.8**).

Hypochondriasis

Hypochondriacs constantly monitor their physical condition, looking for signs of illness. Any tiny alteration from their physical norm leads them to conclude that they have contracted a disease. **Hypochondriasis (more widely known as *hypochondria*) is characterized by excessive preoccupation with health concerns and incessant worry about developing physical illnesses.** The following case illustrates the nature of hypochondria:

Jeff is a middle-aged man who works as a clerk in a drug store. He spends long hours describing his health problems to anyone who will listen. Jeff is an avid reader of popular magazine articles on medicine. He can tell you all about the latest medical discoveries. He takes all sorts of pills and vitamins to ward off possible illnesses. He's the first to try every new product on the market. Jeff is constantly afflicted by new symptoms of illness. His most recent problems were poor digestion and a heartbeat that he thought was irregular. He frequently goes to physicians who can find nothing wrong with him physically. They tell him that he is healthy. He thinks they use "backward techniques." He suspects that his illness is too rare to be diagnosed successfully. (Adapted from Suinn, 1984, p. 236)

When hypochondriacs are assured by their physician that they do not have any real illness, they often are skeptical and disbelieving (Starcevic, 2001). As in Jeff's case, they frequently assume that the physician must be incompetent, and they go shopping for another doctor. Hypochondriacs don't subjectively suffer from physical distress as much as they overinterpret every conceivable sign of illness. Hypochondria frequently appears alongside other psychological disorders, especially anxiety disorders and depression (Iezzi, Duckworth, & Adams, 2001). For example, Howard Hughes's obsessive-compulsive disorder was coupled with profound hypochondria.

Etiology of Somatoform Disorders

Inherited aspects of physiological functioning that promote anxiety reactions may predispose some people to

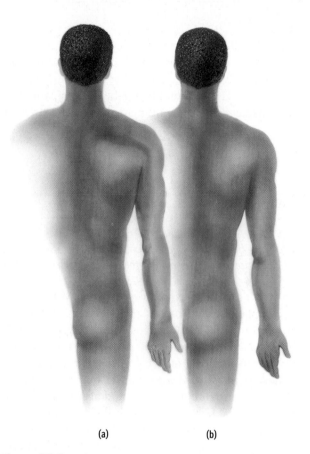

(a)   (b)

Figure 15.8

Glove anesthesia. In conversion disorders, the physical complaints are sometimes inconsistent with the known facts of physiology. Such is the case in *glove anesthesia,* in which the patient complains of losing feeling in a hand. Given the patterns of nerve distribution in the arm shown in **(a)**, a loss of feeling in the hand exclusively as shown in **(b)** is a physical impossibility, indicating that the patient's problem is psychological in origin.

somatoform disorders, but genetic factors do *not* appear to make much of a contribution to the development of these disorders (Hollifield, 2005). The available evidence suggests that these disorders are largely a function of personality and learning.

Personality Factors

People with certain types of personality traits seem to be particularly prone to develop somatoform disorders. The prime candidates appear to be people with *histrionic* personality characteristics (Nemiah, 1985; Slavney, 1990). The histrionic personality tends to be self-centered, suggestible, excitable, highly emotional, and overly dramatic. Such people thrive on the attention that they get when they become ill. The personality trait of *neuroticism* also seems to elevate individuals' susceptibility to somatoform disorders (Noyes et al., 2005). Research also suggests that the pathological care-seeking behavior seen in these disorders may be caused by *insecure attachment styles* (see Chapter 8)

"THE WAY HE MOANS AND GROANS WHEN HE GETS A LITTLE COLD... I CAN'T DECIDE WHETHER HE SHOULD CALL A DOCTOR OR A DRAMA CRITIC."

Reprinted by permission of Edgar Argo.

that are rooted in early experiences with caregivers (Noyes et al., 2003).

Cognitive Factors

In recent years, theorists have devoted increased attention to how cognitive peculiarities might contribute to somatoform disorders. For example, Barsky (2001) asserts that some people focus excessive attention on their internal physiological processes and amplify normal bodily sensations into symptoms of distress, which lead them to pursue unnecessary medical treatment. Recent evidence suggests that people with somatoform disorders tend to draw catastrophic conclusions about minor bodily complaints (Salkovskis & War-

wick, 2001). They also seem to apply a faulty standard of good health, equating health with a complete absence of symptoms and discomfort, which is unrealistic (Barsky et al., 1993).

The Sick Role

As we discussed in Chapter 14, some people grow fond of the role associated with being sick (Hotopf, 2004; Pilowsky, 1993). Their complaints of physical symptoms may be reinforced by indirect benefits derived from their illness (Schwartz, Slater, & Birchler, 1994). One payoff is that becoming ill is a superb way to avoid having to confront life's challenges. Many people with somatoform disorders are avoiding facing up to marital problems, career frustrations, family responsibilities, and the like. After all, when you're sick, others cannot place great demands on you. Another benefit is that physical problems can provide a convenient excuse when people fail, or worry about failing, in endeavors that are critical to their self-esteem (Organista & Miranda, 1991).

Attention from others is another payoff that may reinforce complaints of physical illness. When people become ill, they command the attention of family, friends, co-workers, neighbors, and doctors. The sympathy that illness often brings may strengthen the person's tendency to feel ill. This clearly occurred in Mildred's case of conversion disorder. Her illness paid handsome dividends in terms of attention, consolation, and kindhearted assistance from others.

Dissociative Disorders

LEARNING OBJECTIVES

▶ Describe three types of dissociative disorders.
▶ Summarize what is known about the causes of dissociative disorders.

Dissociative disorders are probably the most controversial set of disorders in the diagnostic system, sparking heated debate among normally subdued researchers and clinicians (Loewenstein & Putnam 2005). *Dissociative disorders* **are a class of disorders in which people lose contact with portions of their consciousness or memory, resulting in disruptions in their sense of identity.** Here we describe three dissociative syndromes—dissociative amnesia, dissociative fugue, and dissociative identity disorder—all of which are relatively uncommon.

Dissociative Amnesia and Fugue

Dissociative amnesia and fugue are overlapping disorders characterized by serious memory deficits. *Dissociative amnesia* **is a sudden loss of memory for**

important personal information that is too extensive to be due to normal forgetting. Memory losses may occur for a single traumatic event (such as an automobile accident or home fire) or for an extended period of time surrounding the event. Cases of amnesia have been observed after people have experienced disasters, accidents, combat stress, physical abuse, and rape, or after they have witnessed the violent death of a parent, among other things (Arrigo & Pezdek, 1997; Loewenstein, 1996). **In** *dissociative fugue,* **people lose their memory for their sense of personal identity.** Having forgotten their name, their family, where they live, and where they work, these people typically wander away from their home area. In spite of this wholesale forgetting, they remember matters unrelated to their identity, such as how to drive a car and how to do math.

Dissociative Identity Disorder

Dissociative identity disorder (DID) **involves the co-existence in one person of two or more largely complete, and usually very different, personalities.** The name for this disorder used to be *multiple personality disorder,* which still enjoys informal usage. In dissociative identity disorder, the divergences in behavior go far beyond those that people normally display in adapting to different roles in life. People with "multiple personalities" feel that they have more than one identity. Each personality has his or her own name, memories, traits, and physical mannerisms. Although rare, this "Dr. Jekyll and Mr. Hyde" syndrome is frequently portrayed in novels, movies, and television shows. In popular media portrayals, the syndrome is often mistakenly called *schizophrenia.* As you will see later, schizophrenic disorders are entirely different and do not involve "split personality."

In dissociative identity disorder, the various personalities generally report that they are unaware of each other (Eich et al., 1997), although doubts have been raised about the accuracy of this assertion (Allen & Iacono, 2001). The alternate personalities commonly display traits that are quite foreign to the original personality. For instance, a shy, inhibited person might develop a flamboyant, extraverted alternate personality. Transitions between identities often occur suddenly. The disparities between identities can be bizarre, as personalities may assert that they are different in age, race, gender, and sexual orientation (Kluft, 1996). Dissociative identity disorder rarely occurs in isolation. Most DID patients also have a history of anxiety, mood, or personality disorders (Ross, 1999).

Starting in the 1970s, there was a dramatic increase in the diagnosis of multiple-personality disorder (Kihlstrom, 2001). Only 79 well-documented cases had accumulated up through 1970, but by the late-1990s about 40,000 cases were estimated to have been reported (Lilienfeld & Lynn, 2003). Some theorists believe that these disorders used to be underdiagnosed—that is, they often went undetected (Maldonado & Spiegel, 2003). However, other theorists argue that a handful of clinicians have begun overdiagnosing the condition and that some clinicians even *encourage and contrib-*

Web Link 15.4 **International Society for the Study of Dissociation**

Dissociative disorders, including dissociative identity disorder, are the focus of this organization of research and clinical professionals. In addition to a selective bibliography and a set of treatment guidelines, the site provides an impressive set of links to other professional groups involved in studying and treating dissociation.

---

ute to the emergence of DID (McHugh, 1995; Powell & Gee, 1999). Consistent with this view, a survey of all the psychiatrists in Switzerland found that 90% of them had never seen a case of dissociative identity disorder, whereas three of the psychiatrists had each seen more than 20 DID patients (Modestin, 1992). The data from this study suggest that 6 psychiatrists (out of 655 surveyed) accounted for two-thirds of the dissociative identity disorder diagnoses in Switzerland.

Etiology of Dissociative Disorders

Dissociative amnesia and fugue are usually attributed to excessive stress. However, relatively little is known about why this extreme reaction to stress occurs in a tiny minority of people but not in the vast majority who are subjected to similar stress. Some theorists speculate that certain personality traits—fantasy-proneness and a tendency to become intensely absorbed in personal experiences—may make some people more susceptible to dissociative disorders, but adequate evidence is lacking on this line of thought (Kihlstrom, Glisky, & Angiulo, 1994).

The causes of dissociative identity disorder are particularly obscure. Some skeptical theorists, such as Nicholas Spanos (1994, 1996) and others (Gee, Allen, & Powell, 2003; Lilienfeld et al., 1999), believe that people with multiple personalities are engaging in intentional role playing to use mental illness as a face-saving excuse for their personal failings. Spanos also argues that a small minority of therapists help create multiple personalities in their patients by subtly encouraging the emergence of alternate personalities. According to Spanos, dissociative identity disorder is a creation of modern North American culture, much as demonic possession was a creation of early Christianity. To bolster his argument, he discusses how DID patients' symptom presentations seem to have been influenced by popular media. For example, the typical patient with dissociative identity disorder used to report having two or three personalities, but since the publication of *Sybil* (Schreiber, 1973) and other books describing patients with many personalities, the average number of alternate personalities has climbed to about 15. In a similar vein, a dramatic upsurge occurred in the number of dissociative patients reporting that they were victims of ritual satanic abuse during childhood after the publication of *Michelle Remembers* (Smith & Pazder, 1980), a book about a DID patient who purportedly was tortured by a satanic cult.

In spite of these concerns, many clinicians are convinced that DID is an authentic disorder (Gleaves, May, & Cardena, 2001). They argue that there is no incentive for either patients or therapists to manufacture cases of multiple personalities, which are often greeted with skepticism and outright hostility. They maintain that most cases of DID are rooted in severe emotional trauma that occurred during childhood (Draijer & Langeland, 1999). A substantial majority of people with DID report a history of disturbed home life, beatings and rejection from parents, and sexual abuse (Scroppo et al., 1998; Foote et al., 2006). However, this abuse typically has not been independently verified (Lilienfeld & Lynn, 2003). Moreover, this link would not be unique to DID, as a history of child abuse elevates the likelihood of *many* disorders, especially among females (MacMillan et al., 2001). In the final analysis, very little is known about the causes of dissociative identity disorder, which remains a controversial diagnosis (Barry-Walsh, 2005). In one survey of American psychiatrists, only one-quarter of the respondents indicated that they felt there was solid evidence for the scientific validity of the DID diagnosis (Pope et al., 1999). Consistent with this finding, a more recent study found that scientific interest in DID has dwindled since the mid-1990s (Pope et al., 2006).

Mood Disorders

LEARNING OBJECTIVES

▶ Describe the two major mood disorders and discuss their prevalence.

▶ Explain how biological factors may be related to the development of mood disorders.

▶ Discuss how cognitive processes may contribute to mood disorders.

▶ Explain how interpersonal behavior and stress may contribute to mood disorders.

What might Abraham Lincoln, Leo Tolstoy, Marilyn Monroe, Vincent Van Gogh, Ernest Hemingway, Winston Churchill, Virginia Woolf, Janis Joplin, Irving Berlin, Kurt Cobain, Francis Ford Coppola, Carrie Fisher, Ted Turner, Sting, Mike Wallace, Larry Flynt, Jane Pauley, and Ben Stiller have in common? Yes, they all achieved great prominence, albeit in different ways at different times. But, more pertinent to our interest, they all suffered from severe mood disorders. Although mood disorders can be terribly debilitating, people with mood disorders may still achieve greatness, because such disorders tend to be *episodic*. In other words, emotional disorders often come and go. Thus, episodes of disturbance are interspersed among periods of normality. These episodes of disturbance can vary greatly in length, but they typically last 3 to 12 months (Akiskal, 2005).

Of course, we all have our ups and downs in terms of mood. Life would be dull indeed if emotional tone were constant. Everyone experiences depression occasionally and has other days that bring an emotional high. Such emotional fluctuations are natural, but some people are prone to extreme distortions of mood. **Mood disorders are a class of disorders marked by emotional disturbances that may spill over to disrupt physical, perceptual, social, and thought processes.**

Mood disorders are common and have afflicted many successful, well-known people, such as Anne Rice, Sheryl Crow and Harrison Ford.

Genetic Vulnerability

The evidence strongly suggests that genetic factors influence the likelihood of developing major depression or a bipolar mood disorder (Kalidindi & McGuffin, 2003; Sullivan, Neale, & Kendler, 2000). In studies that assess the impact of heredity on psychological disorders, investigators look at *concordance rates*. **A *concordance rate* indicates the percentage of twin pairs or other pairs of relatives that exhibit the same disorder.** If relatives who share more genetic similarity show higher concordance rates than relatives who share less genetic overlap, this finding supports the genetic hypothesis. Twin studies, which compare identical and fraternal twins (see Chapter 2), suggest that genetic factors *are* involved in mood disorders (Kelsoe, 2005; Knowles, Kaufmann, & Rieder, 1999). Concordance rates average around 65%–72% for identical twins but only 14%–19% for fraternal twins, who share less genetic similarity. Thus, evidence suggests that heredity can create a *predisposition* to mood disorders. Environmental factors probably determine whether this predisposition is converted into an actual disorder. Research suggests that genetic vulnerability may play a larger role in women's depression than in men's (Kendler et al., 2006). The influence of genetic factors also appears to be stronger for bipolar disorders than for unipolar disorders (Kieseppa et al., 2004). Some promising results have been reported in *genetic mapping* studies that have attempted to pinpoint the specific genes that shape vulnerability to mood disorders (Caspi et al., 2003; Holmans et al., 2007). However, results have been disturbingly inconsistent and scientists do *not* appear to be on the verge of unraveling the genetic code for mood disorders, which probably depend on subtle variations in constellations of many genes (Kendler, 2005a, 2005b; Merikangas & Risch, 2003).

Neurochemical and Neuroanatomical Factors

Heredity may influence susceptibility to mood disorders by creating a predisposition toward certain types of neurochemical abnormalities in the brain. Correlations have been found between mood disorders and abnormal levels of two neurotransmitters in the brain: norepinephrine and serotonin (Sher & Mann, 2003), although other neurotransmitter disturbances may also contribute (Thase, Jindal, & Howland, 2002). The details remain elusive, but low levels of serotonin appear to be a crucial factor underlying most forms of depression (Flores et al., 2004). A variety of drug therapies are fairly effective in the treatment of severe mood disorders. Most of these drugs are known to affect the availability (in the brain) of the neurotransmitters that have been related to mood disorders (Dubovsky et al., 2003). Since this effect is unlikely to be a coincidence, it bolsters the plausibility of the idea that neurochemical

changes produce mood disturbances. That said, after 40 years of enormous research effort, the neurochemical bases of mood disorders remain more mysterious than scientists would like (Delgado & Moreno, 2006).

Studies have also found some interesting correlations between mood disorders and a variety of structural abnormalities in the brain (Flores et al., 2004). Perhaps the best documented correlation is the association between depression and *reduced hippocampal volume* (Campbell et al, 2004; Videbech, 2006). The *hippocampus,* which is known to play a major role in memory (see **Figure 15.12**), tends to be about 8%–10% smaller in depressed subjects than in normal subjects (Videbech & Ravnkilde, 2004). A fascinating new theory of the biological bases of depression may be able to account for this finding. The springboard for this theory is the recent discovery that the human brain continues to generate new neurons in adulthood, especially in the hippocampal formation (Gage, 2002). This process is called *neurogenesis.* Evidence suggests that depression occurs when major life stress causes neurochemical reactions that suppress neurogenesis, resulting in reduced hippocampal volume (Jacobs, 2004; Warner-Schmidt & Duman, 2006). According to this view, the suppression of neurogenesis is the central cause of depression, and antidepressant drugs that relieve depression do so because they promote neurogenesis (Duman & Monteggia, 2006). A great deal of additional research will be required to fully test this innovative new model of the biological bases of depressive disorders.

Cognitive Factors

A variety of theories emphasize how cognitive factors contribute to depressive disorders (Abramson et al., 2002). We will discuss Aaron Beck's (1976, 1987) influential cognitive theory of depression in Chapter 16, where his approach to therapy is described. In this section, we examine Martin Seligman's *learned helplessness model* of depression (see Chapter 4) and its most recent descendant, *hopelessness theory.* Based largely on animal research, Seligman (1974) proposed that depression is caused by *learned helplessness*—passive "giving up" behavior produced by exposure to unavoidable aversive events (such as uncontrollable shock in the laboratory). He originally considered learned helplessness to be a product of conditioning but eventually revised his theory, giving it a cognitive slant. The reformulated theory of learned helplessness postulated that the roots of depression lie in how people explain the setbacks and other negative events that they experience (Abramson, Seligman, & Teasdale, 1978). According to Seligman (1990), people who exhibit a *pessimistic explanatory style* are especially vulnerable to depression (see Chapter 5). These people tend to attribute their setbacks to their personal flaws instead of situational

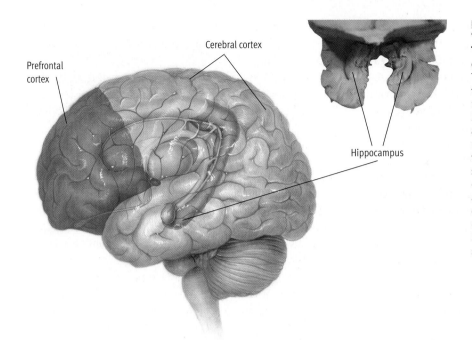

Figure 15.12

The hippocampus and depression. This graphic shows the hippocampus in blue. The photo inset shows a brain dissected to reveal the hippocampus in both the right and left hemispheres. It has long been known that the hippocampus plays a key role in memory, but its possible role in depression has only come to light in recent years. Research suggests that shrinkage of the hippocampal formation due to suppressed neurogenesis may be a key causal factor underlying depressive disorders. This graphic also shows the location of the *prefrontal cortex*, which will be discussed in our upcoming coverage of schizophrenic disorders (see p. 506).

Labels in figure: Cerebral cortex, Prefrontal cortex, Hippocampus

factors, and they tend to draw global, far-reaching conclusions about their personal inadequacies based on these setbacks.

Hopelessness theory builds on these insights by postulating a sense of hopelessness as the "final pathway" leading to depression and by incorporating additional factors that may interact with explanatory style to foster this sense of hopelessness (Abramson, Alloy, & Metalsky, 1995). According to hopelessness theory, a pessimistic explanatory style is just one of several or more factors—along with high stress, low self-esteem, and so forth—that may contribute to hopelessness, and thus depression. Although hopelessness theory casts a wider net than the learned helplessness model, it continues to emphasize the importance of people's *cognitive reactions* to the events in their lives.

In accord with this line of thinking, Susan Nolen-Hoeksema (1991, 2000) has found that people who *ruminate* about their problems and setbacks have elevated rates of depression and tend to remain depressed longer than those who do not ruminate. People who tend to ruminate repetitively focus their attention on their depressing feelings, thinking constantly about how sad, lethargic, and unmotivated they are. According to Nolen-Hoeksema (1995), excessive rumination tends to extend and amplify episodes of depression. She believes that women are more likely to ruminate than men and that this disparity may be a major reason why depression is more prevalent in women.

In sum, cognitive models of depression maintain that negative thinking is what leads to depression in many people. The principal problem with cognitive theories is their difficulty in separating cause from effect (Rehm, Wagner, & Ivens-Tyndal, 2001). Does neg-

ative thinking cause depression? Or does depression cause negative thinking (see **Figure 15.13**)? A *clear* demonstration of a causal link between negative thinking and depression is not possible because it would require manipulating people's explanatory style (which is not easy to change) in sufficient degree to produce full-fledged depressive disorders (which would not be ethical). However, a study by Lauren Alloy and her colleagues (1999) provided impressive evidence consistent with a causal link between negative thinking and vulnerability to depression. They assessed the explanatory style of a sample of first-year college students who were

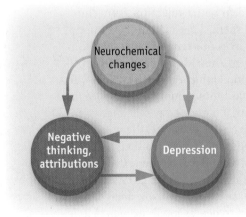

Figure 15.13

Interpreting the correlation between negative thinking and depression. Cognitive theories of depression assert that consistent patterns of negative thinking cause depression. Although these theories are highly plausible, depression could cause negative thoughts, or both could be caused by a third factor, such as neurochemical changes in the brain.

not depressed at the outset of the study. The students were characterized as being at high risk or low risk for depression based on whether they exhibited a negative cognitive style. The follow-up data over the ensuing two and a half years on students who had no prior history of depression showed dramatic differences between the two groups in vulnerability to depression. During this relatively brief period, a major depressive disorder emerged in 17% of the high-risk students in comparison to only 1% of the low-risk students (see **Figure 15.14**). These findings and other data from the study suggest that negative thinking makes people more vulnerable to depression.

Interpersonal Roots

Some theorists suggest that inadequate social skills put people on the road to depressive disorders (Coyne, 1999; Lewinsohn & Gotlib, 1995). According to this notion, depression-prone people lack the social finesse needed to acquire many important kinds of reinforcers, such as good friends, top jobs, and desirable spouses. This paucity of reinforcers could understandably lead to negative emotions and depression (see **Figure 15.15**). Consistent with this theory, researchers have indeed found correlations between poor social skills and depression (Petty, Sachs-Ericsson, & Joiner, 2004).

Another interpersonal factor is that depressed people tend to be depressing (Joiner & Katz, 1999). Individuals suffering from depression often are irritable and pessimistic. They complain a lot and aren't particularly enjoyable companions. They also alienate people by constantly asking for reassurances about their relationships and their worth (Burns et al., 2006). As a consequence, depressed people tend to court rejection from those around them. This alienation of important sources of social support may contribute to their downward spiral into depression (Joiner & Metalsky, 2001). To compound these problems, evidence indicates that depressed people may gravitate to partners who view them unfavorably and hence reinforce their negative views of themselves (Joiner, 2002). Interestingly, recent evidence suggests that lack of social support may make a larger contribution to depression in women than in men (Kendler, Myers, & Prescott, 2005).

Precipitating Stress

Mood disorders sometimes appear mysteriously "out of the blue" in people who appear to be leading benign, nonstressful

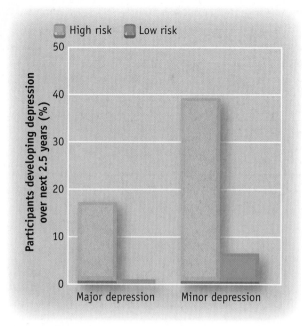

Figure 15.14

Negative thinking and prediction of depression. Alloy and colleagues (1999) measured the explanatory style of first-year college students and characterized them as being high risk or low risk for depression. This graph shows the percentage of these students who experienced major or minor episodes of depression over the next 2.5 years. As you can see, the high-risk students, who exhibited a negative thinking style, proved to be much more vulnerable to depression. (Data from Alloy et al., 1999)

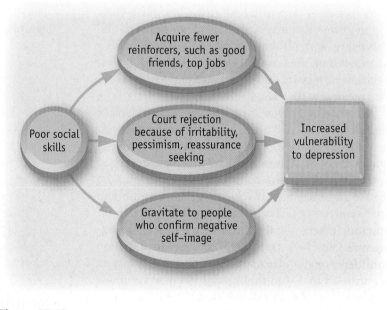

Figure 15.15

Interpersonal factors in depression. Interpersonal theories about the etiology of depression emphasize how inadequate social skills may contribute to the development of the disorder. Recent studies suggest that excessive reassurance-seeking may play a particularly critical role in the social dynamics promoting depression.

lives. For this reason, experts used to believe that mood disorders are relatively uninfluenced by stress. However, recent advances in the measurement of personal stress have altered this picture. The evidence available today suggests a moderately strong link between stress and the onset of mood disorders (Kendler, Kuhn, & Prescott, 2004; Kessler, 1997). Stress also appears to affect how people with mood disorders respond to treatment and whether they experience a relapse of their disorder (Monroe & Hadjiyannakis, 2002).

Of course, many people endure great stress without getting depressed. The impact of stress varies in part because different people have different degrees of *vulnerability* to mood disorders (Lewinsohn, Joiner, & Rohde, 2001). Variations in vulnerability appear to depend primarily on biological makeup. Similar interactions between stress and vulnerability probably influence the development of many kinds of disorders, including those that are next on our agenda: the schizophrenic disorders.

Schizophrenic Disorders

LEARNING OBJECTIVES

▶ Describe the prevalence and general symptoms of schizophrenia.

▶ Describe the subtypes of schizophrenia and distinguish between positive and negative symptoms.

▶ Discuss the course and outcome of schizophrenia.

▶ Summarize how genetic vulnerability and neurochemical factors may contribute to the etiology of schizophrenia.

▶ Discuss evidence relating schizophrenia to structural abnormalities in the brain and neurodevelopmental insults to the brain.

▶ Summarize how expressed emotion and stress may contribute to schizophrenia.

Literally, *schizophrenia* means "split mind." However, when Eugen Bleuler coined the term in 1911, he was referring to the fragmenting of thought processes seen in the disorder—not to a "split personality." Unfortunately, writers in the popular media often assume that the split-mind notion refers to the syndrome in which a person manifests two or more personalities. As you have already learned, this syndrome is actually called *dissociative identity disorder*. Schizophrenia is a much more common, and altogether different, type of disorder.

Schizophrenic disorders are a class of disorders marked by disturbances in thought that spill over to affect perceptual, social, and emotional processes. How common is schizophrenia? Prevalence estimates suggest that about 1% of the population may suffer from schizophrenic disorders (Lauriello, Bustillo, & Keith, 2005). That may not sound like much, but it means that in North American alone there may be several million people troubled by schizophrenic disturbances. Moreover, schizophrenia is an extremely costly disorder for society, because it is a severe, debilitating illness that tends to have an early onset and often requires lengthy hospital care. Because of these considerations, the financial impact of schizophrenia is estimated to exceed the costs of all types of cancers combined (Buchanan & Carpenter, 2005).

General Symptoms

Although there are a number of distinct schizophrenic syndromes, they share some general characteristics that we need to examine before looking at the subtypes. Many of these characteristics are apparent in the following case history (adapted from Sheehan, 1982).

Sylvia was first diagnosed as schizophrenic at age 15. She has been in and out of many types of psychiatric facilities since then. She has never been able to hold a job for any length of time. During severe flare-ups of her disorder, her personal hygiene deteriorates. She rarely washes, wears clothes that neither fit nor match, smears makeup on heavily but randomly, and slops food all over herself. Sylvia occasionally hears voices talking to her. Sylvia tends to be argumentative, aggressive, and emotionally volatile. Over the years, she has been involved in innumerable fights with fellow patients, psychiatric staff members, and strangers. Her thoughts can be highly irrational, as is apparent from the following quotation:

"Mick Jagger wants to marry me. If I have Mick Jagger, I don't have to covet Geraldo Rivera. Mick Jagger is St. Nicholas and the Maharishi is Santa Claus. I want to form a gospel rock group called the Thorn Oil, but Geraldo wants me to be the music critic on Eyewitness News, so what can I do? Got to listen to my boyfriend. Teddy Kennedy cured me of my ugliness. I'm pregnant with the son of God. I'm going to marry David Berkowitz and get it over with. Creedmoor is the headquarters of the American Nazi Party. They're eating the patients here. Archie Bunker wants me to play his niece on his TV show. I work for Epic Records. I'm Joan of Arc. I'm Florence Nightingale. The door between the ward and the porch is the dividing line between New York and California. Divorce isn't a piece of

paper, it's a feeling. Forget about Zip Codes. I need shock treatment." (Sheehan, 1982, pp. 104–105)

Sylvia's case clearly shows that schizophrenic thinking can be bizarre and that schizophrenia is a brutally serious, psychologically disfiguring disorder. Although no single symptom is inevitably present, the following symptoms are commonly seen in schizophrenia (Ho, Black, & Andreasen, 2003; Lindenmayer & Khan, 2006).

Irrational thought. Cognitive deficits and disturbed thought processes are the central, defining feature of schizophrenic disorders (Barch, 2003; Heinrichs, 2005). Various kinds of delusions are common. **Delusions are false beliefs that are maintained even though they clearly are out of touch with reality.** For example, one patient's delusion that he was a tiger (with a deformed body) persisted for 15 years (Kulick, Pope, & Keck, 1990). More typically, affected persons believe that their private thoughts are being broadcast to other people, that thoughts are being injected into their mind against their will, or that their thoughts are being controlled by some external force (Maher, 2001). In *delusions of grandeur,* people maintain that they are extremely famous or important. Sylvia expressed an endless array of grandiose delusions, such as thinking that Mick Jagger wanted to marry her, that she dictated the hobbit stories to Tolkien, and that she was going to win the Nobel Prize for medicine. In addition to delusions, the schizophrenic person's train of thought deteriorates. Thinking becomes chaotic rather than logical and linear. There is a "loosening of associations" as the schizophrenic shifts topics in disjointed ways. The quotation from Sylvia illustrates this symptom dramatically. The entire passage involves a wild "flight of ideas," but at one point (beginning with the sentence "Creedmoor is the headquarters . . .") she rattles off ten consecutive sentences that have no apparent connection to the preceding sentence.

Deterioration of adaptive behavior. Schizophrenia involves a noticeable deterioration in the quality of one's routine functioning in work, social relations, and personal care. Friends will often make remarks such as "Hal just isn't himself anymore." This deterioration is readily apparent in Sylvia's inability to get along with others or function in the work world. It's also apparent in her neglect of personal hygiene.

Distorted perception. A variety of perceptual distortions may occur in schizophrenia, with the most common being auditory hallucinations. *Hallucinations are sensory perceptions that occur in the absence of a real external stimulus or that represent gross distortions of perceptual input.* Schizophrenics frequently

report that they hear voices of nonexistent or absent people talking to them. Sylvia, for instance, heard messages from Paul McCartney. These voices often provide an insulting running commentary on the person's behavior ("You're an idiot for shaking his hand"). The voices may be argumentative ("You don't need a bath"), and they may issue commands ("Prepare your home for visitors from outer space").

Disturbed emotion. Normal emotional tone can be disrupted in schizophrenia in a variety of ways. Although it may not be an accurate indicator of their underlying emotional experience (Kring, 1999), some victims show little emotional responsiveness, a symptom referred to as "blunted or flat affect." Others show inappropriate emotional responses that don't jell with the situation or with what they are saying. People with schizophrenia may also become emotionally volatile. This pattern was displayed by Sylvia, who often overreacted emotionally in erratic, unpredictable ways.

Subtypes

Four subtypes of schizophrenic disorders are recognized, including a category for people who don't fit neatly into any of the first three categories (Ho et al., 2003; Kirkpatrick & Tek, 2005).

Paranoid Type

As its name implies, *paranoid schizophrenia* **is dominated by delusions of persecution, along with delusions of grandeur.** In this common form of schizophrenia, people come to believe that they have many enemies who want to harass and oppress them. They may become suspicious of friends and relatives, or they may attribute the persecution to mysterious, unknown persons. They are convinced that they are being watched and manipulated in malicious ways. To make sense of this persecution, they often develop delusions of grandeur. They believe that they must be enormously important people, often seeing themselves as great inventors or as great religious or political leaders. For example, in the case described at the beginning of the chapter, Ed's belief that he was president of the United States was a delusion of grandeur.

Catatonic Type

Catatonic schizophrenia **is marked by striking motor disturbances, ranging from muscular rigidity to random motor activity.** Some catatonics go into an extreme form of withdrawal known as a catatonic stupor. They may remain virtually motionless and seem oblivious to the environment around them for long periods of time. Others go into a state of catatonic excitement. They become hyperactive and incoherent. Some alternate between these dramatic extremes. The catatonic subtype is not particularly common, and its prevalence seems to be declining.

Disorganized Type

In *disorganized schizophrenia,* **a particularly severe deterioration of adaptive behavior is seen.** Prominent symptoms include emotional indifference, frequent incoherence, and virtually complete social withdrawal. Aimless babbling and giggling are common. Delusions often center on bodily functions ("My brain is melting out my ears").

Undifferentiated Type

People who are clearly schizophrenic but who cannot be placed into any of the three previous categories are said to have *undifferentiated schizophrenia,* **which is marked by idiosyncratic mixtures of schizophrenic symptoms.** The undifferentiated subtype is fairly common.

Positive Versus Negative Symptoms

Many theorists have raised doubts about the value of dividing schizophrenic disorders into these four subtypes (Sanislow & Carson, 2001). Critics note that the catatonic subtype is disappearing and that undifferentiated cases aren't a subtype so much as a hodgepodge of "leftovers." Critics also point out that the classic schizophrenic subtypes do not differ meaningfully in etiology, prognosis, or response to treatment. The absence of such differences casts doubt on the value of the current classification scheme.

Nancy Andreasen

Because of such problems, Nancy Andreasen (1990) and others (Carpenter, 1992; McGlashan & Fenton, 1992) have proposed an alternative approach to subtyping. This scheme divides schizophrenic disorders into just two categories based on the predominance of negative versus positive symptoms (see **Figure 15.16** on the next page). *Negative symptoms* involve behavioral deficits, such as flattened emotions, social withdrawal, apathy, impaired attention, and poverty of speech. *Positive symptoms* involve behavioral excesses or peculiarities, such as hallucinations, delusions, bizarre behavior, and wild flights of ideas.

Theorists advocating this scheme hoped to find consistent differences between the two subtypes in etiology, prognosis, and response to treatment, and some progress along these lines *has* been made. For example, a predominance of positive symptoms is associated with better adjustment prior to the onset of schizophrenia and greater responsiveness to treatment (Fenton & McGlashan, 1994; Galderisi et al., 2002). However, the assumption that patients can be placed into discrete categories based on this scheme now seems untenable. Most patients exhibit both types of symptoms and vary only in the degree to which positive or negative symptoms dominate (Black & Andreasen, 1994). Moreover, there is some debate about which symptoms should be classified as positive and which as negative, and some theorists have proposed a third category of symptoms reflecting *disorganization* of

---

Web Link 15.6   **Doctor's Guide to the Internet: Schizophrenia**

Produced by a communications and medical education consulting company, the free Doctor's Guide site is updated frequently to provide a current overview of the state of research on schizophrenic disorders. A more detailed set of resources for physicians parallels this site, which is intended primarily for patients and their families.

Figure 15.16

Positive and Negative Symptoms in Schizophrenia

Negative symptoms	Percent of patients	Positive symptoms	Percent of patients
Few friendship relationships	96	Delusions of persecution	81
Few recreational interests	95	Auditory hallucinations	75
Lack of persistence at work or school	95	Delusions of being controlled	46
Impaired grooming or hygiene	87	Derailment of thought	45
Paucity of expressive gestures	81	Delusions of grandeur	39
Social inattentiveness	78	Bizarre social, sexual behavior	33
Emotional nonresponsiveness	64	Delusions of thought insertion	31
Inappropriate emotion	63	Aggressive, agitated behavior	27
Poverty of speech	53	Incoherent thought	23

behavior (Toomey et al., 1997; Lindenmayer & Khan, 2006). Although it seems fair to say that the distinction between positive and negative symptoms is enhancing our understanding of schizophrenia, it has not yielded a classification scheme that can replace the traditional subtypes of schizophrenia.

Course and Outcome

Schizophrenic disorders usually emerge during adolescence or early adulthood, with 75% of cases manifesting by the age of 30 (Perkins, Miller-Anderson, & Lieberman, 2006). Those who develop schizophrenia usually have a long history of peculiar behavior and cognitive and social deficits, although most do not manifest a full-fledged psychological disorder during childhood (Walker et al., 2004). The emergence of schizophrenia may be sudden, but it usually is insidious and gradual. Once it clearly emerges, the course of schizophrenia is variable, but patients tend to fall into three broad groups. Some patients, presumably those with milder disorders, are treated successfully and enjoy a full recovery. Other patients experience a partial recovery so that they can return to independent living for a time. However, they experience regular relapses and are in and out of treatment facilities for much of the remainder of their lives. Finally, a third group of patients endure chronic illness that sometimes results in permanent hospitalization. Estimates of the percentage of patients falling in each category vary. Overall, it appears that about 15%–20% of schizophrenic patients enjoy a full recovery, although some long-term studies have yielded higher estimates (Modestin et al., 2003; Robinson et al., 2004).

Etiology of Schizophrenia

Most of us can identify, at least to some extent, with people who suffer from mood disorders, somatoform disorders, and anxiety disorders. You can probably imagine events that might leave you struggling with depression, grappling with anxiety, or worrying about your physical health. But what could possibly have led Ed to believe that he had been fighting space wars and vampires? What could account for Sylvia thinking that she was Joan of Arc, or that she had dictated the hobbit novels to Tolkien? As mystifying as these delusions may seem, you'll see that the etiology of schizo-

John Nash, the Nobel prize–winning mathematician whose story was told in the film A Beautiful Mind, *has struggled with paranoid schizophrenia since 1959.*

phrenic disorders is not all that different from the etiology of other disorders.

Genetic Vulnerability

Evidence is plentiful that hereditary factors play a role in the development of schizophrenic disorders (Sullivan et al., 2006; Tsuang, Glatt, & Faraone, 2003). For instance, in twin studies, concordance rates for schizophrenia average around 48% for identical twins, in comparison to about 17% for fraternal twins (Gottesman, 1991, 2001). Studies also indicate that a child born to two schizophrenic parents has about a 46% probability of developing a schizophrenic disorder (as compared to the probability of about 1% for the population as a whole). These and other findings that demonstrate the genetic roots of schizophrenia are summarized in **Figure 15.17**. Overall, the picture is similar to that seen for mood disorders. Several converging lines of evidence indicate that people inherit a genetically transmitted *vulnerability* to schizophrenia (Riley & Kendler, 2005; Schneider & Deldin, 2001). Although genetic factors may account for more than two-thirds of the variability in susceptibility to schizophrenia, genetic mapping studies have made little progress in identifying the specific genes responsible (Crow, 2007; Owen & O'Donovan, 2003).

Neurochemical Factors

Like mood disorders, schizophrenic disorders appear to be accompanied by changes in the activity of one or more neurotransmitters in the brain (Patel, Pinals, Breier, 2003). Excess *dopamine* activity has been implicated as a likely cause of schizophrenia (Javitt & Laruelle, 2006). This hypothesis makes sense because most of the drugs that are useful in the treatment of schizophrenia are known to dampen dopamine activity in the brain (Tamminga & Carlsson, 2003). However, the evidence linking schizophrenia to high dopamine levels is riddled with inconsistencies, complexities, and interpretive problems (Abi-Dargham, 2004). Researchers are currently exploring how interactions between the dopamine, serotonin, and other neurotransmitter systems may contribute to schizophrenia (Patel et al., 2003). Recent research has also suggested that abnormalities in neural circuits using *glutamate* as a neurotransmit-

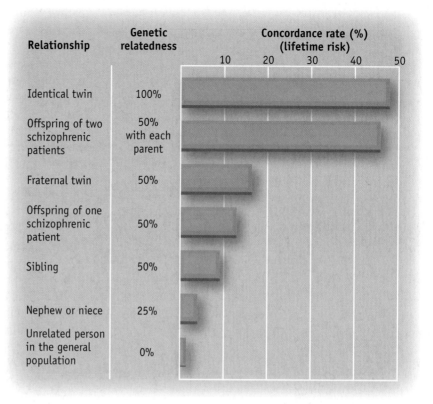

Figure 15.17

Genetic vulnerability to schizophrenic disorders. Relatives of schizophrenic patients have an elevated risk for schizophrenia. This risk is greater among closer relatives. Although environment also plays a role in the etiology of schizophrenia, the concordance rates shown here suggest that there must be a genetic vulnerability to the disorder. These concordance estimates are based on pooled data from 40 studies. (Data from Gottesman, 1991)

ter may play a role in schizophrenic disturbance (Tibbo et al., 2004). Thus, investigators are gradually making progress in their search for the neurochemical bases of schizophrenia.

Structural Abnormalities in the Brain

For decades, studies have suggested that individuals with schizophrenia exhibit a variety of deficits in attention, perception, and information processing (Gold & Green, 2005; Keefe & Eesley, 2006). Impairments in working (short-term) memory are especially prominent (Silver et al., 2003). These cognitive deficits suggest that schizophrenic disorders may be caused by neurological defects. Until recent decades, however, this theory was based more on speculation than on actual research. However, advances in brain-imaging technology have yielded mountains of intriguing data since the mid-1980s. CT scans and MRI scans suggest an association between enlarged brain ventricles (the hollow, fluid-filled cavities in the brain depicted in **Figure 15.18** on the next page) and schizophrenic disturbance (Belger & Dichter, 2006). Enlarged ventricles are assumed to reflect either the degeneration or failure to develop of nearby brain tissue. The significance of

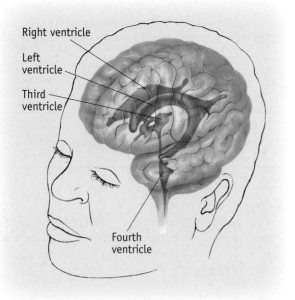

Right ventricle

Left ventricle

Third ventricle

Fourth ventricle

Figure 15.18

Schizophrenia and the ventricles of the brain. Cerebrospinal fluid (CSF) circulates around the brain and spinal cord. The hollow cavities in the brain filled with CSF are called *ventricles*. The four ventricles in the human brain are depicted here. Studies with modern brain-imaging techniques suggest that an association exists between enlarged ventricles in the brain and the occurrence of schizophrenic disturbance.

enlarged ventricles is hotly debated, however. Structural deterioration in the brain could be a contributing *cause* or a *consequence* of schizophrenia.

Brain-imaging studies have also uncovered structural and metabolic abnormalities in the frontal lobes of individuals with schizophrenia. Although the research results are not entirely consistent, schizophrenia appears to be associated with smaller size and reduced metabolic activity in specific areas of the *prefrontal cortex* (consult **Figure 15.12**; Fowles, 2003). Scientists are also intrigued by the fact that a major dopamine

pathway runs through the area in the prefrontal cortex where metabolic abnormalities have been found. A connection may exist between the abnormal dopamine activity implicated in schizophrenia and the dysfunctional metabolic activity seen in this area of the prefrontal cortex (Conklin & Iacono, 2002). Although the research on the prefrontal cortex is intriguing, Ho, Black, and Andreasen (2003) caution that the neural correlates of schizophrenia are complex and that the disease is not likely to be caused by "a single abnormality in a single region of the brain" (p. 408).

The Neurodevelopmental Hypothesis

In recent years, several new lines of evidence have led to the emergence of the *neurodevelopmental hypothesis* of schizophrenia, which posits that schizophrenia is caused in part by various disruptions in the normal maturational processes of the brain before or at birth (Brown, 1999). According to this hypothesis, insults to the brain during sensitive phases of prenatal development or during birth can cause subtle neurological damage that elevates individuals' vulnerability to schizophrenia years later in adolescence and early adulthood (see **Figure 15.19**). What are the sources of these early insults to the brain? Thus far, research has focused on viral infections or malnutrition during prenatal development and obstetrical complications during the birth process.

The evidence on viral infections has been building since Sarnoff Mednick and his colleagues (1988) discovered an elevated incidence of schizophrenia among the children of women who were in their second trimester of prenatal development during a 1957 influenza epidemic in Finland. Several subsequent studies in other locations have also found a link between exposure to influenza during pregnancy and increased prevalence of schizophrenia (Brown et al., 2004). Another study, which investigated the possible impact of prenatal malnutrition, found an elevated incidence

Figure 15.19

The neurodevelopmental hypothesis of schizophrenia. Research suggests that insults to the brain sustained during prenatal development or at birth may disrupt crucial maturational processes in the brain, resulting in subtle neurological damage that gradually becomes apparent as youngsters develop. This neurological damage is believed to increase both vulnerability to schizophrenia and the incidence of minor physical anomalies.

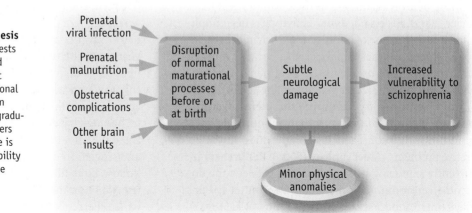

of schizophrenia in a cohort of people who were pre-natally exposed to a severe famine in 1944–45 because of a Nazi blockade of food deliveries in the Netherlands during World War II (Susser et al., 1996). A follow-up study of some schizophrenic patients exposed to this famine found increased brain abnormalities among the patients, as the neurodevelopmental hypothesis would predict (Hulshoff et al., 2000). Other research has shown that schizophrenic patients are more likely than control subjects to have a history of obstetrical complications (Kelly et al., 2004; Murray & Bramon, 2005). Finally, research suggests that minor physical anomalies (slight anatomical defects of the head, hands, feet, and face) that would be consistent with pre-natal neurological damage are more common among people with schizophrenia than in other people (Mc-Neil, Cantor-Graae, & Ismail, 2000; Schiffman et al., 2002). Collectively, these diverse studies argue for a relationship between early neurological trauma and a predisposition to schizophrenia (Mednick et al., 1998).

Expressed Emotion

Studies of expressed emotion have primarily focused on how this element of family dynamics influences the *course* of schizophrenic illness after the onset of the disorder (Leff & Vaughn, 1985). *Expressed emotion (EE)* reflects the degree to which a relative of a schizo-phrenic patient displays highly critical or emotionally overinvolved attitudes toward the patient. Audio-taped interviews of relatives' communication are carefully evaluated for critical comments, hostility toward the patient, and excessive emotional involvement (over-protective, overconcerned attitudes) (Hooley, 2004).

Studies show that a family's expressed emotion is a good predictor of the course of a schizophrenic patient's illness (Hooley & Candela, 1999; Kavanaugh, 1992). After release from a hospital, patients who re-turn to a family high in expressed emotion show re-lapse rates three or four times those of patients who return to a family low in expressed emotion. Part of the problem for patients returning to homes high in expressed emotion is that their families are probably sources of stress rather than of social support (Cutting & Docherty, 2000). However, Rosenfarb et al. (1995) caution against placing all the blame on the families high in expressed emotion. They found that patients returning to high-EE homes exhibited more odd and disruptive behavior than patients returning to low-EE homes. Thus, the more critical, negative attitudes ex-perienced by patients in high-EE homes may be caused in part by their own behavior.

Precipitating Stress

Many theories of schizophrenia assume that stress plays a role in triggering schizophrenic disorders (Walker et al., 2004). According to this notion, various biologi-cal and psychological factors influence individuals' *vul-nerability* to schizophrenia. High stress may then serve to precipitate a schizophrenic disorder in someone who is vulnerable (McGlashan & Hoffman, 2000).

APPLICATION

Understanding Eating Disorders

LEARNING OBJECTIVES

▶ *Describe the symptoms of anorexia nervosa, bulimia nervosa, and binge-eating disorder.*

▶ *Discuss the history, prevalence, and gender distribution of eating disorders.*

▶ *Explain how genetic factors, personality, and culture may contribute to eating disorders.*

▶ *Explain how family dynamics and disturbed thinking may contribute to eating disorders.*

Answer the following "true" or "false."

___ **1.** Although they have attracted attention only in recent years, eating disorders have a long history and have always been fairly common.

___ **2.** Eating disorders are universal problems found in virtually all cultures.

___ **3.** People with anorexia nervosa are much more likely to recognize their eating behavior as pathological than people suffering from bulimia nervosa.

___ **4.** The prevalence of eating disorders is twice as high in women as it is in men.

___ **5.** The binge-and-purge syndrome seen in bulimia nervosa is not common in anorexia nervosa.

All five of these statements are false, as you will see in this Application. The psychological disorders that we discussed in the main body of the chapter have largely been recognized for centuries and generally are found in one form or another in all cultures and societies. Eating disorders, however, present a sharp contrast to this picture: They have only been recognized in recent decades, and initially they were largely confined to affluent, Westernized cultures (Russell, 1995; Szmukler & Patton, 1995). In spite of these fascinating differences, eating disorders have much in common with traditional forms of pathology.

Types of Eating Disorders

Eating disorders **are severe disturbances in eating behavior characterized by preoccupation with weight and unhealthy efforts to control weight.** The vast majority of cases consist of two sometimes overlapping syndromes: *anorexia nervosa* and *bulimia nervosa*. A third syndrome, called *binge-eating disorder,* is described in the appendix of DSM-IV as a potential new disorder, pending further study. We will devote our attention in this Application to the two established eating disorders, but we will briefly outline the symptoms of this new disorder.

Anorexia Nervosa

Anorexia nervosa **involves intense fear of gaining weight, disturbed body image, refusal to maintain normal weight, and dangerous measures to lose weight.** Two subtypes have been distinguished (Herzog & Delinsky, 2001). In *restricting type anorexia nervosa,* people drastically reduce their intake of food, sometimes literally starving themselves. In *binge-eating/ purging type anorexia nervosa,* victims attempt to lose weight by forcing themselves to vomit after meals, by

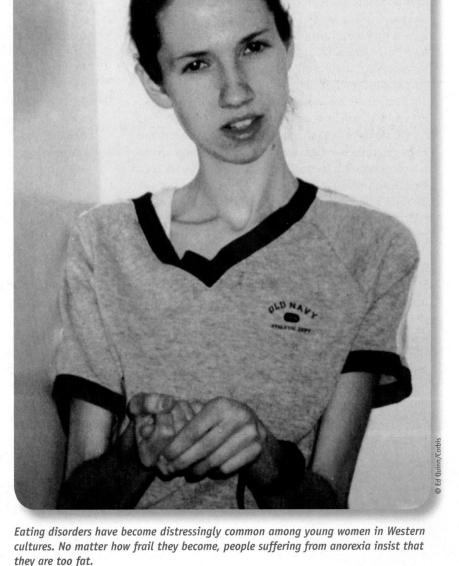

Eating disorders have become distressingly common among young women in Western cultures. No matter how frail they become, people suffering from anorexia insist that they are too fat.

misusing laxatives and diuretics, and by engaging in excessive exercise.

Both types entail a disturbed body image. No matter how frail and emaciated the victims become, they insist that they are too fat. Their morbid fear of obesity means that they are never satisfied with their weight. If they gain a pound or two, they panic. The only thing that makes them happy is to lose more weight. The common result is a relentless decline in body weight—in fact, patients entering treatment for anorexia nervosa are typically 25%–30% below their normal weight (Hsu, 1990). Because of their disturbed body image, people suffering from anorexia generally do *not* appreciate the maladaptive quality of their behavior and

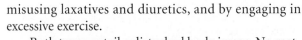

Web Link 15.7 **The Alliance for Eating Disorders Awareness**

This site offers a great deal of information on eating disorders. Visitors can find statistics, suggested readings, information on symptoms and treatments, self-tests, success stories from people who have overcome their eating disorders, and links to other worthwhile websites.

rarely seek treatment on their own. They are typically coaxed or coerced into treatment by friends or family members who are alarmed by their appearance.

Anorexia nervosa eventually leads to a cascade of medical problems, including *amenorrhea* (a loss of menstrual cycles in women), gastrointestinal problems, low blood pressure, *osteoporosis* (a loss of bone density), and metabolic disturbances that can lead to cardiac arrest or circulatory collapse (Pomeroy & Mitchell, 2002; Walsh, 2003). Anorexia is a debilitating illness that leads to death in 5%–10% of patients (Steinhausen, 2002).

Bulimia Nervosa

Bulimia nervosa **involves habitually engaging in out-of-control overeating followed by unhealthy compensatory efforts, such as self-induced vomiting, fasting, abuse of laxatives and diuretics, and excessive exercise.** The eating binges are usually carried out in secret and are followed by intense guilt and concern about gaining weight. These feelings motivate ill-advised strategies to undo the effects of the overeating. However, vomiting prevents the absorption of only about half of recently consumed food, and laxatives and diuretics have negligible impact on caloric intake, so people suffering from bulimia nervosa typically maintain a reasonably normal weight (Beumont, 2002; Kaye et al., 1993).

Medical problems associated with bulimia nervosa include cardiac arrythmias, dental problems, metabolic deficiencies, and gastrointestinal problems (Halmi, 2002, 2003). Bulimia often coexists with other psychological disturbances, including depression, anxiety disorders, and substance abuse (Hudson et al., 2007).

Obviously, bulimia nervosa shares many features with anorexia nervosa, such as a morbid fear of becoming obese, preoccupation with food, and rigid, maladaptive approaches to controlling weight that are grounded in naive all-or-none thinking. The close relationship between the disorders is demonstrated by the fact that many patients who initially develop one syndrome cross over to display the other syndrome (Tozzi et al., 2005). However, the syndromes also differ in crucial ways. First and foremost, bulimia is a less life-threatening condition. Second, although their weight and appearance usually is more "normal" than that seen in anorexia, people with bulimia are much more likely to recognize that their eating behavior is pathological and are more prone to recognize their need for treatment (Striegel-Moore, Silberstein, & Rodin, 1993; Guarda et al., 2007).

Binge-Eating Disorder

Binge-eating disorder **involves distress-inducing eating binges that are not accompanied by the purging, fasting, and excessive exercise seen in bulimia.** Obviously, this syndrome resembles bulimia, but it is a less severe disorder. Still, this disorder creates great distress, as these people tend to be disgusted by their bodies and distraught about their overeating. People with binge-eating disorder are frequently overweight. Their excessive eating is often triggered by stress (Gluck, 2006). Research suggests that this comparatively mild syndrome may be more common than anorexia or bulimia (Hudson et al., 2007). A great deal of additional research is needed to determine whether this syndrome should be recognized as an independent disorder or perhaps a subtype of bulimia nervosa.

History and Prevalence

Historians have been able to track down descriptions of anorexia nervosa that date back centuries, so the disorder is not entirely new, but anorexia nervosa did not become a *common* affliction until the middle of the 20th century (Vandereycken, 2002). Although binging and purging have a long history in some cultures, they were not part of a pathological effort to control weight, and bulimia nervosa appears to be a new syndrome that emerged gradually in the middle of the 20th century and was first recognized in the 1970s (Russell, 1997; Vandereycken, 2002).

Both disorders are a product of modern, affluent Western culture, where food is generally plentiful and the desirability of being thin is widely endorsed. Until recently, these problems were not seen outside of Western cultures (Hoek, 2002). However, in recent years, advances in communication have exported Western culture to farflung corners of the globe, and eating disorders have started showing up in many non-Western societies, especially affluent Asian countries (Lee & Katzman, 2002).

A huge gender gap exists in the likelihood of developing eating disorders. About 90%–95% of individuals who are treated for anorexia nervosa and bulimia nervosa are female (Thompson & Kinder, 2003). This staggering discrepancy appears to be a result of cultural pressures rather than biological ones (Smolak & Murnen, 2001). Western standards of attractiveness emphasize being slender more for females than for males, and women generally experience heavier pressure to be physically attractive than men do (Sobal, 1995). The prevalence of eating disorders is also elevated in certain groups that place an undue emphasis on thinness, such as fashion models, dancers, actresses, and athletes. Eating disorders mostly afflict *young* women. The typical age of onset for anorexia is 14–18, and for bulimia it is 15–21 (see **Figure 15.20** on the next page).

How common are eating disorders in Western societies? The prevalence of these disorders has increased dramatically in recent decades, although this escalation may be leveling off (Steiger & Seguin, 1999). Studies of

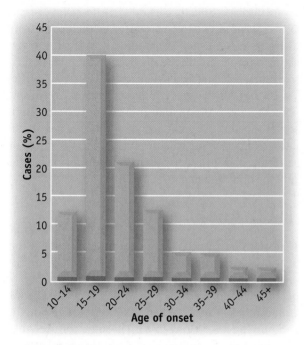

Figure 15.20

Age of onset for anorexia nervosa. Eating disorders emerge primarily during adolescence, as these data for anorexia nervosa show. This graph shows how age of onset was distributed in a sample of 166 female patients from Minnesota. As you can see, over half experienced the onset of their illness before the age of 20, with vulnerability clearly peaking between the ages of 15 and 19. (Data from Lucas, et al., 1991)

young women suggest that about 1% develop anorexia nervosa and about 2%–3% develop bulimia nervosa (Anderson & Yager, 2005). In some respects, these figures may only scratch the surface of the problem. Evidence suggests that as many as 20% of female college students may struggle with transient bulimic symptoms (Anderson & Yager, 2005). And recent community surveys suggest that there may be more undiagnosed eating disorders among men than generally appreciated (Hudson et al., 2007).

Etiology of Eating Disorders

Like other types of psychological disorders, eating disorders are caused by multiple determinants that work interactively. **Figure 15.21** provides an overview of the factors that contribute to the emergence of anorexia nervosa and bulimia nervosa.

Genetic Vulnerability

The scientific evidence is not nearly as strong or complete for eating disorders as it is for many other types of psychopathology (such as anxiety, mood, and schizophrenic disorders), but some people may inherit a genetic vulnerability to these problems (Slof-Op't Landt

et al., 2005). Studies show that relatives of patients with eating disorders have elevated rates of anorexia nervosa and bulimia nervosa (Bulik, 2004). And studies of female twins report higher concordance rates for identical twins than fraternal twins, suggesting that a genetic predisposition may be at work (Steiger, Bruce, & Israël, 2003).

Personality Factors

Strober (1995) has suggested that genetic factors may exert their influence indirectly by fostering certain personality traits that make people more vulnerable to eating disorders. Although there are innumerable exceptions, victims of anorexia nervosa tend to be obsessive, rigid, neurotic, and emotionally restrained, whereas victims of bulimia nervosa tend to be impulsive, overly sensitive, and low in self-esteem (Anderluh, Tchanturia. & Rabe-Hesketh, 2003; Wonderlich, 2002). Recent research also suggests that perfectionism is a risk factor for anorexia (Bulik et al., 2003; Halmi et al., 2000).

Cultural Values

The contribution of cultural values to the increased prevalence of eating disorders can hardly be overestimated (Anderson-Fye & Becker, 2004; Stice, 2001). In Western society, young women are socialized to believe that they must be attractive, and to be attractive, they must be as thin as the actresses and fashion models that dominate the media (Levine & Harrison, 2004). Thanks to this cultural milieu, many young women are dissatisfied with their weight because the societal ideals promoted by the media are unattainable for most of them (Thompson & Stice, 2001). Unfortunately, in a small portion of these women, the pressure to be thin, in combination with genetic vulnerability, family pathology, and other factors, leads to unhealthy efforts to control weight.

The Role of the Family

Many theorists emphasize how family dynamics can contribute to the development of anorexia nervosa and bulimia nervosa in young women (Haworth-Hoeppner, 2000). Some theorists suggest that parents who are overly involved in their children's lives turn the normal adolescent push for independence into an unhealthy struggle (Minuchin, Rosman, & Baker, 1978). Needing to assert their autonomy, some adolescent girls seek extreme control over their bodies, leading to pathological patterns of eating (Bruch, 1978). Other theorists argue that parents of adolescents with eating disorders tend to define their children's needs for them instead of allowing them to define their own needs, thus making the youngsters insensitive to their internal needs (Bruch, 1973; Steiner et al., 1991). In contrast, Pike and Rodin (1991) maintain that some mothers contribute

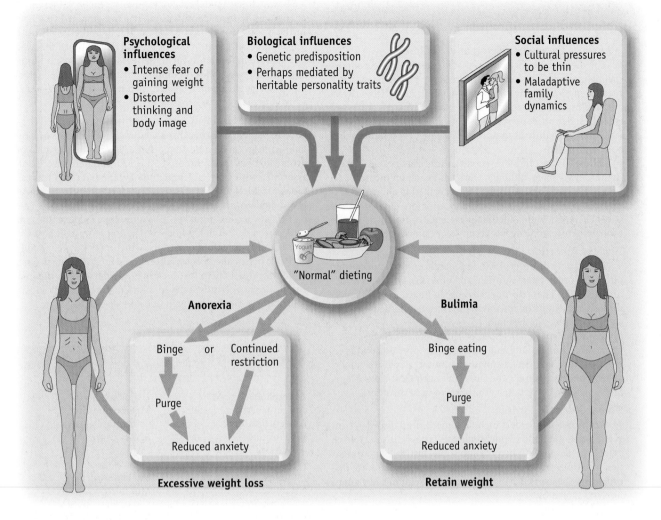

Figure 15.21

The etiology of eating disorders. The causes of eating disorders are complex and multifaceted. Psychological, biological, and social factors often lead people into "normal" dieting, which sometimes spins out of control. Maladaptive weight control efforts temporarily relieve individuals' pathological fear of gaining weight, but this reduced anxiety has a tremendous cost, as anorexia nervosa and bulimia nervosa are dangerous illnesses.

Graphic adapted from Barlow. D. H., & Durand, V. M. (1999). *Abnormal psychology: An integrative approach.* Belmont, CA: Wadsworth. Copyright © 1999 Wadsworth Publishing. Reprinted by permission.

to eating disorders simply by endorsing society's message that "you can never be too thin" and by modeling unhealthy dieting behaviors of their own. Although the hypotheses about the role of family dynamics in eating pathology are speculative, it does appear that families can contribute to eating disorders in a variety of ways.

Cognitive Factors

Many theorists emphasize the role of disturbed thinking in the etiology of eating disorders (Williamson et al., 2001). For example, anorexic patients' typical belief that they are fat when they are really wasting away is a dramatic illustration of how thinking goes awry. Patients with eating disorders display rigid, all-or-none thinking and many maladaptive beliefs, such as "I must be thin to be accepted," "If I am not in complete control, I will lose all control," and "If I gain one pound, I'll go on to gain enormous weight." Additional research is needed to determine whether distorted thinking is a *cause* or merely a *symptom* of eating disorders.

KEY IDEAS

Abnormal Behavior: Myths and Realities

▶ The medical model assumes that it is useful to view abnormal behavior as a disease. There are some problems with the medical model, but the disease analogy is useful. Three criteria are used in deciding whether people suffer from psychological disorders: deviance, personal distress, and maladaptive behavior. Often, it is difficult to draw a clear line between normality and abnormality.

▶ DSM-IV is the official psychodiagnostic classification system in the United States, although work has begun on the next edition (DSM-V). This system asks for information about patients on five axes. Psychological disorders are more common than widely believed, with a lifetime prevalence of roughly 44%, although there is some debate about recent prevalence estimates.

Anxiety Disorders

▶ The anxiety disorders include generalized anxiety disorder, phobic disorder, panic disorder, and obsessive-compulsive disorder (OCD). These disorders have been linked to genetic predisposition, temperament, anxiety sensitivity, and neurochemical abnormalities in the brain.

▶ Many anxiety responses, especially phobias, may be caused by classical conditioning and maintained by operant conditioning. Cognitive theorists maintain that some people are vulnerable to anxiety disorders because they see threat everywhere. Stress may also contribute to the onset of these disorders.

Somatoform Disorders

▶ Somatoform disorders include somatization disorder, conversion disorder, and hypochondriasis. These disorders often emerge in people with highly suggestible, histrionic personalities, who think irrationally about their health. Somatoform disorders may be learned avoidance strategies reinforced by attention and sympathy.

Dissociative Disorders

▶ Dissociative disorders include dissociative amnesia, dissociative fugue, and dissociative identity disorder (DID). These disorders appear to be uncommon, although there is some controversy about the prevalence of DID. Stress and childhood trauma may contribute to DID, but overall, the causes of dissociative disorders are not well understood.

Mood Disorders

▶ The principal mood disorders are major depressive disorder and bipolar disorder. People vary in their genetic vulnerability to mood disorders, which are accompanied by changes in neurochemical activity in the brain. Reduced hippocampal volume and suppressed neurogenesis may be factors in depression.

▶ Cognitive models posit that a pessimistic explanatory style, rumination, and other types of negative thinking contribute to depression. Depression is often rooted in interpersonal inadequacies, as people who lack social finesse often have difficulty acquiring life's reinforcers. Mood disorders are sometimes stress related.

Schizophrenic Disorders

▶ Schizophrenic disorders are characterized by deterioration of adaptive behavior, irrational thought, distorted perception, and disturbed mood. Schizophrenic disorders are classified as paranoid, catatonic, disorganized, or undifferentiated. The distinction between positive and negative symptoms has proven useful, but it has not yielded an effective new classification scheme.

▶ Research has linked schizophrenia to genetic vulnerability, changes in neurotransmitter activity, and enlarged ventricles in the brain. The neurodevelopmental hypothesis attributes schizophrenia to disruptions of normal maturational processes in the brain before or at birth. Patients who return to homes high in expressed emotion tend to have elevated relapse rates. Precipitating stress may also contribute to the emergence of schizophrenia.

Application: Understanding Eating Disorders

▶ The principal eating disorders are anorexia nervosa and bulimia nervosa. Binge-eating disorder is a new diagnostic syndrome that has been proposed. Anorexia and bulimia are both associated with other psychopathology, and both lead to a cascade of medical problems. Eating disorders appear to be a product of modern, affluent, Westernized culture.

▶ Females account for 90%–95% of eating disorders. The typical age of onset is roughly 15 to 20. There appears to be a genetic vulnerability to eating disorders, which may be mediated by heritable personality traits. Cultural pressures on young women to be thin clearly help foster eating disorders. Some theorists emphasize how family dynamics and disturbed thinking can contribute to the development of eating disorders.

KEY TERMS

Agoraphobia   p. 485
Anorexia nervosa   p. 508
Anxiety disorders   p. 485
Binge-eating
  disorder   p. 509
Bipolar disorder   p. 495
Bulimia nervosa   p. 509
Catatonic
  schizophrenia   p. 503
Concordance rate   p. 498
Conversion disorder   p. 489
Delusions   p. 502
Diagnosis   p. 480
Disorganized
  schizophrenia   p. 503
Dissociative amnesia   p. 491
Dissociative
  disorders   p. 491
Dissociative fugue   p. 491
Dissociative identity disorder
  (DID)   p. 492
Eating disorders   p. 508
Epidemiology   p. 482
Etiology   p. 480
Generalized anxiety
  disorder   p. 485
Hallucinations   p. 502

Hypochondriasis   p. 490
Major depressive
  disorder   p. 494
Manic-depressive
  disorder   p. 495
Medical model   p. 479
Mood disorders   p. 493
Multiple-personality
  disorder   p. 492
Neurotransmitters   p. 487
Obsessive-compulsive
  disorder (OCD)   p. 486
Panic disorder   p. 485
Paranoid
  schizophrenia   p. 503
Phobic disorder   p. 485
Prevalence   p. 482
Prognosis   p. 480
Schizophrenic
  disorders   p. 501
Somatization
  disorder   p. 489
Somatoform
  disorders   p. 489
Undifferentiated
  schizophrenia   p. 503

KEY PEOPLE

Nancy Andreasen   p. 503
Susan Nolen-
  Hoeksema   pp. 495, 499

Martin Seligman   p. 498
Thomas Szasz   p. 480

PRACTICE TEST

1. Sergio has just entered treatment for bipolar disorder and he is informed that most patients respond to drug treatment within a month. This information represents:
   a. a prognosis.
   b. an etiology.
   c. a histology.
   d. a concordance.

2. Although Sue always feels high levels of dread, worry, and anxiety, she still meets her daily responsibilities. Sue's behavior:
   a. should not be considered abnormal, since her adaptive functioning is not impaired.
   b. should not be considered abnormal, since everyone sometimes experiences worry and anxiety.
   c. can still be considered abnormal, since she feels great personal distress.
   d. both a and b.

3. Recent epidemiological studies have found that the most common types of psychological disorders are:
   a. mood disorders and anxiety disorders.
   b. anxiety disorders and schizophrenic disorders.
   c. substance-use disorders and anxiety disorders.
   d. substance-use disorders and somatoform disorders.

4. People who repeatedly perform senseless rituals to overcome their anxiety are said to have a(n):
   a. generalized anxiety disorder.
   b. manic disorder.
   c. obsessive-compulsive disorder.
   d. phobic disorder.

5. If a person has a paralyzed arm for which no organic basis can be found, she probably has:
   a. a conversion disorder.
   b. paralytic hypochondriasis.
   c. a dissociative disorder.
   d. a schizophrenic disorder.

6. After several months during which he was always gloomy and dejected, Mario has suddenly perked up. He feels elated and energetic and works around the clock on a writing project. He has also started to bet heavily on sporting events over the Internet, which he never did previously. Mario's behavior is consistent with:
   a. schizophrenia.
   b. obsessive-compulsive disorder.
   c. bipolar disorder.
   d. dissociative identity disorder.

7. A concordance rate indicates:
   a. the percentage of twin pairs or other relatives that exhibit the same disorder.
   b. the percentage of people with a given disorder that are currently receiving treatment.
   c. the prevalence of a given disorder in the general population.
   d. the rate of cure for a given disorder.

8. Which of the following would be a negative symptom of schizophrenia?
   a. Auditory hallucinations
   b. Delusions of persecution
   c. Having virtually no friendships
   d. Delusions of grandeur

9. Jamaal, who works as a projectionist at the local theater, is convinced that everyone is out to get him. He is sure that his phone is tapped by ruthless enemies. He thinks that most of the people in the theater each night are there to spy on him. Worse yet, he is sure people follow him home from work every night. Jamaal is probably suffering from:
   a. paranoid schizophrenia.
   b. catatonic schizophrenia.
   c. bipolar disorder.
   d. dissociative fugue.

10. About _____ % of patients with eating disorders are female.
    a. 40
    b. 50–60
    c. 75
    d. 90–95

Book Companion Website

 Visit the Book Companion Website at **academic.cengage. com/psychology/weiten**, where you will find tutorial quizzes, flash cards, and web links for every chapter, a final exam, and more! You can also link to the Psychology Resource Center (accessible directly at **academic.cengage.com/login**) for a range of psychology-related resources.

Personal Explorations Workbook

The following exercises in your *Personal Explorations Workbook* may enhance your self-understanding in relation to issues raised in this chapter. **Questionnaire 15.1:** Manifest Anxiety Scale. **Personal Probe 15.1:** What Are Your Attitudes on Mental Illness? **Personal Probe 15.2:** Do You Think That We Are All Candidates for a Disorder?

ANSWERS

1. a Page 480
2. c Pages 480–481
3. c Pages 483–484
4. c Page 486
5. a Pages 489–490
6. c Page 495
7. a Page 498
8. c Pages 503–504
9. a Page 503
10. d Page 509

CHAPTER 16

Psychotherapy

What do you picture when you hear the term *psychotherapy*? If you're like most people, you probably envision a troubled patient lying on a couch in a therapist's office, with the therapist asking penetrating questions and providing sage advice. Typically, people believe that psychotherapy is only for those who are "sick" and that therapists have special powers that allow them to "see through" their clients. It is also widely believed that therapy requires years of deep probing into a client's innermost secrets. Many people further assume that therapists routinely tell their patients how to lead their lives. Like most stereotypes, this picture of psychotherapy is a mixture of fact and fiction, as you'll see in the upcoming pages.

In this chapter, we take a down-to-earth look at the process of *psychotherapy,* using the term in its broadest sense to refer to all the diverse approaches to the treatment of psychological problems. We start by discussing some general questions about the provision of treatment. Who seeks therapy? What kinds of professionals provide treatment? How many types of therapy are there? After considering these general issues, we examine some of the more widely used approaches to treating psychological maladies, analyzing their goals, techniques, and effectiveness. The Application at the end of the chapter focuses on practical issues involved in finding a therapist, in case you ever have to advise someone about seeking help.

The Elements of the Treatment Process

LEARNING OBJECTIVES

▶ *Identify the three major categories of therapy.*

▶ *Discuss why people do or do not seek psychotherapy.*

▶ *Describe the various types of mental health professionals involved in the provision of therapy.*

Today people have a bewildering array of psychotherapy approaches to choose from. In fact, the immense diversity of therapeutic treatments makes defining the concept of *psychotherapy* difficult. After organizing a landmark conference that brought together many of the world's leading authorities on psychotherapy, Jeffrey Zeig (1987) commented, "I do not believe there is any capsule definition of psychotherapy on which the 26 presenters could agree" (p. xix). In lieu of a definition, we can identify a few basic elements that the various approaches to treatment have in common. All psychotherapies involve a helping relationship (the treatment) between a professional with special training (the therapist) and another person in need of help (the client). As we look at each of these three elements, you'll see the diverse nature of modern psychotherapy.

Treatments: How Many Types Are There?

In their efforts to help people, mental health professionals use many methods of treatment, including discussion, emotional support, persuasion, conditioning procedures, relaxation training, role playing, drug therapy, biofeedback, and group therapy. Some therapists also use a variety of less conventional procedures, such as rebirthing, poetry therapy, and primal therapy. No one knows exactly how many approaches to treatment there are. One expert (Kazdin, 1994) estimates that there may be over 400 distinct types of psychotherapy! Fortunately, we can impose some order on this chaos. As varied as therapists' procedures are, approaches to treatment can be classified into three major categories:

   1. *Insight therapies.* Insight therapy is "talk therapy" in the tradition of Freud's psychoanalysis. This is probably the approach to treatment that you envision when you think of psychotherapy. In insight therapies, clients engage in complex verbal interactions with their therapists. The goal in these discussions is to pursue increased insight regarding the nature of the client's difficulties and to sort through possible solutions. Insight therapy can be conducted with an individual or with a group.

   2. *Behavior therapies.* Behavior therapies are based on the principles of learning and conditioning, which were introduced in Chapter 2. Instead of emphasizing personal insights, behavior therapists make direct efforts to alter problematic responses (phobic behaviors, for instance) and maladaptive habits (drug use, for instance). Behavior therapists work on changing clients' overt behaviors. They use different procedures for different kinds of problems.

   3. *Biomedical therapies.* Biomedical approaches to therapy involve interventions into a person's physiological functioning. The most widely used procedures are drug therapy and electroconvulsive therapy. As the name bio*medical* therapies suggests, these treatments have traditionally been provided only by physicians with a medical degree (usually psychiatrists). This situation is changing, however, as psychologists have been campaigning for prescription privileges (Norfleet, 2002; Welsh, 2003). To date psychologists have obtained prescription authority in two states (New Mexico and Louisiana), and they have made legislative progress toward this goal in many other states (Long, 2005). Although some psychologists have argued against pursuing the right to prescribe medication (Heiby, 2002; Robiner et al., 2003), the movement is gathering momentum and seems likely to prevail.

   In this chapter we examine approaches to therapy that fall into each of these three categories. Although different methods are used in each, the three major classes of treatment are not entirely incompatible. For example, a client being seen in insight therapy may also be given medication.

Clients: Who Seeks Therapy?

In the therapeutic triad (therapists, treatments, clients), the greatest diversity is seen among the clients. According to the 1999 U.S. Surgeon General's report on mental health (U.S. Department of Health and Human Services, 1999), about 15% of the U.S. population use mental health services in a given year. These people bring to therapy the full range of human problems: anxiety, depression, unsatisfactory interpersonal relations, troublesome habits, poor self-control, low self-esteem, marital conflicts, self-doubt, a sense of emptiness, and feelings of personal stagnation. The two most common presenting problems are excessive anxiety and depression (Narrow et al., 1993).

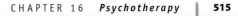

Interestingly, people often delay for many years before finally seeking treatment for their psychological problems (Kessler, Olfson, & Berglund, 1998). One recent large-scale study (Wang, Berglund, et al., 2005) found that the median delay in seeking treatment was 6 years for bipolar disorder and for drug dependence, 8 years for depression, 9 years for generalized anxiety disorder, and 10 years for panic disorder! **Figure 16.1** summarizes data from the same study on the percentage of people with various disorders who seek treatment within the first year after the onset of the disorder. As you can see, the figures are surprisingly low for most disorders.

A client in treatment does *not* necessarily have an identifiable psychological disorder. Some people seek professional help for everyday problems (career decisions, for instance) or vague feelings of discontent (Strupp, 1996). One surprising finding in recent research has been that only about half of the people who use mental health services in a given year meet the criteria for a full-fledged mental disorder (Kessler et al., 2005b).

People vary considerably in their willingness to seek psychotherapy. One study found that even when people perceive a need for professional assistance, only 59% actually seek professional help (Mojtabai, Olfson, & Mechanic, 2002). As you can see in **Figure 16.2**, women are more likely than men to receive treatment, and whites are more likely than blacks or Hispanics to obtain therapy. Treatment is also more likely when people have medical insurance and when they have more education (Olfson et al., 2002; Wang, Lane, et al, 2005). *Unfortunately, it appears that many people who*

Recommended
READING

A Consumer's Guide to Psychotherapy
by Larry E. Beutler, Bruce Bongar, and Joel N. Shurkin
(Oxford University Press, 2001)

This book is a serious, sophisticated work that may be more thoroughly grounded in scientific research than any of its competitors. The character of the book is consistent with the fact that Larry Beutler is one of the leading researchers on the efficacy of psychotherapy. That is *not* to say that this is a research treatise. It is a pragmatic, readable discussion of everyday issues, such as what to look for in choosing a therapist, what questions to ask when you have doubts about your therapy, what role you play in the success of your treatment, how to recognize and deal with unprofessional or unethical behavior on the part of a therapist, and how to recognize when therapy is not working. The greatest strength of the book is its analysis of what research says about the effectiveness of specific therapies for particular problems. The authors carefully summarize the findings on what works best with what problems.

need therapy don't receive it (Kessler et al., 2005b). As **Figure 16.3** (on page 518) shows, only a portion of the people who need treatment get it. People who could benefit from therapy do not seek it for a variety of reasons. Lack of health insurance and cost concerns appear to be major barriers to obtaining needed care for many

Figure 16.1

Treatment seeking for various disorders. In a study of the extent to which people seek treatment for psychological disorders, Wang et al. (2005) found that only a minority of people promptly pursue treatment for their disorder. The data summarized here show the percentage of people who obtain professional treatment within the first year after the onset of various disorders. The percentages vary depending on the disorder, but all the figures are surprisingly low. (Data from Wang et al., 2005).

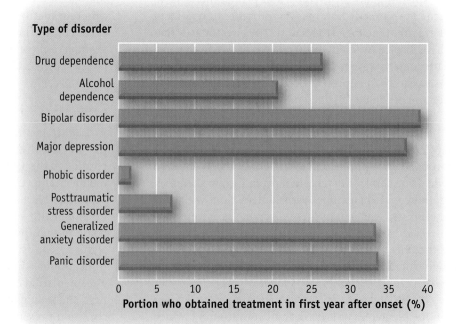

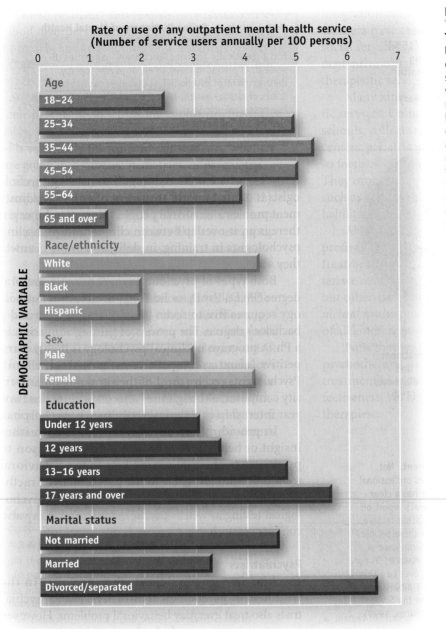

Rate of use of any outpatient mental health service
(Number of service users annually per 100 persons)

Figure 16.2

Therapy utilization rates. Olfson and colleagues (2002) gathered data on the use of nonhospital outpatient mental health services in the United States in relation to various demographic variables. In regard to marital status, utilization rates are particularly high among those who are divorced or separated. The use of therapy is greater among those who have more education and, in terms of age, utilization peaks in the 35–44 age bracket. Females are more likely to pursue therapy than males are, but utilization rates are extremely low among ethnic minorities. (Data from Olfson et al., 2002)

people. According to the Surgeon General's report, the biggest roadblock is the "stigma surrounding the receipt of mental health treatment." Unfortunately, many people equate seeking therapy with admitting personal weakness.

Therapists: Who Provides Professional Treatment?

Friends and relatives may provide excellent advice about personal problems, but their assistance does not qualify as therapy. Psychotherapy refers to *professional* treatment by someone with special training. However, a common source of confusion about psychotherapy is the variety of "helping professions" available to offer

assistance. Psychology and psychiatry are the principal professions involved in psychotherapy, providing the lion's share of mental health care. However, therapy is also provided by social workers, psychiatric nurses, and counselors, as outlined in **Figure 16.4** (on the next page).

Psychologists

Two types of psychologists may provide therapy, although the distinction between them is more theoretical than real. *Clinical psychologists* and *counseling psychologists* specialize in the diagnosis and treatment of psychological disorders and everyday behavioral problems. In theory, the training of clinical psychologists emphasizes treatment of full-fledged

form of therapy. Although only about 8% of psychiatrists administer ECT (Hermann et al., 1998), estimates suggest that about 100,000 people receive ECT treatments each year in the United States (Hermann et al., 1995). Some critics argue that ECT is overused because it is a lucrative procedure that boosts psychiatrists' income while consuming relatively little of their time in comparison to insight therapy (Frank, 1990). Conversely, some advocates argue that ECT is underutilized because the public harbors many misconceptions about its risks and side effects (McDonald et al., 2004). Although ECT was once considered appropriate for a wide range of disorders, in recent decades it has primarily been recommended for the treatment of depression.

Effectiveness of ECT

The evidence on the therapeutic efficacy of ECT is open to varied interpretations. Proponents of ECT maintain that it is a remarkably effective treatment for major depression (Prudic, 2005; Rudorfer, Henry, & Sackeim, 2003). Moreover, they note that many patients who do not benefit from antidepressant medication improve in response to ECT (Nobler & Sackeim, 2006). However, opponents of ECT argue that the available studies are flawed and inconclusive and that ECT is probably no more effective than a placebo (Rose et al., 2003). Overall, enough favorable evidence seems to exist to justify *conservative* use of ECT in treating severe mood disorders in patients who have not responded to medication (Carney & Geddes, 2003;

Metzger, 1999). Unfortunately, relapse rates after ECT are distressingly high. Over 50% of patients relapse within 6 to 12 months, although relapse rates can be reduced by giving ECT patients antidepressant drugs (Sackeim et al., 2001).

The debate about whether ECT works does *not* make ECT unique among approaches to the treatment of psychological disorders. Controversies exist regarding the effectiveness of most therapies. However, this controversy is especially problematic because ECT carries some risks.

Risks Associated with ECT

Even ECT proponents acknowledge that memory losses, impaired attention, and other cognitive deficits are common short-term side effects of electroconvulsive therapy (Lisanby et al., 2000; Nobler & Sackeim, 2006). However, ECT proponents assert that these deficits are mild and usually disappear within a month or two (Glass, 2001). An American Psychiatric Association (2001) task force concluded that there is no objective evidence that ECT causes structural damage in the brain or that it has any lasting negative effects on the ability to learn and remember information. In contrast, ECT critics maintain that ECT-induced cognitive deficits are often significant and sometimes permanent (Breggin, 1991; Frank, 1990; Rose et al., 2003), although their evidence seems to be largely anecdotal. Given the concerns about the risks of ECT and the doubts about its efficacy, it appears that the use of ECT will remain controversial for some time to come.

This patient is being prepared for electroconvulsive therapy. The mouthpiece keeps the patient from biting her tongue during the electrically induced seizures.

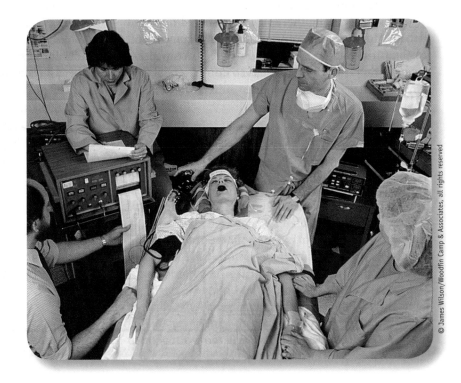

Current Trends and Issues in Treatment

LEARNING OBJECTIVES

▶ Discuss how managed care has affected the provision of therapy.
▶ Discuss the merits of blending approaches to therapy.
▶ Explain why therapy is underutilized by ethnic minorities.

The controversy about ECT is only one of many contentious issues and shifting trends in the world of mental health care. In this section, we discuss the impact of managed care on psychotherapy, the continuing trend toward blending various approaches to therapy, and efforts to respond more effectively to increasing cultural diversity in Western societies.

Grappling with the Constraints of Managed Care

The 1990s brought a dramatic shift in how people in the United States pay for their health care. Alarmed by skyrocketing health care costs, huge numbers of employers and individuals moved from traditional fee-for-service arrangements to managed care health plans (Hogan & Morrison, 2003; Kiesler, 2000). In the *fee-for-service* system, hospitals, physicians, psychologists, and other providers charged fees for whatever health care services were needed, and most of these fees were reimbursed by private insurance or the government (through Medicaid, Medicare, and other programs). In *managed care systems* people enroll in prepaid plans with small co-payments for services, typically run by health maintenance organizations (HMOs), which agree to provide ongoing health care for a specific sum of money. Managed care usually involves a tradeoff: Consumers pay lower prices for their care, but they give up much of their freedom to choose their providers and to obtain whatever treatments they believe necessary. If an HMO's treatment expenses become excessive, it won't turn a profit, so HMOs have powerful financial incentives to hold treatment costs down.

The HMOs originally promised individuals and employers that they would be able to hold costs down without having a negative impact on the quality of care, by negotiating lower fees from providers, reducing inefficiency, and cracking down on medically unnecessary services. During the 1990s, managed care *was* successful in reducing the acceleration of medical costs in the United States (Drum & Sekel, 2003). However, critics charge that managed care systems have squeezed all the savings they can out of the "fat" that existed in the old system and that they have responded to continued inflation in their costs by rationing care and limiting access to medically *necessary* services (Duckworth & Borus, 1999; Giles & Marafiote, 1998; Sanchez & Turner, 2003).

The possibility that managed care is having a negative effect on the quality of care is a source of concern throughout the health care professions, but the issue is especially sensitive in the area of mental health care (Bursztajn & Brodsky, 2002; Campbell, 2000). Critics maintain that mental health care has suffered particularly severe cuts in services because the question of what is "medically necessary" can be more subjective than in other treatment specialties (such as internal medicine or ophthalmology) and because patients who are denied psychotherapy services are relatively unlikely to complain (Duckworth & Borus, 1999). For example, a business executive who is trying to hide his depression or cocaine addiction from his employer will be reluctant to complain to his employer if therapeutic services are denied.

According to critics, the restriction of mental health services sometimes involves outright denial of treatment, but it often takes more subtle forms, such as underdiagnosing conditions, failing to make needed referrals to mental health specialists, and arbitrarily limiting the length of treatment (Bursztajn & Brodsky, 2002; Miller, 1996). Long-term therapy is becoming a thing of the past unless patients can pay for it out of pocket, and the goal of treatment has been reduced to reestablishing a reasonable level of functioning (Zatzick, 1999). Many managed care systems hold down costs by erecting *barriers to access,* such as requiring referrals from primary care physicians who don't have appointments available for weeks or months or authorizing only a few sessions of therapy at a time (Sanchez & Turner, 2003). Another cost-cutting strategy is to reroute patients from highly trained providers, such as psychiatrists and doctoral-level psychologists, to less-well-trained providers, such as masters-level counselors, who may not be adequately prepared to handle serious psychological disorders (Seligman & Levant, 1998).

The extensive utilization review procedures required by managed care have also raised concerns about providers' autonomy and clients' confidentiality (Chambliss, 2000; Plante, 2005). Clinicians who have to "sell" their treatment plans to managed care bureaucrats who may know little about mental health care feel that they have lost control over their professional practice. They also worry that the need to divulge the details of clients' problems to justify treatment may breach the confidentiality of the therapist-client relationship.

Recommended READING

Crazy: A Father's Search Through America's Mental Health Madness
by Pete Earley (G. P. Putnam's Sons, 2006)

This book will make you feel outraged. This book will make you cry. Above all else, this book will educate you about how incredibly difficult it can be to get effective mental health care for people troubled by severe disturbances such as schizophrenia and bipolar mood disorder. You will learn that our mental health system sometimes seems insane. The author is a former *Washington Post* investigative reporter who was suddenly drawn into the quagmire of America's mental health system when his son, Mike, developed bipolar disorder at the age of 23. Mike became seriously psychotic—at one point he wrapped aluminum foil around his head so people wouldn't be able to read his thoughts. His behavior became erratic. He crashed his car while trying to drive with his eyes closed, informed strangers at a coffee shop that he had supernatural powers, and broke into a residence where he ignored a wailing burglar alarm and proceeded to pee on the carpet, turn on all the water faucets, thus flooding the home, and give himself a bubble bath—until the police arrived to detain him. In his disoriented state, Earley's son was not willing to voluntarily cooperate with treatment. Mike was sure that the psychiatrists would attempt to poison him. So, the family repeatedly found themselves in hospital emergency rooms where they were told that their son could not be admitted because—as an adult—he had the right to refuse treatment, even though his judgment obviously was severely impaired. In essence, they were told that their son could not be treated until he seriously hurt himself or someone else. As Earley put it, "I couldn't believe this was happening. My son was crazy and getting worse with each passing moment! Yet I couldn't get anyone to help him" (p. 17).

This frustrating experience was the impetus for Earley's book. It motivated him to conduct a wide-ranging investigation of mental health care in the United States today. His journey took him to mental hospitals, prisons, courts, alternative facilities for the mentally ill, meetings of mental health advocacy groups, and street corners where the homeless mentally ill congregated. He learned that "What was happening to Mike was not an oddity. It was a tiny piece in a bigger story. A major shift had occurred in our country. The mentally ill, who used to be treated in state mental hospitals, were now being arrested. Our nation's jails and prisons were our new asylums" (p. 2).

This book tells two intertwined stories—Earley's personal battle to obtain meaningful treatment for his son and his investigative analysis of modern mental health care. Both stories are compelling, heart-wrenching, and enlightening. And both stories demonstrate that American society is not providing adequate care for a sizable segment of the mentally ill population.

Unfortunately, there are no simple solutions to these problems on the horizon. Restraining the burgeoning cost of health care without compromising the quality of care, consumers' freedom of choice, and providers' autonomy is an enormously complex and daunting challenge. At this juncture, it is difficult to predict what the future holds. However, it is clear that economic realities have ushered in an era of transition for the treatment of psychological disorders and problems.

Blending Approaches to Treatment

In this chapter we have reviewed many approaches to treatment. However, there is no rule that a client must be treated with just one approach. Often, a clinician will use several techniques in working with a client. For example, a depressed person might receive group therapy (an insight therapy), social skills training (a behavior therapy), and antidepressant medication (a biomedical therapy). Multiple approaches are particularly likely when a treatment *team* provides therapy. Studies suggest that combining approaches to treatment has merit (Glass, 2004; Riba & Miller, 2003).

The value of multiple approaches may explain why a significant trend seems to have crept into the field of psychotherapy: a movement away from strong loyalty to individual schools of thought and a corresponding move toward integrating various approaches to therapy (Castonguay et al., 2003; D. Smith, 1999). Most clinicians used to depend exclusively on one system of therapy while rejecting the utility of all others. This era of fragmentation may be drawing to a close. In recent surveys of psychologists' theoretical orientations, researchers have found that one-half to two-thirds of respondents describe themselves as *eclectic* in approach (Lambert, Bergin, & Garfield, 2004). *Eclecticism* in the practice of therapy involves drawing ideas from two or more systems of therapy, instead of committing to just one system.

Increasing Multicultural Sensitivity in Treatment

Research on how cultural factors influence the process and outcome of psychotherapy has burgeoned in recent years, motivated in part by the need to improve mental health services for ethnic minority groups in American society (Lee & Ramirez, 2000; Miranda et al., 2005). The data are ambiguous for a couple of ethnic groups, but studies suggest that American minority groups generally underutilize therapeutic services (Olfson et al., 2002; Vega et al., 1999; Wells et al., 2001). Why? A variety of barriers appear to contribute to this problem, including the following (Snowden & Yamada, 2005; U.S. Department of Health and Human Services, 1999; Zane et al., 2004):

Cultural barriers have emerged in the psychotherapy process. A number of minority groups in the United States shy away from using professional services in this field. Those who do try it also tend to quickly terminate treatment more often than white Americans.

1. *Cultural barriers.* In times of psychological distress, some cultural groups are reluctant to turn to formal, professional sources of assistance. Given their socialization, they prefer to rely on informal assistance from family members, the clergy, respected elders, herbalists, acupuncturists, and so forth, who share their cultural heritage. Many members of minority groups have a history of frustrating interactions with American bureaucracies and are distrustful of large, intimidating, foreign institutions, such as hospitals and community mental health centers (Pierce, 1992).

2. *Language barriers.* Effective communication is crucial to the provision of psychotherapy, yet most hospitals and mental health agencies are not adequately staffed with therapists who speak the languages used by minority groups in their service areas. The resulting communication problems make it awkward and difficult for many minority group members to explain their problems and obtain the type of help they need.

3. *Institutional barriers.* Stanley Sue and Nolan Zane (1987) argue that the "single most important explanation for the problems in service delivery involves the inability of therapists to provide culturally responsive forms of treatment" (p. 37). The vast majority of therapists have been trained almost exclusively in the treatment of middle-class white Americans and are not familiar with the cultural backgrounds and unique characteristics of various ethnic groups. This culture gap often leads to misunderstandings and ill-advised treatment strategies (Hughes, 1993). Unfortunately, there is a grievous shortage of ethnic therapists to meet the needs of various ethnic groups (Mays & Albee, 1992).

What can be done to improve mental health services for American minority groups? Researchers in this area have offered a variety of suggestions (Hong, Garcia, & Soriano, 2000; Miranda et al., 2005; Pedersen, 1994; Sue & Zane, 1987; Yamamoto et al., 1993). Discussions of possible solutions usually begin with the need to recruit and train more ethnic minority therapists. Studies show that ethnic minorities are more likely to go to mental health facilities that are staffed by a higher proportion of people who share their ethnic background (Snowden & Hu, 1996; Sue, Zane, & Young, 1994). Furthermore, clients' satisfaction with therapy tends to be greater when they are treated by therapists from their own culture. Therapists can also be given special training to work more effectively with people from different cultural backgrounds. For example, Wade and Bernstein (1991) found that a cultural sensitivity training program for white therapists working with an African American clientele resulted in improved client satisfaction. Finally, most authorities urge further investigation of how traditional approaches to therapy can be modified and tailored to be more compatible with specific cultural groups' attitudes, values, norms, and traditions (Hwang, 2006).

LEARNING OBJECTIVES

▶ *Discuss where to seek therapy.*

▶ *Evaluate the potential importance of a therapist's gender and professional background.*

▶ *Summarize the evidence on whether therapists' theoretical approaches influence their effectiveness.*

▶ *Discuss what one should expect from therapy.*

Answer the following "true" or "false."

____ **1.** Psychotherapy is an art as well as a science.

____ **2.** The type of professional degree that a therapist holds is relatively unimportant.

____ **3.** Psychotherapy can be harmful or damaging to a client.

____ **4.** Psychotherapy does not have to be expensive.

____ **5.** It is a good idea to shop around when choosing a therapist.

All of these statements are true. Do any of them surprise you? If so, you're in good company. Many people know relatively little about the practicalities of selecting a therapist. The task of finding an appropriate therapist is no less complex than shopping for any other major service. Should you see a psychologist or a psychiatrist? Should you opt for individual therapy or group therapy? Should you see a client-centered therapist or a behavior therapist? The unfortunate part of this decision process is that people seeking psychotherapy often feel overwhelmed by personal problems. The last thing they need is to be confronted by yet another complex problem.

Nonetheless, the importance of finding a good therapist cannot be overestimated. Therapy can sometimes have harmful rather than helpful effects. We have already discussed how drug therapies and ECT can sometimes be damaging, but problems are not limited to these interventions. Talking about your problems with a therapist may sound pretty harmless, but studies indicate that insight therapies can also backfire (Lambert & Ogles, 2004; McGlashan et al., 1990). Although a great many talented therapists are available, psychotherapy, like any other profession, has incompetent practitioners as well. Therefore, you should shop for a skilled therapist, just as you would for a good attorney or a good mechanic.

In this Application, we present some information that should be helpful if you ever have to look for a therapist for yourself or for a friend or family member (based on Beutler, Bongar, & Shurkin, 2001; Bruckner-Gordon, Gangi, & Wallman, 1988; Ehrenberg & Ehrenberg, 1994; Pittman, 1994).

Where Do You Find Therapeutic Services?

Psychotherapy can be found in a variety of settings. Contrary to general belief, most therapists are not in

Finding the right therapist is no easy task. You need to take into account the therapist's training and orientation, fees charged, and personality. An initial visit should give you a good idea of what a particular therapist is like.

private practice. Many work in institutional settings such as community mental health centers, hospitals, and human service agencies. The principal sources of therapeutic services are described in **Figure 16.14**. The exact configuration of therapeutic services available will vary from one community to another. To find out what your community has to offer, it is a good idea to consult your friends, your local phone book, or your local community mental health center.

Is the Therapist's Profession or Sex Important?

Psychotherapists may be trained in psychology, psychiatry, social work, counseling, psychiatric nursing, or marriage and family therapy. Researchers have *not* found any reliable associations between therapists' professional background and therapeutic efficacy (Beutler et al., 2004), probably because many talented therapists can be found in all of these professions. Thus, the kind of degree that a therapist holds doesn't need to be a crucial consideration in your selection process.

Whether a therapist's sex is important depends on your attitude. If *you* feel that the therapist's sex is important, then for you it is. The therapeutic relationship must be characterized by trust and rapport. Feeling uncomfortable with a therapist of one sex or the other could inhibit the therapeutic process. Hence, you should feel free to look for a male or female therapist if you prefer to do so. This point is probably most relevant to female clients whose troubles may be related to the extensive sexism in our society (A. Kaplan, 1985). It is entirely reasonable for women to seek a therapist

Recommended
READING

The Psychotherapy Maze
by Otto and Miriam Ehrenberg
(Aronson, 1994)

This book is billed as a "consumer's guide to the ins and outs of therapy." The Ehrenbergs provide a frank, down-to-earth discussion of practical issues relating to psychotherapy. Most books on therapy are devoted to explaining various theoretical approaches to therapy. The Ehrenbergs go far beyond that in this book. They tackle such practical issues as how to select a therapist, how to help make therapy work for you, and how to judge whether therapy is doing you any good. They also discuss mundane but important details such as fees, insurance, missed sessions, and emergency phone calls. The Ehrenbergs' goal is to make therapy less intimidating and mysterious. They succeed handsomely in this endeavor.

with a feminist perspective if that would make them feel more comfortable.

Speaking of sex, you should be aware that sexual exploitation is an occasional problem in the context of therapy. Studies indicate that a small minority of therapists take advantage of their clients sexually (Pope, Keith-Spiegel, & Tabachnick, 1986). These incidents almost always involve a male therapist making advances to a female client. The available evidence indicates that these sexual liaisons are usually harmful to clients

Principal Sources of Therapeutic Services	
Source	**Comments**
Private practitioners	Self-employed therapists are listed in the Yellow Pages under their professional category, such as psychologists or psychiatrists. Private practitioners tend to be relatively expensive, but they also tend to be highly experienced therapists.
Community mental health centers	Community mental health centers have salaried psychologists, psychiatrists, and social workers on staff. The centers provide a variety of services and often have staff available on weekends and at night to deal with emergencies.
Hospitals	Several kinds of hospitals provide therapeutic services. There are both public and private mental hospitals that specialize in the care of people with psychological disorders. Many general hospitals have a psychiatric ward, and those that do not will usually have psychiatrists and psychologists on staff and on call. Although hospitals tend to concentrate on inpatient treatment, many provide outpatient therapy as well.
Human service agencies	Various social service agencies employ therapists to provide short-term counseling. Depending on your community, you may find agencies that deal with family problems, juvenile problems, drug problems, and so forth.
Schools and workplaces	Most high schools and colleges have counseling centers where students can get help with personal problems. Similarly, some large businesses offer in-house counseling to their employees.

Figure 16.14

Sources of therapeutic services. Therapists work in a variety of organizational settings. Foremost among them are the five described here.

(Gabbard, 1994; Williams, 1992). There are absolutely no situations in which therapist-client sexual relations are an ethical therapeutic practice. If a therapist makes sexual advances, a client should terminate treatment.

Is Therapy Always Expensive?

Psychotherapy does not have to be prohibitively expensive. Private practitioners tend to be the most expensive, charging between $25 and $140 per (50-minute) hour. These fees may seem high, but they are in line with those of similar professionals, such as dentists and attorneys. Community mental health centers and social service agencies are usually supported by tax dollars. Hence, they can charge lower fees than most therapists in private practice. Many of these organizations use a sliding scale, so that clients are charged according to how much they can afford. Thus, most communities have inexpensive opportunities for psychotherapy. Moreover, many health insurance plans provide at least partial reimbursement for the cost of treatment.

Is the Therapist's Theoretical Approach Important?

Logically, you might expect that the diverse approaches to therapy vary in effectiveness. For the most part, that is *not* what researchers find, however. After reviewing the evidence, Jerome Frank (1961) and Lester Luborsky and his colleagues (1975) both quote the dodo bird who has just judged a race in *Alice in Wonderland:* "Everybody has won, and *all* must have prizes." Improvement rates for various theoretical orientations usually come out pretty close in most studies (Lambert & Ogles, 2004; Luborsky et al., 2002; Wampold, 2001). In their landmark review of outcome studies, Smith and Glass (1977) estimated the effectiveness of many major approaches to therapy. As **Figure 16.15** shows, the estimates cluster together closely.

However, these findings are a little misleading, as they have been averaged across many types of patients and many types of problems. Most experts seem to think that *for certain types of problems, some approaches*

Figure 16.15

Efficacy of various approaches to therapy.
Smith and Glass (1977) reviewed nearly 400 studies in which clients who were treated with a specific type of therapy were compared with a control group made up of people with similar problems who went untreated. The bars indicate the percentile rank (on outcome measures) attained by the average client treated with each type of therapy when compared to control subjects. The higher the percentile, the more effective the therapy was. As you can see, the different approaches were fairly close in their apparent effectiveness.

Adapted from Smith, M. L., & Glass, G. V. (1977). Meta-analysis of psychotherapy outcome series. *American Psychologist, 32,* 752–760. Copyright © 1977 by the American Psychological Association. Adapted by permission of the publisher and author.

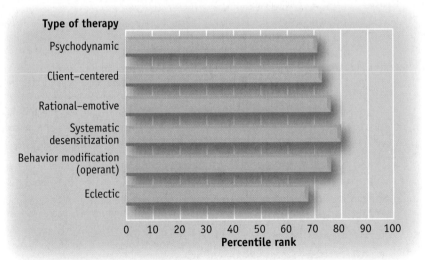

Therapy is both a science and an art. It is scientific in that practitioners are guided in their work by a huge body of empirical research. It is an art in that therapists often have to be creative in adapting their treatment procedures to individual patients and their idiosyncrasies.

pist's theoretical approach *may* make a difference.

It is also important to point out that the finding that various approaches to therapy are roughly equal in overall efficacy does not mean that all *therapists* are created equal. Some therapists unquestionably are more effective than others. However, these variations in effectiveness appear to depend on individual therapists' personal skills rather than on their theoretical orientation (Beutler et al., 2004). Good, bad, and mediocre therapists are found within each school of thought.

The key point is that effective therapy requires skill and creativity. Arnold Lazarus (1989), who devised an approach to treatment called multimodal therapy, emphasizes that therapists "straddle the fence between science and art." Therapy is scientific in that interventions are based on extensive theory and empirical research (Forsyth & Strong, 1986). Ultimately, though, each client is a unique human being, and the therapist has to creatively fashion a treatment program that will help that individual.

What Is Therapy Like?

It is important to have realistic expectations about therapy, or you may be unnecessarily disappointed. Some people expect miracles. They expect to turn their life around quickly with little effort. Others expect their therapist to run their lives for them. These are unrealistic expectations.

Therapy is usually a slow process. Your problems are not likely to melt away quickly. Moreover, therapy is hard work, and your therapist is only a facilitator. Ultimately, *you* have to confront the challenge of changing your behavior, your feelings, or your personality. This process may not be pleasant. You may have to face up to some painful truths about yourself. As Ehrenberg and Ehrenberg (1994) point out, psychotherapy takes time, effort, and courage.

to therapy are more effective than others (Beutler, 2002; Crits-Christoph, 1997; Norcross, 1995). For example, Martin Seligman (1995) asserts that panic disorders respond best to cognitive therapy, that specific phobias are most amenable to treatment with systematic desensitization, and that obsessive-compulsive disorders are best treated with behavior therapy or medication. Thus, for a specific type of problem, a thera-

KEY IDEAS

The Elements of the Treatment Process

▶ Psychotherapy involves three elements: treatments, clients, and therapists. Approaches to treatment are diverse, but they can be grouped into three categories: insight therapies, behavior therapies, and biomedical therapies. People vary considerably in their willingness to seek psychotherapy, and many people who need therapy do not receive it.

▶ Therapists come from a variety of professional backgrounds. Clinical and counseling psychologists, psychiatrists, social workers, psychiatric nurses, and counselors are the principal providers of therapeutic services.

Insight Therapies

▶ Insight therapies involve verbal interactions intended to enhance self-knowledge. In psychoanalysis, free association and dream analysis are used to explore the unconscious. When an analyst's probing hits sensitive areas, resistance can be expected. The transference relationship may be used to overcome this resistance. Classical psychoanalysis is not widely practiced anymore, but Freud's legacy lives on in a rich diversity of modern psychodynamic therapies.

▶ Rogers pioneered client-centered therapy, which is intended to provide a supportive climate in which clients can restructure their self-concepts. This therapy emphasizes clarification of the client's feelings and self-acceptance. Most theoretical approaches to insight therapy have been adapted for use with groups. Group therapy has its own unique strengths and is not merely a cheap substitute for individual therapy.

▶ The weight of the evidence suggests that insight therapies can be effective. The benefits of insight therapies may be due in part to common factors. Repressed memories of childhood sexual abuse recovered through therapy are a new source of controversy in the mental health field. Although many recovered memories of abuse may be the product of suggestion, some probably are authentic.

Behavior Therapies

▶ Behavior therapies use the principles of learning in direct efforts to change specific aspects of behavior. Wolpe's systematic desensitization is a treatment for phobias. It involves the construction of an anxiety hierarchy, relaxation training, and step-by-step movement through the hierarchy.

▶ In aversion therapy, a stimulus associated with an unwanted response is paired with an unpleasant stimulus in an effort to eliminate the maladaptive response. Social skills training can improve clients' interpersonal skills through shaping, modeling, and behavioral rehearsal. Beck's cognitive therapy concentrates on changing the way clients think about events in their lives. Ample evidence shows that behavior therapies are effective.

Biomedical Therapies

▶ Biomedical therapies involve physiological interventions for psychological problems. Two examples of biomedical treatments are drug therapy and electroconvulsive therapy. A great variety of disorders are treated with drugs. The principal types of therapeutic drugs are antianxiety drugs, antipsychotic drugs, antidepressant drugs, and mood stabilizers.

▶ Drug therapies can be effective, but they have their pitfalls. Many drugs produce problematic side effects, and some are overprescribed. Critics are also concerned that the pharmaceutical industry has gained too much influence over drug testing research.

▶ Electroconvulsive therapy (ECT) is used to trigger a cortical seizure that is believed to have therapeutic value for depression. There is contradictory evidence and heated debate about the effectiveness of ECT and about possible risks associated with its use.

Current Trends and Issues in Treatment

▶ Many clinicians and their clients believe that managed care has restricted access to mental health care and undermined its quality. Managed care has also raised concerns about providers' autonomy and clients' confidentiality.

▶ Combinations of insight, behavioral, and biomedical therapies are often used fruitfully in the treatment of psychological disorders. Many modern therapists are eclectic, using ideas and techniques gleaned from a number of theoretical approaches.

▶ Because of cultural, language, and access barriers, therapeutic services are underutilized by ethnic minorities in America. However, the crux of the problem is the failure of institutions to provide culturally sensitive forms of treatment for ethnic minorities.

Application: Looking for a Therapist

▶ Therapeutic services are available in many settings, and such services do not have to be expensive. Excellent and mediocre therapists can be found in all of the mental health professions. Thus, therapists' personal skills are more important than their professional degree. In selecting a therapist, it is reasonable to insist on a therapist of one gender or the other.

▶ The various theoretical approaches to treatment appear to be fairly similar in overall effectiveness. However, for certain types of problems, some approaches to therapy may be more effective than others. Therapy requires time, hard work, and the courage to confront your problems.

KEY TERMS

Antianxiety drugs   p. 534
Antidepressant drugs   p. 535
Antipsychotic drugs   p. 534
Aversion therapy   p. 530
Behavior therapies   p. 528
Biomedical therapies   p. 533
Client-centered
   therapy   p. 522
Clinical psychologists   p. 517
Cognitive-behavioral
   treatments   p. 531
Cognitive therapy   p. 531
Counseling
   psychologists   p. 517
Dream analysis   p. 520
Electroconvulsive therapy
   (ECT)   p. 537

Free association   p. 520
Group therapy   p. 523
Insight therapies   p. 519
Interpretation   p. 520
Mood stabilizers   p. 536
Psychiatrists   p. 518
Psychoanalysis   p. 519
Psychopharmacotherapy
   p. 533
Resistance   p. 521
Social skills training   p. 531
Systematic
   desensitization   p. 529
Tardive dyskinesia   p. 535
Transference   p. 521

KEY PEOPLE

Aaron Beck   pp. 531–533
Sigmund
   Freud   pp. 519–521

Carl Rogers   pp. 522–523
Joseph Wolpe   pp. 529–530

1. Which of the following approaches to psychotherapy is based on the theories of Sigmund Freud and his followers?
   a. Behavior therapies
   b. Client-centered therapy
   c. Biomedical therapies
   d. Psychoanalytic therapy

2. Miriam is seeing a therapist who encourages her to let her mind ramble and say whatever comes up, regardless of how trivial or irrelevant it may seem. The therapist explains that she is interested in probing the depths of Miriam's unconscious mind. This therapist appears to practice _____ and the technique in use is _____.
   a. psychoanalysis; transference
   b. psychoanalysis; free association
   c. cognitive therapy; free association
   d. client-centered therapy; clarification

3. Because Suzanne has an unconscious sexual attraction to her father, she behaves seductively toward her therapist. Suzanne's behavior is most likely a form of:
   a. resistance.
   b. transference.
   c. misinterpretation.
   d. spontaneous remission.

4. Client-centered therapy emphasizes:
   a. interpretation.
   b. probing the unconscious
   c. clarification.
   d. all of the above.

5. With regard to studies of the efficacy of various treatments, research suggests:
   a. insight therapy is superior to no treatment or placebo treatment.
   b. individual insight therapy is effective, but group therapy is not.
   c. group therapy is effective, but individual insight therapy rarely works.
   d. insight therapy is effective, but only if patients remain in therapy for at least three years.

6. According to behavior therapists, pathological behaviors:
   a. are signs of an underlying emotional or cognitive problem.
   b. should be viewed as the expression of an unconscious sexual or aggressive conflict.
   c. can be modified directly through the application of established principles of conditioning.
   d. both a and b.

7. A stimulus that elicits an undesirable response is paired with a noxious stimulus in:
   a. systematic desensitization.
   b. cognitive therapy.
   c. aversion therapy.
   d. psychoanalysis.

8. Bryce's psychiatrist has prescribed both Prozac and lithium for him. Bryce's diagnosis is probably:
   a. schizophrenia.
   b. obsessive-compulsive disorder.
   c. bipolar disorder.
   d. dissociative disorder.

9. Drug therapies have been criticized on the grounds that:
   a. they are ineffective in most patients.
   b. they temporarily relieve symptoms without addressing the real problem.
   c. many drugs are overprescribed and many patients are overmedicated.
   d. both b and c.

10. A therapist's theoretical approach is not nearly as important as his or her:
    a. age.
    b. appearance.
    c. personal characteristics and skills.
    d. type of professional training.

Book Companion Website

Visit the Book Companion Website at **academic.cengage.com/psychology/weiten**, where you will find tutorial quizzes, flash cards, and web links for every chapter, a final exam, and more! You can also link to the Psychology Resource Center (accessible directly at **academic.cengage.com/login**) for a range of psychology-related resources.

Personal Explorations Workbook

The following exercises in your *Personal Explorations Workbook* may enhance your self-understanding in relation to issues raised in this chapter. **Questionnaire 16.1:** Attitudes Toward Seeking Professional Psychological Help. **Personal Probe 16.1:** What Are Your Feelings about Therapy? **Personal Probe 16.2:** Thinking About Therapy.

1. d Pages 519–521
2. b Pages 519–520
3. b Page 521
4. c Page 523
5. a Pages 524–525
6. c Pages 528–529
7. c Page 530
8. c Pages 535–536
9. d Pages 536–537
10. c Page 545

Glossary

acquired immune deficiency syndrome (AIDS) A disorder in which the immune system is gradually weakened and eventually disabled by the human immunodeficiency virus (HIV).

actor-observer effect The tendency to attribute one's own behavior to situational factors and others' behavior to personal factors.

acculturation Changing to adapt to a new culture.

acute stressors Threatening events that have a relatively short duration and a clear end point.

adjustment The psychological processes through which people manage or cope with the demands and challenges of everyday life.

aggression Any behavior intended to hurt someone, either physically or verbally.

agoraphobia A fear of going out to public places.

alcohol dependence *See* alcoholism

alcoholism A chronic, progressive disorder marked by a growing compulsion to drink and impaired control over drinking that eventually interfere with health and social behavior.

ambient stress Chronic environmental conditions that, although not urgent, are negatively valued and place adaptive demands on people.

anal intercourse The insertion of the penis into a partner's anus and rectum.

androcentrism The belief that the male is the norm.

androgens The principal class of male sex hormones.

androgyny The coexistence of both masculine and feminine personality traits in an individual.

anorexia nervosa An eating disorder characterized by intense fear of gaining weight, disturbed body image, refusal to maintain normal weight, and use of dangerous methods to lose weight.

antecedents In behavior modification, events that typically precede a target response.

antianxiety drugs Drugs that relieve tension, apprehension, and nervousness.

antidepressant drugs Drugs that gradually elevate mood and help to bring people out of a depression.

antipsychotic drugs Drugs used to gradually reduce psychotic symptoms, including hyperactivity, mental confusion, hallucinations, and delusions.

anxiety disorders A class of psychological disorders marked by feelings of excessive apprehension and anxiety.

approach-approach conflict A conflict in which a choice must be made between two attractive goals.

approach-avoidance conflict A conflict in which a choice must be made about whether to pursue a single goal that has both attractive and unattractive aspects.

archetypes Emotionally charged images and thought forms that have universal meaning.

assertiveness Acting in one's own best interest by expressing one's feelings and thoughts honestly and directly.

atherosclerosis A disease characterized by gradual narrowing of the coronary arteries.

attachment styles Typical ways of interacting in close relationships.

attitudes Beliefs and feelings about people, objects, and ideas.

attributions Inferences that people draw about the causes of events, others' behavior, and their own behavior.

autonomic nervous system (ANS) That portion of the peripheral nervous system made up of the nerves that connect to the heart, blood vessels, smooth muscles, and glands.

aversion therapy A behavior therapy in which an aversive stimulus is paired with a stimulus that elicits an undesirable response.

avoidance-avoidance conflict A conflict in which a choice must be made between two unattractive goals.

basking in reflected glory The tendency to enhance one's image by publicly announcing one's association with those who are successful.

battering Physical abuse, emotional abuse, and sexual abuse, especially in marriage or relationships.

behavior Any overt (observable) response or activity by an organism.

behavior modification A systematic approach to changing behavior through the application of the principles of conditioning.

behavior therapies The application of the principles of learning to direct efforts to change clients' maladaptive behaviors.

behavioral contract A written agreement outlining a promise to adhere to the contingencies of a behavior modification program.

behaviorism A theoretical orientation based on the premise that scientific psychology should study observable behavior.

bereavement The painful loss of a loved one through death.

binge-eating disorder An eating disorder that involves distress-inducing eating binges that are not accompanied by the purging, fasting, and excessive exercise seen in bulimia.

biomedical therapies Physiological interventions intended to reduce symptoms associated with psychological disorders.

biopsychosocial model The idea that physical illness is caused by a complex interaction of biological, psychological, and socio-cultural factors.

bipolar disorders Psychological disorders marked by the experience of both depressed and manic periods.

bisexuals People who seek emotional-sexual relationships with members of both genders.

body mass index (BMI) Weight (in kilograms) divided by height (in meters) squared (kg/m2).

brainstorming Generating as many ideas as possible while withholding criticism and evaluation.

bulimia nervosa An eating disorder characterized by habitual out-of-control over-eating followed by unhealthy compensatory efforts, such as self-induced vomiting, fasting, abuse of laxatives and diuretics, and excessive exercise.

burnout Physical, mental, and emotional exhaustion that is attributable to work-related stress.

bystander effect The social phenomenon in which individuals are less likely to provide needed help when others are present than when they are alone.

cancer Malignant cell growth, which may occur in many organ systems in the body.

cannabis The hemp plant from which marijuana, hashish, and THC are derived.

case study An in-depth investigation of an individual subject.

catastrophic thinking Unrealistic appraisals of stress that exaggerate the magnitude of one's problems.

catatonic schizophrenia A type of schizophrenia marked by striking motor disturbances, ranging from muscular rigidity to random motor activity.

catharsis The release of emotional tension.

cerebral hemispheres The right and left halves of the cerebrum, which is the convoluted outer layer of the brain.

channel The medium through which a message reaches the receiver.

chronic stressors Threatening events that have a relatively long duration and no readily apparent time limit.

classical conditioning A type of learning in which a neutral stimulus acquires the capacity to evoke a response that was originally evoked by another stimulus.

client-centered therapy An insight therapy that emphasizes providing a supportive emotional climate for clients, who play a major role in determining the pace and direction of their therapy.

Moffat, F. L., Jr., & Clark, K. C. (1993). How coping mediates the effect of optimism on distress: A study of women with early-stage breast cancer. *Journal of Personality and Social Psychology, 65,* 375–390.

Carver, C. S., & Scheier, M. F. (1994). Situational coping and coping dispositions in a stressful transaction. *Journal of Personality and Social Psychology, 66,* 184–195.

Carver, C. S., & Scheier, M. F. (2002). Optimism. In C. R. Snyder & S. J. Lopez (Eds.), *Handbook of positive psychology.* New York: Oxford University Press.

Carver, C. S., & Scheier, M. F. (2005). Optimism. In C. R. Snyder & S. J. Lopez (Eds.), *Foundations of health psychology.* New York: Oxford University Press.

Carver, C. S., Scheier, M. F., & Weintraub, J. K. (1989). Assessing coping strategies: A theoretically based approach. *Journal of Personality and Social Psychology, 56,* 267–283.

Cascio, W. F., & Young, C. E. (2005). Work-family balance: Does the market reward firms that respect it? In D. F. Halpern & S. E. Murphy (Eds.), *From work-family balance to work-family interaction: Changing the metaphor.* Mahwah, NJ: Erlbaum.

Cashdan, E. (1998). Smiles, speech, and body posture: How women and men display sociometric status and power. *Journal of Nonverbal Behavior, 22,* 209–228.

Caspersen, C. J., Bloemberg, B. P., Saris, W. H., Merritt, R. K., & Kromhout, D. (1991). The prevalence of selected physical activities and their relation with coronary heart disease risk factors in elderly men: The Zutphen study, 1985. *American Journal of Epidemiology, 133,* 1078–1092.

Caspi, A., Sugden, K., Moffitt, T. E., Taylor, A., Craig, I. W., Harrington, H., McClay, J., Mill, J., Martin, J., Braithwaite, A., & Poulton, R. (2003). Influence of life stress on depression: Moderation by a polymorphism in the 5-HTT gene. *Science, 301,* 386–389.

Cassata, D. (2005, October 16). The decline of American civilization, or at least its manners. *Statesboro Herald,* p. 9A.

Cassel, R. N. (2000). Third force psychology and person-centered theory: From ego-status to ego-ideal. *Psychology: A Journal of Human Behavior, 37*(3), 44–48.

Castonguay, L. G., Reid Jr., J. J., Halperin, G. S., & Goldfried, M. R. (2003). Psychotherapy integration. In G. Stricker, & T. A. Widiger (Eds.), *Handbook of psychology: Vol. 8. Clinical psychology.* New York: Wiley.

Catalyst. (2007). *Catalyst releases 2006 census of women in Fortune 500 corporate officer and board positions.* Retrieved on June 5, 2007 from http://www.catalyst.org/pressroom/press_releases/2006_Census_Release.pdf.

Catania, J. A., Binson, D., Dolcini, M. M., Moskowitz, J. T., & van der Straten, A. (2001). In A. Baum, T. A. Revenson, & J. E. Singer (Eds.), *Handbook of health psychology.* Mahwah, NJ: Erlbaum.

Cate, R. M., & Lloyd, S. A. (1988). Courtship. In S. Duck (Ed.), *Handbook of personal relationships.* New York: Wiley.

Cates, W., Jr. (2004). Reproductive tract infections. In R. A. Hatcher, J. Trussell, F. H. Stewart, A. L. Nelson, W. Cates Jr., F. Guest, & D. Kowal (Eds.), *Contraceptive technology.* New York: Ardent Media.

Cattell, R. B. (1950). *Personality: A systematic, theoretical and factual study.* New York: McGraw-Hill.

Cattell, R. B. (1966). *The scientific analysis of personality.* Chicago: Aldine.

Cattell, R. B. (1990). Advances in Cattellian personality theory. In L. A. Pervin (Ed.), *Handbook of personality: Theory and research.* New York: Guilford.

Cattell, R. B., Eber, H. W., & Tatsuoka, M. M. (1970). *Handbook of the Sixteen Personality Factor Questionnaire* (16PF). Champaign, IL: Institute for Personality and Ability Testing.

Catz, S. L., & Kelly, J. A. (2001). Living with HIV disease. In A. Baum, T. A. Revenson, & J. E. Singer (Eds.), *Handbook of health psychology.* Mahwah, NJ: Erlbaum.

Cavanaugh, J. C. (1993). *Adult development and aging* (2nd ed.). Pacific Grove, CA: Brooks/Cole.

Cavanaugh, J. C. (2000). Metamemory from a social-cognitive perspective. In D. Park & N. Schwarz (Eds.), *Cognitive aging: A primer.* Philadelphia: Psychology Press.

Cavanaugh, J. C., Feldman, J. M., & Hertzog, C. (1998). Meta-memory as social cognition: A reconceptualization of what memory questionnaires assess. *Review of General Psychology, 2,* 48–65.

Caverly, D. C., Orlando, V. P., & Mullen, J. L. (2000). Textbook study reading. In R. F. Flippo & D. C. Caverly (Eds.), *Handbook of college reading and study strategy research.* Mahwah, NJ: Erlbaum.

Centers for Disease Control. (2002). Youth risk behavior surveillance—United States, 2001. *Morbidity and Mortality Weekly Report,* Retrieved March 19, 2007 from http://www.cdc.gov/mmwr/preview/mmwrhtml/ss5104a1.htm#top.

Centers for Disease Control. (2006). Update: Trends in AIDS incidence-United States. *MMWR, 46*(37), 861–867.

Centers for Disease Control. (2007). *A glance at the HIV/AIDS epidemic.* Retrieved June 24, 2007 from http://www.cdc.gov/hiv/resources/factsheets/pdf/at=a-glance.pdf.

Cerletti, U., & Bini, L. (1938). Un nuovo metodo di shockterapie "L'elettro-shock." Boll. Acad. Med. *Roma, 64,* 136–138.

Cetron, M. J., & Davies, O. (2003, March–April). Trends shaping the future: Technological, workplace, management, and institutional trends. *The Futurist,* pp. 30–43.

Chamberlin, J. (2007, March). Too much information. *GradPSYCH,* pp. 14–16.

Chambless, D. L., & Hollon, S. D. (1998). Defining empirically supported therapies. *Journal of Consulting & Clinical Psychology, 66*(1), 7–18.

Chambless, D. L., & Ollendick, T. H. (2001). Empirically supported psychological interventions: Controversies and evidence. *Annual Review of Psychology, 52,* 685–716.

Chambliss, C. H. (2000). *Psychotherapy and managed care: Reconciling research and reality.* Boston, MA: Allyn & Bacon.

Chan, R. W., Brooks, R. C., Raboy, B., & Patterson, C. J. (1998). Division of labor among lesbian and heterosexual parents: Associations with children's adjustment. *Journal of Family Psychology, 12,* 402–419.

Chandler, M. J., Lalonde, C. E., Sokol, B. W., & Hallett, D. (2003). Personal persistence, identity development, and suicide: A study of native and non-native North American adolescents. *Monographs of the Society for Research in Child Development, 68*(2), viii–130.

Chang, E. C. (1996). Cultural differences in optimism, pessimism, and coping: Predictors of subsequent adjustment in Asian American and Caucasian American college students. *Journal of Counseling Psychology, 43,* 113–123.

Chang, R. Y., & Kelly, P. K. (1993). *Step-by-step problem solving: A practical guide to ensure problems get (and stay) solved.* Irvine, CA: Richard Chang Associates.

Chaplin, W. F., Phillips, J. B., Brown, J. D., Clanton, N. R., & Stein, J. L. (2000). Handshaking, gender, personality, and first impressions. *Journal of Personality and Social Psychology, 79*(1), 110–117.

Charles, S. T., & Carstensen, L. L. (1999). The role of time in the setting of social goals across the life span. In T. M. Hess & F. Blanchard-Fields (Eds.), *Social cognition and aging.* San Diego: Academic Press.

Charlesworth, W. R., & Dzur, C. (1987). Gender comparisons of preschoolers' behavior and resource utilization in group problem-solving. *Child Development, 58,* 191–200.

Chartrand, T., Pinckert, S., & Burger, J. M. (1999). When manipulation backfires: The effects of time delay and requester on the foot-in-the-door technique. *Journal of Applied Social Psychology, 29*(1), 211–221.

Chemers, M. M., Hu, L., & Garcia, B. F. (2001). Academic self-efficacy and first-year college student performance and adjustment. *Journal of Educational Psychology, 93*(1), 55–64.

Chen, Y. Y., Gilligan, S., & Coups, E. J. (2005). Hostility and perceived social support: Interactive effects on cardiovascular reactivity to laboratory stressors. *Annals of Behavioral Medicine, 29,* 37–43.

Cheng, C. (2001). Assessing coping flexibility in real-life and laboratory settings: A multimethod approach. *Journal of Personality and Social Psychology, 80*(5), 814–833.

Cheng, C. (2003). Cognitive and motivational processes underlying coping flexibility: A dual-process model. *Journal of Personality and Social Psychology, 84,* 425–438.

Cheng, C., & Cheung, M. W. L. (2005). Cognitive processes underlying coping flexibility: Differentiation and integration. *Journal of Personality, 73,* 859–886.

Cherlin, A. J. (1999). Going to extremes: Family structure, children's well-being, and social science. *Demography, 36,* 421–428.

Cherlin, A. J. (2004). The deinstitutionalization of American marriage. *Journal of Marriage and Family, 66,* 848–861.

Chia, R. C., Moore, J. L., Lam, K. N., Chuang, C. J., & Cheng, B. S. (1994). Cultural differences in gender role attitudes between Chinese and American students. *Sex Roles, 31,* 23–29.

Chiappelli, F., & Hodgson, D. (2000). Immune suppression. In G. Fink (Ed.), *Encyclopedia of stress* (Vol. 2). San Diego: Academic Press.

Chiappelli, F., & Liu, Q. N. (2000). Immunity. In G. Fink (Ed.), *Encyclopedia of stress.* San Diego: Academic Press.

Chick, J. (1998). Alcohol, health, and the heart: Implications for clinicians. *Alcohol and Alcoholism, 33*(6), 576–591.

Chick, K. A., Heilman-Houserk, R. A., & Hunter, M. W. (2002). The impact of child care on gender role development and gender stereotypes. *Early Childhood Education Journal, 29*(3), 149–154.

Chiriboga, D. A. (1987). Personality in later life. In P. Silverman (Ed.), *The elderly as modern pioneers.* Bloomington: Indiana University Press.

Chiriboga, D. A. (1989). Mental health at the midpoint: Crisis, challenge, or relief? In S. Hunter & M. Sundel (Eds.), *Mid-life myths: Issues, findings, and practical implications.* Thousand Oaks, CA: Sage.

Choi, I., Dalal, R., Kim-Prieto, C., & Park, H. (2003). Culture and judgment of causal relevance. *Journal of Personality and Social Psychology, 84*(1), 46-59.

Choi, I., Nisbett, R. E., & Norenzayan, A. (1999). Causal attribution across cultures: Variation and universality. *Psychological Bulletin, 125*(1), 47–63.

Choice, P., & Lamke, L. K. (1997). A conceptual approach to understanding abused women's stay/leave decisions. *Journal of Family Issues, 18,* 290–314.

Chopra, D. (1993). *Ageless body, timeless mind.* New York: Crown.

Chopra, S. S. (2003). Industry funding of clinical trials: Benefit or bias? *JAMA, 290,* 113–114.

Chou, C., Condron, L., & Belland, J. C. (2005). A review of the research on Internet addiction. *Educational Psychology Review, 17,* 363–388.

Choudhry, N. K., Stelfox, H. T., & Detsky, A. S. (2002). Relationships between authors of clinical practice guidelines and the pharmaceutical industry. *Journal of the American Medical Association, 287*(5), 612–617.

Christensen, A., & Jacobson, N. S. (2000). *Reconcilable differences.* New York: Guilford Press.

Christensen, A. J., & Johnson, J. A. (2002). Patient adherence with medical treatment regimens: An interactive approach. *Current Directions in Psychological Science, 11*(3), 94–97.

Christensen, P., & Kashy, D. (1998). Perceptions of and by lonely people in initial social interaction. *Personality and Social Psychology Bulletin, 24*(3), 322–329.

Christoph, R. T., Schoenfeld, G. A., & Tansky, J. W. (1998). Overcoming barriers to training utilizing technology: The influence of self-efficacy factors on multimedia-based training receptiveness. *Human Resource Development Quarterly, 9*(1), 25–38.

Christophe, V., & Rime, B. (1997). Exposure to the social sharing of emotion: Emotional impact, listener responses and secondary social sharing. *European Journal of Social Psychology, 27,* 37–54.

Christopher, F. S., & Sprecher, S. (2000). Sexuality in marriage, dating, and other relationships: A decade review. *Journal of Marriage and the Family, 62,* 999–1017.

Chua, H. F., Leu, J., & Nisbett, R. E. (2005). Culture and diverging views of social events. *Personality and Social Psychology Bulletin, 31,* 925–934.

Chun, C., Moos, R. H., & Cronkite, R. C. (2006). Culture: A fundamental context for the stress and coping paradigm. In P. T. P. Wong & L. C. J. Wong (Eds.), *Handbook of multicultural perspectives on stress and coping.* New York: Springer.

Cialdini, R. B. (2001). *Influence: Science and practice* (4th ed.). Boston: Allyn & Bacon.

Cialdini, R. B. (2007). *Influence: Science and practice.* New York: HarperCollins.

Cialdini, R. B., Borden, R. J., Thorne, A., Walker, M. R., Freeman, S., & Sloan, L. R. (1976). Basking in reflected glory: Three (football) field studies. *Journal of Personality and Social Psychology, 34,* 366–375.

Cialdini, R. B., & Goldstein, N. J. (2004). Social Influence: Compliance and conformity. *Annual Review of Psychology, 55,* 591–621.

Ciarrochi, J., Dean, F. P., & Anderson, S. (2002). Emotional intelligence moderates the relationship between stress and mental health. *Personality & Individual Differences, 32,* 197–209.

Cicirelli, V. G. (1999). Personality and demographic factors in older adults' fear of death. *Gerontologist, 39*(5), 569–579.

Cicirelli, V. G. (2002). *Older adults' views on death.* New York: Springer.

Claar, R. L., & Blumenthal, J. A. (2003). The value of stress-management interventions in life-threatening medical conditions. *Current Directions in Psychological Science, 12*(4), 133–137.

Clark, D. (2005). *Loving someone gay.* Berkeley, CA: Celestial Arts.

Clark, M. S., & Grote, N. K. (2003). Close relationships. In T. Millon & M. J. Lerner (Eds.) *Handbook of psychology: Vol. 5. Personality and social psychology.* New York: Wiley.

Clark, M. S., & Mills, J. (1993). The difference between communal and exchange relationships: What it is and is not. *Journal of Personality and Social Psychology Bulletin, 19,* 684–691.

Clarke-Stewart, K. A., & Bailey, B. L. (1989). Adjusting to divorce: Why do men have it easier? *Journal of Divorce, 13,* 75–94.

Cleek, M. G., & Pearson, T. A. (1985). Perceived causes of divorce: An analysis of interrelationships. *Journal of Marriage and the Family, 47,* 179–183.

Clements, A. M., Rimrodt, S. L., Abel, J. R., Blankner, J. G., Mostofsky, S. H., Pekar, J. J., et al. (2006). Sex differences in cerebral laterality of language and visuospatial processing. *Brain and Language, 98*(2), 150–158.

Clements, M. L., Stanley, S. M., & Markman, H. J. (2004). Before they said "I do": Discriminating among marital outcomes over 13 years. *Journal of Marriage and Family, 66,* 613–626.

Cloitre, M., Morin, N. A., & Linares, O. (2004, January-February). Children's resilience in the face of trauma. *The New York University Child Study Letter.*

Clow, A. (2001). The physiology of stress. In F. Jones & J. Bright (Eds.), *Stress: Myth, theory and research.* Harlow, England: Pearson Education.

Coates, T. J., & Collins, C. (1998). Preventing HIV infection. *Scientific American, 279*(1), 96–97.

Cochran, S. D. (2001). Emerging issues in research on lesbians' and gay men's mental health: Does sexual orientation really matter? *American Psychologist, 56,* 931–947.

Cohan, C. L., & Kleinbaum, S. (2002). Toward a greater understanding of the cohabitation effect: Premarital cohabitation and marital communication. *Journal of Marriage and Family, 64,* 180–192.

Cohen, C. E. (1981). Person categories and social perception: Testing some boundaries of the processing effects of prior knowledge. *Journal of Personality and Social Psychology, 40,* 441–452.

Cohen, D. (1997). A critique of the use of neuroleptic drugs in psychiatry. In S. Fisher & R. P. Greenberg (Eds.), *From placebo to panacea: Putting psychiatric drugs to the test.* New York: Wiley.

Cohen, D., & McCubbin, M. (1990). The political economy of tardive dyskinesia: Asymmetries in power and responsibility. *The Journal of Mind and Behavior, 11,* 465–488.

Cohen, D. B. (1999). *Stranger in the nest: Do parents really shape their child's personality, intelligence, or character?* New York: Wiley.

Cohen, F. (1979). Personality, stress and the development of physical illness. In G. C. Stone, F. Cohen, N. E. Adler, & associates (Eds.), *Health psychology—A handbook.* San Francisco: Jossey-Bass.

Cohen, F., Solomon, S., Maxfield, M. , Pyszczynski, T., & Greenberg, J. (2004). Fatal attraction: The effects of mortality salience on evaluations of charismatic, task-oriented, and relationship-oriented leaders. *Psychological Science, 15,* 846–851.

Cohen, M. J. M., Kunkel, E. S., & Levenson, J. L. (1998). Associations between psychosocial stress and malignancy. In J. R. Hubbard & E. A. Workman (Eds.), *Handbook of stress medicine: An organ system approach.* Boca Raton: CRC Press.

Cohen, S., Doyle, W. J., Turner, R., Alper, C. M., & Skoner, D. P. (2003). Sociability and susceptibility to the common cold. *Psychological Science, 14*(5), 389–395.

Cohen, S., Evans, G. W., Krantz, D. S., & Stokols, D. (1980). Physiological, motivational, and cognitive effects of aircraft noise on children: Moving from the laboratory to the field. *American Psychologist, 35,* 231–243.

Cohen, S., Hamrick, N., Rodriguez, M. S., Feldman, P. J., Rabin, B. S., & Manuck, S. B. (2002). Reactivity and vulnerability to stress-associated risk for upper respiratory illness. *Psychosomatic Illness, 64,* 302–310.

Cohen, S., Kessler, R. C., & Gordon, L. U. (1995). Strategies for measuring stress in studies of psychiatric and physical disorders. In S. Cohen, R. C. Kessler, & L. U. Gordon (Eds.), *Measuring stress: A guide for health and social scientists.* New York: Oxford University Press.

Cohen, S., Lichtenstein, E., Prochaska, J. O., Rossi, J. S., Gritz, E. R., Carr, C. R., Orleans, C. T., Schoenbach, V. J., Biener, L., Abrams, D., DiClemente, C., Curry, S., Marlatt, G. A., Cummings, K. M., Emont, S. L., Giovino, A., & Ossip-Klein, D. (1989). Debunking myths about self-quitting: Evidence from 10 prospective studies of persons who attempt to quit smoking by themselves. *American Psychologist, 44,* 1355–1365.

Cohen, S., Tyrrell, D. A., & Smith, A. P. (1993). Negative life events, perceived stress, negative affect, and susceptibility to the common cold. *Journal of Personality and Social Psychology, 64,* 131–140.

Cohen-Bendahan, C. C. C., van de Beek, C., & Berenbaum, S. A. (2005). Prenatal sex hormone effects on child and adult sex-typed behavior: Methods and findings. *Neuroscience & Biobehavioral Reviews, 29,* 353–384.

Colder, C. R. (2001). Life stress, physiological and subjective indexes of negative emotionality and coping reasons for drinking: Is there evidence for a self-medication model of alcohol use? *Psychology of Addictive Behaviors, 15*(3), 237–245.

Cole, S. W., Kemeny, M. E., Taylor, S. E., & Visscher, B. R. (1996). Elevated physical health risk among gay men who conceal their homosexual identity. *Health Psychology, 15,* 243–251.

Coles, M. E., Schofield, C. A., & Pietrefesa, A. S. (2006). Behavioral inhibition and obsessive-compulsive disorder. *Journal of Anxiety Disorders, 20,* 1118–1132.

Collaer, M. L., & Hines, M. (1995). Human behavioral sex differences: A role for gonadal hormones during early development? *Psychological Bulletin, 118,* 55–107.

College Entrance Examination Board. (2004). *Writing: a Ticket to Work. . . . Or a Ticket Out: A Survey of Business Leaders.* Retrieved September 4, 2007 from http://www.writingcommission.org/prod_downloads/writingcom/writing-ticket-to-work.pdf

Colley, A., & Todd, Z. (2002). Gender-linked differences in the style and content of e-mails to friends. *Journal of Language and Social Psychology, 21*(4), 380–392.

Colligan, T. W., & Higgins, E. M. (2005). Workplace stress: Etiology and consequences. *Journal of Workplace Behavioral Health, 21*(2), 89–97.

Collins, N. L., & Feeney, B. C. (2004). An attachment theory perspective on closeness and intimacy. In D. J. Mashek & A. Aron (Eds.), *Handbook of closeness and intimacy.* Mahwah, NJ: Erlbaum.

Collins, N. L., & Miller, L. C. (1994). Self-disclosure and liking: A meta-analytic review. *Psychological Bulletin, 116,* 457–475.

Collins, R. L. (1996). For better or worse: The impact of upward social comparison on self-evaluations. *Psychological Bulletin, 119*(1), 51–69.

Collins, W. A., & Madsen, S. D. (2006). Personal relationships in adolescence and early adulthood. In A. L. Vangelisti & D. Perlman (Eds.), *The Cambridge handbook of personal relationships.* New York: Cambridge University Press.

Collins, W. A., Maccoby, E. E., Steinberg, L., Hetherington, E. M., & Bornstein, M. H. (2000). Contemporary research in parenting: The case for nature and nurture. *American Psychologist, 55,* 218–232.

Coltrane, S. (2001). Marketing the marriage "solution": Misplaced simplicity in the politics of fatherhood. *Sociological Perspectives, 44*(4), 387–418.

Coltrane, S., & Adams, M. (2003). The social construction of the divorce "problem": Morality, child victims, and the politics of gender. *Family Relations: Interdisciplinary Journal of Applied Family Studies, 52*(4), 363–372.

Colvin, C. R., & Block, J. (1994). Do positive illusions foster mental health? An examination of the Taylor and Brown formulation. *Psychological Bulletin, 116,* 3–20.

Colvin, C. R., Block, J., & Funder, D. C. (1995). Overly positive self-evaluations and personality: Negative implications for mental health. *Journal of Personality and Social Psychology, 68,* 1152–1162.

Comas-Diaz, L. (1987). Feminist therapy with mainland Puerto Rican women. *Psychology of Women Quarterly, 11,* 461–474.

Condoms—extra protection. (2005, February). *Consumer Reports,* pp. 34–38.

Condon, J. W., & Crano, W. D. (1988). Inferred evaluation and the relation between attitude similarity and interpersonal attraction. *Journal of Personality and Social Psychology, 54*(5), 789–797.

Conklin, H. M., & Iacono, W. G. (2002). Schizophrenia: A neurodevelopmental perspective. *Current Directions in Psychological Science, 11,* 33–37.

Connidis, I. A., & McMullin, J. A. (1999). Permanent childlessness: Perceived advantages and disadvantages among older persons. *Canadian Journal on Aging, 18,* 447–465.

Contrada, R. J., Ashmore, R. D., Gary, M. L., Coups, E., Egeth, J. D., Sewell, A., Ewell, K., Goyal, T. M., & Chasse, V. (2000). Ethnicity-related sources of stress and their effects on well-being. *Current Directions in Psychological Science, 9*(4), 136–139.

Coontz, S. (1997, November 17). Divorcing reality. *The Nation,* pp. 21–24.

Coontz, S. (2000). *The way we never were: American families and the nostalgia trap.* New York: Basic Books.

Cooper, A. (2002). *Sex and the Internet.* Philadelphia: Brunner-Routledge.

Cooper, A., Boies, S., Maheu, M., & Greenfield, D. (2000). Sexuality and the Internet: The next sexual revolution. In L. T. Szuchman & F. Muscarella (Eds.), *Psychological perspectives on human sexuality.* New York: Wiley.

Cooper, A., & Griffin-Shelley, E. (2002). A quick tour of online sexuality: Part 1. *Annals of the American Psychotherapy Association, 5*(6), 11–13.

Cooper, A., Morahan-Martin, J., Mathy, R. M., & Maheu, M. (2002). Toward an increased understanding of user demographics in online sexual activities. *Journal of Sex and Marital Therapy, 28,* 105–129.

Cooper, A., & Sportolari, L. (1997). Romance in cyberspace: Understanding online attraction. *Journal of Sex Education and Therapy, 22,* 7–14.

Cooper, A., Safir, M. P., & Rosenmann, A. (2006). Workplace worries: A preliminary look at online sexual activities at the office—Emerging issues for clinicians and employers. *CyberPsychology & Behavior, 9*(1), 22–29.

Cooper, C. L., & Dewe, P. (2004). *Stress: A brief history.* Malden, MA: Blackwell Publishing.

Cooper, D. C., & Waldstein, S. R. (2004). Hostility differentially predicts risk factors in African American and White young adults. *Journal of Psychosomatic Research, 57,* 491–497.

Cooper, L., & Bright. J. (2001). Individual differences in reactions to stress. In F. Jones & J. Bright (Eds.), *Stress: Myth, theory and research.* Harlow, England: Pearson Education.

Cooper, M. L. (2006). Does drinking promote risky sexual behavior? A complex answer to a simple question. *Current Directions in Psychological Science, 15*(1), 19–23.

Cooper, M. L., Albino, A. W., Orcutt, H. K., & Williams, N. (2004). Attachment styles and intrapersonal adjustment: A longitudinal study from adolescence into young adulthood. In W. S. Rholes & J. A. Simpson (Eds.), *Adult attachment: Theory, research, and clinical implications.* New York: Guilford.

Cooper, M. L., Shapiro, C. M., & Powers, A. M. (1998). Motivations for sex and risky sexual behavior among adolescents and young adults: A functional perspective. *Journal of Personality and Social Psychology, 75,* 1528–1558.

Cooper, P. J. (1995). Eating disorders and their relationship to mood and anxiety disorders. In K. D. Brownell & C. G. Fairburn (Eds.), *Eating disorders and obesity: A comprehensive handbook.* New York: Guilford Press.

Cope, M. B., Fernández, J. R., & Allilson, D. B. (2004). Genetic and biological risk factors. In J. K. Thompson (Ed.), *Handbook of eating disorders and obesity.* New York: Wiley.

Cordova, J. V., Gee, C. B., & Warren, L. Z. (2005). Emotional skillfulness in marriage: Intimacy as a mediator of the relationship between emotional skillfulness and marital satisfaction. *Journal of Social and Clinical Psychology, 24,* 218–235.

Cornell, D. G. (1997). Post hoc explanation is not prediction. *American Psychologist, 52,* 1380.

Corr, C. A. (1993). Coping with dying: Lessons that we should and should not learn from the work of Elisabeth Kübler-Ross. *Death Studies, 17*(1), 69–83.

Correia, I., Vala, J., & Aguiar, P. (2007). Victim's innocence, social categorization, and the threat to the belief in a just world. *Journal of Experimental Social Psychology, 43,* 31–38.

Correll, C. U., Leucht, S., & Kane, J. M. (2004). Lower risk for tardive dyskinesia associated with second-generation antipsychotics: A systematic review of 1-year studies. *American Journal of Psychiatry, 161,* 414–425.

Corsica, J. A., & Perri, M. G. (2003). Obesity. In A. M. Nezu, C. M. Nezu, & P. A. Geller (Eds.), *Handbook of psychology: Vol. 9. Health psychology.* New York: Wiley.

Costa, P. T., Jr., & McCrae, R. R. (1985). *NEO Personality Inventory.* Odessa, FL: Psychological Assessment Resources.

Costa, P. T., Jr., & McCrae, R. R. (1988). Personality in adulthood: A six-year longitudinal study of self-reports and spouse ratings on the NEO Personality Inventory. *Journal of Personality and Social Psychology, 54,* 853–863.

Costa, P. T., Jr., & McCrae, R. R. (1992). *Revised NEO Personality Inventory: NEO PI and NEO Five-Factor Inventory (Professional Manual).* Odessa, FL: Psychological Assessment Resources.

Costa, P. T., Jr., & McCrae, R. R. (1994). Set like plaster? Evidence for the stability of adult personality. In T. F. Heatherton & J. L. Weinberger (Eds.), *Can personality change?* Washington, DC: American Psychological Association.

Costa, P. T., Jr., & McCrae, R. R. (1997). Longitudinal stability of adult personality. In R. Hogan, J. Johnson, & S. Briggs (Eds.), *Handbook of personality psychology.* San Diego: Academic Press.

Cotter, D. A., Hermsen, J. M., Ovadia, S., & Vanneman, R. (2001). The glass ceiling effect. *Social Forces, 80,* 655–682.

Courtenay, W. H. (2000). Behavioral factors associated with disease, injury, and death among men: Evidence and implications for prevention. *Journal of Men's Studies, 9*(1), 81–142.

Covey, S. R. (1989). *The seven habits of highly effective people.* New York: Simon & Schuster.

Cowan, C. P., & Cowan, P. A. (1997). Working with couples during stressful transitions. In S. Dreman (Ed.), *The family on the threshold of the 21st century.* Mahwah, NJ: Erlbaum.

Cowan, C. P., & Cowan, P. A. (2000). *When partners become parents.* Mahwah, NJ: Erlbaum.

Cowley, J., & Murr, A. (2004, December 6). The new face of AIDS. *Newsweek,* pp. 76–78.

Cox, M. J., Paley, B., Burchinal, M., & Payne, C. C. (1999). Marital perceptions and interactions across the transition to parenthood. *Journal of Marriage and the Family, 61,* 611–625.

Coyne, J. C. (1999). Thinking interactionally about depression: A radical restatement. In T. E. Joiner & J. C. Coyne (Eds.), *Interpersonal processes in depression.* Washington, DC: American Psychological Association.

Coyne, S. M., Archer, J., & Eslea, M. (2006). "We're not friends anymore! Unless . . .": The frequency and harmfulness of indirect, relational, and social aggression. *Aggressive Behavior, 32,* 294–307.

Craik, F. I. M., & Tulving, E. (1975). Depth of processing and the retention of words in episodic memory. *Journal of Experimental Psychology. General, 104,* 268–294.

Cramer, P. (2000). Defense mechanisms in psychology today: Further processes for adaptation. *American Psychologist, 55*(6), 637–646.

Crawford, M., & Popp, D. (2003). Sexual double standards: A review and methodological critique of two decades of research. *Journal of Sex Research, 40*(1), 13–26.

Creed, F. (1989). Appendectomy. In G. W. Brown & T. O. Harris (Eds.), *Life events and illness.* New York: Guilford Press.

Creed, P., Prideaux, L., & Patton, W. (2005). Antecedents and consequences of career decisional states in adolescence. *Journal of Vocational Behavior, 67,* 397–412.

Crepaz, N., Hart, T. A., & Marks, G. (2004). Highly active antiretroviral therapy and sexual risk behavior. *Journal of the American Medical Association, 292*(2), 224–236.

Crews, F. (2006). *Follies of the wise: Dissenting essays.* Emeryville, CA: Shoemaker Hoard.

Crick, N. R., Casas, J. F., & Nelson, D. A. (2002). Toward a more comprehensive understanding of peer maltreatment: Studies of relational victimization. *Current Directions in Psychological Science, 11*(3), 98–101.

Crimmins, E. M., & Ingegneri, D. G. (1990). Interaction and living arrangements of older parents and their children. *Research on Aging, 12,* 3–35.

Crisp, R. J., & Hewastone, M. E. (2006). *Multiple social categorization: Processes, models, and applications.* New York: Psychology Press.

Critelli, J. W., & Ee, J. S. (1996). Stress and physical illness: Development of an integrative model. In T. W. Miller (Ed.), *Theory and assessment of stressful life events.* Madison, CT: International Universities Press.

Crits-Christoph, P. (1997). Limitations of the dodo bird verdict and the role of clinical trials in psychotherapy research: Comment on Wampold, et al. (1997). *Psychological Bulletin, 122,* 216–220.

Crocker, J., & Luhtanen, R. (1990). Collective self-esteem and ingroup bias. *Journal of Personality and Social Psychology, 58,* 60–67.

Crocker, J., & McGraw, K. M. (1984). What's good for the goose is not good for the gander: Solo status as an obstacle to occupational achievement for males and females. *American Behavioral Scientist, 27,* 357–370.

Crocker, J., & Nuer, N. (2004). Do people need self-esteem? Comment on Pyszczynski et al. *Psychological Bulletin, 130,* 469–472.

Crocker, J., & Park, L. E. (2004). The costly pursuit of self-esteem. *Psychological Bulletin, 130,* 392–414.

Crohan, S. E. (1992). Marital happiness and spousal consensus on beliefs about marital conflict: A longitudinal investigation. *Journal of Social and Personal Relationships, 9,* 89–102.

Crooks, R., & Baur, K. (2008). *Our sexuality.* Belmont, CA: Wadsworth.

Crosby, F. J., & Sabattini, L. (2006). Family and work balance. In J. Worrell & C. D. Goodheart (Eds.), *Handbook of girls' and women's psychological health.* New York: Oxford University Press.

Crosby, O., & Moncarz, R. (2006, Fall). The 2004–14 job outlook for college graduates. *Occupational Outlook Quarterly,* pp. 42–57.

Crosby, O., Iyer, A., Clayton, S., & Downing, R. A. (2003). Affirmative action: Psychological data and the policy debates. *American Psychologist, 58*(1), 93–115.

Cross, C. K., & Hirschfeld, R. M. A. (1986). Epidemiology of disorders in adulthood: Suicide. In G. L. Klerman, M. M. Weissman, P. S. Appelbaum, & L. H. Roth (Eds.), *Psychiatry: Vol. 5. Social, epidemiologic, and legal psychiatry.* New York: Basic Books.

Cross, P. (1977). Not can but will college teaching be improved? *New Directions for Higher Education, 17,* 1–15.

Cross, S. E., Bacon, P. L., & Morris, M. L. (2000). The relational-interdependent self-construal and relationships. *Journal of Personality and Social Psychology, 78*(4), 791–808.

Cross, S. E., & Gore, J. S. (2003). Cultural models of the self. In M.R. Leary & J. P. Tangney (Eds.), *Handbook of self and identity.* New York: Guilford.

Cross, S. E., & Madson, L. (1997). Models of the self: Self-construal and gender. *Psychological Bulletin, 122*(1), 5–37.

Cross, S. E., & Markus, H. (1991). Possible selves across the life span. *Human Development, 34*(4), 230–255.

Cross, S. E., & Markus, H. R. (1999). The cultural constitution of personality. In L. A. Pervin & O. P. John (Eds.), *Handbook of personality: Theory and research* (2nd ed.). New York: Guilford Press.

Crouter, A. C., & Bumpus, M. F. (2001). Linking parents' work stress to children's and adolescents' psychological adjustment. *Current Directions in Psychological Science, 10*(5), 156–159.

Crouter, A. C., Bumpus, M. F., Maguire, M. C., & McHale, S. M. (1999). Linking parents' work pressure and adolescents' well-being: Insights into dynamics in dual-earner families. *Developmental Psychology, 35,* 1453–1461.

Crow, T. J. (2007). How and why genetic linkage has not solved the problem of psychosis: Review and hypothesis. *American Journal of Psychiatry, 164,* 13–21.

Crowell, J. A., Treboux, D., & Waters, E. (2002). Stability of attachment representations: The transition to marriage. *Developmental Psychology, 38,* 467–479.

Crowley, A. E., & Hoyer, W. D. (1994). An integrative framework for understanding two-sided persuasion. *Journal of Consumer Research, 20,* 561–574.

Crowley, B. J., Hayslip, B. Jr., & Hobdy, J. (2003). Psychological hardiness and adjustment to life events in adulthood. *Journal of Adult Development, 10*(4), 237–248.

Cullen, L. T. (2007, February 22). It's a wrap. You're hired! *Time*, p. 57.

Culpepper, L., Davidson, J. R. T., Dietrich, A. J., Goodman, W. K., Kroenke, K., & Schwenk, T. L. (2004). Suicidality as a possible effect of antidepressant treatment. *Journal of Clinical Psychiatry, 65*(6), 742–749.

Cummings, E. M., Braungart-Rieker, J. M., & du Rocher-Schudlich, T. (2003). Emotion and personality development in childhood. In R. M. Lerner, M. A. Easterbrooks, & J. Mistry (Eds.), *Handbook of psychology: Vol. 6. Developmental psychology.* New York: Wiley.

Cunningham, C. O., & Selwyn, P. A. (2005). HIV-related medical complications and treatment. In J. H. Lowinson, P. Ruiz, R. B. Millman, & J. G. Langrod (Eds.), *Substance abuse: A comprehensive textbook.* Philadelphia: Lippincott/Williams & Wilkins.

Cunningham, M. (2001). The influence of parental attitudes and behaviors on children's attitudes toward gender and household labor in early adulthood. *Journal of Marriage and the Family, 63*(1), 111–122.

Cunningham, M. R., Barbee, A. P., & Pike, C. L. (1990). What do women want? Facialmetric assessment of multiple motives in the perception of male facial physical attractiveness. *Journal of Personality and Social Psychology, 59*, 61–72.

Cunningham, M. R., Druen, P. B., & Barbee, A. P. (1997). Angels, mentors, and friends: Trade-offs among evolutionary, social, and individual variables in physical appearance. In J. A. Simpson & D. T. Kenrick (Eds.), *Evolutionary Social Psychology.* Mahwah, NJ: Erlbaum.

Cunningham, M. R., Roberts, A. R., Barbee, A. P., Druen, P. B., & Wu, C., (1995). "Their ideas of beauty are, on the whole, the same as ours": Consistency and variability in the cross-cultural perception of female physical attractiveness. *Journal of Personality and Social Psychology, 68*, 261–279.

Curioni, C. C., & Lourenco, P. M. (2005). Long-term weight loss after diet and exercise: A systematic review. *International Journal of Obesity, 29*, 1168–1174.

Curtis, R. C., & Miller, K. (1986). Believing another likes or dislikes you: Behaviors making the beliefs come true. *Journal of Personality and Social Psychology, 51*, 284–290.

Cutrona, C. E. (1982). Transition to college: Loneliness and the process of social adjustment. In L. A. Peplau & D. Perlman (Eds.), *Loneliness: A sourcebook of current theory, research, and therapy.* New York: Wiley.

Cutting, L. P., & Docherty, N. M. (2000). Schizophrenia outpatients' perceptions of their parents: Is expressed emotion a factor? *Journal of Abnormal Psychology, 109*(2), 266–272.

Dabbs, J. M., with Dabbs, M. G. (2000). *Heroes, rogues, and lovers: Testosterone and behavior.* New York: McGraw-Hill.

Dainton, M. (2000). Maintenance behaviors, expectations for maintenance, and satisfaction: Linking comparison levels to relational maintenance strategies. *Journal of Social and Personal Relationships, 17*(6), 827–842.

Dallman, M. F., Bhatnagar, S., & Viau, V. (2000). Hypothalamo-pituitary-adrenal axis. In G. Fink (Ed.), *Encyclopedia of stress* (Vol. 2). San Diego: Academic Press.

D'Amico, M. L. (1998). Internet has become a necessity, U.S. poll shows. *CNNinteractive* [Internet magazine],1.

Danieli, Y., Engdahl, B., & Schlenger, W. E. (2004). The psychological aftermath of terrorism. In F. M. Moghaddam & A. J. Marsella (Eds.), *Understanding terrorism: Psychological roots, consequences, and interventions.* Washington, D.C.: American Psychological Association.

Daniels, K., Hartley, R., & Travers, C. J. (2006). Beliefs about stressors alter stressors' impact: Evidence from two experience-sampling studies. *Human Relations, 59*, 1261–1285.

Dantzer, R., & Mormede, P. (1995). Psychoneuro-immunology of stress. In B. E. Leonard & K. Miller (Eds.), *Stress, the immune system and psychiatry.* New York: Wiley.

Das, E. H. H. J., de Wit, J. B. F., & Stroebe, W. (2003). Fear appeals motivate acceptance of action recommendations: Evidence for a positive bias in the processing of persuasive messages. *Personality and Social Psychology Bulletin, 29*(5), 650–664.

D'Augelli, A. R., & Hershberger, S. L. (1993). Lesbian, gay, and bisexual youth in community settings: Personal challenges and mental health problems. *American Journal of Community Psychology, 21*, 421–448.

David, D. H., & Lyons-Ruth, K. (2005). Differential attachment responses of male and female infants to frightening maternal behavior: Tend or befriend versus fight of flight? *Infant Mental Health Journal, 26*(1), 1–18.

Davidson, M. J., & Fielden, S. (1999). Stress and the working woman. In G. N. Powell (Ed.), *Handbook of gender and work.* Thousand Oaks, CA: Sage.

Davies, A. P. C., & Shackelford, T. K. (2006). An evolutionary psychological perspective on gender similarities and differences. *American Psychologist, 32*, 640–641.

Davies, L. (1995). A closer look at gender and distress among the never married. *Women and Health, 23*, 13–30.

Davila, J., & Cobb, R. J. (2003). Predicting change in self-reported and interviewer-assessed adult attachment: Tests of the individual difference and life stress models of attachment change. *Personality and Social Psychology Bulletin, 29*, 859–870.

Davila, J., & Sargent, E. (2003). The meaning of life (events) predicts changes in attachment security. *Personality and Social Psychology Bulletin, 29*, 1383–1395.

Davis, J. L., & Rusbult, C. E. (2001). Attitude alignment in close relationships. *Journal of Personality and Social Psychology, 81*(1), 65–84.

Davis, K. L., Mohs, R. C., Marin, D., Purohit, D. P., Perl, D. P., Lantz, M., Austin, G., & Haroutunian, V. (1999). Cholinergic markers in elderly patients with early signs of Alzheimer's disease. *Journal of the American Medical Association, 281*, 1401–1406.

Davis, L. L., Frazier, E. C., Williford, R. B., & Newell, J. M. (2006). Long-term pharmacotherapy for post-traumatic stress disorder. *CNS Drugs, 20*, 465–476.

Davis, M. H., Morris, M. M., & Kraus, L. A. (1998). Relationship-specific and global perceptions of social support: Associations with well-being and attachment. *Journal of Personality and Social Psychology, 74*, 468–481.

Davis, R. A. (2001). A cognitive-behavioral model of pathological Internet use. *Computers in Human Behavior, 17*(2), 187–195.

Dawkins, K., Golden, R. N., & Fawcett, J. A. (2003). Therapeutic management of the suicidal patient. In A. Tasman, J. Kay, & J. A. Lieberman (Eds.), *Psychiatry.* New York: Wiley.

Dean, L. R., Carroll, J. S., & Yang, C. (2007). Materialism, perceived financial problems, and marital satisfaction. *Family and Consumer Sciences Research Journal, 35*, 260–281.

DeAngelis, T. (2001, December). Are men emotional mummies? *Monitor on Psychology*, pp. 40–41.

DeAngellis, T. (2004). What's to blame for the surge in super-size Americans? *Monitor on Psychology, 35*(1), 46, 62.

Deaux, K., & Hanna, R. (1984). Courtship in the personals column: The influence of gender and sexual orientation. *Sex Roles, 11*, 363–375.

Deaux, K., & Lewis, L. L. (1983). Components of gender stereotypes. *Psychological Documents, 13*, Ms. No. 2583.

Deaux, K., & Lewis, L. L. (1984). Structure of gender stereotypes: Interrelationships among components and gender label. *Journal of Personality and Social Psychology, 46*, 991–1004.

DeCarvalho, R. J. (1991). *The founders of humanistic psychology.* New York: Praeger.

De Cock, K. M., & Janssen, R. S. (2002). An unequal epidemic in an unequal world. *Journal of the American Medical Association, 288*(2), 236–238.

DeFrain, J., & Olson, D. H. (1999). Contemporary family patterns and relationships. In M. B. Sussman, S. K. Steinmetz, & G. W. Peterson (Eds.), *Handbook of marriage and the family.* New York: Plenum Press.

DeGroot, T., & Motowidlo, S. (1999). Why visual and vocal interview cues can affect interviewers' judgments and predict job performance. *Journal of Applied Psychology, 84*, 986–993.

de Jong, P. J., & Merckelbach, H. (2000). Phobia-relevant illusory correlations: The role of phobic responsivity. *Journal of Abnormal Psychology, 109*, 597–601.

de Jong Gierveld, J., van Tilburg, T., & Dykstra, P. A. (2006). Loneliness and social isolation. In A. L. Vangelisti & D. Perlman (Eds.), *The Cambridge handbook of personal relationships.* New York: Cambridge University Press.

de Kloet, E. R., Joels, M., & Holsboer, F. (2005). Stress and the brain: From adaptation to disease. *Nature Reviews Neuroscience, 6*, 463–474.

Delay, J., & Deniker, P. (1952). *Trente-huit cas de psychoses traitees par la cure prolongee et continue de 4560 RP.* Paris: Masson et Cie.

De Leo, D., Bille-Brahe, U., Kerkhof, A., & Schmidke, A. (Eds.). (2004). *Suicidal behavior: Theories and research findings.* Cambridge, MA: Hogrefe & Huber.

Delgado, P. L., & Moreno, F. A. (2006). Neurochemistry of mood disorders. In D. J. Stein, D. J. Kupfer, & A. F. Schatzberg (Eds.), *Textbook of mood disorders.* Washington, DC: American Psychiatric Publishing.

Del Monte, M. M. (2000). Retrieved memories of childhood sexual abuse. *British Journal of Medical Psychology, 73*, 1–13.

DeLongis, A., Folkman, S., & Lazarus, R. S. (1988). The impact of daily stress on health and mood: Psychological and social resources as mediators. *Journal of Personality and Social Psychology, 54*, 486–495.

DeMaris, A., & Swinford, S. (1996). Female victims of spousal violence: Factors influencing their level of fearfulness. *Family Relations, 45*(1), 98–106.

DeMaris, A., Benson, M. L., Fox, G. L., Hill, T., & Van Wyk, J. (2003). Distal and proximal factors in domestic violence: A test of an integrated model. *Journal of Marriage and Family, 65*, 652–667.

Demerouti, E., & Geurts, S. (2004). Towards a typology of work-home interaction. *Community, Work, & Family, 7*, 285–309.

Demo, D. H. (1992). Parent-child relations: Assessing recent changes. *Journal of Marriage and the Family, 54*, 104–117.

Dempster, F. N. (1996). Distributing and managing the conditions of encoding and practice. In E. L. Bjork & R. A. Bjork (Eds.), *Memory.* San Diego: Academic Press.

Denisoff, E., & Endler, N. S. (2000). Life experiences, coping, and weight preoccupation in young adult women. *Canadian Journal of Behavioural Science, 32*(1), 97–103.

Dennerstein, L., Dudley, E., & Guthrie, J. (2002). Empty nest or revolving door? A prospective study of women's quality of life in midlife during the phase of children leaving and re-entering the home. *Psychological Medicine, 32*(3), 545–550.

Dennis, C., & Ross, L. (2005). Relationships among infant sleep patterns, maternal fatigue, and development of depressive symptomatology. *Birth, 32*, 187–193.

Dennis, W. (1966). Creative productivity between the ages of 20 and 80 years. *Journal of Gerontology, 21*, 1–8.

DePaulo, B. M. (1994). Spotting lies: Can humans learn to do better? *Current Directions in Psychological Science, 3*(3), 83–86.

DePaulo, B. M., & Friedman, H. (1998). Nonverbal communication. In D. T. Gilbert, S. T. Fiske, &

Edwards, R., & Hamilton, M. A. (2004). You need to understand my gender role: An empirical test of Tannen's model of gender and communication. *Sex Roles, 50*(7/8), 491–504.

Edwards, S. (2006). Physical exercise and psychological well-being. *South African Journal of Psychology, 36,* 357–373.

Egan, T. (2000, October 23). Technology sent Wall Street into market for pornography. *New York Times,* pp. 1–20.

Egeci, I. S., & Gençöz, T. (2006). Factors associated with relationship satisfaction: Importance of communication skills. *Contemporary Family Therapy: An International Journal, 28,* 383–391.

Ehrenberg, O., & Ehrenberg, M. (1994). *The psychotherapy maze: A consumer's guide to getting in and out of therapy.* Northvale, NJ: Jason Aronson.

Ehrenreich, H., Rinn, T., Kunert, H. J., Moeller, M. R., Poser, W., Schilling, L., Gigerenzer, G., & Hoehe, M. R. (1999). Specific attentional dysfunction in adults following early start of cannabis use. *Psychopharmacology, 142,* 295–301.

Eich, E., Macaulay, D., Loewenstein, R. J., & Dihle, P. H. (1997). Memory, amnesia, and dissociative identity disorder. *Psychological Science, 8,* 417–422.

Einstein, G. O., & McDaniel, M. A. (2004). *Memory fitness: A guide for successful aging.* New Haven, CT: Yale University Press.

Eisenberger, N. I., Kemeny, M. E., & Wyatt, G. E. (2003). Psychological inhibition and CD4 T-cell levels in HIV-seropositive women. *Journal of Psychosomatic, 54,* 213–224.

Eisler, R. M., & Ragsdale, K. (1992). Masculine gender role and midlife transition in men. In V. B. Van Hasselt & M. Hersen (Eds.), *Handbook of social development: A lifespan perspective.* New York: Plenum.

Ekman, P. (1972). Universals and cultural differences in facial expressions of emotion. In J. Cole (Ed.), *Nebraska symposium on motivation, 1971.* Lincoln, NE: University of Nebraska Press.

Ekman, P. (1975, September). The universal smile: Face muscles talk every language. *Psychology Today,* pp. 35–39.

Ekman, P. (1994). Strong evidence for universals in facial expressions: A reply to Russell's mistaken critique. *Psychological Bulletin, 115,* 268–287.

Ekman, P., & Friesen, W. V. (1974). Detecting deception from the body or face. *Journal of Personality and Social Psychology, 29*(3), 288–298.

Ekman, P., & Friesen, W. V. (1984). *Unmasking the face.* Palo Alto, CA: Consulting Psychologists Press.

Ekman, P., & O'Sullivan, M. (1991). Who can catch a liar? *American Psychologist, 44*(9), 913–920.

Ekman, P., O'Sullivan, M., & Frank, M. G. (1999). A few can catch a liar. *Psychological Science, 10*(3), 263–266.

Elfenbein, H. A., & Ambady, N. (2003). Universals and cultural differences in recognizing emotions of a different cultural group. *Current Directions in Psychological Science, 12*(5), 159–164.

Elias, M. F., Elias, J. W., & Elias, P. K. (1990). Biological and health influences on behavior. In J. E. Birren & K. W. Schaie (Eds.), *Handbook of the psychology of aging.* San Diego: Academic Press.

Elkind, D. (1978). *A sympathetic understanding of the child: Birth to sixteen.* Boston: Allyn and Bacon.

Ellington, L., & Wiebe, D. J. (1999). Neuroticism, symptom presentation, and medical decision making. *Health Psychology, 18*(6), 634–643.

Elliot, A. J., & Church, M. A. (2003). A motivational analysis of defensive pessimism and self-handicapping. *Journal of Personality, 71,* 369–393.

Elliot, L., & Brantley, C. (1997). *Sex on campus.* New York: Random House.

Ellis, A. (1973). *Humanistic psychotherapy: The rational-emotive approach.* New York: Julian Press.

Ellis, A. (1977). *Reason and emotion in psychotherapy.* Seacaucus, NJ: Lyle Stuart.

Ellis, A. (1985). *How to live with and without anger.* New York: Citadel Press.

Ellis, A. (1987). The evolution of rational-emotive therapy (RET) and cognitive behavior therapy (CBT). In J. K. Zeig (Ed.), *The evolution of psychotherapy.* New York: Brunner/Mazel.

Ellis, A. (1989). Rational-emotive therapy. In R. J. Corsini & D. Wedding (Eds.), *Current Psychotherapies.* Itasca, IL: Peacock.

Ellis, A. (1993). The advantages and disadvantages of self-help therapy materials. *Professional Psychology: Research and Practice, 24,* 335–339.

Ellis, A. (1994). *Reason and emotion in psychotherapy.* Seacaucus, NJ: Birch Lane Press.

Ellis, A. (1995). Thinking processes involved in irrational beliefs and their disturbed consequences. *Journal of Cognitive Psychotherapy, 9,* 105–116.

Ellis, A. (1996). How I learned to help clients feel better and get better. *Psychotherapy, 33,* 149–151.

Ellis, A. (1999). *How to make yourself happy and remarkably less disturbable.* Atascadero, CA: Impact Publishers.

Ellis, A. (2001a). *Feeling better, getting better, staying better: Profound self-help therapy for your emotions.* Atascadero, CA: Impact Publishers.

Ellis, A. (2001b). *Overcoming destructive beliefs, feelings, and behaviors: New directions for Rational Emotive Behavior Therapy.* Amherst, NY: Prometheus Books.

Ellis, A. (2003). *Ask Albert Ellis: Straight answers and sound advice from America's best-known psychologist.* Atascadero, CA: Impact Publishers.

Ellis, A. (2004). Expanding the ABCs of rational emotive behavior therapy. In A. Freeman, M. J. Mahoney, P. Devito, & D. Martin (Eds.), *Cognition and psychotherapy.* New York: Springer Publishing.

Ellis, J. (2006, January 28). "IM-speak" struggle for teachers. *Statesboro Herald,* pp. 1A, 14A.

Ellison, N., Heino, R., & Gibbs, J. (2006). Managing impressions online: Self-presentation processes in the online dating environment. *Journal of Computer-Mediated Communication, 11,* 415–441.

Emanuel, H. M. (1987). Put time on your side. In A. D. Timpe (Ed.), *The management of time.* New York: Facts On File.

Emavardhana, T., & Tori, C. D. (1997). Changes in self-concept, ego defense mechanisms, and religiosity following seven-day Vipassana meditation retreats. *Journal for the Scientific Study of Religion, 36,* 194–206.

Emmelkamp, P. M. G. (1994). Behavior therapy with adults. In A. E. Bergin & S. L. Garfield (Eds.), *Handbook of psychotherapy and behavior change* (4th ed.). New York: Wiley.

Emmelkamp, P. M. G. (2004). In M. J. Lambert (Ed.), *Bergin and Garfield's handbook of psychotherapy and behavior change.* New York: Wiley.

Emmons, R. A. (2003). Personal goals, life meaning, and virtue: Wellsprings of a positive life. In C. L. M. Keyes & J. Haidt (Eds.), *Flourishing: Positive psychology and the life well-lived.* Washington, DC: American Psychological Association.

Employers bemoan workers' writing skills. (2004, September 15). *The Statesboro Herald,* p. 9.

Emsley, R., Rabinowitz, J., & Medori, R. (2006). Time course for antipsychotic treatment response in first-episode schizophrenia. *American Journal of Psychiatry, 163,* 743–745.

Epel, E. S., Blackburn, E. H., Lin, J., Dhabhar, F. S., Adler, N. E., Morrow, J. D., & Cawthon, R. M. (2004). Accelerated telomere shortening in response to life stress. *Proceedings of the National Academy of Sciences, 101,* 17312–17315.

Epstein, R. (2001). Physiologist Laura. *Psychology Today, 34* (4), 5.

Epstein, R. (2007, February–March). The truth about online dating. *Scientific American Mind, 18,* pp. 28–35.

Erdelyi, M. H. (2001). Defense processes can be conscious or unconscious. *American Psychologist, 56*(9), 761–762.

Erikson, E. H. (1963). *Childhood and society.* New York: Norton.

Erikson, E. H. (1968). *Identity: Youth and crisis.* New York: Norton.

Ernst, C., & Angst, J. (1983). Birth order: Its influence on personality. *Behavioral and Brain Sciences, 10*(1), 55.

Esping-Andersen, G. (2007). Sociological explanations of changing income distributions. *American Behavioral Scientist, 50,* 639–658.

Espiritu, D. A. V., Rashid, H., Mast, B. T., Fitzgerald, J., Steinberg, J., & Lichtenberg, P. A. (2001). Depression, cognitive impairment and function in Alzheimer's disease. *International Journal of Geriatric Psychiatry, 16*(11), 1098–1103.

Esterling, B. A., Kiecolt-Glaser, J. K., Bodnar, J. D., & Glaser, R. (1994). Chronic stress, social support, and persistent alterations in the natural killer cell response to cytokines in older adults. *Health Psychology, 13,* 291–298.

Esterson, A. (1993). *Seductive mirage: An exploration of the work of Sigmund Freud.* Chicago: Open Court.

Esterson, A. (2001). The mythologizing of psychoanalytic history: Deception and self-deception in Freud's accounts of the seduction theory episode. *History of Psychiatry, 7,* 329–352.

Etaugh, C. (1993). Maternal employment: Effects on children. In J. Frankel (Ed.), *The employed mother and the family context.* New York: Springer.

Evans, G. W. (2001). Environmental stress and health. In A. Baum, T. A. Revenson, & J. E. Singer (Eds.), *Handbook of health psychology.* Mahwah, NJ: Erlbaum.

Evans, G. W., Hygge, S., & Bullinger, M. (1995). Chronic noise and psychological stress. *Psychological Science, 6,* 333–338.

Evans, G. W., & Stecker, R. (2004). Motivational consequences of environmental stress. *Journal of Environmental Psychology, 24*(2), 143–165.

Evans, G. W., & Wener, R. E. (2006). Rail commuting duration and passenger stress. *Health Psychology, 25,* 408–412.

Evans, G. W., Lepore, S. J., & Schroeder, A. (1996). The role of interior design elements in human responses to crowding. *Journal of Personality and Social Psychology, 70,* 41–46.

Evans, R. G., & Dinning, W. D. (1982). MMPI correlates of the Bem Sex Role Inventory and Extended Personal Attributes Questionnaire in a male psychiatric sample. *Journal of Clinical Psychology, 38,* 811–815.

Everly, G. S., Jr., & Mitchell, J. T. (2001). America under attack: The "10 commandments" of responding to mass terrorist attacks. *International Journal of Emergency Mental Health, 3,* 133–135.

Everson, S. A., Kauhanen, J., Kaplan, G. A., Goldberg, D. E., Julkunen, J., Tuomilehto, J., & Salonen, J. T. (1997). Hostility and increased risk of mortality and acute myocardial infarction: The mediating role of behavioral risk factors. *American Journal of Epidemiology, 146*(2), 142–152.

Ewart, C. K., & Suchday, S. (2002). Discovering how urban poverty and violence affect health: Development and validation of a neighborhood stress index. *Health Psychology, 21*(3), 254–262.

Exline, J. J., Baumeister, R. F., Bushman, B. J., Campbell, W. K., & Finkel, E. J. (2004). Too proud to let go: Narcissistic entitlement as a barrier to forgiveness. *Journal of Personality and Social Psychology, 87,* 894–912.

Eysenck, H. J. (1959). Learning theory and behaviour therapy. *Journal of Mental Science, 195,* 61–75.

Eysenck, H. J. (1967). *The biological basis of personality.* Springfield, IL: Charles C Thomas.

Eysenck, H. J. (1982). *Personality, genetics and behavior: Selected papers.* New York: Praeger.

Eysenck, H. J. (1991). Dimensions of personality: 16, 5, or 3?—Criteria for a taxonomic paradigm. *Personality and Individual Differences, 12,* 773–790.

Eysenck, H. J. (1993a). Forty years on: The outcome problem in psychotherapy revisited. In T. R. Giles (Ed.), *Handbook of effective psychotherapy.* New York: Plenum.

Eysenck, H. J. (1993b). Prediction of cancer and coronary heart disease: Mortality by means of a personality inventory: Results of a 15-year follow-up study. *Psychological Reports, 72,* 499–516.

Eysenck, M. W., Mogg, K., May, J., Richards, A., & Mathews, A. (1991). Bias in interpretation of ambiguous sentences related to threat in anxiety. *Journal of Abnormal Psychology, 100,* 144–150.

Faber R. J. (2003). Self- control and compulsive buying. In T. Kasser, & A. D. Kanner (Eds.), *Psychology and consumer culture: The struggle for a good life in a materialistic world.* Washington, DC: American Psychological Association.

Fabian, G. (2002). Sequential request and organ donation. *Journal of Social Psychology, 22,* 171–178.

Fagot, B. I., & Hagan, R. (1991). Observations of parent reactions to sex-stereotyped behaviors: Age and sex effects. *Child Development, 62,* 617–628.

Fagot, B. I., Hagan, R., Leinbach, M. D., & Kronsberg, S. (1985). Differential reactions to assertive and communicative acts of toddler boys and girls. *Child Development, 56,* 1499–1505.

Fairbank, J. A., Ebert, L., & Caddell, J. M. (2001). Posttraumatic stress disorder. In P. B. Sunker & H. E. Adams (Eds.), *Comprehensive handbook of psychopathology* (3rd ed.). New York: Kluwer Academic/Plenum Publishers.

Fairbrother, K., & Warn, J. (2003). Workplace dimensions, stress, and job satisfaction. *Journal of Managerial Psychology, 18*(1), 8–21.

Falk, P. (1994). The gap between psychological assumptions and empirical research in lesbian-mother child custody cases. In A. E. Gottfried & A. W. Gottfried (Eds.), *Redefining families: Implications for children's development.* New York: Plenum.

Falsetti, S. A., & Ballenger, J. C. (1998). Stress and anxiety disorders. In J. R. Hubbard & E. A. Workman (Eds.), *Handbook of stress medicine: An organ system approach.* New York: CRC Press.

Families and Work Institute. (2004). *Generation and gender in the workplace.* New York: Families and Work Institute.

Fancher, R. E. (1979). *Pioneers of psychology.* New York: Norton.

Farah, A. (1997). An overview of ECT. *Primary Psychiatry, 4,* 58–62.

Faravelli, C., & Pallanti, S. (1989). Recent life events and panic disorders. *American Journal of Psychiatry, 146,* 622–626.

Farina, A., Burns, G. L., Austad, C., Bugglin, C., & Fischer, E. H. (1986). The role of physical attractiveness in the readjustment of discharged psychiatric patients. *Journal of Abnormal Psychology, 95,* 139–143.

Fassler, D. (2001). *Talking to children about war and terrorism: 20 tips for parents.* Retrieved November 20, 2001 from American Psychiatric Association Web site: http://www.psych.org/disaster/20tipsparents11801.cfm.

Faulkner, G., & Carless, D. (2006). Physical activity in the process of psychiatric rehabilitation: Theoretical and methodological issues. *Psychiatric Rehabilitation Journal, 29,* 258–265.

Faust, K. A., & McKibben, J. N. (1999). Marital dissolution: Divorce, separation, annulment, and widowhood. In M. B. Sussman, S. K. Steinmetz, & G. W. Peterson (Eds.), *Handbook of marriage and the family.* New York: Plenum Press.

Fausto-Sterling, A. (1992). *Myths of gender: Biological theories about women and men* (2nd ed.). New York: Basic Books.

Fava, G. A., Fabbri, S., Sirri, L., & Wise, T. N. (2007). Psychological factors affecting medical condition: A new proposal for DSM-V. *Psychosomatics: Journal of Consultation Liaison Psychiatry, 42*(2), 103–111.

Federal Interagency Forum on Aging-Related Statistics. (2004). *Older Americans 2004: Key indicators of well-being.* Washington, DC: Government Printing Office.

Feeney, J. A. (2004). Adult attachment and relationship functioning under stressful conditions: Understanding partners' responses to conflict and challenge. In W. S. Rholes & J. A. Simpson (Eds.), *Adult attachment: Theory, research, and clinical implications.* New York: Guilford.

Feeney, J. A., & Noller, P. (1990). Attachment style as a predictor of adult romantic relationships. *Journal of Personality and Social Psychology, 58,* 281–291.

Fehr, B. (1996). *Friendship processes.* Thousand Oaks, CA: Sage.

Fehr, B. (2000). The life cycle of friendship. In C. Hendrick & S. S. Hendrick (Eds.), *Close relationships: A sourcebook.* Thousand Oaks, CA: Sage.

Fehr, B. (2004). Intimacy expectations in same-sex friendships: A prototype interaction-pattern model. *Journal of Personality and Social Psychology, 86*(2), 265–284.

Fein, S. (1996). Effects of suspicion on attributional thinking and the correspondence bias. *Journal of Personality and Social Psychology, 70,* 1164–1184.

Feingold, A. (1988). Matching for attractiveness in romantic partners and same-sex friends: A meta-analysis and theoretical critique. *Psychological Bulletin, 104,* 226–235.

Feingold, A. (1992a). Gender differences in mate selection preferences: A test of the parental investment model. *Psychological Bulletin, 112,* 125–139.

Feingold, A. (1992b). Good-looking people are not what we think. *Psychological Bulletin, 111,* 304–341.

Feiring, C., & Lewis, M. (1987). The child's social network: Sex differences from three to six years. *Sex Roles, 17,* 621–636.

Feldman, P. J., Cohen, S., Doyle, W. J., Skoner, D. P., & Gwaltney, J. M., Jr. (1999). The impact of personality on the reporting of unfounded symptoms and illness. *Journal of Personality and Social Psychology, 77*(2), 370–378.

Feldman-Barrett, L., & Swim, J. K. (1998). Appraisals of prejudice and discrimination. In J. K. Swim & C. Stangor (Eds.), *Prejudice: The target's perspective.* New York: Academic Press.

Felker, B., & Hubbard, J. R. (1998). Influence of mental stress on the endocrine system. In J. R. Hubbard & E. A. Workman (Eds.), *Handbook of stress medicine: An organ system approach.* New York: CRC Press.

Felmlee, D. H., Sprecher, S., & Bassin, E. (1990). The dissolution of intimate relationships: A hazard model. *Social Psychology Quarterly,* 513–30.

Felmlee, D. H. (1995). Causes and consequences of women's employment discontinuity, 1967–1973. *Work and Occupation, 22,* 167–187.

Felson, R. B. (1989). Parents and the reflected appraisal process: A longitudinal analysis. *Journal of Personality and Social Psychology, 56,* 965–971.

Felson, R. B. (1992). Coming to see ourselves: Social sources of self-appraisals. *Advances in Group Processes, 9,* 185–205.

Fenton, W. S., & McGlashan, T. H. (1994). Antecedents, symptom progression, and long-term outcome of the deficit syndrome in schizophrenia. *American Journal of Psychiatry, 151,* 351–356.

Fenwick, P. (1987). Meditation and the EEG. In M. A. West (Ed.), *The psychology of meditation.* Oxford: Clarendon Press.

Ferguson, J. M. (2001). SSRI antidepressant medications: Adverse effects and tolerability. *Primary Care Companion Journal of Clinical Psychiatry, 3,* 22–27.

Feroli, K., & Burstein, G. (2003). Adolescent sexually transmitted diseases. *American Journal of Maternal/Child Nursing, 28,* 113–118.

Ferrari, J. R. (1992). Psychometric validation of two adult measures of procrastination: Arousal and avoidance measures. *Journal of Psychopathology & Behavioral Assessment, 14,* 97–100.

Ferrari, J. R. (2001). Getting things done on time: Conquering procrastination. In C. R. Snyder (Ed.), *Coping with stress: Effective people and processes.* New York: Oxford University Press.

Ferrari, J. R., Johnson, J. L., & McCown, W. G. (1995). *Procrastination and task avoidance: Theory research and treatment.* New York: Plenum Press.

Ferriss, A. L. (2002). Religion and the quality of life. *Journal of Happiness Studies, 3,* 199–215.

Festinger, L. (1954). A theory of social comparison processes. *Human Relations, 7,* 117–140.

Fiatrone, M. A., O'Neill, E. F., Doyle, N., Clements, K. M., Roberts, S. B., Kehayias, J. J., Lipsitz, L. A., & Evans, W. J. (1993). The Boston FICSIT study: The effects of resistance training and nutritional supplementation on physical frailty in the oldest old. *Journal of the American Geriatrics Society, 41,* 333–337.

Fiedler, K., Schmid, J., & Stahl, T. (2002). What is the current truth about polygraph lie detection? *Basic & Applied Social Psychology, 24,* 313–324.

Fiese, B. H., & Skillman, G. (2000). Gender differences in family stories: Moderating influence of parent gender role and child gender. *Sex Roles, 43*(5–6), 267–283.

Figueredo, A. J., Sefcek, J. A., Vasquez, G., Brumbach, B. H., King, J. E., & Jacobs, W. J. (2005). Evolutionary personality psychology. In D. M. Buss (Ed.), *The handbook of evolutionary psychology.* New York: Wiley.

Fincham, F. D. (2001). Attributions in close relationships: From Balkanization to integration. In G. J. O. Fletcher, & M. S. Clark (Eds.), *Blackwell handbook of social psychology: Vol. 2. Interpersonal processes.* Oxford: Blackwell.

Fincham, F. D. (2003). Marital conflict: Correlates, structure, and context. *Current Directions in Psychological Science, 12*(1), 23–27.

Fincham, F. D., & Beach, S. R. H. (2006). Relationship satisfaction. In A. L. Vangelisti & D. Perlman (Eds.), *The Cambridge handbook of personal relationships.* New York: Cambridge University Press.

Fine, R. (1990). *The history of psychoanalysis.* New York: Continuum.

Finkelhor, D., Mitchell, K., & Wolak, J. (2000). *Online victimization: A report on the nation's youth.* Washington, DC: National Center for Missing and Exploited Children.

Finkenauer, C., & Hazam, H. (2000). Disclosure and secrecy in marriage: Do both contribute to marital satisfaction? *Journal of Social and Personal Relationships, 17*(2), 245–263.

First, M. B. (2003). Psychiatric classification. In A. Tasman, J. Kay, & J. A. Lieberman (Eds.), *Psychiatry.* New York: Wiley.

Fischer, K. W., & Bidell, T. R. (1998). Dynamic development of psychological structures in action and thought. In R. M. Lerner (Ed.), *Handbook of child psychology: Vol. 1. Theoretical models of human development.* New York: Wiley.

Fischer, P., Greitemeyer, T., & Pollozek, F. (2006). The unresponsive bystander: Are bystanders more responsive in dangerous emergencies? *European Journal of Social Psychology, 36,* 267–278.

Fisher, E. B., Brownson, R. C., Heath, A. C., Luke, D. A., & Sumner II, W. (2004). Cigarette smoking. In J. M. Raczynski & L. C. Leviton (Eds.), *Handbook of clinical health psychology: Vol. 2. Disorders of behavior and health.* Washington, DC: American Psychological Association.

Fisher, S., & Greenberg, R. P. (1996). *Freud scientifically reappraised: Testing the theories and therapy.* New York: Wiley.

Fishman, D. B., & Franks, C. M. (1992). Evolution and differentiation within behavior therapy: A theoretical epistemological review. In D. K. Freedheim (Ed.), *History of psychotherapy: A century of change.* Washington, DC: American Psychological Association.

Fiske, S. T. (1993). Social cognition and social perception. *Annual Review of Psychology, 44,* 155–194.

Fiske, S. T. (1998). Stereotyping, prejudice, and discrimination. In D. T. Gilbert, S. T. Fiske, & G. Lindzey (Eds.), *The handbook of social psychology.* New York: McGraw-Hill.

Fiske, S. T. (2002). What we know now about bias and intergroup conflict, the problem of the century. *Current Directions in Psychological Science, 11*(4), 123–128.

Fiske, S. T. (2004). *Social beings: A core motives approach to social psychology.* New York: Wiley.

Fiske, S. T., Harris, L. T., & Cuddy, A. J. C. (2004). Why ordinary people torture enemy prisoners. *Science, 36*, 1482–1483.

Fiske, S. T., & Ruscher, J. B. (1993). Negative interdependence and prejudice: Whence the affect? In D. M. Mackie & D. L. Hamilton (Eds.), *Affect, cognition, and stereotyping: Interactive processes in group perception.* New York: Academic.

Fiske, S. T., & Taylor, S. E. (1991). *Social cognition.* New York: McGraw-Hill.

Fitch, S. A., & Adams, G. R. (1983). Ego identity and intimacy status: Replication and extension. *Developmental Psychology, 19*, 839–845.

Fitness, J., Fletcher, G., & Overall, N. (2007). Interpersonal attraction and intimate relationships. In M. A. Hogg & J. Cooper (Eds.), *The Sage handbook of social psychology.* Los Angeles: Sage.

Flaks, D. K., Ficher, I., Masterpasqua, M., & Joseph, G. (1995). Lesbians choosing motherhood: A comparative study of lesbians and heterosexual parents and their children. *Developmental Psychology, 31*, 105–114.

Flannagan, D., & Perese, S. (1998). Emotional references in mother-daughter and mother-son dyads' conversations about school. *Sex Roles, 39*(5–6), 353–367.

Flannery, R. B., Jr. (1999). Psychological trauma and posttraumatic stress disorder: A review. *International Journal of Mental Health, 1*(2), 135–140.

Flavell, J. H., Miller, P. H., & Miller, S. A. (2001). *Cognitive development.* Upper Saddle River, NJ: Prentice-Hall.

Flavin, C., & Dunn, S. (1999). Reinventing the energy system. In L. R. Brown, C. Flavin, H. French, J. Abramovitz, S. Dunn, G. Gardner, A. Mattoon, A. P. McGinn, M. O'Meara, M. Renner, D. Roodman, P. Sampat, L. Starke, & J. Tuxill (Eds.), *State of the world 1999.* New York: Norton.

Fleeson, W. (2004). Moving personality beyond the person-situation debate: The challenge and the opportunity of within-person variability. *Current Directions in Psychological Science, 13*(2), 83–87.

Fleeson, W., Malanos, A. B., & Achille, N. M. (2002). An intraindividual process approach to the relationship between extraversion and positive affect: Is acting extraverted as "good" as being extraverted? *Journal of Personality and Social Psychology, 83*(6), 1409–1422.

Fletcher, G. (2002). *The new science of intimate relationships.* Malden, MA: Blackwell Publishers.

Fletcher, G. J. O., Overall, N. C., & Friesen, M. D. (2006). Social cognition in intimate relationships. In A. L. Vangelisti & D. Perlman (Eds.), *The Cambridge handbook of personal relationships.* New York: Cambridge University Press.

Fletcher, G. J. O., & Thomas, G. (2000). Behavior and on-line cognition in marital interaction. *Personal Relationships, 7*(1), 111–130.

Fletcher, G. J. O., Tither, J. M., O'Loughlin, C., Friesen, M., & Overall, N. (2004). Warm and homely or cold and beautiful? Sex differences in trading off traits in mate selection. *Personality and Social Psychology Bulletin, 30*, 659–672.

Fletcher, G. J. O., & Ward, C. (1988). Attribution theory and processes: A cross-cultural perspective. In M. H. Bond (Ed.), *The cross-cultural challenge to social psychology.* Newbury Park, CA: Sage.

Flett, G. L., Hewitt, P. L., & Martin, T. R. (1995). Dimensions of perfectionism and procrastination. In J. R. Ferrari, J. L. Johnson, & W. G. McCown (Eds.), *Procrastination and task avoidance: Theory, research, and treatment.* New York: Plenum Press.

Flippen, C., & Tienda, M. (2000). Pathways to retirement: Patterns of labor force participation and labor market exit among pre-retirement population by race, Hispanic orgin, and sex . *Journals of Gerontology: Series B: Psychological Sciences and Social Sciences, 55B*(1), S14–S27.

Flores, B. H., Musselman, D. L., DeBattista, C., Garlow, S. J., Schatzberg, A. F., & Nemeroff, C. B. (2004). Biology of mood disorders. In A. F. Schatzberg & C. B. Nemeroff (Eds.), *Textbook of psychopharmacology.* Washington, DC: American Psychiatric Publishing.

Floyd, F. J., & Bakeman, R. (2006). Coming-out across the life course: Implications of age and historical context. *Archives of Sexual Behavior, 35*, 287–297.

Floyd, M. (2003). Bibliotherapy as an adjunct to psychotherapy for depression in older adults. *Journal of Clinical Psychology, 59*(2), 187–195.

Flynn, F. J., Reagans, R. E., Amanatullah, E. T., & Ames, D. R. (2006). Helping one's way to the top: Self-monitors achieve status by helping others and knowing who helps whom. *Journal of Personality and Social Psychology, 91*, 1123–1137.

Foa, E. B. (1998). Rape and posttraumatic stress disorder. In E. A. Blechman & K. D. Brownell (Eds.), *Behavioral medicine and women: A comprehensive handbook.* New York: Guilford Press.

Foa, E. B., Hembree, E. A., Riggs, D., Rauch, S., & Franklin, M. (2001). *Common reactions to trauma.* Retrieved November 21, 2001 from U.S. Department of Veterans Affairs National Center for PTSD Web site: http:www.ncptsd.org/facts/disasters/fs_foa_handout.html.

Folkman, S. (1997). Positive psychological states and coping with severe stress. *Social Science and Medicine, 45*, 1207–1221.

Folkman, S., & Moskowitz, J. T. (2000). Positive affect and the other side of coping. *American Psychologist, 55*(6), 647–654.

Folkman, S., Moskowitz, J. T., Ozer, E. M., & Park, C. L. (1997). Positive meaningful events and coping in the context of HIV/AIDS. In B. H. Gottlieb (Ed.), *Coping with chronic stress.* New York: Plenum.

Foote, B., Smolin, Y., Kaplan M., Legatt, M. E., & Lipschitz, D. (2006). Prevalence of dissociative disorders in psychiatric outpatients. *American Journal of Psychiatry, 163*, 623–629.

Forbes, G. B., Adams-Curtis, L. E., & White, K. B. (2004). First- and second-generation measures of sexism, rape, myths and related beliefs, and hostility toward women: Their interrelationships and associations with college students' experience with dating aggression and sexual coercion. *Violence Against Women, 10*(3), 236–261.

Formicelli, L. (2001, March/April). Baby blues. *Psychology Today*, p. 24.

Forrest, J. A., & Feldman, R. S. (2000). Detecting deception and judge's involvement: Lower task involvement leads to better lie detection. *Personality and Social Psychology Bulletin, 26*(1), 118–125.

Forstein, M. (2004). The pseudoscience of sexual orientation change therapy. *BMJ USA, 4*, 143–144.

Forsyth, D. R., & Strong, S. R. (1986). The scientific study of counseling and psychotherapy: A unificationist view. *American Psychologist, 41*, 113–119.

Foster, J. D., Kuperminc, G. P., & Price, A. W. (2004). Gender differences in posttraumatic stress related symptoms among inner-city minority youth exposed to community violence. *Journal of Youth and Adolescence, 33*, 59–69.

Fouad, N. A. (2007). Work and vocational psychology: Theory, Research, and applications. *Annual Review of Psychology, 58*, 543–564.

Fouad, N. A., & Mohler, C. J. (2004). Cultural validity of Holland's theory and the Strong Interest Inventory for five racial/ethnic groups. *Journal of Career Assessment, 12*, 423–439.

Fouts, G., & Burggraf, K. (1999). Television situation comedies: Female body images and verbal reinforcements. *Sex Roles, 40*(5/6), 473–481.

Fouts, G., & Vaughan, K. (2002). Television situation comedies: Male weight, negative references, and audience reactions. *Sex Roles, 46*(11/12), 439–442.

Fowers, B. J. (2000). *Beyond the myth of marital happiness: How embracing the virtues of loyalty, generosity, justice, and courage can strengthen your relationship.* San Francisco: Jossey-Bass.

Fowers, B. J., Applegate, B., Olson, D. H., & Pomerantz, B. (1994). Marital conventionalization as a measure of marital satisfaction: A confirmatory factor analysis. *Journal of Family Psychology, 8*, 98–103.

Fowers, B. J., Lyons, E., Montel, K. H., & Shaked, N. (2001). Positive illusions about marriage among married and single individuals. *Journal of Family Psychology, 15*(1), 95–109.

Fowles, D. C. (2003). Schizophrenia spectrum disorders. In G. Stricker & T. A. Widiger (Eds.), *Handbook of psychology: Vol. 8. Clinical psychology.* New York: Wiley.

Fox, G. L., & Chancey, D. (1998). Sources of economic distress: Individual and family outcomes. *Journal of Family Issues, 19*, 725–749.

Fox, G. L., Bruce, C., & Combs-Orme, T. (2000). Parenting expectations and concerns of fathers and mothers of newborn infants. *Family Relations, 49*(2), 123–131.

Fox, R. (1996). Bisexuality in perspective: A review of theory and research. In B. Firestein (Ed.), *Bisexuality: The psychology and politics of an invisible minority.* Thousand Oaks, CA: Sage.

Fraley, R. C. (2002). Attachment stability from infancy to adulthood: Meta-analysis and dynamic modeling of developmental mechanisms. *Personality and Social Psychology Review, 6*(2), 123–151.

Fraley, R. C., & Brumbaugh, C. C. (2004). A dynamical systems approach to conceptualizing and studying stability and change in attachment security. In W. S. Rholes & J. A. Simpson (Eds.), *Adult attachment: Theory, research, and clinical implications.* New York: The Guilford.

Frank, E., Anderson, C., & Rubinstein, D. (1978). Frequency of sexual dysfunction in "normal" couples. *New England Journal of Medicine, 299*, 111–115.

Frank, J. D. (1961). *Persuasion and healing.* Baltimore: John Hopkins University Press.

Frank, J. D., & Frank, J. B. (1991). *Persuasion and healing: A comparison study of psychotherapy.* Baltimore: Johns Hopkins University Press.

Frank, L. R. (1990). Electroshock: Death, brain damage, memory loss, and brainwashing. *The Journal of Mind and Behavior, 11*, 489–512.

Frank, M. G., & Ekman, P. (1997). The ability to detect deceit generalizes different types of high-stake lies. *Journal of Personality and Social Psychology, 72*, 1429–1439.

Frank, R. H. (1999). *Luxury fever: Why money fails to satisfy in an era of excess.* New York: Free Press.

Frankel, F. H. (1993). Adult reconstruction of childhood events in the multiple personality literature. *American Journal of Psychiatry, 150*, 954–958.

Franzoi, S. L., & Herzog, M. E. (1987). Judging personal attractiveness: What body aspects do we use? *Personality and Social Psychology Bulletin, 13*, 19–33.

Frasure-Smith, N., Lesperance, F., & Talajic, M. (1995). The impact of negative emotions on prognosis following myocardial infarction: Is it more than depression? *Health Psychology, 14*, 388–398.

Frazier, P. A., Mortensen, H., & Steward, J. (2005). Coping strategies as mediators of the relations among perceived control and distress in sexual assault survivors. *Journal of Counseling Psychology, 52*, 267–278.

Frederick, S., & Loewenstein, G. (1999). Hedonic adaptation. In D. Kahneman, E. Diener, & N. Schwarz (Eds.), *Well-being: The foundations of hedonic psychology.* New York: Sage.

Fredrickson, B. L. (1998). What good are positive emotions? *Review of General Psychology, 2*, 300–319.

Fredrickson, B. L. (2001). The role of positive emotions in positive psychology: The broaden-and-build theory of positive emotions. *American Psychologist, 56*, 218–226.

Fredrickson, B. L. (2006). The broaden-and-build theory of positive emotions. In M. Csikszentmihalyi & I. S. Csikszentmihalyi (Eds.), *A life worth living: Contributions to positive psychology.* New York: Oxford University Press.

Fredrickson, B. L., & Branigan, C. (2005). Positive emotions broaden the scope of attention and thought-action repertoires. *Cognition and Emotion, 19*, 313–332.

Fredrickson, B. L., & Losada, M. F. (2005). Positive affect and the complex dynamics of human flourishing. *American Psychologist, 60,* 678–686.

Fredrickson, B. L., Roberts, T., Noll, S. M., Quinn, D. M., & Twenge, J. M. (1998). That swimsuit becomes you: Sex differences in self-objectification, restrained eating, and math performance. *Journal of Personality and Social Psychology, 75,* 269–284.

Fredrickson, B. L., Tugade, M. M., Waugh, C. E., & Larkin, G. R. (2003). What good are positive emotions in crises? A prospective study of resilience and emotions following the terrorist attacks on the United States on September 11th, 2001. *Journal of Personality and Social Psychology, 84*(2), 365–376.

Freedberg, K., Losina, E., Weinstein, M., Paltiel, A., Cohen, C., Seage, G., Craven, D., Zhang, H., Kimmel, A., & Goldie, S. (2001). The cost effectiveness of combination antiretroviral therapy for HIV disease. *New England Journal of Medicine,* 824–831.

Freedman, J. L., & Fraser, S. C. (1966). Compliance without pressure: The foot-in-the-door technique. *Journal of Personality and Social Psychology, 4,* 195–202.

Freeman, E., Bloom, D., & McGuire, E. (2001). A brief history of testosterone. *Journal of Urology, 165,* 371–373.

Freese, J., Powell, B., & Steelman, L. C. (1999). Rebel without a cause or effect: Birth order and social attitudes. *American Sociological Review, 64,* 207–231.

Fremouw, W. J., de Perczel, M., & Ellis, T. E. (1990). *Suicide risk: Assessment and response guidelines.* New York: Pergamon.

French, S. A., Harnack, L., & Jeffrey, R. W. (2000). Fast food restaurant use among women in the Pound of Prevention study: Dietary, behavioral and demographic correlates. *International Journal of Obesity, 24,* 1353–1359.

Freud, S. (1901/1960). *The psychopathology of everyday life* (Standard ed., Vol. 6.) London: Hogarth. (Original work published 1901)

Freud, S. (1920/1924). *A general introduction to psychoanalysis.* New York: Boni and Liveright. (Original work published 1920)

Freud, S. (1923). *The ego and the id* (Standard ed., Vol. 19.) London: Hogarth.

Freud, S. (1935). *A general introduction to psychoanalysis* (J. Rivere, Trans.). New York: Liveright.

Frey, B. S., & Stutzer, A. (2002). What can economists learn from happiness research? *Journal of Economic Literature, 40,* 402–435.

Fried, S. B., & Schultis, G. A. (1995). *The best self-help and self-awareness books: A topic-by-topic guide to quality information.* Chicago: American Library Association.

Friedan, B. (1964). *The feminine mystique.* New York: Dell.

Friedman, H. S. (1991). *The self-healing personality: Why some people achieve health and others succumb to illness.* New York: Holt.

Friedman, H. S. (2007). Personality, disease, and self-healing. In H. S. Friedman & R. C. Silver (Eds.), *Foundations of health psychology.* New York: Oxford University Press.

Friedman, H. S., & Adler, N. E. (2007). The history and background of health psychology. In H. S. Friedman & R. C. Silver (Eds.), *Foundations of health psychology.* New York: Oxford University Press.

Friedman, J. (1989). The impact of homophobia on male sexual development. *Siecus Report, 17,* 8–9.

Friedman, M. (1996). *Type A behavior: Its diagnosis and treatment.* New York: Plenum Press.

Friedman, M., & Rosenman, R. F. (1974). *Type A behavior and your heart.* New York: Knopf.

Friedman, M. J. (2006). Posttraumatic stress disorder among military returnees from Afghanistan and Iraq. *American Journal of Psychiatry, 163,* 586-593.

Friedrich, M. J. (2004). To "E" or not to "E," vitamin E's role in health and disease is the question. *Journal of the American Medical Association, 292*(6), 671–673.

Friend, R., Rafferty, Y., & Bramel, D. (1990). A puzzling misinterpretation of the Asch "conformity"

study. *European Journal of Social Psychology, 20,* 29–44.

Fromholt, P., & Bruhn, P. (1998). Cognitive dysfunction and dementia. In I. H. Nordus, G. R. VandenBos, S. Berg, & P. Fromholt (Eds.), *Clinical geropsychology.* Washington, DC: American Psychological Association.

Fromm, E. (1963). *Escape from freedom.* New York: Holt.

Fromm, E. (1981). *Sane society.* New York: Fawcett.

Fuligni, A. J., & Eccles, J. S. (1993). Perceived parent-child relationships and early adolescents' orientation toward peers. *Developmental Psychology, 29,* 622–632.

Fullerton, C. S., Ursano, R. J., & Wang, L. (2004). Acute stress disorder, posttraumatic stress disorder, and depression in disaster or rescue workers. *American Journal of Psychiatry, 161,* 1370–1376.

Fullerton, H. N., Jr. (1997). Labor force 2006: Slowing down and changing composition. *Monthly Labor Review, 120,* 23–38.

Funder, D. C. (2001). Personality. *Annual Review of Psychology, 52,* 197–221.

Furman, E. (1984). Children's patterns in mourning the death of a loved one. In H. Wass & C. A. Corr (Eds.), *Childhood and death.* Washington, DC: Hemisphere.

Furnham, A., & Cheng, H. (2000). Perceived parental behavior, self-esteem and happiness. *Social Psychiatry and Psychiatric Epidemiology, 35*(10), 463–470.

Furnham, A., & Mak, T. (1999). Sex-role stereotyping in television commercials: A review and comparison of fourteen studies done on five continents over 25 years. *Sex Roles, 41,* 413–437.

Furnham, A., & Procter, E. (1989). Belief in a just world: Review and critique of the individual difference literature. *British Journal of Social Psychology, 28*(4), 365–384.

Furstenberg, F. F., Jr. (2001). The sociology of adolescence and youth in the 1990s: A critical commentary. In R. M. Milardo (Ed.), *Understanding families into the new millennium: A decade in review.* Minneapolis, MN: National Council on Family Relations.

Furstenberg, F. F., Jr., & Kiernan, K. E. (2001). Delayed parental divorce: How much do children benefit? *Journal of Marriage and Family, 63,* 446–457.

Fyer, A. J. (2000). Anxiety disorders: Genetics. In B. J. Sadock & V. A. Sadock (Eds.), *Kaplan and Sadock's comprehensive textbook of psychiatry* (7th ed., Vol. 1). Philadelphia: Lippincott/Williams & Wilkins.

Gabbard, G. O. (1994). Reconsidering the American Psychological Association's policy on sex with former patients: Is it justifiable? *Professional Psychology: Research and Practice, 25,* 329–335.

Gable, S. L., Gonzaga, G. C., & Strachman, A. (2006). Will you be there for me when things go right? Supportive responses to positive event disclosures. *Journal of Personality and Social Psychology, 91,* 904–917.

Gabrel, C. S. (2000). *Advance data from Vital and Health Statistics of the Centers for Disease Control and Prevention.* Washington, DC: U.S. Department of Health and Human Services.

Gabriel, S., & Gardner, W. L. (1999). Are there "his" and "hers" types of interdependence? The implications of gender differences in collective versus relational interdependence for affect, behavior, and cognition. *Journal of Personality and Social Psychology, 77*(3), 642–655.

Gaertner, S. L., & Dovidio, J. F. (1986). The aversive form of racism. In J. F. Dovidio & S. L. Gaertner (Eds.), *Prejudice, discrimination, and racism: Theory and research.* Orlando, FL: Academic Press.

Gaertner, S. L., & Dovidio, J. F. (2005). Understanding and addressing contemporary racism: From aversive racism to the common ingroup identity model. *Journal of Social Issues, 61,* 615–639.

Gaertner, S. L., Dovidio, J. F., & Banker, B. S. (2000). Reducing intergroup conflict: From superordinate goals to decategorization, and mutual

differentiation. *Group Dynamics: Theory, Research and Practice, 4,* 98–114.

Gage, F. H. (2002). Neurogenesis in the adult brain. *Journal of Neuroscience, 22,* 612–613.

Galambos, N. L., Barker, E. T., & Krahn, H. J. (2006). Depression, self-esteem, and anger in emerging adulthood: Seven-year trajectories. *Developmental Psychology, 42,* 350–365.

Galderisi, S., Maj, M., Mucci, A., Cassano, G. B., Invernizzi, G., Rossi, A., Vita, A., Dell'Osso, L., Daneluzzo, E., & Pini, S. (2002). Historical, psychopathological, neurological, and neuropsychological aspects of deficit schizophrenia: A multicenter study. *American Journal of Psychiatry, 159,* 983–990.

Galinsky, E., Bond, J. T., Kim, S. S., Backon, L., Brownfield, E., & Sakai, K. (2005). *Overwork in America.* New York: Families and Work Institute.

Gall, T. L., Evans, D. R., & Howard, J. (1997). The retirement adjustment process: Changes in the well-being of male retirees across time. *Journal of Gerontology: Psychological Sciences, 52,* 110–117.

Gallagher, R., & Chase, A. (2002). *Building resilience in children in the face of fear and tragedy.* Retrieved January 11, 2005 From the New York University Child Study Center Website: Http://www.Aboutourkids.Org/Aboutour/Articles/Crisis_Resilience. html.

Gambone, J. C., Reiter, R. C., & DiMatteo, M. R. (1994). *The PREPARED provider: A guide for improved patient communication.* Beaverton, OR: Mosybl Great Performance.

Gana, K., Alaphilippe, D., & Bailly, N. (2004). Positive illusions and mental and physical health in later life. *Aging and Mental Health, 8*(1), 58–64.

Ganahl, D. J., Prinsen, T. J., & Netzley, S. B. (2003). A content analysis of prime time commercials: A contextual framework of gender representation. *Sex Roles, 49,* 545–551.

Gangestad, S. W. (1993). Sexual selection and physical attractiveness: Implications for mating dynamics. *Human Nature, 4,* 205–235.

Gangestad, S. W., & Snyder, M. (2000). Self-monitoring appraisal and reappraisal. *Psychological Bulletin, 126*(4), 530–555.

Gantt, W. H. (1975, April 25). Unpublished lecture, Ohio State University. Cited in D. Hothersall (1984), *History of psychology.* New York: Random House.

Gao, G. (2001). Intimacy, passion and commitment in Chinese and U.S. American romantic relationships. *International Journal of Intercultural Relations, 25*(3), 329–342.

Garb, H. N., Florio, C. M., & Grove, W. M. (1998). The validity of the Rorschach and the Minnesota Multiphasic Personality Inventory: Results from meta-analysis. *Psychological Science, 9,* 402–404.

Garland, A. F., & Zigler, E. (1993). Adolescent suicide prevention: Current research and social policy implications. *American Psychologist, 48,* 169–182.

Garnets, L. D., & Kimmel, D. C. (1991). Lesbian and gay male dimensions in the psychological study of human diversity. In J. D. Goodchilds (Ed.), *Psychological perspectives on human diversity in America.* Washington, DC: American Psychological Association.

Garnets, L. D., & Kimmel, D. C. (2003a). Identity development and stigma management. In L. D. Garnets & D. C. Kimmel (Eds.), *Psychological perspectives on lesbian, gay, and bisexual experiences.* New York: Columbia University Press.

Garnets, L. D., & Kimmel, D. C. (2003b). Lesbian, gay male, and bisexual dimensions in the psychological study of human diversity. In L. D. Garnets & D. C. Kimmel (Eds.), *Psychological perspectives on lesbian, gay and bisexual experiences.* New York: Columbia University Press.

Gartrell, N., Banks, A., Hamilton, J., Reed, N., Bishop, H., & Rodas, C. (1999). The national lesbian family study: Interviews with mothers of toddlers. *American Journal of Orthopsychiatry, 69,* 362–369.

Gates, G. J., & Sell, R. (2007). Measuring gay and lesbian couples. In S. L. Hofferth & L. M. Casper (Eds.), *Handbook of measurement issues in family research.* Mahwah, NJ: Erlbaum.

Myers, D. G., & Diener, E. (1995). Who is happy? *Psychological Science, 6*, 10–19.

Myers, D. G., & Diener, E. (1997). The pursuit of happiness. *Scientific American, Special Issue 7*, 40–43.

Myrtek, M. (2007). Type A behavior and hostility as independent risk factors for coronary heart disease. In J. Jochen, B. Barde, & A. M. Zeiher (Eds.), *Contributions toward evidence-based psychocardiology: A systematic review of the literature*. Washington, DC: American Psychological Association.

Nabi, R. L., & Sullivan, J. L. (2001). Does television viewing relate to engagement in protective action against crime? A cultivation analysis from a theory of reasoned action perpective. *Communication Research, 28*(6), 802–825.

Nakonezny, P. A., Reddick, R., & Rodgers, J. L. (2004). Did divorces decline after the Oklahoma City bombing? *Journal of Marriage and Family, 66*, 90–100.

Nalwa, K., & Anand, A. P. (2003). Internet addiction in students: A cause of concern. *CyberPsychology and Behavior, 6*(6), 653–656.

Narrow, W. E., Rae, D. S., Robins, L. N., & Regier, D. A. (2002). Revised prevalence based estimates of mental disorders in the United States: Using a clinical significance criterion to reconcile 2 surveys' estimates. *Archives of General Psychology, 59*(2), 115–123.

Narrow, W. E., Regier, D. A., Rae, D. S., Manderscheid, R. W., & Locke, B. Z. (1993). Use of services by persons with mental and addictive disorders: Findings from the National Institute of Mental Health Epidemiologic Catchment Area Program. *Archives of General Psychiatry, 50*, 95–107.

Nash, M. (1997). Gift of love. *Time*, 80–82.

Nathan, P. E., & Langenbucher, J. (2003). Diagnosis and classification. In G. Stricker & T. A. Widiger (Eds.), *Handbook of psychology: Vol. 8. Clinical psychology*. New York: Wiley.

National Center for Health Statistics. (2006). *National Vital Statistics Reports*, Vol. 54, No. 14, pp. 34–35.

National Institute of Mental Health. (2001). *Helping children and adolescents cope with violence and disasters*. Bethesda, MD: National Institute of Mental Health.

Naveh-Benjamin, M., Lavi, H., McKeachie, W. J., & Lin, Y. (1997). Individual differences in students' retention of knowledge and conceptual structures learned in university and high school courses: The case of test anxiety. *Applied Cognitive Psychology, 11*, 507–526.

Naylor, T. H., Willimon, W. H., & Naylor, M. R. (1994). *The search for meaning*. Nashville: Abingdon Press.

Neese, R. M., & Young, E. A. (2000). Evolutionary origins and functions of the stress response. In G. Fink (Ed.), *Encyclopedia of stress* (Vol. 2). San Diego: Academic Press.

Neimeyer, R. A., & Van Brunt, D. (1995). Death anxiety. In H. Wass & R. A. Neimeyer (Eds.), *Dying: Facing the facts* (3rd ed.). Washington, DC: Taylor & Francis.

Neiss, R. (1988). Reconceptualizing arousal: Psychobiological states in motor performance. *Psychological Bulletin, 103*, 345–366.

Neiss, R. (1990). Ending arousal's reign of error: A reply to Anderson. *Psychological Bulletin, 107*, 101–105.

Nelson, C., & Demas, G. E. (2004). Seasonal patterns of stress, disease, and sickness responses. *Current Directions in Psychological Science, 13*, 198–201.

Nelson, R. J., Franks, S., & Brose, A. (2005). The influence of hostility and family history of cardiovascular disease on autonomic activation in response to controllable versus uncontrollable stress, anger imagery reduction, and relaxation therapy. *Journal of Behavioral Medicine, 28*, 213–221.

Nemiah, J. C. (1985). Somatoform disorders. In H. I. Kaplan & B. J. Sadock (Eds.), *Comprehensive textbook of psychiatry/IV*. Baltimore: Williams & Wilkins.

Nettle, D. (2006). The evolution of personality variation in humans and other animals. *American Psychologist, 61*(6), 622–631.

Neupert, S. D., Almeida, D. M., Mroczek, D. K., & Spiro, A. (2006). Daily stressors and memory failures in a naturalistic setting: Findings from the VA normative aging study. *Psychology and Aging, 21*, 424–429.

Newcomb, M. D. (1990). Social support and personal characteristics: A developmental and interactional perspective. *Journal of Social and Clinical Psychology, 9*, 54–68.

Newell, G. R. (1991, May). Stress and cancer. *Primary Care and Cancer*, 29–30.

Newman, M., & Berkowitz, B. (1976). *How to be awake and alive*. Westminster, MD: Ballantine.

Nezu, A. M., Nezu, C. M., Felgoise, S. H., & Zwick, M. L. (2003). Psychosocial oncology. In A. M. Nezu, C. M. Nezu, & P. A. Geller (Eds.), *Handbook of psychology: Vol. 9. Health psychology*. New York: Wiley.

Ng, D. M., & Jeffery, R. W. (2003). Relationships between perceived stress and health behaviors in a sample of working adults. *Health Psychology, 22*, 638–642.

Niaura, R., & Abrams, D. B. (2002). Smoking cessation: Progress, priorities, and prospectus. *Journal of Consulting & Clinical Psychology, 70*(3), 494–509.

Niaura, R., Todaro, J. F., Stroud, L., Spiro, A., Ward, K. D., & Weiss, S. (2002). Hostility, the metabolic syndrome, and incident coronary heart disease. *Health Psychology, 21*(16), 588–593.

NICHD Early Child Care Research Network. (1997). The effects of infant child care on infant-mother attachment security: Results of the NICHD Study of Early Child Care. *Child Development, 68*, 860–879.

Nichols, B. (2006). Violence against women: The extent of the problem. In P. K. Lundberg-Love & S. L. Marmion (Eds.), *"Intimate" violence against women: When spouses, partners, or lovers attack*. Westport, CT: Praeger.

Nicholson, C. (2006). Freedom and choice, culture, and class. *APS Observer, 19*(8), 31, 45.

Nickerson, C., Schwarz, N., Diener, E., & Kahneman, D. (2003). Zeroing in on the dark side of the American dream: A closer look at the negative consequences of the goal for financial success. *Psychological Science , 14*(6), 531–536.

Nickerson, R. S. (1998). Confirmation bias: A ubiquitous phenomenon in many guises. *Review of General Psychology, 2*, 175-220.

Nie, N. H., & Erbring, L. (2002). Internet and society: A preliminary report. *IT & Society, 1*(1), 275–283.

Niederhoffer, K. G., & Pennebaker, J. W. (2005). Sharing one's story: On the benefits of writing or talking about emotional experience. In C. R. Snyder & S. J. Lopez (Eds.), *Handbook of positive psychology*. New York: Oxford University Press.

Nielsen Media Research. (2005). *Nielsen reports Americans watch TV at record levels*. Retrieved May 3, 2007 from http://www.nielsenmedia.com.

Nielsen Media Research. (2006). *Nielsen media research reports television's popularity is still growing*. Retrieved May 3, 2007 from http://www.nielsenmedia.com/nc/portal/site.Public/menuitem.55dc65b4a.

Nielsen, J. M. (1990). *Sex and gender in society: Perspective on stratification* (2nd ed.). Prospect Heights, IL: Waveland.

Niemann, Y. F., Jennings, L., Rozelle, R. M., Baxter, J. C., & Sullivan, E. (1994). Use of free responses and cluster analysis to determine stereotypes of eight groups. *Personality and Social Psychology Bulletin, 20*, 379–390.

Ninan, P. T., & Muntasser, S. (2004). Buspiron and gepirone. In A. F. Schatzberg & C. B. Nemeroff (Eds), *Textbook of psychopharmacology*. Washington, DC: American Psychiatric Publishing.

Nisbett, R. E., & Miyamoto, Y. (2005). The influence of culture: Holistic versus analytic perception. *Trends in Cognitive Science, 9*, 467–473.

Nisbett, R. E., Peng, K., Choi, I., & Norenzayan, A. (2001). Culture and systems of thought: Holistic versus analytic cognition. *Psychological Review, 108*(2), 291–310.

Nobler, M. S., & Sackeim, H. A. (2006). Electroconvulsive therapy and transcranial magnetic stimulation. In D. J. Stein, D. J. Kupfer, & A. F. Schatzberg (Eds.), *Textbook of mood disorders*. Washington, DC: American Psychiatric Publishing.

Nobre, P. J., & Pinto-Gouveia, J. (2006). Dysfunctional sexual beliefs as vulnerability factors for sexual dysfunction. *Journal of Sex Research, 43*(1), 68–75.

Nock, S. L. (1995). A comparison of marriages and cohabitating relationships. *Journal of Family Issues, 13*, 53–76.

Nolen-Hoeksema, S. (1991). Responses to depression and their effects on the duration of depressive episodes. *Journal of Abnormal Psychology, 100*, 569–582.

Nolen-Hoeksema, S. (1995). Gender differences in coping with depression across the lifespan. *Depression, 3*, 81–90.

Nolen-Hoeksema, S. (2000). The role of rumination in depressive disorders and mixed anxiety/depressive symptoms. *Journal of Abnormal Psychology, 109*(3), 504–511.

Nolen-Hoeksema, S. (2001). Gender differences in depression. *Current Directions in Psychological Science, 10*, 173–176.

Nolen-Hoeksema, S. (2002). Gender differences in depression. In I. H. Gotlib & C. L. Hammen (Eds.), *Handbook of depression*. New York: Guilford.

Nolen-Hoeksema, S., & Davis, C. G. (2005). Positive responses to loss: Perceiving benefits and growth. In C. R. Snyder & S. J. Lopez (Eds.), *Handbook of positive psychology*. New York: Oxford University Press.

Nolen-Hoeksema, S., & Keita, G. P. (2003). Women and depression: An introduction. *Psychology of Women Quarterly, 27*, 89–90.

Noller, P. (1985). Negative communications in marriage. *Journal of Social and Personal Relationships, 2*, 289–301.

Noller, P. (1987). Nonverbal communication in marriage. In D. Perlman & S. Duck (Eds.), *Intimate relationships: Development, dynamics, and deterioration*. Newbury Park, CA: Sage.

Noller, P. (2006). Bringing it all together: A theoretical approach. In A. L. Vangelisti & D. Perlman (Eds.), *The Cambridge handbook of personal relationships*. New York: Cambridge University Press.

Noller, P., & Fitzpatrick, M. A. (1990). Marital communication in the eighties. *Journal of Marriage and the Family, 52*, 832–843.

Noller, P., & Gallois, C. (1988). Understanding and misunderstanding in marriage: Sex and marital adjustment differences in structured and free interaction. In P. Noller & M. A. Fitzpatrick (Eds.), *Perspectives on marital interaction*. Clevedon, England: Multilingual Matters.

Nomaguchi, K. M. (2006). Maternal employment, nonparental care, mother-child interactions and child outcomes during preschool years. *Journal of Marriage and Family, 68*, 1341–1369.

Nomaguchi, K. M., & Milkie, M. A. (2003). Costs and rewards of children: The effects of becoming a parent on adults' lives. *Journal of Marriage and Family, 65*, 356–374.

Noom, M. J., Dekovic, M., & Meeus, W. (2001). Conceptual analysis and measurement of adolescent autonomy. *Journal of Youth and Adolescence, 30*, 577–595.

Norcross, J. C. (1995). Dispelling the dodo bird verdict and the exclusivity myth in psychotherapy. *Psychotherapy, 32*, 500–504.

Norcross, J. C., Santrock, J. W., Campbell, L. F., Smith, T. P., Sommer, R., & Zuckerman, E. L. (2003). *Authoritative guide to self-help resources in mental health*. New York: Guilford.

Norem, J. K. (1989). Cognitive strategies as personality: Effectiveness, specificity, flexibility, and chance. In D. M. Buss & N. Cantor (Eds.), *Personal-

ity psychology: Recent trends and emerging directions. New York : Springer-Verlag.

Norem, J. K. (2001). *The positive power of negative thinking: Using defensive pessimism to manage anxiety and perform at your peak.* New York: Basic Books.

Norem, J. K. (2002). Defensive self-deception and social adaptation among optimists. *Journal of Research in Personality, 36,* 549–555.

Norem, J. K., & Smith, S. (2006). Defensive pessimism: Positive past, anxious present, and pessimistic future. In L. J. Sanna & E. C. Chang (Eds.), *Judgments over time: The interplay of thoughts, feelings, and behaviors.* New York: Oxford University Press.

Norenzayan, A., Choi, I., & Nisbett, R. E. (2002). Cultural similarities and differences in social inference: Evidence from behavioral predictions and lay theories of behavior. *Personality and Social Psychology Bulletin, 28,* 109–120.

Norfleet, M. A. (2002). Responding to society's needs: Prescription privileges for psychologists. *Journal of Clinical Psychology, 58,* 599–610.

Norman, C., & Aron, A. (2003). Aspects of possible self that predict motivation to achieve or avoid it. *Journal of Experimental Social Psychology, 39,* 500–507.

Norris, F. H., & Kaniasty, K. (1996). Received and perceived social support in times of stress: A test of the social support deterioration deterrence model. *Journal of Personality and Social Psychology, 71*(3), 498–511.

Norton, P. G. W. (2004, February 1). Low-fat foods helped fuel obesity epidemic. *Family Practice News,* p. 22.

Norton, S. (2002). Women exposed: Sexual harrassment and female vulnerability. In L. Diamant & J. Lee (Eds.), *The psychology of sex, gender, and jobs.* Westport, CT: Praeger.

Notarius, C., & Markman, H. (1993). *We can work it out: Making sense of marital conflict.* New York: G. P. Putnam's Sons.

Nowell, A., & Hedges, L. V. (1998). Trends in gender differences in academic achievement from 1960–1994: An analysis of differences in mean, variance, and extreme scores. *Sex Roles, 39*(1/2), 21–43.

Noyes, R. Jr., Stuart, S. P., Lanbehn, D. R., Happel, R., Longley, S. L., Muller, B. A., & Yagla, S. J. (2003). Test of an interpersonal model of hypochondriasis. *Psychosomatic Medicine, 65,* 292–300.

Noyes, R. Jr., Watson, D. B., Letuchy, E. M., Longley, S. L., Black, D. W., Carney, C. P., & Doebbeling, B. N. (2005). Relationship between hypochondriacal concerns and personality dimensions and traits in a military population. *Journal of Nervous and Mental Disease, 193*(2), 110–118.

Nurminen, E., Malmivaara, A., Ilmarinen, J., Ylöstalo, P., Mutanen, P., Ahonen, G., & Aro, T. (2002). Effectiveness of a worksite exercise program with respect to perceived work ability and sick leaves among women with physical work. *Scandinavian Journal of Work, Environment and Health, 28*(2), 85–93.

Nurnberger, J. I., & Zimmerman, J. (1970). Applied analysis of human behavior: An alternative to conventional motivational inferences and unconscious determination in therapeutic programming. *Behavior Therapy, 1,* 59–69.

Oakes, P. (2001). The root of all evil in intergroup relations? Unearthing the categorization process. In R. Brown & S. L. Gaertner (Eds.), *Blackwell handbook of social psychology: Intergroup processes.* London: Blackwell.

Oaten, M., & Cheng, K. (2005). Academic examination stress impairs self-control. *Journal of Social and Clinical Psychology, 24,* 254–279.

Oaten, M., & Cheng, K. (2006). Longitudinal gains in self-regulation from regular physical exercise. *British Journal of Health Psychology, 11,* 717–733.

O'Brien, B. (1996). Economic evaluation of pharmaceuticals. *Medical Care, 34,* 99–108.

O'Brien, C. P., Volkow, N., & Li, T.-K. (2006). What's in a word? Addiction versus dependence

in DSM-V. *American Journal of Psychiatry, 163,* 764–765.

O'Brien, S. J., & Vertinsky, P. A. (1991). Unfit survivors: Exercise as a resource for aging women. *The Gerontologist, 31,* 347–357.

O'Callahan, M., Andrews, A. M., & Krantz, D. S. (2003). Coronary heart disease and hypertension. In A. M. Nezu, C. M. Nezu, & P. A. Geller (Eds.), *Handbook of psychology: Vol. 9. Health psychology.* New York: Wiley.

Ocon, R. (2006). *Issues on gender and diversity in management.* Lanham, MD: University Press of America.

O'Donohue, W., & Crouch, J. L. (1996). Marital therapy and gender-linked factors in communication. *Journal of Marital and Family Therapy, 22,* 87–101.

Oesterman, K., Bjoerkqvist, K., Lagerspetz, K. M. J., Kaukiainen, A., Landau, S. F., Fraczek, A., & Caprara, G. V. (1998). Cross-cultural evidence of female indirect aggression. *Aggressive Behavior, 24*(1), 1–80.

Oettingen, G., & Gollwitzer, P. M. (2001). Goal setting and goal striving. In A. Tesser & N. Schwarz. (Eds.), *Blackwell handbook of social psychology: Intraindividual processes.* Malden, MA: Blackwell.

Offer, D., Ostrov, E., & Howard, K. I. (1981). *The adolescent.* New York: Basic Books.

Ohman, A., & Mineka, S. (2003). The malicious serpent: Snakes as a prototypical stimulus for an evolved module of fear. *Current Directions in Psychological Science, 12,* 5–9.

O'Keefe, D. J., & Hale, S. L. (2001). An odds-ratio based meta-analysis of research on the door-in-the-face influence strategy. *Communication Reports, 14*(1), 31–38.

Olff, M., Langeland, W., Draijer, N., & Gersonons, B. P. R. (2007). Gender differences in posttraumatic stress disorder. *Psychological Bulletin, 133,* 183–204.

Olfson, M., Marcus, S. C., Druss, B. , & Pincus, H. A. (2002). National trends in the use of outpatient psychotherapy. *American Journal of Psychiatry, 159,* 1914–1920.

Olfson, M., Shaffer, D., Marcus, S. C., & Greenberg, T. (2003). Relationship between antidepressant medication treatment and suicide in adolescents. *Archives of General Psychiatry, 60*(10), 978–982.

Olio, K. (1994). Truth in memory. *American Psychologist, 49,* 442–443.

Olivardia, R., Pope, H. G., & Phillips, K. A. (2000). *The Adonis complex: The secret crisis of male body obsession.* New York: Free Press.

Oliver, M. B., & Hyde, J. S. (1993). Gender differences in sexuality: A meta-analysis. *Psychological Bulletin, 114,* 29–51.

O'Neil, J. M., & Egan, J. (1992). Men's and women's gender role journeys: A metaphor for healing, transition, and transformation. In B. Wainrib (Ed.), *Gender issues across the life cycle.* New York: Springer.

O'Neill, N., & O'Neill, G. (1972). *Open marriage.* New York: Evans.

Ong, A. D., Bergeman, C. S., Bisconti, T. L., & Wallace, K. A. (2006). Psychological resilience, positive emotions, and successful adaptation to stress in later life. *Journal of Personality and Social Psychology, 91,* 730–749.

Ono, H. (1998). Husbands' and wives' resources and marital dissolution. *Journal of Marriage and the Family, 60,* 674–689.

Ono, H. (2006). Homogamy among the divorced and never married on marital history in recent decades: Evidence from vital statistics data. *Social Science Research, 35,* 356–383.

Orenstein, P. (1994). *School girls: Young women, self-esteem, and the confidence gap.* New York: Doubleday.

Organista, P. B., & Miranda, J. (1991). Psychosomatic symptoms in medical outpatients: An investigation of self-handicapping theory. *Health Psychology, 10,* 427–431.

Orlofsky, J. L., Marcia, J. E., & Lesser, I. M. (1973). Ego identity status and the intimacy versus isolation

crisis of young adulthood. *Journal of Personality and Social Psychology, 27,* 211–219.

Orth-Gomer, K., Wamala, S. P., Horsten, M., Schenck-Gustafsson, K., Schneiderman, N., & Mittleman, M. A. (2000). Marital stress worsens prognosis in women with coronary heart disease: The Stockholm female coronary risk study. *Journal of the American Medical Association, 284*(23), 3008–3014.

Oskamp, S. (2000). A sustainable future for humanity? How psychology can help. *American Psychologist, 55*(5), 496–508.

Osman, S. L. (2003). Predicting men's rape perceptions based on the belief that "no" really means "yes." *Journal of Applied Social Psychology, 33*(4), 683–692.

O'Sullivan, L. F., McCrudden, M. C., & Tolman, D. L. (2006). To your sexual health! Incorporating sexuality into the health perspective. In J. Worrell & C. D. Goodheart (Eds.), *Handbook of girls' and women's psychological health.* New York: Oxford University Press.

Otto, M. W., Pollack, M. H., Jenike, M. A., & Rosenbaum, J. F. (1999). Anxiety disorders and their treatment. In A. M. Nicholi (Ed.), *The Harvard guide to psychiatry* (3rd ed.). Cambridge, MA: Harvard University Press.

Ouellette, S. C. (1993). Inquiries into hardiness. In L. Goldberger & S. Breznitz (Eds.), *Handbook of stress: Theoretical and clinical aspects* (2nd ed.). New York: Free Press.

Ouellette, S. C., & DiPlacido, J. (2001). Personality's role in the protection and enhancement of health: Where the research has been, where it is stuck, how it might move. In A. Baum, T. A. Revenson, & J. E. Singer *Handbook of health psychology.* Mahwah, NJ: Erlbaum.

Owen, M. J., & O'Donovan, M. C. (2003). Schizophrenia and genetics. In R. Plomin, J. C. Defries, I. W. Craig & P. McGuffin (Eds.), *Behavioral genetics in the postgenomic era.* Washington, DC: American Psychological Association.

Oyserman, D., Bybee, D., & Terry, K. (2006). Possible selves and academic outcomes: How and when possible selves impel action. *Journal of Personality and Social Psychology, 91,* 188–204.

Ozer, D. J., & Reise, S. P. (1994). Personality assessment. *Annual Review of Psychology, 45,* 357–388.

Ozer, E. J., Best, S. R., Lipsey, T. L., & Weiss, D. S. (2003). Predictors of posttraumatic stress disorder and symptoms in adults: A meta-analysis. *Psychological Bulletin, 129*(1), 52–73.

Ozer, E. J., & Weiss, D. S. (2004). Who develops posttraumatic stress disorder? *Current Directions in Psychological Science, 13,* 169–172.

Ozer, E. M., & Bandura, A. (1990). Mechanisms governing empowerment effects: A self-efficacy analysis. *Journal of Personality and Social Psychology, 58,* 472–486.

Padgett, D. A., & Sheridan, J. F. (2000). Herpesviruses. In G. Fink (Ed.), *Encyclopedia of stress.* San Diego: Academic Press.

Paivio, A. (1986). *Mental representations: A dual coding approach.* New York: Oxford University Press.

Papalia, D. E., & Olds, C. W. (1995). *Human Development* (6th ed.). New York: McGraw-Hill.

Papp, L. M., Cummings, E. M., & Schermerhorn, A. C. (2004). Pathways among marital distress, parental symptomatology, and child adjustment. *Journal of Marriage and Family, 66,* 368–384.

Park, C. W., & Young, S. M. (1986). Consumer response to television commercials: The impact of involvement and background music on brand attitude formation. *Journal of Marketing Research, 23* 11–24.

Park, K. (2005). Choosing childlessness: Weber's typology of action and motives of the voluntarily childless. *Sociological Inquiry, 75,* 372–402.

Parker, R. (2000). Health literacy: A challenge for American patients and their health care providers. *Health Promotion International, 15,* 277–283.

Parrott, A. C. (2000). Human research on MDMA (3,4-Methylenedioxymethamphetamine) neurotoxicity: Cognitive and behavioural indices of change. *Neuropsychobiology, 42*(1), 17–24.

Parrott, D. J., & Zeichner, A. (2006). Effect of psychopathy on physical aggression toward gay and heterosexual men. *Journal of Interpersonal Violence, 21,* 390–410.

Parsons, T., & Bales, R. F. (1995). *Family, socialization, and interaction process.* Glencoe, IL: Free Press.

Pasley, K., & Moorefield, B. S. (2004). Stepfamilies: Changes and challenges. In M. Coleman, & L. H. Ganong (Eds.), *Handbook of contemporary families: Considering the past, contemplating the future.* Thousand Oaks, CA: Sage.

Pasterski, V. L., Geffner, M. E., Brain, C., Hindmarsh, P., Brook, C., & Hines, M. (2005). Prenatal hormones and postnatal socialization by parents as determinants of male-typical toy play in girls with congenital adrenal hyperplasia. *Child Development, 76,* 264–278.

Patel, J. K., Pinals, D. A., & Breier, A. (2003). Schizophrenia and other psychoses. In A. Tasman, J. Kay, & J. A. Lieberman (Eds.), *Psychiatry.* New York: Wiley.

Pato, M. T., Eisen, J. L., & Phillips, K. A. (2003). Obsessive-compulsive disorder. In A. Tasman, J. Kay, & J. A. Lieberman (Eds.), *Psychiatry.* New York: Wiley.

Patterson, C. J. (2001). Family relationships of lesbians and gay men. In R. M. Milardo (Ed.), *Understanding families into the new millennium: A decade in review.* Minneapolis: National Council on Family Relations.

Patterson, C. J. (2003). Children of lesbian and gay parents. In L. D. Garnets & D. C. Kimmel (Eds.), *Psychological perspectives on lesbian, gay, and bisexual experiences.* New York: Columbia University Press.

Patterson, C. J. (2006). Children of lesbian and gay parents. *Current Directions in Psychological Science, 15,* 241–254.

Patterson, C. J., & Redding, R. E. (1996). Lesbian and gay families with children: Implications of social science research for policy. *Journal of Social Issues, 52*(3), 29–50.

Patterson, G. R., DeBaryshe, B. D., & Ramsey, E. (1989). A developmental perspective on antisocial behavior. *American Psychologist, 44*(2), 329–335.

Patterson, M. L. (1988). Functions of nonverbal behavior in close relationships. In S. Duck (Ed.), *Handbook of personal relationships: Theory, research, and interventions.* New York: Wiley.

Paul, A. M. (2001). Self-help: Shattering the myths. *Psychology Today, 34*(2), 60.

Paul, E. L., McManus, B., & Hayes, A. (2000). "Hookups": Characteristics and correlates of college students' spontaneous and anonymous sexual experiences. *Journal of Sex Research, 37*(1), 76–88.

Paulhus, D. L. (1991). Measurement and control of response bias. In J. P. Robinson, P. Shaver, & L. S. Wrightsman (Eds.), *Measures of personality and social psychological attitudes.* San Diego: Academic Press.

Paulhus, D. L., Fridhandler, B., & Hayes, S. (1997). Psychological defense: Contemporary theory and research. In R. Hogan, J. Johnson, & S. Briggs (Eds), *Handbook of personality psychology.* San Diego: Academic Press.

Paulhus, D. L., Trapnell, P. D., & Chen, D. (1999). Birth order effects on personality and achievement within families. *Psychological Science, 10,* 482–488.

Paunonen, S. V. (1998). Hierarchical organization of personality and prediction of behavior. *Journal of Personality and Social Psychology, 74*(2), 538–556.

Paunonen, S. V. (2003). Big five factors of personality and replicated predictions of behavior. *Journal of Personality and Social Psychology, 84,* 411–424.

Paunonen, S. V., & Ashton, M. C. (1998). The structured assessment of personality across cultures. *Journal of Cross-Cultural Psychology, 29,* 150–170.

Pavlov, I. P. (1906). The scientific investigation of psychical faculties or processes in the higher animals. *Science, 24,* 613–619.

Paxton, S. J., Norris, M., Wertheim, E. H., Durkin, S. J., & Anderson, J. (2005). Body dissatisfaction,

dating, and importance of thinness to attractiveness in adolescent girls. *Sex Roles, 53,* 663–675.

Payne, B. K. (2006). Weapon bias: Split-second decisions and unintended sterotyping. *Current Directions in Psychological Science, 15,* 287–291.

Payne, D. G., & Wenger, M. J. (1996). Practice effects in memory: Data, theory, and unanswered questions. In D. J. Herrmann, C. McEvoy, C. Hertzog, P. Hertel, & M. K. Johnson (Eds.), *Basic and applied memory research: Practical applications* (Vol. 2). Mahwah, NJ: Erlbaum.

Pearce, L. (1974). Duck! It's the new journalism. *New Times, 2,* 40–41.

Pearson, P. (1998). *When she was bad: Violent women and the myth of innocence.* New York: Viking.

Pearson, Q. M. (1998). Job satisfaction, leisure satisfaction, and psychological health. *Career Development Quarterly, 46*(4), 416–426.

Pechacek, T. F., & Babb, S. (2004). Commentary: How acute and reversible are the cardiovascular risks of secondhand smoke? *British Medical Journal, 328,* 980–983.

Pechnick, R. N., & Ungerleider, T. J. (2005). Hallucinogens. In J. H. Lowinson, P. Ruiz, R. B. Millman, & J. G. Langrod (Eds.), *Substance abuse: A comprehensive textbook.* Philadelphia: Lippincott/Williams & Wilkins.

Pedersen, P. (1994). A culture-centered approach to counseling. In W. J. Lonner & R. Malpass (Eds.), *Psychology and culture.* Boston: Allyn & Bacon.

Pedersen, W., & Skrondal, A. (1999). Ecstasy and new patterns of drug use: A normal population study. *Addiction, 94*(11), 1695–1706.

Pegula, S., & Marsh, S. M. (2007). Fatal occupational injuries—United States, 2005. *Journal of the American Medical Association, 297,* 2193–2194.

Peirce, R. S., Frone, M. R., Russell, M., & Cooper, M. L. (1996). Financial stress, social support, and alcohol involvement: A longitudinal test of the buffering hypothesis in a general population survey. *Health Psychology, 15,* 38–47.

Peladeau, N., Forget, J., & Gagne, F. (2003). Effect of paced and unpaced practice on skill application and retention: How much is enough? *American Educational Research Journal, 40,* 769–801.

Pennebaker, J. W. (1997). *Opening up: The healing power of expressing emotions.* New York: Guilford.

Pennebaker, J. W., Colder, M., & Sharp, L. K. (1990). Accelerating the coping process. *Journal of Personality and Social Psychology, 58,* 528–537.

Peplau, L. A. (1988). Research on homosexual couples: An overview. In J. P. De Cecco (Ed.), *Gay relationships.* New York: Harrington Park Press.

Peplau, L. A. (1991). Lesbian and gay relationships. In J. C. Gonsiorek & J. D. Weinrich (Eds.), *Homosexuality: Research implications for public policy.* Newbury Park, CA: Sage.

Peplau, L. A. (2003). Human sexuality: How do men and women differ? *Current Directions in Psychological Science, 12*(2), 37–40.

Peplau, L. A., & Cochran, S. D. (1990). A relational perspective on homosexuality. In D. P. McWhirter, S. A. Sanders, & J. M. Reinisch (Eds.), *Homosexuality/heterosexuality: Concepts of sexual orientation.* New York: Oxford University Press.

Peplau, L. A., & Fingerhut, A. W. (2007). The close relationships of lesbians and gay men. *Annual Review of Psychology, 58,* 405–424.

Peplau, L. A., Fingerhut, A., & Beals, K. P. (2004). Sexuality in the relationships of lesbians and gay men. In J. H. Harvey, A. Wenzel, & S. Sprecher (Eds.), *The handbook of sexuality in close relationships.* Mahwah, NJ: Lawrence Erlbaum.

Peplau, L. A., & Garnets, L. D. (2000). A new paradigm for understanding women's sexuality and sexual orientation. *Journal of Social Issues, 56*(2), 329–350.

Peplau, L. A., & Gordon, S. L. (1985). Women and men in love: Gender differences in close heterosexual relationships. In V. E. O'Leary, R. K. Unger, & B. S. Wallston (Eds.), *Women, gender, and social psychology.* Hillsdale, NJ: Erlbaum.

Peplau, L. A., Hill, C. T., & Rubin, Z. (1993). Sex role attitudes in dating and marriage: A 15-year follow-up of the Boston couples study. *Journal of Social Issues, 49,* 31–52.

Peplau, L. A., & Spalding, L. R. (2000). The close relationships of lesbians, gay men, and bisexuals. In C. Hendrick & S. S. Hendrick (Eds.), *Close relationships: A sourcebook.* Thousand Oaks, CA: Sage.

Peplau, L. A., & Spalding, L. R. (2003). The close relationships of lesbians, gay men, and bisexuals. In L. D. Garnets & D. C. Kimmel (Eds.), *Psychological perspectives on lesbian, gay, and bisexual experiences.* New York: Columbia University Press.

Peretti, P. O., & Abplanalp, R. R., Jr. (2004). Chemistry in the college dating process: Structure and function. *Social Behavior and Personality, 32*(2), 147–154.

Perkins, D. F., & Borden, L. M. (2003). Positive behaviors, problem behaviors, and resiliency in adolescence. In R. M. Lerner, M.A. Easterbrooks, & J. Mistry (Eds.), *Handbook of psychology: Vol. 6. Developmental psychology.* New York: Wiley.

Perkins, D. O., Miller-Anderson, L., & Lieberman, J. A. (2006). Natural history and predictors of clinical course. In J. A. Liberman, T. S. Stroup, & D. O. Perkins (Eds.), *Textbook of schizophrenia.* Washington, DC: American Psychiatric Publishing.

Perlis, R. H., Perlis, C. S., Wu, Y., Hwang, C., Joseph, M., & Nierenberg, A. A. (2005). Industry sponsorship and financial conflict of interest in the reporting of clinical trials in psychiatry. *American Journal of Psychiatry, 162,* 1957–1960.

Perloff, R. M. (1993). *The dynamics of persuasion.* Hillsdale, NJ: Erlbaum.

Perreault, S., & Bourhis, R. Y. (1999). Ethnocentrism, social identification, and discrimination. *Personality and Social Psychology Bulletin, 25*(1), 92–103.

Perrett, D. I., Lee, K. J., Penton-Voak, I., Rowland, D., Yoshikawa, S., Burt, D. M., Henzi, S. P., Castles, D. L., & Akamatsu, S. (1998). Effects of sexual dimorphism on facial attractiveness. *Nature, 394,* 884–887.

Perri, M. G., Anton, S. D., Durning, P. E., Ketterson, T. U., Sydeman, S. J., Berlant, N. E., Kanasky Jr., W. F., Newton Jr., R. L., Llimacher, M. C., & Martin, A. D. (2002). Adherence to exercise prescriptions: Effects of prescribing moderate versus higher levels of intensity and frequency. *Health Psychology, 21*(5), 452–458.

Perry-Jenkins, M., Repetti, R. L., & Crouter, A. C. (2001). Work and family in the 1990s. In R. M. Milardo (Ed.), *Understanding families into the new millennium: A decade in review.* Minneapolis, MN: National Council on Family Relations.

Perry-Jenkins, M., & Turner, E. (2004). Jobs, marriage, and parenting: Working it out in dual-earner families. In M. Coleman, & L. H. Ganong (Eds.), *Handbook of contemporary families: Considering the past, contemplating the future.* Thousand Oaks, CA: Sage.

Person, E. S. (1990). The influence of values in psychoanalysis: The case of female psychology. In C. Zanardi (Ed.), *Essential papers in psychoanalysis.* New York: New York University Press.

Pervin, L. A. (1994). Personality stability, personality change, and the question of process. In T. F. Heatherton & J. L. Weinberger (Eds.), *Can personality change?* Washington, DC: American Psychological Association.

Pervin, L. A., & John, O. P. (2001). *Personality: Theory and research.* New York: Wiley.

Petersen, A. C. (1987, September). Those gangly years. *Psychology Today,* pp. 28–34.

Petersen, A. C. (1988). Adolescent development. *Annual Review of Psychology, 39,* 583–607.

Petersen, R. C., Ed. (2003). *Mild cognitive impairment.* Oxford, England: Oxford University Press.

Peterson, B. E., & Lane, M. D. (2001). Implications of authoritarianism for young adulthood: Longitudinal analysis of college experiences and future goals. *Personality and Social Psychology Bulletin, 27*(6), 678–690.

Peterson, C., & Bossio, L. M. (2001). Optimism and physical well-being. In E. C. Chang (Ed.), *Optimism and pessimism: Implications for theory, research, and practice*. Washington, DC: American Psychological Association.

Peterson, C., Maier, S. F., & Seligman, M. E. P. (1993). *Learned helplessness: A theory for the age of personal control*. New York: Oxford University Press.

Peterson, C., & Seligman, M. E. P. (2004). *Character strengths and virtues: A handbook and classification*. Washington, DC: American Psychological Association/New York: Oxford University Press.

Peterson, C., & Vaidya, R. S. (2001). Explanatory style, expectations, and depressive symptoms. *Personality and Individual Differences, 31*, 1217–1223.

Peterson, C., Seligman, M. E. P., & Vaillant, G. E. (1988). Pessimistic explanatory style is a risk factor for physical illness: A thirty-five-year longitudinal study. *Journal of Personality and Social Psychology, 55*, 23–27.

Peterson, C., Seligman, M. E. P., Yurko, K. H., Martin, L. R., & Friedman, H. S. (1998). Castastrophizing and untimely death. *Psychological Science, 9*, 127–130.

Peterson, J. L., & Bakeman, R. (2006). Impact of beliefs about HIV treatment and peer condom norms on risky sexual behavior among gay and bisexual men. *Journal of Community Psychology, 34*(1), 37–46.

Peterson, N., & González, R. (2005). *The role of work in people's lives: Applied career counseling and vocational psychology*. Belmont, CA: Wadsworth.

Petit, J. W., & Joiner, T. E. (2006). *Chronic depression: Interpersonal sources, therapeutic solutions*. Washington, DC: American Psychological Association.

Petras, R., & Petras, K. (1993). *The 776 stupidest things ever said*. New York: Doubleday.

Petrill, S. A. (2005). Behavioral genetics and intelligence. In O. Wilhelm & R. W. Engle (Eds.), *Handbook of understanding and measuring intelligence*. Thousand Oaks, CA: Sage Publications.

Petticrew, M., Fraser, J. M., & Regan, M. F. (1999). Adverse life-events and risk of breast cancer: A meta-analysis. *British Journal of Health Psychology, 4*, 1–17.

Pettigrew, T. F. (2001). The ultimate attribution error: Extending Allport's cognitive analysis of prejudice. In M. A. Hogg & D. Abrams (Eds.), *Intergroup relations: Essential readings*. New York: Psychology Press.

Pettigrew, T. F., & Tropp, L. R. (2000). Does intergroup contact reduce prejudice: Recent meta-analytic findings. In S. Oskamp (Ed.), *Reducing prejudice and discrimination*. Mahwah, NJ: Erlbaum.

Pettigrew, T. F., & Tropp, L. R. (2006). A meta-analytic test of intergroup contact theory. *Journal of Personality and Social Psychology, 90*, 751–783.

Petty, R. E., & Cacioppo, J. T. (1986). The elaboration likelihood model of persuasion. In L. Berkowitz (Ed.), *Advances in experimental social psychology* (Vol. 19). Orlando, FL: Academic Press.

Petty, R. E., & Cacioppo, J. T. (1990). Involvement and persuasion: Tradition versus integration. *Psychological Bulletin, 107*, 367–374.

Petty, R. E., Fleming, M. A., Priester, J. R., & Feinstein, A. H. (2001). Individual versus group interest violation: Surprise as a determinant of argument scrutiny and persuasion. *Social Cognition, 19*(4), 418–442.

Petty, R. E., Priester, J. R., & Wegener, D. T. (1994). Cognitive processes in attitude change. In R. S. Wyer & T. K. Srull (Eds.), *Handbook of social cognition* (Vol. 2). Hillsdale, NJ: Erlbaum.

Petty, R. E., & Wegener, D. T. (1998). Attitude change: Multiple roles for persuasion variables. In D. T. Gilbert, S. T. Fiske, & G. Lindzey (Eds.), *The handbook of social psychology* (4th ed., Vol. 1). New York: McGraw-Hill.

Petty, R. E., Wegener, D. T., & Fabrigar, L. R. (1997). Attitudes and attitude change. *Annual Review of Psychology, 48*, 609–647.

Petty, S. C., Sachs-Ericsson, N., & Joiner, T. E., Jr. (2004). Interpersonal functioning deficits: Temporary or stable characteristics of depressed individuals. *Journal of Affective Disorders, 81*(2), 115–122.

Phillips, W. T., Kiernan, M., & King, A. C. (2001). The effects of physical activity on physical and psychological health. In A. Baum, T. A. Revenson, & J. E. Singer (Eds.), *Handbook of health psychology*. Mahwah, NJ: Erlbaum.

Pi, E. H., & Simpson, G. M. (2001). Medication-induced movement disorders. In B. J. Sadock & V. A. Sadock (Eds.), *Kaplan and Sadock's comprehensive textbook of psychiatry* (7th ed., Vol. 2). Philadelphia: Lippincott/ Williams & Wilkins.

Pierce, C. M. (1992). Contemporary psychiatry: Racial perspectives on the past and future. In A. Kales, C. M. Pierce, & M. Greenblatt (Eds.), *The mosaic of contemporary psychiatry in perspective*. New York: Springer-Verlag.

Pietromonaco, P. R., Greenwood, D., & Barrett, L. F. (2004). Conflict in adult close relationships: An attachment perspective. In W. S. Rholes & J. A. Simpson (Eds.), *Adult attachment: Theory, research, and clinical implications*. New York: Guilford.

Piferi, R. L., & Lawler, K. A. (2006). Social support and ambulatory blood pressure: An examination of both receiving and giving. *International Journal of Psychophysiology, 62*, 328–336.

Pike, A., Manke, B., Reiss, D., & Plomin, R. (2000). A genetic analysis of differential experiences of adolescent siblings across three years. *Social Development, 9*, 96–114.

Pike, K. M., & Rodin, J. (1991). Mothers, daughters, and disordered eating. *Journal of Abnormal Psychology, 100*, 198–294.

Pillow, D. R., Zautra, A. J., & Sandler, I. (1996). Major life events and minor stressors: Identifying mediational links in the stress process. *Journal of Personality and Social Psychology, 70*, 381–394.

Pilowsky, I. (1993). Aspects of abnormal illness behaviour. *Psychotherapy and Psychosomatics, 60*, 62–74.

Pine, D. S., & McClure, E. B. (2005a). Anxiety disorders: Clinical features. In B. J. Sadock & V. A. Sadock (Eds.), *Kaplan & Sadock's comprehensive textbook of psychiatry*. Philadelphia: Lippicott Williams & Wilkins.

Pine, D. S., & McClure, E. B. (2005b). Anxiety disorders: Genetics. In B. J. Sadock & V. A. Sadock (Eds.), *Kaplan & Sadock's comprehensive textbook of psychiatry*. Philadelphia: Lippincott Williams & Wilkins.

Pinel, J. P. J., Assanand, S., & Lehman, D. R. (2000). Hunger, eating, and ill health. *American Psychologist, 55*, 1105–1116.

Pines, A. M. (1993). Burnout. In L. Goldberger & S. Breznitz (Eds.), *Handbook of stress: Theoretical and clinical aspects* (2nd ed.). New York: Free Press.

Pink, D. H. (2001). *Free agent nation: The future of working for yourself*. New York: Warner Business Books.

Pinquart, M. (2003). Loneliness in married, widowed, divorced, and never-married older adults. *Journal of Social and Personal Relationships, 20*(1), 31–53.

Pinquart, M., & Sorensen, S. (2001). Influences on loneliness in older adults: A meta-analysis. *Basic and Applied Social Psychology, 23*, 245–266.

Pipher, M. (1994). *Reviving Ophelia: Saving the selves of adolescent girls*. New York: Ballantine.

Pi-Sunyer, F. X. (2002). Medical complications of obesity in adults. In C. G. Fairburn & K. D. Brownell (Eds.), *Eating disorders and obesity: A comprehensive handbook*. New York: Guilford.

Pittman, F., III. (1994, January/February). A buyer's guide to psychotherapy. *Psychology Today*, pp. 50–53, 74–81.

Piver, S. (2000). *The hard questions: 100 questions to ask before you say "I do."* New York: Jeremy P. Tarcher/Putnam.

Planalp, S., Fitness, J., & Fehr, B. (2006). Emotion in theories of close relationships. In A. L. Vangelisti & D. Perlman (Eds.), *The Cambridge handbook of personal relationships*. New York: Cambridge University Press.

Plante, T. G. (2005). *Contemporary clinical psychology*. New York: Wiley.

Plante, T. G., Caputo, D., & Chizmar, L. (2000). Perceived fitness and responses to laboratory induced stress. *International Journal of Stress Management, 7*(1), 61–73.

Pleck, J. H. (1981). *The myth of masculinity*. Cambridge, MA: MIT Press.

Pleck, J. H. (1995). The gender role strain paradigm: An update. In R. F. Levant & W. S. Pollack (Eds.), *A new psychology of men*. New York: Basic Books.

Plomin, R. (1994). Nature, nurture, and development. In R. J. Sternberg (Ed.), *Encyclopedia of human intelligence*. New York: Macmillan.

Plomin, R., & Caspi, A. (1999). Behavioral genetics and personality. In L. A. Pervin & O. P. John (Eds.), *Handbook of personality: Theory and research* (2nd ed.). New York: Guilford Press.

Plomin, R., & Spinath, F. M. (2004). Intelligence: Genetics, genes, and genomics. *Journal of Personality & Social Psychology, 86*, 112–129.

Plous, S. L., & Zimbardo, P. G. (2004, September 10). How social science can reduce terrorism. *The Chronicle of Higher Education*, pp. B9–B10.

Polivy, J., & Herman, C. P. (2002). Causes of eating disorder. *Annual Review of Psychology, 53*, 187–213.

Pollak, L. (2007). *Getting from college to career: 90 things to do before you join the real world*. New York: HarperCollins.

Pomeroy, C., & Mitchell, J. E. (2002). Medical complications of anorexia nervosa and bulimia nervosa. In C. G. Fairburn & K. D. Brownell (Eds.), *Eating disorders and obesity: A comprehensive handbook*. New York: Guilford.

Pope, E., & Shouldice, M. (2001). Drugs and sexual assault: A review. *Trauma Violence and Abuse, 2*(1), 51–55.

Pope, H. G., Barry, S., Bodkin, A., & Hudson, J. I. (2006). Tracking scientific interest in the dissociative disorders: A study of scientific publication output 1984–2003. *Psychotherapy and Psychosomatics, 75*, 19–24.

Pope, H. G., Gruber, A. J., Hudson, J. I., Huestis, M. A., & Yurgelun-Todd, D. (2001). Neuropsychological performance in long-term cannabis users. *Archives of General Psychiatry, 58*, 909–915.

Pope, H. G., Gruber, A. J., & Yurgelun-Todd, D. (2001). Residual neuropsychologic effects of cannabis. *Current Psychiatry Report, 3*, 507–512.

Pope, H. G., Oliva, P. S., Hudson, J. I., Bodkin, J. A., & Gruber, A. J. (1999). Attitudes toward DSM-IV dissociative disorders diagnoses among board-certified American psychiatrists. *American Journal of Psychiatry, 156*(2), 321–323.

Pope, K. S., Keith-Spiegel, P., & Tabachnick, B. G. (1986). Sexual attraction to clients. *American Psychologist, 41*, 147–158.

Popenoe, D. (1993). American family decline, 1960–1990: A review and appraisal. *Journal of Marriage and the Family, 55*, 527–555.

Popenoe, D. (1999). *Life without father: Compelling new evidence that fatherhood and marriage are indispensable for the good of children and society*. Cambridge, MA: Harvard University Press.

Potenza, M. N. (2006). Should addictive disorders include non–substance-related conditions? *Addiction, 101*(Suppl 1), 142–151.

Potter, W. Z., Padich, R. A., Rudorfer, M. V., & Krishnan, K. R. R. (2006). Tricyclics, tetracyclics, and monoamine oxidase inhibitors. In D. J. Stein, D. J. Kupfer, & A. F. Schatzberg (Eds.), *Textbook of mood disorders*. Washington, DC: American Psychiatric Publishing.

Powell, J. L., & Drucker, A. D. (1997). The role of peer conformity in the decision to ride with an intoxicated driver. *Journal of Alcohol and Drug Education, 43*(1), 1–7.

Powell, R. A., & Gee, T. L. (1999). The effects of hypnosis on dissociative identity disorder: A reexamination of the evidence. *Canadian Journal of Psychiatry, 44,* 914–916.

Pratt, L. A., Ford, D. E., Crum, R. M., Armenian, H. K., Gallo, J. J., & Eaton, W. W. (1996). Depression, psychotropic medication, and risk of myocardial infarction: Prospective data from the Baltimore ECA follow-up. *Archives of Internal Medicine, 94,* 3123–3129.

Pratto, F., Sidanius, J., Stallworth, L. M., & Malle, B. F. (1994). Social dominance orientation: A personality variable predicting social and political attitudes. *Journal of Personality and Social Psychology, 67,* 741–763.

Pratto, F., & Walker, A. (2004). The bases of gendered power. In A. H. Eagly, A. E. Beall, & R. J. Sternberg (Eds.), *The psychology of gender.* New York: Guilford Press.

Presser, H. B. (2000). Nonstandard work schedules and marital instability. *Journal of Marriage and the Family, 62,* 93–110.

Pressman, S. (1993). *Outrageous betrayal: The real story of Werner Erhard, EST and the Forum.* New York: St. Martin's Press.

Preto, N. G. (1999). Transformation of the family system during adolescence. In B. Carter & M. McGoldrick (Eds.), *The expanded family life cycle: Individual, family, and social perspectives* (3rd ed.). Boston: Allyn & Bacon.

Pruchno, R., & Rosenbaum, J. (2003). Social relationships in adulthood and old age. In R. M. Lerner, M. A. Easterbrooks, & J. Mistry (Eds.), *Handbook of psychology: Vol. 6. Developmental psychology.* New York: Wiley.

Prudic, J. (2005). Electroconvulsive therapy. In B. J. Sadock & V. A. Sadock (Eds.), *Kaplan and Sadock's comprehensive textbook of psychiatry.* Philadelphia: Lippincott Williams & Wilkins.

Pryor, F. L., & Schaffer, D. (1997, July). Wages and the university educated: A paradox resolved. *Monthly Labor Review,* 3–14.

Pryor, J. B., Giedd, J. L., & Williams, K. B. (1995). A social psychological model for predicting sexual harassment. *Journal of Social Issues, 51,* 69–84.

Puetz, T. W., O'Connor, P. J., & Dishman, R. K. (2006). Effects of chronic exercise on feelings of energy and fatigue: A quantitative synthesis. *Psychological Bulletin, 132,* 866–876.

Putnam, R. D. (1996). The strange disappearance of civic America. *The American Prospect, 24,* 34–46.

Pyszczynski, T., Greenberg, J., & Goldenberg, J. L. (2003). Freedom versus fear: On the defense, growth, and expansion of the self. In M. R. Leary & J. P. Tangney (Eds.), *Handbook of self and identity.* New York: Guilford.

Pyszczynski, T., Greenberg, J., & Solomon, S. (1999). A dual-process model of defense against conscious and unconscious death-related thoughts: An extension of terror management theory. *Psychological Review, 106*(4), 835–845.

Pyszczynski, T., Greenberg, J., Solomon, S., Arndt, J., & Schimel, J. (2004). Why do people need self-esteem? A theoretical and empirical review. *Psychological Bulletin, 130*(3), 435–468.

Pyszczynski, T., Solomon, S., & Greenberg, J. (2003a). Giving peace a chance. In T. Pyszczynski, S. Solomon, & J. Greenberg (Eds.), *In the wake of 9/11: The psychology of terror.* Washington, DC: American Psychological Association.

Pyszczynski, T., Solomon, S., & Greenberg, J. (2003b). *In the wake of 9/11: The psychology of terror.* Washington, DC: American Psychological Association.

Quinn, K. A., Macrae, C. N., & Bodenhausen, G. V. (2003). Stereotyping and impression formation: How categorical thinking shapes person perception. In M. A. Hogg & J. Cooper (Eds.), *The Sage handbook of social psychology.* Thousand Oaks, CA: Sage Publications.

Rabkin, J. G. (1993). Stress and psychiatric disorders. In L. Goldberger & S. Breznitz (Eds.), *Handbook of stress: Theoretical and clinical aspects* (2nd ed.). New York: Free Press.

Rachman, S. J. (1990). *Fear and courage.* New York: Freeman.

Rachman, S. J. (1992). Behavior therapy. In L. R. Squire (Ed.), *Encyclopedia of learning and memory.* New York: Macmillan.

Ragins, B. R., Cornwell, J. M., & Miller, J. S. (2003). Heterosexism in the workplace: Do race and gender matter? *Group & Organization Management, 28*(1), 45–74.

Ragland, D. R., & Brand, R. J. (1988). Type A behavior and mortality from coronary heart disease. *The New England Journal of Medicine, 318,* 65–69.

Rahe, R. H., & Arthur, R. H. (1978). Life change and illness studies. *Journal of Human Stress, 4,* 3–15.

Rahe, R. H., Veach, T. L., Tolles, R. L., & Murakami, K. (2000). The stress and coping inventory: An educational and research instrument. *Stress Medicine, 16,* 199–208.

Rahim, M. A., & Magner, N. R. (1995). Confirmatory factor analysis of the styles of handling interpersonal conflict: First-order factor model and its invariance across groups. *Journal of Applied Psychology, 80,* 122–132.

Rahman, Q. (2005). Fluctuating asymmetry, second to fourth finger length and human sexual orientation. *Psychoneuroendocrinology, 30,* 382–391.

Raines, L. (2006, June 4). For interviews, rein in your fashion freedom. *Atlanta Journal/Constitution,* p. 3.

Raj, A., & Sheehan, D. (2004). Benzodiazepines. In A. F. Schatzberg & C. B. Nemeroff (Eds.), *Textbook of psychopharmacology.* Washington, DC: American Psychiatric Publishing.

Raloff, J. (1996). Breakfast trends. *Science News, 150,* 90–91.

Ramadan, N. M. (2000). Migraine. In G. Fink (Ed.), *Encyclopedia of stress.* San Diego: Academic Press.

Ramaekers, J. G., Robbe, H. W. J., & O'Hanlon, J. F. (2000). Marijuana, alcohol and actual driving performance. *Human Psychopharmacology Clinical & Experimental, 15*(7), 551–558.

Randhawa, B. S., & Hunter, D. M. (2001). Validity of performance assessment in mathematics for early adolescents. *Canadian Journal of Behavioral Science, 33,* 14–24.

Rank, M. R. (2004). The disturbing paradox of poverty in American families: What we have learned over the past four decades. In M. Coleman & L. H. Ganong (Eds.), *Handbook of contemporary families: Considering the past, contemplating the future.* Thousand Oaks, CA: Sage.

Ransome, P. (2005). *Work, consumption and culture: Affluence and social change in the twenty-first century.* Thousand Oaks, CA: SAAR.

Rapee, R. M., & Barlow, D. H. (2001). Generalized anxiety disorders, panic disorders, and phobias. In P. B. Sutker & H. E. Adams (Eds.), *Comprehensive handbook of psychopathology* (3rd ed.). New York: Kluwer Academic/Plenum Publishers.

Raphael, B., & Dobson, M. (2000). Effects of public disasters. In G. Fink (Ed.), *Encyclopedia of stress* (Vol. 1). San Diego: Academic Press.

Raskin, P. M. (1986). The relationship between identity and intimacy in early adulthood. *Journal of Genetic Psychology, 147,* 167–181.

Ray, G. E., Cohen, R., Secrist, M. E., & Duncan, M. K. (1997). Relating aggressive and victimization behaviors to children's sociometric status and friendships. *Journal of Social and Personal Relationships, 14*(1), 95–108.

Read, C. R. (1991). Achievement and career choices: Comparisons of males and females. *Roeper Review, 13* 188–193.

Reddy, B. S. (1999). Role of dietary fiber in colon cancer: An overview. *American Journal of Medicine, 106*(1A), 16S–19S.

Reed, G. M., Kemeny, M. E., Taylor, S. E., & Visscher, B. R. (1999). Negative HIV-specific expectancies and AIDS-related bereavement as predictors of symptom onset in asymptomatic HIV-positive gay men. *Health Psychology, 18,* 354–363.

Rees, C. J., & Metcalfe, B. (2003). The faking of personality questionnaire results: Who's kidding whom. *Journal of Managerial Psychology, 18,* 156–165.

Regan, P. C. (2003). *The mating game: A primer on love, sex, and marriage.* Thousand Oaks, CA: Sage Publications.

Regan, P. C., & Berscheid, E. (1997). Gender differences in characteristics desired in potential sexual and marriage partners. *Journal of Psychology and Human Sexuality, 9*(1), 25–37.

Regier, D. A., & Burke, J. D. (2000). Epidemiology. In B. J. Sadock & V. A. Sadock (Eds.), *Kaplan and Sadock's comprehensive textbook of psychiatry.* Philadelphia: Lippincott/Williams & Wilkins.

Regier, D. A., Narrow, W. E., & Rae, D. S. (2004). For DSM-V, It's the "disorder threshold," stupid. *Archives of General Psychiatry, 61,* 1051.

Rehm, L. P., Wagner, A., & Ivens-Tyndal, Co. (2001). Mood disorders: Unipolar and bipolar. In P. B. Sutker & H. E. Adams (Eds.), *Comprehensive handbook of psychopathology* (3rd ed.). New York: Kluwer Academic/Plenum.

Reibel, D. K., Greeson, J. M., Brainard, G. C., & Rosenzweig, S. (2001). Mindfulness-based stress reduction and health-related quality of life in a heterogeneous patient population. *General Hospital Psychiatry, 23*(4), 183–192.

Reid, M., Miller, W., & Kerr, B. (2004). Sex-based glass ceilings in U. S. state-level bureaucracies, 1987-1997. *Administration and Society, 36,* 377–405.

Reid, P. T., & Paludi, M. A. (1993). Developmental psychology of women: Conception to adolescence. In F. L. Denmark & M. A. Paludi (Eds.), *Psychology of women: A handbook of issues and theories.* Westport, CT: Greenwood Press.

Reimann, R. (1997). Does biology matter?: Lesbian couples' transition to parenthood and their division of labor. *Qualitative Sociology, 20*(2), 153–185.

Reinisch, J. M. (1990). *The Kinsey Institute new report on sex: What you must know to be sexually literate.* New York: St. Martin's.

Reis, H. T. (1998). Gender differences in intimacy and related behaviors: Context and processes. In D. Canary & K. Dindia (Eds.), *Sex and gender in communication: Similarities and differences.* Mahwah, NJ: Erlbaum.

Reis, H. T., & Patrick. B. C. (1996). Attachment and intimacy: Component processes. In E. T. Higgins & A. Kruglanski (Eds.), *Social psychology: Handbook of basic principles.* New York: Guilford.

Reis, H. T., & Shaver, P. (1988). Intimacy as an interpersonal process. In S. W. Duck (Ed.), *Handbook of personal relationships.* New York: Wiley.

Reis, H. T., & Wheeler, L. (1991). Studying social interaction with the Rochester Interaction Record. *Advances in Experimental Social Psychology, 24,* 269–318.

Reis, T. J., Gerrard, M., & Gibbons, F. X. (1993). Social comparison and the pill: Reactions to upward and downward comparison of contraceptive behavior. *Personality and Social Psychology Bulletin, 19,* 13–21.

Reisner, A. D. (1998). Repressed memories: True and false. In R. A. Baker (Ed.), *Child sexual abuse and false memory syndrome.* Amherst, NY: Prometheus Books.

Reiss, S. (1991). Expectancy model of fear, anxiety and panic. *Clinical Psychology Review, 11,* 141–154.

Reissman, C., Aron, A., & Bergen, M. R. (1993). Shared activities and marital satisfaction: Causal direction and self-expansion versus boredom. *Journal of Social and Personal Relationships, 10,* 243–254.

Renaud, C. A., & Byers, E. S. (2001). Positive and negative sexual cognitions: Subjective experience and relationships to sexual adjustment. *Journal of Sex Research, 38*(3), 252–262.

Rennie, D., & Luft, H. S. (2000). Making them transparent, making them credible. *Journal of the American Medical Association, 283,* 2516–2521.

Rennison, C. M., & Welchans, S. (2000). *Intimate partner violence.* Washington, DC: U.S. Department of Justice, Office of Justice Programs, Bureau of Justice Statistics.

Renshaw, D. C. (2005). Premature ejaculation revisited–2005. *Family Journal, 13,* 150–152.

Renzetti, C. (1995). Violence in gay and lesbian relationships. In R. J. Gelles (Ed.), *Vision 2010: Families and violence, abuse and neglect.* Minneapolis: National Council on Family Relations.

Repetto, M., & Gold, M. S. (2005). Cocaine and crack: Neurobiology. In J. H. Lowinson, P. Ruiz, R. B. Millman, & J. G. Langrod (Eds.), *Substance abuse: A comprehensive textbook.* Philadelphia: Lippincott/Williams & Wilkins.

Rhodewalt, F., Sanbonmatsu, D. M., Tschanz, B., Feick, D. L., & Waller, A. (1995). Self-handicapping and interpersonal trade-offs: The effects of claimed self-handicaps on observers' performance evaluations and feedback. *Personality and Social Psychology Bulletin, 21,* 1042–1050

Rhodewalt, F., Tragakis, M. W., & Finnerty, J. (2006). Narcissism and self-handicapping: Linking self-aggrandizement to behavior. *Journal of Research in Personality, 40,* 573–597.

Riba, M. B., & Miller, R. R. (2003). Combined therapies: Psychotherapy and pharmacotherapy. In A. Tasman, J. Kay, & J. A. Lieberman (Eds.), *Psychiatry.* New York: Wiley.

Rice, J. K., & Else-Quest, N. (2006). The mixed messages of motherhood. In J. Worrell & C. D. Goodheart (Eds.), *Handbook of girls' and women's psychological health.* New York: Oxford University Press.

Rice, L. N., & Greenberg, L. S. (1992). Humanistic approaches to psychotherapy. In D. K. Freedheim (Ed.), *History of psychotherapy: A century of change.* Washington, DC: American Psychological Association.

Richardson, C. R., Kriska, A. M., Lantz, P. M., & Hayward, R. A. (2004). Physical activity and mortality across cardiovascular disease risk groups. *Medicine and Science in Sports and Exercise, 36*(11), 1923–1929.

Richardson, J. G., & Simpson, C. H. (1982). Children, gender and social structure: An analysis of the contents of letters to Santa Claus. *Child Development, 53* 429–436.

Richmond, V. P., & McCroskey, J. C. (1995). *Communication: Apprehension, avoidance, and effectiveness* (5th ed.). Boston: Allyn & Bacon.

Richter, H. (2007, May 7). Lights, camera, hired! *Newsweek,* p. 65.

Ridge, S. R., & Feeney, J. A. (1998). Relationship history and relationship attitudes in gay males and lesbians: Attachment style and gender differences. *Australian and New Zealand Journal of Psychiatry, 32*(6), 848–859.

Ridgeway, C. L., & Bourg, C. (2004). Gender as status: An expectation states theory approach. In A. H. Eagly, A. E. Beall, & R. J. Sternberg (Eds.), *The psychology of gender.* New York: Guilford Press.

Ridker, P. M. (2001). High-sensitivity C-reactive protein: Potential adjunct for global risk assessment in the primary prevention of cardiovascular disease. *Circulation, 103,* 1813–1818.

Rief, W., Henningsen, P., & Hiller, W. (2006). Classification of somatoform disorders. *American Journal of Psychiatry, 163,* 746–747.

Riemann, R., Angleitner, A., & Strelau, J. (1997). Genetic and environmental influences on personality: A study of twins reared together using the self- and peer report NEO-FFI scales. *Journal of Personality, 65,* 449–476.

Rierdan, J., & Koff, E. (1991). Depressive symptomatology among very early maturing girls. *Journal of Youth and Adolescence, 20,* 415–425.

Rifkin, J. (1989). *Time wars: The primary conflict in human history.* New York: Simon & Schuster.

Rigotti, N. A., Lee, J. E., & Wechsler, H. (2000). U.S. college students' use of tobacco products: Results of a national survey. *Journal of the American Medical Association, 284,* 699–705.

Rihmer, Z. (2003). Do SSRI's increase the risk of suicide among depressives even if they are only tak-

ing placebo? *Psychotherapy & Psychosomatics, 72*(6), 357–358.

Rihmer, Z., & Angst, J. (2005). Mood disorders: Epidemiology. In B. J. Sadock & V. A. Sadock (Eds.), *Kaplan & Sadock's comprehensive textbook of psychiatry.* Philadelphia: Lippicott Williams & Wilkins.

Riis, J., Loewenstein, G., Baron, J. , Jepson, C., Fagerlin, A., & Ubel, P. A. (2005). Ignorance of hedonic adaptation to hemodialysis: A study using ecological momentary assessment. *Journal of Experimental Psychology: General, 134,* 3–9.

Riley, B. P., & Kendler, K. S. (2005). Schizophrenia: Genetics. In B. J. Sadock & V. A. Sadock (Eds.), *Kaplan & Sadock's comprehensive textbook of psychiatry.* Philadelphia: Lippincott Williams & Wilkins.

Riley, L. D., & Bowen, C. (2005). The sandwich generation: Challenges and coping strategies of multigenerational families. *Family Journal: Counseling and Therapy for Couples and Families, 13,* 52–58.

Rimal R. N. (2001). Longitudinal influences of knowledge and self-efficacy on exercise behavior: Tests of a mutual reinforcement model. *Journal of Health Psychology, 6,* 31–46.

Rindfuss, R. R. (1991). The young adult years: Diversity, structural change, and fertility. *Demography, 28,* 493–512.

Riskey, D. R., & Birnbaum, M. H. (1974). Compensatory effects in moral judgment: Two rights don't make up for a wrong. *Journal of Experimental Psychology, 103,* 171–173.

Riskind, J. H. (2005). Cognitive mechanisms in generalized anxiety disorder: A second generation of theoretical perspectives. *Cognitive Therapy & Research, 29*(1), 1–5.

Riso, L. P., du Toit, P. L., Blandino, J. A., Penna, S., Dacey, S., Duin, J. S., Pacoe, E. M., Grant, M. M., & Ulmer, C. S. (2003). Cognitive aspects of chronic depression. *Journal of Abnormal Psychology, 112*(1), 72–80.

Ritskes, R., Ritskes-Hoitinga, M., Stodkilde-Jorgensen, H., Baerentsen, K. , & Hartman, T. (2003). MRI scanning during Zen meditation: The picture of enlightenment. *Constructivism in the Human Sciences, 8*(1), 85–90.

Ritz, T., Steptoe, A., DeWilde, S., & Costa, M. (2000). Emotions and stress increase respiratory resistance in asthma. *Psychosomatic Medicine, 62*(3), 401–412.

Rivas-Vazquez, R. A. (2001). Antidepressants as first-line agents in the current pharmacotherapy of anxiety disorders. *Professional Psychology: Research & Practice, 32*(1), 101–104.

Robbins, A., & Wilner, A. (2001). *Quarterlife crisis: The unique challenges of life in your twenties.* New York: Putnam.

Roberts, A. R. (2002). Myths, facts, and realities regarding battered women and their children: An overview. In A. R. Roberts (Ed.), *Handbook of domestic violence intervention strategies: Policies, programs, and legal remedies.* New York: Oxford University Press.

Roberts, B. W., & DelVecchio. W. F. (2000). The rank-order consistency of personality traits from childhood to old age: A quantitative review of the longitudinal studies. *Psychological Bulletin, 126,* 3–25.

Roberts, B. W., & Pomerantz, E. M. (2004). On traits, situations, and their integration: A developmental perspective. *Personality and Social Psychology Review, 8*(4), 402–416.

Roberts, D. F., Foehr, U. G., Rideout, V. J., & Vrodie, M. (1999). Kids and media @ the new millennium. Menlo Park, CA: Kaiser Family Foundation.

Roberts, L. J. (2000). Fire and ice in marital communication: Hostile and distancing behaviors as predictors of marital distress. *Journal of Marriage and the Family, 62,* 693–707.

Roberts, L. J., & Krokoff, L. J. (1990). A time series analysis of withdrawal, hostility, and displeasure in satisfied and dissatisfied marriages. *Journal of Marriage and the Family, 52,* 95–105.

Roberts, P., & Newton, P. M. (1987). Levinsonian studies of women's adult development. *Psychology and Aging, 2,* 154–163.

Roberts, S. (2006, October 15). It's official: To be married means to be outnumbered. *New York Times.*

Robertson, J. M., Lin, C., Woodford, J., Danos, K. K., & Hurst, M. A. (2001). The (un)emotional male: Physiological, verbal and written correlates of expressiveness. *Journal of Men's Studies, 9,* 393–412.

Robiner, W. N., Bearman, D. L., Berman, M., Grove, W. M., Colon, E., Armstrong, J., Mareck, S., & Tanenbaum, R. L. (2003). Prescriptive authority for psychologists: Despite deficits in education and knowledge. *Journal of Clinical Psychology in Medical Settings, 10*(3), 211–212.

Robins, L. N., Locke, B. Z., & Regier, D. A. (1991). An overview of psychiatric disorders in America. In L. N. Robins & D. A. Regier (Eds.), *Psychiatric disorders in America: The epidemiologic catchment area study.* New York: Free Press.

Robins, R. W., & Trzesniewski, K. H. (2005). Self-esteem development across the lifespan. *Current Direction in Psychological Science, 14,* 158–162.

Robinson, B., Frye, E. M., & Bradley, L. J. (1997). Cult affiliation and disaffiliation: Implications for counseling. *Counseling and Values, 41,* 166–173.

Robinson, B. E., Flowers, C., & Ng, K. (2006). The relationship between workaholism and marital disaffection: Husband's perspective. *Family Journal: Counseling and Therapy for Couples and Families, 14,* 213–220.

Robinson, D. G., Woerner, M. G., McMeniman, M., Mendelowitz, A., & Bilder, R. M. (2004). Symptomatic and functional recovery from a first episode of schizophrenia or schizoaffective disorder. *American Journal of Psychiatry, 161,* 473–479.

Robinson, F. P. (1970). *Effective study* (4th ed.). New York: HarperCollins.

Robinson, J. P., & Godbey, G. (1997). *Time for life: The surprising ways Americans use their time.* University Park, PA: Pennsylvania State University Press.

Robinson, M. D., Johnson, J. T., & Shields, S. A. (1995). On the advantages of modesty: The benefits of a balanced self-presentation. *Communication Research, 22,* 575–591.

Robles, T. F., Glaser, R., & Kiecolt-Glaser, J. K. (2005). Out of balance: A new look at chronic stress, depression, and immunity. *Current Directions in Psychological Science, 14,* 111–115.

Rodger, C. (2004). Aging male syndrome, andropause, androgen decline or mid-life crisis? *Journal of Men's Health & Gender, 1,* 55–59.

Rodin, J., Schank, D., & Striegel-Moore, R. H. (1989). Psychological features of obesity. *Medical Clinics of North America, 73* 47–66.

Rodrigues, A. E., Hall, J. H., & Fincham, F. D. (2006). What predicts divorce and relationship dissolution. In M. A. Fine & J. H. Harvey (Eds.), *Handbook of divorce and relationship resolution.* Mahwah, NJ: Erlbaum.

Roediger, H. L., III, & McDermott, K. B. (1995). Creating false memories: Remembering words not presented in lists. *Journal of Experimental Psychology: Learning, Memory, and Cognition, 21,* 803–814.

Roediger, H. L., III, & McDermott, K. B. (2000). Tricks of memory. *Current Directions in Psychological Science, 9,* 123–127.

Rogers, C. R. (1951). *Client-centered therapy: Its current practice, implications, and theory.* Boston: Houghton Mifflin.

Rogers, C. R. (1961). *On becoming a person: A therapist's view of psychotherapy.* Boston: Houghton Mifflin.

Rogers, C. R. (1977). *Carl Rogers on personal power.* New York: Delacorte.

Rogers, C. R. (1980). *A way of being.* Boston: Houghton Mifflin.

Rogers, C. R. (1986). Client-centered therapy. In I. L. Kutash & A. Wolf (Eds.), *Psychotherapist's casebook.* San Francisco: Jossey-Bass.

Rogers, M. P., Fricchione, G., & Reich, P. (1999). Psychosomatic medicine and consultation-liaison psychiatry. In A. M. Nicholi (Ed.), *The Harvard guide to psychiatry* (3rd ed.). Cambridge, MA: Harvard University Press.

Rogers, R. W., & Prentice-Dunn, S. (1997). Protection motivation theory. In D. Gochman (Ed.), *Handbook of health behavior research* (Vol. 1). New York: Plenum.

Rogers, S. J., & White, L. K. (1998). Satisfaction with parenting: The role of marital happiness, family structure, and parents' gender. *Journal of Marriage and the Family, 60,* 293–308.

Rogge, R. D., Bradbury, T. N., Hahlweg, K., Engl, J., & Thurmaier, F. (2006). Predicting marital distress and dissolution: Refining the two-factor hypothesis. *Journal of Family Psychology, 20,* 156–159.

Rohde, P. A., Atzwanger, K., Butovskayad, M., Lampert, A., Mysterud, I., Sanchez-Andres, A., & Sulloway, F. J. (2003). Perceived parental favoritism, closeness to kin and the rebel of the family: The effects of birth order and sex. *Evolution & Human Behavior, 24,* 261–276.

Rohner, R. P., & Veneziano, R. A. (2001). The importance of father love: History and contemporary evidence. *Review of General Psychology, 5*(4), 382–405.

Rohrer, D., Taylor, K., Pashler, H., Wixted, J. T., & Capeda, N. J. (2005). The effect of overlearning on long-term retention. *Applied Cognitive Psychology, 19,* 361–374.

Rojewski, J. W. (2005). Occupational aspirations: Constructs, meanings, and application. In S. D. Brown & R. W. Lent (Eds.), *Career development and counseling: Putting theory and research to work.* New York: Wiley.

Rokach, A. (2000). Perceived causes of loneliness in adulthood. *Journal of Social Behavior and Personality, 15,* 67–84.

Rollie, S. S., & Duck, S. (2006). Divorce and dissolution of romantic relationships. In M. A. Fine & J. H. Harvey (Eds.), *Handbook of divorce and relationship resolution.* Mahwah, NJ: Erlbaum.

Rook, K. S. (1998). Investigating the positive and negative sides of personal relationships: Through a lens darkly? In B. H. Spitzberg & W. R. Cupach (Eds.), *The dark side of close relationships.* Mahwah, NJ: Lawrence Erlbaum.

Rook, K. S., & Pietromonaco, P. (1987). Close relationships: Ties that heal or ties that bind? In W. H. Jones & D. Perlman (Eds.), *Advances in personal relationships.* Greenwich, CT: JAI Press.

Rose, D., Wykes, T., Leese, M., Bindman, J., & Fleischmann, P. (2003). Patient's perspectives on electroconvulsive therapy: Systematic review. *British Medical Journal, 326,* 1363–1365.

Rose, D. P. (1997). Dietary fatty acids and cancer. *American Journal of Clinical Nutrition, 66*(4), 998S–1003S.

Rosen, D. H. (1974). *Lesbianism: A study of female homosexuality.* Springfield, IL: Charles C Thomas.

Rosen, E., Ackerman, L., & Zosky, D. (2002). The sibling empty nest syndrome: The experience of sadness as siblings leave the family home. *Journal of Human Behavior in the Social Environment, 6,* 65–80.

Rosen, G. M. (1993). Self-help or hype? Comments on psychology's failure to advance self-care. *Professional Psychology: Research and Practice, 24,* 340–345.

Rosen, G. M., Glasgow, R. E., & Moore, T. E. (2003). Self-help therapy: The science and business of giving psychology away. In S. O. Lilienfeld, S. J. Lynn, & J. M. Lohr (Eds.), *Science and pseudoscience in clinical psychology.* New York: Guilford Press.

Rosen, R. (2000). Medical and psychological interventions for erectile dysfunction. In S. Leiblum & R. Rosen (Eds.), *Principles and practice of sex therapy.* New York: Guilford.

Rosen, R. D. (1977). *Psychobabble.* New York: Atheneum.

Rosenbaum, M., Lakin, M., & Roback, H. B. (1992). Psychotherapy in groups. In D. K. Freedheim (Ed.), *History of psychotherapy: A century of change.* Washington, DC: American Psychological Association.

Rosenberg, M. (1956). *Society and the adolescent self-image.* Princeton, NJ: Princeton University Press.

Rosenblatt, A., Greenberg, J., Solomon, S., Pyszczynski, T., & Lyon, D. (1989). Evidence for terror management theory: I. The effects of mortality salience on reactions to those who violate or uphold cultural values. *Journal of Personality and Social Psychology, 57,* 681–690.

Rosenbluth, S. C. (1997). Is sexual orientation a matter of choice? *Psychology of Women Quarterly, 21,* 595–610.

Rosenfarb, I. S., Goldstein, M. J., Mintz, J., & Nuechterlein, K. H. (1995). Expressed emotion and subclinical psychopathology observable within the transactions between schizophrenic patients and their family members. *Journal of Abnormal Psychology, 104,* 259–267.

Rosenfield, S. (1999). Splitting the difference: Gender, the self and mental health. In C. S. Aneshensel & J. C. Phelan (Eds.), *Handbook of the sociology of mental health.* New York: Kluwer Academic.

Rosenheck, R. A. (2006). Outcomes, costs, and policy caution. *Archives of General Psychiatry, 63,* 1074–1076.

Rosenman, R. H. (1993). Relationships of the Type A behavior pattern with coronary heart disease. In L. Goldberger & S. Breznitz (Eds.), *Handbook of stress: Theoretical and clinical aspects* (2nd ed.). New York: Free Press.

Rosenthal, H. (1988). *Not with my life I don't: Preventing suicide and that of others.* Muncie, IN: Accelerated Development.

Rosenthal, R. (1985). From unconscious experimenter bias to teacher expectancy effects. In J. B. Dusek, V. C. Hall & W. J. Meyer (Eds.), *Teacher expectancies.* Hillsdale, NJ: Erlbaum.

Rosenthal, R. (2003). Covert communication in laboratories, classrooms, and the truly real world. *Current Directions in Psychological Science, 12*(5), 151–154.

Rosier, K. B., & Feld, S. L. (2000). Covenant marriage: A new alternative for traditional families. *Journal of Comparative Family Studies, 31,* 385–394.

Ross, C. A. (1999). Dissociative disorders. In T. Millon, P. H. Blaney, & R. D. Davis (Eds.), *Oxford textbook of psychopathology.* New York: Oxford University Press.

Ross, C. E., & Van Willigen, M. (1997). Education and the subjective quality of life. *Journal of Health & Social Behavior, 38,* 275–297.

Ross, L. D. (1977). The intuitive psychologist and his shortcomings: Distortions in the attribution process. In L. Berkowitz (Ed.), *Advances in experimental social psychology* (Vol. 10). New York: Academic Press.

Ross, L., & Nisbett, R. E. (1991). *The person and the situation: Perspectives of social psychology.* New York: McGraw-Hill.

Ross, L., & Ward, A. (1996). Naive realism: Implications for social conflict and misunderstanding. In T. Brown, E. Reed, & E. Turiel (Eds.), *Values and knowledge.* Hillsdale, NJ: Erlbaum.

Ross, M., & Conway, M. (1986). Remembering one's own past: The construction of personal histories. In R. M. Sorrentino & E. T. Higgins (Eds.), *Handbook of motivation and cognition: Foundations of social behavior.* New York: Guilford Press.

Ross, M., & Wilson, A. E. (2002). It feels like yesterday: Self-esteem, valence of personal past experiences, and judgments of subjective distance. *Journal of Personality and Social Psychology, 82,* 792–803.

Ross, M. W. (2005). Typing, doing, and being: Sexuality and the Internet. *Journal of Sex Research, 42,* 342–352.

Roter, D. L., Hall, J. A., Merisca, R., Nordstrom, B., Cretin, D., & Svarstad, B. (1998). Effectiveness of interventions to promote patient compliance. *Medical Care, 36,* 1138–1161.

Rothblum, E. D., Solomon, L. J., & Albee, G. W. (1986). A sociopolitical perspective on DSM-III. In T. Million & G. L. Klerman (Eds.), *Contemporary directions in psychopathology: Toward the DSM-IV.* New York: Guilford Press.

Rotter, J. B. (1982). *The development and application of social learning theory.* New York: Praeger.

Roughton, B. (2001, May 27). In Europe, workers time off adds up. *The Atlanta Journal-Constitution,* pp. D1–D2.

Rowe, D. (1994). *The limits of family influence: Genes, experience, and behavior.* New York: Guilford.

Rowe, D., & van den Oord, E. J. C. G. (2005). Genetic and environmental influences. In V. A. Derlega, B. A. Winstead, & W. H. Jones (Eds.), *Personality: Contemporary theory and research.* Belmont, CA: Wadsworth.

Rozanski, A., Blumenthal, J. A., & Kaplan, J. (1999). Impact of psychological factors on the pathogenesis of cardiovascular disease and implications for therapy. *Circulation, 99*(16), 2192–2197.

Rozee, P. D., Bateman, P., & Gilmore, T. (1991). The personal perspective of acquaintance rape prevention: A three-tier approach. In A. Parrot & L. Bechhofer (Eds.), *Acquaintance rape: The hidden crime.* New York: Wiley.

Rubenstein, C. M., & Shaver, P. (1982). The experience of loneliness. In L. A. Peplau & D. Perlman (Eds.), *Loneliness: A sourcebook of current theory, research and therapy.* New York: Wiley.

Rubin, R. H. (2001). Alternative lifestyles revisited, or whatever happened to swingers, group marriages, and communes? *Journal of Family Issues, 22,* 711–726.

Rubin, Z., Peplau, L. A., & Hill, C. T. (1981). Loving and leaving: Sex differences in romantic attachments. *Sex Roles, 7,* 821–835.

Rudisch, B., & Nemeroff, C. B. (2003). Epidemiology of comorbid coronary artery disease and depression. *Biological Psychiatry, 54*(3), 227–240.

Rudorfer, M. V., Henry, M. E., & Sackeim, H. A. (2003). Electroconvulsive therapy. In A. Tasman, J. Kay, & J. A. Lieberman (Eds.), *Psychiatry.* New York: Wiley.

Rush, A. J. (1984). Cognitive therapy. In T. B. Karasu (Ed.), *The psychiatric therapies.* Washington, DC: American Psychiatric Association.

Rush, A. J., & Beck, A. T. (2000). Cognitive therapy. In B. J. Sadock & V. A. Sadock (Eds.), *Kaplan and Sadock's comprehensive textbook of psychiatry* (7th ed., Vol. 1). Philadelphia: Lippincott/Williams & Wilkins.

Russell, G. F. M. (1995). Anorexia nervosa through time. In G. Szmukler, C. Dare, & J. Treasure (Eds.), *Handbook of eating disorders: Theory, treatment, and research.* New York: Wiley.

Russell, G. F. M. (1997). The history of bulimia nervosa. In D. M. Garner & P. E. Garfinkel (Eds.), *Handbook of treatment for eating disorders* (2nd ed.). New York: Guilford Press.

Russo, N. F. (1979). Overview: Sex roles, fertility, and the motherhood mandate. *Psychology of Women Quarterly, 4,* 7–15.

Rutledge, T., & Hogan, B. E. (2002). A quantitative review of prospective evidence linking psychological factors with hypertension development. *Psychosomatic Medicine, 64,* 758–766.

Ruzek, J. (2001). *Coping with PTSD and recommended lifestyle changes for PTSD patients.* Retrieved November 28, 2001 from U.S. Department of Veterans Affairs National Center for PTSD Website: http://www.ncptsd.org/facts/treatment/fs_coping. html.

Ryan, C., & Futterman, D. (1997). Lesbian and gay youth: Care and counseling. *Adolescent Medicine, 8,* 221.

Ryan, R. M., & Deci, E. L. (2001). On happiness and human potentials: A review of research on hedonic and eudaimonic well-being. *Annual Review of Psychology, 52,* 141–166.

Rye, M. S., Folck, C. D., Heim, T. A., Olszewski, B. T., Traina, E. (2004). Forgiveness of an ex-spouse: How does it relate to mental health following a divorce? *Journal of Divorce and Remarriage, 41,* 31–51.

Saad, L. (1999, September 3). *American workers generally satisfied, but indicate their jobs leave much to be desired.* Princeton, NJ: Gallup News Service.

Saad, L. (2007). *Americans rate the morality of 16 social issues.* Retrieved June 23, 2007 from http://www.galluppoll.com/content/?ci=27757&p=1.

Sabatelli, R. M., & Ripoll, K. (2004). Variations in marriage over time: An ecological/exchange perspective. In M. Coleman & L. H. Ganong (Eds.), *Handbook of contemporary families: Considering the past, contemplating the future.* Thousand Oaks, CA: Sage.

Sackeim, H. A., Haskett, R. F., Mulsant, B. H., Thase, M. E., Mann, J. J., Pettinati, H. M., Greenberg, R. M., Crowe, R. R., Cooper, T. B., & Prudic, J. (2001). Continuation pharmacotherapy in the prevention of relapse following electroconvulsive therapy: A randomized controlled trial. *Journal of the American Medical Association, 285*(10), 1299–1307.

Sadker, M., & Sadker, D. (1994). *Failing at fairness: How America's schools cheat girls.* New York: Scribners.

Sadler, J. Z. (2005). *Values and psychiatric diagnosis.* New York: Oxford University Press.

Sagiv, L., Roccas, S., & Hazan, O. (2004). Value pathways to well-being: Healthy values, valued goal attainment, and environmental congruence. In P. A. Linley & S. Joseph (Eds.), *Positive psychology in practice.* New York: Wiley.

Sagrestano, L. M., Heavey, C. L., & Christensen, A. (2006). Individual differences versus social structural approaches to explaining demand-withdraw and social influence behaviors. In K. Dindia, & D. J. Canary (Eds.), *Sex differences and similarities in communication.* Mahwah, NJ: Erlbaum.

Saks, A. M. (2006). Multiple predictions and criteria of job search success. *Journal of Vocational Behavior, 68*, 400–415.

Salerno, S. (2005). *Sham: How the self-help movement made America helpless.* New York: Crown Publishers.

Salkovskis, P. M., & Warwick, H. M. C. (2001). Meaning, misinterpretations, and medicine: A cognitive-behavioral approach to understanding health anxiety and hypochondriasis. In V. Starcevic & D. R. Lipsitt (Eds.), *Hypochondriasis: Modern perspectives on an ancient malady.* New York: Oxford University Press.

Salovey, P., & Mayer, J. D. (1990). Emotional intelligence. *Imagination, Cognition, and Personality, 9*, 185–211.

Salovey, P., Mayer, J. D., & Caruso, D. (2002). The positive psychology of emotional intelligence. In C. R. Synder & S. J. Lopez (Eds.), *Handbook of positive psychology.* New York: Oxford University Press.

Salovey, P., Mayer, J. D., & Caruso, D. (2005). The positive psychology of emotional intelligence. In C. R. Snyder & S. J. Lopez (Eds.), *Handbook of positive psychology.* New York: Oxford University Press.

Salovey, P., Rothman, A. J., Detweiler, J. B., & Steward, W. T. (2000). Emotional states and physical health. *American Psychologist, 55*(1), 110–121.

Salthouse, T. A. (2000). Steps toward the explanation of adult age differences in cognition. In T. Perfect & E. Maylor (Eds.), *Theoretical debate in cognitive aging.* Oxford, UK: Oxford University Press.

Salthouse, T. A. (2004). What and when of cognitive aging. *Current Directions in Psychological Science, 13*(4), 140–144.

Salvendy, J. T. (1993). Selection and preparation of patients and organization of the group. In H. I. Kaplan & B. J. Sadock (Eds.), *Comprehensive group psychotherapy.* Baltimore: Williams & Wilkins.

Samberg, E., & Marcus, E. R. (2005). Process, resistance, and interpretation. In E. S. Person, A. M. Cooper, & G. O. Gabbard (Eds.), *Textbook of psychoanalysis.* Washington, DC: American Psychiatric Publishing.

Samovar, L. A., & Porter, R. E. (2004). *Communication between cultures.* Belmont, CA: Wadsworth.

Samovar, L. A., Porter, R. E., & McDaniel, E. R. (2007). *Communication between cultures.* Belmont, CA: Wadsworth.

Samovar, L. A., Porter, R. E., & Stefani, L. A. (1998). *Communication between cultures* (2nd ed.). Belmont, CA: Wadsworth.

Sampson, R. (2003). *Acquaintance rape of college students. Problem-oriented guides for police: Problem specific guides series, No. 17.* Washington, DC: U.S. Department of Justice.

Sanchez, L. M., & Turner, S. M. (2003). Practicing psychology in the era of managed care: Implications for practice and training. *American Psychologist, 58*(2), 116–129.

Sande, M. A., & Ronald, A. (2004). Treatment of HIV/AIDS: Do the dilemmas only increase? *Journal of the American Medical Association, 292*(2), 224–236.

Sanders, G. (2000). Men together: Working with gay couples in contemporary times. In P. Papp (Ed.), *Couples on the fault line.* New York: Guilford Press.

Sanderson, W. C., & Barlow, D. H. (1990). A description of patients diagnosed with DSM-III-R generalized anxiety disorder. *Journal of Nervous and Mental Disease, 178*, 588–591.

Sandin, B., Chorot, P., Santed, M. A., & Valiente, R. M. (2004). Differences in negative life events between patients with anxiety disorders, depression and hypochondriasis. *Anxiety, Stress & Coping: An International Journal, 17*(1), 37–47.

Sandnabba, N. K., & Ahlberg, C. (1999). Parents' attitudes and expectations about children's cross-gender behavior. *Sex Roles, 40*(3–4), 249–263.

Sandoz, J. (2004). Internet addiction. *Annals of the American Psychotherapy Association, 7*(1), 34.

Sanislow, C. A., & Carson, R. C. (2001). Schizophrenia: A critical examination. In P. B. Sutker & H. E. Adams (Eds.), *Comprehensive handbook of psychopathology* (3rd ed.). New York: Kluwer Academic/Plenum.

Santelli, J. S., Morrow, B., Anderson, J. E., & Lindberg, L. D. (2006). Contraceptive use and pregnancy risk among U. S. high school students, 1991–2003. *Perspectives on Sexual and Reproductive Health, 38*(2), 106–111.

Sanz de Acedo, M. L., & Garcia Ganuza, J. M. (2003). Improvement of mental rotation in girls and boys. *Sex Roles, 49*(5–6), 277–286.

Sapolsky, R. M. (2004). *Why zebras don't get ulcers: The acclaimed guide to stress, stress-related diseases, and coping.* New York: Holt.

Sarason, I. G., Johnson, J. H., & Siegel, J. M. (1978). Assessing the impact of life changes: Development of the Life Experiences Survey. *Journal of Consulting and Clinical Psychology, 46*, 932–946.

Sarason, I. G., Pierce, G. R., & Sarason, B. R. (1994). General and specific perceptions of social support. In W. R. Avison & I. H. Gotlib (Eds.), *Stress and mental health: Contemporary issues and prospects for the future.* New York: Plenum.

Sarwer, D. B., Foster, G. D., & Wadden, T. A. (2004). Treatment of obesity I: Adult obesity. In J. K. Thompson (Ed.), *Handbook of eating disorders and obesity.* New York: Wiley.

Savin-Williams, R. C. (2001). *Mom, dad. I'm gay.* Washington, D. C.: American Psychological Association.

Savin-Williams, R. C. (2006). Who's gay? Does it matter? *Current Directions in Psychological Science, 15*, 40–44.

Saxena, S., van Ommeren, M., Tang K. C., & Armstrong, T. P. (2005). Mental health benefits of physical activity. *Journal of Mental Health, 14*, 445–451.

Sayer, L. C. (2005). Gender, time, and inequality: Trends in women's and men's paid work, unpaid work, and free time. *Social Forces, 84*, 285–303.

Sayer, L. C. (2006). Economic aspects of divorce and relationship dissolution. In M. A. Fine & J. H. Harvey (Eds.), *Handbook of divorce and relationship dissolution.* Mahwah, NJ: Erlbaum.

Sayers, S. L. (2004). Depression and heart disease: The interrelationship between these two common disorders is complex and requires careful diagnostic and treatment methods. *Psychiatric Annals, 34*(4), 282–288.

Scanzoni, J. (2004). Household diversity: The starting point for healthy families in the new century. In M. Coleman & L. H. Ganong (Eds.), *Handbook of contemporary families: Considering the past, contemplating the future.* Thousand Oaks, CA: Sage.

Schaalma, H. P., Abraham, C., Gillmore, M. R., & Kok, G. (2004). Sex education as health promotion: What does it take? *Archives of Sexual Behavior, 33,*, 259–269.

Schachner, D. A., Shaver, P. R., & Mikulincer, M. (2005). Patterns of nonverbal behavior and sensitivity in the context of attachment relations. *Journal of Nonverbal Behavior, 29*(3), 141–169.

Schachter, S. (1959). *The psychology of affiliation.* Stanford, CA: Stanford University Press.

Schaie, K. W. (1994). The course of adult development. *American Psychologist, 49*(4), 304–313.

Schaninger, C. M., & Buss, W. C. (1986). A longitudinal comparison of consumption and finance handling between happily married and divorced couples. *Journal of Marriage and the Family, 48*, 129–136.

Scheidlinger, S. (1993). History of group psychotherapy. In H. I. Kaplan & B. J. Sadock (Eds.), *Comprehensive group psychotherapy.* Baltimore: Williams & Wilkins.

Scheier, M. F., & Carver, C. S. (1985). Optimism, coping, and health: Assessment and implications of generalized outcome expectancies. *Health Psychology, 4*, 219–247.

Scheier, M. F., Carver, C. S., & Bridges, M. W. (2001). Optimism, pessimism, and psychological well-being. In E. C. Chang (Ed.), *Optimism and pessimism: Implications for theory, research, and practice.* Washington, DC: American Psychological Association.

Scheier, M. F., Matthews, K. A., Owens, J. F., Magovern, G. J., Sr., Lefebvre, R. C., Abbott, R. A., & Carver, C. S. (1989). Dispositional optimism and recovery from coronary artery bypass surgery: The beneficial effects on physical and psychological well-being. *Journal of Personality and Social Psychology, 57*, 1024–1040.

Scherwitz, L., Perkins, L., Chesney, M., & Hughes, G. (1991). Cook-Medley Hostility Scale and subsets: Relationship to demographic and psychosocial characteristics in young adults in the CARDIA study. *Psychosomatic Medicine, 53*, 36–49.

Schiappa, E., Gregg, P. B., & Hewes, D. E. (2006). Can one TV show make difference? Will & Grace and the parasocial contact hypothesis. *Journal of Homosexuality, 51*(4), 15–37.

Schiffman, J., Ekstrom, M., LaBrie, J., Schulsinger, F., Sorenson, H., & Mednick, S. (2002). Minor physical anomalies and schizophrenia spectrum disorders: A prospective investigation. *American Journal of Psychiatry, 159*, 238–243.

Schilit, W. K. (1987). Thinking about managing your time. In A. D. Timpe (Ed.), *The management of time.* New York: Facts On File.

Schimel, J., Simon, L., Greenberg, J., Pyszczynski, T., Solomon, S., Waxmonsky, J., & Arndt, J. (1999). Stereotypes and terror management: Evidence that mortality salience enhances stereotypic thinking and preferences. *Journal of Personality and Social Psychology, 77*(5), 905–926.

Schirmer, L. L., & Lopez, F. G. (2001). Probing the social support and work strain relationship among adult workers: Contributions of adult attachment orientations. *Journal of Vocational Behavior, 59*(1), 17–33.

Schlegel, A., & Barry, H., III. (1991). *Adolescence: An anthropological inquiry.* New York: Free Press.

Schlenger, W. E., Kulka, R. A., Fairbank, J. A., Hough, R. L., et al. (1992). The prevalence of post-traumatic stress disorder in the Vietnam generation: A multimethod, multisource assessment of psychiatric disorder. *Journal of Traumatic Stress, 5*, 333–363.

Schlenker, B. R. (2003). Self-presentation. In M.R. Leary & J. P. Tangney (Eds.), *Handbook of self and identity.* New York: Guilford.

Schlenker, B. R., & Pontari, B. A. (2000). The strategic control of information: Impression management and self-presentation in daily life. In A. Tesser, R. B. Felson, & J. M. Suls (Eds.), *Psychological perspectives on self and identity.* Washington, DC: American Psychological Association.

Schmidt, N. B., Zvolensky, M. J., & Maner, J. K. (2006). Anxiety sensitivity: Prospective prediction of panic attacks and Axis I pathology. *Journal of Psychiatric Research, 40*, 691–699.

Schmitz, J. M., & DeLaune, K. A. (2005). Nicotine. In J. H. Lowinson, P. Ruiz, R. B. Millman, & J. G. Langrod (Eds.), *Substance abuse: A comprehensive textbook*. Philadelphia: Lippincott/Williams & Wilkins.

Schneider, D. J. (2004). *The psychology of stereotyping*. New York: Guilford.

Schneider, F., & Deldin, P. J. (2001). Genetics and schizophrenia. In P. B. Sutker & H. E. Adams (Eds.), *Comprehensive handbook of psychopathology* (3rd ed.) New York: Kluwer Academic/Plenum.

Schneider, J. P. (2003). The impact of compulsive cybersex behaviors on the family. *Sexual and Relationship Therapy, 18*(3), 329–354.

Schneider, T. R. (2004). The role of neuroticism on psychological and physiological stress responses. *Journal of Experimental Social Psychology, 40*, 795–804.

Schooler, D., Ward, L. M., Merriwether, A., & Caruthers, A. (2004). Who's that girl: Television's role in the body image development of young white and black women. *Psychology of Women Quarterly, 28*, 38–47.

Schoon, I., & Parsons, S. (2002). Teenage aspirations for future careers and occupational outcomes. *Journal of Vocational Behavior, 60*(2), 262–288.

Schottenbauer, M. A., Arnkoff, D. B., Glass, C. R., & Gray, S. H. (2006). Psychotherapy for PTSD in the community: Reported prototypical treatments. *Clinical Psychology & Psychotherapy, 13*(2), 108–122.

Schramm, D. G., Marshall, J. P., Harris, V. W., & Lee, T. R. (2005). After "I do": The newlywed transition. *Marriage & Family Review, 38*, 45–67.

Schraw, G., Wadkins, T., & Olafson, L. (2007). Doing the things we do: A grounded theory of academic procrastination. *Journal of Educational Psychology, 99*(1), 12–25.

Schreiber, F. R. (1973). *Sybil*. New York: Warner.

Schroeder, D. H., & Costa, P. T., Jr. (1984). Influence of life events stress on physical illness: Substantive effects or methodological flaws? *Journal of Personality and Social Psychology, 46*, 853–863.

Schuckit, M. A. (2000). Alcohol-related disorders. In B. J. Sadock & V. A. Sadock (Eds.), *Kaplan and Sadock's comprehensive textbook of psychiatry* (7th ed.). Philadelphia: Lippincott/Williams & Wilkins.

Schunk, D. H. (2003). Self-efficacy for reading and writing: Influence of modeling, goal setting, and self-evaluation. *Reading and Writing Quarterly: Overcoming Learning Difficulties, 19*(2), 159–172.

Schutte, N. S., Malouff, J. M., Thorsteinsson, E. B., Bhullar, N., & Rooke, S. E. (2007). A meta-analytic investigation of the relationship between emotional intelligence and health. *Personality and Individual Differences, 42*, 921–933.

Schwartz, B. (2004). *The paradox of choice: Why more is less*. New York: Ecco.

Schwartz, J. E., Neale, J., Marco, C., Shiffman, S. S., & Stone, A. A. (1999). Does trait coping exist? A momentary assessment approach to the evaluation of traits. *Journal of Personality and Social Psychology, 77*(2), 360–369.

Schwartz, J. P., Waldo, M., & Higgins, A. J. (2004). Attachment styles: Relationship to masculine gender role conflict in college men. *Psychology of Men & Masculinity, 5*(2), 143–146.

Schwartz, L., Slater, M. A., & Birchler, G. R. (1994). Interpersonal stress and pain behaviors in patients with chronic pain. *Journal of Consulting and Clinical Psychology, 62*, 861–864.

Schwarz, N., & Strack, F. (1999). Reports of subjective well-being: Judgmental processes and their methodological implications. In D. Kahneman, E. Diener, & N. Schwarz (Eds.), *Well-being: The foundations of hedonic psychology*. New York: Russell Sage Foundation.

Schwarzer, R., & Schulz, U. (2003). Stressful life events. In A. M. Nezu, C. M. Nezu, & P. A. Geller (Eds.), *Handbook of psychology: Vol. 9. Health psychology*. New York: Wiley.

Scroppo, J. C., Drob, S. L., Weinberger, J. L., & Eagle, P. (1998). Identifying dissociative identity disorder: A self-report and projective study. *Journal of Abnormal Psychology, 107*, 272–284.

Scully, J. A., Tosi, H., & Banning, K. (2000). Life event checklists: Revisiting the social readjustment rating scale after 30 years. *Educational & Psychological Measurement, 60*(6), 864–876.

Seabrook, R., Brown, G. D. A., & Solity, J. E. (2005). Distributed and massed practice: From laboratory to classroom. *Applied Cognitive Psychology, 19*(1), 107–122.

Searle, A., & Bennett, P. (2001). Psychological factors and inflammatory bowel disease: A review of a decade of literature. *Psychology, Health and Medicine, 6*(2), 121–135.

Seccombe, K. (1987). Children: Their impact on the elderly in declining health. *Research on Aging, 9*, 312–326.

Seccombe, K. (2001). Families in poverty in the 1990s: Trends, causes, consequences, and lessons learned. In R. M. Milardo (Ed.), *Understanding families into the new millennium: A decade in review.* Minneapolis: National Council on Family Relations.

Sedikides, C. (1993). Assessment, enhancement, and verification determinants of the self-evaluation process. *Journal of Personality and Social Psychology, 65*(2), 317–338.

Sedikides, C. (1995). Central and peripheral self-conceptions are differently influenced by mood: Tests of the differential sensitivity hypothesis. *Journal of Personality and Social Psychology, 69*, 759–777.

Sedikides, C., & Strube, M. J. (1997). Self-evaluation: To thine own self be good, to thine own self be sure, to thine own self be true, and to thine own self be better. In M. P. Zanna (Ed.), *Advances in experimental social psychology* (Vol. 29). New York: Academic Press.

Segal, M. W. (1974). Alphabet and attraction: An unobtrusive measure of the effect of propinquity in a field setting. *Journal of Personality and Social Psychology, 30*, 654–657.

Segall, A. (1997). Sick role concepts and health behavior. In D. S. Gochman (Ed.), *Handbook of health behavior research I: Personal and social determinants*. New York : Plenum Press.

Segerstrom, S. C., Taylor, S. E., Kemeny, M. E., & Fahey, J. L. (1998). Optimism is associated with mood, coping and immune change in response to stress. *Journal of Personality and Social Psychology, 74*, 1646–1655.

Self, D. W. (1998). Neural substrates of drug craving and relapse in drug addiction. *Annals of Medicine, 30*, 379–389.

Seligman, M. E. P. (1971). Phobias and preparedness. *Behavior Therapy, 2*, 307–321.

Seligman, M. E. P. (1974). Depression and learned helplessness. In R. J. Friedman & M. M. Katz (Eds.), *The psychology of depression: Contemporary theory and research*. New York: Wiley.

Seligman, M. E. P. (1990). *Learned optimism: How to change your mind and your life*. New York: Pocket Books.

Seligman, M. E. P. (1991). *Learned optimism*. New York: Alfred A. Knopf.

Seligman, M. E. P. (1992). *Helplessness: On depression, development, and death*. New York: Freeman.

Seligman, M. E. P. (1994). *What you can change and what you can't*. New York: Knopf.

Seligman, M. E. P. (1995). The effectiveness of psychotherapy. *American Psychologist, 50*, 965–974.

Seligman, M. E. P. (2003). The past and future of positive psychology. In C. L. M. Keyes & J. Haidt (Eds.), *Flourishing: Positive psychology and the life well-lived*. Washington, DC: American Psychological Association.

Seligman, M. E. P., & Csikszentmihalyi, M. (2000). Positive psychology: An introduction. *American Psychologist, 55*(1), 5–14.

Seligman, M. E. P., & Isaacowitz, D. M. (2000). Learned helplessness. In G. Fink (Ed.), *Encyclopedia of stress* (Vol. 2). San Diego: Academic Press.

Seligman, M. E. P., & Levant, R. F. (1998). Managed care policies rely on inadequate science. *Professional Psychology: Research and Practice, 29*, 211–212.

Seligman, M. E. P., Schulman, P., DeRubeis, R. J., & Hollon, S. D. (1999). The prevention of depression and anxiety. *Prevention and Treatment*, http://journals.apa.org/prevention/volume2/pre0020008a.html

Sellers, R. M., Copeland-Linder, N., Martin, P. P., & Lewis, R. L. (2006). Racial identity matters: The relationship between racial discrimination and psychological functioning in African American adolescents. *Journal of Research on Adolescence, 16*, 187–216.

Seltzer, J. A. (2001). Families formed outside of marriage. In R. M. Milardo (Ed.), *Understanding families into the new millennium: A decade in review*. Minneapolis: National Council on Family Relations.

Seltzer, J. A. (2004). Cohabitation and family change. In M. Coleman & L. H. Ganong (Eds.), *Handbook of contemporary families: Considering the past, contemplating the future*. Thousand Oaks, CA: Sage.

Selye, H. (1936). A syndrome produced by diverse nocuous agents. *Nature, 138*, 32.

Selye, H. (1956). *The stress of life*. New York: McGraw-Hill.

Selye, H. (1974). *Stress without distress*. New York: Lippincott.

Selye, H. (1982). History and present status of the stress concept. In L. Goldberger & S. Breznitz (Eds.), *Handbook of stress: Theoretical and clinical aspects*. New York: Free Press.

Semans, J. H. (1956). Premature ejaculation: A new approach. *Journal of Southern Medicine, 79*, 353–361.

Senecal, C., Lavoie, K., & Koestner, R. (1997). Trait and situational factors in procrastination: An interactional model. *Journal of Social Behavior and Personality, 12*, 889–903.

Serido, J., Almeida, D. M., & Wethington, E. (2004). Chronic stressors and daily hassles: Unique and interactive relationships with psychological distress. *Journal of Health and Social Behavior, 45*, 17–33.

Servan-Schreiber, D., Kolb, R., & Tabas, G. (1999). The somatizing patient. *Primary Care, 26*(2), 225–242.

Servin, A., Nordenstrom, A., Larsson, A., & Bohlin, G. (2003). Prenatal androgens and gender-typed behavior: A study of girls with mild and server forms of congenital hyperplasia. *Developmental Psychology, 39*, 440–450.

Sesso, H. D., Buring, J. E., Rifai, N., Blake, G. J., Gaziano, J. M., & Ridker, P. M. (2003). C-reactive protein and the risk of developing hypertension. *Journal of the American Medical Association, 290*(22), 2945–2951.

Seta, J. J., Seta, C. E., & McElroy, T. (2002). Strategies for reducing the stress of negative life experiences: An averaging/summation analysis. *Personality and Social Psychology Bulletin, 28*(11), 1574–1585.

Settersten, R. A., & Hagestad, G. (1996). What's the latest? Cultural deadlines for educational and work transitions. *Gerontologist, 36*, 602–613.

Settles, I. H., Cortina, L. M., Malley, J., & Stewart, A. J. (2006). The climate for women in academic science: The good, the bad, and changeable. *Psychology of Women Quarterly, 30*, 47–58.

Shaffer, D. R. (1989). *Developmental psychology: Childhood and adolescence*. Pacific Grove, CA: Brooks/Cole.

Shah, J., & Higgins, E. T. (2001). Regulatory concerns and appraisal efficiency: The general impact of promotion and prevention. *Journal of Personality and Social Psychology, 80*, 693–705.

Shalev, A. Y. (2001). Posttraumatic stress disorder. *Primary Psychiatry, 8*(10), 41–46.

Shapira-Berman, O. (2004). Why do married mothers choose to do all house tasks? Re-examining feminist agenda and its implications for therapy. *Journal of Feminist Family Therapy, 16*(3), 51–70.

Shapiro, A. F., Gottman, J. M., & Carrère. (2000). The baby and marriage: Identifying factors that buffer against decline in marital satisfaction after the first baby arrives. *Journal of Family Psychology, 14*(1), 59–70.

Shapiro, D. H., Jr. (1984). Overview: Clinical and physiological comparison of meditation with other self-control strategies. In D. H. Shapiro, Jr. & R. N. Walsh (Eds.), *Meditation: Classic and contemporary perspectives.* New York: Aldine.

Shapiro, S. L., Schwartz, G. E. R., & Santerre, C. (2002). Meditation and positive psychology. In C. R. Snyder & S. J. Lopez (Eds.), *Handbook of positive psychology.* New York: Oxford University Press.

Shavelson, R. J., Hubner, J. J., & Stanton, G. C. (1976). Self-concept: Validation of construct interpretations. *Review of Educational Research, 46,* 407–411.

Shaver, P. R., & Brennan, K. A. (1992). Attachment styles and the "Big Five" personality traits: Their connections with each other and with romantic relationship outcomes. *Personality and Social Psychology Bulletin, 18,* 536–545.

Shaver, P. R., & Hazan, C. (1993). Adult attachment: Theory and research. In W. Jones & D. Perlman (Eds.), *Advances in personal relationships* (Vol. 4). London: Jessica Kingsley.

Shaver, P. R., & Mikulincer, M. (2006). Attachment theory, individual psychodynamics, and relationship functioning. In A. L. Vangelisti & D. Perlman (Eds.), *The Cambridge handbook of personal relationships.* New York: Cambridge University Press.

Shaver, P. R., Wu, S., & Schwartz, J. C. (1991). Cross-cultural similarities and differences in emotion and its representation: A prototype approach. In M. S. Clark (Ed.), *Review of personality and social psychology* (Vol. 13). Newbury Park, CA: Sage.

Shaw, L. H., & Gant, L. M. (2002). In defense of the Internet: The relationship between Internet communication and depression, loneliness, self-esteem, and perceived social support. *CyberPsychology, 5*(2), 157–171.

Shear, M. K., & Beidel, D. C. (1998). Psychotherapy in the overall management strategy for social anxiety disorder. *Journal of Clinical Psychiatry, 59,* 39–46.

Sheehan, S. (1982). *Is there no place on earth for me?* Boston: Houghton Mifflin.

Sheese, B. E., Brown, E. L., & Graziano, W. G. (2004). Emotional expression in cyberspace: Searching for moderators of the Pennebacker disclosure effect via e-mail. *Health Psychology, 23,* 457–464.

Sheldon, J. P. (2004). Gender stereotypes in educational software for young children. *Sex Roles, 51,* 433–444.

Sheldon, K. M., & Kasser, T. (2001a). Getting older, getting better? Personal strivings and psychological maturity across the life span. *Developmental Psychology, 37*(4), 491–501.

Sheldon, K. M., & Kasser, T. (2001b). Goals, congruence, and positive well-being: New empirical support for humanistic theories. *Journal of Humanistic Psychology, 41*(1), 30–50.

Shelton, R. C., & Lester, N. (2006). Selective serotonin reuptake inhibitors and newer antidepressants. In D. J. Stein, D. J. Kupfer, & A. F. Schatzberg (Eds.), *Textbook of mood disorders.* Washington, DC: American Psychiatric Publishing.

Shepperd, J. A., & McNulty, J. K. (2002). The affective consequences of expected and unexpected outcomes. *Psychological Science, 13,* 85–88.

Sher, L. (2003). Daily hassles, cortisol, and depression. *Australian and New Zealand Journal of Psychiatry, 37*(3), 383–384.

Sher, L., Kandel, I., & Merrick, J. (2006). Editorial: Alcohol and suicidal behavior in adolescents: A medical and social problem. *International Journal of Adolescent Medicine and Health, 18,* 1–2.

Sher, L., & Mann, J. J. (2003). Psychiatric pathophysiology: Mood disorders. In A. Tasman, J. Kay, & J. A. Lieberman (Eds.), *Psychiatry.* New York: Wiley.

Sher, T. G., & Baucom, D. H. (1993). Marital communication: Differences among maritally distressed, depressed, and nondistressed-nondepressed couples. *Journal of Family Psychology, 7,* 148–153.

Sherif, M. (1936). *The psychology of social norms.* New York: Harper.

Sherman, A. M., de Vries, B., & Lansford, J. E. (2000). Friendship in childhood and adulthood: Lessons across the life span. *International Journal of Aging and Human Development, 51*(1), 31–51.

Shike, M. (1999). Diet and lifestyle in the prevention of colorectal cancer: An overview. *American Journal of Medicine, 106*(1A), 11S–15S, 50S–51S.

Shiota, M. N. (2006). Silver linings and candles in the dark: Differences among positive coping strategies in predicting subjective well-being. *Emotion, 6,* 335–339.

Shneidman, E. S. (1985). *At the point of no return.* New York: Wiley.

Shneidman, E. S., Farberow, N. L., & Litman, R. E. (1994). *The psychology of suicide: A clinician's guide to evaluation and treatment.* Northvale, NJ: J. Aronson.

Shobe, K. K., & Schooler, J. W. (2001). Discovering fact and fiction: Case-based analyses of authentic and fabricated discovered memories of abuse. In G. M. Davies & T. Dalgleish (Eds.), *Recovered memories: Seeking the middle ground.* Chichester, England: Wiley.

Shoda, Y., Mischel, W., & Peake, P. K. (1990). Predicting adolescent cognitive and self-regulatory competencies from preschool delay of gratification: Identifying diagnostic conditions. *Developmental Psychology, 26,* 978–986.

Shors, T. J. (2004). Learning during stressful times. *Learning and Memory, 11*(2), 137–144.

Shotland, R. L., & Hunter, B. A. (1995). Women's "token resistant" and compliant sexual behaviors are related to uncertain sexual intentions and rape. *Personality and Social Psychology Bulletin, 21,* 226–236.

Shuchter, S. R., & Zisook, S. (1993). The course of normal grief. In M. S. Stroebe, W. Stroebe, & R. O. Hansson (Eds.), *Handbook of bereavement: Theory, research, and intervention.* Cambridge, England: Cambridge University Press.

Shulman, R. B. (2001). Response versus remission in the treatment of depression: Understanding residual symptoms. *Primary Psychiatry, 8*(5), 28–30, 34.

Shuval, J. T. (1993). Migration and stress. In L. Goldberger & S. Breznitz (Eds.), *Handbook of stress: Theoretical and clinical aspects* (2nd ed.). New York: Free Press.

Sidanius, J., & Pratto, P. (1999). *Social dominance: An intergroup theory of social hierarchy and oppression.* New York: Cambridge University Press.

Sidanius, J., & Pratto, P. (2004). Ethnic enclaves and the dynamics of social identity on the college campus: The good, the bad, and the ugly. *Journal of Personality and Social Psychology, 87,* 96–110.

Sidanius, J., Van Laar, C., & Levin, S. (2004). Ethnic enclaves and the dynamics of social identity on the college campus: The good, the bad, and the ugly. *Journal of Personality and Social Psychology, 87,* 96–110.

Siddiqui, R. N., & Pandey, J. (2003). Coping with environmental stressors by urban slum dwellers. *Environment and Behavior, 35,* 589–604.

Siebert, A. (1995). *Student success: How to succeed in college and still have time for your friends.* Fort Worth, TX: Harcourt Brace.

SIECUS. (2004, Fall). SIECUS Fact Sheet: Public support for comprehensive sexuality education. Retrieved January 25, 2005 from http://63.73.227.69/Pubs/Fact/Fact0017.html.

Siegel, O. (1982). Personality development in adolescence. In B. B. Wolman (Ed.), *Handbook of developmental psychology.* Englewood Cliffs, NJ: Prentice-Hall.

Siegler, I. C., & Brummett, B. H. (2000). Associations among NEO personality assessments and well-being at mid-life: Facet-level analyses. *Psychology & Aging, 15,* 710–714.

Siegler, I. C., Bosworth, H. B., & Poon, L. W. (2003). Disease, health and aging. In R. M. Lerner, M.A. Easterbrooks, & J. Mistry (Eds.), *Handbook of psychology: Vol. 6. Developmental psychology.* New York: Wiley.

Siegler, I. C., Peterson, B. L., Barefoot, J. C., & Williams, R. B. (1992). Hostility during late adolescence predicts coronary risk factors at mid-life. *American Journal of Epidemiology, 136*(2), 146–154.

Signorielli, N., & Bacue, A. (1999). Recognition and respect: A content analysis of prime-time television characters. *Sex Roles, 40*(7/8), 527–544.

Silberman, E. K. (1998). Psychiatrists' and internists' beliefs. *Primary Psychiatry, 5,* 65–71.

Silke, A. (2003). *Terrorists, victims, and society: Psychological perspectives on terrrorism and its consequences.* New York: Wiley.

Silver, H., Feldman, P., Bilker, W., & Gur, R. C. (2003). Working memory deficit as a core neuropsychological dysfunction in schizophrenia. *American Journal of Psychiatry, 160,* 1809–1816.

Silver, M. (2002, June 10). What they're seeing. *U.S. News & World Report,* p. 41.

Silverman, P. R., & Worden, J. M. (1992). Children's reactions in the early months after the death of a parent. *American Journal of Orthopsychiatry, 62,* 93–104.

Simmons, T., & Dye, J. L. (2004). What has happened to the median age at first marriage data? Paper presented at the meeting of the American Sociological Association, San Francisco, CA.

Simmons, T., & O'Connell, M. (2003). *Married-couple and unmarried-partner households: 2000.* U.S. Census Bureau, Census 2000 Special Reports. Washington, DC: U.S. Department of Commerce.

Simon, G. E., Savarino, J., Operskalski, B., & Wang, P. S. (2006). Suicide risk during antidepressant treatment. *American Journal of Psychiatry, 163,* 41–47.

Simonton, D. K. (1997). Creative productivity: A predictive and explanatory model of career trajectories and landmarks. *Psychological Review, 104*(1), 66–89.

Sinclair, R. C., Mark, M. M., & Clore, G. L. (1994). Mood-related persuasion depends on (mis)attributions. *Social Cognition, 12,* 309–326.

Singer, A. R., Cassin, S. E., & Dobson, K. S. (2005). The role of gender in the career aspirations of professional psychology graduates: Are there more similarities than differences? *Canadian Psychology, 46*(4), 215–222.

Singh, D. (1993). Adaptive significance of female physical attractiveness: Role of waist-to-hip ratio. *Journal of Personality and Social Psychology, 65,* 293–307.

Singh, D. (1995). Female judgment of male attractiveness and desirability for relationships: Role of waist-to-hip ratio and financial status. *Journal of Personality and Social Psychology, 69,* 1089–1101.

Sinkkonen, J., Anttila, R., & Siimes, M. A. (1998). Pubertal maturation and changes in self-image in early adolescent Finnish boys. *Journal of Youth and Adolescence, 27,* 209–218.

Sinnott, J. D. (1989). A model for solution of ill-structured problems: Implications for everyday and abstract problem solving. In J. D. Sinnott (Ed.), *Everyday problem solving: Theory and application.* New York: Praeger.

Sirois, F. M., Melia-Gordon, M. L., & Pychyl, T. A. (2003). "I'll look after my health, later": An investigation of procrastination and health. *Personality and Individual Differences, 35*(5), 1167–1184.

Skinner, A. E. G. (2001). Recovered memories of abuse: Effects on the individual. In G. M. Davies & T. Dalgleish (Eds.), *Recovered memories: Seeking the middle ground.* Chichester, England: Wiley.

Skinner, B. F. (1953). *Science and human behavior.* New York: Macmillan.

Skinner, B. F. (1974). *About behaviorism.* New York: Knopf.

Skinner, B. F. (1987). Whatever happened to psychology as the science of behavior? *American Psychologist, 42,* 780–786.

Skinner, B. F. (1990). Can psychology be a science of mind? *American Psychologist, 45,* 1206–1210.

Skinner, E. A., Edge, K., Altman, J. , & Sherwood, H. (2003). Searching for the structure of coping: A review and critique of category systems for classifying ways of coping. *Psychological Bulletin, 129,*216–269.

Skinner, N. F. (2003). Birth order effects in dominance: Failure to support Sulloway's view. *Psychological Reports, 92,* 387–388.

Skinner, P. H., & Shelton, R. L. (1985). *Speech, language, and hearing: Normal processes and disorders* (2nd ed.). New York: Wiley.

Skolnick, P. (2003). Psychiatric pathophysiology: Anxiety disorders. In A. Tasman, J. Kay, & J. A. Lieberman (Eds.), *Psychiatry.* New York: Wiley.

Skowronski, J. J., & Carlston, D. E. (1989). Negativity and extremity biases in impression formation: A review of explanation. *Psychological Review, 105,* 131–142.

Skowronski, J. J., & Carlston, D. E. (1992). Caught in the act: When impressions are based on highly diagnostic information behaviours are resistant to contradiction. *European Journal of Social Psychology, 22,* 435–452.

Slashinki, M. J., Coker, A. L., & Davis, K. E. (2003). Physical aggression, forced sex, and stalking victimization by a dating partner: An analysis of the National Violence Against Women Survey. *Violence & Victims, 18*(6), 595–617.

Slaski, M., & Cartwright, S. (2003). Emotional intelligence training and its implications for stress, health and performance. *Stress and Health: Journal of the International Society for the Investigation of Stress, 19*(4), 233–239.

Slavney, P. R. (1990). *Perspectives on hysteria.* Baltimore: John Hopkins University Press.

Sloan, D. M., & Marx, B. P. (2004). A closer examination of the structured written disclosure procedure. *Journal of Consulting and Clinical Psychology, 72*(2), 165–175.

Slof-Op't Landt, M. C. T., van Furth, E. F., Meulenbelt, I., Slagboom, P. E., Bartels, M., Boomsma, D. I., & Bulik, C. M. (2005). Eating disorders: From twin studies to candidate genes and beyond. *Twin Research and Human Genetics, 8,* 467–482.

Slonim-Nevo, V., & Al-Krenawi, A. (2006). Success and failure among polygamous families: The experience of wives, husbands, and children. *Family Process, 45,* 311–330.

Slovic, P., Fischhoff, B., & Lichtenstein, S. (1982). Facts versus fears: Understanding perceived risk. In D. Kahneman, P. Slovic, & A. Tversky (Eds.), *Judgment under uncertainty: Heuristics and biases.* Cambridge, England: Cambridge University Press.

Smiler, A. P. (2004). Thirty years after the discovery of gender: Psychological concepts and measures of masculinity. *Sex Roles, 50*(1–2), 15–26.

Smith, A. K. (2000, November 6). Charting your own course. *U.S. News & World Report,* 56–60, 62, 64–65.

Smith, C. A., & Lazarus, R. S. (1993). Appraisal components, core relational themes, and the emotions. *Cognition and Emotion, 7,* 233–269.

Smith, D. A. (1999). The end of theoretical orientations? *Applied & Preventative Psychology, 8,* 269–280.

Smith, D. M., & Gates, G. J. (2001) *Gay and lesbian families in the United States: Same-sex unmarried partner households: Preliminary analysis of 2000 U.S. census data, a human rights campaign report* [Web Page]. URL www.hrc.org.

Smith, D. M., Langa, K. M., Kabeto, M. U., & Ubel, P. A. (2005). Health, wealth, and happiness: Financial resources buffer subjective well-being after the onset of a disability. *Psychological Science, 16,* 663–666.

Smith, G., Bartlett, A., & King, M. (2004). Treatments of homosexuality in Britain since the 1950s—an oral history: The experience of patients. *BMJ USA, 4,* 143–144.

Smith, G. S., Branas, C. C., & Miller, T. R. (1999). Fatal nontraffic injuries involving alcohol: A meta-analysis. *Annals of Emergency Medicine, 33*(6), 659–668.

Smith, J. C. (1975). Meditation and psychotherapy: A review of the literature. *Psychological Bulletin, 32,* 553–564.

Smith, M., & Pazder, L. (1980). *Michelle remembers.* New York: Pocket Books.

Smith, M. L., & Glass, G. V. (1977). Meta-analysis of psychotherapy outcome studies. *American Psychologist, 32,* 752–760.

Smith, P. B., & Bond, M. H. (1999). *Social psychology across cultures.* Boston: Allyn & Bacon.

Smith, R. E. (1989). Effects of coping skills training on generalized self-efficacy and locus of control. *Journal of Personality and Social Psychology, 56,* 228–233.

Smith, T. W. (1999). *The emerging 21st century American family.* University of Chicago: National Opinion Research Center.

Smith, T. W. (2003). Hostility and health: Current status of a psychosomatic hypothesis. In P. Salovey & A. J. Rothman (Eds.), *Social psychology of health.* New York: Psychology Press.

Smith, T. W. (2006). Personality as risk and resilience in physical health. *Current Directions in Psychological Science, 15,* 227–231.

Smith, T. W., & Gallo, L. C. (1999). Hostility and cardiovascular reactivity during marital interaction. *Psychosomatic Medicine, 61,* 436–445.

Smith, T. W., & Gallo, L. C. (2001). Personality traits as risk factors for physical illness. In A. Baum, T. A. Revenson, & J. E. Singer (Eds.), *Handbook of health psychology.* Mahwah, NJ: Erlbaum.

Smith, T. W., Glazer, K., & Ruiz, J. M. (2004). Hostility, anger, aggressiveness, and coronary heart disease: An interpersonal perspective on personality, emotion, and health. *Journal of Personality, 72,* 1217–1270.

Smith, T. W., Pope, M. K., Sanders, J. D., Allred, K. D., & O'Keefe, J. L. (1988). Cynical hostility at home and work: Psychosocial vulnerability across domains. *Journal of Research in Personality, 22,* 525–548.

Smith, W. P., Compton, W. C., & West, W. B. (1995). Meditation as an adjunct to a happiness enhancement program. *Journal of Clinical Psychology, 51,* 269–273.

Smock, P. J. (2000). Cohabitation in the United States: An appraisal of research themes, findings, and implications. *Annual Review of Sociology, 26,* 1–20.

Smock, P. J., Manning, W. D., & Gupta, S. (1999). The effect of marriage and divorce on women's economic well-being. *American Sociological Review, 64,* 794–812.

Smolak, L. (2006). Body image. In J. Worrell & C. D. Goodheart (Eds.), *Handbook of girls' and women's psychological health.* New York: Oxford University Press.

Smolak, L., & Murnen, S. K. (2001). Gender and eating problems. In R. H. Striegel-Moore & L. Smolak (Eds.), *Eating disorders: Innovative directions in research and practice.* Washington, DC: American Psychological Association.

Smoll, F. L., & Schutz, R. W. (1990). Quantifying gender differences in physical performance: A developmental perspective. *Developmental Psychology, 26,* 360–369.

Smyth, J., Litcher, L., Hurewitz, A., & Stone, A. (2001). Relaxation training and cortisol secretion in adult asthmatics. *Journal of Health Psychology, 6*(2), 217–227.

Smyth, J. M., & Pennebaker, J. W. (1999). Sharing one's story: Translating emotional experiences into words as a coping tool. In C. R. Snyder (Ed.), *Coping: The psychology of what works.* New York: Oxford Univer-sity Press.

Smyth, J. M., & Pennebaker, J. W. (2001). What are the health effects of disclosure? In A. Baum, T. A. Revenson, & J. E. Singer (Eds.), *Handbook of health psychology.* Mahwah, NJ: Erlbaum.

Snowden, L. R., & Yamada, A. (2005). Cultural differences in access to care. *Annual Review of Clinical Psychology, 1,* 143–166.

Snowdon, D. (2001). *Aging with grace: What the nun study teaches us about leading longer, healthier, and more meaningful lives.* New York: Bantam Books.

Snyder, M. (1979). Self-monitoring processes. In L. Berkowitz (Ed.), *Advances in experimental social psychology* (Vol. 12). New York: Academic Press.

Snyder, M. (1986). *Public appearances/Private realities: The psychology of self-monitoring.* New York: Freeman.

Snyder, M., & Swann, W. B., Jr. (1978). Hypothesis testing processes in social interaction. *Journal of Personality and Social Psychology, 36*(11), 1202–1212.

Sobal, J. (1995). Social influences on body weight. In K. D. Brownell & C. G. Fairburn (Eds.), *Eating disorders and obesity: A comprehensive handbook.* New York: Guilford Press.

Solberg, E. C., Diener, E., & Robinson, M. (2004). Why are materialists less satisfied? In T. Kasser & A. D. Kanner (Eds.). *Psychology and consumer culture: The struggle for a good life in a materialistic world.* Washington, DC: American Psychological Association.

Solberg, E. C., Diener, E., Wirtz, D., Lucas, R. E., & Oishi, S. (2002). Wanting, having, and satisfaction: Examining the role of desire discrepancies in satisfaction with income. *Journal of Personality and Social Psychology, 83*(3), 725–734.

Solms, M. (2004). Freud returns. *Scientific American, 290*(5), 83–88.

Solomon, S., Greenberg, J. L., & Pyszczynski, T A. (1991). A terror management theory of social behavior: The psychological functions of self-esteem and cultural worldviews. In M. Zanna (Ed.), *Advances in experimental social psychology* (Vol. 24). Orlando, FL: Academic Press.

Solomon, S., Greenberg, J., & Pyszczynski, T. (2004a). The cultural animal: Twenty years of terror management. In J. Greenberg, S. L. Koole, & T. Pyszczynski (Eds.), *Handbook of experimental existential psychology.* New York: Guilford Press.

Solomon, S., Greenberg, J., & Pyszczynski, T. (2004b). Lethal consumption: Death-denying materialism. In T. Kasser, & A. D. Kanner (Eds.), *Psychology and consumer culture: The struggle for a good life in a materialistic world.* Washington, DC: American Psychological Association.

Solomon, S. E., Rothblum, E. D., & Balsam, K. F. (2004). Pioneers in partnership: Lesbian and gay male couples in civil unions compared with those not in civil unions and married heterosexual siblings. *Journal of Family Psychology, 18,* 275–286.

Solowij, N., Stephens, R. S., Roffman, R. A., Babor, T., Kadden, R., Miller, M., Christiansen. K., McRee, B., & Vendetti, J. (2002). Cognitive functioning of long-term heavy cannabis users seeking treatment. *Journal of the American Medical Association, 287,* 1123–1131.

Sommer, B. R., Hoff, A. L., & Costa, M. (2003). Folic acid supplementation in dementia: A preliminary report. *Journal of Geriatric Psychiatry and Neurology, 16,* 156–159.

Sommers-Flanagan, R., Sommers-Flanagan, J., & Davis, B. (1993). What's happening on music television? A gender-role content analysis. *Sex Roles, 28,* 745–753.

Son Hing, L. S., Bobocel, D. R., & Zanna, M. P. (2007). Authoritarian dynamics and unethical decision making: High social dominance orientation leaders and high right wing authoritarianism followers. *Journal of Personality and Social Psychology, 92,* 67–81.

Son Hing, L. S., Li, W., & Zanna, M. P. (2002). Inducing hypocrisy to reduce prejudicial responses among aversive racists. *Journal of Experimental Social Psychology, 38,* 71–78.

Sonnentag, S., & Frese, M. (2003). Stress in organizations. In W. C. Borman , D. R. Ilgen, & R. J. Klimoski (Eds.), *Handbook of psychology: Vol. 12. Industrial and organizational psychology.* New York: Wiley.

Sonstroem, R. J. (1997). Physical activity and self-esteem. In W. P. Morgan (Ed.), *Physical activity and mental health.* Washington, DC: Taylor & Francis.

Sorensen, J. L., Haug, N. A., & Batki, S. L. (2005). Psychosocial issues of HIV/AIDS among drug users in treatment. In J. H. Lowinson, P. Ruiz, R. B. Millman, & J. G. Langrod (Eds.), *Substance abuse: A comprehensive textbook.* Philadelphia: Lippincott/Williams & Wilkins.

Sotiriou, P. E. (2002). *Integrating college study skills: Reasoning in reading, listening, and writing.* Belmont, CA: Wadsworth.

South, S. J. (1993). Racial and ethnic differences in the desire to marry. *Journal of Marriage and the Family, 55,* 357–370.

South, S. J., Bose, S., & Trent, K. (2004). Anticipating divorce: Spousal agreement, predictive accuracy, and effects on labor supply and fertility. *Journal of Divorce and Remarriage, 40*(3–4), 1–22.

South, S. J., & Lloyd, K. M. (1995). Spousal alternatives and marital dissolution. *American Sociological Review, 60,* 21–35.

Spada, M. M., & Wells, A. (2006). Metacognitions about alcohol use in problem drinkers. *Clinical Psychology & Psychotherapy, 13*(2), 138–143.

Spanos, N. P. (1994). Multiple identity enactments and multiple personality disorder: A sociocognitive perspective. *Psychological Bulletin, 116,* 143–165.

Spanos, N. P. (1996). *Multiple identities and false memories.* Washington, DC: American Psychological Association.

Spector, I., & Carey, M. (1990). Incidence and prevalence of the sexual dysfunctions: A critical review of the empirical literature. *Archives of Sexual Behavior, 19,* 389–408.

Spelke, E. S. (2005). Sex differences in intrinsic aptitude for mathematics and science? *American Psychologist, 60,* 950–958.

Spence, J. T. (1983). Comment on Lubinski, Tellegen, and Butcher's "Masculinity, femininity, and androgyny viewed and assessed as distinct concepts." *Journal of Personality and Social Psychology, 44,* 440–446.

Spence, J. T., & Buckner, C. E. (2000). Instrumental and expressive traits, trait stereotypes, and sexist attitudes. *Psychology of Women Quarterly, 24,* 44–62.

Spence, J. T., & Robbins, A. S. (1992). Workaholism: Definition, measurement, and preliminary results. *Journal of Personality Assessment, 58,* 160–178.

Spencer, P. T. (1990). Exercise as psychotherapy. *Counseling Psychology Quarterly, 3*(3), 291–293.

Sperry, L. (2006). *Psychological treatment of chronic illness: The biopsychosocial therapy approach.* Washington, DC: American Psychological Association.

Sperry, R. W. (1982). Some effects of disconnecting the cerebral hemispheres. *Science, 217,* 1223–1226, 1250.

Spiegel, D., Bloom, J. R., Kraemer, H. C., & Gottheil, E. (1989). Psychological support for cancer patients. *Lancet, 2,* 1447.

Spiegler, M. D., & Guevremont, D. C. (1998). *Contemporary behavior therapy.* Pacific Grove, CA: Brooks/Cole.

Spiegler, M. D., & Guevremont, D. C. (2003). *Contemporary behavior therapy.* Belmont, CA: Wadsworth.

Spitzberg, B. H. (1999). An analysis of empirical estimates of sexual aggression victimization and perpetration. *Violence and Victims, 14*(3), 241–260.

Spitzer, R. L., First, M. B., & Wakefield, J. C. (2007). Saving PTSD from itself in DSM-V. *Journal of Anxiety Disorders, 21,* 233–241.

Spokane, A. R., & Cruza-Guet, M. C. (2005). Holland's theory of vocational personalities in work environments. In S. D. Brown & R. W. Lent (Eds.), *Career development and counseling: Putting theory and research to work.* New York: Wiley.

Sporer, S. L., & Schwandt, B. (2007). Moderators of nonverbal indicators of deception: A meta-analytic synthesis. *Psychology, Public Policy, and Law, 13,* 1–34.

Sprecher, S. (1994). Two sides to the breakup of dating relationships. *Personal Relationships, 1,* 199–222.

Sprecher, S. (2002). Sexual satisfaction in premarital relationships: Associations with satisfaction, love, commitment, and stability. *The Journal of Sex Research, 39*(3), 190–196.

Sprecher, S., & Cate, R. M. (2004). Sexual satisfaction and sexual expression as predictors of relationship satisfaction and stability. In J. H. Harvey, A. Wenzel, & S. Sprecher (Eds.), *The handbook of sexuality and close relationships.* Mahwah, NJ: Lawrence Erlbaum.

Sprecher, S., Christopher, F. S., & Cate, R. (2006). Sexuality in close relationships. In A. L. Vangelisti & D. Perlman (Eds.), *The Cambridge handbook of personal relationships.* New York: Cambridge University Press.

Sprecher, S., & Duck, S. (1994). Sweet talk: The importance of perceived communication for romantic and friendship attraction experienced during a get-acquainted date. *Personality and Social Psychology Bulletin, 20*(4), 391–400.

Sprecher, S., & Regan, P. C. (1998). Passionate and companionate love in courting and young married couples. *Sociological Inquiry, 68*(2), 163–185.

Sprecher, S., Sullivan, Q., & Hatfield, E. (1994). Mate selection preferences: Gender differences examined in a national sample. *Journal of Personality and Social Psychology, 66,* 1074–1080.

Springen, K. (2004, November 1). Under the knife. *Newsweek,* pp. 59–60.

Springer, S. P., & Deutsch, G. (1998). *Left brain, right brain.* New York: Freeman.

Stack, S. (1998). Marriage, family and loneliness: A cross-national study. *Sociological Perspectives, 41,* 415–432.

Stack, S., & Eshleman, J. R. (1998). Marital status and happiness: A 17-nation study. *Journal of Marriage and the Family, 60,* 527–536.

Stafford, L., & Canary, D. J. (1991). Maintenance strategies and romantic relationship type, gender and relational characteristics. *Journal of Social and Personal Relationships, 8,* 217–242.

Stajkovic, A. D., & Luthans, F. (1998). Self-efficacy and work-related performance: A meta-analysis. *Psychological Bulletin, 124*(2), 240–261.

Stamler, J., Daviglus, M. L., Garside, D. B., Dyer, A. R., Greenland, P., & Neaton, J. D. (2000). Relationship of baseline serum cholesterol levels in 3 large cohorts of younger men to long-term coronary, cardiovascular, and all-cause mortality and to longevity. *Journal of the American Medical Association, 284,* 311–318.

Stanley, S. M., Whitton, S. W., & Markman, H. J. (2004). Maybe I do? Interpersonal commitment and premarital or nonmarital cohabitation. *Journal of Family Issues, 25,* 496–519.

Stanton, A. L., Lobel, M., Sears, S., & DeLuca, R. S. (2002). Psychosocial aspects of selected issues in women's reproductive health: Current status and future directions. *Journal of Consulting & Clinical Psychology, 70*(3), 751–770.

Starcevic, V. (2001). Clinical features and diagnosis of hypochondriasis. In V. Starcevic & D. R. Lipsitt (Eds.), *Hypochondriasis: Modern perspectives on an ancient malady.* New York: Oxford University Press.

Starker, S. (1990). Self-help books: Ubiquitous agents of health care. *Medical Psychotherapy: An International Journal, 3* 187–194.

Starker, S. (1992). Characteristics of self-help book readers among VA medical outpatients. *Medical Psychotherapy: An International Journal, 5,* 89–93.

Starrels, M. E., Ingersoll-Dayton, B., Dowler, D. W., & Neal, M. B. (1997). The stress of caring for a parent: Effects of the elder's impairment on an employed adult child. *Journal of Marriage and the Family, 59,* 860–872.

Statt, D. A. (1994). *Psychology and the world of work.* New York: New York University Press.

Stattin, H., & Magnusson, D. (1990). *Pubertal maturation in female development.* Hillsdale, NJ: Erlbaum.

Staudinger, U. M., & Bluck, S. (2001). A view on midlife development from a life-span theory. In M. E. Lachman (Ed.), *Handbook of midlife development.* New York: Wiley.

Steel, P. (2007). The nature of procrastination: A meta-analytic and theoretical review of quintessential self-regulatory failure. *Psychological Bulletin, 133*(1), 65–94.

Steele, C. M. (1988). The psychology of self-affirmation: Sustaining integrity of the self. In L. Berkowitz (Ed.), *Advances in experimental social psychology.* New York: Academic Press.

Steele, C. M. (1997). A threat in the air: How stereotypes shape intellectual identity and performance. *American Psychologist, 52,* 613–629.

Steiger, H., Bruce, K. R., & Israël, M. (2003). Eating disorders. In G. Stricker & T. A. Widiger (Eds.), *Handbook of psychology: Vol. 8. Clinical psychology.* New York: Wiley.

Steiger, H., & Seguin, J. R. (1999). Eating disorders: Anorexia nervosa and bulimia nervosa. In T. Millon, P. H. Blaney, & R. D. Davis (Eds.), *Oxford textbook of psychopathology.* New York: Oxford University Press.

Stein, M. B., Forde, D. R., Anderson, G., & Walker, J. R. (1997a). Obsessive-compulsive disorder in the community: An epidemiologic survey with clinical reappraisal. *American Journal of Psychiatry, 154,* 1120–1126.

Stein, M. B., Walker, J. R., Hazen, A. L., & Forde, D. R. (1997b). Full and partial posttraumatic stress disorder: Findings from a community survey. *American Journal of Psychiatry, 154,* 1114–1119.

Stein, N., Marshall, N. L., & Tropp, L. R. (1993). *Secrets in public: Sexual harassment in our schools.* Wellesley, MA: Center for Research on Women at Wellesley College and the NOW Legal Defense and Education Fund.

Stein, P. J. (1975). Singlehood: An alternative to marriage. *Family Coordinator, 24,* 489–503.

Stein, P. J. (1976). *Single.* Englewood Cliffs, NJ: Prentice-Hall.

Stein, R. J., O'Byrne, K. K., Suminski, R. R., & Haddock, C. K. (1999). Etiology and treatment of obesity in adults and children: Implications for the addiction model. *Drugs and Society, 15*(1–2), 103–121.

Steinberg, L. (2001). We know some things: Parent-adolescent relationships in retrospect and prospect. *Journal of Research on Adolescence, 11*(1), 1–19.

Steinberg, L. (2004). *The ten basic principles of good parenting.* New York: Simon & Schuster.

Steinberg, L., Blatt-Eisengart, I., & Cauffman, E. (2006). Patterns of competence and adjustment among adolescents from authoritative, authoritarian, indulgent, and neglectful homes: A replication in a sample of serious juvenile offenders. *Journal of Research on Adolescence, 16,* 47–58.

Steinberg, L., & Levine, A. (1997). *You and your adolescent: A parents' guide for ages 10 to 20.* New York: Harper Perennial.

Steiner, H., Smith, C., Rosenkranz, R. T., & Litt, I. (1991). The early care and feeding of anorexics. *Child Psychiatry and Human Development, 21,* 163–167.

Steinhausen, H. (2002). The outcome of anorexia nervosa in the 20th century. *American Journal of Psychiatry, 159,* 1284–1293.

Steinmetz, H., Staiger, J. F., Schluag, G., Huang, Y., & Jancke, L. (1995). Corpus callosum and brain volume in women and men. *Neuroreport, 3,* 1002–1004.

Stephens, R. S. (1999). Cannabis and hallucinogens. In B. S. McCrady, & E. E. Epstein (Eds.), *Addictions: A comprehensive guidebook.* New York: Oxford University Press.

Sternberg, R. J. (1986). A triangular theory of love. *Psychological Review, 93* 119–135.

Sternberg, R. J. (1988). Triangulating love. In R. J. Sternberg & M. L. Barnes (Eds.), *The psychology of love.* New Haven, CT: Yale University Press.

Sternberg, R. J., Grigorenko, E. L., & Kidd, K. K. (2005). Intelligence, race, and genetics. *American Psychologist, 60,* 45–69.

Stevens, D. P., Minnotte, K. L., Mannon, S. E., & Kiger, G. (2007). Examining the "neglected side of the work-family interface": Antecedents of positive and negative family-to-work spillover. *Journal of Family Issues, 28,* 242–262.

Stewart, A. J., & Ostrove, J. M. (1998). Women's personality in middle age: Gender, history, and midcourse corrections. *American Psychologist, 53*, 1185–1194.

Stewart, A. J., Ostrove, J. M., & Helson, R. (2001). Middle aging in women: Patterns of personality change from the 30's to the 50's. *Journal of Adult Development, 8*(1), 23–37.

Stewart, F. H., Ellertson, C., & Cates, W. Jr. (2004). Abortion. In R. A. Hatcher, J. Trussell, F. H. Stewart, A. L. Nelson, W. Cates Jr., F. Guest, & D. Kowal (Eds.), *Contraceptive technology* (18th rev. ed.). New York: Ardent Media.

Stice, E. (2001). Risk factors for eating pathology: Recent advances and future directions. In R. H. Striegel-Moore & L. Smolak (Eds.), *Eating disorders: Innovative directions in research and practice.* Washington, DC: American Psychological Association.

Stice, E., Spangler, D., & Agras, W. S. (2001). Exposure to media-portrayed thin-ideal images adversely affects vulnerable girls: A longitudinal experiment. *Journal of Social and Clinical Psychology, 20*, 270–288.

Stillion, J. M. (1995). Death in the lives of adults: Responding to the tolling of the bell. in H. Wass & R. A. Neimeyer (Eds.), *Dying: Facing the facts.* New York: Taylor & Francis.

Stith, S. M., Rosen, K. H., Middleton, K. A., Busch, A. L., Lundeberg, K., & Carlton, R. P. (2000). The intergenerational transmission of spouse abuse: A meta-analysis. *Journal of Marriage and the Family, 62*, 640–654.

Stith, S. M., Smith, D. B., Penn, C. E., Ward, D. B., & Tritt, D. (2004). Intimate partner physical abuse perpetration and victimization risk factors: A meta-analytic review. *Aggression and Violent Behavior, 10*, 65–98.

Stoffer, G. R., Davis, K. E., & Brown, J. B., Jr. (1977). The consequences of changing initial answers on objective tests: A stable effect and a stable misconception. *Journal of Educational Research, 70*, 272–277.

Stoll, B. M., Arnaut, G. L., Fromme, D. K., & Felker-Thayer, J. A. (2005). Adolescents in stepfamilies: A qualitative analysis. *Journal of Divorce & Remarriage, 44*, 177–189.

Stone, L. (1977). *The family, sex and marriage in England 1500–1800.* New York: Harper & Row.

Stone, P., & Lovejoy, M. (2004, November). Fast-track women and the "choice" to stay home. *Annals of the American Academy of Political and Social Science, 596*, 62–83.

Stone, W. N. (2003). Group psychotherapy. In A. Tasman, J. Kay, & J. A. Lieberman (Eds.), *Psychiatry.* New York: Wiley.

Stoney, C. M. (2003). Gender and cardiovascular disease: A psychobiological and integrative approach. *Current Directions in Psychological Science, 12*(4), 129–133.

Strauman, T. J., Vookles, J., Berenstein, V., Chaiken, S., & Higgins, E. T. (1991). Self-discrepancies and vulnerability to body dissatisfaction and disordered eating. *Journal of Personality and Social Psychology, 61*, 946–956.

Strickland, C. J. (1997). Suicide among American Indian, Alaskan Native, and Canadian Aboriginal youth: Advancing the research agenda. *International Journal of Mental Health, 25*, 11–32.

Striegel-Moore, R. H., McMahon, R. P., Biro, F. M., Schreiber, G., Crawford, P. B., & Voorhees, C. (2001). Exploring the relationship between timing of menarche and eating disorder symptoms in black and white adolescent girls. *International Journal of Eating Disorders, 30*(4), 421–433.

Striegel-Moore, R. H., Silberstein, L. R., & Rodin, J. (1993). The social self in bulimia nervosa: Public self-consciousness, social anxiety, and perceived fraudulence. *Journal of Abnormal Psychology, 102*, 297–303.

Strober, M. (1995). Family-genetic perspectives on anorexia nervosa and bulimia nervosa. In K. D. Brownell & C. G. Fairburn (Eds.), *Eating disorders and obesity: A comprehensive handbook.* New York: Guilford Press.

Stroebe, K., Lodewijkx, H. F. M., & Spears, R. (2005). Do unto others as they do unto you: Reciprocity and social identification as determinants of ingroup favoritism. *Personality and Social Psychology Bulletin, 31*, 831–845.

Stroebe, W., Stroebe, M., Abakoumkin, G., & Schut, H. (1996). The role of loneliness and social support in adjustment to loss: A test of attachment versus stress theory. *Journal of Personality and Social Psychology, 70*(6), 1241–1249.

Stroup, T. S., Kraus, J. E., & Marder, S. R. (2006). Pharmacotherapies. In J. A. Lieberman, T. S. Stroup, & D. O. Perkins (Eds.), *Textbook of schizophrenia.* Washington, DC: American Psychiatric Publishing.

Strupp, H. H. (1996). The tripartite model and the *Consumer Reports* study. *American Psychologist, 51*, 1017–1024.

Stuart, P. (1992). Murder on the job. *Personnel Journal, 71*, 72–84.

Stubbe, J. H., Posthuma, D., Boomsma, D. I., & De Geus, E. J. C. (2005). Heritability of life satisfaction in adults: A twin-family study. *Psychological Medicine, 35*, 1581–1588.

Stunkard, A. J., Harris, J. R., Pederson, N. L., & McClearn, G. E. (1990). The body-mass index of twins who have been reared apart. *New England Journal of Medicine, 322*, 1483–1487.

Stunkard, A. J., Sorensen, T., Hanis, C., Teasdale, T. W., Chakraborty, R., Schull, W. J., & Schulsinger, F. (1986). An adoption study of human obesity. *New England Journal of Medicine, 314*, 193–198.

Suarez, E. C. (2004). C-reactive protein is associated with psychological risk factors of cardiovascular disease in apparently healthy adults. *Psychosomatic Medicine, 66*(5), 684–691.

Suarez, E. C., Kuhn, C. M., Schanberg, S. M., Williams, R. B., Jr., & Zimmermann, E. A. (1998). Neuroendocrine, cardiovascular, and emotional responses of hostile men: The role of interpersonal challenge. *Psychosomatic Medicine, 60*(1), 78–88.

Suarez-Orozco, C., & Suarez-Orozco, M. M. (1995). *Transformation: Immigration, family life, and achievement motivation among Latino adolescents.* Stanford, CA: Stanford University Press.

Suchday, S., Kapur, S., Ewart, C. K., & Friedberg, J. P. (2006). Urban stress and health in developing countries: Development and validation of a neighborhood stress index for India. *Behavioral Medicine, 32*(3), 77–86.

Sudak, H. S. (2005). Suicide. In B. J. Sadock & V. A. Sadock (Eds.), *Kaplan & Sadock's comprehensive textbook of psychiatry.* Philadelphia: Lippincott Williams & Wilkins.

Sue, D. (1979). Erotic fantasies of college students during coitus. *Journal of Sex Research, 15*, 299–305.

Sue, S., & Zane, N. (1987). The role of culture and cultural techniques in psychotherapy: A critique and reformulation. *American Psychologist, 42*, 37–45.

Sue, S., Zane, N., & Young, K. (1994). Research on psychotherapy with culturally diverse populations. In A. E. Bergin & S. L. Garfield (Eds.), *Handbook of psychotherapy and behavior change* (4th ed.). New York: John Wiley.

Suicide Awareness Voices of Education. (2007). *Someone you know is suicidal.* Retrieved April 12, 2007 from http://www.save.org/prevention/someone_you_know.html.

Suinn, R. M. (1984). *Fundamentals of abnormal psychology.* Chicago: Nelson-Hall.

Sullivan, G. M., & Coplan, J. D. (2000). Anxiety disorders: Biochemical aspects. In B. J. Sadock & V. A. Sadock (Eds.), *Kaplan and Sadock's comprehensive textbook of psychiatry,* (7th ed., Vol. 1). Philadelphia: Lippincott/Williams & Wilkins.

Sullivan, P. F., Neale, M. C., & Kendler, K. S. (2000). Genetic epidemiology of major depression: Review and meta-analysis. *American Journal of Psychiatry, 157*, 1552–1562.

Sullivan, P. F., Owen, M. J., O'Donovan, M. C., & Freedman, R. (2006). Genetics. In J. A. Lieberman, T. S. Stroup, & D. O. Perkins (Eds.), *Textbook of schizophrenia.* Washington, DC: American Psychiatric Publishing.

Sulloway, F. J. (1991). Reassessing Freud's case histories: The social construction of psychoanalysis. *ISIS, 82*, 245–275.

Sulloway, F. J. (1995). Birth order and evolutionary psychology: A meta-analytic overview. *Psychological Inquiry, 6*, 75–80.

Sulloway, F. J. (1996). *Born to rebel: Birth order, family dynamics, and creative lives.* New York: Pantheon Books.

Sullum, J., Clark, M. M., & King, T. K. (2000). Predictors of exercise relapse in a college population. *Journal of American College Health, 48*, 175–180.

Suls, J., & Bunde, J. (2005). Anger, anxiety, and depression as risk factors for cardiovascular disease: The problems and implications of overlapping affective dispositions. *Psychological Bulletin, 131*, 260–300.

Suls, J., & Rothman, A. (2004). Evolution of the biopsychosocial model: Prospects and challenges for health psychology. *Health Psychology, 23*(2), 119–125.

Summers, G., & Feldman, N. S. (1984). Blaming the perpetrator: An attributional analysis of spouse abuse. *Journal of Social and Clinical Psychology, 2*, 339–347.

Super, D. E. (1957). *The psychology of careers.* New York: HarperCollins.

Super, D. E. (1985). Career and life development. In D. Brown & L. Brooks (Eds.), *Career choice and development.* San Francisco: Jossey-Bass.

Super, D. E. (1988). Vocational adjustment: Implementing a self-concept. *The Career Development Quarterly, 36*, 351–357.

Surra, C. A., Gray, C. R., Boettcher, T. M. J., Cottle, N. R., & West, A. R. (2006). From courtship to universal properties: Research on dating and mate selection, 1950 to 2003. In A. L. Vangelisti & D. Perlman (Eds.), *The Cambridge handbook of personal relationships.* New York: Cambridge University Press.

Susman, E. J., Dorn, L. D., & Schiefelbein, V. L. (2003). Puberty, sexuality, and health. In R. M. Lerner, M.A. Easterbrooks, & J. Mistry (Eds.), *Handbook of psychology: Vol. 6. Developmental psychology.* New York: Wiley.

Susser, E., Neugebauer, R., Hoek, H. W., Brown, A. S., Lin, S., Labovitz, D., & Gorman, J. M. (1996). Schizophrenia after prenatal famine: Further evidence. *Archives of General Psychiatry, 53*, 25–31.

Sutherland, V. J. (2000). Understimulation/boredom. In G. Fink (Ed.), *Encyclopedia of stress* (Vol. 3). San Diego: Academic Press.

Swan, G. E., Hudmon, K. S., & Khroyan, T. V. (2003). Tobacco dependence. In A. M. Nezu, C. M. Nezu , & P. A. Geller (Eds.), *Handbook of psychology: Vol. 9. Health psychology.* New York: Wiley.

Swan, S. C., & Snow, D. L. (2006). The development of a theory of women's use of violence in intimate relationships. *Violence Against Women, 12*, 1026–1045.

Swanger, N. (2006). Visible body modification (VBM): Evidence from human resource managers and recruiters and the effects on employment. *International Journal of Hospitality Management, 25*(1), 154–158.

Swann, W. B., Rentfrow, P. J., & Guinn, J. S. (2003). Self-verification: The search for coherence. In M. R. Leary & J. P. Tangney (Eds.), *Handbook of self and identity.* New York: Guilford.

Swann, W. B., Stein-Seroussi, A., & Giesler, R. B. (1992). Why people self-verify. *Journal of Personality and Social Psychology, 62*, 392–401.

Swann, W. B., Stein-Seroussi, A., & McNulty, S. E. (1992). Outcasts in a white-lie society: The enigmatic worlds of people with negative self-conceptions. *Journal of Personality and Social Psychology, 62*, 618–624.

Swanson, J. L., & D'Achiardi, C. (2005). Beyond interests, needs/values, and abilities: Assessing other important career constructs over the life span. In S. D. Brown & R. W. Lent (Eds.), *Career development and counseling: Putting theory and research to work.* New York: Wiley.

Swap, W. C. (1977). Interpersonal attraction and repeated exposure to rewarders and punishers. *Personality and Social Psychology Bulletin, 3,* 248–251.

Swim, J. K., Aikin, K. J., Hall, W. S., & Hunter, B. A. (1995). Sexism and racism: Old-fashioned and modern prejudices. *Journal of Personality and Social Psychology, 68,* 199–214.

Sygnatur, E. F., & Toscano, G. A. (2000, Spring). Work-related homicides: The facts. *Compensation and Working Conditions,* 3–8.

Szasz, T. S. (1974). *The myth of mental illness.* New York: HarperCollins.

Szasz, T. S. (1993). *A lexicon of lunacy: Metaphoric malady, moral responsibility, and psychiatry.* New Brunswick, NJ: Transaction.

Szmukler, G. I., & Patton, G. (1995). Sociocultural models of eating disorders. In G. Szmukler, C. Dare, & J. Treasure (Eds.), *Handbook of eating disorders: Theory, treatment and research.* New York: Wiley.

Tajfel, H. (1982). *Social identity and intergroup relations.* London: Cambridge University Press.

Takanishi, R. (1993). The opportunities of adolescence—Research, interventions, and policy. *American Psychologist, 48,* 85–87.

Tamminga, C. A., & Carlsson, A. (2003). Psychiatric pathophysiology: Schizophrenia. In A. Tasman, J. Kay, & J. A. Lieberman (Eds.), *Psychiatry.* New York: Wiley.

Tang, M. (2002). A comparison of Asian American, Caucasian American, and Chinese college students: An initial report. *Journal of Multicultural Counseling and Development, 30*(2), 124–134.

Tannen, D. (1990). *You just don't understand: Women and men in conversation.* New York: Ballantine.

Tannen, D. (1998). *The argument culture: Moving from debate to dialogue.* New York: Random House.

Tanner, J. M. (1990). *Fetus into man: Physical growth from conception to maturity.* Cambridge, MA: Harvard University Press.

Tashiro, T., Frazier, P., & Berman, M. (2006). Stress-related growth following divorce and relationship dissolution. In M. A. Fine & J. H. Harvey (Eds.), *Handbook of divorce and relationship resolution.* Mahwah, NJ: Erlbaum.

Tasker, F. (2005). Lesbian mothers, gay fathers, and their children: A review. *Journal of Developmental & Behavioral Pediatrics, 26,* 224–240.

Tavris, C. (1982). *Anger: The misunderstood emotion.* New York: Simon & Schuster.

Tavris, C. (1989). *Anger: The misunderstood emotion* (2nd ed.). New York: Simon & Schuster.

Taylor, D. A., & Altman, I. (1987). Communication in interpersonal relationships: Social penetration processes. In M. E. Roloff & G. R. Miller (Eds.), *Interpersonal processes: New directions in communication research.* Newbury Park, CA: Sage.

Taylor, E. (2001). Positive psychology and humanistic psychology: A reply to Seligman. *Journal of Humanistic Psychology, 41*(1), 13–29.

Taylor, L. D. (2005). Effects of visual and verbal sexual television content and perceived realism on attitudes and beliefs. *Journal of Sex Research, 42*(2), 130–137.

Taylor, M. C. (1995). White backlash to workplace affirmative action: Peril or myth? *Social Forces, 73,* 1385–1414.

Taylor, R. J., Chatters, L. M., Tucker, M. B., & Lewis, E. (1990). Developments in research on black families: A decade review. *Journal of Marriage and the Family, 52,* 993–1014.

Taylor, S. (2004). Amnesia, folklore and folks: Recovered memories in clinical practice. *Cognitive Behaviour Therapy, 33*(2), 105–108.

Taylor, S. E. (1981a). A categorization approach to stereotyping. In D. H. Hamilton (Ed.), *Cognitive processes in stereotyping and intergroup relations.* Hillsdale, NJ: Erlbaum.

Taylor, S. E. (1981b). The interface of cognitive and social psychology. In J. Harvey (Ed.), *Cognition, social behavior, and the environment.* Hillsdale, NJ: Erlbaum.

Taylor, S. E. (2006). Tend and befriend: Biobehavioral bases of affiliation under stress. *Current Directions in Psychological Science, 15*(6), 273–277.

Taylor, S. E. (2007). Social support. In H. S. Friedman & R. C. Silver (Eds.), *Foundations of health psychology.* New York: Oxford University Press.

Taylor, S. E., & Brown, J. D. (1988). Illusion and well-being: A social psychological perspective on mental health. *Psychological Bulletin, 103,* 193–210.

Taylor, S. E., & Brown, J. D. (1994). Positive illusions and well-being revisited: Separating fact from fiction. *Psychological Bulletin, 116,* 21–27.

Taylor, S. E., Klein, L. C., Lewis, B. P., Gruenewald, T. L., Gurung, R. A. R., & Updegraff, J. A. (2000). Biobehavioral responses to stress in females: Tend-and-befriend, not fight-or-flight. *Psychological Review, 107*(3), 411–429.

Taylor, S. E., Lerner, J. S., Sherman, D. K., Sage, R. M., & McDowell, N. K. (2003). Are self-enhancing cognitions associated with healthy or unhealthy biological profiles? *Journal of Personality and Social Psychology, 85*(4), 605–615.

Taylor, S. E., Sherman, D. K., Kim, H. S., Jarcho, J., Takagi, K., & Dunagan, M. S. (2004). Culture and social support: Who seeks it and why? *Journal of Personality, 87,* 354–362.

Teachman, J. D. (2003). Premarital sex, premarital cohabitation, and the risk of subsequent marital dissolution among women. *Journal of Marriage and Family, 65,* 444–445.

Teachman, J. D., Polonko, K. A., & Scanzoni, J. (1999). Demography and families. In M. B. Sussman, S. K. Steinmetz, & G. W. Peterson (Eds.), *Handbook of marriage and the family.* New York: Plenum.

Teachman, J. D., Tedrow, L. M., & Crowder, K. D. (2001). The changing demography of America's families. In R. M. Milardo (Ed.), *Understanding families into the new millennium: A decade in review.* Minneapolis: National Council on Family Relations.

Teachman, J., Tedrow, L., & Hall, M. (2006). The demographic future of divorce and dissolution. In M. A. Fine & J. H. Harvey (Eds.), *Handbook of divorce and relationship resolution.* Mahwah, NJ: Erlbaum.

Tedeschi, R. G., & Calhoun, L. G. (1996). The traumatic growth inventory: Measuring the positive legacy of trauma. *Journal of Traumatic Stress, 9,* 455–471.

Tedeschi, R. G., & Calhoun, L. G. (2004). Posttraumatic growth: Conceptual foundations and empirical evidence. *Psychological Inquiry, 15*(1), 1–18.

Tellegen, A., Lykken, D. T., Bouchard, T. J., Jr., Wilcox, K. J., Segal, N. L., & Rich, S. (1988). Personality similarity in twins reared apart and together. *Journal of Personality and Social Psychology, 54,* 1031–1039.

Tennen, H., & Affleck, G. (2002). Benefit-finding and benefit-reminding. In C. R. Synder & S. J. Lopez (Eds.), *Handbook of positive psychology.* New York: Oxford University Press.

Tennen, H., & Affleck, G. (2005). Benefit-finding and benefit-reminding. In C. R. Snyder & S. J. Lopez (Eds.), *Handbook of positive psychology.* New York: Oxford University Press.

Terracciano, A., Abdel-Khalak, A. M., Adam, N., Adamovova, L., Ahn, C., Ahn, H., & et al. (2005). National character does not reflect mean personality trait levels in 49 cultures. *Science, 310,* 96–100.

Terracciano, A., Costa, P. T., & McCrae, R. R. (2006). Personality plasticity after age 30. *Personality and Social Psychology Bulletin, 32,* 999–1009.

Tesch, S. A., & Whitbourne, S. K. (1982). Intimacy and identity status in young adults. *Journal of Personality and Social Psychology, 43,* 1041–1051.

Tesser, A. (2001). Self-esteem. In A. Tesser & N. Schwarz (Eds.), *Blackwell handbook of social psychology: Intraindividual processes.* Malden, MA: Blackwell.

Testa, K. (1996). Church to pay $1 million in false-memory case. *San Jose Mercury News,* 8A.

Thase, M. E., Jindal, R., & Howland, R. H. (2002). Biological aspects of depression. In I. H. Gotlib & C. L. Hammen (Eds.), *Handbook of depression.* New York: Guilford.

Theisen, T. (2002, March 17). Too many are lying to get the job. *Atlanta Journal-Constitution,* p. R5.

Thibaut, J. W., & Kelley, H. H. (1959). *The social psychology of groups.* New York: Wiley.

Thomas, A. J., Kalaria, R. N., & O'Brien, J. T. (2004). Depression and vascular disease: What is the relationship? *Journal of Affective Disorders, 79*(1–3), 81–95.

Thomas, K. M. (2005). *Diversity dynamics in the workplace.* Belmont, CA: Wadsworth.

Thompkins, C. D., & Rando, R. A. (2003). Gender role conflict and shame in college men. *Psychology of Men and Masculinity, 4*(1), 79–81.

Thompson, J. K., & Kinder, B. (2003). Eating disorders. In M. Hersen & S. Turner (Eds.), *Handbook of adult psychopathology.* New York: Plenum Press.

Thompson, J. K., & Stice, E. (2001). Thin-ideal internalization: Mounting evidence for a new risk factor for body-image disturbance and eating pathology. *Current Directions in Psychological Science, 10*(5), 181–183.

Thompson, T., & Massat, C. R. (2005). Experiences of violence, post-traumatic stress, academic achievement and behavior problems of urban African-American children. *Child and Adolescent Social Work Journal, 22,* 367–393.

Thompson, T. L., & Zerbinos, E. (1995). Gender roles in animated cartoons: Has the picture changed in 20 years? *Sex Roles, 32,* 651–673.

Thornton, A., & Young-DeMarco, L. (2001). Four decades of trends in attitudes toward family issues in the United States: The 1960s through the 1990s. *Journal of Marriage and Family, 63,* 1009–1037.

Thorson, J. A., & Powell, F. C. (2000). Death anxiety in younger and older adults. In A. Tomer (Ed.), *Death attitudes and the older adult: Theories, concepts, and applications.* Philadelphia: Brunner-Routledge.

Thune, I., & Furberg, A. (2001). Physical activity and cancer risk: Dose-response and cancer, all sites and site specific. *Medicine and Science in Sports and Exercise, 33*(6), S530–S550.

Tibbo, P., Hanstock, C., Valiakalayil, A., & Allen, P. (2004). 3-T proton MRS investigation and glutamine in adolescents at high genetic risk for schizophrenia. *American Journal of Psychiatry, 161,* 1116–1118.

Tice, D. M., & Baumeister, R. F. (1997). Longitudinal study of procrastination, performance, stress, and health: The cost and benefits of dawdling. *Psychological Science, 8,* 454–458.

Tice, D. M., Bratslavsky, E., & Baumeister, R. F. (2001). Emotional distress regulation takes precedence over impulse control: If you feel bad, do it! *Journal of Personality and Social Psychology, 80*(1), 53–67.

Tice, D. M., Butler, J. L., Muraven M. B., & Stillwell A. M. (1995). When modesty prevails: Differential favorability of self-presentation to friends and strangers. *Journal of Personality and Social Psychology, 69,* 1120–1138.

Tice, D. M., & Wallace, H. M. (2003). The reflected self: Creating yourself as (you think) others see you. In M. R. Leary & J. P. Tangney (Eds.), *Handbook of self and identity.* New York: Guilford.

Tigner, R. B. (1999). Putting memory research to good use: Hints from cognitive psychology. *College Teaching, 47*(4), 149–151.

Titsworth, B. S., & Kiewra, K. A. (2004). Spoken organizational lecture cues and student notetaking as facilitators of student learning. *Contemporary Educational Psychology, 29,* 447–461.

Tjaden, P., & Thoennes, N. (2000). Prevalence and consequences of male-to-female and female-to-male intimate partner violence as measured by the National Violence Against Women Survey. *Violence Against Women, 6,* 142–161.

Toffler, A. (1970). *Future shock.* New York: Random House.

Toffler, A. (1980). *The third wave.* New York: Bantam Books.

Tolin, D. F., & Foa, E. B. (2006). Sex differences in trauma and posttraumatic stress disorder: A quantitative review of 25 years of research. *Psychological Bulletin, 132,* 959–992.

Tolman, D. L. (2002). *Dilemmas of desire: Teenage girls talk about sexuality.* Cambridge, MA: Harvard University Press.

Toomey, R., Kremen, W. S., Simpson, J. C., Samson, J. A., Seidman, L. J., Lyons, M. J., Faraone, S. V., & Tsuang, M. T. (1997). Revisiting the factor structure for positive and negative symptoms: Evidence from a large heterogeneous group of psychiatric patients. *American Journal of Psychology, 154,* 371–377.

Torres, A. R., Prince, M. J., Bebbington, P. E., Bhugra, D., Brugha, T. S., Farrell, M., Jenkins, R., Lewis, G., Meltzer, H., & Singleton, N. (2006). Obsessive-compulsive disorder: Prevalence, comorbidity, impact, and help-seeking in the British national psychiatric morbidity survey of 2000. *American Journal of Psychiatry, 163,* 1978–1985.

Torrey, E. F. (1992). *Freudian fraud: The malignant effect of Freud's theory on American thought and culture.* New York: Harper Perennial.

Torrey, E. F., Bowler, A. E., Taylor, E. H., & Gottesman, I. I. (1994). *Schizophrenia and manic-depressive disorder.* New York: Basic Books.

Toufexis, A. (1990, December 17). Drowsy America. *Time,* pp. 78–85.

Tozzi, F., Thornton, L. M., Klump, K. L., Fichter, M. M., Halmi, K. A., Kaplan, A. S., Strober, M., Woodside, D. B., Crow, S., Mitchell, J., Rotondo, A., Mauri, M., Cassano, G., Keel, P., Plotnicov, K. H., Pollice, C., Lilenfeld, L. R., Berrettini, W. H., Bulik, C. M., & Kaye, W. H. (2005). Symptom fluctuation in eating disorders: Correlates of diagnostic crossover. *American Journal of Psychiatry, 162,* 732–740.

Trachtenberg, J. D., & Sande, M. A. (2002). Emerging resistance to nonnucleoside reverse transcriptase inhibitors: A warning and a challenge. *Journal of the American Medical Association, 288*(2), 239–241.

Travis, F. (2001). Autonomic and EEG patterns distinguish transcending from other experiences during Transcendental Meditation practice. *International Journal of Psychophysiology, 42,* 1–9.

Travis, L. A., Bliwise, N. G., Binder, J. L., & Horne-Moyer, H. L. (2001). Changes in clients' attachment style over the course of time-limited dynamic psychotherapy. *Psychotherapy: Theory, Research, Practice, Training, 38*(2), 149–159.

Treas, J., & Lawton, L. (1999). Family relations in adulthood. In M. B. Sussman, S. K. Steinmetz, & G. W. Peterson (Eds.), *Handbook of marriage and the family.* New York: Plenum Press.

Triandis, H. C. (1994). *Culture and social behavior.* New York: McGraw-Hill.

Triandis, H. C. (2001). Individualism-collectivism and personality. *Journal of Personality, 69*(6), 907–924.

Trope, Y. (1983). Self-assessment in achievement behavior. In J. Suls & A. Greenwald (Eds.), *Psychological perspectives* (Vol. 2). Hillsdale, NJ: Erlbaum.

Trope, Y. (1986). Self-enhancement and self-assessment in achievement behavior. In R. Sorrentino & E. T. Higgins (Eds.), *Handbook of motivation and cognition* (Vol. 2). New York: Guilford Press.

Trope, Y., & Gaunt, R. (2003). Attribution and person perception. In M. A. Hogg & J. Cooper (Eds.), *The Sage handbook of social psychology.* Thousand Oaks, CA: Sage Publications.

Troy, A. B., Lewis-Smith, J., & Laurenceau, J. (2006). Interracial and intraracial romantic relationships: The search for differences in satisfaction, conflict, and attachment style. *Journal of Social & Personal Relationships, 23,* 65–80.

Trussell, J. (2004). Contraceptive efficacy. In R. A. Hatcher, J. Trussell, F. H. Stewart, A. L. Nelson, W. Cates Jr., F. Guest, & D. Kowal *Contraceptive technology.* New York: Ardent Media.

Trussell, J., Brown, S., & Hogue, C. (2004). Adolescent sexual behavior, pregnancy, and childbearing. In R. A. Hatcher, J. Trussell, F. H. Stewart, A. L. Nelson, W. Cates Jr., F. Guest, & D. Kowal (Eds.), *Contraceptive technology.* New York: Ardent Media.

Trzesniewski, K. H., Donnellan, M. B., & Robins, R. W. (2003). Stability of self-esteem across the life

span. *Journal of Personality and Social Psychology, 84*(1), 205–220.

Tsai, M., & Uemera, A. (1988). Asian Americans: The struggles, the conflicts, and the successes. In P. Bronstein & K. Quina (Eds.), *Teaching a psychology of people.* Washington, DC: American Psychological Association.

Tsuang, M. T., Glatt, S. J., & Faraone, S. V. (2003). Genetics and genomics in schizophrenia. *Primary Psychiatry, 10*(3), 37–40, 50.

Tugade, M. M., & Fredrickson, B. L. (2004). Resilient individuals use positive emotions to bounce back from negative emotional experiences. *Journal of Personality and Social Psychology, 86*(2), 320–333.

Turkheimer, E., & Waldron, M. (2000). Nonshared environment: A theoretical, methodological, and quantitative review. *Psychological Bulletin, 126,* 78–108.

Turner, J. C. (1987). *Rediscovering the social group: A self-categorization theory.* Oxford, England: Basil Blackwell.

Turner, J. C., & Reynolds, K. J. (2004). The social identity perspective in intergroup relations: Theories, themes, and controversies. In M. B. Brewer & M. Hewstone (Eds.), *Self and social identity.* Malden, MA: Blackwell.

Turner, J. R., & Wheaton, B. (1995). Checklist measurement of stressful life events. In S. Cohen, R. C. Kessler, & L. U. Gordon (Eds.), *Measuring stress: A guide for health and social scientists.* New York: Oxford University Press.

Turner, S. M., Beidel, D. C., Stanley, M. A., & Heiser, N. (2001). Obsessive-compulsive disorder. In P. B. Sutker & H. E. Adams (Eds.), *Comprehensive textbook of psychiatry* (3rd ed.). New York: Kluwer Academic/Plenum.

Turner-Bowker, D. M. (2001). How can you pull yourself up by your bootstraps if you don't have boots? Work appropriate clothing for women. *Journal of Social Issues, 57,* 311–322.

Twenge, J. M. (2000). The age of anxiety? Birth cohort change in anxiety and neuroticism, 1952–1993. *Journal of Personality and Social Psychology, 79*(6), 1007–1021.

Twenge, J. M., & Campbell W. K. (2003). Isn't it fun to get the respect that we're going to deserve? Narcissism, social rejection, and aggression. *Personality and Social Psychology, 29*(2), 261–272.

Twenge, J. M., Campbell, W. K., & Foster, C. A. (2003). Parenthood and marital satisfaction: A meta-analytic review. *Journal of Marriage and Family, 65,* 574–83.

Twenge, J. M., & Crocker, J. (2002). Race and self-esteem: Meta-analyses comparing whites, blacks, Hispanics, Asians, and American Indians and comment on Gray-Little and Hafdahl (2000). *Psychological Bulletin, 128*(3), 371–408.

Uchino, B. N., Cacioppo, J. T., & Kiecolt-Glaser, J. K. (1996). The relationship between social support and physiological processes: A review with emphasis on underlying mechanisms and implications for health. *Psychological Bulletin, 119,* 488–531.

Uhlmann, E., & Swanson, J. (2004). Exposure to violent video games increases automatic aggressiveness. *Journal of Adolescence, 27,* 41–52.

Uleman, J. S., Hon, A., Roman, R. J., & Moskowitz, G. B. (1996). Online evidence for spontaneous trait inferences at encoding. *Personality and Psychology Bulletin, 22*(4), 377–394.

Ullman, S. E. (2004). Sexual assault victimization and suicidal behavior in women: A review of the literature. *Aggression and Violent Behavior, 9*(4), 331–351.

Ulrich, M., & Weatherall, A. (2000). Motherhood and infertility: Viewing motherhood through the lens of infertility. *Feminism & Psychology, 10,* 323–336.

Umberson, D., Wortman, C. B., & Kessler, R. C. (1992). Widowhood and depression: Explaining long-term gender differences in vulnerability. *Journal of Health and Social Behavior, 33,* 10–24.

Unger, R. (2006). Untangling the web: Threat, ideology, and political behavior. In P. R. Kimmel & C. E. Stout (Eds.), *Collateral damage: The psychological consequences of America's war on terrorism.* Westport, CT: Praeger.

Ursano, R. J., Fullerton, C. S., Vance, K., & Kao, T. C. (1999). Posttraumatic stress disorder and identification in disaster workers. *American Journal of Psychiatry, 156,* 353–359.

Ursano, R. J., & Silberman, E. K. (2003). Psychoanalysis, psychoanalytic psychotherapy, and supportive psychotherapy. In R. E. Hales & S. C. Yudofsky (Eds.), *Textbook of clinical psychiatry.* Washington, DC: American Psychiatric Publishing.

U.S. Bureau of Labor Statistics. (1998). *Occupational outlook handbook: 1998–1999.* Washington, DC: U.S. Government Printing Office.

U.S. Bureau of Labor Statistics. (2003). Highlight of women's earnings in 2002. Retrieved December 12, 2004 from http://www.bls.gov/cps/cpswom2002.pdf.

U.S. Bureau of Labor Statistics. (2004). *Occupational outlook handbook: 2004–2005.* Washington, DC: U.S. Government Printing Office.

U.S. Bureau of Labor Statistics. (2005). *Workers on flexible and shift schedules in 2004 summary.* Retrieved June 4, 2007 from http://www.bls.gov/news.release/flex.nr0.htm.

U.S. Bureau of Labor Statistics. (2006). *Occupational outlook handbook, 2006–2007 edition.* Washington, D.C.: U. S. Government Printing Office.

U.S. Bureau of Labor Statistics. (2007). *Employment characteristics of families in 2006.* Washington, D.C: Department of Labor.

U.S. Bureau of the Census. (2000). *Statistical abstract of the United States: 2000.* Washington, DC: U.S. Government Printing Office.

U.S. Bureau of the Census. (2003). *Statistical abstract of the United States: 2003.* Washington, DC: U.S. Government Printing Office.

U.S. Bureau of the Census. (2004a). *Statistical abstract of the United States: 2004–2005.* Washington, DC: U.S. Government Printing Office.

U.S. Bureau of the Census. (2004b). *America's families and living arrangements: 2003.* Washington, DC: U.S. Government Printing Office.

U.S. Bureau of the Census. (2005). *Occupation by sex and median earnings in the past 12 months.* Retrieved May 7, 2007 from http://factfinder.census.gov.servlet/STTable?_bm=y&-geo.

U.S. Bureau of the Census. (2006a). *Americans marrying older, living alone more, see households shrinking, Census Bureau reports* (CB06-83). Retrieved May 15, 2007 from http://www.census.gov/Press-Release/www/releases/archives/families_households/006840.html.

U.S. Bureau of the Census. (2006b). *Statistical abstract of the United States: 2007.* Washington, DC: U.S. Government Printing Office.

U.S. Department of Health and Human Services. (1990). *The health benefits of smoking cessation: A report of the surgeon general.* Washington, DC: U.S. Government Printing Office.

U.S. Department of Health and Human Services. (1995). *Healthy people 2000 review, 1994.* Washington, DC: U.S. Government Printing Office.

U.S. Department of Health and Human Services. (1999). *Mental health: A report of the Surgeon General.* Washington, DC: U.S. Government Printing Office.

U.S. Department of Health and Human Services. (2002, June 10). Preventing teenage pregnancy. Retrieved January 30, 2005 From http://www.Hhs.Gov/News/Press/2002pres/Teenpreg.html.

U.S. Department of Health and Human Services. (2003). *Profile of older Americans: 2003.* Washington, DC: U.S. Government Printing Office.

U.S. Department of Health and Human Services. (2006a). Trends in sexual risk behaviors among high school students--United States, 1991–2005. *Morbidity and Mortality Weekly Report, 55,* 851–854.

U.S. Department of Health and Human Services. (2006b). Youth risk behavior surveillance—United States, 2006. *Morbidity and Mortality Weekly Report, 55*(SS-5), 1–112.

U.S. Department of Health and Human Services. (2007). *Impacts of four Title V, Section 510 abstinence education programs, final report.* Retrieved June 16, 2007 from http://aspe.hhs.gov/hsp/abstinence07/index.htm.

U.S. Department of Justice. (2003). *Crime in the United States— 2003: Uniform crime reports.* Washington, DC: U.S. Government Printing Office.

U.S. Department of Justice. (2007). *Criminal offenders statistics.* Retrieved April 22, 2007 from http://www.ojp.usdoj.gov/bjs/crimoff.htm.

U.S. Department of Labor. (1992). *Pipelines of progress: An update on the glass ceiling initiative.* Washington, DC: U.S. Government Printing Office.

U.S. Department of Labor. (2000, Summer). Futurework: Trends and challenges for work in the 21st century. *Occupational Outlook Quarterly,* pp. 31–36.

U.S. Department of Labor. (2003). *Facts on women workers.* Washington, DC: U.S. Government Printing Office.

U.S. Department of Labor. (2006). High-paying occupations with many job openings, projected 2004–14. *Occupational Outlook Quarterly* (Spring), p. 56.

U.S. Equal Employment Opportunity Commission. (2007). *Occupational employment in private industry by race/ethnic group/sex, and by industry, United States, 2005.* Retrieved June 4, 2007 from http://www.eeoc.gov/stats/jobpat/2005/national.html.

U.S. General Accounting Office. (2003). *Women's earnings: Work patterns partially explain difference between men's and women's earnings.* Washington, DC: General Accounting Office.

U.S. Small Business Administration. (2006). *Women in business, 2006: A demographic review of women's business ownership.* Retrieved June 4, 2007 from http://www.sba.gov/advo/research/rs280tot.pdf.

Vaillant, G. E. (2000). Adaptive mental mechanisms: Their role in a positive psychology. *American Psychologist, 55*(1), 89–98.

Valent, P. (2000). Disaster syndrome. In G. Fink (Ed.), *Encyclopedia of stress* (Vol. 1). San Diego: Academic Press.

Vallone, R. P., Ross, L., & Lepper, M. R. (1985). The hostile media phenomenon: Biased perception and perceptions of bias in coverage of the Beirut massacre. *Journal of Personality and Social Psychology, 50,* 482–491.

Van Boven, L. (2005). Experientialism, materialism, and the pursuit of happiness. *Review of General Psychology, 9*(2), 132–142.

Vandenberg, S. G. (1987). Sex differences in mental retardation and their implications for sex differences in ability. In J. M. Reinisch, L. A. Rosenblum, & S. A. Sanders (Eds.), *Masculinity/Femininity: Basic perspectives.* New York: Oxford University Press.

Vandereycken, W. (2002). History of anorexia nervosa and bulimia nervosa. In C. G. Fairburn & K. D. Brownell (Eds.), *Eating disorders and obesity.* New York: Guilford Press.

Vandewater, E. A., Bickham, D. S., Lee, J. H., Cummings, H. M., Wartella, E. A., & Rideout, V. J. (2005). When the television is always on. *American Behavioral Scientist, 48,* 562–577.

van Griensven, F., Chakkraband, M. L. S., Thienkrua, W., Pengjuntr, W., Cardozo, B. L., Tantipiwatanaskul, P., & et al. (2007). Mental health problems among adults in tsunami-affected areas in Southern Thailand. *JAMA, 296,* 537–548.

van Kammen, D. P., & Marder, S. R. (2005). Serotonin-dopamine antagonists (atypical or second-generation antipsychotics). In B. J. Sadock & V. A. Sadock (Eds.), *Kaplan and Sadock's comprehensive textbook of psychiatry.* Philadelphia: Lippincott Williams & Wilkins.

van Wel, F., Linssen, H., & Abma, R. (2000). The parental bond and the well-being of adolescents and young adults. *Journal of Youth and Adolescence, 29,* 307–318.

Vartanian, L. R., Giant, C. L., & Passino, R. M. (2001). "Ally McBeal vs. Arnold Schwarzenegger": Comparing mass media, interpersonal feedback and gender as predictors of satisfaction with body thinness and masculinity. *Social Behavior and Personality, 29*(7), 711–723.

Vazire, S., & Gosling, S. D. (2004). e-Perceptions: Personality impressions based on personal websites. *Journal of Personality and Social Psychology, 87*(1), 123–132.

Veenhoven, R. (1993). *Happiness in nations.* Rotterdam, Netherlands: Risbo.

Veevers, J. E., Gee, E. M., & Wister, A. V. (1996). Homeleaving age norms: Conflict or consensus? *International Journal of Aging and Human Development, 43*(4), 277–295.

Vega, W. A., Kolody, B., Aguilar-Gaxiola, S., & Catalano, R. (1999). Gaps in service utilization by Mexican Americans with mental health problems. *American Journal of Psychiatry, 156,* 928–934.

Venturello, S., Barzega, G., Maina, G., & Bogetto, F. (2002). Premorbid conditions and precipitating events in early-onset panic disorder. *Comprehensive Psychiatry, 43,* 28–36.

Verderber, K. S., Verderber, R. F., & Berryman-Fink, C. (2007). *Inter-Act: Interpersonal communication concepts, skills, and contexts.* New York: Oxford University Press.

Verderber, R. F., & Verderber, K. S. (2004). *Inter-Act: Interpersonal communication concepts, skills, and contexts.* New York: Oxford University Press.

Verderber, R. F., Verderber, K. S., & Berryman-Fink, C. (2008). *Communicate.* Belmont, CA: Wadsworth.

Verona, E., & Curtin, J. J. (2006). Gender differences in the negative affective priming of aggressive behavior. *Emotion, 6*(1), 115–124.

Vgontzas, A. N., Bixler, E. O., & Kales, A. K. (2000). Sleep, sleep disorders, and stress. In G. Fink (Ed.), *Encyclopedia of stress* (Vol. 3, p. 449–457). San Diego: Academic Press.

Videbech, P. (2006). Hippocampus and unipolar depression. *Directions in Psychiatry, 26*(3), 183–194.

Videbech, P., & Ravnkilde, B. (2004). Hippocampal volume and depression: A meta-analysis of MRI studies. *American Journal of Psychiatry, 161,* 1957–1966.

Viglione, D. J., & Rivera, B. (2003). Assessing personality and psychopathology with projective methods. In J. R. Graham, & J. A. Naglieri (Eds.), *Handbook of psychology: Vol. 10. Assessment psychology.* New York: Wiley.

Vinogradov, S., Cox, P. D., & Yalom, I. D. (2003). Group therapy. In R. E. Hales & S. C. Yudofsky (Eds.), *Textbook of clinical psychiatry.* Washington, DC: American Psychiatric Publishing.

Vinokur, A. D., Price, R. H., & Caplan, R. D. (1996). Hard times and hurtful partners: How financial strain affects depression and relationship satisfaction of unemployed persons and their spouses. *Journal of Personality and Social Psychology, 71,* 166–179.

Vittengl, J. R., & Holt, C. S. (2000). Getting acquainted: The relationship of self-disclosure and social attraction to positive affect. *Journal of Social and Personal Relationships, 17*(1), 53–56.

Volavka, J., Czobor, P., Sheitman, B., Lindenmayer, J. P., Citrome, L., McEvoy, J. P., Cooper, T. B. , Chakos, M., & Lieberman, J. A. (2002). Clozapine, olanzapine, risperidone, haloperidol in the treatment of patients with chronic schizophrenia and schizoaffective disorder. *American Journal of Psychiatry, 159,* 255–262.

Vollmer, W. M., Sacks, F. M., Ard, J., Appel, L. J., Bray, G. A., Simons-Morton, D. G., & et al. (2001). Effects of diet and sodium intake on blood pressure: Subgroup analysis of the DASH-sodium trial. *Annals of Internal Medicine, 18,* 1019–1028.

Von Baeyer, C. L., Sherk, D. L., & Zanna, M. P. (1981). Impression management in the job interview: When the female applicant meets the male (chauvinist) interviewer. *Personality and Social Psychology Bulletin, 7,* 45–51.

Vonk, R. (1993). The negativity effect in trait rating and in open-ended descriptions of persons. *Personality and Social Psychology Bulletin, 19,* 269–278.

Vorauer, J. D., Cameron, J. J., Holmes, J. G., & Pearce, D. G. (2003). Invisible overtures: Fears of rejection and the signal amplification bias. *Journal of Personality and Social Psychology, 84*(4), 793–812.

Voydanoff, P. (2005). Consequences of boundary-spanning demands and resources for work-to-family conflict and perceived stress. *Journal of Occupational Health Psychology, 10,* 491–503.

Voydanoff, P., & Donnelly, B. W. (1999). Multiple roles and psychological distress: The intersection of the paid worker, spouse, and parent roles with the role of the adult child. *Journal of Marriage and the Family, 61,* 725–738.

Voyer, D., & Hou, J. (2006). Type of items and the magnitude of gender differences on the mental rotations test. *Candian Journal of Experimental Psychology, 60*(2), 91–100.

Vrugt, A., & Luyerink, M. (2000). The contribution of bodily posture to gender stereotypical impressions. *Social Behavior and Personality, 28*(1), 91–103.

Wachtel, P. L. (1989). *The poverty of affluence: A psychological portrait of the American way of life.* Philadelphia: New Society.

Wade, C., & Tavris, C. (1990). *Learning to think critically: A handbook to accompany psychology.* New York: HarperCollins.

Wade, P., & Bernstein, B. (1991). Culture sensitivity training and counselor's race: Effects on black female clients' perceptions and attrition. *Journal of Counseling Psychology, 38,* 9–15.

Wagner, D. M. (1998, Feb 1). Divorce reform: New directions. *Current,* pp. 7–10.

Waite, L. (2000). Trends in men's and women's well-being in marriage. In L. J. Waite (Ed.), *The ties that bind.* New York: Aldine de Gruyter.

Waite, L. J. (1995). Does marriage matter? *Demography, 32,* 483–507.

Waite, L., & Gallagher, M. (2000). *The case for marriage: Why married people are happier, healthier, and better off financially.* New York: Doubleday.

Wakabayashi, C., & Donato, K. M. (2006). Does caregiving increase poverty among women in later life? Evidence from health and retirement survey. *Journal of Health and Social Behavior, 47,* 258–274.

Wakefield, J. C. (1999). The measurement of mental disorder. In A. V. Horvitz & T. L. Scheid (Eds.), *A handbook for the study of mental health: Social contexts, theories, and systems.* New York: Cambridge University Press.

Wakefield, J. C., & Spitzer, R. L. (2002). Lowered estimates—but of what? *Archives of General Psychiatry, 59*(2), 129–130.

Waldrop, D., Lightsey, O. R., Ethington, C. A., Woemmel, C. A., & Coke, A. L. (2001). Self-efficacy, optimism, health competence, and recovery from orthopedic surgery. *Journal of Counseling Psychology, 48,* 233–238.

Walker, E., Kestler, L., Bollini, A., & Hochman, K. M. (2004). Schizophrenia: Etiology and course. *Annual Review of Psychology, 55,* 401–30.

Walker, K. (1994). Men, women, and friendship: What they say, what they do. *Gender & Society, 8,* 246–265.

Walker, L. S., Claar, R. L., & Garber, J. (2002). Social consequences of children's pain: When do they encourage symptoms of maintenance? *Journal of Pediatric Psychology, 27*(8), 689–698.

Wallace, H. M., Baumeister, R. F., & Vohs, K. D. (2005). Audience support and choking under pressure: A home disadvantage? *Journal of Sports Sciences, 23,* 429–438.

Waller, M. R., & McLanahan, S. S. (2005). "His" and "her" marriage expectations: Determinants and consequences. *Journal of Marriage and Family, 67,* 53–67.

Wallerstein, J. S. (2005). Growing up in the divorced family. *Clinical Social Work Journal, 33,* 401–418.

Wallerstein, J. S., & Blakeslee, S. (1989). *Second chances: Men, women, and children a decade after divorce.* Boston: Houghton Mifflin.

Wallerstein, J. S., & Kelly, J. B. (1980). *Surviving the breakup: How children and parents cope with divorce.* New York: Basic Books.

Wallerstein, J. S., Lewis, J. M., & Blakeslee, S. (2000). *The unexpected legacy of divorce: A 25-year landmark study.* New York: Hyperion.

Wallis, C. (2003, December 15). Does kindergarten need cops? *Time,* pp. 52–53.

Wallis, C. (2004, March 22). The case for staying home. *Time,* pp. 51–59.

Walsh, B. T. (2003). Eating disorders. In A. Tasman, J. Kay, & J. A. Lieberman (Eds.), *Psychiatry.* New York: Wiley.

Walsh, F. (1999). Families in later life: Challenges and opportunities. In B. Carter & M. McGoldrick (Eds.), *The expanded family life cycle: Individual, family, and social perspectives* (3rd ed.). Boston: Allyn & Bacon.

Walsh, J. K., Dement, W. C., & Dinges, D. F. (2005). Sleep medicine, public safety, and public health. In M. H. Kryger, T. Roth, & W. C. Dement (Eds.), *Principles and practice of sleep medicine.* Philadelphia: Elsevier Saunders.

Walster, E., Aronson, E., Abrahams, D., & Rottman, L. (1966). Importance of physical attractiveness in dating behavior. *Journal of Personality and Social Psychology, 4,* 508–516.

Walter, C. A. (2000). The psychosocial meaning of menopause: Women's experiences. *Journal of Women and Aging, 12*(3–4), 117–131.

Wampold, B. E. (2001). *The great psychotherapy debate.* Mahwah, NJ: Erlbaum.

Wang, H., & Amato, P. R. (2000). Predictors of divorce adjustment: Stressors, resources, and definitions. *Journal of Marriage and the Family, 62,* 655–668.

Wang, P. S., Berglund, P., Olfson, M., Pincus, H. A., Wells, K. B., & Kessler, R. C. (2005). Failure and delay in initial treatment contact after first onset of mental disorders in the National Comorbidity Survey Replication. *Archives of General Psychiatry, 62,* 603–613.

Wang, P. S., Lane, M., Olfson, M., Pincus, H. A., Wells, K. B., & Kessler, R. C. (2005). Twelve-month use of mental health services in the United States: Results from the National Comorbidity Survey Replication. *Archives of General Psychiatry, 62,* 629–640.

Wannamethee, G., Shaper, A. G., & MacFarlane, P. W. (1993). Heart rate, physical activity, and mortality from cancer and other noncardiovascular disease. *American Journal of Epidemiology, 137,* 735–748.

Ward, A., & Brenner, L. (2006). Accentuate the negative: The positive effects of negative acknowledgement. *Psychological Science, 17,* 959–962.

Ward, C. N., & Lundberg-Love, P. K. (2006). Sexual abuse of women. In P. K. Lundberg-Love & S. L. Marmion (Eds.), *"Intimate" violence against women: When spouses, partners, or lovers attack.* Westport, CT: Praeger.

Wardle, J., Robb, K. A., Johnson, F., Griffith, J., et al. (2004). Socioeconomic variations in attitudes to eating and weight in female adolescents. *Health Psychology, 23,* 275–282.

Warner, L., Hatcher, R. A., & Steiner, M. J. (2004). Male condoms. In R. A. Hatcher, J. Trussell, F. H. Stewart, A. L. Nelson, W. Cates Jr., F. Guest, & D. Kowal (Eds.), *Contraceptive technology* (18th rev. ed.). New York: Ardent Media.

Warner-Schmidt, J. L., & Duman, R. S. (2006). Hippocampal neurogenesis: Opposing effects of stress and antidepressant treatment. *Hippocampus, 16,* 239–249.

Warr, P. (1999). Well-being and the workplace. In D. Kahneman, E. Diener, & N. Schwarz (Eds.), *Well-being: The foundations of hedonic psychology.* New York: Sage.

Warren, R. (2002). *The purpose driven life: What on Earth am I here for?* Grand Rapids, MI: Zondervan.

Waters, E., Merrick, S., Treboux, D., Crowell, J., & Albersheim, L. (2000). Attachment security in infancy and early adulthood: A twenty-year longitudinal study. *Child Development, 71*(3), 684–689.

Watkins, P. L., Ward, C. H., & Southard, D. R. (1992). The Type A belief system: Relationship to hostility, social support, and life stress. *Behavioral Medicine, 18,* 27–32.

Watson, D., & Clark, L. A. (1997). Extraversion and its positive emotional core. In R. Hogan, J. Johnson, & S. Briggs (Eds), *Handbook of personality psychology.* San Diego: Academic Press.

Watson, D., David, J. P., & Suls, J. (1999). Personality, affectivity, and coping. In C. R. Snyder (Ed.), *Coping: The psychology of what works.* New York: Oxford University Press.

Watson, D., Klohnen, E. C., Casillas, A., Nus Simms, E., Haig, J., & Berry, D. S. (2004). Match makers and deal breakers: Analyses of assortative mating in newlywed couples. *Journal of Personality, 72,* 1029–1068.

Watson, D., & Pennebaker, J. W. (1989). Health complaints, stress, and distress: Exploring the central role of negative affectivity. *Psychological Review, 96,* 234–254.

Watson, D., Suls, J., & Haig, J. (2002). Global self-esteem in relation to structural models of personality and affectivity. *Journal of Personality and Social Psychology, 83,* 185–197.

Watson, D. L., & Tharp, R. G. (2007). *Self-directed behavior: Self-modification for personal adjustment.* Belmont, CA: Wadsworth.

Watson, J. B. (1913). Psychology as the behaviorist views it. *Psychological Review, 20,* 158–177.

Weaver, A. D., & Byers, E. S. (2006). The relationships among body image, body mass index, exercise, and sexual functioning in heterosexual women. *Psychology of Women Quarterly, 30,* 333–339.

Weaver, M. F., & Schnoll, S. H. (1999). Stimulants: Amphetamines and cocaine. In B. S. McCrady & E. E. Epstein (Eds.), *Addictions: A comprehensive guidebook.* New York: Oxford University Press.

Weber, L. J. (2006). *Profits before people?* Bloomington, IN: Indiana University Press.

Webster, D. M. (1993). Motivated augmentation and reduction of the overattribution bias. *Journal of Personality and Social Psychology, 65,* 261–271.

Webster, D. M., Richter, L., & Kruglanski, A. W. (1996). On leaping to conclusions when feeling tired: Mental fatigue effects on impressional primacy. *Journal of Experimental Social Psychology, 32,* 181–195.

Wechsler, H., Lee, J. E., Kuo, M., Seibring, M., Nelson, T. F., & Lee, H. (2002). Trends in college binge drinking during a period of increased prevention efforts. *Journal of American College Health, 50*(5), 203–217.

Wegener, D. T., & Petty, R. E. (1994). Mood management across affective states: The hedonic contingency hypothesis. *Journal of Personality and Social Psychology, 66,* 1034–1048.

Weil, M. M., & Rosen, L. D. (1997). *TechnoStress: Coping with technology @ home @ work @ play.* New York: Wiley.

Weimer, B. L., Kerns, K. A., & Oldenburg, C. M. (2004). Adolescents' interactions with a best friend: Associations with attachment style. *Journal of Experimental Child Psychology, 88*(1), 102–120.

Weinberg, C. (1979). *Self-creation.* New York: Avon.

Weinberger, D. A. (1990). The construct validity of the repressive coping style. In J. L. Singer (Ed.), *Repression and dissociation.* Chicago: University of Chicago Press.

Weinberger, J. (1995). Common factors aren't so common: The common factors dilemma. *Clinical Psychology: Science and Practice, 2,* 45–69, 1915–1933.

Weiner, B. (1986). *An attribution theory of emotion and motivation.* New York: Springer-Verlag.

Weiner, B. (1994). Integrating social and personal theories of achievement striving. *Review of Educational Research, 64,* 557–573.

Weiner, B. (2006). *Social motivation, justice, and the moral emotions: An attributional approach.* Mahwah, NJ: Erlbaum.

Weinfield, N., Sroufe, L. A., & Egeland, B. (2000). Attachment from early infancy to early adulthood in a high-risk sample: Continuity, discontinuity, and their correlates. *Child Development, 71*(3), 695–702.

Weinstein, N. D. (1980). Unrealistic optimism about future life events. *Journal of Personality and Social Psychology, 39,* 806–820.

Weinstein, N. D. (1982). Unrealistic optimism about susceptibility to health problems. *Journal of Behavioral Medicine, 5,* 441–460.

Weinstein, N. D. (2003). Exploring the links between risk perceptions and preventive health behavior. In J. Suls & K. A. Wallston (Eds.), *Social psychological foundations of health and illness.* Malden, MA: Blackwell Publishing.

Weinstein, N. D., & Klein, W. M. (1996). Unrealistic optimism: Present and future. *Journal of Social and Clinical Psychology, 15*(1), 1–8.

Weinstein, N. D., Slovic, P., & Gibson, G. (2004). Accuracy and optimism in smokers' beliefs about quitting. *Nicotine & Tobacco Research, 6*(Suppl3), 375–380.

Weisaeth, L. (1993). Disasters: Psychological and psychiatric aspects. In L. Goldberger & S. Breznitz (Eds.), *Handbook of stress: Theoretical and clinical aspects* (2nd ed.). New York: Free Press.

Weisler, R. H., Barbee, J. G., & Townsend, M. H. (2007). Mental health and recovery in the Gulf Coast after Hurricanes Katrina and Rita. *JAMA, 296,* 585–588.

Weiss, E. M., Kemmler, G., Deisenhammer, E. A., Fleischhacker, W. W., & Delazer, M. (2003). Sex differences in cognitive functions. *Personality and Individual Differences, 35,* 863–875.

Weiss, R. (1973). *Loneliness: The experience of emotional and social isolation.* Cambridge, MA: MIT Press.

Weiss, R. S. (1975). *Marital separation.* New York: Basic Books.

Weisz, J. R., Rothbaum, F. M., & Blackburn, T. C. (1984). Standing out and standing in: The psychology of control in America and Japan. *American Psychologist, 39,* 955–969.

Weiten, W. (1988). Pressure as a form of stress and its relationship to psychological symptomatology. *Journal of Social and Clinical Psychology, 6,* 127–139.

Weiten, W. (1998). Pressure, major life events, and psychological symptoms. *Journal of Social Behavior and Personality, 13,* 51–68.

Weiten, W., Guadagno, R. E., & Beck, C. A. (1996). Students' perceptions of textbook pedagogical aids. *Teaching of Psychology, 23,* 105–107.

Weitzman, L. (1996). The economic consequences of divorce are still unequal: Comment on Peterson. *American Sociological Review, 61,* 537–538.

Wells, K., Klap, R., Koike, A., & Sherbourne, C. (2001). Ethnic disparities in unmet need for alcoholism, drug abuse, and mental health care. *American Journal of Psychiatry, 158,* 2027–2032.

Welsh, R. S. (2003). Prescription priveleges: Pro or con. *Clinical Psychology: Science & Practice, 10,* 371–372.

Wessely, S., & Kerwin, R. (2004). Suicide risk and the SSRI's. *Journal of the American Medical Association, 292*(3), 379–381.

Wesson, D. R., Smith, D. E., Ling, W., & Seymour, R. B. (2005). Sedatives–hypnotics. In J. H. Lowinson, P. Ruiz, R. B. Millman, & J. G. Langrod (Eds.), *Substance abuse: A comprehensive textbook.* Philadelphia: Lippincott/Williams & Wilkins.

West, D. S., Harvey-Berino, J., & Raczynski, J. M. (2004). Behavioral aspects of obesity, dietary intake, and chronic disease. In J. M. Raczynski & L. C. Leviton (Eds.), *Handbook of clinical health psychology: Vol. 2. Disorders of behavior and health.* Washington, DC: American Psychological Association.

Westefeld, J. S., Maples, M. R., Buford, B., & Taylor, S. (2001). Gay, lesbian, and bisexual college students: The relationship between sexual orientation and depression, loneliness and suicide. *Journal of College Student Psychotherapy, 15*(3), 71–82.

Westen, D. (1998). The scientific legacy of Sigmund Freud: Toward a psychodynamically informed psychological science. *Psychological Bulletin, 124*(3), 333–371.

Westen, D., & Gabbard, G. O. (1999). Psychoanalytic approaches to personality. In L. A. Pervin & O. P. John (Eds.), *Handbook of personality: Theory and research* (2nd ed.). New York: Guilford Press.

Wester, S. R., Pionke, D. R., & Vogel, D. L. (2005). Male gender role conflict, gay men, and same-sex romantic relationships. *Psychology of Men and Masculinity, 6*, 195–208.

Wester, S. R., Vogel, D. L., Wei, M., & McLain, R. (2006). African American men, gender role conflict, and psychological distress: The role of racial identity. *Journal of Counseling & Development, 84*, 419–429.

Wethington, E. (2002). The relationship of turning points at work to perceptions of psychological growth and change. In R. A. Settersten & T. J. Owens (Eds.), *New frontiers in socialization*. Amsterdam: JAI.

Wethington, E., Kessler, R., & Pixley, J. (2004). Turning points in adulthood. In O. G. Brim, C. D. Ryff, & R. Kessler (Eds.), *How healthy are we: A national study of well-being in midlife*. Chicago: University of Chicago Press.

Wheaton, B. (1994). Sampling the stress universe. In W. R. Avison & I. H. Gotlib (Eds.), *Stress and mental health: Contemporary issues and prospects for the future*. New York: Plenum Press.

Wheeler, L., Koestner, R., & Driver, R. (1982). Related attributes in the choice of comparison others: It's there, but it isn't all there is. *Journal of Experimental Social Psychology, 18*, 489–500.

Wheeler, L., & Suls, J. (2005). Social comparison and self-evaluations of competence. In A. J. Elliot & C. S. Dweck (Eds.), *Handbook of competence and motivation*. New York: Guilford.

Whipple, B. (2000). Beyond the G spot. *Scandinavian Journal of Sexology, 3*(2), 35–42.

Whiston, S. C., & Keller, B. K. (2004). The influences of the family of origin on career development: A review and analysis. *Counseling Psychologist, 32*(4), 493–568.

Whitaker, R. (2002). *Mad in America: Bad science, bad medicine, and the enduring mistreatment of the mentally ill*. New York: Perseus Publishing.

Whitbourne, S. K. (1996). *The aging individual: Physical and psychological perspectives*. New York: Springer.

Whitbourne, S. K. (2001). The physical aging process in midlife: Interactions with psychological and sociocultural factors. In M. E. Lachman (Ed.), *Handbook of midlife development*. New York: Wiley.

Whitbourne, S. K. (2002). *The aging individual: Physical and psychological perspectives*. New York: Springer.

Whitbourne, S. K., Zuschlag, M. K., Elliot, L. B., & Waterman, A. S. (1992). Psychosocial development in adulthood: A 22-year sequential study. *Journal of Personality and Social Psychology, 63*, 260–271.

White, L. K., & Edwards, J. N. (1990). Emptying the nest and parental well-being: An analysis of national panel data. *American Sociological Review, 55*(2), 235–242.

White, L. K., & Rogers, S. J. (1997). Strong support but uneasy relationships: Coresident and adult children's relationships with their parents. *Journal of Marriage and the Family, 59*, 62–76.

White, L. K., & Rogers, S. J. (2001). Economic circumstances and family outcomes: A review of the 1990s. In R. M. Milardo (Ed.), *Understanding families into the new millennium: A decade in review*. Minneapolis: National Council on Family Relations.

White, O. K. Jr., & White, D. (2005). Polygamy and Mormon identity. *Journal of American Culture, 28*, 165–177.

Whitehead, B. D., & Popenoe, D. (2001). *The state of our unions: The social health of marriage in America, 2001*. Piscataway, NJ: The National Marriage Project.

Whitehouse, W. G., & Dinges, D. F., Orne, E. C., & Orne, M. T. (1988). Hypnotic hyperamnesia: Enhanced memory accessibility or report bias? *Journal of Abnormal Psychology, 97*, 298–295.

Whiteman, S. D., McHale, S. M., & Crouter, A. C. (2003). What parents learn from experience: The first child as a first draft? *Journal of Marriage and Family, 65*, 608–621.

Whitley, B. E. (1999). Right-wing authoritarianism, social dominance orientation, and prejudice. *Journal of Personality and Social Psychology, 77*(1), 126–134.

Whitley, B. E. (2001). Gender-role variables and attitudes toward homosexuality. *Sex Roles, 45*, 691–721.

Whitley, B. E., & Kite, M. E. (2006). *The psychology of prejudice and discrimination*. Belmont, CA: Wadsworth.

Whitty, M. T. (2005). The realness of cybercheating: Men's and women's representations of unfaithful internet relationships. *Social Science Computer Review, 23*(1), 57–67.

Whybrow, P. C. (2005). *American mania: When more is not enough*. New York: Norton.

Wickrama, K. A. S., Lorenz, F. O., Conger, R. D., & Elder, G. H. (1997). Marital quality and physical illness: A latent growth curve analysis. *Journal of Marriage and Family, 59*, 143–155.

Widiger, T. A., & Sankis, L. M. (2000). Adult psychopathology: Issues and controversies. *Annual Review of Psychology, 51*, 377–404.

Widiger, T. A., & Simonsen, E. (2005). Introduction to the special section: The American psychiatric association's research agenda for the DSM-V. *Journal of Personality Disorders, 19*(2), 103–109.

Wiederman, M. W. (1993). Evolved gender differences in mate preferences: Evidence from personal advertisements. *Ethology and Sociobiology, 14*, 331–352.

Wiederman, M. W. (1997). Extramarital sex: Prevalence and correlates in a national survey. *Journal of Sex Research, 34*, 167–174.

Wiederman, M. W. (2004). Methodological issues in studying sexuality in close relationships. In J. H. Harvey, A. Wenzel, & S. Sprecher (Eds.), *The handbook of sexuality in close relationships*. Mahwah, NJ: Lawrence Erlbaum.

Wielawski, I. (1991, October 3). *Unlocking the secrets of memory*. Los Angeles Times, p. 1.

Wilfong, J. D. (2006). Computer anxiety and anger: The impact of computer use, computer experience, and self-efficacy beliefs. *Computers in Human Behavior, 22*, 1001–1011.

Wilgosh, L. (2001). Enhancing gifts and talents of women and girls. *High Ability Studies, 12*(1), 45–59.

Wilkaitis, J., Mulvhill, T., & Nasrallah, H. A. (2004). Classic antipsychotic medications. In A. F. Schatzberg & C. B. Nemeroff (Eds), *Textbook of psychopharmacology*. Washington, DC: American Psychiatric Publishing.

Willets, M. C., Sprecher, S., & Beck, F. D. (2004). Overview of sexual practices and attitudes within relationship contexts. In J. H. Harvey, A. Wenzel, & S. Sprecher (Eds.), *The handbook of sexuality in close relationships*. Mahwah, NJ: Lawrence Erlbaum.

Willett, W. C., & Stampfer, W. J. (2003). Rebuilding the food pyramid. *Scientific American, 288*(1), 64–71.

Williams, C. G., Gagne, M., Ryan, R. M., & Deci, E. L. (2002). Facilitating autonomous motivation for smoking cessation. *Health Psychology, 21*, 40–50.

Williams, C. L. (1998). The glass escalator: Hidden advantages for men in the female professions. In M. S. Kimmel & M. A. Messner (Eds.), *Men's lives*. Boston: Allyn & Bacon.

Williams, J. E., & Best, D. L. (1982). *Measuring sex stereotypes: A thirty-nation study*. Newbury Park, CA: Sage.

Williams, J. E., & Best, D. L. (1990). *Measuring sex stereotypes: A multination study* (Rev. ed.). Newbury Park, CA: Sage Publications.

Williams, J. E., Paton, C. C., Siegler, I. C., Eigenbrodt, M. L., Neito, F. J., & Tyroler, H. A. (2000). Anger proneness predicts coronary heart disease risk. *Circulation, 101*, 2034–2039.

Williams, J. E., Satterwhite, R. C., & Best, D. L. (1999). Pancultural gender stereotypes revisited: The five-factor model. *Sex Roles, 40*, 513–526.

Williams, J. M. G., Watts, F. N., MacLeod, C., & Mathews, A. (1997). *Cognitive psychology and emotional disorders* (2nd ed.). Chichester, UK: Wiley.

Williams, K. B., Radefeld, P. S., Binning, J. F., & Sudak, J. R. (1993). When job candidates are "hard-" versus "easy-to-get": Effects of candidate availability on employment decisions. *Journal of Applied Social Psychology, 23*(3), 169–198.

Williams, K. E., & Bond, M. J. (2002). The roles of self-efficacy, outcome expectancies and social support in the self-care behaviors of diabetics. *Psychology, Health & Medicine, 7*(2), 127–141.

Williams, M. H. (1992). Exploitation and inference: Mapping the damage from therapist-patient sexual involvement. *American Psychologist, 47*, 412–421.

Williams, N. A., & Deffenbacher, J. L. (1983). Life stress and chronic yeast infections. *Journal of Human Stress, 9*, 26–31.

Williams, P. (2005). What is psychoanalysis? What is a psychoanalyst? In E. S. Person, A. M. Cooper, & G. O. Gabbard (Eds.), *Textbook of psychoanalysis*. Washington, DC: American Psychiatric Publishing.

Williams, R. B. (1996). Hostility and the heart. In D. Goleman & J. Gurin (Eds.), *Mind-body medicine: How to use your mind for better health*. Yonkers, NY: Consumer Reports Books.

Williams, R. B. (2001). Hostility (and other psychosocial risk factors): Effects on health and the potential for successful behavioral approaches to prevention and treatment. In A. Baum, T. A. Revenson, & J. E. Singer (Eds.), *Handbook of health psychology*. Mahwah, NJ: Erlbaum.

Williams, R. B., & Williams, V. P. (1993). *Anger kills: Seventeen strategies for controlling the hostility that can harm your health*. New York: Times Books/Random House.

Williams, R. L., & Eggert, A. (2002). Notetaking predictors of test performance. *Teaching of Psychology, 29*, 234–237.

Williams, S. L. (1995). Self-efficacy, anxiety, and phobic disorders. In J. E. Maddux (Ed.), *Self-efficacy, adaptation, and adjustment: Theory, research, and application*. New York: Plenum Press.

Williamson, D. A., Zucker, N. L., Martin, C. K., & Smeets, M. A. M. (2001). Etiology and management of eating disorders. In P. B. Sutker & H. E. Adams (Eds.), *Comprehensive handbook of psychopathology* (3rd ed.). New York: Kluwer Academic/Plenum.

Willis, S. L., & Reid, J. E. E. (1999). *Life in the middle: Psychological and social development in middle age*. San Diego: Academic Press.

Wills, T. A., & Fegan, M. (2001). Social networks and social support. In A. Baum, T. A. Revenson, & J. E. Singer (Eds.), *Handbook of health psychology*. Mahwah, NJ: Erlbaum.

Wilpert, B. (1995). Organizational behavior. *Annual review of psychology, 46*, 59–90

Wilsnack, S. C., Wonderlich, S. A., Kristjanson, A. F., Vogeltanz-Holm, N. D., & Wilsnack, R. W. (2002). Self-reports of forgetting and remembering childhood sexual abuse in a nationally representative sample of U.S. women. *Child Abuse and Neglect, 26*(2), 139–147.

Wilson, A. E., & Ross, M. (2000). The frequency of temporal-self and social comparisons in people's personal appraisals. *Journal of Personality and Social Psychology, 78*, 928–942.

Wilson, J. P., Drozdek, B., & Turkovic, S. (2006). Posttraumatic shame and guilt. *Trauma, Violence and Abuse, 7*(2), 122–141.

Wilson, R. S., & Bennett, D. A. (2003). Cognitive activity and the risk of Alzheimer's disease. *Current Directions in Psychological Science, 12*(3), 87–91.

Wilson, T. D. (2002). *Strangers to ourselves: Discovering the adaptive unconscious*. Cambridge: Belknap Press.

Wilson, T. D., & Gilbert, D. T. (2005). Affective forecasting: Knowing what to want. *Current Directions in Psychological Science, 14*(3), 131–134.

Credits

Photo Credits

This page constitutes an extension of the copyright page. We have made every effort to trace the ownership of all copyrighted material and to secure permission from copyright holders. In the event of any question arising as to the use of any material, we will be pleased to make the necessary corrections in future printings. Thanks are due to the following authors, publishers, and agents for permission to use the material indicated.

Chapter 1

2: © AP Images/Suzanne Plunkett 3: © Carlos Spottorno/Taxi/Getty Images 5: left, © Christopher J. Morris/Corbis 5: right, © Reuters/HO 7: bottom, © AP Images/Stephen Chernin 18: inset, © David Young-Wolff/Photo Edit 23: left, © Anderson Ross/Digital Vision/Getty Images 23: right, © Javier Pierini/Taxi/Getty Images 24: © Dana White/PhotoEdit 26: © JFB/Stone/Getty Images

Chapter 2

35: right, National Library of Medicine 35: bottom, © Peter Aprahamian/Corbis 40: © Creatas/Jupiter Images 41: left, © Bettmann/Corbis 41: right, © Bettmann/Corbis 44: © Bettmann/Corbis 46: Courtesy of B. F. Skinner 47: © Big Shots/Digital Vision/Getty Images 48: Courtesy, Albert Bandura 51: Carl Rogers Memorial Library 52: Courtesy, Abraham Maslow 55: right, Courtesy, Hans Eysenck, photo by Mark Gerson 55: bottom right, © Michael Nichols/Magnum Photos 55: bottom left, © Michael Nichols/Magnum Photos 61: right, © Joe Raedle/Getty Images 61: left, © Jack Carey/Alamy

Chapter 3

71: Courtesy, Richard Lazarus 73: left, © AP Images/Reed Saxon 73: right, © Richard Lord/PhotoEdit 76: Courtesy, Neal Miller 79: left, © Allen Birnbach/Masterfile 79: right, © Kelvin Murray/Stone/Getty Images 82: Courtesy, Susan Folkman 84: © Bettmann/Corbis 90: © AP Images/Ben Sklar 94: right, Courtesy, Suzanne C. Ouelette 95: © Paula Bronstein/Getty Images 97: Courtesy, Eleanor Holmes Williams

Chapter 4

106: Courtesy, Dr. Martin Seligman 108: © Paul Thomas/The Image Bank/Getty Images 111:

© Rachel Epstein/The Images Works 113: Courtesy, Shelley Taylor 115: Courtesy, Albert Ellis Institute 119: left, © Radhika Chalasani/Getty Images 123: © Bruce Ayres/Stone/Getty Images 128: © Altrendo Images/Getty Images 129: © Acey Harper/Time Life Pictures/Getty Images 134: © Nicola Sutton/Life File/Photodisc Green/Getty Images 137: © Mark Richards/PhotoEdit

Chapter 5

141: Stanford University News Service, photo by L. A. Cicero 144: © Zigzag Images/Alamy 145: © Pat Bruno/Positive Images 146: © David Young-Wolff/Photo Edit 148: Courtesy, Roy Baumeister 153: © Blend Images/Alamy 159: © GDT/Stone/Getty Images 162: Courtesy, Albert Bandura 163: © Mary Kate Denny/Photo Edit 164: © Marc Vaughn/Masterfile 167: Courtesy, Mark Snyder 168: © Jo Hale/Getty Images

Chapter 6

174: bottom, Courtesy, Susan Fiske 174: top, © Spencer Grant/PhotoEdit 180: © Andrew Holbrooke/The Image Works 185: © Bill Aaron/PhotoEdit 190: © Mychal Watts/WireImage/Getty Images 191: bottom, Courtesy, John T. Cacioppo 191: top, Courtesy, Richard E. Petty 192: © David McNew/Getty Images 193: © Royalty Free-Masterfile 195: right, © 1981 Eric Kroll, courtesy of Alexandra Milgram 196: inset, Photos copyright 1965 by Stanley Milgram. From the film *Obedience*, distributed by The Pennsylvania State University. Obedience, distributed by The Pennsylvania State University. Reprinted by permission of Alexandra Milgram. 198: Courtesy, Robert Cialdini 200: © Bob Daemmrich/PhotoEdit 201: © Tony Freeman/Photo Edit

Chapter 7

207: © Richard Flood/DK Stock/Getty Images 209: © AP Images/Ron Edmonds 210: © AP Images/Greg Baker 211: Photos from *Unmasking the Face*, © 1975 by Paul Ekman, photographs courtesy of Paul Ekman 212: right, © Tony Freeman/Photo Edit 212: left, © Walter Hodges/Corbis 213: © Bob Daemmrich/The Image Works 214: Courtesy, Bella DePaulo 215: © Bob Daemmrich/The Image Works 219: © Mary Kate Denny/PhotoEdit 221: © Dana Hursey/Masterfile 223: © Michael Newman/Photo Edit 225: © Radius Images/Alamy 226: Photo by Sara Barrett, courtesy of Random House

Chapter 8

237: top, © Earl & Nazima Kowalt/Corbis 237: bottom, © Royalty-Free/Masterfile 239: © David Young-Wolff/PhotoEdit 243: © Ephraim Ben-Shimon/Corbis 244: Courtesy of David M. Buss 245: © Hepp/Stone/Getty Images 253: right, Michael Marsland/Yale University 253: © AP Images/Winslow Townson 254: Photo by Bill Warren/*Ithaca Journal* 255:

Photo provided by Philip Shaver 260: © Ronnie Kaufman/Corbis 262: © Royalty-Free/Masterfile

Chapter 9

272: © Michael Newman/PhotoEdit 277: © AP Images/Susan Walsh 283: Photo by Sharon M. Fentiman 285: © Matthew McVay/Corbis Saba 288: Courtesy, E. Mavis Hetherington 289: right, © David Young-Wolff/Photo Edit 292: © Ron Chapple/Thinkstock/Alamy 295: © AP Images/Ben Margot 297: © AP Images/Ed Andriesky

Chapter 10

303: Courtesy, Janet Shibley Hyde 310: Courtesy, Alice Eagly 312: Wadsworth Collection 314: © David W. Hamilton/Alamy 315: © Hill Street Studios/Blend/Getty Images 316: © Michelle D. Bridwell/Photo Edit 327: © Paul Wood/Alamy 328: Courtesy, Sandra Bem 330: Photo by Sara Barrett, courtesy of Random House

Chapter 11

339: © David Young-Wolff/Photographer's Choice/Getty Images 341: © Ted Streshinsky/Corbis 343: © Peter Byron/PhotoEdit 346: © Red Chopsticks/Getty Images 351: © Jutta Klee/Stone/Getty Images 352: © Hill Street Studios/Blend Images/Getty Images 353: Courtesy, Susan Whitbourne 357: © Siphiwe Sibeko/Reuters 360: © Ken Ross 362: © AP Images/Evan Vucci 363: © Arko Datta/Reuters/Corbis 364: Courtesy, Diana Baumrind 365: © David Young-Wolff/Photo Edit 367: Courtesy, Laurence Steinberg

Chapter 12

375: left, © AP Images/Richard Drew 375: right, © Bonnie Kamin/PhotoEdit 377: © Bill Aron/PhotoEdit 379: top, Columbia University Archives-Columbiana Library 381: © Yellow Dog Productions/Stone/Getty Images 384: © Peter Macdiarmid/Getty Images 387: © AP Images/Steve Ruark 390: © AP Images/Gregory Bull 403: © JupiterImages/Creatas/Alamy

Chapter 13

410: Courtesy, Letitia Anne Peplau 412: right, © AP Images/HO 412: left, © Michael Newman/Photo Edit 414: © AP Images/Reed Saxon 415: bottom left, Courtesy, Douglas C Kimmel 415: top left, Courtesy, Linda Doris Garnets 415: right, © AP Images/Chris Pizzello 424: © Mario Tama/Getty Images 426: © AP Images/Seth Wenig 435: © Marc Romanelli/The Image Bank/Getty Images 436: © Bettmann/Corbis

Chapter 14

446: © Annabella Bluesky/Photo Researchers, Inc. 449: Courtesy, Janice Kiecott-Glaser 454: © Topham/The Image Works 464: © Jim Cummings/Taxi/Getty Images 467: Courtesy, M. Robin DiMatteo 468: © JupiterImages 470: © image100/Alamy Images

from Bushman, B. J. & Anderson, C. A. (2001), "Media violence and the American public: Scientific facts versus media misinformation," *American Psychologist, 56,* 477–489. Copyright © 2001 American Psychological Association. Reprinted by permission of the publisher and author. **110:** Figure 4.4: From Young, K. S. (1998) *Caught in the net: How to recognize the signs of Internet addiction—and a winning strategy for recovery,* copyright © 1998 John Wiley & Sons, Inc. Reprinted with permission of John Wiley & Sons, Inc. **112:** Figure 4.5: Adapted From Carson, Robert C., Butcher, J. N., & Coleman, J. C. (1988), *Abnormal Psychology and Modern Life, 8th Edition,* pp 64–65. Published by Allyn and Bacon, Boston, MA, Copyright © 1988 by Pearson Education. Adapted by permission of the publisher. **112:** Cartoon CALVIN AND HOBBES © Watterson. Reprinted with permission of UNIVERSAL PRESS SYNDICATE. All rights reserved. **115:** Cartoon SALLY FORTH Copyright © 1984 News Group Chicago, reprinted by permission of North America Syndicate. **119:** Figure 4.8: Adapted from Martin, R. A. and Lefcourt, H. M. (1983) "Sense of humor as a moderator of the relation between stressors and moods," *Journal of Personality and Social Psychology, 45 (6),* 1313–1324. Copyright © 1983 by the American Psychological Association. Adapted by permission of the publisher and author. **119:** Cartoon Copyright © by Dan Piraro. Reprinted by permission of King Features Syndicate. **122:** Figure 4.10: From M. LeBoeuf, "Managing Time Means Managing Yourself," Questionnaire, p. 45. Reprinted from *Business Horizons Magazine,* February 1980. Copyright by the Foundation for the School of Business at Indiana University. Used with permission from Elsevier. **129:** Figure 4.14: Excerpt from "Sharing One's Story," [J. M. Smyth and J. W. Pennebaker,] pg. 84 from *Coping: The Psychology of What Works,* edited by C. R. Snyder, copyright © 1999 by Oxford University Press. Inc.. Used by permission of Oxford University Press, Inc. **131:** Figure 4.15: Page 114–115 from *The Relaxation Response* by Herbert Benson, M.D. with Miriam Z. Klipper. Copyright © 1975 by William Morrow & Company, Inc. Reprinted by permission of HarperCollins Publishers, Inc. **134:** Figure 4.18: From D. L. Watson & R. L. Tharp, *Self-Directed Behavior: Self-Modification for Personal Adjustment, Fourth Edition,* pp. 213–214. Copyright © 1972, 1977, 1981, 1985, 1993 by Brooks/Cole Publishing Company.

Chapter 5

144: Figure 5.3: From Hull J. G. and Young, R. D. (1983) "Self-consciousness, self-esteem, and success-failure as determinants of alcohol consumption in male social drinkers," *Journal of Personality and Social Psychology, 44 (6),* 1097–1109. Copyright © 1983 American Psychological Association. Reprinted by permission of the publisher and author. **147:** Figure 5.5: Adapted from Markus, H. R. and Kitayama, S. (1991) "Culture and the self: Implications for cognition, emotion, and motivation," *Psychological Review, 98 (2)* 224–253. Copyright © 1991 American Psychological Association.

Adapted by permission of the publisher and author. **149:** Figure 5.7 Adapted from Rosenberg, M. (1965), Society and the adolescent self-image, Princeton University Press. Copyright © 1965 by Princeton University Press. http://www.bsos.umd.edu/socy/grad/socpsy_rosenberg.html **150:** Figure 5.8: Adapted from Sharon S. Brehm and Saul M. Kassin, (1993), *Social Psychology, 2nd Edition.* Copyright © 1993 Houghton-Mifflin Company. Adapted by permission. **158:** Cartoon PEANUTS © United Feature Syndicate, Inc. **160:** Figure 5.13 Adapted from Norem, J. K. (2001), *The Positive Power of Negative Thinking: Using Defensive Pessimism to Manage Anxiety and Perform at Your Peak.* Copyright © 2001 by Julie K. Norem. Reprinted by permission of Basic Books, a member of Perseus Book Group. **166:** Figure 5.17: Based on Jones, E. E. (1990) *Interpersonal Perception,* Table 703, p. 198. W. H. Freeman & Company. **169:** Cartoon FRANK & ERNEST Thaves/Dist. by Newspaper Enterprise Association, Inc.

Chapter 6

175: Figure 6.1: Adapted from Sharon S. Brehm and Saul M. Kassin, *Social Psychology,* Second Edition. Copyright © 1993 by HoughtonMifflin Company. Adapted with permission. **176:** Cartoon DILBERT © Scott Adams/Dist. by United Feature Syndicate, Inc **177:** Figure 6.3: Adapted from Smith, E. R. and Mackie, D. M. (1995) *Social Psychology,* p. 103. Copyright © 1995 Worth Publishing. Reprinted by permission. **179:** Figure 6.4: Data from 1999, September 15: Americans Agree That Being Attractive is a Plus in American Society. Taken from 2001, June 10, from http://gallup.com/poll/releases/pr990915. **183:** Figure 6.8: Statements from Swim, J. K. Aikin, K. J., Hall, W. S. & Hunter, B. A. (1995) "Sexism and racism: Old-fashioned and modern prejudices," *Journal of Personality and Social Psychology, 68 (2),* 199–214 (adapted from McConahay, J. B. (1986) "Modernism, ambivalence, and the Modern-Racism-Scale." In J. F. Dovidio & S. L. Gaerther (Eds.), Prejudice, discrimination, and racism (pp. 91–25). Academic Press). Copyright © 1995 American Psychological Association. Reprinted by permission of the publisher and author. **184:** Figure 6.9: Adapted from Pratto, F. Sidanius, J. Stallworth, L. M., & Mlle, B. F. (1994), "Social dominance orientation: A personality variable predicting social and political attitudes," *Journal of Personality and Social Psychology, 67,* 741–763 Copyright © 1994 by the American Psychological Association. Adapted by permission of the publisher and author. **187:** Figure 6.10: Adapted from Sharon S. Brehm and Saul M. Kassin, *Social Psychology,* Second Edition. Copyright © 1993 by Houghton Mifflin Company. Adapted with permission. **193:** Figure 6.13: Adapted from an illustration by Sarah Love on p. 35, *Scientific American, November 1955,* from "Opinion and Social Pressure," by Solomon Asch. Copyright © 1955 by Scientific American, Inc. All rights reserved. **194:** Figure 6.14: Adapted from an illustration by Sarah Love on p. 32, *Scientific American, November 1955,* from "Opinion and

Social Pressure," by Solomon Asch. Copyright © 1955 by Scientific American, Inc. All rights reserved. **195:** Cartoon ZITS © Jerry Scott and Jim Borgman. Reprinted by permission of King Features Syndicate. **200:** Cartoon CALVIN AND HOBBES © Watterson. Reprinted with permission of UNIVERSAL PRESS SYNDICATE. All rights.

Chapter 7

207: Figure 7.2 Copyright © 1994–2006. NetLingo# The Internet Dictionary at http://www.netlingo.com **213:** Figure 7.7: "Where friends touch each other," page 89, [adapted] *from Eye to Eye: How People Interact,* by Peter Marsh. Copyright © 1988 by Andromeda Oxford Ltd. Reprinted by permission of HarperCollins, Publishers, Inc. and Andromeda Oxford Ltd. **218:** Cartoon DAVE © 1993 Dave Miller. Reprinted with permission of the artist. All rights reserved. **221:** Cartoon DILBERT © 2004 Scott Adams. Reprinted by permission of United Features Syndicate, Inc **231:** Excerpts from *Asserting Yourself: A Practical Guide for Positive Change* by Sharon Anthony Bower and Gordon H. Bower, pp 8, 9, 11. Copyright © 2004, 1991 by Sharon Anthony Bower and Gordon H. Bower. Reprinted by permission of Perseus DA CAPO PRESS, a member of Perseus Books. **231:** Cartoon by Marlette: KUDZU © Tribune Media Services, Inc. All Rights Reserved. Reprinted with permission. **232:** Figure 7.13: From *Asserting Yourself: A Practical Guide for Positive Change* by Sharon Anthony Bower and Gordon H. Bower. Copyright © 2004, 1991 by Sharon Anthony Bower and Gordon H. Bower, p. 100. Reprinted by permission of DA CAPO PRESS, a member of Perseus Books. **233:** Figure 7.14: From *Asserting Yourself: A Practical Guide for Positive Change* by Sharon Anthony Bower and Gordon H. Bower, p. 68. Copyright © 2004, 1991 by Sharon Anthony Bower and Gordon H. Bower. Reprinted by permission of DA CAPO PRESS, a member of Perseus Books.

Chapter 8

238: Figure 8.1: Adapted from R. Levine, S. Sato, T. Hashimoto, J. Verma, "Love and marriage in eleven cultures," 1995, *Journal of Cross-Cultural Psychology 26(5),* 561, 564. Copyright © 1995 by Sage Publications, Inc. Adapted by permission of Sage Publications. **239:** Figure 8.1 Adapted from Madden, M. & Lenhart, A. (2006), "Online dating," retrieved April 29, 2007 from http://www.pewinternet.org/pdfs/PIP_Online_Dating.pdf (Dating-Related Activities Online table, p. 5. Reprinted by permission of PEW Internet & American Life Project. Washington, D.C. **241:** Cartoon CATHY © 1993 by Cathy Guisewite. Reprinted with permission of UNIVERSAL PRESS SYNDICATE. All rights reserved. **242:** Figure 8.3: From Buss, D. M. (1989) "Sex differences in human mate preferences: Evolutionary hypotheses tested in 37 cultures," 1989, *Behavioral and Brain Sciences, 12,* 1–14. Copyright © 1989 by Cambridge University Press. Reprinted with the permission of Cambridge University Press and the author. **244:** Figure 8.4: Adapted from Buss,

D. M. (1988) "The evolution of human intrasexual competition: Tactics of mate attraction," *Journal of Personality and Social Psychology, 54(4)*, 616–628. Copyright © 1988 by the American Psychological Association. Adapted by permission of the publisher and author. **246:** Cartoon BIZARRO © Dan Piraro. Reprinted by permission of King Features Syndicate. **247:** Figure 8.7: Adapted from Gonzales, M. H. Davis, J. M. Loeny, G. L. Lukens, C. K. & Junghans, C. H. (1983) "Interactional approach to interpersonal attraction," *Journal of Personality and Social Psychology, 44*, 1191–1197. Copyright © 1983 by the American Psychological Association. Adapted by permission of the publisher and author. **247:** Figure 8.8: Based on Regan, P.C. & Berscheid, E. "Gender differences in characteristics desired in a potential sexual marriage partner," 1997, *Journal of Psychology and Human Sexuality, 9*, Table 1, p. 32. Haworth Press, Inc. **249:** Figure 8.10: Adapted from Sharon S. Brehm and Saul M. Kassin, *Social Psychology, Second Edition*. Copyright © 1993 by Houghton Mifflin Company. Reprinted with permission. **254:** Figure 8.12: From Sternberg, R. J. (1986) "A triangular theory of love," *Psychological Review, 93*, 119–135. Copyright © 1986 by the American Psychological Association. Reprinted by permission of the publisher and author. **258:** Cartoon FOR BETTER OR FOR WORSE® © Lynn Johnston Productions, Inc./Distributed by Universal Press Syndicate. Reprinted with permission. All rights reserved. **259:** Figure 8.16: Adapted from Hill, C. T. Rubin, Z. & Peplau, L. A. (1976) "Breakups before marriage: The end of 103 affairs," *Journal of Social Issues, 32*, 147–168. © Society for the Psychological Study of Social Issues. Adapted by permission of the author. All rights reserved. **263:** Figure 8.18: From *Shyness: What Is It, What To Do About It*, by Philip Zimbardo. Copyright © 1977 by Philip Zimbardo, Inc. Reprinted by permission of DA CAPO PRESS, a member of Perseus Books. **264:** Figure 8.19: From a paper presented at the annual convention of the American Psychological Association, 9/2/79. An expanded version of this paper appears in *New Directions in Cognitive Therapy*, edited by Emery, Hollan, and Bedrosian, Guilford Press, 1981 and in *Loneliness: A Sourcebook of Current Theory, Research and Therapy*, by L. A. Peplau and D. Perlman (Eds.). Copyright © 1982 by John Wiley & Sons, Inc., and Jeffrey Young. **265:** Figure 8.20 Based on Shaver, P. & Rubenstein, C. (1980). "Childhood attachment experience and adult loneliness." In L. Wheeler (Ed.), *Review of Personality and Social Psychology, Vol. 1*, pp. 42–73. Thousand Oaks, CA: Sage Publications.

Chapter 9

271: Figure 9.3: Adapted from Peter J. Stein, "Singlehood: An alternative to marriage," *The Family Coordinator, 24(4)*, 500. Copyrighted © 1975 by the National Council on Family Relations, 3989 Central Ave. N. E., Suite 550, Minneapolis, MN 55421. Reprinted by permission. **278:** Cartoon CATHY © 1994 by Cathy Guisewite. Reprinted with permission of UNIVERSAL PRESS SYNDICATE. All rights reserved. **280:** Cartoon SALLY FORTH © by Howard and Mac. Reprinted with special permission of King Features Syndicate. **284:** Cartoon CATHY © 1996 Cathy Guisewite. Reprinted with permission of UNIVERSAL PRESS SYNDICATE. All rights reserved. **287:** Cartoon © 1992 The New Yorker Collection 1992 Michael Maslin from cartoonbank.com. All rights reserved. **293:** Figure 9.13: From Peplau, L. A. "What homosexuals want," March 1981, *Psychology Today, 3*, 28–38. Reprinted with permission from Psychology Today Magazine. Copyright © 1981 (Sussex Publishers, LLC.). **297:** Figure 9.14: From I. M. Johnson, J. Crowley, and R. T. Sigler, "Agency response to domestic violence: Services provided to battered women," 1992. In E. C. Viano (Ed.), *Intimate Violence: Interdisciplinary Perspectives*, pp. 191–202 (Table on p. 199). Copyright © 1992 Hemisphere Publishing. Reprinted with permission of Taylor & Francis, Inc.

Chapter 10

304: Figure 10.2: Adapted from Ruble, T. L. (1983) "Sex stereotypes: Issues of change in the 70s," *Sex Roles, 9*, 397–402. Copyright © 1983 Plenum Publishing Co. Adapted by permission of Springer Science and *Business Media* and the author. **304:** Cartoon CATHY © 1986 Cathy Guisewite. Reprinted with permission of UNIVERSAL PRESS SYNDICATE. All rights reserved. **305:** Cartoon Six Chix © by Isabella Bannerman, Margaret Shulock, Rina Piccolo, Ann C. Telnaes, Kathryn LeMieux and Stephanie Piro. Reprinted by permission of King Features Syndicate. **307:** Figure 10.4: Adapted from Shepard, R. N. and Metzler, J. N. (1971) "Mental rotation of three-dimensionl objects," *Science, 171*, 701–703. Copyright © 1971 by American Association for the Advancement of Science. Adapted by permission of the publisher and author. **309:** Figure 10.6: Adapted from Kring, A. M., and Gordon, A. H. (1998) "Sex differences in emotions: Expression, experience and physiology," *Journal of Personality and Social Psychology, 74 (3)*, 686–703. Copyright © 1998 American Psychological Association. Adapted by permission of the publisher and author. **315:** Figure 10.8: Adapted from Richardson, J. G., & Simpson, C. H. (1982) "Children, gender and social structure: An analysis of the contents of letters to Santa Claus," *Child Development, 53*, 429–436. Copyright © 1982 by the Society for Research in Child Development, Inc. Adapted by permission. **317:** Figure 10.9: Adapted from Robert M. Liebert & Joyce Sprafkin, *The Early Window: Effects of Television on Children and Youth, 3/e*. Published by Allyn and Bacon, Boston, Ma. Copyright © 1988 by Pearson Education. Adapted by permission of the publisher. **319:** Cartoon © The New Yorker Collection, Robert Weber 2002 from cartoonbank.com. All rights reserved. **322:** Cartoon DOONSBURY © 1975 G. B. Trudeau. Reprinted with permission of UNIVERSAL PRESS SYNDICATE. All rights reserved. **326:** Figure 10.13: Adapted from Stein, N., Marshall, N. L., and Tropp, L. R. (1993) *Secrets in Public: Sexual Harassment in Our Schools*, p. 4. Copyright © 1993 Center for Research on Women at Wellesley College and the NOW Legal Defense and Education Fund. Adapted by permission. **333:** Figure 10.15: Based on insights from *You Just Don't Understand: Women and Men in Conversation*, by Deborah Tannen, 1990. New York: William Morrow & Company, Inc.

Chapter 11

339: Cartoon *FOR BETTER OR FOR WORSE*® cartoon © 1988 Lynn Johnston Productions, Inc./Distributed by Universal Press Syndicate. Reprinted with permission. All rights reserved. **340:** Figure 11.2: Adapted from Tobin-Richards, M. H., Boxer, A. M., and Petersen, A. C. (1983) from "The psychological significance of pubertal change: Sex differences in perceptions of self during early adolescence." In J. Brooks-Gunn and A. C. Petersen (Eds.), *Girls at Puberty: Biological and Psychosocial Perspectives*, p. 137. Copyright © 1983 Plenum Publishing Inc. Adapted by permission of Springer Science and Business Media and the author. **341:** Figure 11.3: Figure [adapted] of Erikson's "Stages of Personality Development," from *Childhood and Society* by Erik H. Erikson. Copyright 1950 © 1963 by W. W. Norton & Co. Inc., renewed © 1978, 1991 by Erik H. Erikson. Used by permission of W. W. Norton & Company, Inc. Further permission from Hogarth Press (UK distribution). Reprinted by permission of The Random House Group Ltd. **342:** Figure 11.4: Adapted from Marcia, J. E. (1980) "Identity in Adolescence." In J. Adelson (Ed.), *Handbook of Adolescent Psychology*, pp. 159–210. Copyright © 1980 by John Wiley & Sons, Inc. Adapted by permission of John Wiley & Sons, Inc. **344:** Figure 11.5: Based on American Foundation for Suicide Prevention: When You Fear Someone May Take Their Life 9n.d.) Retrieved January 10, 2005 from http://www.afsp.org/about/whattodo.htm **349:** Figure 11.8: Adapted from Montepare, J., and Lachman, M. (1989) "You're only as old as you feel: Self-perceptions of age, fears of aging, and life satisfaction," *Psychology and Aging, 4*, 73–78. Copyright © 1989 American Psychological Association. Adapted by permission of the publisher and author. **349:** Cartoon ZITS © Jerry Scott and Jim Borgman. Reprinted by permission of King Features Syndicate. **350:** Cartoon CATHY © Cathy Guisewite. Reprinted with permission of UNIVERSAL PRESS SYNDICATE. All rights reserved. **357:** Figure 11.10. Reprinted from "Intellectual development in adulthood," by K. W. Schaie in *Handbook of the Psychology of Aging, Third Edition*, edited by J. E. Birren and K. W. Schaie, copyright © 1990 (Academic Press) reproduced with permission of Elsevier. **358:** Figure 11.11 Based on data from Dennis, W. (1966) "Creative productivity between the ages of 20 and 80 years." *Journal of Gerontology, 2(1)*, 1–8. **365:** Figure 11.13: Based on data from "Socialization determinants of personal agency," a paper presented at the biennial meeting of the Society for Research in Child Development, New Orleans, 1977. **368:** Figure 11.14: Data from Lamborn, S. D., Mounts, N. S., Steinberg, L. &

Dornbusch, S. M. (1991), "Patterns of competence and adjustment among adolescents from authoritative, authoritarian, indulgent, and neglectful families." *Child Development, 62*, p 1060. Copyright © 1991 by the Society for Research in Child Development, Inc. Used with permission of SRCD.

Chapter 12

378: Figure 12.2: From John L. Holland, *Making Vocational Choices: A Theory of Vocational Personalities and Work Environments (2nd ed.).* © 1985, pp. 19–23, 36–40. Adapted by permission of Prentice-Hall, Inc. Englewood Cliffs, NJ. **379:** Figure 12.3: Adapted from J. Zaccaria, *Theories of Occupational Choice and Vocational Development,* pp. 51–52. Houghton Mifflin. Copyright © 1970 by Time Share Corporation, New Hampshire. **385:** Figure 12.7: Adapted from Maume, D. J. (2004), "Is the glass ceiling a unique form of inequality?," *Work and Occupations, 31(2),* 250–274. Copyright © 2004 by Sage Publications, Inc. Adapted by permission of Sage Publications. **387:** Cartoon CATHY copyright © 2001Cathy Guisewite. Reprinted with permission of UNIVERSAL PRESS SYNDICATE. All rights reserved. **388:** Figure 12.8: Adapted from Landy, F. J. (1989) *Psychology of Work Behavior (4th ed.),* p. 638. Copyright © 1989 by Wadsworth, Inc. Reprinted by permission of Brooks/Cole Publishing Company. **389:** Cartoon SALLY FORTH © Reprinted with special permission of King Features Syndicate. **389:** Figure 12.9: Redrawn from Karasek, R. A., Baker, D. Marxer, F., Ahlbom, A., Theorell, T. (1981), "Job decision latitude, job demands, and cardiovascular disease: A prospective study of Swedish men," *American Journal of Public Health, 71,* 694–705. Reprinted with permission from the American Public Heath Association. **391:** Figure 12.10: From Bowes-Sperry, L., and Tata, J. (1999) "A Multi-perspective framework of sexual harassment," in G. N. Powell (Ed.), *Handbook of Gender and Work,* pp. 263–280. © 1999 by Sage Publications. Reprinted with permission of Sage Publications, Inc. **395:** Cartoon DILBERT © 2005 Scott Adams/Dist. by United Feature Syndicate, Inc. **396:** Figure 12.12: From Table 4 on page 10 in Families and Work Institute (2004 October). Generation and gender in the workplace. New York: Author **396:** Figure 12.13: Adapted from Lawrence Mishel, Jared Bernstein, John Schmitt, and Economic Policy Institute, *The State of Working America 2000–2001,* p. 401. Copyright © 2001 by Cornell University. Adapted by permission of the publisher, Cornell University Press. **400:** Figure 12.15: Adapted from Lock, R. D. (2005) *Job search: Career Planning Guidebook, Book II.* Belmont, CA: Brooks/Cole Publishing Company. **400:** Cartoon DILBERT © 2006 Scott Adams/Dist. by United Feature Syndicate, Inc.

Chapter 13

409: Figure 13.1: Adapted from Holt, T., Greene, L., & Davis, J. (2003) "National survey of adolescents and young adults: Sexual health knowledge, attitudes, and experience," Kaiser Family Foundation, Question 2, p. 97. Henry J. Kaiser Family Foundation. **410:** Figure 13.2:

From Kunkel, D., Eyal, K., Finnerty, K., Biely, E. & Donnerstein, E. (2005), A Biennial Report of the Kaiser Family Foundation: Sex on TV 4, Executive Summary," (#7399), The Henry J. Kaiser Family Foundation, November 2005. This information was reprinted with permission the Henry J. Kaiser Family Foundation. The Kaiser Family Foundation, based in Menlo Park, California, is a nonprofit, independent national health care philanthropy and is not associated with Kaiser Permanente or Kaiser Industries. **418:** Figure 13.7: From Elaine Hatfield and Richard L. Rapson, *Love, Sex and Intimacy: Their Psychology, Biology and History,* Table 3.10, p. 92. Published by Allyn and Bacon, Boston, MA. Copyright © 1997 by Pearson Education. Reprinted by permission of the publisher. **420:** Figure 13.9: From Laumann, E. O. Gagnon, J. H. Michael, R. T. and Michaels, S. (1994), *The Social Organization of Sexuality: Sexual Practices in the United States,* 1994. Copyright © 1994 University of Chicago Press. Reprinted by permission. **421:** Figure 13.10: From David Sue, "The Erotic fantasies of college students during coitus," 1979, *The Journal of Sex Research, 15,* p. 303. Copyright © 1979 Society for the Scientific Study of Sexuality. Reprinted by permission. **425:** Figure 13.12: From Lambert, T. A., Kahn, A. S. & Apple, K. J., (2003), "Pluralistic ignorance and hooking up," *The Journal of Sex Research,* 40(2) 129–133. Copyright © 1979 Society for the Scientific Study of Sexuality. Reprinted by permission. **425:** Figure 13.13: From *Sex in America* by Robert T. Michael, John H. Gagnon, Edward D. Laumann, and Gina Kolata. Copyright © 1994 by CSG Enterprises, Inc., Edward O. Lauman, Robert T. Michael, and Gina Kolata. By permission of Little, Brown & Co., Publishers, and Brockman, Inc. **427:** Figure 13.14: From Handy, B. (1998), "How We Really Feel About Infidelity," *Time,* August 3, 1998, pp. 52–53. Copyright © 1998 Time Inc. Reprinted by permission. **428:** Cartoon by Wasserman © 1986 Tribune Media Services, Inc. All Rights Reserved. Reprinted with permission. **434:** Figure 13.17: Adapted from Frank, E., Anderson, C., & Rubenstein, D. (1978) "Frequency of sexual dysfunction in 'normal' couples," *The New England Journal of Medicine, 299,* 111–115. **435:** Figure 13.18: From Laumann, E. O., Gagnon, J. H., Michael, R. T., and Michaels, S. (1994), *The Social Organization of Sexuality: Sexual Practices in the United States,* p. 369. Copyright © 1994 University of Chicago Press. Reprinted by permission. **437:** Figure 13.19: Adapted from William H. Masters, Virginia E. Johnson, and Robert C. Kolodny, *Human Sexuality, 3rd Edition* © 1988, p. 527. Published by Allyn and Bacon, Boston, MA. Copyright © 1998 by Pearson Education. Adapted by permission of the publisher.

Chapter 14

444: Figure 14.4: Adapted from Ridker, P. M. (2002). "High sensitivity C-reactive protein: Potential adjunct for global risk assessment in primary prevention of cardiovascular disease," *Circulation, 103,* 1813–1818. Copyright © 2002 American Heart Association. Adapted by permission of the publisher Lippincott Williams &

Willams and the author. **451:** Cartoon © Jim Borgman. Reprinted with permission of UNIVERSAL PRESS SYNDICATE. All rights reserved **453:** Figure 14.11 Data from *Smoking and Health* (1990). Rockville, MD: Health and Human Services; Graph from *Healthy for Life: Wellness and the Art of Living* by B. K. Williams and S. M. Knight, p. 4.12, Brooks/Cole Publishing Company, 1994. **453:** Figure 14.11: Adapted from Hafen, B. Q., and Hoeger, W. W. K. (1998) *Wellness: Guidelines for a Healthy Lifestyle.* Copyright © 1998 by Morton Publishing Company. **454:** Cartoon © Roger Bollen **456:** Figure 14.14: From Edlin G., and Golanty, E., *Health and Wellness, Third Edition,* p. 294. Copyright © 1992, Jones & Bartlett Publishers, Sudbury, MA. www.jbpub.com. Reprinted with permission. **459:** Cartoon CATHY copyright © 1982 Cathy Guisewite. Reprinted with permission of UNIVERSAL PRESS SYNDICATE. All rights reserved. **461:** Figure 14.18: From Hales, D. *Invitation to Health, 9/e* p. 169. Copyright © 2000 by Wadsworth Publishing. **462:** Figure 14.19: Reprinted (adapted) with the permission of Simon & Schuster Adult Publishing Group from *Eat, Drink, and Be Healthy* by Walter C. Willett, M.D. Copyright © 2001, 2006 by President and Fellows at Harvard College. **464:** Figure 14.21: Adapted from Conrad, C. C., "How different sports rate in promoting physical fitness," *Medical Times, May 1976,* 4–5. Copyright © 1976 by Romaine Pierson Publishers. Reprinted by permission. **466:** Figure 14.22: Adapted from Kalichman, S. C. (1995) Understanding AIDS: A Guide for Mental Health Professionals, Appendix C, pp. 391–392. Copyright © 1995 by the American Psychological Association. Adapted with permission of the publisher and author.

Chapter 15

483: Figure 15.3: Adapted with permission from the *Diagnostic and Statistical Manual of Mental Disorders, Fourth Edition,* Text Revision Copyright © 2000 American Psychiatric Association. **486:** Figure 15.5: From I. M. Marks, *Fears & Phobias,* 1969, Academic Press. Copyright © 1969 by Isaac Marks. Reprinted by permission. **486:** Cartoon by Harris © 1990 ScienceCartoonsPlus.com **491:** Cartoon © Egar Argo. Reprinted by permission. **494:** Figure 15.10: From I. G. Sarason and B. R. Sarason, *Abnormal Psychology: The Problem of Maladaptive Behavior (5th Ed.),* © 1987, p. 283. Reprinted by permission of Prentice-Hall, Inc., Englewood Cliffs, NJ. **495:** Cartoon © The New Yorker Collection Cheney 1996. All rights reserved. From *The New Yorker,* Feb. 12, 1996. **497:** Figure 15.11: From Figure 6-1 (p. 132) "Age of onset for bipolar mood disorder," from *Manic-Depressive Illness,* by Frederick K. Goodwin and Kay R. Jamison, copyright © 1990 by Oxford University Press, Inc. Used by permission of Oxford University Press, Inc.

Chapter 16

525: Figure 16.6: Adapted from Lambert, M. J., Hansen, N. B., & Finch A. E. (2001), "Patient-focused research: Using patient outcome data to enhance treatment effects," *Journal of Consulting and Clinical Psychology, 69,* 159–172. Copyright © 2001 by the American Psychological Association. Adapted by permission of the publisher and author. **527:** Figure 16.7: From "Lies of the Mind" *Time,* 11/29/93. Copyright © 1993 Time Inc. Reprinted by permission **526:** Cartoon DOONESBURY © 1994 G. B. Trudeau. Reprinted with permission of UNIVERSAL PRESS SYNDICATE. All rights reserved. **529:** Cartoon © ScienceCartoonsPlus. com **530:** Figure 16.9: From K. E. Rudestam, *Methods of Self-Change: An ABC Primer,*

pp. 42–43, 1980. Brooks/Cole Publishing Company. Copyright © 1980 by Wadsworth, Inc. **531:** Figure 16.11: Adapted from Beck, A. T. (1976) *Cognitive Therapy and the Emotional Disorders,* International Universities Press. Copyright © 1976 by International Universities Press, Inc. Adapted by permission of the publisher. **535:** Cartoon © The New Yorker Collection 2001, Barbara Smaller from cartoonbank .com. All rights reserved. **535:** Figure 16.13: From data in NIMH-PSC Collaborative Study I and reported in "Drugs in the Treament of Psychosis," by Cole, J. O., Goldberg, S. C., and Davis, J. M. (1966). In P. Solomon (Ed.) *Psychi-

atric Drugs,* Grune & Stratton. Additional data added from J. M. Davis, 1985. By permission of the author. **537:** Cartoon DILBERT © Scott Adams/Dist. by United Feature Syndicate, Inc. **544:** Figure 16.15: Adapted from Smith, M. L., & Glass, G. V. (1977), "Meta analysis of psychotherapy outcome series," *American Psychologist, 32 (September),* 752–760. Copyright © 1977 by the American Psychological Association. Adapted by permission of the publisher and author. **544:** Cartoon INSIDE WOODY ALLEN by Stuart Hample. Reprinted by permission. © King Features Syndicate, Inc., 1977. World rights reserved.

Name Index

Ko, D., 121
Kobasa, S. C., 94–95
Kobrynowicz, D., 319
Koestner, R., 123, 145, 246
Koff, E., 339
Kolb, R., 489
Kolodny, R. C., 437
Konnert, C., 276
Konrad, A. M., 321
Koopman, C., 90
Kop, W. J., 446
Kopta, S. M., 524
Koran, L. M., 1
Koren, D., 90
Koriat, A., 28
Kornspan, A. S., 380
Koss, M. P., 296, 297, 298
Kouzma, N. M., 79
Kowalski, R. M., 321
Kozlowski, S. W. J., 374
Kraaij, V., 111
Krahn, H. J., 308
Kramer, P. D., 43
Kransny, L., 531
Krantz, D. S., 446, 449
Kraus, J. E., 535
Kraus, L. A., 93
Krause, N., 353
Kraut, R., 220
Kreider, R. M., 285, 289
Kressin, M. R., 352
Kring, A. M., 309, 502
Kroger, J., 342
Krokoff, L. J., 260
Krueger, R. F., 19, 20
Krueger, W. C. F., 28
Kruger, J., 164
Kruglanski, A. W., 182
Krupat, E., 467
Kübler-Ross, E., 360–361, 393
Kudo, E., 159
Kuhn, J., 501
Kulick, A. R., 502
Kulik, L., 392
Kunkel, D., 409, 410
Kunkel, E. S., 448
Kuperminc, G. P., 73
Kurdek, L. A., 207, 249, 252, 253, 257, 285, 293, 294, 329, 396, 426, 427
Kutcher, E. J., 403
Kutchins, H., 481

L

L'Engle, K. L., 409
Lachman, M. E., 349, 350, 351
LaFrance, M., 211
Lakein, A., 123, 124, 125, 25
Lakin, M., 523
Lam, L. T., 127
Lambert, J. D., 278
Lambert, M. J., 180, 524, 525, 540, 542, 544
Lambert, T. A., 424, 425
Lamborn, S. D., 368
Lamke, L. K., 296
Lammers, C., 424
Lamon, S. J., 306
Lampe, A., 448, 449
Lanares, O., 366
Landabaso, M. A., 530
Landau, M. J., 61
Landrine, H., 74
Landsberger, S. A., 257
Landsman, T., 113
Lane, C. J., 358
Lane, M., 516
Lane, M. D., 184
Lang, P. J., 177
Langeland, W., 493
Langenbucher, J., 481

Langer, E., 154–155, 158, 187
Langlois, J. H., 178, 242
Lanphear, B. P., 460
Lansford, J. E., 353
Lanza, S. T., 339
LaPiere, R. T., 183
LaPierre, Y. D., 536
Larson, R., 332, 343
Laruelle, M., 505
Larzelere, R. E., 369
Laskoff, M. B., 393
Lasley, E. N., 92
Lassiter, G. D., 214
Latané, B., 195
Lating, J. M., 532
Lauer, J., 259
Lauer, R., 259
Laughlin, H., 112, 485
Laumann, E. O., 412, 420, 422, 423, 426, 434, 435
Laurenceau, J. P., 218, 219, 272
Lauriello, J., 501
Laursen, B., 343
Lauzen, M. M., 318
Lavalle, L. F., 148
Lavin, C., 270
Lavin, M. J., 265
Lavine, H., 323
La Violette, A. D., 296
Lavoie, K., 123
Lawler, K. A., 94
Lawton, L., 278
Lay, C. H., 124
Lazarus, A., 545
Lazarus, R. S., 71, 72, 81, 85
Le, B., 249
Le, K., 164
Leahy, J. M., 363
Leana, C. R., 393
Leaper, C., 317
Leary, M. R., 150, 152, 153, 236
Leatham, G., 263
Leavitt, F., 470, 472, 528
LeBeau, L. S., 216
LeBlanc, M. M., 392
Le Boeuf, M., 122
Leckman, J. F., 486
Lee, C. M., 67
Lee, D., 120
Lee, F. R., 271, 272
Lee, G. R., 278, 353
Lee, I.-M., 463
Lee, J. E., 452
Lee, R. M., 540
Lee, S., 509
Lee, Y. T., 159
Lefcourt, H. M., 119, 120
Leff, J., 507
Lefkowitz, E. S., 329
Lehman, C. M., 226
Lehman, D., 457
Lehrer, P., 449
Lehrer, R. M., 131
Leibel, R. L., 458
Leigh, G. K., 273
Leitenberg, H., 421, 434
Leiter, M. P., 88
Lemack, G. E., 91
LeMay, C. S., 209
Lemelle, A. J., Jr., 293
Lemieux, R., 254
Lemme, B. H., 351
Lengua, L. J., 72
Lenhart, A., 239
Lenton, R. L., 240
Leo, J., 55
LePore, S. J., 73
Lepper, M. R., 186
Lerman, H., 43
Lerner, M. J., 180
Letherby, G., 276

Lett, H. S., 447
Leu, J., 180
Leucht, S., 535
Levant, R. F., 2, 318, 319, 320, 539
Le Vay, S., 292
Levenson, J. L., 92, 448
Levenstein, S., 448, 449
Leventhal, E. A., 467
Leventhal, H., 467
Lever, J., 423
Levin, S., 186, 250
Levine, A., 277
Levine, M. P., 243, 510
LeVine, R. A., 62
Levine, R. V., 195, 237, 238
Levine, S. B., 435
Levinson, D., 350–351
Levinthal, C. E., 471, 472
Levis, D. J., 487
Levitt, J. G., 376
Levy, S. R., 185
Lewandowski, C. A., 75
Lewin, E., 269
Lewin, K., 76
Lewinsohn, P. M., 500, 501
Lewis, B. P., 87
Lewis, J. M., 288
Lewis, L. L., 305
Lewis, M., 330, 361
Lewis, R. A., 350
Lewis, R. J., 74
Lewis, S., 448, 449
Lewis-Smith, J., 272
Leyens, J., 304
Li, T.-K., 482
Li, W., 49, 184
Li, Y., 537
Libby, P., 443
Licata, N., 286
Lichtenstein, S., 117
Lichtenthal, W.G., 482
Lichter, D. T., 282, 291
Lickey, M. E., 534
Lieberman, J. A., 504, 535
Lieberman, M. D., 179
Liebert, L. L., 50
Liebert, R. M., 50, 317
Lilienfeld, S. O., 6, 8, 67, 492, 493
Lim, G. Y., 298
Lin, L. W., 350
Lin, Y., 220
Linde, J. A., 49
Lindenberger, U., 354
Lindenmayer, J. P., 502, 504
Linder, D. E., 87
Lindren, H. C., 27
Lindsay, D. S., 526, 527, 528
Link, B. G., 77, 98
Linley, P. A., 120
Linton, R., 62
Lipkus, I. M., 180
Lippa, R. A., 306, 311, 312, 314, 316, 318
Lisanby, S. H., 538
Litman, R. E., 496
Litz, B. T., 107
Litzinger, S., 283
Liu, Q. N., 448
Liu, R. X., 79
Liu, T., 449
Livanou, M., 532
Liverant, G. I., 107
Livesley, W. J., 56
Lloyd, K. M., 259, 282
Lloyd, M., 375
Lloyd, S. A., 274
Lock, R. D., 381, 383, 393, 400, 401, 403
Locke, B. Z., 482
Lockwood, P., 145
Lodewijkx, H. F. M., 187
Loehlin, J. C., 56, 57

Subject Index

loss
  as source of stress, 75
  coping with, 363
  of job, 393
  of spouse, 362–363
love
  as attachment, 254–257
  course of, 257–258
  cultural differences in, 238
  happiness and, 22
  romantic, 252–258
  sex and, 417
  triangular theory of, 253–254
  unconditional, 51
Loving Someone Gay, 416
lowball technique, 199
LSD, 471, 473
lung cancer, smoking and, 452
lying, 214–215
  in online communications, 240
  see also deception

M

macho sexual image, 321
mailing lists, 206
makeover culture, 4
maladaptive behavior, 480
male role, 319–321
malingering, 489
malnutrition, 461
managed care health plans, 539
Mandela, Nelson, 357
mania, 494, 495, 497
manipulation, 230
MAO inhibitors, 535–536
marijuana, 471, 474
marital bliss, 276
marital satisfaction
  in early years, 276
  in later years, 278–279, 350
  predictors of, 248
  sexual satisfaction and, 18, 425
  work and, 280, 281
marital success, predictors of, 273–274
marriage, 269
  abuse in, 295–296
  adjusting to, 347
  age at first, 273–274, 347
  alternatives to, 290–294
  arranged, 237, 238
  based on romantic love, 237
  communication problems in, 283–284
  conflict in, 274, 278, 283–284
  covenant, 286
  cultural differences in, 237–238
  division of labor in, 280
  financial problems in, 282–283
  gay, 414
  government promotion of, 286
  happiness and, 22
  health benefits of, 290–291
  infidelity in, 426–427
  interracial, 272
  masturbation in, 422
  motivation for, 271
  moving toward, 270–274
  open, 426
  postponing, 275
  sex before, 424–425
  sexual activity in, 425–426
  trends in, 269–270
  see also divorce
marriage mandate, 321
marriage squeeze, 272
Masculine Self, The (Kilmartin), 320
masculinities, 319
masculinity, 304, 328

masturbation, 420, 422
matching hypothesis, 243–244
mate selection, 271–273
  cultural differences in, 242–243
materialism, 1–2, 4, 20, 61
mathematical abilities, gender differences in, 306–307
Mating Game, The (Regan), 258
Mayer-Salovey-Caruso Emotional Intelligence Test, 127
MDMA, 475
"me first" philosophy, 8
meaning, search for, 4
media
  aggression in, 226
  for messages, 188
  health information in, 452
  sexual content of, 409–410
  as source of gender-role socialization, 317–318
  violence in, 108, 109
medical advice, adherence to, 468–469
Medical College Admissions Test (MCAT), 113
medical treatment, seeking, 467
meditation, 130–131
Mellaril, 534
memorization, 28, 29
memory
  aging and, 355, 358–359
  improving, 27–29
  loss of, 491
  marijuana use and, 475
  recovered, 525–528
  stress and, 88
menarche, 338
menopause, 355–356
menstruation, 338, 412
mental abilities/processes
  aging and, 356–359
  behavioral perspective on, 43
  study of, 11
mental health professions, 517–519
mental health services, 539, 541, 543
mental hospitals, declining populations in, 533, 534
mental illness. *See* psychological disorders
mentoring, 348
mentors, 386
mere exposure effect, 241
mescaline, 47, 4731
messages, 205
  persuasive, 188, 190
Messages: The Communication Skills Book (McKay, Davis, & Fanning), 217
meta-analysis, 306
methamphetamine, 473
method of loci, 29
Michelle Remembers (Smith & Pazder), 492
midlife crisis, 350–351
mifepristone, 430
mindfulness, 155, 187
minding, of relationships, 248
mindlessness, 155, 187, 191
minerals, 461
Minnesota Multiphasic Personality Inventory (MMPI), 65
minorities
  discrimination against, 183
  stresses for, 74
  use of psychotherapy by, 517
  therapeutic services for, 540–541
  in workforce, 384, 385
  workplace harassment of, 326
miscommunication, 206
Mismeasure of Woman (Tavris), 324
mnemonics, 29
mobility, geographic, 77–78
modal personality, 62
modeling (models), 162

of assertive communication, 232
of gender roles, 314
in observational learning, 48–49
in social skills training, 531
money
  happiness and, 19–20
  as marital problem, 282–283
monogamy, 271–272
mood disorders, 483, 484, 493–501
  biological causes of, 498
  cognitive factors in, 498–499
  drug therapy for, 535–536
  etiology of, 497–501
  gender differences in, 309
  interpersonal roots of, 500
  prevalence of, 495
  seeking treatment for, 516
  stress and, 500–501
  suicide and, 496
  types of, 494–497
mood stabilizers, 536
moods, in adolescence, 343
Morgan Stanley, 385
Mormon Church, 271–272
morphine, 471, 472
mortality
  acknowledging, 349
  from health-impairing behaviors, 450, 451
  obesity and, 457
  physical fitness and, 463
mortality rates
  for diseases, 441
  for smokers, 452, 453
mortality salience, 60, 61, 152
motherhood mandate, 321
mothers, in workforce, 323–324
motivational distortion, 223
motives
  guiding self-understanding, 147
  sexual, 416–417
motor vehicle accidents, 451
multiaxial system of classification, 482, 483
Multicultural Manners (Dresser), 206
multimodal therapy, 545
multiple-choice tests, changing answers on, 16, 17
multiple sclerosis, stress and, 92
multiple-personality disorder, 492–493
Mundugamor, 314
murder
  of spouse, 296
  in workplace, 392
music videos, 318, 410
mutual gaze, 211
My Lai incident, 197
myocardial infarction, 443
myocardial ischemia, 443, 446
MySpace, 238

N

narcissism, 151
narcotics, 471, 472
Nardil, 535
Nash, John, 504
National Alliance for the Mentally Ill, 482
National Business Employment Weekly, 401
national character, 62–63
National Comorbidity Study, 484
National Council on Family Relations, 281
National Institute on Drug Abuse, 470
nations, subjective well-being of, 19, 20
Native Americans, 230
  health of, 356
  suicide by, 344
natural resources, depletion of, 3
natural selection, 58, 244, 311
naturalistic observation, 16
Nazi war crimes, 197

TO THE OWNER OF THIS BOOK

We hope that you have found *Psychology Applied to Modern Life,* Ninth Edition useful. So that this book can be improved in a future edition, would you take the time to complete this sheet and return it? Thank you.

School and address: _____

_____

Department: _____

Instructor's name: _____

1. What I like most about this book is: _____

_____

_____

2. What I like least about this book is: _____

_____

_____

3. My general reaction to this book is: _____

_____

_____

4. The name of the course in which I used this book is: _____

_____

5. Were all of the chapters of the book assigned for you to read?_____

    If not, which ones weren't? _____

6. In the space below, or on a separate sheet of paper, please write specific suggestions for improving this book and anything else you'd care to share about your experience in using this book.

_____

_____

_____

_____

_____

_____

_____

WADSWORTH
CENGAGE Learning

BUSINESS REPLY MAIL
FIRST-CLASS MAIL   PERMIT NO. 34   BELMONT CA

POSTAGE WILL BE PAID BY ADDRESSEE

Attn: Michele Sordi, Psychology Editor

Wadsworth Cengage Learning
10 Davis Dr
Belmont CA 94002-98001

OPTIONAL:

Your name: _____ Date _____

May we quote you, either in promotion for *Psychology Applied to Modern Life,* Ninth Edition,
or in future publishing ventures?

Yes: _____ No: _____